Routledge History of Philosophy
Volume I

Volume I of the *Routledge History of Philosophy* covers one of the most remarkable periods in human thought. In the space of two and a half centuries, philosophy developed from quasi-mythological speculation to a state in which many of the most fundamental questions about the universe, the mind and human conduct had been vigorously pursued and some of the most enduring masterworks of Western thought had been written.

The essays present the fundamental approaches and thinkers of Greek philosophy in chronological order. Each is written by a recognized authority in the particular field, and takes account of the large amount of high-quality work done in the last few decades on Platonic and pre-Platonic philosophy. All write in an accessible style, meeting the needs of the non-specialist without loss of scholarly precision. Topics covered range from early Greek speculative thought and its cultural and social setting, to the Sophists and Socrates, culminating in three chapters on Plato's lasting contribution to all central areas of philosophy.

Supplemented with a chronology, a glossary of technical terms and an extensive bibliography, this volume will prove an invaluable and comprehensive guide to the beginnings of philosophy.

C. C. W. Taylor is Professor of Philosophy in the University of Oxford and a Fellow of Corpus Christi College. He is the author of *Plato, Protagoras* (1976, 1996), *Socrates* (1998) and *The Atomists: Leucippus and Democritus* (1999), co-author of *The Greeks on Pleasure* (1982) and co-editor of *Human Agency: Philosophical Essays in Honor of J. O. Urmson* (1988). He was editor of *Oxford Studies in Ancient Philosophy* from 1993 to 1998.

Routledge History of Philosophy
General Editors – G. H. R. Parkinson and S. G. Shanker

The *Routledge History of Philosophy* provides a chronological survey of the history of Western philosophy, from its beginnings in the sixth century BC to the present time. It discusses all the major philosophical developments in depth. Most space is allocated to those individuals who, by common consent, are regarded as great philosophers. But lesser figures have not been neglected, and together the ten volumes of the *History* include basic and critical information about every significant philosopher of the past and present. These philosophers are clearly situated within the cultural and, in particular, the scientific context of their time.

The *History* is intended not only for the specialist, but also for the student and general reader. Each chapter is by an acknowledged authority in the field. The chapters are written in an accessible style and a glossary of technical terms is provided in each volume.

Each volume contains 10–15 chapters by different contributors.

Routledge History of Philosophy
Volume I

From the Beginning to Plato

EDITED BY
C. C. W. Taylor

Routledge
Taylor & Francis Group

LONDON AND NEW YORK

First published 1997
by Routledge
11 New Fetter Lane, London EC4P 4EE

Simultaneously published in the USA and Canada
by Routledge
29 West 35th Street, New York, NY 10001

Reprinted 2000, 2001

First published in paperback 2003

Routledge is an imprint of the Taylor & Francis Group

Selection and editorial matter © 1997 C. C. W. Taylor
Individual chapters © 1997 the contributors

Typeset in Garamond by RefineCatch Ltd, Bungay, Suffolk
Printed and bound in Great Britain by
TJ International Ltd, Padstow, Cornwall

British Library Cataloguing in Publication Data
A catalogue record for this book is available from the British Library

Library of Congress Cataloging in Publication Data

ISBN 0-415-06272-1 hbk
ISBN 0-415-30873-9 pbk

Contents

Preface to the paperback edition

The success of the first edition of the **Routledge History of Philosophy**, which has led to the publication of this new paperback edition, fully justifies the thinking behind this project. Our view at the time that we planned this collection was that the history of philosophy has a special importance for contemporary philosophers and philosophy students. For the discipline demands that one develop the rigorous techniques required to grasp the significance of a philosopher's ideas within their historical framework, while constantly assessing the relevance of the problems or theories discussed to contemporary issues. The very persistence of these "perennial problems in philosophy" is an indication, not just of their enduring relevance, but equally, of how important it is to be thoroughly grounded in their history in order to grasp their full complexity. We would like to take this opportunity to thank once again all of the authors involved, each of whom has produced such a lasting contribution to the history of philosophy, and also, our editors Richard Stoneman and Muna Khogali, for their role in making the **History** such an indispensable resource.

G. H. R. P. Reading, 2002
S. G. S. Toronto, 2002

General editors' preface

The history of philosophy, as its name implies, represents a union of two very different disciplines, each of which imposes severe constraints upon the other. As an exercise in the history of ideas, it demands that one acquire a 'period eye': a thorough understanding of how the thinkers whom it studies viewed the problems which they sought to resolve, the conceptual frameworks in which they addressed these issues, their assumptions and objectives, their blind spots and miscues. But as an exercise in philosophy, we are engaged in much more than simply a descriptive task. There is a crucial critical aspect to our efforts: we are looking for the cogency as much as the development of an argument, for its bearing on questions which continue to preoccupy us as much as the impact which it may have had on the evolution of philosophical thought.

The history of philosophy thus requires a delicate balancing act from its practitioners. We read these writings with the full benefit of historical hindsight. We can see why the minor contributions remained minor and where the grand systems broke down: sometimes as a result of internal pressures, sometimes because of a failure to overcome an insuperable obstacle, sometimes because of a dramatic technological or sociological change and, quite often, because of nothing more than a shift in intellectual fashion or interests. Yet, because of our continuing philosophical concern with many of the same problems, we cannot afford to look dispassionately at these works. We want to know what lessons are to be learnt from the inconsequential or the glorious failures; many times we want to plead for a contemporary relevance in the overlooked theory or to reconsider whether the 'glorious failure' was indeed such or simply ahead of its time: perhaps even ahead of its author.

We find ourselves, therefore, much like the mythical 'radical translator' who has so fascinated modern philosophers, trying to understand an author's ideas in his and his culture's eyes, and at the same time, in our own. It can be a formidable task. Many times we fail in the historical undertaking because our philosophical interests are so strong, or lose sight of the latter because we are so enthralled by the former. But the nature of philosophy is such that we are compelled to master both techniques. For learning about the history of philosophy is not just a challenging and engaging pastime: it is an essential element in learning about the nature of philosophy – in grasping how philosophy is intimately connected with and yet distinct from both history and science.

The *Routledge History of Philosophy* provides a chronological survey of the history of Western philosophy, from its beginnings up to the present time. Its aim is to discuss all major philosophical developments in depth, and with this in mind, most space has been allocated to those individuals who, by common consent, are regarded as great philosophers. But lesser figures have not been neglected, and it is hoped that the reader will be able to find, in the ten volumes of the *History*, at least basic information about any significant philosopher of the past or present.

Philosophical thinking does not occur in isolation from other human activities, and this *History* tries to situate philosophers within the cultural, and in particular the scientific, context of their time. Some philosophers, indeed, would regard philosophy as merely ancillary to the natural sciences; but even if this view is rejected, it can hardly be denied that the sciences have had a great influence on what is now regarded as philosophy, and it is important that this influence should be set forth clearly. Not that these volumes are intended to provide a mere record of the factors that influenced philosophical thinking; philosophy is a discipline with its own standards of argument, and the presentation of the ways in which these arguments have developed is the main concern of this *History*.

In speaking of 'what is now regarded as philosophy', we may have given the impression that there now exists a single view of what philosophy is. This is certainly not the case; on the contrary, there exist serious differences of opinion, among those who call themselves philosophers, about the nature of their subject. These differences are reflected in the existence at the present time of two main schools of thought, usually described as 'analytic' and 'continental' philosophy. It is not our intention, as general editors of this *History*, to take sides in this dispute. Our attitude is one of tolerance, and our hope is that these volumes will contribute to an understanding of how philosophers have reached the positions which they now occupy.

One final comment. Philosophy has long been a highly technical subject, with its own specialized vocabulary. This *History* is intended not only for the specialist but also for the general reader. To this end, we have tried to ensure that each chapter is written in an accessible style; and since technicalities are unavoidable, a glossary of technical terms is provided in each volume. In this way these volumes will, we hope, contribute to a wider understanding of a subject which is of the highest importance to all thinking people.

G. H. R. Parkinson
S. G. Shanker

Notes on contributors

Hugh H. Benson is Professor and Chair of the Department of Philosophy at the University of Oklahoma. He is the author of *Socratic Wisdom* (2000), *Plato's Charmides* (2001: Archelogos Project) and of articles on Socrates, Plato and Aristotle, and is the editor of *Essays on the Philosophy of Socrates* (1992).

Robert Heinaman is Reader in Philosophy at University College, London. He is the author of articles on Plato and Aristotle, and editor of *Aristotle and Moral Realism* (1995).

Edward Hussey is Lecturer in Ancient Philosophy in the University of Oxford and a Fellow of All Souls College. He is the author of *The Presocratics* (1972) and *Aristotle Physics III and IV* (1982).

G. B. Kerferd, who died in 1998, was Professor of Greek at the University of Manchester from 1973 to 1982. He was the author of *The Sophistic Movement* (1981) and of many articles on the history of Greek philosophy, and editor of *The Sophists and Their Legacy* (1981). He was editor of *Phronesis* from 1973 to 1979.

Ian Mueller is Professor of Philosophy at the University of Chicago and a member of the Académie internationale d'histoire des sciences. He is the author of *Philosophy of Mathematics and Deductive Structure in Euclid's Elements* (1981), and editor of *PERI TON MATHEMATON: Essays on Greek Mathematics and Its Later Development* (1991).

Catherine Osborne is Reader in Ancient Greek Culture at the University of Liverpool. She is the author of *Rethinking Early Greek Philosophy* (1987), *Eros Unveiled* (1994) and *Presocratic Philosophy: A Very Short Introduction* (in preparation).

Robin Osborne is Professor of Ancient History in the University of Cambridge, and a Fellow of King's College. He is the author of *Demos: The Discovery of Classical Attika* (1985), *Classical Landscape with Figures: The*

Ancient Greek City and its Countryside (1987) and *Greece in the Making, 1200–479 BC* (1996).

A. W. Price is Reader in Philosophy at Birkbeck College, London. He is the author of *Love and Friendship in Plato and Aristotle* (1989) and *Mental Conflict* (1995).

Christopher Rowe is Professor of Greek at the University of Durham. He is the author of *The Eudemian and Nicomachean Ethics: A Study of the Development of Aristotle's Thought* (1971) and of commentaries on *Plato's Phaedrus* (1986, with translation), *Phaedo* (1993), *Statesman* (1995, with translation) and *Symposium* (1998, with translation). He is the editor of *Reading the Statesman: Proceedings of the Third Symposium Platonicum* (1995), co-editor (with M. Schofield) of *The Cambridge History of Greek and Roman Political Thought* (2000) and (with J. Annas) of *New Perspectives on Plato, Modern and Ancient* (2002), and translator of *Aristotle, Nicomachean Ethics* (2002, with commentary by S. Broadie).

Malcolm Schofield is Professor of Ancient Philosophy in the University of Cambridge and a Fellow of St. John's College. He is the author of *An Essay on Anaxagoras* (1980), *The Stoic Idea of the City* (1991, expanded edition 1999) and *Saving the City* (1999), co-author (with G. S. Kirk and J. E. Raven) of *The Presocratic Philosophers* (2nd edition 1983), and co-editor (with A. Laks) of *Justice and Generosity: Studies in Hellenistic Social and Political Philosophy* (Proceedings of the Sixth Symposium Hellenisticum, 1995) and (with C. Rowe) of *The Cambridge History of Greek and Roman Political Thought* (2000). He was editor of *Phronesis* from 1987 to 1992.

C. C. W. Taylor is Professor of Philosophy in the University of Oxford and a Fellow of Corpus Christi College. He is the author of *Plato, Protagoras* (Clarendon Plato Series 1976, revised edition 1991, World's Classics edition 1996), *Socrates* (1998) and *The Atomists: Leucippus and Democritus* (Phoenix Presocratics Series 1999), co-author (with J. C. B. Gosling) of *The Greeks on Pleasure* (1982) and co-editor (with J. Dancy and J. M. E. Moravcsik) of *Human Agency: Philosophical Essays in Honor of J. O. Urmson* (1988). He was editor of *Oxford Studies in Ancient Philosophy* from 1993 to 1998.

M. R. Wright is Professor of Classics at the University of Wales, Lampeter. Her publications include *Empedocles: The Extant Fragments* (1981, revised edition 1995), *Cicero, On Stoic Good and Evil* (1991) and *Cosmology in Antiquity* (1995).

Chronology
C. C. W. Taylor and Robin Osborne

We have comparatively few precise and reliable dates for the biography of individuals (including birth, death and composition of individual works). In some cases approximate dates can be given, but in others all that can be said is that the person was active during a certain period, e.g. in the first third or half of a particular century. Dramatic works are dated by the year of their performance at one of the Athenian dramatic festivals, of which official records were preserved.

All dates are BC. Dates of the form 462/1 designate years of the official Athenian calendar, in which the year began in June. (Hence 462/1 is the year from June 462 BC to June 461 BC.) Dates of the form 750–700 designate periods of several years.

Politics and religion		The arts	
776	First Olympiad	800	Geometric pottery produced throughout Greece
c.750–c.700	Foundation of Greek colonies in S. Italy and Sicily		
		c. mid-cent.	Earliest Greek alphabetic inscriptions
		2nd half of cent.	Figurative decoration developed on Late Geometric pottery Composition of Homeric poems
		c.700	Hesiod active Earliest certain scenes of myths on Greek pottery
		c.700–c.650	Oriental influence manifest in Greek pottery and metalwork
		c.650	Archilochus, Semonides, Tyrtaeus active
c.650–c.600	Age of tyrants and lawgivers Laws of Draco at Athens 621	630–600	Alcman active
		c.610–c.600	Earliest black-figure vase painting at Athens
		c.600	First monumental kouroi Sappho, Alcaeus active
594/3	Archonship of Solon at Athens	c.600–c.550	Earliest Doric temples (Olympia, Corinth, Syracuse, Corcyra, Selinus)
		c.560	Earliest Ionic temples (Samos, Ephesus)
		c.550	Theognis active Mythological cosmogony of Pherecydes of Syros Amasis Painter and Exekias active at Athens
c.550–c.500	Earliest Orphic poems written		
546	Persian conquest of Lydia		
c.540–c.522	Tyranny of Polycrates at Samos	540–520	Anacreon active Temple of Hera at Samos
		535	Traditional date of first dramatic competition at Athens
		520–10	Invention of red-figure technique of vase painting at Athens
		c.510–480	Technique for making large hollow-cast bronze statues perfected
508/7	Reforms of Cleisthenes: full democracy established at Athens		
500–494	Ionian revolt against Persia	c.500	Kleophrades Painter and Berlin Painter active at Athens
		500–490	Temple of Athena Aphaia, Aegina

Science and technology		Philosophy	
early 6th cent.	Geometrical discoveries attributed to Thales (see Ch. 8) Anaximander's world map	585	Eclipse allegedly predicted by Thales Anaximander, Anaximenes active
c.575–560	Earliest electrum coins minted in Ionia	c.570–c.550	Birth of Pythagoras
		546 (?)	Xenophanes goes into exile
c.540–c.522	Polycrates' tunnel	c.540–c.520	Foundation of Pythagorean community at Croton
c.520	Earliest Athenian owl coinage	c.540	Foundation of Elea
		c.515	Birth of Parmenides
Late 6th–early 5th cent.	Hecataeus, *Journey Round the World*, world map and work on mythology and genealogy	c.500	Heraclitus active Birth of Anaxagoras Birth of Protagoras

Politics and religion		The arts	
		494	Phrynichus, *Capture of Miletus*
		500–440	Pindar (d. 438) active Bacchylides active Simonides (d. 468) active Building of temples at Acragas
490	First Persian invasion: Battle of Marathon (Aeschylus a combatant)		
		485	Comedy added to City Dionysia
		484	Aeschylus' first victory
480–79	Second Persian invasion: Battles of Thermopylae, Salamis and Plataea Battle of Himera: Carthaginian invasion of Sicily defeated	c.480	Critian boy
		472	Aeschylus, *Persians*
		470	Sophocles' first victory
		468	Aeschylus, *Seven Against Thebes*
c.465	Battle of Eurymedon	470–60	Painted Stoa at Athens: paintings by Polygnotus and others
c.463	Establishment of democracy at Syracuse		
462/1	Ostracism of Kimon Reforms of Ephialtes at Athens		
459–4	Athenian expedition to Egypt		
		458	Aeschylus, *Oresteia*
		456	Death of Aeschylus Completion of Temple of Zeus at Olympia
454	Tranfer of treasury of Delian League to Athens: beginning of Athenian empire Pericles elected general for first time		
		c.450	Piraeus replanned by Hippodamus of Miletus
		450–30	Polyclitus active
448	Pericles re-elected general (and annually thereafter till his death)	447	Parthenon begun
443	Foundation of Thurii Ostracism of Thucydides son of Melesias		Herodotus among the colonists of Thurii: city laid out by Hippodamus Sophocles, *Antigone*
441	Revolt of Samos from Athens	441	Euripides' first victory
		438	Euripides, *Alcestis* Phidias, statue of Athena in Parthenon

Science and technology		Philosophy	
		469	Birth of Socrates
		467	Fall of meteorite at Aegospotamoi said to have been predicted by Anaxagoras
		c.460	Birth of Democritus
5th cent.	Pythagorean discovery of mathematical basis of musical intervals		
		454	Destruction of Pythagorean communities in S. Italy
2nd half of 5th cent.	Hippocrates of Chios, *Elements* Hippocrates of Cos active Early Hippocratic treatises	450	Dramatic date of Plato, *Parmenides* Parmenides c.65 yrs old, Zeno c.40 yrs old
		443	Protagoras writes laws for Thurii. Anaxagoras active in Athens
		441	Melissus commands Samian fleet against Athens.
		mid 5th. cent.	Empedocles, Leucippus, Alcmaeon of Croton active

Politics and religion		The arts	
432	Outbreak of Peloponnesian War	c.432	Parthenon sculptures completed Zeuxis at outset of his career Thucydides begins his history.
		431	Euripides, *Medea*
		c.430	Sophocles, *Oedipus Tyrannus* Phidias, statue of Zeus at Olympia Birth of Xenophon
429	Plague at Athens: death of Pericles		
		428	Euripides, *Hippolytus*
427	Leontinoi seeks help from Athens against Syracuse, (Gorgias an ambassador)		
		425	Aristophanes, *Acharnians*
424	Battle of Delium (Socrates distinguishes himself.) Capture of Amphipolis by Brasidas: exile of Thucydides	424	Aristophanes, *Knights*
		423	Aristophanes, *Clouds*
		422	Aristophanes, *Wasps*
421	Peace of Nicias	421	Aristophanes, *Peace* Eupolis, *Flatterers*
420	Alcibiades elected general Introduction of cult of Asclepius to Athens	c.420	Herodotus active
418	Renewal of war between Athens and Sparta		
416	Destruction of Melos by Athens	416	Agathon's first victory (celebrated by Plato, *Symposium*)
415	Sicilian expedition: Mutilation of the Hermai: Alcibiades goes over to Sparta	415	Euripides, *Trojan Women*
		414	Aristophanes, *Birds*
413	Defeat of Sicilian expedition		
413/12	Introduction of cult of Bendis to Athens (mentioned at beginning of Plato, *Republic*)		
		412	Euripides, *Helen*

Science and technology		Philosophy	
late 5th cent.	Hippias discovers quadratrix, compiles list of Olympic victors	c.433	Dramatic date of Plato, *Protagoras* Protagoras, Hippias, Prodicus active
		c.430	Anaxagoras exiled from Athens
		c.428	Death of Anaxagoras
		427	Birth of Plato
		423	Diogenes of Apollonia active (doctrines caricatured in *Clouds*).
		c.420	Death of Protagoras
		late 5th cent.	Democritus, Philolaus active
		2nd half of 5th cent.	Democritus states without proof that volumes of cone and pyramid are 1/3 respectively of volumes of cylinder and prism.

Politics and religion		The arts	
411	Rule of 400 at Athens		Aristophanes, *Lysistrata* and *Thesmophoriazusai*
		409	Sophocles, *Philoctetes*
		408	Euripides, *Orestes*
407	Return of Alcibiades to Athens Spartan treaty with Persia		
406	Battle of Arginusai and trial of generals (Socrates a member of presiding board) Carthaginian invasion of Sicily	406	Death of Sophocles Death of Euripides
405	Defeat of Athenian fleet at Aegospotamoi Dionysius I establishes tyranny at Syracuse	405	Aristophanes, *Frogs* Euripides, *Bacchae* and *Iphigenia in Aulis* (produced posthumously)
405–4	Siege of Athens		
404	Surrender of Athens		
404–3	Rule of Thirty Tyrants at Athens: Lysias goes into exile: Socrates refuses to take part in arrest of Leon of Salamis Death of Alcibiades		
403	Restoration of democracy at Athens: death of Critias		
		401	Sophocles, *Oedipus at Colonus* (produced posthumously)
		c.400	Death of Thucydides Temple of Apollo, Bassai
395–3	Rebuilding of Long Walls at Athens	1st, half of 4th cent.	Lysias active (d. *c.*380) Xenophon active (d. *c.*354) Isocrates active (d.338)
		392	Aristophanes, *Ecclesiazusai*
		389	Aristophanes, *Plutus*
386	King's Peace		

Science and technology		Philosophy	
late 5th cent.	Basic work on irrationals by Theodorus of Cyrene		
1st half of 4th cent.	Theaetetus (d. 369) generalizes Theodorus' work on irrationals and describes five regular solids.	399	Trial and death of Socrates
	Eudoxus (d. c.340) invents general theory of proportion and proves Democritus' discoveries of volumes of cone and pyramid; invents mathematical model of cosmos as set of nested spheres to explain movements of heavenly bodies.	1st half of 4th cent.	Associates of Socrates active: Antisthenes (d. c.360) Aristippus (reputed founder of Cyrenaic school) Aeschines Eucleides (d. c.380: founder of Megarian school) Phaedo
	Archytas solves problem of duplication of the cube, carries further Pythagorean work on mathematical determination of musical intervals and is first to apply mathematical principles to mechanics.		
		387	Plato's first visit to Sicily Foundation of Academy

Politics and religion		The arts	
377	Foundation of Second Athenian Confederacy		
371	Battle of Leuctra		
370–69	Liberation of Messenia		
367	Death of Dionysius I of Syracuse: succession of Dionysius II		
360	Accession of Philip II of Macedon: beginning of rise of Macedon to hegemony in Greece		
		c.356	Praxiteles, altar of Artemis at Ephesus
		352–1	Mausoleum at Halicarnassus
351	Demosthenes, *First Philippic*		

Science and technology	Philosophy	
	384	Birth of Aristotle
	367	Plato's second visit to Sicily Aristotle joins Academy
	361	Plato's third visit to Sicily
	c.360	Birth of Pyrrho, founder of Scepticism
	c. mid-cent.	Diogenes the Cynic comes to Athens.
	347	Death of Plato: Speusippus succeeds as head of Academy: Aristotle leaves Athens.

List of Sources

The following ancient authors and works are cited as sources, chiefly for pre-Socratic philosophy, in this volume. Many of these works are available in original language editions only; details of these may be found (for Greek authors) in Liddell and Scott, *A Greek–English Lexicon*, 9th edn, revised H. S. Jones and R. McKenzie, Oxford, Clarendon Press, 1940 (many reprints), pp. xvi–xli. This list indicates English translations where available; (L) indicates that the works cited are available, in the original with facing English translation, in the Loeb Classical Library (Harvard University Press). Where details of a translation are given in the bibliography of any chapter, the appropriate reference is given. There is a helpful discussion of the sources for pre-Socratic philosophy in G. S. Kirk, J. E. Raven and M. Schofield, *The Presocratic Philosophers*, 2nd edn, Cambridge, Cambridge University Press, 1983 ([1.6], pp. 1–6.

Achilles. Astronomer; 3rd c. AD.

Aetius. Conjectured author of a history of philosophy, believed to have lived 1st or 2nd c. AD. His work survives in two summaries, the *Epitome* of [Plutarch] (1) (q.v.) and the *Selections* of Stobaeus (q.v.), with some excerpts also preserved by Theodoretus (q.v.); these versions are edited by H. Diels in *Doxographi Graeci* [2.1].

Albert the Great (St). Theologian and scientist; 13th c. AD. Work cited; *On Vegetables*, ed. E. Meyer and C. Jessen, Berlin, 1867.

Alexander of Aphrodisias. Philosopher and Aristotelian commentator; 2nd–3rd c. AD. Works cited; *On Fate* (trans. R. Sharples, London, Duckworth, 1983), commentaries on *Meteorology* and *Topics*.

Ammonius. Neoplatonist philosopher; 5th c. AD. Work cited; commentary on Porphyry's *Introduction*.

Aristotle. 4th c. BC. All works cited are translated in J. Barnes (ed.) *The Complete Works of Aristotle*, 2 vols, Princeton, NJ, Princeton University Press, 1984 (also (L)).

Asclepius. Aristotelian commentator; 6th c. AD. Work cited: commentary on *Metaphysics A–Z*.

Boethius. Roman statesman and philosopher; 5th c. AD. See [8.29].

Censorinus. Roman grammarian; 3rd c. AD. Work cited: *On the Day of Birth* ed. N. Sallman, Leipzig, Teubner, 1983.

Cicero. Roman statesman and philosopher; 1st c. BC. Works cited; *Academica, On the Nature of the Gods, Tusculan Disputations* (L).

Clement. Bishop of Alexandria; 3rd c. AD. Works cited: *Protrepticus, Miscellanies* (L).

Columella. Roman writer on agriculture; 1st c. AD. Work cited: *On Agriculture* (L).

Diogenes Laertius. Biographer; 3rd *c.* AD(?). Work cited: *Lives of the Philosophers* (L).

Epicurus. Philosopher, founder of Epicurean school; 4th–3rd c. BC. Works cited: *Letter to Menoeceus, On Nature.* Ed. G. Arrighetti, *Epicure, Opere*, Turin, Giulio Einaudi, 1960. Trans. in C. Bailey, *Epicurus*, Oxford, Clarendon Press, 1926, repr. Hildesheim and New York, Georg Olms Verlag, 1970, and in A. A. Long and D. N. Sedley, *The Hellenistic Philosophers*, Cambridge: Cambridge University Press, 1987, Vol. 1.

Etymologicum Magnum. 12th c. AD Greek dictionary.

Eusebius. Historian and chronologist; 3rd–4th c. AD. Works cited: *Preparation for the Gospel, Chronicles.*

Eutocius. Mathematician; 6th c. AD. See [8.44].

Heraclitus. Interpreter of Homer; 1st c. AD.

Hesychius. Lexicographer; 5th c. AD(?).

Hippolytus. Bishop of Rome; 3rd c. AD. Work cited: *Refutation of All Heresies* (see [3.13]).

Iamblichus. Neoplatonist philosopher; 4th c. AD. See [8.52].

Lactantius. Ecclesiastical writer; 3rd–4th c. AD. Work cited: *Divine Institutions*, (in *Corpus Scriptorum Ecclesiasticorum Latinorum*, Vol. 19).

Lucretius. Epicurean philosopher and poet; 1st c. BC. Work cited: *De Rerum Natura* (L).

Marcus Aurelius. Roman emperor and Stoic philosopher; 2nd c. AD. Work cited: *Meditations* (L).

Maximus of Tyre. Moralist and lecturer; 2nd c. AD.

Nicomachus of Gerasa. Mathematician; 1st–2nd c. AD. See [8.55-8].

Olympiodorus. Neoplatonist philosopher; 6th c. AD. Work cited: commentary on Aristotle's *Categories*.

Origen. Theologian; 2nd–3rd c. AD. Work cited: *Against Celsus*, trans. H. Chadwick, Oxford, Clarendon Press, 1953.

Pappus. Mathematician; 4th c. AD. See [8.60].

Pausanias. Geographer and antiquarian; 2nd c. AD. Work cited: *Description of Greece* (L).

Philoponus (John). Aristotelian commentator; 6th c. AD. Works cited: commentaries on *Physics* and on *On Generation and Corruption.*

Philostratus. Biographer; 2nd–3rd c. AD. Work cited: *Lives of the Sophists* (L).

Plotinus. Neoplatonist philosopher; 3rd. c. AD. Work cited: *Enneads* (L).

Plutarch. Philosopher, historian and essayist; 1st–2nd c. AD. The various works cited, apart from the *Lives*, are all included in his collected works, entitled *Moralia* (L). (*Lives* also (L)).

[Plutarch] (1) *Epitome*, a summary of philosophical history; 2nd c. AD. See Aetius.

[Plutarch] (2) *Miscellanies*, a collection of miscellaneous scientific information preserved by Eusebius (q.v.).

[Plutarch] (3) *Consolation to Apollonius.* Date uncertain.

Porphyry. Philosopher and polymath; 3rd c. AD. Works cited: *Homeric Questions*, commentary on Ptolemy *Harmonics* (see [8.73]).

Proclus. Neoplatonist philosopher; 3rd c. AD. Works cited: commentary on Euclid *Elements* Book 1 (see [8.75]), commentary on Plato *Parmenides*, commentary on Plato, *Alcibiades I.*

scholium (pl. **scholia**). A marginal note in an ancient manuscript. **Scholiast.** A writer of scholia.

Sextus Empiricus. Sceptical philosopher; 2nd c. AD. Works cited: *Outlines of Pyrrhonism, Adversus Mathematicos* (L).

Simplicius. Aristotelian commentator; 6th c. AD. Works cited: commentaries on *On the Heavens* and *Physics.*

Stobaeus (John of Stobi). Anthologist; 5th c. AD.

Suda, The (also known as **Suidas**). 10th c. AD Greek lexicon. See [8.87].

Themistius. Rhetorician and Aristotelian commentator; 4th c. AD. Works cited: *Orations*, commentary on *Physics.*

Theodoretus. Ecclesiastical writer; 5th c. AD.

Theodorus Prodromos. Polymath; 12th c. AD.

Theon of Smyrna. Mathematician; 1st c. AD. See [8.93].

Theophrastus. Aristotle's successor as head of the Lyceum; 4th–3rd c. BC. Work cited: *On the Senses*, Trans. in G. M. Stratton, *Theophrastus and the Greek Physiological Psychology Before Aristotle*, London, Allen and Unwin, 1917, repr. Bonset/P. Schippers, Amsterdam, 1964 [2.43].

Tzetzes (John). Commentator on Homer and polymath; 12th c. AD.

Introduction
C. C. W. Taylor

In the two and a half centuries covered by this volume, from the beginning of the sixth century BC to the death of Plato in 347, Western philosophy developed from infancy to adulthood, from the earliest stage at which it can be recognized as an intellectual activity in its own right to a state in which most of its principal branches had been articulated from one another, major advances had been made in some of those branches, and some enduring masterpieces had already been written. The several chapters in this volume describe this astonishing process in detail; it is the task of this introduction to attempt an overview of the main developments.

The tradition of beginning the history of Western philosophy with the Ionian theorists of the sixth century (see Chapter 2) is as old as the history of philosophy itself; Aristotle, the earliest historian of philosophy whose work survives, describes Thales (*Metaphysics* 983b20–1) as 'the founder of that kind of philosophy', i.e. the enquiry into the basic principles of the physical world. Yet in the same passage Aristotle admits some uncertainty as to whether 'the men of very ancient times who first told stories about the gods' should not be counted as pioneers of that kind of enquiry (b27–30). This brings out the fact that Ionian speculation about the nature and origins of the physical world itself arises from an older tradition of cosmology, represented in Greek thought by Homer, Hesiod and the so-called 'Orphic' poems, a tradition which has considerable affinities with the mythological systems of Egypt and the Near Eastern civilizations (see Chapter 1, and, for detailed discussion KRS [1.6], ch. 1). While it is traditional to contrast the 'mythological' thought of the poets, who explained the genesis and nature of the world via the activities of divinities, with the 'physical' or 'materialistic' thought of the Ionians, who appealed to observable stuffs such as water or air, that contrast is somewhat misleading, since on the one hand many of the divinities of the poets were

1

themselves identified with components of the world such as the sea or the earth, while on the other the Ionians appear to have regarded their basic components as alive, and to have given them some of the attributes of divinity, such as immortality. None the less there are certain features of Ionian cosmological speculation which justify the traditional claim that it marks an unprecedented step in human thought. While the mythical cosmologies mix up the cosmic deities with fairy-tale figures such as giants, Titans and monsters without distinction, and have no explanatory resources beyond the sexual and other psychological motivations of these beings, the Ionians eliminate the purely personal element, seeking to explain the world in terms of a minimum number of basic stuffs (e.g. water, air) and processes (e.g. condensation and rarefaction), and subjecting these accounts to the control both of primitive observation (as in Aristotle's account of Thales' reasons for identifying his principle with water) and of a priori reasoning (e.g. in Anaximander's treatment of the problem of the stability of the earth). Their speculations were thus subjected to norms of rationality, as those of their mythologizing precedessors were not, and in satisfying those norms they pioneered the crucial concepts of a theoretical entity (Anaximander's *apeiron*) and of a world organized in accordance with natural law (in the single fragment of Anaximander). (For a fuller discussion see Hussey [2.36].)

The Ionian cosmological tradition was an active element in the development of philosophy throughout the period covered by this volume, and beyond. But other strands soon become discernible in the fabric. The fragments of the poet Xenophanes, an Ionian writing later in the sixth century and probably well into the fifth, contain, in addition to some cosmological material, a number of criticisms of traditional theology. One element in this criticism is the rejection, on moral grounds, of the traditional tales of quarrels, adultery and other misdeeds on the part of the gods; the demand for a conception of the divine which represents it as a paradigm of moral perfection is from Xenophanes onwards a recurrent theme in Greek thought, particularly important in Plato, and is one of the elements which was taken over in the Christianization of Greek philosophy. More radical was Xenophanes' ridicule of anthropomorphic representations of gods, which looks forward to the cultural relativism of the fifth century and thereby to an important aspect of the thought of the sophists. But Xenophanes' contribution to theological speculation was not wholly negative; the fragments also provide evidence of belief in a non-anthropomorphic, perhaps incorporeal deity, which undertakes no physical activity, but controls everything by the power of thought. While there is disagreement among scholars as to whether Xenophanes was a monotheist, and whether he identified the deity with the cosmos, there can be no doubt that he is a pioneer of a theological tradition whose influence can be discerned in thinkers as diverse as Anaxagoras, Aristotle and the Stoics. He is also the earliest thinker who provides evidence of engagement with epistemological problems, initiating a tradition which was developed in different ways by the Eleatics, Plato and the Hellenistic schools.

The Ionian tradition was further diversified in the later sixth century by Pythagoreanism and by Heraclitus. The former movement, which had at least as much of the character of an esoteric religion as of a philosophical or scientific system, might appear altogether remote from the Ionians, but Aristotle's evidence suggests that the early Pythagoreans thought of themselves rather as offering alternative answers to the same fundamental questions about the physical world as the Ionians had posed than as taking an altogether new direction. Their fundamental insight, which was to have a profound influence on Plato and thereby on later developments, was that understanding of the physical world was to be attained by grasping the mathematical principles of its organization, but those principles do not appear to have been, at this early stage, clearly distinguished from the physical principles which the Ionians had posited. Another important aspect of early Pythagoreanism was its development of a theory of the nature of the soul, and in particular of the view that the soul is akin to the world as a whole, and therefore to be explained via the application of the same mathematical conceptions as make the world intelligible. While Heraclitus' thought was closer to that of his Ionian predecessors, lacking the peculiarly mathematical slant of the Pythagoreans, it none the less has certain affinities with the latter. He too seeks to identify an intelligible structure underlying the apparent chaos of phenomena, and thinks that that structure has to be ascertained by the intellect, rather than directly by observation. He too is interested in the nature of the soul, and stresses its continuity with the rest of the physical world. He shows greater consciousness than the Pythagoreans of epistemological questions, including the relation of theory to observation, and is the first thinker to show an interest in the nature of language and its relation to reality, a set of problems which came to dominate much fifth-century thought, which were central to the thought of Plato, Aristotle and their successors, and which, it is no exaggeration to say, have remained at the centre of philosophical enquiry to the present day.

Undoubtedly the two most significant figures in the thought of the fifth century were Parmenides and Socrates, each of whom not only reshaped his immediate philosophical environment but influenced, indirectly yet decisively, the whole subsequent development of western thought. In his total rejection, not merely of Ionian cosmology, but of the senses as sources of knowledge, Parmenides initiated the conception of a purely a priori investigation of reality, and may thus be said to have begun the debate between empiricism and rationalism which has been central to much subsequent philosophy. More immediately, he challenged those who accepted the reality of the observable world to show how plurality, change, coming-to-be and ceasing-to-be are possible, and the subsequent history of fifth-century cosmology, represented by Empedocles, Anaxagoras and the Atomists, is that of a series of attempts to meet that challenge. Plato's response to Parmenides was more complex. While the fifth-century pluralists sought to defend the reality of the observable world against the challenge of Parmenidean monism, Plato accepted one of Parmenides' fundamental theses, that only the objects of thought, as distinct from perceptible things, are fully real. But rather than drawing the conclusion that the observable world is mere illusion, with the corollary that the language that we apply to that world is mere empty sound, he sought to show how the observable world is an approximation to, or imperfect copy of, the intelligible world, and to develop an appropriate account of language, in which words whose primary application is to the intelligible world apply derivatively to the sensible. An important part of that enterprise was to show how, *contra* Parmenides, it is possible to speak intelligibly of what is not. Holding that strict monism is self-refuting, Plato was committed to positing a plurality of intelligible natures constituting the intelligible world, to describing the structure of that world and to defending that construction against Parmenidean arguments against the possibility of non-being. Some of the central themes of Platonic metaphysics and philosophy of language can thus be seen to have developed at least partially in response to the challenge of Parmenides' logic.

In one way the influence of Socrates on subsequent philosophy is incalculable. Had Socrates not lived, and more particularly had he not died as he did, it is doubtful if Plato would have become a philosopher rather than a statesman, and had Plato not become a philosopher the whole development of Western philosophy would have been unimaginably different. (For a start, Aristotle would not have been trained in the Academy; hence his philosophical development, assuming it to have occurred at all, would have been altogether different, and so on.) Aside from the general influence of his personality on Plato, Socrates' principal contribution to philosophy seems to have been twofold, first in focusing on fundamental questions of conduct, as distinct from physical speculation, and second in applying to those questions a rigorous agumentative method. The effect of the application of this method to that subject-matter was the creation of ethics as a distinct area of philosophy. It would, however, be quite misleading to think of Socrates as having single-handedly given philosophy this new direction,

4

for in concentrating on questions of conduct and treating them with his characteristic method of argument he was responding in part to developments instituted by certain of his contemporaries, known collectively as 'The Sophists'.

The so-called 'Sophistic Movement' was a complex phenomenon. In the fifth century BC the increasing intellectual sophistication, economic prosperity and political development of a number of Greek states, particularly Athens, created a demand for education going beyond the traditional elementary grounding in music and literature (especially poetry), arithmetic and physical training which was all that was then available. To a certain extent this took the form of the popularization of the Ionian tradition of cosmological speculation, which was extended into areas such as history, geography and the origins of civilization. The demand for success in forensic and political oratory, fostered by the increase in participatory democracy which was a feature of political life, especially in Athens, led to the development of specialized techniques of persuasion and argument, associated in particular with the names of Gorgias and Protagoras. Finally, the sophists were associated with a rationalistic and critical attitude to things in general, with implications, unwelcome to those of conservative views, for matters of morality and religion. One feature of this attitude was cultural relativism, leading to a view of moral and religious beliefs as tied to the particular norms of different peoples, with no claim to universal validity. Beliefs of this kind were said to arise purely by convention (*nomos*), and hence to lack the objective authority that was supposed to reside in nature (*phusis*); a typical example of the use of this contrast was the claim (maintained by Callicles in Plato's *Gorgias*) that since by nature the strong prevail over the weak (as can be observed, for example, from the behaviour of animals), that is how things should be, and that conventional rules constraining the aggression of the strong lack any legitimacy. This complex of activities and attitudes was transmitted throughout the Greek world by a new profession, that of itinerant teachers who travelled from city to city lecturing and giving other kinds of instruction to those who were prepared to pay. It was essentially an individualistic activity, an extension to new areas of the older tradition of the itinerant rhapsode (i.e. reciter of poems). The sophists belonged to no organization, nor did they all share a common body of specific belief (though the attitudes mentioned above were sufficiently widespread to be regarded as characteristic of them), and they founded no schools, either in the sense of academic institutions or in that of groups of individuals committed to the promulgation of specific philosophical doctrines.

None of these aspects of the sophists' activity was without some impact on Socrates, according to Plato's portrayal of him. He was at one time deeply interested in physical speculation, though he appears to have abandoned it in favour of concentration on ethical questions. This shift of interest seems to have been motivated by the rationalistic assumption that mechanistic explanations are in general inadequate, since they can provide no account of the reasons for which things happen. For that it is necessary to show how things happen as a rational agent would arrange them, i.e. for the best. An application of that rationalistic assumption is at the heart of Plato's version of Socratic morality. Every rational agent is uniformly motivated to seek what is best, understood in self-interested terms as what is best for the agent; given that constant motivation, understanding of what is in fact for the best is sufficient to guarantee conduct designed to achieve it. But rather than leading to the abandonment of conventional morality, as in the case of some of his sophistic opponents, this rationalism presents Plato's Socrates with the task of showing that adherence to the traditional virtues of courage, self-control, etc. are in fact beneficial to the agent. In so doing Socrates rejects the antithesis between *nomos* and *phusis*; so far from conflicting with the promptings of nature, morality is necessary for humans to achieve what nature (i.e. rational organization) has designed them to seek, namely, what is best for them. As regards techniques of argument, Socrates indeed relied on a technique which was one of those pioneered by the sophists, that of subjection of a hypothesis, proposed by a participant in debate, to critical questioning, with a view to eliciting a contradiction in the set of beliefs held by the proponent of the hypothesis. In this case the difference was not in method, but in aim. Plato consistently represents the sophists as treating argument as a competitive game in which victory was achieved by reducing one's opponent to self-contradiction, whereas Socrates regarded argument as a co-operative enterprise in which the participants are not opponents but partners in the search for truth. Reduction of one's interlocutor to self-contradiction is not the end of the game, as it is for the sophists, but a necessary stage on the path of discovery.

Inevitably, discussion of the role of Socrates in the development of philosophy in the fifth century has merged insensibly into discussion of Plato. This reflects the fact that Plato's earliest writings take the form of imaginative representations of conversations between Socrates and others, which, while remaining faithful to the personality of Socrates and the spirit of his philosophizing, present him as the ideal philosopher. At this stage it is not possible to draw any clear line between doctrines maintained, possibly in inchoate form, by the historical Socrates and those developed by Plato under the stimulus of Socratic argumentation. Gradually Plato develops his independent voice, both in widening the range of his interests from Socrates' concentration on ethics and in articulating his own doctrines, in particular the Theory of Forms (see Chapter 10). The range of Plato's interests is formidable, including virtually all the areas dealt with by his predecessors, as well as areas in which his pioneering ventures set the agenda for future generations. His cosmology in the *Timaeus* blends a basically Pythagorean conception of the organization of the cosmos with a great deal of detail derived from Empedocles and others; his metaphysics, which includes pioneering work in the theory of language and of definition and classification (primarily in the *Sophist* and *Statesman*), is a sustained dialogue with Parmenides (and to a lesser extent Heraclitus) and his ethics is in large part a response to the challenge of the sophists. In many areas the depth and comprehensiveness of his vision takes him beyond his predecessors to make new connections and develop new fields. For instance, taking over from the Pythagoreans and Empedocles the theory of the survival of the soul through a series of embodiments, he applies it not merely in the context of arguments for immortality, but in a novel account of a priori knowledge (in the *Meno*) and of the ability to apply universal concepts (in the *Phaedo*). Again, while in the early dialogues he had followed Socrates in arguing that observance of morality is in accordance with the natural drive towards self-interest, he had provided no convincing argument to show that the social goods promoted by morality always coincide with the individual's own good. In the *Republic* he seeks to bridge that gap by nothing less than the integration of psychology with political theory; the individual personality is itself organized on a social model and its best state consists in a certain form of social organization which mirrors that of the good society. Finally, while the sophists and their younger contemporary Democritus had indeed touched on some of the political implications of ethical questions, it was Plato who, in systematically exploring these connections in a series of major works, not only created political philosophy but in the *Republic* wrote what is still acknowledged to be one of the masterpieces of that subject, and indeed of philosophy as a whole.

That work more than any exhibits the synoptic character of Plato's genius. In addition to the attempted integration of politics and psychology just mentioned, it encompasses virtually all the major areas of philosophy. A well-organized society must be founded on knowledge of what is best for its citizens; hence the dialogue embraces the nature of knowledge and its relation to belief. Knowledge is a grasp of reality, and in particular of the reality of goodness; hence basic metaphysics is included. The account of the training of the rulers to achieve that knowledge constitutes a fundamental treatment of the philosophy of education, literature and art. Some of these topics are explored by Plato in other dialogues, some of which individually excel the *Republic* in their particular fields (see the discussions in Chapters 10–12). No single work, however, better encapsulates Plato's unique contribution to the development of Western philosophy.

CHAPTER 1

The polis and its culture

Robin Osborne

❦

'We love wisdom without becoming soft', Thucydides has the Athenian politician Pericles claim, using the verb *philosophein*.[1] Claims to, and respect for, wisdom in archaic Greece were by no means restricted to those whom the western tradition, building on Aristotle's review of past thinkers in *Metaphysics* Book 1, has effectively canonized as 'philosophers'. This chapter has two functions: to reveal something of the social, economic and political conditions of the world in which Greek philosophy, as we define it, was created; and to indicate some of the ways in which issues which we would classify as 'philosophical', or which have clear philosophical implications, were raised and discussed by those whose work is nowadays classed as 'literature' or 'art' rather than 'philosophy', and thus to put *philosophia* back into the wider context of *sophia* – 'wisdom'.

Discussions of the background to early Greek philosophy frequently stress the intimate link between philosophical and political developments.[2] Part of my aim in this chapter is to make the case for the importance of other factors, and to stress the extent to which self-conscious articulation of ethical, political, epistemological and indeed metaphysical questions precedes the development of large-scale political participation in practice. It is for this reason, as well as because of their subsequent importance as texts universally familiar throughout the Greek world, that the longest section of this chapter is devoted to a detailed discussion of certain themes in the works of Homer and Hesiod. Greek philosophy as we define it is, I argue, simply one remarkable fruit of a cultural sophistication which is the product of the rich contacts between Greece and the world of the eastern Mediterranean and of the somewhat precarious conditions of human life within

9

Greece itself, conditions which demanded both determined independence and access to, and relations with, others.

The Greece of the archaic and classical polis belonged to, and was intimately linked with, a wider eastern and central Mediterranean world. The Minoan and Mycenaean palaces of the late Bronze Age had had strong links with Cyprus and with southern Italy; it is increasingly clear that during the period which we know as the Dark Ages, from c.1100 to c.800 BC, when archaeological evidence suggests that human activity in Greece was restricted to a very small number of sites, those wider contacts were maintained, albeit at a rather low level of intensity. During the eighth century that contact seems to have focused upon the exchange of goods, whether by trade or by what might rather be termed piracy, but during the following centuries Greeks were persistently involved in direct hostilities in the eastern Mediterranean, hostilities which culminated, but by no means ended, with the 'Persian Wars' of the early fifth century. Contact with that wider world played a major part during the eighth and seventh centuries in stimulating many essential features of the culture of the Greek polis, including alphabetic writing and the development of narrative and figurative art; during the period from 600 to 370 BC direct borrowings from the East are more difficult to detect, but the perceived need for self-definition in the face of the 'barbarian' came to be one of the most important factors in shaping the nature and ideology of the Greek city and was an undeniable ingredient in late-sixth and fifth century sensitivity to cultural relativism.

But the Greek polis and its culture were also shaped by conditions that were closely bound up with the lands where Greeks lived, Mediterranean lands which are marginal for the cultivation of some cereals and many vegetable crops, but which also enjoy widely varying ecological conditions within restricted geographical areas. To farm is to run serious risks of crop failure, and the farmer who isolates himself ends by starving himself.[3] These, then, are lands which compel people to move and make contact with others if they are to survive, but they are also lands (and this is particularly true of the Greek mainland itself) in which mountainous terrain renders movement difficult. The political history of Greece is marked by a constant tension between isolation and independence on the one hand – the Greek world as a world made up of hundreds of self-governing cities tiny in area and in population – and a sense of a common identity and dependence on the other – a world where cities are linked for survival, in empires, leagues, and confederacies which are often at war with one another. This tension between independence and common identity also marks the cultural history of Greece.

❧ GREEKS AND THE EAST ❧

Greeks of the late Bronze Age wrote in a syllabary, known as Linear B, the decipherment of which in the 1950s has enormously increased our knowledge of the political and social organization of Mycenaean palace society, of the Mycenaean economy, and of Mycenaean religion. Linear B was, however, a means by which scribes could keep detailed records rather than a means of general, let alone mass, communication. Like all syllabaries it required a large number of separate symbols; with the fall of the palaces the motivation for record-keeping disappeared, and Linear B disappeared with it, although a (different) syllabary is found in use in classical Cyprus. As far as we know, between c.1200 and a little after 800 BC Greeks possessed no means of written communication. Then in the eighth century writing reappears in the Greek world, but now it is alphabetic rather than syllabic and the letters of the alphabet are largely those of the Semitic alphabet used by the Phoenicians. There is no doubt that Greeks borrowed not only the idea but the very means of alphabetic writing from the East. However, the Greek alphabet differs crucially from its eastern Mediterranean model: Greek from the beginning represents vowels, as well as consonants, with full letters. The invention of the vowel made Greek writing both more flexible and more straightforward than Phoenician, but it did not, as is sometimes claimed, mean that there was a different symbol for every different sound; the earliest alphabets do not, for instance, distinguish between long and short vowels. Given this limitation, it is unclear whether representing vowels was a stroke of individual genius on the part of the Greek who first took up the idea of an alphabet, or was simply a happy accident of someone who translated the initial sounds of some Phoenician letter names into Greek vowel sounds.[4]

The distinction between Phoenician and Greek alphabets rests not simply on the representation of vowels, but also on what the alphabet was used for. Many of the earliest examples of writing in Greek are metrical, their purpose more to entertain than to inform. So a graffito on a pottery jug from Athens of c.750 BC declares that jug to be a prize for the person 'who dances most friskily', another, of slightly later date, on a cup found in a grave of the Greek community on Ischia, plays on the epic tradition about Nestor and declares itself to be Nestor's cup, expressing the wish that whoever drinks from it might be visited with desire by the goddess of love, Aphrodite. The frequency with which verse occurs in early Greek writing has led some to suggest that it was the desire to make a permanent record of oral epic poetry that led to the invention of the Greek alphabet.[5] That the script local to Ionia, the homeland of epic poetry, was the earliest to distinguish long and short vowels might be held to suggest that the first Greek scripts needed adaptation to be truly useful for quantitative verse. But in any case it is clear that early Greek uses of writing were not at all limited by Phoenician practice.

Early Greek writing illustrates well the unity and at the same time the diversity of the Greek world. Writing is early attested from a very large number of cities in the Greek world, and always the fundamental character of the alphabet, the representation of vowel sounds, is the same; indeed the use of the Greek alphabet served as one way of defining who was and who was not Greek (Crete is, Cyprus not). But the symbols that were added to the core of twenty-two symbols borrowed directly from Phoenician, and the symbols adopted for particular sounds, differ, showing particular localized groupings. What is more, the purposes to which writing was put varied from area to area: written laws (on which see below) figure prominently in Crete, for example, but not at all in Attica. Greek cities had common interests, but they also had differing priorities and were as little constrained by what neighbours were doing as by what Phoenicians did.[6]

A similar picture can be painted with regard to artistic innovation. That archaic and classical Greek art owed a great deal to the Near East there can be no doubt. One of the skills lost at the end of the Mycenaean era was figurative art. We have little Dark Age sculpture (all we have are small bronzes) and decoration on pottery vessels took the form of geometric decoration, initially dominated by circular motifs against a dark background and then increasingly dominated by rectilinear patterns over the whole surface of the pot. When animal and human figures made their appearance they too took on very geometric shapes. Near-Eastern art of this period had no such devotion to geometric patterns: it was rich in motifs drawn from the natural world. These natural motifs, and with them a much more curvilinear and living approach to the depiction of animal and human figures, came to take the place of the geometric in Greek art, but they were not adopted wholesale and they were adopted in different media and in different places at different times. Purely geometric designs were first supplemented and then largely replaced with motifs drawn from the natural world by the potters of Crete in the second half of the ninth century BC, plausibly under the influence of the Phoenician goldsmiths for whose products and residence on Crete there is some evidence; on the Greek mainland too, at Athens, metalwork showed oriental borrowings, and perhaps oriental presence, by the middle of the eighth century, although it was another fifty years before potters found a use for and took up the possibilities offered by the eastern artists.

With the motifs which Greek artists took up from the East came whole new possibilities for art as a means of communication. The geometric figures of eighth-century pottery from the Greek mainland could very satisfactorily conjure up scenes of a particular type, with many figures involved in identical or similar activities, and were used in particular to conjure up funerary scenes and battle scenes. But the stick figures were not well adapted to telling a particular story or highlighting individual roles in group activities. The richer evocation of natural forms in Near-Eastern art made possible the portrayal of particular stories, stories which can be followed by the viewer even in the absence of guidance from a text. With the adoption of such richer forms the Greek artist took on this possibility of creating a sense of the particular unique combination of circumstances. But again, the Near-Eastern means were not used simply to replicate Near-Eastern narrative techniques, rather the most ambitious of seventh-century Greek artists chose to exploit the fact that invoking a story by pictorial means demands the viewer's interpretative involvement and to juxtapose quite different scenes in ways which challenge the viewer to make, or to resist making, a particular interpretation. Even when we may suspect that particular compositional gambits have been taken over wholesale from Near-Eastern precedents, the application of the gambit to a different story context produces very different effects.

One further, striking, instance of Greek adaptation of ideas from the East deserves mention because of its religious significance. At the end of the seventh century the Greeks began, for the first time, to produce monumental sculpture in stone. There can be no doubt, from analysis of the proportions of these statues, that the ancient tradition that Greek sculptures of standing male figures were based on Egyptian prototypes is correct.[7] But where the Egyptian figures which serve as models are figures of rulers and are clothed in loin cloths, the Greek male figures, known as *kouroi*, are from the beginning naked, and beardless, and stand in no simply representative relationship to any particular man. And from the beginning too, Greeks sculpt figures of (clothed) women (*korai*) as well as men. *Kouroi* and *korai* are primarily found in sanctuaries and although (or perhaps better because) they do not themselves simply represent either the gods or their worshippers, there is little doubt that they came to be a way of thinking about relations between men and gods: the variable scale of these statues (some *kouroi* are monumental, reaching 3, 6, or almost 10 metres in height) drew attention to human inability to determine their own physical bulk; the unvarying appearance of the statues raised issues of human, and divine, mutability; the way their frontal gaze mirrored that of the viewer insistently turned these general questions of the limits of human, and divine, power back on the individual viewer, and, in the case of *korai*, their nubile status and gestures of offering served to query whether exchanges of women and of fruitfulness within human society were images for men's proper relationship with the gods. Such questions about the form of the gods and the ways in which men relate to them are questions which exercised such thinkers as Heraclitus and Xenophanes also. Both *kouroi* and *korai*, in versions of human scale, came to be used also in cemeteries, figuring the life that had been lost, sometimes with epitaphs explicitly inviting the viewer whose gaze met that of the statue to 'stand and mourn', using the mirroring gaze of the statue to emphasize the life shared by viewer and deceased. Conventions which in Egypt translated political power into permanent images of domination were thus adapted in the Greek world to stir up reflection about what people shared with each other and with the gods, and about how people should relate to gods.[8]

This consistent pattern in which Greeks borrow the means from the East but use those means to distinctly different ends, is one that can be seen in the realm of the history of ideas also, where a case can be made for Ionian thinkers taking advantage of the new proximity of the Iranian world with the Persian conquest of Lydia in order to take up ideas and use them in their arguments against each other. Extensive cosmological and cosmogonical writings are known from various peoples in the Near East which can plausibly be held to date from the early first millennium BC or before. The case for taking up eastern ideas is perhaps clearest in the work of Pherecydes of Syros, active in the middle of the sixth century, who wrote a book obscurely entitled 'Seven (or Five) Recesses' (*Heptamukhos* or *Pentemukhos*). His account of creation and of struggles for mastery among the gods, although in some ways in the tradition of Hesiod's *Theogony* (see below), differs crucially in the order of presentation of material and may have been directly indebted to oriental sources.[9] Similar claims have also been made for the Milesian Anaximander whose order of the heavenly bodies, with the stars nearest to the earth, is found in the East but not otherwise in Greece, and whose view of the heavenly bodies as turning on wheels has similarities with the visions of the Old Testament prophet Ezekiel. Pherecydes was individualist in his treatment of traditional stories, Anaximander highly eclectic in any borrowings; such eclectic, individualist, and often directly critical, attitudes towards the ideas of others, other Greeks as well as non-Greeks, is indeed a remarkable feature of the Greek world.[10] But this is not to suggest that transformation in the borrowing is unique to Greeks: it is found too in what later cultures have done with the Greeks themselves. Milton's epics, to take but one example, depend upon the classical epic tradition yet use that tradition to convey a religious and theological world entirely alien to that tradition; so too the cultural achievements of archaic and classical Greece are unthinkable without Near Eastern resources to draw upon, but the different economic, social and political circumstances of the Greek world bring about transformations which result in something entirely different.[11]

This critical assimilation of ideas is only comprehensible against a pattern of extraordinary mobility. It is often unclear from the archaeological record who carried eastern goods to Greece or Greek goods to other parts of the Mediterranean, but that Greeks were themselves frequently on the move, even during the Dark Ages, there can be no doubt. The culture of the Greek polis is not a culture found simply within the boundaries of what is present-day Greece, nor is it limited to those places described by the second century AD traveller Pausanias in his 'Guide to Greece'; it is a culture which grew up as much in communities found on the coasts of Asia Minor, the Black Sea, Italy, Sicily, southern France, Spain and Cyrenaica as in mainland Greece itself. Historians sometimes talk of the 'age of Greek colonization', but the truth of the matter is that Greeks migrated to, and formed or took over settlements in, coastal districts of other parts of the mainland at every period known to us. Greek presence in coastal Asia Minor seems to have been established, or in some places perhaps rather reinforced, during the early Dark Ages, at the same time as other Greeks founded settlements in the northern part of the Aegean. Settlement on the coasts of Sicily and Italy began in the eighth century, the Black Sea and Africa followed in the seventh. Scope for Greek settlement in the eastern Mediterranean was more limited, but there is no doubt that Greek enclaves existed at a number of settlements in the Levant, and the town of Naukratis was set aside for Greeks in Egypt.

Greek settlements abroad generally laid claim not just to a particular 'founder' but also to a particular 'mother city' but models of colonization drawn from the Roman or the modern world are unhelpful for an understanding of what was happening. The population of the new settlements abroad was almost invariably drawn from a number of cities. Movement across the Greek world in the archaic period seems to have been easy: the poet Hesiod tells us that his father moved back from the 'new' Greek world of Asia Minor to mainland Boiotia, craftsmen migrated, temporarily or permanently, from Athens to Corinth, from Corinth to Etruria, and so on. Economic opportunities were one factor causing men to move, local crises, as frequently of a political as of an economic nature, were another. Underpopulation was at least as common a worry for cities as was overpopulation and newcomers were often welcome. Intermarriage with non-Greeks was frequent: the philosopher Thales is said by Herodotus to have had Phoenician ancestry; Pherecydes' father seems to have come from southern Anatolia; the historian Herodotus himself came from Halikarnassos, a mixed Greek and Carian community within the Persian empire; the historian Thucydides' father's line came from Thrace.

15

Sparta, perhaps already in the archaic period, and Athens, from the mid fifth century, were unusual in the way in which they prevented men or women from other Greek cities from acquiring the same rights as, or even marrying, existing members of the community.

➳ HESIOD AND HOMER ➳

Greek literature starts with a bang with the monumental *Theogony* and *Works and Days* of Hesiod and the *Iliad* and *Odyssey* ascribed to 'Homer'. All four works are the products of oral traditions with long histories of which traces remain, but the nature of the oral traditions behind the works of Hesiod is rather less clear than that behind 'Homer', and Hesiod may owe his unique position in part to being able to plug in to both mainland, and, perhaps through his father, Aeolian traditions. That it is these poems that survive to represent the oral traditions may be connected not just to their high quality but to the way in which they gave a pan-Hellenic appeal to what had previously been local traditions, at the moment when the Greek world was significantly expanding its horizons.[12] Hesiod's works are not epic adventure stories but didactic poems aiming directly to teach: morality and practical wisdom in the case of the *Works and Days*, and the structure of the world of the gods in the case of the *Theogony*. Neither of Hesiod's poems has any real successor extant in the corpus of Greek literature or any obvious impact on the imagination of visual artists, but comments and complaints in later writers, both philosophers and others, make it clear that knowledge of his works was widespread and that public views of the gods owed much to them. Herodotus (II.53.1–2) wrote that,

> It was only the day before yesterday, so to speak, that the Greeks came to understand where the gods originated from, whether they all existed always, and what they were like in their visible forms. For Hesiod and Homer, I think, lived not more than four hundred years ago. These are they who composed a theogony for the Greeks, gave epithets to the gods, distinguished their spheres of influence and of activity, and indicated their visible forms.

Hesiod's influence on poets is clearest not in the immediately succeeding period but in Hellenistic times.

The *Works and Days* belongs to the genre of wisdom literature familiar from Near Eastern examples and well represented in the Old Testament. The end of the poem consists of a succession of maxims about what to do, or not do, and when ('Don't piss standing and facing the sun'; 'On the eighth of the month geld the boar and loud-bellowing bull, but hard-working mules on the twelfth'). But the beginning of the poem structures its advice on how to live around a more specific situation, a dispute, whether real or invented, between Hesiod and his brother Perses over sharing out the land inherited from their father. Not only does this introduce us to Hesiod's expectations about dispute settlement – it is clear that local rulers, 'bribe-devouring princes', decide such matters – and about agricultural life,[13] but it gives scope for a mythological explanation of the need for labour in terms of two separate myths, the myth of the 'five ages' and that of Prometheus and Pandora. Through these myths Hesiod ties issues of justice to theological issues, and attempts to make the arbitrary features of the natural world, so manifest in the collection of maxims with which this poem ends, comprehensible within a systematic structure. In doing so Hesiod actually takes over the function of the king as the authority who by his judgements determines what is and what is not right, implicitly raising the issue of how, and by whom, political decisions should be made.[14]

The myth of the five ages (*Works and Days*, lines 109–201) explains both the current state of the world and also the existence of beings between humans and gods. It tells how once the gods made a race of gold, who lived in happiness, plenty and leisure, but when this generation died it was replaced by a race of silver who respected neither each other nor the gods, to whom they did not sacrifice as they should, and were short-lived; these two generations have become two orders of *daimones*. The third generation was a strong race of bronze, smitten with war and destroyed by their own hands, which was replaced by a more just, godlike, race of heroes, including the heroes who fought at Troy, demigods who were taken to dwell in the isles of the blest. After the heroes came the current generation, the race of iron, marked by the disappearance of youth and destined itself for destruction after lives marked by injustice. The interest of this myth lies in the way in which it is not simply a story of decline from a golden age: Hesiod's picture of the race of silver is extremely negative, that of the race of heroes rather more positive. What is more, the neat sequence of metals in order of value is upset by the introduction of the generation of heroes. Hesiod exploits the structures offered by the ageing processes of the natural world and the value-system of exchange of metal to provide a model for a hierarchy of powers between humanity and gods, but at the same time he introduces systematic contrasts between just and unjust behaviour, between good competition and evil strife, which tie this myth into the overall concerns of his poem. He is doing ethics as well as theology.[15]

Hesiod's concern not just with theology but, as it were, with its practical consequences, emerges still more clearly in the myth of Prometheus and Pandora, a myth which he explores not only in *Works and Days* (lines 42–105) but also in the *Theogony* (lines 507–616). In *Works and Days* Hesiod tells how Prometheus (whose name means 'Forethought') stole fire from the gods, hiding it in a fennel stalk, and Zeus in punishment had the other gods fashion Pandora who is given as wife to Prometheus' brother Epimetheus (Afterthought); with her she brings a jar from which comes all the mischief in the world. In the *Theogony* Hesiod tells how when gods and mortals were separated from one another at Mekone Prometheus divided up an ox unequally and tricked Zeus into taking the part consisting merely of fat and bones. In revenge Zeus withholds fire from humanity (so rendering possession of meat useless), but Prometheus then steals fire and Zeus has Pandora, and through her the race of women, made as a punishment (no mention of a jar or of Epimetheus), and Prometheus himself is fastened in torment, his liver perpetually devoured by a bird, until Zeus agrees to have Herakles free him in order to glorify Herakles, his bastard son. Both these stories turn on concealment and trickery: Prometheus makes Zeus take a worthless gift that looks good, and then runs away with a good gift (fire) that looks worthless (a fennel stalk); Zeus makes men take a gift that looks good (woman in her finery) but turns out to be full of trouble.

In the context of the *Works and Days* Hesiod's telling of the myth emphasizes that there are no free gifts in this world and no avoiding hard labour. In the context of the *Theogony* his telling of the myth not only explains Greek sacrificial practice but emphasizes both the parallelism and the divide between humanity and the gods. Human life as we know it depends on women and on the fact that men, like Epimetheus, find them desirable and only think about the consequences later; in that way human life depends on men's 'bad faith' in giving the gods the worthless portion of the sacrifice. At the same time human life as we know it also depends upon sharing all the gifts of the gods, including the fire which makes tricking the gods out of meat worthwhile. The deceitful relationship of humans to gods itself mirrors the deceitful relationship of humans to beasts which is required by arable agriculture, which needs the labour input of oxen but must reduce to a minimum the number of appetites satisfied during the winter, and which is most dramatically demonstrated in feeding up domestic animals for sacrificial slaughter: human life both depends on perpetuating, but also concealing, acts of bad faith to beasts, and suffers from the gods' concealment of good things (the grain concealed in the ground) and from their bad faith (producing irregular fruitfulness in plant and beast).[16]

The use of these myths by Hesiod reveals a concern to find some way of understanding how humanity relates to the world and some reason behind human ritual activities. The course of the mythical narrative assumes that actions are reasonably responded to by like actions, assumes the principle of reciprocity, while recognizing also that bad faith may be ongoing. The place of the myth in the *Works and Days*, in particular, constitutes an argument that recognition of the way reciprocity operates involves a commitment to labour, as well as a commitment to justice. Although never spelt out by Hesiod in those terms, the whole structure of his account of the gods presupposes that justice is a principle respected among gods as well as mortals.

Hesiod generally appears in histories of early Greek philosophy for his cosmogony and cosmology, and indeed the account near the beginning of the *Theogony* (lines 116ff.) of 'Chaos' ('Gap') coming to be first and then Earth, Tartaros (Hell), Eros (Desire), Night and Day, etc. being successively created does seem to represent an important conceptual leap by comparison with Near Eastern cosmologies or indeed with the highly anthropomorphic succession myth which follows in the *Theogony*.[17] I have dwelt here, at some length and in some detail, on rather different aspects of Hesiod's poetry in order to bring out something of the importance of his overall enterprise in the history of Greek thought. Hesiod's poems are not simply rag-bags in which genealogies and maxims are collected, they employ genealogical myths in order to support not just maxims but a set of social priorities.[18] The struggles between successive generations of gods, in the *Theogony*, struggles which have been argued to owe something, perhaps at some rather earlier stage of the oral tradition, to Near Eastern succession myths, are used to put both order and hierarchy into the divine pantheon. The *Works and Days* constitutes an argument that the struggle between Hesiod and Perses should be settled in the light of the principles which emerge from the Prometheus myth. The congruence of human and divine worlds, which is implicit within any anthropomorphic religion, is here being used to establish consequences for human society. This mode of argument, not to be found in the Near Eastern literature, is an important forerunner for some early Ionian philosophy, one might note in particular Anaximander's claim that things in the material world 'pay penalty and retribution to each other for their injustice according to the assessment of time'.

Homer's place in and influence on the culture of the Greek polis is more manifest than that of Hesiod, no doubt in part because the *Iliad* and *Odyssey* had an institutionalized place in the Greek city through their festival performance by rhapsodes. Although neither artists nor dramatists choose, on the whole, to make their works dependent on the details of Homer's texts, the spirit of the Homeric poems comes to pervade classical Athenian art and drama. The extent to which modes of thought and argument characteristic of later philosophical thought, and particularly arguments about ethical and moral values on the one hand and self-conscious analysis of the means of persuasion on the other, are also anticipated in the Homeric poems has, however, frequently been underestimated, and it is to those aspects of the Homeric poems that most attention will be given in what follows.

Much work on Homer during this century has been devoted to exploring the oral tradition out of which *Iliad* and *Odyssey* were created. This work has made it clear, on the one hand, that the techniques and building blocks required to create these monumental poems were forged over a long period. The *Iliad* and *Odyssey* are built upon a skeleton of repeated name–epithet combinations and repeated scenes, which constitute about a third of the poems, which enabled a poet to reconstruct, rather than simply repeat from memory, a poem in performing it. Those repeated phrases and scenes made possible monumental composition, and to some extent shaped the subject-matter, personnel, and the sorts of things said about them; but they did not foreclose on the poet's free choice at any point or determine the order of scenes or development of the narrative. It is likely that many of the stories told in *Iliad* and *Odyssey* were stories that had been told before, but telling them in the particular context in which *Iliad* and *Odyssey* (re)tell them is the decision of the monumental composer(s) responsible for these poems.

As strife is at the centre of *Theogony* and *Works and Days* so also it is at the centre of *Iliad* and *Odyssey*. The *Iliad* relates the quarrel between Achilles and Agamemnon, the commander of the Greek expedition against Troy, over whether Agamemnon had the right to claim a captive girl, Briseis, who had initially been awarded to Achilles, when the girl awarded to himself had been reclaimed by her father. Achilles withdraws his labour from the battlefield in protest at Agamemnon's seizure of the girl, and is deaf to an appeal made to him to rejoin the fray after the Greeks have proceeded to have the worst of it. Finally he agrees to let his companion Patroclus enter battle, wearing his armour, Patroclus is killed by the Trojan champion Hector and Achilles himself re-enters battle to take revenge on Hector whom he kills and mercilessly drags round the walls of Troy. The poem ends with Achilles agreeing to ransom the body of Hector to his aged father Priam who comes alone to the Greek camp for the purpose. The *Odyssey* tells the story of Odysseus' homecoming to Ithaca, with its many violent and remarkable encounters with fabulous creatures, both vicious and virtuous, on the way, and his violent resolution of the struggle for control in Ithaca between his son Telemachus and the suitors assembled to claim the hand of Odysseus' wife Penelope.

The *Iliad* is not the story of a war and its topic is not the sack of Troy. The struggle upon which it focuses is not the struggle between Greeks and Trojans – indeed it has recently been stressed that the *Iliad* does not treat Trojans as barbarians, as a people inferior in nature or morals to the Greeks[19] – but that between Achilles and Agamemnon. This struggle raises issues of authority, allegiance, of conflict between different virtues, and of glory as a zero-sum game: one man's glory is bought at the cost of others' suffering and death. Although scholars have often written as if the *Iliad* simply illustrates the 'heroic code' of behaviour, in fact the struggle between Agamemnon and Achilles is based on a disagreement about ethics and value, and both in the case of the attempts to persuade Achilles to change his mind and in the case of his final agreement to ransom the body of Hector issues of ethics and value are argued about and decisions are made on the basis of changing judgements about them.[20] But the poem is not simply about morality; basic political and theological issues are subject to debate too. In what follows I will indicate briefly some of the major issues that are raised.

The quarrel between Agamemnon and Achilles questions the limits of Agamemnon's authority: Achilles has come to Troy to please Agamemnon and with the promise of honour to be won, and the question is what Agamemnon can do without forfeiting that loyalty, without outweighing the honour with dishonour. Early in the quarrel Achilles raises the question of Agamemnon's own abilities in war, claiming that he never goes out to fight, with the implication that his claims to leadership and booty are thereby compromised: status and office, on this view, are not enough. The aged Nestor responds to this by urging Agamemnon not to pull rank and Achilles to respect Agamemnon's office, on the grounds that their dispute does good only to their enemies, as if office should command authority even if it is unable to assert itself. Nestor himself is heard but ignored. The issue of who has and who speaks with authority is sharply raised again in Book II: when Thersites joins in the attack on Agamemnon, using terms which are generally milder than those employed by Achilles, he is smartly treated to physical punishment by Odysseus, who goes on to call for loyalty not because of who Agamemnon is but because to depart from Troy empty-handed would be to lose face. In Book IX the issue of Agamemnon's authority is once more raised, over his shortcomings as a deviser of counsel revealed in his desire to abandon the expedition: Diomedes questions Agamemnon's authority on the grounds that Agamemnon lacks courage – so turning back on Agamemnon an allegation he had once made about Diomedes – only to have Nestor, once more, intervene with rival advice which he presses on the grounds that his age gives him authority. Nestor goes on to urge that Agamemnon's authority requires that he be prepared to receive as well as give advice.

Exploration of the techniques of persuasion is closely tied into the issue of authority.[21] When, in Book IX, Nestor again urges Agamemnon to placate Achilles he adopts a formal mode of address: 'Most glorious son of Atreus, lord of men Agamemnon, I will finish with you and start from you because you are lord of many men and Zeus has entrusted you with the sceptre and power to decide what is law, in order that you might take counsel for them.' This rhetoric successfully softens the critical sentiments which follow, and makes it possible for Agamemnon to admit that he was wrong. When, as a result, an embassy is sent to Achilles, the opening speech of Odysseus is marked by arguments deployed in a sequence showing consummate skill. He begins by explaining the dire need that the Greeks have of him, and goes on to appeal to Achilles' father's advice to and expectations of his son, and to enumerate the immediate and prospective rewards Achilles will receive if he re-enters battle, including the prospect of political authority back in Greece, before reiterating the appeal to pity the Greeks, this time adding the imminent prospect of killing Hector. Achilles' response is very different in kind, an outpouring whose effect is created not by any carefully reasoned sequence of points but by vivid similes ('I have been like a bird bringing her unfledged nestlings every morsel that she takes, however badly off she is herself'), by urgent rhetorical questions, by the increasingly direct and passionate way in which he reacts to what Odysseus has said, and by the way in which he spells out himself what Odysseus diplomatically left unsaid. The tension between logic and passion, and indeed the impossibility of ethical argument which does not involve both, is brilliantly highlighted by this interchange, and further explored in the exchanges which follow between Achilles and his old tutor, Phoenix.

Gods frequently intervene directly in the course of events throughout the *Iliad*, and issues of the powers and morality of the gods are repeatedly in play. Human characters express the view that the gods support morality, but the debates and decisions on Olympus reveal no such moral imperative; so Menelaus (*Iliad* XIII.620–22) assumes that Zeus will destroy Troy because of Paris's abuse of hospitality, but Zeus shows no awareness of this responsibility in the Council of the Gods in *Iliad* IV. Indeed what debates on Olympus reveal is that divine interests are in conflict and that there is a constant bargaining between gods as to whose interest is to prevail. Disputes among the gods are conducted much as are human disputes, although in the *Iliad* trickery is predominantly a divine attribute. But gods differ from mortals in two important respects: first, among gods there *is* an all powerful figure who can insist that his will be done; Agamemnon may be better than other men (*Iliad* I.281) but Zeus is best (*Iliad* I.581) and when Zeus warns that the consequences of resisting him are terrible (*Iliad* I.563) we know that that means something rather different from when Agamemnon says the same thing (*Iliad* I.325); second, gods are immortal and the divine perspective is longer than the human perspective, so that major events in human life can be seen to be resolved over the longer course of time. Through conflicting divine interests and powerful divine oversight the *Iliad* explores and explains the existence of evil and moral dilemmas.[22]

The struggle at the heart of the *Odyssey* also raises issues of authority and theology, but it raises further issues too upon which I wish to focus here.[23] Plato has Socrates quote the father of his friend Eudicus as saying that 'the *Iliad* is a finer poem than the *Odyssey* by as much as Achilles is a better man than Odysseus' (*Hippias Minor* 363b), and it is Odysseus' cautious, secretive and deceitful behaviour that introduces a whole new set of issues into the *Odyssey*.

The poem traces Odysseus' return from his long enforced residence with the nymph Calypso to his eventual triumph, against all the odds, over the suitors on Ithaca to reclaim his wife and his political control – although we are told of further wanderings to come. The story of how Odysseus came to be stranded with Calypso, which Odysseus tells to the Phaeacians with whom he is next washed up, the stories of the homecomings of other Greek heroes told in the course of the epic, and the episode of the slaughter of the suitors are all strongly moral: in every case before disaster strikes warnings are given about the consequences of behaviour which breaks the rules. Although magic plays a larger part in this poem than in the *Iliad*, it is the logic of morality rather than any supernatural force or arbitrary intervention of the gods that governs events. Even Odysseus brings disaster upon himself and his companions by ignoring wise advice or by arrogant behaviour – as in the foolish bravado which reveals his identity to the Cyclops when he mocks him as he departs. By the end of the poem Odysseus himself is generally more circumspect, but he retains a tendency to be so excessively cautious about revealing more than he has to that, as his failure to reveal what was in the bag of winds led his companions to ruin by opening it, so his reluctance to reveal his identity to his own father Laertes leads to Laertes' unnecessary grief. Reticence as well as rashness can be a fault, and getting it right in every circumstance demands powers of foresight which are greater than even Odysseus' accumulated experience of human feelings and motives can supply.

Odysseus' deception of others, as he spins false tales of his identity to all he meets, not only raises moral issues, it also raises issues about language and representation. Odysseus' briefest deceptive tale is also the most famous: his claim to the Cyclops Polyphemos that 'No One is my name; my mother and father and all other companions call me No One' (IX.366–7), a claim which leads Polyphemos to tell the other Cyclopes that 'No One is killing me'. There are two jokes here, not just one, for according to the rules of Greek syntax 'No One' appears in two forms, *Ou tis* and *Mē tis*, and the latter form is indistinguishable from the word *mētis*, meaning 'guile' or 'deceit' (as also in the repeated phrase *Polymētis Odysseus*, 'Odysseus of the many wiles'). This brief demonstration of the way in which to name is to tell or imply a story, and not simply to refer to some object, of the way in which the name is 'inscribed in the network of differences which makes up social discourse'[24] paves the way to the repeated deceptive tales of the second half of the *Odyssey*.

Six times in the second half of the *Odyssey* Odysseus spins long false tales about his past, in all but the last to Laertes claiming to be a Cretan. These tales, which are closely akin to the tales told of their own past by such figures as Eumaios and Theoclymenos, themselves tell of acts of deception. They draw from those who hear them concrete reactions, reactions which reveal the qualities of listener (as Penelope's deceitful tale to Odysseus about their bed is what draws Odysseus to reveal himself), and also concrete actions (Odysseus gets a cloak out of Eumaios for one of his tales, having failed to get the promise of one out of an earlier tale). But they also reveal Odysseus himself: the tales are not merely 'like the truth' (XIX.203), they are telling about Odysseus, literally (the fictive characters he claims to be claim various things about Odysseus), in the sense that the fictive characters do resemble Odysseus, and in the sense that part of what it is to be Odysseus is to be a teller of tales. But Odysseus' fictions do something still more dramatic: they raise the question of how we distinguish truth and falsehood. If Odysseus' tales in the second half of the *Odyssey* are deceptive, how can we be sure that the tale he tells in Phaeacia, the tale of his wanderings, of Circe, the Cyclops, Calypso and the rest, is not also partly or wholly deceptive? In raising this question, the boundary between fact and fiction, and the role which fiction, including works such as the *Odyssey* itself, plays, are themselves opened up for scrutiny. It is impossible to read the *Odyssey* without having your attention drawn to the way in which people create themselves by creating their own past, by telling their own story, and without appreciating the power which stories about the past have to determine action in the present. It is perhaps not surprising that while it is hard to find a Greek before Alexander the Great who had a life-story modelled on Achilles, many politicians, perhaps most notably Themistocles, seem to have had one modelled on Odysseus.

To grow up with Hesiod and Homer, as the children of the Greek polis did from the seventh century onwards, was to grow up familiar, among other things, with moral dilemmas, with questions of how political authority is earned and jeopardized, with issues of the relationship between individual and group, with sensitivity to the theological basis for human action, and with an awareness of the tricky way in which language creates people and events even as it represents them. Although in their course these poems tell many 'myths', it is not as a repository of myths that they made their mark on later generations, but as introductions to modes of thought and of argument, and to the ways in which language represents issues. Such discussions of what sort of life a person should lead continue to dominate Greek poetry (and drama) from Homer and Hesiod onwards, in a culture where the poet both aspired to, and was expected to, offer moral instruction.[25]

RELIGION: RITUALS, FESTIVALS AND IMAGES OF THE GODS

Concentration on the Homeric poems as exemplary explorations of moral, ethical and rhetorical problems can make it seem as if moral and ethical issues arose only out of struggles for power. As we will see, struggles for political power were indeed important in the archaic city, but it would be wrong to imagine the political to be the only context for debate. To grow up in the Greek city was to grow up in a world where life was shaped from the beginning by rituals, rituals in which encountering the gods was regular and important. The entry for the year 776 BC in Eusebius' *Chronology* notes both that this was the year of the first Olympiad and that, 'From this time Greek history is believed accurate in the matter of chronology. For before this, as anyone can see, they hand down various opinions.' That the history of the Greek city should be deemed to be reliable from the time of the first Olympic games is highly appropriate, for it was indeed festal events which gave cultured regularity to the natural seasons of the year, and festal events even claimed priority over the irregular events of war and politics; wars between Greek cities respected truces for the Olympic games, meetings of the Athenian citizen body avoided festival days. Cities and groups within cities produced and displayed calendars of their ritual activities, and the conflicting claims of traditional piety and of economy might give scope for political argument.

Greek religious life was markedly communal.[26] The sacrifice of an animal to a god was not a solitary action, but involved – created, reflected, and defined – a group, the group of those who shared the meat. Processions, and every act of sacrifice involved at least a minimal procession, displayed the sacrificing group. In many cities the markers of growing up were ceremonies at festivals at which the young person was formally enrolled in the celebrating group. Competitions, which honoured the god for whom the festival was held by displaying the best of physical or mental prowess, as often glorified the group to which the winner belonged (his city if the victory was pan-Hellenic, his tribe in an event limited to local competitors) as the individual himself. In its festival life a city displayed itself and its divisions and citizens observed their own social as well as political place in it. It is not by chance that for many cities the surviving records are dominated by sacred laws and other records to do with sanctuaries and their running of festivals.

Festivals displayed the city at leisure, however. It was not just that to compete in pan-Hellenic competitions at Olympia demanded the leisure to spare the compulsory thirty days before the event when all had to be at the site training; the competitive events, in local as well as pan-Hellenic festivals, although large in number and wide in variety, all involved achievements of little direct practical value: chariot-racing, running, physical beauty, singing and dancing, etc. There were indeed beneficial consequences of an indirect sort from such events, and even more obviously from such things as armed dancing, but neither craft skills nor mainstream fighting skills were ever displayed or tested: the drinking competition at the Athenian Anthesteria, for instance, was about speed of consumption, not quality of production. At the Olympic games victory brought honour but no tangible rewards beyond an olive wreath, but in other places there might be considerable profits to be had from victory, or even from coming second or third in an event. And the home city might add to the honours both marks of respect (Spartan Olympic victors fought next to the king in war) and further material rewards, in particular free meals.[27] These rewards constituted a recognition that there was more to the city than the practical skills that directly sustained it.

If their festivals dominated the calendar of the city, their temples, which housed the gods and the dedications which they attracted, dominated its buildings and often, given prominent placing on an acropolis, its skyline. In a city such as Sparta, which did not go in for monumental buildings for public business, it is the temples in and around the town which dominate the archaeological record. Cities devoted enormous resources of money and energy to temples and to the cult statues which they housed, and competition between cities is visible in the competing dimensions of temples (the Athenian Parthenon just outdoes the temple of Zeus at Olympia, for instance). Unlike festivals, temples were permanent; when the glorious processions or elaborate dramas were gone the temples remained as symbols of the devotion of resources to the gods. But not just the temples. Sanctuaries also accumulated dedications, many of them humble but others precious gold and silver plate, marble and bronze statues. Victors, and this is particularly a mark of the classical city, dedicated sculptures of athletes either at the sanctuary which was the scene of their victory, as with Gelon's monument at Delphi, known as the Delphic Charioteer, or in their home city.

It is easy to make Greek religious activities seem essentially political, contrived to enable elite groups to show off to each other and to those effectively subject to them their wealth and the prowess acquired in leisure. Festivals, on this view, sugared the pill of elite political domination by promoting solidarity through their processions, by inducing feelings of well-being through their pomp, and by rewarding attendance through nourishing with a meat meal those who gathered. But there was another side. Modern sensibilities may find it hard to see scope for religious feeling in the ritual cutting of a domestic animal's throat, but the symbolic importance of this slaughter in an agrarian economy, where animal labour is vital but where draught animals threaten to eat up all too much of the harvest, is considerable, and the combination of elaborate ritual with the smell of fresh blood is likely to have made this a memorable and evocative sensory experience.[28] More accessible to us, perhaps, is the other side of cult activity, the confrontation with the god involved in viewing the cult statue. Cult statues, and this is true of statues such as the Herms (pillars with stump arms, erect phalluses and heads of the god Hermes) found in places other than temples as well as of statues in temples, regularly stare straight forward towards viewer/worshipper, and some temples certainly used external sculpture or other devices to enhance the revelation of the god. So, at Lykosoura in Arcadia, Pausanias tells us that as you come out of the temple of Despoina and Demeter 'there is a mirror fitted to the wall; when you look into this mirror you see yourself very dimly or not at all, but you have a clear view of the goddesses and their throne' (VIII.37.7).[29] This stress on revelation is something which seems to have been further developed in certain 'mystery' cults into which, unlike normal sacrificial cult, specific initiation was required, though what was revealed seems not normally to have been images of the deity. Without awareness of this intensity of religious experience, the theological speculations of Empedocles or of the Pythagoreans (see Chapters 4, 5) can only seem inexplicably eccentric.

It is likely that animal sacrifice was a feature of cult in the Greek world from an early date, but the presentation of the god in sculptural form developed, along with the canonical schemes of Greek temple architecture, during the archaic period. Clay figurines that may have functioned as cult statues in Crete are known from the Dark Ages, and from the eighth century the Cretan site of Dreros has yielded some hammered bronze statues that may have been cult images. But the nature of the divine presence in the temple changed markedly with the development of monumental stone sculpture in the late seventh and the sixth centuries, and the gold and ivory excesses of the Athenian Parthenon and the temple of Zeus at Olympia took yet further advantage of the overpowering force of large-scale sculpture. Even more liable to change were the dedications with which the gods and their temples were surrounded: the nature of dedications in any single sanctuary changes over time (so at Olympia dedications of animal figurines are extremely common during the eighth century but decrease dramatically in number in the seventh century), and one sanctuary differs from another even within the confines of the same city.[30] Certain differences in dedicatory assemblage seem determined by the identity and interests of the deity involved, but it is clear that even within a polytheistic system there was no neat compartmentalization of interests restricting the invocation of specific deities to specific areas of life. Not that the influence of political factors can be ruled out, even here: that 'exclusive' Sparta has many dedications at the sanctuary of Artemis Orthia that are influenced by oriental products but few actual oriental dedications seems more than coincidental.

❧ POLITICS, CONSTITUTIONS, LAWS: ❧ THE CONSEQUENCES OF LITERACY?

It is exclusive Sparta that provides some of our earliest detailed data about constitutional arrangements. In the world of Homer and Hesiod the basis for the power of particular rulers may be disputed and the way they carry out their rule despised but there is no sign that there are formal rules within which they operate. Beginning from the seventh century, however, there is epigraphic and literary evidence for quite widespread concern to define and limit the role of those in authority.[31] The Spartan evidence is literary: Plutarch quotes, almost certainly from Aristotle's work *The Constitution of the Lakedaimonians*, an enactment known as the Great Rhetra which, having referred rather obscurely to two subdivisions of the citizen body, tribes and obes, enjoins that the Kings and Council of Elders are to hold a regular assembly at a specified site and that the people in the assembly should have the right to speak and to decide to do or not to do things; crooked decisions by the people, however, may be laid aside by the kings and elders. The antiquity of this enactment seems guaranteed because the seventh-century poet Tyrtaeus paraphrases it in an elegy also quoted by Plutarch. The precise circumstances in which these rules were formulated are irrecoverable, as is the manner in which they were preserved in a city which later prided itself on not writing down laws, but despite this uncertainty the Great Rhetra is of central importance because of its concern with the authority of offices and the role it grants the people as a whole.

A similar concern with defining the authority of named office holders appears on laws preserved on stone from other parts of the Greek world in the seventh century. At Dreros, in Crete, a single enactment was passed stipulating that when a man had held the (annual) office of *kosmos* he could not hold it again for ten years, and that if he did arrogate to himself the judicial powers of the *kosmos* after the end of his term of office then he should be punished with a double fine, loss of the right to hold office again, and the invalidation of his actions. At Tiryns in the Argolid recently discovered fragments of a series of injunctions reveal a whole network of officials: *platiwoinoi*, who are perhaps pourers of libations of wine, *platiwoinarchoi*, the officials in charge of the *platiwoinoi*, a *hieromnemon* or sacred remembrancer, who is a man with powers to impose fines and not just a repository of traditional knowledge, a popular court and an *epignomon*, who has authority to order the whole people about.[32]

Without the onset of literacy we would not have all this evidence about detailed legal arrangements. But was literacy actually a factor in enabling law to happen in the first place? It has certainly been suggested in the past that literacy encourages, if it does not require, certain intellectual operations which an oral culture manages to do without: logical deduction and exercises in classification, it is claimed, feed upon, if they do not rely upon, written lists, and writing allows more thorough analysis of the modes of communication.[33] The ancients themselves certainly thought that writing, and in particular the writing down of law, made a difference. Euripides has Theseus in the *Suppliant Women* (lines 433–4) say, 'When the laws have been written down, both the weak and the rich have equal justice', a view echoed by Aristotle. No one would argue for widespread ability either to write or to read in archaic Greece, so how plausible are these views that the *existence* of writing changed how people thought or how they interacted with each other? Whether or not one believes that the Homeric poems, which only once refer to writing (*Iliad* VI.168–9), were themselves written down shortly after 700 BC, they reveal that the oral culture in which they were created was distinctly capable of analysing techniques of communication and making play with subtle variations in wording. Equally, it is clear that law did not have to be written to be fixed: 'remembrancers', who continue to exist even when law is written, seem to have been charged with the precise recall of enactments, and references to early law being sung suggest that music was one means by which precision of memory was ensured. Nor does the fixing of law at all guarantee 'equal justice', for, as the procedural emphasis of so much early written law itself emphasizes, power remains with the interpreters of the law.[34] What writing does enable is communication *at a distance*, something with considerable consequences for the general dissemination of information. Even once writing was available, much that might have been written down continued to be unwritten, and it is not clear that communications which were of their nature dependent upon writing developed before the invention of the architectural treatise, giving the precise 'rules' according to which a particular building was created, in the sixth century BC

There might be a stronger case for believing that law codes, rather than simply law itself, were literacy dependent, but although later tradition talks of early lawgivers inventing whole codes of laws for cities, the earliest laws look to have been single enactments brought in to deal with particular problems. And it is significant that while the disputes to be settled in *Iliad* XVIII, where Achilles' new shield's scene of city life includes a dispute being settled, and in Hesiod's *Works and Days* are personal, disputes over property and homicide, these early laws are dominated by broadly 'constitutional' issues.

Other evidence too suggests that political arrangements were very much under discussion in the seventh century, and that the question of the authority of particular offices and officials was a crucial one. The situation which is imagined in the Dreros law, that a magistrate takes advantage of the possibilities for popular support which an office with a judicial role offers in order to ignore the time limit set upon the holding of that office, is precisely the situation which one late source alleges enabled Cypselos to become tyrant in Corinth: he gained popular support by the way in which he settled the cases which came to him as polemarch and then refused to hand on the office. Such seizures of power by individuals are a mark of the archaic period in the Greek cities, but tyrants were not at all restricted to the archaic period; they can be found, and not just in Sicily, throughout the classical period. Greek tyrants were not necessarily despotic, though most later accumulated some tales about a 'reign of terror', and they did not necessarily take all powers into their own hands, many simply overseeing the continued functioning of the existing constitution but controlling access to and the execution of magistracies.[35]

It was not simply magisterial authority which gave the opportunity to the ambitious individual to seize power. Disputes between groups within a city might equally give an individual a chance to insert himself as a person who could bring stability. At Athens factional disputes, fuelled by popular discontent with the unequal distribution of resources, not only produced an attempted *coup* in the late seventh century, when an Olympic victor endeavoured to cash in that glory for political power, but led in the first decade of the sixth century to the granting of extraordinary powers to one man, Solon, to reform the laws and the constitution. So much is later falsely ascribed to Solon that it is unclear what exactly the limits of his legal reforms were, but there is no reason to doubt that he not only took a stand on major social and economic issues such as debt-bondage, but also reformed legal procedure to make recourse to law more practical, and regulated all aspects of citizens' lives, including agricultural practice, verbal abuse, testamentary disposition, and funerals. Although even in the case of Solon it is probably an exaggeration to talk of a 'law code', he seems to have attempted to deal with sources of discontent over a very wide range. Without success. Within a few years one magistrate had attempted to keep his powers beyond their allotted span, and within half a century protracted factional disputes gave an opportunity for Peisistratos, backed by mercenary troops, to establish himself as tyrant.

Possession of overriding power by a particular individual was rarely popular with all, and much of the continued foundation of settlements elsewhere by Greeks should probably be seen as prompted by dissatisfaction with the regime in the home city, if it was not occasioned by actual expulsion of a group. Two episodes of colonization by Sparta, the colonization of Taras in south Italy c.700 and the two attempts to found a city by Dorieus at the end of the sixth century, are traditionally held to belong to these categories. Taras was founded by a group called the Partheniai whom the Spartans had expelled; Dorieus went off to colonize of his own accord to get away from his half-brother Cleomenes when the latter succeeded to the throne.

Although one early tyrant, Pheidon of Argos, was later associated with military reform, most tyrants seem to have left war on one side, not seeking to create empires for themselves, and to have devoted more time and resources to the buildings and institutions of the city. It was indeed during the period of the Cypselids at Corinth that Corinth acquired one of the earliest Doric temples and that Corinthian pottery became most elaborate in design and reached its widest market. But the outstanding example of the tyrant who monumentalized his city is Polycrates of Samos who was reputedly responsible for a massive mole protecting the harbour, a great tunnel more than a kilometre long dug nderneath a mountain, and an enormous temple, never completed, measuring 55 by 112 metres. Other tyrants concentrated on enterprises which more directly involved the citizens as a whole. Cleisthenes of Sikyon insisted on altering the whole internal organization of the citizen body, thereby breaking up traditional groupings and destroying old associations. The Peisistratids in Athens devoted considerable resources to the development of civic festivals, being particularly concerned with putting the performance of the Homeric poems at the Panathenaic festival in order, inviting poets from other Greek cities to their court, and perhaps developing dramatic festivities at the festival of the Great Dionysia.[36]

Individual cities, once they had removed their tyrants, tended to remember them as repressive, perhaps in part to cover the truth about widespread collaboration with a regime no longer regarded as politically correct.[37] But one of those subject to the nastiest tales, Periander son of Cypselos and tyrant of Corinth, came, along with certain men now regarded as philosophers and such mediator figures as Solon, to be regarded as a 'sage' and found his way on to a list of 'seven sages' (in fact seventeen men figure on some list or other of seven sages in antiquity). A variety of anecdotes accumulated around these figures, but the source of their reputation for wisdom seems to lie with their poetic compositions (even Periander is said to have written a didactic poem of some 2,000 lines), their reputation for political astuteness (Thales is said to have advised the Milesians not to ally themselves with Croesus the king of Lydia), and their prominence as performers of effective practical gestures (Bias of Priene got good terms for his city from Alyattes of Lydia by producing fat donkeys and sand heaps covered in grain to suggest enormous prosperity).[38] The probable falsity of most of the stories, and indeed the quasi-fictional nature of some of the sages themselves, is unimportant: what these stories show is the particular characterization of worldly wisdom in the culture of the Greek polis. In many of the stories, the sage does not himself say anything but simply points to the relevance of an everyday scene: in a single transferable anecdote one tyrant is said to have advised another on how to control his city by walking into a cornfield and slashing off the ears of those stalks of grain that grew taller than the rest. It is the ability to take advantage of ambiguity and deceptive appearance and to see the parallelism between disparate situations that marks out the wise man.

The admiration for the 'practical joker' embodied in Homer's image of Odysseus and in the tradition of the seven sages is a central feature of that characteristic aristocratic form of association, the symposium. From the classical period we have selective descriptions of symposia from both Xenophon and Plato but our knowledge of the archaic symposium is largely dependent on the literature and pottery produced for it.[39] It was a setting for performance both formal and extemporized (where song passed round the circle of guests and each was expected to cap the previous singer's lines), accompanied by the *aulos*. A favourite ploy of the singer is to imagine himself as a character, not necessarily male, in a particular situation which has some analogical relevance to the actual situation; the listeners are invited to see their environment as if it were another, and so to see it with new eyes. Much sympotic poetry is explicitly political, with storms and shipwrecks

32

proving images as appropriate to turmoil within the city as to inebriation, much also is personal and concerned in particular with the life of love, and much is self-reflexive. The personal side dominated the games of the symposium, such as the game of *kottabos* in which the last drops of wine were flung from the flat cup and aimed at or dedicated to one's lover, and that side is most evident in sympotic pottery. Sympotic pottery reflects the symposium both directly, with images of reclined symposiasts, singers at the symposium, and so on, and also indirectly: it is full of jokes. There are explicitly joke vases, vases with hidden compartments which enable them to be filled as if by magic, dribble vases, and so on. Many cups have eyes painted on them, but some take the analogy with the body further, replacing the standard round foot, which the drinker grips to raise the cup for drinking, by male genitalia. The images on the vases take the jokes further, extending the sea imagery of the poetry by having ships or sea creatures swimming on the wine, concealing images of inebriation at the bottom of the cup, or exploring the limits of acceptable sympotic behaviour by representing satyrs behaving unacceptably.

The cultural importance of the symposium lies in part in the context which it provided for poetic and artistic creativity: almost all surviving archaic elegaic poetry, including the poetry of the 'philosopher' Xenophanes, was written for the symposium; and whether or not directly made for use at symposia, the imagery of much archaic Athenian pottery presupposes and exploits the sympotic context. But the symposium is important too for the way in which it provided a microcosm of the city itself in which the issues of city life were explored in an intensely self-critical milieu. Drinking at the symposium was strictly regulated by rule and convention, political positions were explored, personal relations were exposed and the boundary between private and public behaviour both tested and patrolled. As there was no room for inhibitions, so also there was no room for pomposity. Dominated by the elite, and often closely linked with official or religious events, the symposium was nevertheless always oppositional, a forum for disagreement rather than laudation. In the symposium the competitive ethos encouraged in religious festivals was internalized and intellectualized.

❧ MYTHOLOGY: INVENTION, ❧ MANIPULATION

The world of sympotic poetry is largely the present world of everyday experience; the world of epic and of temple sculpture is a world of the mythological past; archaic painted pottery shares in each of these worlds, and also in the timeless world of the fantastic. The observed world of shipwrecks, of political struggles, and of wolves surrounded by hunting dogs, and the fabulous world inhabited by centaurs and the heroes of epic tales, are taken up by writers and artists of the archaic age as equally good to think with. Solon finds an image for his own political stance in the battlefield: 'I threw a strong shield around both parties and did not allow either unjustly to get the upper hand' (fr. 5 West); Sappho finds an image for the power of desire in Helen's desertion of Menelaus (fr. 27 Diehl);[40] Pindar repeatedly invokes the world of myth to promote thinking about the glorious achievements of the athletes whom his victory odes celebrate. What is notable is that the immediate past, what we would call 'history', has little or no exemplary role in archaic Greek art or literature.

The distinction between 'myth' and 'history' with which we operate is not a distinction made by any Greek writer before the late fifth century.[41] The terms which come, in the hands of Thucydides, Plato and others, to stand for the opposing poles of 'myth' and 'reason', *muthos* and *logos*, are used virtually interchangeably by earlier writers. Even Herodotus, 'the father of history', writing in the 430s or 420s BC happily regards Homer, Hesiod, and the Trojan War as having the same status. This is important not because it shows how 'unsophisticated' even fifth-century Greeks continued to be, but because it reveals that despite the possibilities of written records, the past had not yet become something fixed. Pindar's First Olympian Ode, with its explicit rejection of one version of the story of Pelops for another less gruesome one, shows that different 'versions' of the 'same' myth coexisted; and so too different versions of the past. Herodotus' *Histories* are distinguished from most later histories in the ancient world (as well as from what most modern historians write) by their willingness to give more than one version of a past event – we have the Theran and the Cyrenaean version of the colonization of Cyrene from Thera – and by Herodotus' declared indifference to the truth of the versions he relates: 'It is my duty to record what is said, but not my duty to give it complete credence' (VII.152.3). Aristotle calls Herodotus a 'mythologist', a teller of exemplary tales (*On the Generation of Animals* 756b6).

Many subsequent readers of Herodotus have found his apparent indifference to the truth of the stories which he repeats incomprehensible or even scandalous. In doing so they have followed the lead given by Thucydides who points to the lack of *muthos* in his account of the war between Athens and Sparta, which dominated the last thirty years of the fifth century, and claims that his carefully researched account of what actually happened will be a surer guide to the future than the 'easier listening' which traditional story-telling produced.[42] The invention of 'mythology' and the invention of 'history' went together,

together with each other but also together with the invention of the category of metaphor and the scientific and philosophical revolution which that entailed.[43] They also went together with a new attitude towards stories detectable in both art and literature: in art, where previously it had been the general story that had been evoked, particular texts are now illustrated; in literature, explorations of the dilemmas of myth characteristic of tragedy go out of fashion and in Hellenistic poetry (very little poetry survives from between 390 and 330) myths are now told in ways which draw attention to the art of the teller and play with a reader who is assumed to be learned enough to detect and respond to copious allusions to earlier literature.

The separation of 'myth' from 'history' and the insistence that 'metaphor' has a distinct status can both be seen as part of a move to be more precise about the status of comparisons by directing attention at the effect of context. The issues of truth and falsehood, already explored in the *Odyssey* and enthusiastically taken up by the sophists as part of their interest in rhetoric, are now relentlessly pursued in the course of an attempt to find the undeceptive 'truth', and not merely to be aware of the ever deceptive nature of words and images. But it is tempting to see the creation of mythology as political, too.

Herodotus begins his work by stating that his aim is to ensure that past events do not grow faint, to record the great achievements of Greek and barbarian, and in particular to explain how they came to fight each other. Herodotus treats the conflict between Greeks and Persians broadly, not concentrating simply on the actual battles of 490 and 480–79 BC, but taking every opportunity to delve back into the past history of the Greek cities. He ends his work, however, at the end of the Persian invasion of the Greek mainland, at a point when armed conflict between Greeks and Persians to remove the Persians from the Aegean and Asia Minor had many years still to run, years during which he himself had been alive and with whose story he must himself have been particularly familiar. By ending in 479 BC Herodotus limited himself to that part of the conflict between Greece and Persia when Greece could be presented as pursuing a broadly united course of action; from the point at which he stops the Athenians took over the leadership of the campaign, to increasingly divided reactions among other cities, and, within relatively few years, turned the pan-Hellenic 'crusade' into what was, they admitted, blatant imperial rule.

The Persian wars, and the imperialism which they brought in their wake, changed history. This is most graphically illustrated by the contrasting role which stories of the past play in Herodotus and Thucydides. Characters in Herodotus do, from time to time at least, invoke examples from the past in order to influence present action, but they do so in a way which is only in the broadest sense political. So,

Socles the Corinthian tries to discourage the Spartans from restoring tyranny to Athens by telling of the increasingly terrifying rule of the Cypselids at Corinth (Herodotus V.92): any story will do, it is the aptness of the analogy that matters, not the particular example chosen. When characters in Thucydides invoke the past it is in order to justify a present claim or excuse a past blemish, in order to determine others' attitudes to themselves in the present, and the failures of the past are visited upon the present. So the Plataeans, when they succumb to the Spartan siege, are asked at their trial what good they have done Sparta in the past, and when they cannot come up with anything are executed: any story won't do, it is what (you can convince others) actually happened that matters.

In the archaic world of the independent city-state it was possible to live in the present. Reputations were established, friends and political power won and lost. Appeal might be made to the achievements of ancestors, and the misdeeds of ancestors used against current opponents, but few owed their current position entirely to parading past actions. Cities threatened by their neighbours tended to come to battle once a generation, and when peace was made it was for an equally short term. Persia's intervention in Greek affairs changed that. The resistance to Persian invasion showed that uniting the military resources of many cities could give previously unimagined power; the continued threat of Persian return, reinforced by the determined 'barbarization' of the Persians, especially on the stage (another trend which Herodotus equally determinedly resists), prevented cities from opting out of collective action against Persia for long enough to enable the Athenians to transform the earlier voluntary union into their own empire. Sparta too, who in the sixth century had built up her Peloponnesian League by treaties of mutual advantage, found herself in the twenty years after the Persian invasion repeatedly at war with her allies; for them too independence was no option. Unlike individuals' histories, those of cities lasted more than a generation; what actually happened, whose citizen actually betrayed the mountain path to the Persians (cf. Herodotus VII.213–14), now mattered. Where previously different people might happily tell different versions of the same events – the Therans telling one version of the colonization of Cyrene in order to keep their claims to a stake in the colony alive, the Cyrenaeans telling another to reinforce their own independence and their monarchy (Herodotus IV.150–6)[44] – now, getting your version accepted as true was likely to be of considerable political importance. Herodotean history focused on how Greeks constructed themselves and others through the stories they told; that sort of history of events after 479 BC was impossible, and Thucydides' insistence that there was a single true version was inevitable in an Athenian. Not surprisingly, it is the Athenian version of events after 479 BC that Thucydides gives.

The role which the essentially transferable story about the past plays in Herodotus came to be left to the now distinct world of 'myth' and to be at the centre of tragic drama, not prose histories.[45] Aeschylus did write about the historical battle of Salamis in his *Persians*, and got away with it, but even before that Phrynichus, attempting to replay the Persian capture of Miletus on stage, was fined for 'recalling to the Athenians their own misfortunes' (Herodotus VI.21). Otherwise fifth-century tragedy exploits a rather limited selection of myths, myths predominantly centred not on Athens but on other cities, and particularly on Thebes. Political issues are aired in these plays in generalized terms and specific items of domestic or foreign policy are rarely alluded to (scholars debate the extent to which Aeschylus' *Eumenides* is an exception to this rule). Although tragedy avoids replaying Homeric stories, its explorations of clash between individual and group, of religious duty and political expediency, of deceptive means to worthwhile ends, and of representation, blindness, and the problems of communication, are very much extensions of the Homeric task.[46] Tragedy takes further the self-analysis present already in the Homeric poems, with extensive exploration of the way in which people are persuaded and of the power and problems of linguistic communication. Like the Homeric poems, tragedy was for a mass audience in a festival context, as thousands of Athenians sat through three days of tragic drama, each day featuring three tragedies and a satyr play by a single playwright, possibly followed by a comedy – some eight hours or more of performance. Even once divorced from 'history' it was myth that continued to dominate the cultural life of the polis.

❧ POLITICAL AND CULTURAL ❧ IMPERIALISM

Both Athens and Sparta engaged in imperialistic activities in the wake of the Persian Wars, so creating the possibility of what Thucydides, with some justification, regarded as the greatest war ever to have engulfed the Greek world, the long struggle which eventually reduced Athens, if only briefly, to being tied to Spartan foreign policy, no stronger than any other Greek city. But it was Athens, not Sparta nor any other Greek city, which was the home of Thucydides, of the great tragedians Aeschylus, Sophocles and Euripides, of Socrates and of Plato. Although a leading centre of the visual arts in the sixth century, Athens can boast only one significant literary figure before the fifth century – Solon. I have suggested above that we should not neglect the importance of the Persian Wars in changing the way in which cities related one to another and changing how cities related to their own past, but the Persian invasions and their consequences will not of themselves explain the way in which Athens became the cultural centre of the Greek world, both attracting leading intellectuals from elsewhere – men like Anaxagoras or Protagoras in the fifth century, Aristotle and Theophrastus in the fourth – and also herself nurturing innovative thinkers.

Contemporary observers had little doubt about the secret of Athenian success: Herodotus (V.78) observes that the military transformation of Athens which followed the expulsion of the tyrant Hippias in 510 demonstrates what an important thing it is that people should have an equal say in the running of their city. The Athenians themselves turned the annual ceremony to mark those who had died in war into the occasion for a heavily stylized speech in praise of Athenian democracy and liberty, attributing Athenian foreign policy successes and cultural hegemony alike to her constitution.[47] 'Democracy' currently carries with it a self-satisfied glow very like that which Athenian funeral orations for the war dead evoked, yet historically Athens has more frequently been held up as an example of how not to run a constitution than how to do so, and the principles upon which Athenian democracy was constructed and the principles on which modern western democracies are founded have relatively little in common.[48] How justified are claims that Athens's constitution had a transformative effect upon her cultural life and, through it, upon the history of philosophy?

Herodotus is unusual among ancient writers in the importance which he ascribes to the reforms introduced by Cleisthenes in 508/7 BC. The Athenians themselves were more inclined to claim that their democratic constitution was owed to Solon, or even to Theseus.[49] Cleisthenes left much unchanged, and his reforms were in any case very much in the tradition of earlier Greek constitutions. Strict controls on the duration and powers of magistracies, insistence on one magistrate checking another, the existence of popular courts and a large council, are all features that can be paralleled in the early laws and constitutions discussed above.[50] The power of the mass of the people, both in assembly and in riot, is likely to have played an important part both in Peisistratos' success in factional politics, paving the way for his tyranny, and in Cleisthenes' own ability to bring in major reforms. Nor did Cleisthenes significantly increase the range of those in fact participating in politics. It was only in the fifth century that property qualifications for office were almost all lifted, that magistrates came to be chosen largely by lot, and that pay was introduced for those serving in Council and Courts. Cleisthenes' achievement was not to invent new principles, or even to apply old principles more rigorously, it was to change the way Athenians related to one another.

Athenian politics in the sixth century had frequently been marked by divisions on family and local lines, and Cleisthenes himself belonged to one of the families with the longest continuous history of political involvement at the highest level, the Alcmaeonidae. Cleisthenes added a whole new network of citizen groupings to the existing network, and ensured that his new groups could not be dominated by family or local ties, as the old had been. Where citizenship had previously effectively been controlled by the kin group known as the phratry, now it depended on being registered in a village community or deme; each deme returned a fixed number of representatives to the Council; the men of each deme fought in war as part of one of ten new tribal units which were made up of men from demes drawn from three different areas of Athens' territory; villages bound to their neighbours in cult units were frequently ascribed to different tribes. The old phratries, old tribes, and old cult units were not abolished, but they could no longer dominate the lives of individuals.[51] Individuals found themselves part of many different groups, there was no common denominator between the level of the individual citizen and the level of the city as a whole. Together with this removal of the individual from the dominance of the kin group went the deliverance of the city from structures founded upon the gods. Modern scholars have stressed how Cleisthenes' demes, unlike the phratries, were not primarily cult groups, how laws now came to be regarded not as 'given' but as 'made' (*nomoi* rather than *thesmoi*) and how a whole new, secular, calendar, dividing the year into ten equal periods, was developed to run alongside the sacred calendar.[52] Cleisthenes' aims in making these changes may have been narrowly political – destroying existing power bases in order to give himself more chance of lasting political influence – but the effect was far from narrow: the citizen was effectively empowered as a rational individual.

Athens's cultural achievements were not, however, simply the product of Cleisthenic social engineering; the success of Athenian democracy was also dependent on social and economic factors, and prime among them, slavery. Just as the precocious constitutional developments in Sparta are inseparable from her exploitation of a subject population of helots who were responsible for all agricultural production, so the democratic equality of citizens in Athens was sustained only because it was possible to get 'dirty jobs', tasks which clearly showed up the worker's dependent status, performed by slaves.[53] Outstanding among those jobs was the mining at Laurium of the silver; this silver enabled Athens to build, in the first decades of the fifth century, the fleet by which the Persian threat was repulsed, and that victory bolstered the self-confidence vital to individual political participation, to a willingness to allow critical and speculative thought, and to the maintenance of democracy itself.

The practice of democracy further stimulated critical thought.[54] One measure of this is the way in which classical Greek political thought is dominated by works critical of democracy. The process of turning issues over to a mass meeting of some 6,000 or so people for debate and immediate decision raised very sharply epistemological issues of the place of expertise and of how right answers could be reached; it also raised more generally the question of natural and acquired skills. The ways in which officials carried out their duties and the reactions of the people to this raised questions about responsibility and the relationship of individual and group interests. The importance of not simply saying the right thing but saying it in the right way raised questions of rhetoric and persuasion and the ethics of dressing up bad arguments well.

Critical reaction to, and exploitation of, the world in which they lived had been characteristic of the Greeks of both archaic and classical periods. Both the natural conditions of life in an area marginal for agriculture and the accident of contact with sophisticated peoples in the eastern Mediterranean can be seen to stimulate Greek cultural products from the eighth century onwards. Theological speculation in Homer, Hesiod, and embodied in the sculptural presentation of divinities, tries to make sense of the arbitrariness of human fortunes and the nature of human experience in terms of the nature of the gods; ethical issues concerning the place of the individual in the community and political issues concerning the basis of and limits to authority in *Iliad* and *Odyssey* seem directly related to cities' concern with self-determination and constitutional experimentation; those constitutional experiments themselves show a willingness to tackle problems by emphasizing the question rather than the answer. It is in this cultural milieu that western philosophy, that the conscious asking of 'second order questions', is born and it is by the transformations of this milieu, as a result of the developments in internal and external politics in the Greek city, that the Sophistic Movement and the Socratic revolution grew. Just as the Greeks themselves saw poets, statesmen, and those whom we call philosophers as all 'wise men' (*sophoi*) so, I have tried to demonstrate in this chapter, it is a mistake to think that it was some particular feature of the Greek city that gave rise to 'philosophers', for asking philosophical questions was never the exclusive prerogative of philosophers, and it is only in the context of the culture of the Greek city as a whole that we can properly understand the development of philosophical discourse.[55]

❧ NOTES ❧

1 Thucydides II.40.1, part of the Funeral Oration.
2 So the pioneering work of Vernant [1.14]. For a classic statement see Lloyd [1.7], ch. 4 and compare [1.9], 60–7.
3 Osborne [1.12].
4 Thomas [1.59].
5 Powell [1.20].
6 On the invention of the Greek alphabet see Jeffery [1.18], which contains the definitive study of the local scripts of archaic Greece.
7 See Guralnick [1.17].
8 See generally Hurwit [1.4].
9 See especially West [1.21], and, on Pherecydes also KRS [1.6], 50–71.
10 See Lloyd [1.7], 229–34; [1.8], ch. 2.
11 Much work on relations between Greece and the East has been stimulated in recent years by Martin Bernal's books. For two different approaches to the problem see Morris [1.19] and Burkert [1.16].
12 See particularly the work of Nagy [1.30, 1.31, 1.32].
13 Millett [1.29].
14 Nagy [1.31].
15 My treatment here closely follows J.-P. Vernant [1.38], chs 1–2.
16 Again the pioneering analysis of the myth is by Vernant in Gordon [1.25], chs 3–4.
17 KRS 34–46. At p. 45 n. 1 the authors aptly draw attention to the similar double succession myth in Genesis: 1 and 2.
18 See West [1.41], ch. 1, [1.39], 31–9.
19 See Hall [1.27].
20 For the view that the 'heroic code' is simple and unambiguous see Finley [1.23], and cf. Adkins [1.22]. Against, among many, Schofield [1.36], Taplin [1.37].
21 I take the examples which follow from Rutherford [1.35]; 60–1.
22 On the gods in the *Iliad* see Griffin [1.26], Redfield [1.33].
23 For what follows see Rutherford [1.34] and [1.35].
24 Goldhill [1.24], 36. My discussion of deception in the *Odyssey* owes much to Goldhill.
25 See Aristophanes *Frogs* 1008–112, Plato *Protagoras* 325e, and Heath [1.28], ch. 2.
26 On Greek religion in general see Burkert [1.43], and Bruit Zaidman and Schmitt Pantel [1.42].
27 See Kurke [1.44].
28 Osborne [1.12], ch. 8.
29 In general see Gordon [1.45]. For another example of elaborate preparation of the worshipper see Osborne [1.47].
30 Morgan [1.46], esp. ch. 6.
31 On early Greek law see Gagarin [1.51] and Hölkeskamp [1.54].
32 The Dreros law is Meiggs and Lewis [1.10], no. 2, the Tiryns laws *SEG* (*Supplementum Epigraphicum Graecum*) 30 (1980): 380.
33 For this view see Goody and Watt [1.53], modified somewhat in Goody's later

work (e.g. Goody [1.52]). For critiques of Goody's position see Lloyd [1.7], Thomas [1.59].

34 On written law see Thomas [1.60].

35 On tyranny Andrewes [1.48] is still classic.

36 Shapiro [1.58].

37 For this case argued in detail for Athens see Lavelle [1.55].

38 On the sages see Martin [1.57].

39 For what follows see Bowie [1.49] and [1.50], Lissarrague [1.56].

40 The standard numbering of the fragments of Solon follows M. L. West *Iambi et Elegi Graeci* II, Oxford, 1972. Likewise, the now-usual numbering of Sappho follows E. Diehl *Anthologia Lyrica Graeca*, I. Leipzig, 1922.

41 For what follows see Detienne [1.62].

42 For an introduction to Herodots see Gould [1.64]; for Thucydides, Hornblower [1.65].

43 On the invention of metaphor see Lloyd [1.8], esp. ch. 4. See also Padel [1.67], esp. 9–19.

44 See Davies [1.61].

45 See generally Goldhill [1.63], Winkler and Zeitlin [1.68].

46 Knox [1.66], ch. 1.

47 Loraux [1.75].

48 See Hansen [1.72], Dunn [1.69], [1.70], Roberts [1.79].

49 Hansen [1.72].

50 Cf. Hornblower [1.73], 1, 'The history of European democracy begins, arguably, not in Athens but in Sparta.'

51 The classic exposition of Cleisthenes' reforms is Lewis [1.74]. See also Ostwald [1.77].

52 Ostwald [1.77], Vidal-Naquet and Levêque [1.80].

53 Osborne [1.76].

54 See Farrar [1.71], Raaflaub [1.78].

55 I am grateful to Christopher Taylor for the invitation to write this chapter and to him, Simon Goldhill, Catherine Osborne, Richard Rutherford and Malcolm Schofield for improving an earlier draft.

❧ BIBLIOGRAPHY ❧

General

1.1 Davies, J. K. *Democracy and Classical Greece*, 2nd edn, London, Fontana, 1993.

1.2 Dougherty, C. and Kurke, L. (eds) *Cultural Poetics in Archaic Greece*, Cambridge, Cambridge University Press, 1993.

1.3 Hornblower, S. *The Greek World 479–323 BC*, 2nd edn, London, Routledge, 1991.

1.4 Hurwit, J. *The Art and Culture of Early Greece*, Ithaca, NY, Cornell University Press, 1985.

1.5 Jeffery, L. H. *Archaic Greece: The City-States c. 700–500 BC*, London, Benn, 1976.

1.6 Kirk, G. S., Raven, J. E. and Schofield, M. *The Presocratic Philosophers*, 2nd edn, Cambridge, Cambridge University Press, 1983. For this work we use the universally accepted abbreviation KRS. The numbers following that abbreviation in citations are those of the excerpts in KRS; where the reference is to pages of KRS, rather than excerpts, the form of citation is 'KRS p. xx'.

1.7 Lloyd, G. E. R. *Magic, Reason and Experience*, Cambridge, Cambridge University Press, 1979.

1.8 —— *The Revolutions of Wisdom*, Berkeley, Calif., University of California Press, 1987.

1.9 —— *Demystifying Mentalities*, Cambridge, Cambridge University Press, 1990.

1.10 Meiggs, R. and Lewis, D. M. *A Selection of Greek Historical Inscriptions to the End of the Fifth Century* BC, rev. edn, Oxford, Oxford University Press, 1988.

1.11 Murray, O. *Early Greece*, 2nd edn, London, Fontana, 1993.

1.12 Osborne, R. G. *Classical Landscape with Figures: The Ancient Greek City and its Countryside*, London, George Philip, 1987.

1.13 Snodgrass, A. M. *Archaic Greece: The Age of Experiment*, London, Dent, 1980.

1.14 Vernant, J.-P. *The Origins of Greek Thought*, London, Methuen, 1982.

Greeks and the East

1.15 Boardman, J. *The Greeks Overseas*, 2nd edn, London, Thames and Hudson, 1980.

1.16 Burkert, W. *The Orientalizing Revolution: Near Eastern Influence on Greek Culture in the Early Archaic Age*, Cambridge, Mass., Harvard University Press, 1992.

1.17 Guralnick, E. 'Proportions of kouroi', *American Journal of Archaeology* 82 (1978): 461–72.

1.18 Jeffery, L. H. *Local Scripts of Archaic Greece*, 2nd edn rev. by A. W. Johnston, Oxford, Oxford University Press, 1990.

1.19 Morris, S. P. *Daidalos and the Origins of Greek art*, Princeton, NJ, Princeton University Press, 1992.

1.20 Powell, B. B. *Homer and the Origin of the Greek Alphabet*, Cambridge, Cambridge University Press, 1991.

1.21 West, M. L. *Early Greek Philosophy and the Orient*, Oxford, Oxford University Press, 1971.

Hesiod and Homer

1.22 Adkins, A. W. H. *Merit and Responsibility*, Oxford, Oxford University Press, 1960.

1.23 Finley, M. I. *The World of Odysseus*, 2nd edn, Harmondsworth, Penguin, 1972.

1.24 Goldhill, S. D. *The Poet's Voice: Essays on Poetics and Greek Literature*, Cambridge, Cambridge University Press, 1991.

1.25 Gordon, R. L. (ed.) *Myth, Religion and Society*, Cambridge, Cambridge University Press, 1981.

1.26 Griffin, J. *Homer on Life and Death*, Oxford, Oxford University Press, 1980.

1.27 Hall, E. *Inventing the Barbarian*, Oxford, Oxford University Press, 1989.

1.28 Heath, M. *The Poetics of Greek Tragedy*, London, Duckworth, 1987.

1.29 Millett, P. C. 'Hesiod and his world', *Proceedings of the Cambridge Philological Society* 30 (1984): 84–115.

1.30 Nagy, G. *The Best of the Achaeans*, Baltimore, Md., Johns Hopkins University Press, 1979.

1.31 —— 'Hesiod', in T. J. Luce (ed.) *Ancient Writers*, vol. 1, New York, Charles Scribners Sons, 1982, pp. 43–72.

1.32 —— *Pindar's Homer*, Baltimore, Md., Johns Hopkins University Press, 1990.

1.33 Redfield, J. M. *Nature and Culture in the* Iliad, 2nd edn, Durham and London, Duke University Press, 1994.

1.34 Rutherford, R. B. 'The Philosophy of the *Odyssey*', *Journal of Hellenic Studies* 106 (1986): 143–62.

1.35 —— *Homer*, Odyssey *Books XIX and XX*, Cambridge, Cambridge University Press, 1992.

1.36 Schofield, M. '*Euboulia* in the *Iliad*', *Classical Quarterly* 36 (1986): 6–31.

1.37 Taplin, O. P. *Homeric Soundings: The Shaping of the* Iliad, Oxford, Oxford University Press, 1992.

1.38 Vernant, J.-P. *Myth and Thought among the Greeks*, London, Routledge, 1983.

1.39 West, M. L. *Hesiod* Theogony, Oxford, Oxford University Press, 1966.

1.40 —— *Hesiod* Works and Days, Oxford, Oxford University Press, 1978.

1.41 —— *The Hesiodic Catalogue of Women: Its Nature, Structure and Origins*, Oxford, Oxford University Press, 1985.

Religion: Rituals, Festivals and Images of the Gods

1.42 Bruit Zaidman, L. and Schmitt Pantel, P. *Religion in the Ancient Greek City*, Cambridge, Cambridge University Press, 1992.

1.43 Burkert, W. *Greek Religion*, Oxford, Blackwell, 1985.

1.44 Kurke, L. 'The economy of *kudos*', in Dougherty and Kurke [1.2], pp. 131–63.

1.45 Gordon, R. L. 'The real and the imaginary: production and religion in the Graeco–Roman world', *Art History* 2 (1979): 5–34.

1.46 Morgan, C. A. *Athletes and Oracles: The Transformation of Olympia and Delphi in the Eighth Century* BC, Cambridge, Cambridge University Press, 1990.

1.47 Osborne, R. 'The viewing and obscuring of the Parthenon Frieze', *Journal of Hellenic Studies* 105 (1985): 94–105.

Politics, Constitutions, Laws and the Consequences of Literacy

1.48 Andrewes, A. *The Greek Tyrants*, London, Hutchinson University Library, 1956.

1.49 Bowie, E. 'Early Greek elegy, symposium, and public festival', *Journal of Hellenic Studies* 106 (1986): 13–35.

1.50 —— 'Greek table-talk before Plato', *Rhetorica* 11 (1993): 355–71.

1.51 Gagarin, M. *Early Greek Law*, New Haven, Conn. Yale University Press, 1986.

1.52 Goody, J. *The Logic of Writing and the Organisation of Society*, Cambridge, Cambridge University Press, 1986.

1.53 Goody, J. and Watt, I. 'The Consequences of Literacy', in J. Goody (ed.) *Literacy in Traditional Societies*, Cambridge, Cambridge University Press, 1968, pp. 27–68.

1.54 Hölkeskamp, K. 'Written Law in Archaic Greece', *Proceedings of the Cambridge Philological Society* 38 (1992): 87–117.

1.55 Lavelle, B. M. *The Sorrow and the Pity: A Prolegomenon to a History of Athens under the Peisistratids, c.560–510 BC*, Historia Einzelschriften 80, Stuttgart, Franz Steiner, 1993.

1.56 Lissarrague, F. *The Aesthetics of the Greek Banquet*, Princeton, NJ, Princeton University Press, 1990.

1.57 Martin, R. P. 'The Seven Sages as performers of wisdom', in Dougherty and Kurke [1.2], pp. 108–28.

1.58 Shapiro, H. A. 'Hipparchos and the rhapsodes', in Dougherty and Kurke [1.2]; pp. 92–107.

1.59 Thomas, R. *Literacy and Orality in Ancient Greece*, Cambridge, Cambridge University Press, 1992.

1.60 —— 'Written in stone: Liberty, equality, orality and the codification of law', *Bulletin of the Institute of Classical Studies* 40(1995):59–74.

Mythology: Invention, Manipulation

1.61 Davies, J. K. 'The reliability of the oral tradition', in J. K. Davies and L. Foxhall (eds) *The Trojan War: Its Historicity and Context*, Bristol, Bristol Classical Press, 1984, pp. 87–110.

1.62 Detienne, M. *The Creation of Mythology*, Chicago, Chicago University Press, 1986.

1.63 Goldhill, S. D. *Reading Greek Tragedy*, Cambridge, Cambridge University Press, 1986.

1.64 Gould, J. *Herodotus*, London, Weidenfeld and Nicholson, 1989.

1.65 Hornblower, S. *Thucydides*, London, Duckworth, 1987.

1.66 Knox, B. *Word and Action*, Baltimore, Md., Johns Hopkins University Press, 1979.

1.67 Padel, R. *In and Out of the Mind: Greek Images of the Tragic Self*, Princeton, NJ, Princeton University Press, 1992.

1.68 Winkler, J. J. and Zeitlin, F. I. (eds) *Nothing to Do with Dionysos? Athenian*

Drama in its Social Context, Princeton, NJ, Princeton University Press, 1990.

Political and Cultural Imperialism

1.69 Dunn, J. (ed.) *Democracy: The Unfinished Journey*, Oxford, Oxford University Press, 1992.

1.70 —— 'The transcultural significance of Athenian democracy', in M. B. Sakellariou (ed.) *Athenian Democracy and Culture*, Athens, forthcoming.

1.71 Farrar, C. *The Origins of Democratic Thinking*, Cambridge, Cambridge University Press, 1988.

1.72 Hansen, M. H. 'The 2500th anniversary of Cleisthenes' reforms and the tradition of Athenian democracy', in R. Osborne and S. Hornblower (eds) *Ritual, Finance, Politics: Athenian Democratic Accounts Presented to David Lewis*, Oxford, Oxford University Press, 1994, pp. 25–37.

1.73 Hornblower, S. 'Creation and development of democratic institutions in ancient Greece', in Dunn [1.69], pp. 1–16.

1.74 Lewis, D. M. 'Cleisthenes and Attica', *Historia* 12 (1963): 22–40.

1.75 Loraux, N. *The Invention of Athens*, Cambridge, Mass, Harvard University Press, 1986.

1.76 Osborne, R. 'The economics and politics of slavery at Athens', in C. A. Powell (ed.) *The Greek World*, London, Routledge, 1995, pp. 27–43.

1.77 Ostwald, M. *Nomos and the Beginnings of Athenian Democracy*, Oxford, Oxford University Press, 1969.

1.78 Raaflaub, K. 'Contemporary perceptions of democracy in fifth-century Athens', in J. R. Fears (ed.) *Aspects of Athenian Democracy*, Classica et Mediaevalia: Dissertationes XI, Copenhagen, Museum Tusculanum Press, 1990.

1.79 Roberts, J. T. *Athens on Trial: The Antidemocratic Tradition in Western Thought*, Princeton, NJ, Princeton University Press, 1994.

1.80 Vidal-Naquet, P. and Levêque, P. *Cleisthenes the Athenian*, Ithaca, NY, Cornell University Press, 1993.

CHAPTER 2

The Ionians
Malcolm Schofield

❧❖❧

The Greeks agreed that philosophy had begun with Thales. However they did not know much about his views.[1]

What survives is mostly a potent legend. Herodotus tells stories of his practical ingenuity, political vision and most famously the skill and learning which enabled him to predict a solar eclipse datable to 585 BC. This feat has been doubted by some modern scholars, but it was not an impossible one for someone familiar with the use of eclipse cycles and fondness for prediction among Babylonian astronomers, as an inhabitant of Miletus on the coast of Asia Minor might have become. In Aristophanes the astronomer and inventor Meton – introduced as a character in the drama – dreams up a hare-brained scheme for employing mathematical instruments to measure the air which inspires the comment, 'the man's a Thales' (*Birds* 1009).[2]

The use of instruments in determining the behaviour of heavenly bodies constitutes in fact Thales' best-documented claim to a place in the history of rational enquiry about the natural world. He was believed to have worked out the variable period of the solstices, and to have calculated the height of the pyramids from their shadows and the distance of ships out at sea. Callimachus credits him with 'measuring' the Little Bear, as a navigational aid. The name of his associate Anaximander is likewise associated with the 'discovery' of the equinox and solstices, or more plausibly with the use of a *gnomon* or stable vertical rod to mark them, as also with that of 'hour-markers'. Anaximander is also said to have published the first map of the earth. Some of the accounts supplying this information may embellish or distort. For example, Eudemus' attempts to attribute knowledge of particular geometrical theorems to Thales on the strength of his efforts at mensuration probably represent (under the guise of Aristotelian history) nothing more than a determination to furnish the geometry of his own day with a suitably ancient and distinguished intellectual pedigree. But the reports on Thales' and Anaximander's endeavours in this field are numerous and various enough in date and provenance, and in their gist sufficiently unfanciful, for it to be unreasonable to press doubts about the truth of the picture they convey. These two thinkers were evidently fascinated with measurement, and with the idea of putting to nature – and more especially the heavens – questions which instruments could be employed to answer.[3]

One other scientific puzzle (as we might now term it) which Thales is reported to have tried to solve is the behaviour of the magnet. Here his style of enquiry was very different. He claimed that magnets have soul: they have the power of moving other bodies without them-selves being moved by anything – but that is a characteristic only of things that have soul, i.e. are alive. Heady speculation, not ingenious observation, is now the order of the day. Perhaps the phenomenon of magnetism was presented as one piece of evidence for the more general thesis, 'All things are full of gods', which Aristotle at any rate is inclined to interpret in terms of the proposition that there is soul in the universe (i.e. not just in animals).[4]

In cosmological speculation Thales is presented by Aristotle as a champion of the primacy of water as an explanatory principle. Aristotle writes as though Thales meant by this that water was the material substrate of everything that exists. But the authority on whom he relies for his information, the sophist Hippias of Elis, seems to have men-tioned Thales' view in the context of a survey of opinions about the *origin* of things. With one exception, to be discussed at length shortly, Aristotle knows nothing else about the water principle. He contents himself with the guess that Thales opted for it because warmth, sperm, nutriment and the life they foster or represent are all functions of moisture.[5]

The most definite claim Aristotle makes in this connection appears in *On the Heavens* (II.13, 294a28–32 [KRS 84]).

> Others say that the earth rests on water. For this is the most
> ancient account we have received, which they say was given by
> Thales the Milesian, that it stays put through floating like a log
> or some other such thing.

To come to terms with this unappealing version of flat-earthism we need to consider two pieces of information relating to Thales' intellectual grandchild Anaximenes, pupil of Anaximander, both also of Miletus:

> Anaximenes and Anaxagoras and Democritus say that its [the
> earth's] flatness is responsible for it staying put: for it does not cut

the air beneath but covers it like a lid, which is evidently what those bodies characterized by flatness do.

> (Aristotle *On the Heavens* II.13, 294b13ff. [KRS 150])

The earth is flat, riding upon air; and similarly also sun, moon and the other stars, although they are all fiery, ride upon air on account of their flatness.

> (Hippolytus *Refutation* I.7.4 [KRS 151])

Anaximenes is usually reckoned one of the least interesting of the pre-Socratics. What we are told of his cosmological system indicates a theorist deaf to the imaginative a priori reasonings which appear to have motivated many of the ideas of his mentor Anaximander; and Anaximander's own mentor, Thales, was – as we have been seeing – the pioneer who initiated the whole Ionian tradition of physical speculation, so far as we can tell from the inadequate surviving evidence of his views. Yet in some respects at least Anaximenes was a more influential figure than either of his two predecessors. And this is of crucial importance for our evaluation of the evidence relating to them. Hence the decision to start our enquiry into Thales' flat-earthism with what we are told about Anaximenes.

Anaximenes' influence is apparent from Aristotle's testimony about his account of the earth. The two great Ionian cosmologies of the fifth century were propounded by Anaxagoras and the atomists Leucippus and Democritus. There are radical and systematic differences in the explanatory foundations of the two theories. But despite their sophistication in responding to metaphysical and epistemological challenges posed by Parmenides and (at least in the atomists' case) Zeno, both endeavour to account for a world conceived in terms defined by Anaximenes, as Aristotle's report (KRS 150, quoted above) makes clear. It is a world in which (a) the earth is taken to be a flat body surrounded by air above and below, (b) bodies fall through the air unless there is some special cause of their not doing so, and (c) flatness is just such a cause. This is a picture of the world far removed from our own heliocentric model, where the earth is (roughly speaking) a spherical object spinning in an elliptical orbit round the sun. In Anaximenes' version it is not even a geocentric model, because while he imagines the earth as occupying a position between above and below, there is no implication that it is at the centre of a system: the heavenly bodies do not revolve about it, but turn in a circle above it.[6]

There can be little doubt of the importance Anaximenes attached to theses (a) to (c). As Hippolytus' evidence in KRS 151 suggests, he applied the same kind of reasoning to account for the appearance of the sun and moon in the heavens. Just as the earth does not fall

downwards, so they too are supported by air and hence stay aloft –
even when they are not apparent:

> He says that the stars do not move under the earth, as others
> have supposed, but round it, just as if a felt cap is being turned
> round our head; and that the sun is hidden not by passing under
> the earth, but through being covered by the higher parts of the
> earth and through its increased distance from us.
>
> (Hippolytus *Refutation* I.7.6 [KRS 156])

Probably the sun and moon at least are conceived of by Anaximenes
as bodies.[7] That is, though fiery they are forms of earth, just as in
Anaxagoras: Anaxagoras notoriously claimed that sun, moon and stars
were themselves bodies made of compressed earth, fiery stones
(Hippolytus *Refutation* I.8.6 [KRS 502]), while the atomists make them
ignited complexes of atoms and void (Diogenes Laertius IX.32 [KRS
563]). However these later thinkers agreed in finding in the vortex a
mechanism to explain projected revolutions of these bodies, and so
without abandoning Anaximenes' assumption (b) about downward
motion could unlike him account for their passing below the earth.[8]

Another piece of information about Anaximenes' views on the
sun indicates how he supported his thesis (c) that their flatness keeps
flat things from falling:[9] 'Anaximenes says that the sun is flat like a
leaf' (Aetius II.22.1 [KRS 155]). Floating leaves, of course, move about,
just as Anaximenes' sun does. Their flatness prevents not lateral but
downward movement. Why the sun, moon and stars rotate but the
earth does not is not discussed in the surviving evidence.

Now back to Thales: his reported view on the stability of the
earth has to be seen within the context of the general theoretical
framework we have been describing. Two features of the state of the
evidence dictate this conclusion. First, Aristotle's citation of Thales'
idea comes in a chapter which represents him, Anaximenes, Anaxagoras
and Democritus as all upholding one side of the argument in a pre-
Socratic debate about the subject (Anaximenes' ultimate achievement is
to have persuaded Aristotle that it *was* a key subject for the pre-
Socratics and his stance the standard one taken by them). Second,
Thales himself seems not to have written a book. So the likeliest way
for his opinion to have survived will be via a reference to it in the
writings of someone close to him in time: presumably either a member
of his own circle such as Anaximander or Anaximenes, or – as I shall
be suggesting later – a critic such as Xenophanes.[10] To put the point a
bit more sharply, we can perceive how Thales' view about the earth
was received, both around his own time and in the pages of Aristotle,
a lot better than we can form reliable conjectures as to how it fitted

into whatever intellectual schemes he himself elaborated. In large part this is a function of the elusiveness in history of the merely oral.

One guess might be that Thales had already anticipated Anaximenes in conceiving of the earth and the sun, moon and stars as comparable phenomena requiring to have their differing patterns of motion and stability explained by the same sorts of physical mechanisms. At the other extreme he might be interpreted as a figure much closer to the myth-tellers of the ancient Near East, preoccupied as they were with the origin of the earth and its physical relationship with primeval water, but not seeing a need to ask analogous physical questions about the heavenly bodies, despite his intense interest in determining and measuring their behaviour.[11] The psalmist believes that Jahweh 'stretched out the earth above the waters' (136:6), 'founded it upon the seas, and established it upon the floods' (24:2). Similarly, in the epic of Gilgamesh Marduk builds a raft on the surface of the original waters, and on it in turn a hut of reeds, which is what the earth is. Perhaps Thales' originality consisted only in introducing an opinion borrowed from sources such as these into Greece, Homer having had the earth surrounded by the river Oceanos but stretching down into murky Tartarus, and Hesiod being certain that its creation as 'firm seat of all things for ever' (*Theogony* 117 [KRS 31]) precedes that of heaven and sea.

It is not clear on this second construction of Thales' view how much relative importance he himself need have attached to the issue of the stability of the earth. His main concern might well have been the general primacy of water in the explanation of things, with the suggestion that it is what supports the earth simply one among several consequential proposals, and conceivably accorded no special significance. Certainly the broad idea of water as first principle is what Aristotle focuses on in his more fundamental presentation of pre-Socratic physical theories in *Metaphysics* A, following a tradition of interpretation already visible in Plato and apparently established by the sophist Hippias.[12]

The evidence is rather stronger that Anaximander took the question of the stability of the earth to be a major problem. It consists principally of an extraordinarily interesting but frustratingly controversial passage of Aristotle from the same chapter of *On the Heavens* that we have been exploiting already. Aristotle takes Anaximander to be a proponent of an entirely different kind of position from that represented in different ways by Thales and Anaximenes:

> There are some who say, like Anaximander among the ancients, that it [the earth] stays put because of likeness. For it is appropriate for that which is established in the middle and

is related all alike to the extremities not to move up rather than down or sideways; but it is impossible for it to make a motion in opposite directions; so of necessity it stays put.

(Aristotle *On the Heavens* II.13, 295b10ff. [KRS 123])

The theory Aristotle ascribes to Anaximander has been described as 'a brilliant leap into the realms of the mathematical and the *a priori*' [KRS p. 134]. It is often taken to constitute the first recorded appeal to a Principle of Sufficient Reason. There is apparently no preoccupation with the propensity of bodies to fall, or with the conditions – flatness, buoyancy of the medium – under which that propensity can be counteracted. It looks instead as though Anaximander subscribes to a fully-fledged geocentric conception of the universe, and in appealing to a sophisticated indifference principle makes the explicit and equally sophisticated assumption that any body at the centre of a sphere will have no propensity to move from it in any particular direction. The result – if we can trust what Aristotle says – was a highly ingenious and original solution to what must presumably have been perceived as an important puzzle.[13]

But doubt has been cast on Aristotle's reliability on this occasion.[14] There are two principal reasons for the doubt. First is that Anaximander was, like Thales and Anaximenes, a flat-earther. Although he abandoned Thales' log analogy, he compared the shape of the earth to the drum of a column, much wider than it is deep, emphasizing – presumably against the Homeric picture – that it has both an upper and a lower surface.[15] But the hypothesis of a *spherical* earth is what would fit much more comfortably with the theory Aristotle is reporting.[16] Flat-earthism more naturally presupposes the flat earth dynamics expressed in Anaximenes' theses (a) to (c). Second, Aristotle makes it clear that it was not just Anaximander who subscribed to the indifference theory. On one guess only the initial claim that the earth stays put because of 'likeness' reflects Anaximander's own formulation. Attention is often drawn to the probability that Aristotle also has in mind a much later and no doubt more readily accessible text, namely the account of the earth put in Socrates' mouth at the end of Plato's *Phaedo*. Socrates is there made to claim that he has been convinced by 'someone': presumably a tacit acknowledgement of a pre-Socratic source, although scholars have never been able to agree on the likeliest candidate. The key sentences are these:

> Well, I have been persuaded first that, if it is in the middle of the heavens, being round in shape, then it has no need of air to prevent it from falling, nor of any other similar necessity. The likeness of the heaven itself to itself everywhere and the equal balance of the earth itself are sufficient to hold it fast. For

something equally balanced, set in the middle of something all alike, will be unable to tilt any more or any less in any direction, but being all alike it will stay put untilted.

(Plato *Phaedo* 108e–109a)

Should we accept that Aristotle is mostly drawing on Plato, not Anaximander?

These arguments against ascribing the indifference theory – and with it rejection of the dynamics of flat-earthism – to Anaximander are to be resisted. I consider first the idea that Aristotle's formulation of the theory derives largely from the *Phaedo* text.

There are clearly similarities in language and thought between it and Aristotle's account of the indifference theory, notably the stress on 'likeness' as a cause. There is equally a striking divergence. Plato makes the stability of the earth a function of two things, its position at the centre of a spherical heaven and its equilibrium in that position. Aristotle by contrast speaks only of the earth's position relative to the extremities, but makes what in Plato functions as an indifference inference from equilibrium serve as the argument that it cannot move position.

At first sight it may look as though the lack of fit between the two formulations has no effect on the character or cogency of the reasoning, with Aristotle simply extracting its essentials in economical fashion. There is in fact a very significant difference.

Consider first the Platonic argument from equilibrium. This makes crucial appeal to the *weight* of the earth. It supposes that a rigid body which is 'like' – in the sense that its weight is equally distributed throughout its mass – will stay put in balance under certain conditions, namely if poised about a central fulcrum. Then its weight on one side of the fulcrum will give it the same reason to tilt in that direction as its weight on the other side to tilt in the other direction. It cannot tilt in both directions at once. So it cannot tilt at all. Plato's claim is that the earth is just such a body, and that because it occupies a position at the centre of a symmetrical cosmos, it is indeed poised about a central fulcrum. He infers that it will not tilt.

So Plato is clearly presenting a *physical* argument. Aristotle's version of the indifference theory, by contrast, is abstractly conceived, and makes no specific physical assumptions. It assumes only something equidistant from its extremities; and then claims that such a thing could have no sufficient reason to travel in one plane towards the extremities that was not a sufficient reason for it to travel there in the same plane in the opposite direction. Nothing is said about what sort of reason might count as a sufficient reason. We might think of physical reasons, e.g. gravitational attraction of the heavens; but nothing precludes the possibility that something purely mathematical, e.g. asymmetry, is envisaged. Perhaps this possibility is positively favoured by the mathematical language in which the assumption underpinning this version of the theory is couched and by the absence of reference to physical considerations.

If Aristotle is basing himself principally on the *Phaedo* passage, he can only be offering a vague and general summary of Plato's reasoning. It is more plausible to supposed that he is actually relying more on a quite different formulation of the indifference theory – in Anaximander's book. At this point it is appropriate to mention an important further piece of evidence about Anaximander's view of why the earth stays put:

> The earth is in mid-air [lit. 'aloft', *meteōron*] not controlled by anything,[17] but staying put because of its like distance from all things.

> (Hippolytus *Refutation* I.6.3 [KRS 124])

Scholars are in agreement that Hippolytus in this part of his work is following Theophrastus' account of early Greek physics, and that Theophrastus' treatment of the subject follows Aristotle in general approach. Theophrastus was often more accurate, however, when it came to details. In the present instance it is clear that Hippolytus' testimony broadly supports Aristotle's interpretation. It suggests that Anaximander spoke not just of 'likeness' in general terms, which might be compatible with *either* an argument from symmetry *or* an equilibrium argument. The more specific expression 'like distance from all things' definitely favours the Aristotelian account. Its similarity to Aristotle's phrase 'related all alike to the extremities' suggests that at this point Aristotle was recalling something in Anaximander rather than in Plato. And while it does not preclude the possibility that Anaximander appealed to equilibrium, it gives it no support. (Equally Hippolytus does not attest explicit use of indifference reasoning on his part; perhaps this was one element in Aristotle's report derived from Plato alone, even if it was reasonable to think it implicit in what Anaximander said.)

Against the testimony of Aristotle and Hippolytus there is some actual counter-evidence. It consists in a claim apparently deriving from the Aristotelian commentator Alexander of Aphrodisias which implies that Anaximander did indeed subscribe to flat-earthist dynamics:

> But Anaximander was of the opinion that the earth stays put both because of the air that holds it up and because of equal balance and likeness.

> (Simplicius *On the Heavens* 532.13–14)

54

This comment, at the end of Simplicius' discussion of Aristotle's introduction of the indifference theory, is usually taken as representing his own account of Anaximander. But the context suggests rather a tendentious bit of argumentation by Alexander in support of his view that Plato is Aristotle's main target in this passage of the *Physics*. There is no reason to think that Alexander's claim has any real authority.[18]

None the less from his representation of Anaximander an ingenious account of why the earth stays put could be constructed. An Alexandrian Anaximander shares the view natural to flat-earthers that the earth must rest on something. He conceives reasons for thinking that it must also be positioned mid-air. And he infers that so positioned it must be in equilibrium. The difficulty is then to explain how a heavy body, the earth, *can* be supported by a light body, the air. The idea of the fulcrum of a balance gives an elegant solution to the problem. For a fulcrum can support a body many times heavier than itself.[19]

How are we to choose between Aristotle's more radical indifference theorist, who abandons the idea of a support for the earth in favour of the mathematics of symmetry, and the mainstream Ionian physicist I have just reconstructed on the basis of Alexander via Plato's equilibrium theory?

A single sentence in Hippolytus is little enough to help decide the issue of whether it was Anaximander's flat-earthism or his fascination with symmetry and a priori thinking which determined his view on what kept the earth stable. But follow Hippolytus we should. Of course, Anaximander ought on this story to have seen that a spherical, not a cylindrical, earth was what suited his position. This does not however constitute much of an objection to the truth of the story. We have simply to concede that Anaximander is a revolutionary who carries some old-fashioned baggage with him. That is the general way with revolutions.

ANAXIMANDER

Anaximander wrote a book in prose – one of the first books in prose ever composed – which contained an ambitious narrative of the origins of the world, beginning with the earth and the heavens, and ending with the emergence of animal and particularly human life. It was evidently conceived as a sort of naturalistic version of Hesiod's *Theogony*. His act of committing his thoughts to papyrus was enormously influential. It effectively defined the shape and contents of Greek philosophical cosmology for centuries to come, establishing a tradition which might be regarded as culminating in Plato's *Timaeus* or – translated to Rome – in Lucretius' *On the Nature of Things*.[20]

Anaximander made the originating principle of things something he called the *apeiron*, the boundless or (as some would prefer to translate) the indefinite. His possible reasons for selecting the *apeiron* for this role were the one Anaximandrian topic which really interested Aristotle.[21] Aristotle's influence on Theophrastus and through him on subsequent ancient accounts of Anaximander's views was, as on so many other topics, enormous; so the issue dominates important parts of the doxography also.[22] Much modern scholarship in its turn has responded by making the *apeiron* the principal focus of its own struggles to understand Anaximander and the one surviving fragment of his work. What has been amassed is largely a tapestry of unrewarding and controversial guesswork – unsurprisingly, when as likely as not Aristotle himself was just guessing.

There is accordingly a lot to be said for beginning (or rather continuing) an account of Anaximander's thought by looking at evidence which offers a more direct insight into his characteristic intellectual style. Two reports that pay particular dividends in this regard are the following:

> He says that something capable of generating hot and cold from
> the eternal was separated off at the genesis of this world, and
> that a sphere of flame grew round the air surrounding the earth,
> like bark round a tree. When this was torn off and closed off into
> certain circles, the sun and the moon and the stars were
> constituted.
>
> (Eusebius' extract 2 from [Plutarch] *Miscellanies* [KRS 121])

> Anaximander says the first animals were born in moisture,
> enclosed in thorny barks; but as their age increased they came
> out on the drier part, and when the bark had broken all round
> they lived a different kind of life for a short time.
>
> (Aetius V.19.4 [KRS 133])

These texts, by different late authors, are thought to depend ultimately on Theophrastus. They contain much that is obscure, but exhibit a patent similarity, which must be due to Anaximander himself.[23] Although one concerns happenings at the beginning of his story, the other a process near its end, both exploit a common analogy: the formation of bark round a tree. Moreover the production of two significant but utterly different features of the world – sun, moon and stars in the heavens, and animal life on earth – is explained by essentially the same mechanism. First one kind of stuff encloses another in the manner of bark, then the bark-like material breaks off or around and new forms develop or appear. Despite the biological character of the analogy, the explanatory pattern itself appears to be conceived in terms of the interplay of elemental *physical* forces.[24] At the origins of the world the hot (in the form of flame) encases the cold (air), and the breaking of the casing is presumably to be understood as due to the pressure caused by the expansion of a gas increasing in temperature. Whether the actual designation of the forces in question in abstract language as hot and cold derives from Anaximander himself or (more probably) is the work of Peripatetic commentary does not much affect the diagnosis. It is not so clear from the Aetius passage that the emergence of animals in their mature forms is the outcome of a similar process. But fortunately another text (Hippolytus *Refutation*, I.6.6 [KRS 136]) informs us that the sun's activity in evaporating moisture is what brings animals into being. If as seems likely this relates to the phenomenon described by Aetius, we are perhaps to think of the drying out of the casing in which animals are first enclosed. The claim will be that this physical effect of heat then makes it break up all around.

From the evidence of KRS 121 and 133 we can already infer that Anaximander sees the world as a systematic unity sustained by dynamic transformations that are thoroughly intelligible to the human mind. This must be why he assumes that momentous events, veiled in obscurity, such as the origins of the cosmos itself and of life within it, can be reconstructed as versions of the more local physical processes with which we are familiar from our own experience. This too must be why he expects two such different sorts of originating event to exhibit similar patterns; and why he believes not just that the transformations involved will be aptly illustrated by analogy, but that one and the same analogy, albeit differently treated in the two cases, will provide that illumination.

Consideration of further evidence confirms the picture of Anaximander's *Weltanschauung* that is beginning to emerge. Here are two texts which give more details of the circles that account for the sun, moon and stars:

> The stars come into being as a circle of fire separated off from
> the fire in the world, and enclosed by air. There are breathing-
> holes, certain pipe-like passages, at which the stars show
> themselves. So when the breathing-holes are blocked off eclipses
> occur; and the moon appears now to be waxing, now waning,
> according to the blocking or opening of the passages. The circle
> of the sun is 27 times the earth, that of the moon 18 times. The
> sun is highest, the circles of the fixed stars lowest.
>
> (Hippolytus *Refutation* I.6.4–5 [KRS 125])

Anaximander says there is a circle 28 times the earth, like a chariot wheel, with its rim hollow and full of fire. It lets the

57

fire appear through an orifice at one point, as through the nozzle of a bellows; and this is the sun.

(Aetius II.20.1 [KRS 126])

Again there is much that is opaque and puzzling in these reports, as well as a number of features that by now will not be unexpected.

The search for system is immediately evident in the ingenious hypothesis of a nested sequence of concentric circles, which reduces the apparently chaotic variety of the heavens to the simplest scheme of geometrical and arithmetical relationships: circles and multiples of the number 9. Once again the idea of one stuff (air) enclosing another (fire) is fundamental to explanation of the transformations Hippolytus mentions, namely eclipses and the phases of the moon. Making the sun and moon functions of *circles* of air and fire is, of course, designed primarily to account for their diurnal revolutions and the alternation of day and night. Making them circles of *air and fire*, not bodies, enables Anaximander to avoid the puzzle of why they do not fall, which Anaximenes and his successors were obliged to address. All in all it is a beautifully economical theory. As with his account of origins, Anaximander recommends it by vivid analogy, taken in this case from the familiar contexts of forge and stadium: a bellows and its nozzle, the wheel and its rim.

The physical if not the mathematical patterns Anaximander has so far invoked are specified also in his accounts of wind, rain (deficiently preserved), thunder and lightning:

Winds come about when the finest vapours of the air are separated off, and move when massed together; rains from the vapour sent up from the earth, as a result of [?] their being [?] [melted] by the sun; lightnings when wind breaks out and divides the clouds.

(Hippolytus *Refutation* I.6.7 [KRS 129])

Anaximander says wind is a flow of air, when the finest and the wettest parts of it are set in motion or melted [producing rain] by the sun.

(Aetius III.7.1)

On thunder, lightning, thunderbolts, whirlwinds and typhoons: Anaximander says these all occur as a result of the wind. When it is enclosed in thick cloud and bursts out forcibly because of its fineness and lightness, then the tearing makes the noise and the rift the flash, in contrast to the blackness of the cloud.

(Aetius III.1.2 [KRS 130])

Fundamental to this explanatory scheme is once again the interaction of fire (here in particular the sun) and air (conceived of as moist vapour). The process of separation off had earlier been identified as the cause of the formation from the *apeiron* of an air-enclosing ball of fire, which then in turn separated off to be enclosed in rings of air. Now it is made responsible for the production of winds. They are themselves taken to be the root cause of a further range of meteorological phenomena, involving further enveloping and subsequent rupturing of envelopes. If as we would expect analogies were introduced to reinforce the persuasiveness of the explanations, these are now lost to us. The action of wind, conceived of as fine dry air bursting through the wet dark air of cloud to generate the bright flash of lightning, has understandably provoked the comment that, in Anaximander's system, the sun and moon resemble a lightning flash of indefinite duration.[25]

More generally, Anaximander's ideas tend to prompt in Whiggish readers a reaction compounded of admiration and incredulity. For example, his conjectures about the origins of life (on which more later) are regularly felt to be 'brilliant' or 'remarkable'.[26] By contrast his meteorology now seems merely quaint, while it is his astronomical system which strikes the modern mind as more grandly and perversely inadequate.

Some of the gaps or implausibilities in Anaximander's explanations in this area are no doubt due to the deficiencies of the surviving evidence. Thus given the efforts he and Thales seem to have made to measure the solstices, it is improbable that he had nothing to say about the annual movement of the sun in the ecliptic (to use a later vocabulary).[27] We do in fact have a report going back to Theophrastus, but queried by some scholars, which suggests that he attributed the solstices to the sun-circle's need for replenishment from rising vapours: when these become now too dense in the north, now too depleted in the south, then – we may imagine – periodic changes of direction occur in the motion of the circle.[28] Anaximander's views on the 'stars' other than the sun and moon are incompletely and inconsistently recorded. For example, one text talks implausibly, in terms reminiscent of Aristotelian astronomy, of *spheres* carrying stars, not just of circles; another suggests that the circles nearest the earth accounted for the planets as well as the fixed stars. It is obscure what Anaximander had in mind by talking of circles in the plural with regard to the fixed stars. One attractive interpretation proposes, for example, three celestial belts or zones dividing up the night sky, as in Baylonian astronomy. There is difficulty, however, in understanding how he could accommodate the circumpolar stars – which do not set – in his scheme, where all circles are to be construed as revolving round the earth. This may be one of the reasons why Anaximenes preferred his 'felt cap' model of the heavens.[29]

It is a feature of Anaximander's system itself, not lacunae in the doxography, which inflicts the most dramatic damage to his standing as even a primitive astronomer. This is his decision to put the fixed stars closer to earth than the moon and the sun. It is not an unintelligible position. The sequence sun-moon-stars-earth is found in Persian religious texts perhaps roughly contemporaneous in origin. In the Avesta the soul of an infant comes down from the 'beginningless lights' through a series of lights decreasing in size and intensity to be born on earth.[30] This corresponds with the implications of Anaximander's own view of physical process as a constant interaction between fire and cold moisture: if the earth is the principal location of one of these forces, it makes sense that the sun, as the main concentration of the other, should be positioned further from the earth than the lesser fires of the stars. Yet how can Anaximander account for the fact that the moon hides any constellation it passes across? Charitable answers have been attempted by scholars on his behalf, but perhaps it is better just to recall that speculation's negotiations with experience have always been a tricky and often an embarrassing matter for science.

The biggest disputed and unanswered questions in Anaximander's system are those to do with his identification of the *apeiron* as first principle and its relationship with the world. His silences here do him rather more credit. Caution about the big bang and what preceded it seems a thoroughly rational stance. I guess that Anaximander conceives the *apeiron* as the beyond: what necessarily lies outside our experience of space and time, pictured as stretching away boundlessly outside the limits of the cosmos which it encloses.[31] If that cosmos came into being, the natural supposition would be that it did so *from* the *apeiron*. How and why are another matter, on which – as also on the essential nature of the *apeiron* itself – it would inevitably be more difficult to find reasonable things to say.

None the less it is clear that Anaximander did say something on these issues. On one of the rare occasions when Aristotle mentions Anaximander by name he attributes to him the thesis that the *apeiron* is immortal and indestructible. These were traditionally the attributes of divinity, and in fact the same passage strongly implies that the *apeiron* not only encloses but also governs (literally 'steers') all things:

> The infinite is thought to be principle of the rest, and to enclose all things and steer all, as all those say who do not postulate other causes over and above the infinite, such as mind or love. This is the divine. For it is immortal and indestructible, as Anaximander says and most of the physicists.
>
> (Aristotle *Physics* 203b7ff. [KRS 108])

Presumably Anaximander relies on the inference: no cosmic order without an ordering intelligence. On *how* it exercises its directive role he seems to have made no guesses.

From Theophrastan sources we learn further that there is eternal motion in or of the *apeiron*, which is what causes the separation from it of opposite physical forces (namely those forces that are invoked in the astronomy, meteorology, etc.). Again we may detect an inference to the best explanation: no creation without activity before creation. Aristotle finds here a clue to the nature of the *apeiron*. If opposites are separated from it, then it must itself be something intermediate in character, and indeed on that account a suitable choice of first principle. This is a conclusion dictated by Aristotle's enthusiasm for pigeon-holing his predecessors' opinions. It is not attested as Anaximander's view by the more careful Theophrastus.[32]

The thesis about eternal motion is sometimes formulated in the sources as the proposition that it causes the separation off of the world, or rather of worlds in the plural; in Theophrastus' words, probably reproducing Anaximander's own language: 'the worlds (*ouranoi*) and the orderings (*kosmoi*) within them'. The doxographers assimilate his view to the atomist theory of an infinity of worlds all subject to destruction as well as creation. This is probably anachronistic, but – contrary to what some interpreters have argued – right in general thrust.[33] We should suppose that the hypothesis of eternal motion generates in its turn a further bold conjecture, exploiting indifference reasoning of just the kind the atomists were to make their own speciality:

1 Eternal motion in the *apeiron* is necessary to generate a universe.
2 But its activity provides no more reason for a universe to be generated here and now than for one to be generated there and then.
3 So if it generates a universe here and now, it also generates a universe there and then.
4 Therefore it generates a plurality of universes.

One strain in the doxography suggests that Anaximander did not merely say that the first principle *is* the infinite, but that it *must* be the infinite – otherwise coming into being would give out. This carries conviction: Aetius introduces the report as his *evidence* for the more far-reaching and dubious claim that Anaximander posited (like the atomists) the birth and death of an infinite number of worlds. Without mentioning Anaximander, Aristotle too cites the need for an infinite supply as one of the reasons people give for introducing the infinite as a principle. He objects:

> Nor, in order that coming into being may not give out, is it necessary for perceptible body to be *actually* infinite. It is

possible for the destruction of one thing to be the generation of
another, the sum of things being limited.

(Aristotle *Physics* 208a8ff. [KRS 107])

This excellent point ought to tell *against* the idea, parroted by the
doxographers, that Anaximander envisaged the *destruction* of worlds as
well as their generation, at any rate if he did endorse the infinite supply
argument. Only if worlds are *not* recycled is there a requirement for
the *apeiron* to meet an infinite need.

It looks in fact as if Theophrastus, in assimilating Anaximander
to the atomists, specifically searched for evidence that he like them
believed in the ultimate destruction of all worlds, and found it hard
to discover any. His citation of the famous surviving fragment of
Anaximander's book is best interpreted as a misguided attempt to
produce such evidence. The relevant passage of Simplicius, reproducing
his account, runs as follows:

> He says that the principle is neither water nor any other of the
> so-called elements, but some different boundless nature, from
> which all the worlds come to be and the orderings within them.
> And out of those things from which the generation is for
> existing things, into these again their destruction comes about
> 'according to what is right and due, for they pay penalty and
> retribution to each other for their injustice, according to the
> ordinance of time' – using these rather poetical terms to speak
> of them.

(Simplicius *Physics* 24.16ff. [KRS 101, 110])

A great deal of scholarly ink has been spilled over this text, and there
is little to show by way of definitive results. The one important thing
the best critical work has established is that the fragment (indicated
above by the quotation marks) refers to a stable *reciprocal* relationship
between opposites *within* a developed or developing cosmos, not to
the cataclysmic reabsorption of a world or its constituents back into the
apeiron.[34] Most interpreters also believe that Theophrastus, however,
vainly attempts to *make* the fragment serve just such a cataclysmic
function, so as to be applicable to the relationship between a world
and the *apeiron*. Quite how he hoped to work the trick is less clear.
The diagnosis I am suggesting notes that whereas Simplicius' first
sentence concerns generation of worlds from the *apeiron*, the second
is introduced by a remark focused on *destruction*, which despite its
plurals ('out of those . . . into these') looks designed to furnish a balancing comment on the death of worlds. Yet the plurals give the game
away: the only evidence Theophrastus can actually offer to support the

implication of cosmic destruction is a statement of Anaximander about the effect of opposites on *each other*.[35]

No one who has worked their way through Anaximander's astronomy, meteorology and biology will have any difficulty in identifying the forces which 'pay retribution to each other for their injustice'. Simplicius takes it that these are the four elements. This Aristotelian analysis is, as often, anachronistic and over-schematic. What Anaximander must principally have in mind is the alternating domination of moisture over fire and fire over moisture which he makes the key to his account of origins, and which he probably thought exemplified above all by the regular pattern of the seasons in the world as it has now developed. This essentially stable pattern, while giving no basis for expectation of cosmic destruction, can accommodate the possibility of further fundamental changes, as it has admitted of them in the past. The clearest example is supplied by Anaximander's less than satisfactorily documented views on the changing relationship of land and sea.

In his *Meteorology* Aristotle sketches a theory of the gradual evaporation of the moisture on the earth's surface by the sun (353b6ff. [KRS 132]). Originally the whole surface of the earth was wet. Then the drying action of the sun produced the present state of things: part of the surface remains wet and constitutes sea, but the moisture elsewhere is subject to evaporation into the atmosphere. In future the same process will cause the sea to shrink in extent and eventually to dry up completely. Alexander's commentary on the *Meteorology* tells us (67.11) that Theophrastus attributed this theory to Anaximander (and subsequently Diogenes of Apollonia), so making him look to a Whiggish eye like a precursor of modern geology. It is tempting to connect the account of the original state of the earth with Anaximander's conjectures about the beginnings of animal life in general and human life in particular:

> Anaximander of Miletus gave it as his view that, when water and earth had been heated, there arose from them fish or animals very like fish. In these men were formed and kept within as embryos until puberty. Then at last the creatures burst open, and out came men and women who were already able to feed themselves.
>
> (Censorinus *On the Day of Birth* 4.7 [KRS 135])

As in the science of our day, the hypotheses of geology and evolutionary biology seem to reinforce each other. Indeed like Xenophanes after him, Anaximander may have based his geological inferences in part on the fossil record. What matters for present purposes, however, is that the whole geological process envisaged by Anaximander constitutes an 'injustice' committed by one elemental force upon another, and as such will presumably, 'according to the ordinance of time', win compensation by 'retribution' in the form of a new inundation of the earth, again as explicitly attested for Xenophanes (unfortunately no similar prediction by Anaximander survives). We can only speculate on whether the language of justice the fragment uses to describe this kind of process is trying to capture the directive operation of the *apeiron*, or whether it is a metaphor for an entirely physical self-regulatory process, or whether Anaximander would have thought that a false dichotomy.

Anaximander's all-embracing vision of the natural world is the first and for many readers the most unforgettable of the pre-Socratic physical systems. Despite its individuality, it established the framework of a common world picture, shared (although sometimes transformed) by them all. This is above all due to its very invention of the idea of a cosmos, a world ordered by law, which was then worked out along lines that guided both the substance and the method of future enquiry. The cosmos and its major features, including life on earth, are conceived as the outcome of evolving interactions between two fundamental but opposed physical forces. It emerges somehow from something infinite and eternal which surrounds and controls it. Despite the welter of specific detail about this world supplied by Anaximander, he sets a high premium on general explanatory patterns, which he couches exclusively in mathematical and naturalistic terms – except for the overarching conception of cosmic justice. Subsequent pre-Socratics will vary or challenge the recipe in one way or another. But his is the theme, theirs the variations.

❦ ANAXIMENES ❦

Anaximander's theoretical silences evidently grated on Anaximenes' ear.[36] His inability to say what sort of thing the *apeiron* is, and his failure to explain how or why opposite forces emerge from it, contrast with Anaximenes' explicitness on both issues, and may be supposed to be what prompted the junior thinker to engage with them. In any event the result is a cosmology resembling Anaximander's in many respects, but at these key points advancing substantive theses. It is succinctly summed up by Simplicius in a passage deriving from Theophrastus:

> Anaximenes son of Eurystratus, of Miletus, a companion of Anaximander, also says, like him, that the underlying nature is one and infinite, yet not indefinite as Anaximander said, but determinate – for he identifies it as air. It differs in thinness and thickness according to the substances which it constitutes, and if

thinned becomes fire, if thickened wind, then cloud, then (thickened further) water, then earth, then stones. Other things come from these. He, too, makes motion eternal, and says that change, as well, comes about because of it.

(Simplicius *Physics* 24.26ff. [KRS 140])

The hypothesis that the first principle is air in eternal motion enables Anaximenes to fill both the principal lacunae in Anaximander's theory. It ventures a definite characterization of the *apeiron*; and in so doing it facilitates an explanation of the emergence of the chief phenomena studied by natural philosophy: the opposite processes of thinning and thickening to which air is subject are what produce fire, on the one hand, and a series – to become canonical in subsequent Ionian thought – of more and more condensed forms of matter, on the other.

It has often been thought that a text of Aetius reports an analogical argument presented by Anaximenes for the claim that air is the first principle. The passage in question begins with the information that this was his principle, and then, on the traditional interpretation, continues with the words:

As (*hoion*) our soul, he says, being air controls us, so (*kai*) *pneuma* and air enclose the whole world. (Air and *pneuma* are synonymous here.)

(Aetius I.3.4 [KRS 160])

This statement has usually been given prominence in reconstructions of Anaximenes' philosophy. It has even been taken as an actual fragment of his book. Its precise logic and overall point have been much discussed, but (assuming always that the translation given above is correct) the context would favour an interpretation which finds some kind of inference from microcosm to macrocosm: as air is the principle of human life, so it is the principle of the cosmos at large.

On further examination Aetius' sentence proves unable to bear such a weight of interpretation. To begin with, it cannot be an actual quotation from Anaximenes. His book was written 'in simple and economical Ionic'. Aetius' sentence is not in Ionic. It also includes at least one word coined much later than the sixth century BC. The Greek is very likely corrupt, too. It looks as if '*pneuma*', as 'breath', should be substituted for 'air' in the first clause and omitted in the second. Most important of all, a more probable translation of the sentence (so emended) would run:

For example (*hoion*), it is as breath, he says, that our soul controls us, and (*kai*) air encloses the whole world.

The only expressions here which can be inferred to be authentically

Anaximenes' are the two Aetius specifically mentions: 'air' and 'breath', although there is no reason to doubt that he talked of 'soul' in this context.[37]

What on this alternative reading was Aetius' point in making the remark? It will have been to furnish two independent grounds for believing that Anaximenes did indeed, as he has just contended, make air the principle. The clause about the cosmos will then not express the conclusion of any inference, but simply express a version of that fundamental Anaximenian thesis: the *apeiron* (as what encloses the world) is air. The first clause is more interesting. Even though it no longer launches an argument from analogy, it may still suggest that Anaximenes himself appealed to the physiological role of *pneuma* as *evidence* that air is the principle. Certainly the claim about human physiology would then parallel some evidence, again from the phenomenon of breath, which he is said to have adduced for the connected idea that thinnings and thickenings of air are what cause the appearance of *other* properties or things:

> He says that matter which is compressed and condensed is cold, while that which is thin and 'relaxed' (he used this very word) is hot. This is why it is not unreasonable to say that a person releases both hot and cold from the mouth. The breath is chilled when it is pressed and condensed by the lips, but when the mouth is loosened it escapes and becomes hot because of its thinness. This opinion Aristotle puts down to the man's ignorance.
> (Plutarch *The Primary Cold* 947F [KRS 143])[38]

What is most interesting in these texts is the attempt to use familiar features of human existence to think about the cosmos at large. Anaximander had had a penchant for analogy and discussed the origins of man, but there is no sign that his theorizing accorded any similar primacy to consideration of things human for this purpose. It seems unlikely, however, that Anaximenes got close to formulating a conception of man as microcosm. It is just as doubtful how far his cosmology was vitalist. There is some evidence, unfortunately rather vague and of doubtful authority, that Anaximenes laid more stress on the divinity of the *apeiron* than Anaximander did. Hippolytus, for instance, says that from air were generated *inter alia* 'gods and things divine' (*Refutation* I.7.1 [KRS 141]). Is this a recrudescence of Thales' notion that 'all things are full of gods'? Or is it an insistence that everything popularly recognized as divine is in one way or another a form of the one true divinity, the infinite air?

If we continue the comparison of Anaximenes with Anaximander, we find much less evidence of an interest on his part in speculative evolutionary hypotheses, whether cosmological or biological, than there is for Anaximander, although he too propounded a cosmogony. We catch little sense of the world as a theatre occupied by opposing powers acting reciprocally on one another, despite the importance accorded to the contrary processes of compression and expansion. Nor does indifference reasoning or mathematical schematism seem to belong in Anaximenes' explanatory repertoire. What the doxography mostly records is firstly the detail of his astronomical system, which was at once closer to the primitive Homeric picture of the heavens and also more influential on subsequent Ionian thinkers like Anaxagoras, the atomists, and Diogenes of Apollonia; and then information about his explanations of meteorological phenomena, where he seems largely to have followed Anaximander. There are some apparently new topics, such as the rainbow, but even here Anaximenes' view is reminiscent of Anaximander's explanation of lightning (to which he too subscribes): the rays of the sun strike against thick, dark cloud, and being unable to penetrate it are reflected off it, the different colours consequences of different interactions between light and cloud.[39]

The major general idea which the surviving reports make their focus, however, is Anaximenes' proposal that progressive stages of thickening or compression account for the formation of different sorts of bodies and other stuffs. There are traces of an alternative interpretation (as with Anaximander) which tries to make hot and cold the primary explanatory categories for Anaximenes, more as they are in Aristotle.[40] Plutarch's passage on breath suggests that Anaximenes was certainly interested in this pair of opposites; but at the same time it clearly indicates the primacy of thick and thin. A basic statement of the theory has already been quoted [KRS 140]. Some further applications occur in the following passage, where incidentally it is noteworthy how there is no reference to cold in the analyses of hail and snow; compression is evidently responsible for their coldness:

> Anaximenes says that clouds occur when the air is further
> thickened [more so than it is in wind]. When it is compressed
> further rain is squeezed out. Hail occurs when the descending
> water coalesces, snow when something windy is caught up with
> the moisture.
>
> (Aetius II.4.1 [KRS 158])

At some points air is treated as occurring in a relatively dense form while still remaining just air. This is referred to in some sources as 'felting', a word which conceivably goes back to Anaximenes himself. One instance is the air that supports the flat earth, another that forcing the sun to change direction at the solstice.[41]

It is hard from our perspective to understand how anyone should have found the compression theory or its many particular applications credible. Yet it is taken for granted as the standard physical account by Melissus a century later, when he says, 'We think that earth and stone are made out of water' (fragment 8 [KRS 537]), probably recalling Anaxagoras's restatement in his fragment 16 [KRS 490]. Slightly later in the fifth century Diogenes of Apollonia would give an even more thoroughgoing re-endorsement of Anaximenes' original version of the idea. What attracted cosmologists to it was doubtless the core thought that the transformations different forms of matter undergo are intelligible only if those transformations are really just variants of one and the same pair of contrary processes, and if what is transformed is ultimately just a single matter. This is a profound thought. It seems to be Anaximenes' achievement, not that of the shadowy Thales nor of Anaximander. For Anaximander the *apeiron* is the source of things, not what they are made of. Anaximenes appears to have been the first to have had the simplifying and unifying notion that their source *is* what they are made of.[42]

∾ XENOPHANES ∾

Xenophanes presents us with a new phenomenon: lots of actual extracts of pre-Socratic writing. We know the sound of Xenophanes' voice.[43]

Interpretation is not therefore plain sailing. In fact Xenophanes is the subject of more disagreement than Anaximander or Anaximenes. The disputes are not just over what specific positions he took nor what his key problems were, but on whether he should count as a substantial thinker at all, or merely as an intellectual gadfly without a systematic set of ideas of his own. One of the difficulties is that the scraps of Xenophanes which are preserved are mostly just that: isolated lines or pairs of lines or quatrains torn from their original context by a quoting authority. Another is that he was to become the focus of different kinds of interest by a variety of later writers. Thus while Heraclitus speaks of him as a typical practitioner of fruitless Ionian curiosity, Plato and Aristotle (followed by the faithful Theophrastus) see him as an obscure precursor of Parmenides, and Timon of Phlius as more than half anticipating the scepticism he attributed to Pyrrho. In subsequent periods the story gets still more complicated, with Xenophanes portrayed, for example, as an exponent of an elaborate Eleatic negative theology. Excavating the real Xenophanes from the *mélange* of different versions of his thought preserved in the sources is accordingly a good deal trickier than reconstructing Milesian cosmology, which never enjoyed comparable resurrection.[44]

Xenophanes wrote verse, not prose, and that too made him more durable. Diogenes Laertius sums up his output in these words:

He wrote in epic metre, also elegiacs and iambics, against Hesiod and Homer, reproving them for what they said about the gods. But he himself also recited his own poems. He is said to have held contrary opinions to Thales and Pythagoras, and to have rebuked Epimenides too.

(Diogenes Laertius IX.18 [KRS 161])

This account corresponds pretty much with the surviving fragments. Many of them are indeed clearly satirical, and the poems from which these are taken – in all three metres mentioned by Diogenes – were known in antiquity as *silloi*: 'squints' or lampoons. It has been conjectured that even fragments dealing with physical phenomena belonged not to a philosophical poem on nature like Empedocles' (as is implied in some unconvincing very late sources), but to his critique of the traditional theology of Homer and Hesiod, which is well represented among the fragments in any case.[45] Among the other butts of his wit Pythagoras is the certain target of some surviving verses:

On the subject of reincarnation Xenophanes bears witness in an elegy which begins: 'Now I will turn to another tale and show the way.' What he says about Pythagoras runs thus: 'Once they say that he was passing by when a puppy was being whipped, and he took pity and said: "Stop, do not beat it; for it is the soul of a friend that I recognised when I heard it giving tongue." '

(Diogenes Laertius VIII.36: fr. 7 [KRS 260])

But it may also be that Xenophanes' attack on Thales was the original home of the following snippet:

Of the earth this is the upper limit, seen by our feet neighbouring the air. But its underneath reaches on indefinitely.

(Achilles *Introduction* 4: fr. 28 [KRS 180])

Aristotle refers to this passage in his chapter on the different explanations theorists have given for the stability of the earth. He accuses Xenophanes of not trying hard enough. We may think his revulsion from speculation on this question gives him the better of the argument with Thales.[46]

Diogenes seems to suggest that the lampoons, in the fashion of lampoons, mostly had their effect by being circulated and repeated by others. By contrast Xenophanes himself performed his own non-satirical poems, evidently as a travelling entertainer at festivals and other aristocratic gatherings. We are told that after exile from his native city of Colophon he emigrated to Sicily. The 'exile' is generally associated by scholars with the capture of the city by the Persians in 546/5 BC, an event to which he himself refers in some verses where he speaks of the coming of the Mede (fr. 22). This probably occurred when he was 25 years of age, if we may so interpret some further verses which boast of an extraordinarily long life, and which incidentally indicate a career pursued all over Greece:

> Already there are seven and sixty years tossing my thought up and down the land of Greece. And from my birth there were another twenty five to add to these, if I know how to speak truly about these things.
> (Diogenes Laertius IX.18: fr. 8 [KRS 161])[47]

We possess two substantial elegiac poems, each a little over twenty lines long, representing Xenophanes' activity as performer at dinner parties and the like. Both contain a critical strain. One (fr. 2) begins with a famous assault on the Olympic games and the conventional view that victory in any of its athletic events brings a benefit to the victor's city which rightly entitles him to great honours from it. No, says Xenophanes: such a person 'is not my equal in worth – better than the strength of men and horses is my wisdom'. For athletic prowess does not contribute to the good government of the city, nor does it fill the city's coffers. Xenophanes implies that his own moral teaching, on virtue and piety (fr. 1) and against luxury (fr. 3), is by contrast oriented towards the public good. The other poem (fr. 1) is about the proper conduct of a symposium. Its main focus is on the nature of true piety. The first half stresses physical preparations: everything must be clean and pure, fragrant with flowers and incense, with pure water to hand. The wine is to be served with the simplest of foods: bread, cheeses, honey. Then Xenophanes gives instructions about what is to be said. 'Reverent words and pure speech' hymning the god is to precede talk of virtue, of right and noble deeds – not tales of giants, Titans and centaurs, nor of conflicts between men in which there is no profit: nothing, presumably, at all like the *Theogony* or the *Iliad*.[48]

Xenophanes' explicit attacks on Homer and Hesiod in his lampoons are not merely critical but – in a sense I shall explain – self-critical. The Milesians had implicitly questioned traditional assumptions about the natural world. In subjecting what the great poets say about the gods to overt scrutiny and condemnation Xenophanes' focus is not reality but how we conceive of it. Philosophy, one might say, now for the first time takes a reflexive turn.

This is immediately apparent from the key fragments on anthropomorphic theology, which constitute Xenophanes' principal claim to a significant niche in the history of philosophy:

> Homer and Hesiod have attributed to the gods everything that

is a shame and reproach among men, stealing and committing adultery and deceiving one another.

> (Sextus Empiricus *Adversus Mathematicos* IX.193: fr. 11 [KRS 166])

But mortals consider that the gods are born, and that they have clothes and speech and bodies like their own.

> (Clement *Miscellanies* V.109.2: fr. 14 [KRS 167])

The Ethiopians say that their gods are snub-nosed and black, the Thracians that theirs have light blue eyes and red hair.

> (Clement *Miscellanies* VII.22.1: fr. 16 [KRS 168])

But if horses or cattle or lions had hands, or were able to draw with their hands and do the works that men can do, horses would draw the forms of the gods like horses, and cattle like cattle, and they would make their bodies such as they had themselves.

> (Clement *Miscellanies* V.109.3: fr. 15 [KRS 169])

We could already have guessed from fragment 1 that Xenophanes would have found the picture of the gods in Homer and Hesiod unacceptable because inconsistent with 'reverent words and pure speech', i.e. with the requirements of proper worship. The passages quoted above indicate two separate grounds for such a view. First, in fragment 11, Xenophanes objects that they make the gods immoral, or more particularly liars and cheats, a line of objection borrowed by Plato in *his* critique of Homer in *Republic* II. Second and more fundamentally, fragment 14 implies that the poets are just like men in general in casting the gods in their own image: self-projection is the basis for their conceptions of divinity. This charge is then brilliantly substantiated in fragments 15 and 16. Fragment 16 reflects the Ionian fascination with ethnography which reaches its fullest expression in Herodotus and fuels the cultural relativism developed by the sophists with the help of the famous nature/culture (*nomos/phusis*) polarity. On its own fragment 16 would not get Xenophanes far enough towards his eventual destination. From the premiss that what *particular* human features we ascribe to the gods is a function of what features different ones among us happen to possess ourselves, it is still some way to the conclusion that the very idea of god's possessing human features of *any* kind is nothing but a projection by humans of their own characteristics on to the divine. This conclusion is mediated by the thought-experiment of fragment 15, which is simply a counter-factual extension of the argument of fragment 16: if the conception of god varies among men according to race, it is reasonable to conjecture that, if *other* animals could conceive of god, their conceptions would vary according to species. So our idea of what god is like is nothing but a similarly speciesist exercise in self-projection.

The account of Xenophanes' thought presented so far has discussed those parts of the remains of his oeuvre whose interpretation is not controversial. When we move beyond them fierce disagreement breaks out. On each of the three main areas covered by the rest of the fragments – god as he *should* be conceived, the natural world, the prospects for knowledge – the evidence is evaluated very differently by scholars of different casts of mind.

A small group of fragments explains what god is really like. Xenophanes does not argue the case. He simply declares the truth as he sees it:

> One god is greatest among gods and men, in no way similar to mortals either in body or thought.
> (Clement *Miscellanies* V.109.1: fr. 23 [KRS 170])

> All of him sees, all thinks, all hears.
> (Sextus Empiricus *Adversus Mathematicos* IX.144: fr. 24 [KRS 172])

> Always he remains in the same place, moving not at all; nor is it fitting for him to go to different places at different times, but without toil he shakes all things with the thought of his mind.
> (Simplicius *Physics* 23. 11 and 20: frs 26 and 25 [KRS 171])

Is fragment 23 an enunciation of monotheism, the first in Western thought? Views are divided.[49] The best comparison with Xenophanes' couplet is a line of Homer:

> One omen is best, to defend the fatherland.
> (Homer *Iliad* XII.243)

Here Hector is rejecting a warning against fighting from his adviser Polydamas, who has inferred a bad omen from the appearance of an eagle to the left, flying with a snake in its beak which it then savaged and dropped into the midst of the Trojan host. Hector's memorably sceptical reply does two things. It *says* that there is only one good omen, much better than all the rest, namely patriotic action. But in suggesting that the other sorts of omens, on which the likes of Polydamas rely, are worthless as a basis for decision and action, it *implies* a radical reinterpretation of the very idea of an omen, removing from it any connotation of divine revelation, and reducing – or elevating – it to a human moral imperative. So Hector's assertion is in effect much stronger: not just that there is only one *good* omen, but that there is only one *real* omen, which is obeying the appropriate human imperative. Xenophanes' thesis works in exactly the same way. It *says* there is only one supreme god. It *implies* there is only one *real* god. For the very idea of god has to be reconceived. Fragments 23–6 show what this theoretical revolution is to consist in. We must rid ourselves of the notion that a god needs limbs and sense organs like a human being (cf. fragments 14–16). He can cause things to happen by thought alone, without moving a muscle; all of him sees, hears, thinks. Is he then a pure bodiless mind? Xenophanes writes as though the issue is not whether but *how* to think of god's body. So while it is tempting to diagnose a further radical implication, questioning whether god needs a body at all, interpretation is probably not justified in going that far. This is to find some measure of agreement with Aristotle (*Metaphysics* 986b22–3) that Xenophanes made nothing clear about 'the one' (i.e. the Eleatic one, which is what Aristotle took his god to be).

Did fragments 23–6 belong to the satirical attack on the views of Homer and Hesiod which constituted the context of fragments 11 and 14–16? Or were they extracted from a quite different poem devoted to philosophy of nature, as Diels supposed? Diels' conjecture seems an improbable one. Leaving aside the vexed issue of whether there *was* a separate poem about nature, we should note: (a) Clement quotes fragments 23, 14 and 15 consecutively in that order, as though they were all part of the same piece of writing. Certainly it is more plausible and economical to postulate reliance on an excerptor plundering *one* original source, not two. (b) The idea that gods make journeys, rejected at fragment 26, exactly matches the conception of the gods in Homer. (c) Fragments 23–6 are interested in exactly the same general question about the divine as fragments 11 and 14–16: how should it be conceived? They say nothing on the other hand about the cosmic role of god. Theophrastus, who thought with Aristotle that Xenophanes might be meaning to identify god with the universe, none the less observed that mention of Xenophanes' view is not appropriate in an enquiry into nature, but is a subject for another branch of philosophy, presumably 'first philosophy' or metaphysics. No doubt he made this comment because he could find in Xenophanes no actual *discussion* of god's relation to the universe. This assessment is pretty well irresistible given his professed inability to decide whether Xenophanes held that the sum of things is one or alternatively that there is a single principle of things.[50]

I infer that Xenophanes said all that he said about god in his lampoon against Homer and Hesiod, and that not unexpectedly his instructions there on how we *should* think of god did not extend very much beyond the few lines which survive as fragments 23–6. Later doxographical reports are confident that Xenophanes claimed much more: notably that god is spherical in shape. We know the ultimate source of these reports. It is a remarkable reconstruction of Xenophanes as an Eleatic monist, employing metaphysical argumentation in the style of Melissus and Gorgias, and known to us in a version preserved in the pseudo-Aristotelian treatise *On Melissus, Xenophanes and Gorgias*. The important thing about this presentation of Xenophanes for our present concerns is precisely that it *is* a reconstruction, in a later idiom involving techniques and assumptions unthinkable before Parmenides.[51]

The basis of the proposition that Xenophanes made god a sphere is clear enough. It derives its main inspiration from Parmenides' lines arguing that what is is 'perfected, like the bulk of a ball (*sphairē*) well-rounded on every side, equally balanced in every direction from the centre' (fr. 8. 42–4). The actual piece of argument ascribed to Xenophanes goes as follows:

> Being one, it is like all over, seeing and hearing and having the other senses all over. Otherwise if there were parts of god they would control and be controlled by each other, which is impossible. But being like all over, it is spherical: for it is not such here but not there, but all over.
>
> ([Aristotle] *On Melissus, Xenophanes and Gorgias* 977a36–b2)

This extract gives a good impression of how the writer works. It looks very unlikely that he has any more to go on in his construction of Xenophanes' reasoning than fragments 23 and 24. He gets the unity of god from fragment 23 (cf. 977a23–4). That Xenophanes believes god is like all over is inferred from fragment 24, and then made the consequence of his unity, in line with a similar inference attributed to Melissus by this same author (974a12–14). The key move to the conclusion that god is therefore spherical is finally worked out by application of reasoning borrowed from fragment 8.22–4, 42–5 of Parmenides.[52]

Despite the preoccupation of many of our sources for Xenophanes with his theology, there is little doubt that his discussions of questions about the heavenly bodies and meteorological phenomena were in fact more extensive. As well as a number of fragments on these topics, a considerable amount of information about his views relating to them is preserved in the doxography. What is missing, however, is evidence of a cosmogony, or of the associated drive towards a comprehensive narrative characteristic for example of Anaximander. Thus the general survey of his thought in the *Miscellanies* attributed to Plutarch sticks mostly to a summary of the pseudo-Aristotelian Xenophanes, interrupted and then completed by a disjointed sequence of reports about specific theses of Xenophanes' physics or epistemology. Hippolytus' overview is better organized, but on physical questions very brief and selective until a final section on large-scale changes in the relation of earth and sea.[53]

We should therefore conclude that there probably never was a single poem devoted to natural philosophy. It is less easy to conjecture what form Xenophanes' writing on the various natural questions which interested him would have taken. Indeed we are in a position of total ignorance on the issue. One thing clear from the few surviving fragments, however, is that many of his verses echoed lines of Homer and Hesiod, invariably to subvert the picture of the natural world they conveyed.

Consider for example the following pair of lines attributed to Xenophanes:

All things that come to be and grow are earth and water.
(Simplicius *Physics* 189.1: fr. 29 [KRS 181])

For we have all come to be from earth and water.
(Sextus Empiricus *Adversus Mathematicos* IX.34: fr. 33 [KRS 182])

These verses recall Menelaus' words in the *Iliad*, cursing the Achaeans:

May you all become earth and water.
(Homer *Iliad* VII.99)

Perhaps Xenophanes' point against Homer would have been that everything alive already *is* earth and water. Whether or not that is how he began his presentation of the idea, his further development of it probably included his remarkable argument for the cyclical process of alternate domination of the earth's surface by earth and sea:

Xenophanes thinks that a mixture of the earth with the sea is going on, and that in time the earth is dissolved by the moist. He says that he has demonstrations of the following kind: shells are found inland and in the mountains, and in the quarries in Syracuse he says that an imprint of a fish and seals were found; and in Paros an imprint of coral in the depth of the rock, and in Malta slabs of rock containing all sorts of sea creatures. These, he says, were produced when everything was long ago covered with mud, and the imprint was dried in the mud. All mankind is destroyed whenever the earth is carried down into the sea and becomes mud; then there is another beginning of coming into being, and this is the foundation for all worlds.
(Hippolytus *Refutation* I.14.5 [KRS 184])

The idea of a cycle of this kind had probably been anticipated by Anaximander, who certainly held that the earth was once much wetter than it is now. But Xenophanes thought the world was at a different phase of the cycle: the earth is not drying out, but reverting to sea. And although Anaximander may have appealed to the evidence of fossils, this is actually attested only for Xenophanes. Whether Xenophanes collected the evidence himself or relied on the reports of others, his assemblage of examples and conception of their significance constitute one of the high points of Ionian *historiē* (enquiry).

The longest physical fragment is also about the sea:

> Sea is the source of water, and source of wind. For neither <would there be the force of wind blowing forth from> inside clouds without the great ocean, nor streams of rivers nor shower water from the air above: but the great ocean is begetter of clouds and winds and rivers.
>
> (Geneva scholium on the *Iliad* XXI.196: fr.30 [KRS 183])

These lines may have belonged to the same poem as did the verses about earth and water. On the other hand there is reason to conjecture a separate poem directed explicitly or implicitly against traditional conceptions of the heavenly bodies as divinities with marvellous properties.[54]

The striking description of the ocean (*pontos*) as 'begetter' already recalls, yet simultaneously rationalizes, Hesiod's account of how it 'begat' Nereus, the old man of the sea, and other mythical figures (*Theogony* 233–9). But the mention of clouds among the offspring of ocean is particularly significant, for the doxographical evidence makes it clear that Xenophanes explained virtually all astronomical and meteorological phenomena in terms of cloud. On these subjects his thinking was both relentlessly systematic and at the same time satirical: the object was to reduce mystery and grandeur to something familiar and homely.[55] Thus the moon is a compressed ('felted') cloud that is on fire. But it 'does no work in the boat', i.e. unlike the sun it does not sustain life.[56] Comets, shooting stars and meteors are groups or movements of burning clouds. St Elmo's fire occurs when cloudlets glimmer owing to a particular sort of movement, and lightning is very similar. A fragment survives which explains that,

> What they call Iris, this too is cloud: purple and red and yellow to behold.
>
> (Scholium bT on the *Iliad* XI.27: fr. 32 [KRS 178])

Here Xenophanes is undoubtedly attempting to demystify and demythologize the rainbow. Iris is no goddess, nor is it a 'marvel to behold' (*thauma idesthai*, in Homeric language), merely a variety of colours 'to behold' (*idesthai*).

The most intriguing of Xenophanes' astronomical explanations are those he gives for the stars and the sun. Here the basic identification as burning cloud is reiterated. But much more detail is given by the doxography. The stars are quenched each morning but flicker again at night like coals. The sun is generated anew each day by the collection of widely scattered flaming particles. This extraordinary idea was probably supported with the claim that the phenomenon can actually be observed at dawn from the heights of Mount Ida above Homer's Troy, when rays originally separate are seen to coalesce into a single ball.[57] It would seem to follow that the process of coalescence must happen again and again every day at different longitudes. Xenophanes was not afraid to draw the logical and undignified conclusion:

> Xenophanes says that there are many suns and moons according to regions, sections and zones of the earth, and that at a particular moment the disc is banished into some section of the earth not inhabited by us – and so, tumbling into a hole, as it were, produces the phenomenon of an eclipse. He also says that the sun goes onward indefinitely, but is thought to move in a circle because of the distance.
>
> (Aetius II.24.9 [KRS 179])

We have specific reason to think that Xenophanes' account of the sun occurred in the same poem as fragment 30: it is quoted by a doxographer who explains that the vapour from the sea which turns eventually into clouds, showers and winds is drawn up by the action of the sun (Aetius III.4.4 [DK 21 A 46]).

What epistemological status did Xenophanes accord to these speculations? A famous and much discussed quatrain gives us his answer, which sounds as though it might have served as a prologue to one of the physical poems:

> No man knows, or ever will know, the clear truth about the gods and about all the things I speak of. For even if someone happened to say something exactly so, he himself none the less does not know it, but opinion is what is the outcome [lit. 'is constructed'] in all cases.
>
> (Sextus Empiricus *Adversus Mathematicos* VII.49 and 110: fr. 34 [KRS 186])

These are the lines which later writers fastened upon in their determination to find ancient antecedents for a radically sceptical stance on the prospects for human knowledge.[58] Certainly Xenophanes is claiming that there is *something* that man does not nor ever will know. But the claim is qualified in two ways. First, the subject-matter is restricted to truths about the gods and 'all the things I speak of': presumably astronomical and meteorological phenomena. Second, when Xenophanes says that no human will ever know the *clear* truth about them, he appears to allow that a person might attain the *truth* on these matters. This idea is amplified in the final clause of the fragment, where translation is unfortunately disputed. On the version given here, Xenophanes states that *opinion* is what is the outcome for everyone. Opinion must therefore be precisely a state of belief (true or false) that does *not* put a person in the position of knowing the truth. The claim is then that no human can be in any other condition so far as concerns the nature of gods and of the heavens.

Xenophanes does not say *why* this is so. There are a number of different ingredients in his concept of knowledge which may indicate the explanation he envisages. First, what the gods or the heavens are like is something inaccessible to direct human experience. Second, when he suggests that someone might 'happen' to say what is true on this subject, he implies that humans have no unfailingly reliable means of establishing the truth – as would be required if knowledge were to be achieved. Finally, the introduction of the notion of clarity suggests that Xenophanes thinks knowledge would be transparent: a knower would know that he knows.[59]

So interpreted Xenophanes' scepticism is limited to a denial that in theology, astronomy and meteorology there can ever be a direct, unfailingly reliable or transparent grasp of the truth even on the part of a person who is in fact in possession of it. On this reading (indeed on most readings) fragment 34 constitutes another instance of the relexive, self-critical turn philosophy takes in his hands. Its point is doubtless to indicate that the claims he is advancing about nature and the divine are modest so far as regards their epistemological status. Other evidence tends to confirm that the object is not to imply any actual *doubt* that those claims are true. The other principal surviving remark on knowledge attributed to Xenophanes says:

> Yet the gods have not revealed all things to mortals from the
> beginning; but by seeking they find out better with time.
>
> (Stobaeus I.8.2: fr. 18 [KRS 188])

This fragment is optimistic about the prospects for discovering the truth. Take the question: is the sea gradually inundating the earth? The gods have not revealed to us the answer just like that – but fragment 18 indicates that by observing for example the fossil record we can find out what it is reasonable to regard as the truth of the matter.[60] The first words of an injunction of Xenophanes (unfortunately truncated) ran:

> Let these be accepted, certainly, as like the realities . . .
>
> (Plutarch *Symposium* 746B: fr. 35 [KRS 187])

This might be interpreted as saying: you are justified in your belief that this is what reality is like (. . . even if you cannot know it).

For Heraclitus Xenophanes was one of those thinkers whose far-flung learning had not brought them understanding. Yet Heraclitus' own ideas about god and knowledge and the heavenly bodies seem to owe much to Xenophanes'. Nor were Plato and Aristotle wrong to perceive his influence on Parmenides, even if he was no Eleatic monist. Without our evidence relating to Xenophanes it would in fact be difficult to understand how philosophy made the transition from Milesian cosmology to the metaphysical and epistemological orientation shared by Heraclitus and Parmenides. Some of his speculations look naïve beyond belief. But he had witty and subtle things to say on all manner of topics. He cherished a healthy regard for evidence: the naïveté is in good part the consequence of his rigour in refusing to go much beyond it. And so far as western thought is concerned, he invented both monotheism and critical theology.

 NOTES

1 A good general account of Thales: KRS ch. 2. For a more ambitious view of what we may reasonably conjecture about his cosmology see West [2.59].

2 Cf. Herodotus I.74–5, 170 [KRS 74, 66, 65]. Solar eclipse: best discussion still Heath [2.33], ch. 3; also e.g. Panchenko [2.53]. That any eclipse Thales predicted was visible in Asia Minor must have been due to luck. Probably it is largely on account of this feat that he came to be credited with views on the causes of eclipses, the nature of the heavenly bodies, and the zones of the heavens [DK 11 A 13c, 17, 17a and b].

3 Texts and discussion: KRS, pp. 81–6, 100–5. On the map see Kahn [2.49], 82–4; on early Greek astronomical knowledge Dicks [2.47]; Kahn [2.50]; Burkert [2.25], ch. 4, sect. 1.

4 See Aristotle *On the Soul* 405a19–21, 411a7–8, Diogenes Laertius I.24, with discussion in KRS pp. 95–8.

5 See Aristotle *Metaphysics* 983b6–984a3. Discussion in KRS, pp. 89–95 On Hippias: Snell [2.57]; Mansfeld [2.40], chs 3, 5.

6 On the physics of flat-earthism see Furley [2.32], chs 1, 2, 18.

7 The doxographical evidence is confused. One source ([Plutarch] *Miscellanies* 3 [KRS 148]) states explicitly that the sun is earth; and Hippolytus' evidence that it is flat and rides on air makes sense only on that assumption (KRS 150, quoted above). However the doxography seems generally to have understood 'fiery' as '*composed* of fire' (cf. Runia [2.67]); and one suspect passage (Hippolytus *Refutation* I.7.5 [KRS 149]) is explicit on the point. Perhaps the ambiguity of 'stars' as heavenly bodies in general or the fixed stars in particular added to the confusion.

8 Anaximenes also posited earthy bodies in the region of the 'stars', envisaged as being carried round with them (Hippolytus *Refutation* I.7.5; Aetius II.13.10

[KRS 152]). These were presumably introduced to account for eclipses: (cf. Hippolytus *Refutation* I.8. 6, 9 on Anaxagoras [KRS 502]).

9 Aristotle's comparison with a lid probably derives not from Anaximenes but from Anaxagoras' version of flat-earthism. Note the reference in the sequel to the *clepsydra* (294b18–21), elsewhere associated by him with Anaxagoras (*Physics* 213a22–7 [KRS 470]).

10 Pre-Socratics seem not to have mentioned predecessors or contemporaries by name except to attack them. An explicit critique of Thales is not attested nor likely for Anaximander or Anaximenes, but is attributed to Xenophanes (Diogenes Laertius IX.18 [KRS 161]). No book: various writings are ascribed to Thales, notably a 'Nautical star-guide' (Simplicius *Physics* 23.25–9, Diogenes Laertius I.23 [KRS 81–2]). But already in antiquity their authenticity was doubted: for a cautiously sceptical review of the evidence see KRS, pp. 86–8.

11 The few mentions in the doxography of physical theses about the constitution and behaviour of the heavenly bodies which Thales is supposed to have advanced (texts at DK 11 A 17a and b) are either inconsistent with better evidence or merely isolated assertions. E.g. the claim that Thales knew the moon derived its light from the sun is at odds with the strong evidence that Anaximander and Anaximenes did not. Such knowledge is first credibly associated with Parmenides (fr. 14, KRS 308) or Anaxagoras (Plato *Cratylus* 409a–b; Hippolytus *Refutation* I.8.8 [KRS 502]) among philosophers.

12 See Mansfeld [2.40], ch. 5.

13 Geocentric conception: Anaximander famously located the earth in the middle of a symmetrical cosmos, with the sun, moon and stars conceived as circling round it in a sequence of concentric rings. For a treatment of Anaximander's logic as represented by Aristotle see Barnes [2.8], 23–9; also Makin [2.52].

14 So Robinson [2.55]; Furley [2.32], ch. 2. Their views are very effectively criticized by Panchenko [2.54].

15 Texts on the shape of the earth and the celestial rings are collected and discussed in KRS, pp. 133–7.

16 Interestingly, a claim that Anaximander's earth 'moves round the middle of the cosmos' is ascribed to Eudemus (Theon of Smyrna p. 198H [DK 12 A 26]). Its truth and provenance are generally doubted: Kahn [2.49], 54–5. But it may originate from an attempt to work out what would be the behaviour of a *cylinder* in unstable equilibrium at the centre of the universe: this would be rotation about its own axis.

17 'Not controlled by anything' is unclear. Perhaps a contrast with the sun, moon and stars is intended: their behaviour *is* controlled by the misty rings which envelope the fire which constitutes them.

18 The sentence about Anaximander seems unmotivated in context, unless seen as completing Alexander's argument that he is not the primary focus of the Aristotelian passage which names him (Simplicius *On the Heavens* 532.7–12). So construed its point will be to suggest that because the theory Aristotle mentions does not really represent Anaximander's position, he must actually have another proponent of it in mind.

19 Simplicius complains that Alexander's presentation of the indifference theory substitutes considerations about equilibrium (derived from Plato) for an argu-

ment from likeness (which is what Aristotle's text actually gives us): *On the Heavens* 535.4–8.

20 The major study of Anaximander: Kahn [2.49]. On Anaximander's book and its significance: Kahn [2.49], 6–8, 199–208; Burkert [2.25], 239–40. Although he is said to have been the first to write 'on nature' (see KRS, pp. 102–3), the claim of the strange Pherecydes of Syros to be the first prose author is stronger if not overwhelming: evidence in KRS, pp. 51–2; discussion e.g. in Kahn [2.49], 240; Schibli [2.56], 4.

21 See especially *Physics* III.4, 5. Modern discussions of the *apeiron*: KRS, pp. 105–17, Kahn [2.49], App. II; Guthrie [2.13] I: 83–9.

22 See in general Diels [2.1]; for Anaximander in particular Kahn [2.49], 11–71. A brief statement in KRS, pp. 1–6.

23 Often observed by readers, but particularly well discussed by Kahn [2.49], 112 n.1.

24 For a contrary view see e.g. Guthrie [2.13] I ch. 3 (esp. pp. 89–91), who holds that Anaximander conceived of the emergence of the world as the development of a cosmic organism; see also West [2.59]. On Anaximander's analogies: Lloyd [2.37].

25 Tannery [2.58], 92 (quoted by Kahn [2.49], 102).

26 So e.g. KRS, pp. 141–2; Kahn [2.49], 112–13.

27 One text attests Anaximander's recognition of the ecliptic: the circles of the sun and moon 'lie aslant' (Aetius II.25.1 [DK 12 A 22]).

28 See Aristotle *Meteorology* 353b5–11 [KRS 132], with Alexander *Meteorology* 67. 3–12 [DK 12 A 27]. Well discussed by Kahn [2.49], 66–7.

29 Spheres: Aetius II.16.5; planet circle: Aetius II.15.6 [DK 12 A 18]. Zones: Kahn [2.49], 88–9.

30 See West [1.21], 89–91.

31 So Kahn [2.49], App. II.

32 Eternal motion: Hippolytus *Refutation* I.6.2 [KRS 101, 115]; intermediate character: Aristotle *On the Heavens* 303b10–13 [KRS 109], *On Generation and Corruption* 332a19–25 [KRS 103], with discussion in KRS, pp. 111–13; Kahn [2.49], 44–6.

33 Theophrastus' words: Simplicius *Physics* 24.17–18 [KRS 101]. Assimilation to atomist theory: Simplicius *Physics* 1121.5–9, [Plutarch] *Miscellanies* 2 [KRS 101], Aetius I.3.3 [DK 12 A 14]. Right in general thrust: so Conche [2.46], ch.5 (cf. also Guthrie [2.13] I: 106–15), against, e.g. KRS, pp. 122–6; Kahn [2.49], 46–53.

34 See above all Kahn [2.49], ch. 3 (but his suggestion that the fragment may extend back to 'And out of those things . . .' is idiosyncratic and unpersuasive).

35 For this interpretation see Barnes [2.8], 33–4.

36 Good general accounts of Anaximenes in KRS and Guthrie [2.13] I.

37 For the later coinage (*sunkratein*) and substitution of *pneuma* see KRS, pp. 158–62. For *hoion* as 'for example' see Longrigg [2.51]. Barnes notes the absence of a connecting particle, common with this use of *hoion* ([2.8], 55).

38 Cf. Barnes [2.8], 46–7, 55.

39 A selection of relevant texts (with discussion) at KRS, pp. 154–8. Anaximenes seems to have suggested a fresh simile to recommend the Anaximandrian account of thunder and lightning: the flashing of oars cleaving the water (Aetius III.3.2 [KRS 158]).

40 Cf. Hippolytus *Refutation* I.7.2–3 [KRS 141]; for Anaximander cf. [Plutarch] *Miscellanies* 2[KRS 121].

41 [Plutarch] *Miscellanies* 3 [KRS 148]; Aetius II.23.1 [KRS 153].

42 Attribution of the notion to Anaximenes is generally accepted, but denied by Stokes [2.42], 43–8. For an elegant logical articulation of it and defence of its Anaximenian credentials see Barnes [2.8], 38–44.

43 A sound and useful edition with translation – of the doxography as well as the fragments – and commentary: Lesher [2.60].

44 Heraclitus: fr.40 [KRS 255]; Plato: *Sophist* 242c–d [KRS 163]; Aristotle: *Metaphysics* 986b18–12 [KRS 164, 174]; Theophrastus: Simplicius *Physics* 22.26–31 [KRS 165]; Timon: Sextus Empiricus *Outlines of Pyrrhonism* I.223–4 [DK 21 A 35]. According to Diogenes Laertius (IX.111), he had a function in Timon's *Silloi* analogous to Virgil's in Dante's *Divine Comedy*. For the later episodes of the story see e.g. Mansfeld [2.40], chs 6–8.

45 So Burnet [2.11], 115–16, in what remains a sparkling treatment of Xenophanes' work. A more recent statement of the same view: Steinmetz [2.69], 54–73.

46 A good discussion of Xenophanes' attitude to Thales in Lesher [2.60], 120–4.

47 On Xenophanes' chronology: Steinmetz [2.69], 13–34.

48 For further discussion see Lesher [2.60], 47–77.

49 Monotheist: e.g. Barnes [2.8], 82–99; polytheist: e.g. Stokes [2.42], ch. 3.

50 For Aristotle's view see *Metaphysics* 986b24–5 [KRS 174] (but his meaning is disputed); Theophrastus' view is preserved at Simplicius *Physics* 22.26–31 [KRS 165].

51 The key modern study of the Xenophanes doxography and its relation to Theophrastus and *On Melissus, Xenophanes and Gorgias* (*MXG*) is Mansfeld [2.40], ch. 6. It has often been supposed that because Hippolytus (*Refutation* I.14.2) says that Xenophanes' god is spherical, it can be inferred that this was Theophrastus' view too (e.g. Burnet [2.11], 125, n.1). But the supposition is incompatible with evidence that Xenophanes did not in his opinion make god limited or unlimited (Simplicius *Physics* 22.26–9 [KRS 165]) unless it is supposed that he is reflecting contradictory remarks by Xenophanes made presumably in different places (so Steinmetz [2.69], 48–54). The date of *MXG* itself is uncertain, although the presentation of Xenophanes it contains – on which see the excellent brief discussion by Lesher [2.60], 192–4 – may go back to the early third century BC. Some scholars continue to defend the credibility of the *MXG* version of Xenophanes: e.g. Barnes [2.8], 84–94; Finkelberg [2.62]. See also Cassin [2.61].

52 It is sometimes suggested (e.g. Steinmetz [2.69], 35–40) that e.g. *homoiēn*, 'like', is an authentically Xenophanean divine attribute, on the strength of Timon, fr.59 (preserved in Sextus Empiricus *Outlines of Pyrrhonism* I. 223 [DK 21 A 35]). But Timon already reads Xenophanes in the fashion of Aristotle and Theophrastus as an Eleatic monist. It seems likelier that he is in fact drawing on a version of the *MXG* account of Xenophanes' theology.

53 See [Plutarch] *Miscellanies* 4 [DK 21 A 32]; Hippolytus *Refutation* I.14 [DK 21 A 33]. No cosmogony: one fragment reads 'All things are from earth and to earth all things come in the end' (fr. 27). In the doxography where this line is quoted it is taken as committing Xenophanes to a cosmogony (Theodoretus, *Therapy for Greek Malaises* IV.5 [DK 21 A 36]). But this conflicts with Xeno-

phanes' stress elsewhere on sea as a source of things, and with Aristotle's denial that any pre-Socratic monist made earth the first principle (*Metaphysics* 989a5–6). Probably Xenophanes meant only that the earth was the origin of all living things: so Guthrie [2.13] I: 383–7; Lesher [2.60], 124–8. The intricacies of the doxography are indicated in Mansfeld [2.40], 150–5.

54 This is the standard interpretation: cf. e.g. Guthrie [2.13] I: 386–7. That popular beliefs are the target of the whole body of Xenophanes' physical fragments is well argued by Lesher [2.60], 124–48. For texts and discussion see also KRS, pp. 172–8.

55 The main modern disagreement about Xenophanes' handling of physical topics is whether he treats them as intrinsically ludicrous, deserving only opportunistic flights of fancy or brief debunking, or works out a serious systematic and comprehensive theory, albeit mocking popular misconceptions at the same time. The first view: Burnet [2.11], 121–5; Guthrie [2.13] I: 387–94; Steinmetz [2.69], 54–68. The second: Fränkel [2.63], 119–21; [2.30], 334 (which complains however of 'poverty-stricken' empiricism); Hussey [2.35], 26 (who credits Xenophanes with a more admirable ontological and methodological 'parsimony'); Lesher [2.60], 145–8.

56 On the moon see Runia [2.67].

57 So Keyser [2.64]. The doxographical evidence about Xenophanes' sun is complex and confusing; for discussion see Runia [2.68].

58 On ancient interpretations of Xenophanes' epistemology, see Mansfeld [2.40], 156–9; on modern see Lesher [2.60], 159–69 (summarizing Lesher [2.65]). A good recent treatment: Hussey [2.35].

59 For knowledge as direct (not a matter of sign-inference), cf. Alcmaeon, fr.1 [KRS 439]; as transparent, cf. Hippocrates *On Ancient Medicine* 1. Not everyone would agree that Xenophanes incorporates all three notions in his concept of knowledge.

60 So Lesher [2.66]. But this may be a text relating rather to the origins of civilization and discovery of the arts: so e.g. Guthrie [2.13] I: 399–401. Note also that fr.35 is 'fraught with ambiguity and uncertainty': Lesher [2.60], 171. The limitations of human understanding are probably the focus of another famous Xenophanean remark: 'If god had not made yellow honey, they would think figs were much sweeter' (fr.38 [KRS 189]).

❧ GENERAL BIBLIOGRAPHY ❧ FOR CHAPTERS 2–6

Texts

Original language editions

2.1 Diels, H. *Doxographi Graeci*, Berlin, G. Reimer, 1879 (repr. de Gruyter 1965). Original texts of the main doxographers, with Latin prolegomena.

2.2 Diels, H. rev. W. Kranz *Die Fragmente der Vorsokratiker*, 3 vols, 6th edn, Berlin, Weidmannsche Verlagsbuchhandlung, 1951. Original texts of fragments and testimonia, with German translation of fragments. This standard work is cited as DK. References are by chapter, each of which is divided into testimonia (A) and fragments (B). Numbered fragments mentioned in the text are found under that number in DK.

2.3 KRS [1.6]. Original texts with English translation and commentary.

2.4 Mansfeld, J. *Die Vorsokratiker*, Stuttgart, Philipp Reclam, 1987. Original texts with German translation and notes.

2.5 Wright, M. R. *The Presocratics*, Bristol, Bristol Classical Press, 1985. Original texts with notes for readers with elementary Greek.

Collections of texts in translation

2.6 Barnes, J. *Early Greek Philosophy*, Harmondsworth, Penguin, 1987.

2.7 McKirahan, R. D., Jr. *Philosophy Before Socrates*, Indianapolis, Ind. and Cambridge, Hackett, 1994. Contains substantial commentary.

General Surveys of Pre-Socratic Philosophy

2.8 Barnes, J. *The Presocratic Philosophers*, rev. edn, London, Routledge, 1982.

2.9 Brun, J. *Les Présocratiques*, 2nd edn, (Que sais-je? no. 1319) Paris, Presses Universitaires de France, 1973.

2.10 Burnet, J. *Greek Philosophy: Thales to Plato*, London, Macmillan, 1914 (numerous reprints).

2.11 —— *Early Greek Philosophy*, 4th edn, London, A. & C. Black, 1930.

2.12 Cornford, F. M. *From Religion to Philosophy*, London, Edward Arnold, 1957, repr. New York, Harper, 1957.

2.13 Guthrie, W. K. C. *A History of Greek Philosophy*, vols I–III, Cambridge, Cambridge University Press, 1962–9.

2.14 Hussey, E. *The Presocratics*, London, Duckworth, 1972.

Collections of articles

2.15 Allen, R. E. and Furley, D. J. (eds) *Studies in Presocratic Philosophy*, 2 vols, London, Routledge and Kegan Paul, 1970 and 1975.

2.16 Anton, J. P. and Kustas, G. L. (eds) *Essays in Ancient Greek Philosophy*, Albany, NY, SUNY Press, 1971.

2.17 Anton, J. P. and Preus, A. (eds) *Essays in Ancient Greek Philosophy*, vol. II, Albany, NY, SUNY Press, 1983.

2.18 Boudouris, K. (ed.) *Ionian Philosophy*, Athens, International Association for Greek Philosophy, 1989.

2.19 Mourelatos, A. P. D. (ed.) *The Pre-Socratics*, New York, Anchor Press/ Doubleday, 1974; rev. edn., Princeton, NJ, Princeton University Press, 1993.

2.20 Robb, K. (ed.) *Language and Thought in Early Greek Philosophy*, La Salle, Ill., Hegeler Institute, 1983.

2.21 Shiner, R. A. and King-Farlow, J. (eds) *New Essays on Plato and the Pre-Socratics, Canadian Journal of Philosophy*, suppl. vol. 2, 1976.

Bibliography

Mourelatos [2.19] contains a bibliography.

2.22 Navia, L. E. *The Presocratic Philosophers: An Annotated Bibliography*, New York and London, Garland Publishing, 1993.

2.23 Paquet, L., Roussel, M. and Lanfrance, Y. *Les Présocratiques: Bibliographie analytique (1879–1980)*, 2 vols, Montreal, Bellarmin, 1988–9.

General studies

2.24 Beare, J. I. *Greek Theories of Elementary Cognition*, Oxford, Clarendon Press, 1906.

2.25 Burkert, W. *Lore and Science in Ancient Pythagoreanism*, Cambridge, Mass. Harvard University Press, 1972 (German original Nuremberg, Verlag Hans Carl, 1962).

2.26 Cherniss, H. *Aristotle's Criticism of Presocratic Philosophy*, Baltimore, Md., Johns Hopkins University Press, 1935; repr. New York, Octagon Books, 1964, 1971.

2.27 Dicks, D. R. *Early Greek Astronomy to Aristotle*, Ithaca, NY, Cornell University Press, 1970.

2.28 Dodds, E. R. *The Greeks and the Irrational*, Berkeley, Calif., University of California Press, 1951.

2.29 Fränkel, H. *Wege und Formen frügriechischen Denkens*, Munich, C. H. Beck, 1968.

2.30 —— *Early Greek Poetry and Philosophy*, New York, Harcourt Brace Jovanovich, 1973 (German original Munich, C. H. Beck, 1969).

2.31 Furley, D. J. *The Greek Cosmologists*, vol. I, Cambridge, Cambridge University Press, 1987.

2.32 —— *Cosmic Problems*, Cambridge, Cambridge University Press, 1989.

2.33 Heath, T. L. *Aristarchus of Samos*, Oxford, Clarendon Press, 1913, repr. 1959.

2.34 —— *A History of Greek Mathematics*, 2 vols, Oxford, Clarendon Press, 1921.

2.35 Hussey, E. 'The beginnings of epistemology: from Homer to Philolaus', in S. Everson (ed.) *Companions to Ancient Thought I: Epistemology*, Cambridge, Cambridge University Press, 1990, pp. 11–38.

2.36 —— 'Ionian inquiries: on understanding the Presocratic beginnings of science', in A. Powell (ed.) *The Greek World*, London and New York, Routledge, 1995, pp. 530–49.

2.37 Lloyd, G.E.R. *Polarity and Analogy*, Cambridge, Cambridge University Press, 1966.

2.38 —— *Early Greek Science: Thales to Aristotle*, London, Chatto and Windus, 1970.

2.39 —— [1.7].

2.40 Mansfeld, J. *Studies in the Historiography of Greek Philosophy*, Assen and Maastricht, Van Gorcum, 1990.

2.41 Sambursky, S. *The Physical World of the Greeks*, London, Routledge and Kegan Paul, 1956.

2.42 Stokes, M. C. *One and Many in Presocratic Philosophy*, Cambridge, Mass., Harvard University Press, 1971.

2.43 Stratton, G. M. *Theophrastus and the Greek Physiological Psychology before Aristotle*, London, Allen and Unwin, and New York, Macmillan, 1917.

2.44 Thomson, G. *The First Philosophers*, 2nd edn, London, Lawrence and Wishart, 1961.

2.45 West [1.21].

Texts and studies of individual philosophers are listed in the bibliographies to the respective chapters.

BIBLIOGRAPHY
FOR CHAPTER 2

Milesians

Text

2.46 Conche, M. *Anaximandre, fragments et témoignages: Texte grec, traduction, introduction et commentaire*, Paris, Presses Universitaires de France, 1991.

Studies

2.47 Dicks, D. R. 'Solstices, equinoxes and the Presocratics', *Journal of Hellenic Studies* 86 (1966): 26–40.

2.48 Furley [2.32], esp. ch. 2, 'The dynamics of the earth: Anaximander, Plato and the centrifocal theory'.

2.49 Kahn, C. H. *Anaximander and the Origins of Greek Cosmology*, New York, Columbia University Press, 1960; repr. Indianapolis, Ind., and Cambridge, Hackett, 1994.

2.50 —— 'On early Greek astronomy', *Journal of Hellenic Studies* 90 (1970): 99–116.

2.51 Longrigg, J. 'A note on Anaximenes fragment 2', *Phronesis* 9 (1964): 1–5.

2.52 Makin, S. *Indifference Arguments*, Oxford, Blackwell, 1994.

2.53 Panchenko, D. 'Thales' prediction of a solar eclipse', *Journal for the History of Astronomy* 25 (1994): 275–88.

2.54 —— '"Ομοιος and ὁμοιότης in Anaximander and Thales', *Hyperboreus* 1 (1994): 28–55.

2.55 Robinson, J. M. 'Anaximander and the problem of the earth's immobility', in Anton and Kustas [2.16].

2.56 Schibli, H. S. *Pherekydes of Syros*, Oxford, Clarendon Press, 1990.

2.57 Snell, B. 'Die Nachrichten über die Lehren des Thales', *Philologus* 96 (1944): 170–82, repr with additions in Snell, *Gesammelte Schriften*, Göttingen, Vandenhoeck and Rupprecht, 1966, pp. 119–28.

2.58 Tannery, P., *Pour l'histoire de la science Hellène*, 2nd edn, Paris, Gauthier-Villars, 1930.

2.59 West, M. L. 'Ab ovo', *Classical Quarterly* NS 44 (1994): 289–307.

Xenophanes

Text

2.60 Lesher, J. H. *Xenophanes of Colophon: Fragments*: a text and translation with commentary (*Phoenix* suppl vol 32), Toronto, Toronto University Press, 1992. Includes substantial bibliography.

Studies

2.61 Cassin, B. *Si Parménide: le traité anonyme De Melisso Xenophane Gorgia*, Lille and Paris, Presses Universitaires de France, 1980.

2.62 Finkelberg, A. 'Studies in Xenophanes', *Harvard Studies in Classical Philology* 93 (1990): 103–67.

2.63 Fränkel, H. 'Xenophanes' empiricism and his critique of knowledge', in Mourelatos [2.19], pp. 118–31.

2.64 Keyser, P. 'Xenophanes' sun on Trojan Ida', *Mnemosyne* 45 (1992): 299–311.

2.65 Lesher, J. H. 'Xenophanes' scepticism', *Phronesis* 23 (1978): 1–21; repr in Anton and Preus [2.17].

2.66 —— 'Xenophanes on enquiry and discovery', *Ancient Philosophy* 11 (1991): 229–48.

2.67 Runia, D. 'Xenophanes on the moon: a *doxographicum* in Aetius', *Phronesis* 34 (1989): 245–69.

2.68 —— 'Xenophanes or Theophrastus? An Aëtian *doxographicum* on the sun', in W. W. Fortenbaugh and D. Gutas (eds) *Theophrastus: His Psychological, Doxographical and Scientific Writings*, New Brunswick, NJ, Rutgers University Press, 1992: pp. 112–40.

2.69 Steinmetz, P. 'Xenophanesstudien', *Rheinisches Museum* 109 (1966): 13–73.

CHAPTER 3

Heraclitus

Catherine Osborne

❧

No philosopher before Socrates can have had such a profound influence on so many generations of subsequent thinkers as Heraclitus. Nor can any thinker, probably in the whole history of philosophy, have inspired such a wide range of different ideas, all claiming in some way to be true to his authentic genius. Yet the sparsity of his written remains, and the richly obscure or even mystical style of his sayings, leave us with no grounds for concluding that one, rather than another of the great variety of Heracliteanisms on offer in the history of thought is more accurate than another. This fact is probably as it should be; for if I am right in the interpretation that I shall try to present in this chapter, Heraclitus' most important observation was that the significance of things changes with the time and place and context of the observer, and of the speaker; that what is the same differs from day to day; and that what one says, and the words one says it in, will mean different and even opposed things to different people, and for different purposes. Heraclitus, the purveyor of an eternal doctrine that is both familiar to all and obscure to most, illustrates in himself the very doctrine that he tried to present: that what counts as the same and what counts as opposed is decided by a significance acquired in a social or temporal context, and is not determined absolutely by a fixed nature or material constitution in the entities we observe.

❧ PROBLEMS OF INTERPRETATION ❧

The problems of interpretation that are characteristic of pre-Socratic thinkers are all the more acute for Heraclitus. Firstly, we have little reliable evidence about his life,[1] though much that is unreliable; but that scarcely seems to matter when we consider the much more severe difficulties involved in reconstructing his thought. None of his work is preserved directly in its own right, a situation that is normal for thinkers of this period. The texts that we have are collected from the quotations in later writers, some of them far removed in time from Heraclitus. Although we have more of these 'fragments' than we have of any of the earlier Ionian thinkers, two factors make Heraclitus' work peculiarly difficult to reconstruct. (1) Heraclitus seems to have expressed his views in the form of short pithy sayings, largely disconnected, in prose rather than poetry.[2] The disconnected brevity of the sayings may be true to the original style of his thought, or may be the effect of the extraction of memorable quotations by subsequent generations. For our purposes, what we have to work with are primarily extracts which include minimal connected argument.[3] As a result it is difficult to determine how to string these 'fragments' together, and indeed how to decide which words are attributed to Heraclitus in the quoting authority. (2) Because Heraclitus has been a peculiarly rich source of inspiration for subsequent generations of thinkers from Plato to Heidegger, the use made of him by thinkers of Sceptic, Stoic, Christian and Platonist persuasions has coloured the resources from which we have to reconstruct his thought. This means that although we have some versions of his own words which can be culled from these later thinkers, all those versions carry with them some preoccupations and interests from the later thinkers, both in the selection of texts that are preserved and the interpretations that are put upon them in the sources we are using.

Ideally, to work on Heraclitus a scholar will need to engage in detailed work on the context within which each of his sayings is preserved. None of us is in a position to read his work independently of the later thinkers who reconstructed his ideas on their own lines. This remains equally true of recent scholarship on the subject, which clearly shows that linking fragments together in support of a particular interpretation itself brings out resonances between the fragments.[4] Which resonances emerge depends on which fragments we juxtapose, and each reading validates itself by constructing a sequence of texts suited to its theme.[5] For our own part, the best that we can do in this chapter is to remind ourselves of the profound effect we create by placing a fragment in a particular context, and to take note wherever possible of the readings of those writers who preserve the fragments for us.[6] In this chapter the footnote included each time a new fragment is introduced will provide some minimal background regarding the quoting authority, and indicate whether the context prompts a particular reading. The reader who requires a quick and superficial grasp of the interpretation I am putting forward can afford to ignore these notes, but anyone who wishes to engage critically with the views presented here may need to pursue the suggestions made in the notes.

❧ RITUAL AND THE GODS ❧

Where, if at all, do the gods need to enter into the explanation of human and natural events? What should the divine nature be taken to be? These questions can be seen to underlie many of the concerns of thinkers before Parmenides. On a conventional view, the task engaging the earliest thinkers might be seen as a rationalist project to prise away the explanation of apparently mysterious phenomena from unpredictable divine beings and to ascribe them instead to predictable physical laws and patterns of behaviour. But the philosophers still sometimes speak of their own principles and causes as divine, and this indicates that their project is not an atheist drive to exclude the gods from the picture altogether. Indeed atheism is effectively unknown in antiquity.[7] The presence of the divine in the systematic explanations offered by the early thinkers should not be taken as merely a figure of speech. It suggests a revised account of the work of the gods, in which what is truly divine is a cause outside and beyond the humdrum decisions of unpredictable individuals. Hence the conventional picture of the gods in those terms is being rejected, but that is not to make the gods redundant, nor to say that the world is independent of any divine influence. Physics and theology are still closely linked, even in Xenophanes.

Heraclitus' analysis of religious practice and belief needs to be understood before we go any further. Perhaps religion is not peculiarly significant for Heraclitus, but it provides a classic illustration of his account of the complex significance of things in general.[8] Several of his sayings have been routinely taken as critical of established religious rites, and of conventional ideas of what gods are. But although Heraclitus clearly has *some* point to make about the rites and beliefs that he mentions, careful attention to his ideas suggests that the sayings usually taken to ridicule religion are better read as observations about the significance of the religious context: although these sayings argue against simple-minded misunderstanding of conventional piety, they do not condemn such piety in itself. Instead they offer a more sophisticated theological picture, one that belongs with Heraclitus' famous commitment to the unity of opposites.[9]

We may start by looking at a group of fragments concerned with conventional rituals. In fragment B5 people ('they') who are polluted with blood are said to purify themselves with blood.[10] Heraclitus compares the procedure with using mud to wash off mud and observes (quite correctly) that in ordinary life such a procedure would be thought insane:

Tainted with blood they purify themselves in a different way[11] as

90

if someone who stepped into mud were cleansed with mud. But any human who claimed that the person was doing that would be considered insane.[12]

This is the first part of an unusually long piece of Heraclitus' prose. On the standard interpretation[13] it is taken as a mocking reductio: what good is a purification of that sort? It can't work any more than a mud bath! Heraclitus, like a modern logical positivist, stands for no nonsense: look at the ritual in the cold light of reason, he says, and it cannot possibly produce the results that it claims to produce.

But is this right? Heraclitus says that in the ritual purification they 'purify themselves in a different way'. The word *allōs* is ambiguous: its basic meaning is 'differently' (the participants in the religious ritual are 'differently purified') but it can also mean 'pointlessly', and that is how it is usually taken when the saying is read as a reductio of religious practice. The ambiguity, as generally in Heraclitus, is surely not accidental.[14] The comparison with washing in mud demonstrates not the absurdity of the rite but the different logic that applies in the sacred context. Ritual purification is a different kind of washing, a kind that would be nonsensical or 'pointless' in the secular context where it would be like bathing in mud, and the claim to have been cleansed by a human agent in that way would be insane. Hence we shall read *allōs* as 'differently' if we see it from the religious point of view (the purification works in a different way), and as 'pointlessly' if we see it from the human point of view (the purification is no use at all).[15] The word itself changes its significance depending on the context or viewpoint of the reader, just as the rite of purification changes its significance when viewed as a sacred rite, or as a secular attempt at hygiene. Heraclitus implies that it is not insane for *god* to claim to cleanse us of the taint of blood that way, though the same claim from a human would be mad.

The second part of fragment B5 is about prayer. The worshippers, we are told, pray to the statues in a manner that is somehow analogous to talking to houses:

And they pray to these statues, as if someone, who knew nothing of what gods or heroes are like, were to converse with the houses.[16]

Once again the analogy has been taken as a reductio of religious practice. Praying to statues, Heraclitus would be saying, is about as effective as talking to houses.

But again it can be read another way. Notice that it is the one who does not understand the nature of gods and heroes who talks to the houses. This implies that if we understand what a god is we shall understand how the ritual of praying to statues works and why it is not a matter of talking to some old stones, whether sacred or secular. Heraclitus observes that what we do when we pray *is absurd* if considered from a non-religious viewpoint: someone who had no understanding of religion might try to achieve the same effect by talking to houses, and that would be to miss the point. Talking to stones makes sense if you understand about the gods, and not if you do not.

Both parts of fragment B5 can thus be taken to suggest that the meaning of religious rites is given by their religious context and cannot be judged on the logic of everyday secular practices. The same actions are either sense or nonsense depending on whether they are sacred or secular. This kind of observation about the contextual dependence of significance is familiar in many other Heraclitean sayings:[17] sea water is pure for fish and impure for humans;[18] the road up and the road down is one and the same;[19] the actions of cutting, burning and inflicting pain are good when performed in a case of surgery, and bad in a case of torture.[20]

In fragment B5 the one who does not understand what gods and heroes are will try to converse with stones. Conversation is, of course, part of the human way of life, and we know exactly what will be involved in making a successful job of it. One prerequisite will be that the conversation takes place with another living human person, and not a stone wall or an empty dwelling. Similarly washing is part of the human way of life, and it is essential that we wash away the dirt with something other than the very dirt we are removing. The parallels drawn in fragment B5 presuppose that the divine way of life is the same as the human way of life, and they point out that it does not make any sense when treated like that. So the theological error of one who takes the religious rite as a confused attempt to perform a simple human task is that of transferring human expectations into the divine context in which a different kind of behaviour makes sense. It is a kind of anthropomorphism. The ordinary people take the human way of life as a standard by which to judge activities that belong to religion. That may be what Heraclitus is saying when he cryptically comments, in B119,

ēthos anthrōpōi daimōn: 'the way of life for humanity is humanity's god'.[21]

In other words ordinary people fail to see that religious rituals operate in a different way from secular (human) habits and tasks, and that religious activities belong to another ethos in which those activities make sense. Failure to understand 'what the gods and heroes are' makes them see the religious activity as another human activity, but one that emerges as nonsense in the context of the human ethos that has become their god.

There are, then, two ways of life, that of religion in which we wash off blood with blood, and that of the human in which we do not converse with stones. In fragment B78 Heraclitus observes that the human way of looking at it has no sense:

> The human way [*ethos*] has no sense [*gnōmai*] but the divine way does.[22]

We might take this as a comment directly attached to fragment B5 in which case it concludes that washing off blood with blood does make sense so long as we recognize the divine way of life that gives it its sense; but there is no sense in the practice if it is viewed within the ethos of human activities. This leaves open the possibility that Heraclitus means that each kind of activity makes equally good sense, provided it is seen in its context, and the rationale of that ethos is respected. That position accords with Heraclitus' idea that a unified rationale (the *logos*) can be seen to underlie all our shared life and language, and to be in agreement with itself even where it appears to be different.[23]

Less satisfactory is an alternative interpretation which would give fragment B78 general significance, as an observation that in every circumstance the practices that depend upon the human or secular way of doing things are senseless, and that sense lies only in the divine way of doing things. The divine way of doing things is the religious or sacred rationale of ritual and sacrifice, in which we wash off blood with blood. Then Heraclitus would be saying that whereas ordinary people judge on the basis of the human ethos and find the sacred rituals to be nonsense, in fact the *sacred* is where sense is primarily located: those rites are not pointless but significant. On that account any sense that human practices have must be parasitic or derivative from the sacred practices that belong to the divine custom or *logos* and are expressed in shared human customs; yet it becomes unclear then why the secular practices should develop a different way of doing things, since, as Heraclitus says in B114, all human customs are nourished by the one divine way of doing things.[24] It therefore seems more appropriate to read fragment B78 with fragment B5, as saying that neither the sacred nor the secular is a privileged context: both are equally good reflections of the one underlying rationale that makes sense of all things, but an action only makes sense within its own context. What we must not do is forget the difference, and judge an action in the terms of the wrong ethos.

Fragment B15 is an observation about the rites held in honour of Dionysus, a divinity associated with an exuberant style of religious experience:

If it were not Dionysus for whom they held the procession and sang the hymn to the shameful parts, they would be performing the most shameless deeds . . .[25]

The festivals of Dionysus included a number of rituals that might be considered shocking. Heraclitus mentions particularly the procession of the phallus and the associated hymn, though the rest of the fragment also mentions the Dionysiac frenzy. But here it is not that such action would be shocking in a *secular* context but that the propriety of the actions is restricted, even within the religious sphere, to the honour of a particular deity: what is appropriate for Dionysus would not be done for Hades, god of the dead. Hence the context in which the same action is shameful or shameless is given not by whether we do it in a religious context but whether it is the right religious context.

In fact, however, Heraclitus goes on to say that Hades and Dionysus are one and the same:

But Hades is the same as the Dionysus for whom they rave and celebrate Lenaia.[26]

Now we cannot infer that one kind of rite suits one god and another another. The two gods in this case are one and the same. So is Heraclitus objecting to the variety of rituals? I think not, for elsewhere Heraclitus tells us that two things are 'one and the same':[27] not only the road up and the road down,[28] but also day and night[29] and the beginning and the end of a circle.[30] In none of these cases do we have to suppose that because two things are 'one and the same' they must demand the same response. We approach the uphill struggle differently from the same road taken as a downhill stroll, and what we do at night differs from what we do in the day, however much it simply depends on whether the sun is in our part of the sky whether the same hours are night or day.[31] Heraclitus' point is rather that, as he claims in B51,[32] things can differ while agreeing with themselves: something that is fundamentally the same is viewed under different aspects (as day and night, as up or down) and consequently merits and receives different responses appropriate to each.

So what are we to learn? The procession they perform for Dionysus is appropriate to Dionysus and would be inappropriate in the funerary contexts we associate with Hades.[33] You cannot do for Hades what you do for Dionysus. But that need not mean that Hades and Dionysus are two different deities. One and the same god, viewed under two different aspects, may merit two wholly different kinds of rite and response and Heraclitus may be denying that the deities thus worshipped are themselves different entities, (or he may be simply observing that we can and do regard them as a unity without difficulty).[34]

Thus Heraclitus does not ridicule the religious practices that belong within religion and to particular deities within religion; he argues that they make sense only within their context, and that the judgement of what is or is not right depends on understanding that context. Nevertheless the tone of his sayings is mocking, particularly in its use of the third person plural: 'they purify themselves', 'they pray to statues', 'they perform the procession'. Heraclitus does not say 'we' do these things. Evidently Heraclitus, as elsewhere, is claiming that the ordinary people are confused over the most obvious things, even when the evidence is before their very eyes.[35] If it is 'they' who do these things, then Heraclitus plainly thinks that 'they' are in a muddle.

However we need not suppose that the muddle is in the religious practices themselves. The muddle is apparently in people's understanding of the significance of the ritual: they do not see that the rationale of the ritual is distinct and peculiar to the sacred. Someone who fails to understand what gods and heroes are fails to see that the same action is a different action, with a different kind of point, in a sacred ritual, or in the rites of one particular god. Ordinary religion may be confused, not in its recognition of the sacred as a distinctive context, for that is quite proper, but because it fails to appreciate that it is the distinction of context itself which accounts for the distinctive significance of religious rites. The failure in religion would then be the failure of its adherents to appreciate what they were actually doing;[36] and that fits with Heraclitus' view that ordinary mortals generally fail to see what they are doing in the common way they live their lives, use their language and perceive what is obvious and familiar.[37] They go through life as though they were asleep.[38] They engage in the religious rituals, but they fail to grasp what gives them significance.[39]

CUSTOM AND SHARED PRACTICE

Those who speak with sense [xun noōi legontas] ought to rely
on what is common [xunos] among all things, just as a city
relies on custom – and much more reliably; for all human
customs are nourished by one custom, the divine one. It
exercises as much power as it likes, and is sufficient for all and
more besides.

(B114)[40]

Therefore one should follow what is xunos – that is, what is

common, for *xunos* means 'common' – but although the *logos*
is *xunos* most people live as though they had their own wisdom.

(B2)[41]

Custom and established practice is a shared feature of the life of mortals,
and with language (*logos*) it contains the key to understanding the
rationale (*logos*) of everything, according to Heraclitus.[42] There is no
reason to suppose that customary religious practice is excluded from
the shared customs to which people should owe allegiance and for
which they should fight as a city fights for its defending wall.[43] It seems
highly unlikely that Heraclitus is suggesting any kind of rejection of
the customary beliefs and practices; it is far more in keeping with his
ideas to suggest that we should look at those practices in a new light
and see for ourselves how they illustrate the universal principle that
what is fundamentally the same acquires significance in a variety of
contexts.

This is perhaps one aspect of the notion that human customs,
which rightly command our allegiance, are nourished by a single universal divine custom (or law, *nomos*):[44]

For all human customs are nourished by one custom, the divine
one . . .

(B114)

Human practices and customs may vary from city to city, but that
again will be simply a feature of the unity in diversity, the context-
dependent significance of human practices. It need not mean that they
do not cohere with a single underlying rationale that accounts for
the significance of everything, however apparently diverse. The 'divine
custom' here seems to be that universal rationale, and, as was suggested
in the identification of Hades and Dionysus, so here too, in B114, it is
said to be one.[45] This point precisely coheres with the sense of B67
which claims that God is 'day, night, winter, summer, war, peace, satiety,
hunger . . . all the opposites . . . and it changes like when [something]
is combined with spices and is named according to the savour of each'.[46]
There may be one god, but we give the one god a name according to
the context we encounter it in – a context which is not in any way
illusory or mistaken, but which quite properly transforms the significance we find in it and the name we consequently apply to that god.
Heraclitus shares with Xenophanes an interest in the varieties of ritual
representations of the gods. Perhaps he is not far from Xenophanes
when he wants to say that what are named as two are ultimately just
one god; but he does not think that recognizing this truth will involve
rejecting the variety of religious practices, although people may sometimes mistake their significance.

Thus adherence to shared practices and forms of life, whether religious, linguistic or any other kind of human custom, need not, in Heraclitus' view, be rejected, nor need it undermine his fundamental claim that there is just one common rationale that underpins the sense of the whole system. Indeed it is by adhering to, and defending, the shared life of the religious and linguistic community that we shall avoid turning aside into a private world of our own in which nothing has any sense. 'Heraclitus says that for those who are awake there is one common world, but among the sleepers each one turns to a private world' (B89).[47] It is clear that being awake to the significance of shared customs and practices is the same thing as being awake to Heraclitus' own message.

◆◆ THE LOGOS ◆◆

With this *logos* which is for ever human people are out of touch
[*axunetoi*] both before they hear it and once first they have
heard it; for although all things take place in accordance with
this *logos*, they are like beginners experimenting with both
words and practices such as these that I am going through as I
divide each thing according to nature and say how it is. But it
eludes other people what they are doing when they are awake,
just as it eludes them what they do when asleep.

(B1)[48]

This important text, which stood near the beginning of Heraclitus' work, suggests that ordinary people are unaware of what is going on, or indeed of what they are themselves doing, as though they were going through life asleep. What they are missing out on is 'this *logos*', but what exactly that might be is something of a mystery. We are told that it 'is for ever (or always)' and that all things take place in accordance with it; but it is also something that people hear, and yet fail to appreciate even when they have heard it. The word *logos*, which is etymologically linked to the word *legein* (to speak), can carry a range of meanings connected both with speech, rational discourse, sentence or word, and with logical reasoning, proportion, system, calculation, definition or explanation. It seems that Heraclitus has a point to make both about the rational coherence underlying our customary experiences of the world: their point or meaning, their explanation (something that is true and explanatory independently of Heraclitus' own verbal expression of it) *and* about his own attempt to present that explanation as a discourse in words. It is Heraclitus' presentation of the rationale underlying our shared world that we hear and yet fail to grasp; yet that rationale is something that we encounter in any case in all our actions and words, the actions and words that we fumble with as though we were beginners coming to a new subject. It is not really a new experience: it is the significance that has lain behind everything that has taken place so far in our lives. But we have encountered it in our sleep, so to speak, unable to take its meaning on board.

The *logos* is the objective explanatory rationale of the world, which is presented in Heraclitus' own *logos*, or discourse. It seems plain that it figures in that discourse both as the explicit subject (sometimes) of the argument and as the implicit message of it; for language and discourse is, like other shared practices, expressive of the common *logos* in its very structure. Thus we can 'hear' the *logos*, simply in virtue of hearing and understanding the language that Heraclitus and all the rest of us speak; though the understanding that would put us in touch with the *logos* is distinct from the understanding of the overt meaning of a text:

> Those who are out of touch [*axunetoi*], having heard, are just
> like deaf people; it is to them that the saying testifies that though
> present they are absent.
>
> (B34)[49]

Heraclitus distinguishes himself from the *logos* in a famous text:

> It is wise for those who have listened not to me but to the *logos*
> to agree that all things are one, Heraclitus says.
>
> (B50)[50]

The word for 'agree' (*homologein*) has often been recognized as a play on the notion of *logos*, together with the notion of sameness given by the root *homo*. One effect of understanding or hearing the *logos* is that wisdom follows and the hearer grants the coherence of the one universal *logos*. But why does hearing the *logos* not involve listening to Heraclitus himself? The point seems to be that we need to hear not merely what he says, but also the language in which he says it; the rational linguistic structure or form of life in which his discourse belongs, and which it implicitly expresses, can be 'heard' in what he says. It is that which tells us that *what* he says about the unity of the *logos* must be true. We could almost translate the text 'If you listen to the way the language works, rather than to what I say, you will rightly acknowledge all things to be one.'[51]

❧ EVERYTHING FLOWS ❧

It may be that the *logos* also has an explanatory role in the physical behaviour of the world. There is a long-standing tradition, from Plato onwards, that associates Heraclitus with a particular interest in change. In Plato's *Cratylus* he is said to be committed to the thesis that every-thing flows and nothing stays still;[52] in the *Theaetetus* he is caricatured as committed to such a radical thesis of total universal flux, that nothing whatever, neither a substance nor any of its attributes, stays stable long enough to be mentioned correctly by name, or to be said to 'be' rather than to 'flow' or 'become'.[53] In this situation truth becomes a meaningless notion and discourse is impossible. It is unlikely that the extreme flux doctrine developed in the *Theaetetus* is, or was even meant to be, true to Heraclitus' own views. But this need not mean that there was nothing authentically Heraclitean behind the notion that everything flows.

The most obviously relevant texts are a set known as the 'River fragments'. These may be variants of a single Heraclitean saying or he may have said several similar things.

> For it is not possible to step twice into the same river, according to Heraclitus, nor twice to touch a mortal being in the same condition . . .
>
> (B91)[54]

> Onto those who step into the same rivers different and different waters flow; and souls are exhaled from moistures.
>
> (B12)[55]

> We step and do not step into the same rivers, we are and we are not.
>
> (B49a)[56]

The interpretations offered by those who quote the texts imply that Heraclitus was making an observation about the continuing identity of the human soul; there need not be material identity in the waters flowing down a river, yet we shall say that it is the same river. There is a sense in which we encounter the same individual twice, but if the individual is not in the same condition what is it that makes it the same person? The point may not have been linked to other change, but there is no doubt that Heraclitus also thought that other parts of nature underwent similar processes of change:

> Cold things warm up, the warm gets cold, the moist dries up, the parched gets damp.
>
> (B126)[57]

In particular he focused on some changes in which the material components did not remain:

> Always remember Heraclitus' view that the death of earth is to be born as water, and the death of water to be born air, and of air fire, and the reverse. Bear in mind as well the one who has forgotten whither the road leads; and that people are at odds with the thing with which they are most constantly associating, the *logos* that directs all things, and the things they encounter daily seem strange to them; and we should not act and speak as if asleep . . .[58]

The first part of this extract seems to refer to processes of change in the natural world, processes in which, to Heraclitus at least, it appeared that the prior stuff was eliminated ('died') and a new stuff came into existence ('was born'[59]); the second part again alludes to the inability of ordinary people to detect the *logos* in the everyday things they encounter. It seems that one aspect of the systematic and coherent *logos* appears in the regularity of systematic change in the natural world, even where discontinuity seems evident.

> This system, one and the same system of all things, no god, nor any human being made it, but it always was and is and will be an ever-living fire, catching light in measures and extinguished in measures.
>
> (B30)[60]
>
> Sea is poured off and is measured out to the same proportion [*logos*] as it was formerly, before the birth of earth.
>
> (B31b)[61]
>
> All things are in return for fire and fire for all things, like goods for gold and gold for goods.
>
> (B90)[62]

Two important features emerge from these texts: first, there is a *logos*, a measure or proportion, which is fixed and regular in the processes of natural change; and second, this measure is independent of material continuity and is based on some kind of continuity of exchange value, as in the image of the buying and selling of goods for gold. When we purchase something for money we do not retain anything of the same product that we owned before. We no longer have the gold; we have the purchased item instead. But the purchased item can then be returned, and we can get the money back. What remains through the exchange is not the material item, but the value of the goods measured by an independent standard. Thus Heraclitus can maintain that the discontinuity in the changes observed in the world is structured by a system of measured proportion, the *logos* that ensures that what we have after the change is, in the sense that matters, the same value: it is measured to the same *logos*. He can affirm that everything flows in radical change where no material substance remains, and yet there is a coherence and unity to the changing world.

The suggestion that no material substance persists marks a radical break with the older Ionian tradition which sought to find unity behind the changing processes in the form of a single underlying stuff that was preserved through change, manifesting itself in different forms but essentially retaining its identity. For Anaximenes everything is a form of air, varying only in its density. For Heraclitus it does not matter if air 'dies' completely and fire is born from its ashes. We can still retain a sense that the world has a continuing identity, like the identity of a river whose constant flow of new water is what makes it a river.

None of the fragments implies that fire persists through the changes. In B30 the fire is said to be regularly being extinguished in measures: presumably those parts are then not fire. Thus to say that the system as a whole always is a fire is only to say that all of its material serves as fuel, and some parts of it are periodically alight, not that all of it is continuously fire, even the parts currently extinguished. The role of fire is as a standard measure (as we use gold for currency) and this gives it a fundamental or basic place in Heraclitus' system without committing him to the view that every part is always fire, just as our use of gold as a standard monetary measure means only that the paper money, the numbers on the bank statement, or the purchased goods, can all be cashed in for gold, not that they are all gold in disguise. The widespread assumption that Heraclitus believed that fire was an element or substrate of all things is, I believe, a mistaken inference from its role as the canonical measure.

It is therefore important to observe that Heraclitus' theory is not like the modern notion of 'energy', which corresponds much more closely with the ideas of Anaximander and Anaximenes.[63] For Heraclitus the things we meet with are not manifestations of a universal stuff (energy) which we encounter in its various guises and never gets destroyed but is always 'conserved'. For Heraclitus the important point is that the elements do get destroyed. They are not just fire in another guise. In fact it is important that they are not fire, just as it is important when I buy bread with my copper coins that I do not keep my copper coins in any form. I get a *different* item in return. The purchase of bread differs from the process of making bread out of flour, water and yeast, because I do not get back what I put in. What remains is not in any respect a material ingredient, or energy transmuted into another form. The only constant is the measure or value, the *logos*, which means that my coins could have purchased your large loaf just as well as they purchased mine; nothing in the matter paid in will determine which item is acquired, nor will I get precisely the same coins back if I return my goods.

❧ THE UNITY OF OPPOSITES ❧

In his comments on the significance of religion Heraclitus drew attention to the significance of context in accounting for the variety of practice in the sacred and secular spheres. One and the same action can be either insane or sensible, depending on where it belongs; and an action that is shameful in one context may be proper and pious for another purpose. When we say that it is one and the same action, we need not, of course, mean that it is numerically identical: the action of washing off blood with blood may occur at one time in one context and at another time in another. They are two examples of the same kind of action. But as Heraclitus observes, the two examples may carry very different significance; so we might ask whether they are the same action. In other cases, however, a single example may be perceived to have two different kinds of significance. We saw with the word *allōs* in B5 that an ambiguous term may mean two different things depending on the way the reader takes it: for the unbeliever it means 'pointlessly'; for the believer it means 'differently'. The same is true of the road uphill and the road downhill: for a traveller at the top of the hill the road is a downhill stroll; for the traveller at the bottom it is an uphill struggle: 'The road up and down is one and the same' (B60).[64]

It seems clear that Heraclitus' interest in context-dependent significance is linked to his interest in continuity and identity through change. In both he is concerned to show that the kind of unity or identity that is determined by the *logos* does not depend upon material continuity, nor does opposition or diversity of significance depend upon material discontinuity. The same item, such as the road, can carry a different significance to another observer, while on the other hand a significant continuity can be preserved for two items that elicit varied responses, such as the day and the night, or sea and earth. The explanation of identity must be sought not in a material substrate, but in a more complex account of observer-related or context-dependent significance.

Some of the opposites mentioned by Heraclitus are substantive nouns, such as those attached to god in fragment B67 (day, night, winter, summer, hunger, satiety); others are expressed as adjectives expressing relations or attributes or evaluations of things, such as up, down, good, bad, pure, impure, straight, crooked and the like. We might think that these were two different kinds of items, since nouns name things while adjectives say something about the properties of things, and it might be tempting to suppose that the kind of opposites that are attributes or relations or values would be more likely to be context-dependent. But it should be noticed that neither set is a set of material entities; nor are the ones identified by nouns more absolute or objective than the others: the classification of hours as day or night, or the classification of months as winter or summer, implies a certain response or attitude to the significance of those items for our own activities and for our lives.[65] The connection between the two sets of opposites can be seen if we look at the notion of slave and free:

> War is both father and king of all, and it has revealed some to be gods, some human; it has made some slaves and some free.
>
> (B53)[66]

To be human is to be a slave or a free person. But which you are depends upon your status, your position in society. In this respect you are made a slave or free: it is war that makes us slaves or free. So does the term 'slave' identify what the individual is, or some attribute or evaluation of the person? The term can be either a noun or an adjective; it can point out a person, or it can say something about the person. But what is there to the person, other than an identity within a particular society? Where you belong and who you are seem to be defined by a range of roles that acquire their significance in your relations to others. Indeed perhaps we cannot ask who you are, or whether you are the same person, unless we have in mind some society within which your identity matters. Thus your identity is defined not by your physical constitution but by the significance of your place in society. What and who you are is context-dependent, determined by the circumstances of a human way of life, the conventions of warfare and of society. It is not a fact given independently of the value judgements of social convention, but is itself wholly bound up with those forms of significance. Hence it seems that there is no independent set of self-identical entities. Identity, similarity, difference, opposition are all determined by the significance acquired in context.

> The doctors, Heraclitus says, while cutting, and burning, and torturing sick people badly in every way, demand a fee from the sick, unworthy though they be of anything, engaging in the very same practice – both good things and diseases.
>
> (B58)[67]

In so far as we can grasp the general gist of this saying, it appears that the activities of the surgeons and doctors, carried out in the sick-room for the cure of diseases, are regarded as a benefit and merit a fee from the victim, while the same practices carried out in the torture room or in any other day-to-day context, would certainly not be worth paying for. Indeed we should disapprove all the more if the deeds were inflicted upon a weak or sickly individual. In these circumstances the surgeon's techniques would actually produce an illness, not cure one. Thus just as ritual purification makes sense only within the ritual context, so the action of the doctor is worthy only in the sick-room. The same actions cannot be judged out of their proper context. What they are, and what they achieve, depends entirely on that acquired significance.

What counts as good and worthwhile depends upon who we are: donkeys prefer rubbish to gold (B9);[68] pigs wash in mud; farmyard birds wash in dust (B37);[69] cows are most happy with vetch (B4).[70] Something similar may lie behind the curious observation that corpses are more to be discarded than dung.[71] Whether dung is worth saving depends on what you need it for; most of us have good uses for it. But we are less likely to put our dead bodies to good use, so why do we treat them with such respect? Transferred out of context the value placed on dead bodies looks inappropriate; but they do have a place in our ritual lives. We see here the same kind of analysis of ritual practice as we identified in fragment B5: an attempt to show the significance of the ritual context by pointing to the incongruity of the practice if viewed in the context of the ordinary secular or human ethos.

For cases of natural change Heraclitus uses the language of living and dying to express the transformation that brings an end to one stuff and introduces another. We have seen that that must mark a total material discontinuity, with the constant factor lying in the measure of exchange governed by *logos*. Does the same apply in the case of the human individual? If we are right in suggesting that the important continuity is not material identity, we shall not expect Heraclitus to mention a material soul. What interests him more is the changing significance attached to an individual in the course of life and death:

> The same [inside] living and dead, and what is awake and what
> is asleep, and young and old: for those change and are these
> and these change again and are those.

(B88)[72]

In these circumstances we need not expect Heraclitus to be bothered by the discontinuity evident in the death or decay of an individual body. The changing significance of life and death, for the individual concerned, is no different from the change from winter to summer, or from Hades to Dionysus: our response will be different, because we are encountering a different experience, just as adding a new spice to something makes it taste different (B67). But the significance varies with the change of context, and the discontinuity is less important than the continuing pattern ensured by the underlying *logos*, which is the essence of identity and continuity in a world of material flux, and context-dependent significance. Indeed if we are constantly breathing out a new soul,[73] it clearly will not be the material continuity of an enduring soul that ensures our continuing identity, even within life. So it seems that what we are, if indeed we are a single individual through the changes from young to old, slave to free, and living to dead, is neither an unchanging body, nor an unchanging soul.[74] Evidently we must find our identity in a pattern of changing experiences that is systematic, and ultimately secured by the unity of the *logos*, for which there need not be any one essential item that remains to constitute the identity.

My experiences as a youngster were not your experiences, and my life is not like yours now; but my story fits together as a continuous sequence, and although my story will be different from yours, like yours it will be unbroken through to death. The sequence of that story is a sequence of changing events, but it is uninterrupted; it has no gaps; there are no absences, except in sleep and those are filled by the experiences of sleep and dreams. Thus we can envisage that story going on, still uninterrupted into death, since there is no reason to suppose that the changes will cease, just as the cosmic story of the world continues uninterrupted, even though the elements change from one to another. Hence Heraclitus can maintain that there is continuity under the systematic measured rule of the *logos*, even where no permanent item remains.

What we eventually encounter in death will not, of course, be more of the same experiences as we encounter in life; for then it would be life, not death. Whatever the events might be, they would have a totally distinct significance for us, just as what we encounter in our sleep has a different significance for us from our waking experiences, and what we do in religious rites differs in its rationale from what belongs to secular human behaviour.

> What remains for humans when they die are things such as they neither hoped for nor thought of.
>
> $\qquad\qquad\qquad\qquad\qquad\qquad\qquad\qquad$ (B27)[75]

We cannot imagine what it would be like to be dead, placed as we are in the context of a life in which all the thoughts and experiences have their significance defined by that life, the absence of which would be death.

While life and death are contrasted in this way there is still, for Heraclitus, a fundamental connection between them. This connection is expressed in the structure of language, in the fact that the word for life (*bios*) is also one of the names for the bow, an instrument of death. The coherence of these opposites is thus evident in the systematic ambiguity of language, one of the shared practices that expresses the systematic *logos*: 'The name of the bow is life, its function death' (B48).[76] Whether the word carries implications of life or death will be determined by its context in language, and that fact reflects the context-dependent significance of life and death as features of our human ethos.

Aristotle knows of a tradition which suggests that Heraclitus denied the law of non-contradiction:

> It is impossible for anyone to suppose that the same thing both is and is not, as some people think Heraclitus said. For it is not necessarily the case that what someone says is what he supposes.[77]

In Aristotle's view it is not possible seriously to believe in a contradiction. He does not deny that that might be the effect of something Heraclitus says, but he denies that Heraclitus could seriously have held it to be so. Subsequently Heraclitus seems to have been adopted as an authority by the Sceptic Aenesidemus, and although it is unclear exactly what Aenesidemus found in Heraclitus that led him to suggest that the Sceptical method of doubt led ultimately to Heracliteanism, it is possible that his point was that the Sceptic will ultimately need to question even the law of non-contradiction, on which all earlier doubts were founded.[78] What these traditions draw on seems to be the sayings we possess that stress the importance of seeing one and the same thing under opposed descriptions. Heraclitus was indeed concerned to draw attention to the contrasting significance of words and practices, and to say that we need not then suppose that what we thus perceived as opposed was not a unity. But Aristotle was probably right that, in stressing that aspect, he did not mean to say that there was a contradiction involved; rather he wants to say that the context is sufficient to give us opposition; indeed that it is the sole source of the contrasting significance of what is in other respects one and the same.[79]

❧ HARMONY AND THE RECOGNITION ❧ OF WHAT IS OBSCURE

The internal relation between features of apparently opposite significance is sometimes linked to the notion of 'agreement' and '*logos*':

> It is wise for those who have listened not to me but to the *logos* to agree that all things are one, Heraclitus says.
>
> (B50)[80]

But another way of expressing the same idea is that of a harmony, or connection among things:

They do not understand how in differing it agrees with itself: a backward-turning structure like that of a bow or a lyre.

(B51)[81]

Exactly how the structure (*harmoniē*) of a bow or lyre illustrates the agreement in difference has been the subject of some discussion. One possibility is the equilibrium of tension between two opposing forces, another the technique of plucking or drawing the string in such a way that it springs back to the original position. The former is a more static image: a world in which equilibrium ensures continuity without radical change; the latter is more dynamic, capturing the idea of a world engaged in reciprocal change between opposing states.

Hippolytus, after quoting this passage, goes on to tell us that for Heraclitus a harmony or connection that is not apparent is more powerful than one that is apparent (B54).[82] Hippolytus' discussion is concerned with the use of sense perception and the value placed upon empirical evidence, but it seems clear that Heraclitus had some claim to make about the internal connection between things that are, at the superficial level, unconnected, or indeed opposed. Indeed his point seems to be that that is the more important relation: that what appears obvious is not always the locus of the most profound and telling connections.[83] It is not always by looking at things that appear immediately promising or rich in significance that we shall discover what is really important: those who search for gold dig up a great deal of earth and discover little (B22).[84]

A number of other matters are said to be particularly obscure or hidden: the *logos* of the soul, which we have seen cannot be located in a material identity, is one of them:

You would not discover the limits of soul if you traversed every path; that is how profound its *logos* is.

(B45)[85]

Nature is another.[86] Discovering the truth is a matter of looking for something that is not obvious or expected, where you least anticipate it:

You will not discover what is unexpected unless it is expected, because it is impossible to deduce and obscure.

(B18)[87]

This is a connection or harmony among things that are not related by empirically observed continuity of material entities, the sort of continuity that we might deduce from accumulating data and predicting similar patterns. It is a connection that is context-bound, producing a varied significance of things that is not evidently predictable but derives from an obscure relation among words and things.

In these circumstances the senses are not the most obvious tools for achieving an understanding of what matters; or rather the senses alone are not adequate for the job. The testimony of the senses can be positively misleading unless we can grasp the significance of the evidence they give. This seems to be the claim expressed in the curious saying

> The eyes and ears of those who have foreign souls are bad
> witnesses for people.
>
> (B107)[88]

A foreign ('barbarian') soul is one who cannot understand the message; perhaps one who cannot grasp the *logos*, the lingo, in which the sense perceptions are coded. This person, as it were, hears the sounds, but misinterprets what is said, so that the witness that is given turns out to be a false testimony, leading the hearer to believe a false account rather than the true *logos* that is actually encoded in the message of the senses when correctly understood. The message is some kind of riddle which, in the imagery of another fragment, cannot be understood by the blind:

> People are taken in as regards knowledge of things that are
> apparent, like Homer, who was wiser than all the Greeks. For
> some children killing lice fooled him by saying: the ones we saw
> and caught, those we left behind; but the ones we neither
> saw nor caught, those we are taking with us.
>
> (B56)[89]

The language of this riddle is rich with epistemological significance. Homer, who was traditionally blind, unfamiliar with what is apparent to the senses, is also blind to the significance of the riddle, because he cannot see that it is lice that the children are busy catching. But other people are also blind to the significance of the riddle, which is that the superficial evidence, that we see and grasp, is worthless and can be discarded; while the less obvious significance, what we carry with us in the internal structure of our language, our rituals, and the shared customs that we use but do not observe, is what is worth grasping, if only we could.

❧ THE ERRORS OF OTHER PEOPLE ❧

Much of the material that we have considered so far has included disparaging remarks about the inability of ordinary mortals to comprehend what is before their eyes. In fragment B1 the word for 'out of touch' (*axunetoi*), describing those who fail to comprehend the *logos*, appears to pun with the texts that stress the importance of what is 'common' (*xunos*). The word also occurs in B34:

> Those who are out of touch [*axunetoi*], having heard, are just
> like deaf people; it is to them that the saying testifies that though
> present they are absent.[90]

What the ordinary observer is out of touch with is that which is common, on which those who speak with sense (*xun noōi*) rely absolutely (B114).[91] As in the case of those who blindly use their eyes and fail to grasp what is really important, so those who listen but fail to hear are like the deaf. It is possible, and indeed usual, according to Heraclitus, to use the senses but to fail to make contact with what is common, to go through life asleep, and to be out of touch with what one has heard.

How, then, can one improve or gain understanding? Not, it appears, by means of learning from other supposedly wise people, for it is not only Homer who fails to live up to his reputation for wisdom, but also Hesiod:

> Hesiod is the teacher of a great many; they understand that he
> knew a great many things, though he did not recognize day and
> night. For they are one.
>
> (B57)[92]

and all the other well-respected authorities:

> Quantity of learning does not teach sense, otherwise it would
> have taught Hesiod and Pythagoras, and again Xenophanes and
> Hecataeus.
>
> (B40)[93]

> Pythagoras, son of Mnesarchus, was the most assiduous
> researcher of all mankind, and by excerpting from these writings
> he made his own wisdom: quantity of learning, bad practice.
>
> (B129)[94]

A consistent theme in these criticisms of the teachers respected by most is the notion that the quantity of things known is no guarantee of wisdom. Yet Heraclitus also seems to have said that 'philosophical men have to be researchers of a very great quantity of things' (B35).[95] If the 'philosopher' here is a man of true wisdom there seems to be some conflict with the claim that the quantity of things known is no guide in the attainment of sense. An alternative way of taking this last text would be to suppose that Heraclitus is scornful of 'philosophical men'; the term 'philosopher', if genuinely Heraclitus' own, makes its first known appearance here. Such people, he might be saying, must, if they are to attain that status, engage in the kind of research that brings learning but no understanding. But that is not the kind of thinker that Heraclitus himself respects.

It might be thought that Heraclitus respects only his own judgement: 'I searched myself' (B101);[96] 'Of those whose theories I have heard, none has attained this: to recognize that the wise is distinct from all things' (B108).[97] Only one thinker is mentioned with respect, and that is Bias, one of the seven sages, but since little is known of him nothing can be deduced as to the grounds on which Heraclitus observes that 'his *logos* is greater than the rest'.[98]

What can safely be deduced? Heraclitus does not hold that research of the normal sort practised by philosophers and poets offers a way to an understanding of the significant truth. There is one truth that all but a few fail to appreciate, and that is the independence of the one thing that is wise: its detachment from the great plurality of things into which these other thinkers enquire and the knowledge of which they amass with such enthusiasm.

> One thing, what is wise, to understand the sense in the way in which it controls all things through all things.
>
> (B41)[99]

❧ POLITICS, VIRTUE AND GLORY ❧

> Diodotus . . . says that the treatise is not about nature but about politics and what it says concerning nature is included as illustrative examples.
>
> (Diogenes Laertius *Lives* IX.15)

Even if we do not subscribe to Diodotus' extreme view, it is evident that Heraclitus expressed some opinions on political matters. Predictably something goes wrong with politics if the choice of leader lies with those who are out of touch with what matters; Heraclitus explodes about the action of his own citizens in expelling the one man who was worth having:

> It would be worthwhile if the Ephesians were all hanged from the young men upwards, and left the city to the boys, since they expelled Hermodorus who was the most valuable man of them all, saying: Let not one among us be the most valuable; or else let him be elsewhere and among other people.
>
> (B121)[100]

What does Heraclitus mean by the 'most valuable'? The point seems to be that the citizens have rejected the person who was most effective at the job, purely out of a concern that he should not stand out from the rest of them. Heraclitus' observation that they might as well be hanged suggests not simply that they have done wrong, but that their life will now be not worth living, and the city would be as well off in the hands of youngsters.

The faintly anti-democratic sentiment of this observation accords well with Heraclitus' general estimate of the capacity of ordinary mortals to understand what matters, and is borne out by some of his other reflections:

> Have they any mind or intelligence? They believe the popular singers and take the crowd as their teacher, unaware that the common people are bad and few are good.
>
> (B104)[101]

Nevertheless it would probably be wrong simply to infer that Heraclitus is expressing a standard prejudice against popular rule. We need first to discover what it is that makes a man 'good' and why the rejection of such a man from the city is a major disaster. Heraclitus' view of who counts as good or worthy of respect is developed along the lines of his own understanding of things. It is tied up with his estimate of what gives significance to justice, and value to the things that we ordinarily find choiceworthy in life. Value and significance depend upon a context in which the good things can be recognized and appreciated: 'It is sickness that has made health pleasant and good, hunger satisfaction, toil release' (B111).[102] We value these things precisely because they come as an exchange from another situation, and it is the context of release from something unpleasant that makes those conditions desirable and appreciated. The opposites are related in such a way that we could not have the one without the other: release would not be release from anything if there were no toil or pain to be released from. We value it in those circumstances and in no others.

It seems to follow that having too much of these 'good' things can result in the absence of any appreciable value at all. This probably explains Heraclitus' enthusiasm for self-restraint: 'It is not preferable for people to get whatever they want' (B110);[103] 'Moderation is the greatest virtue, and wisdom is speaking the truth and acting knowingly in accordance with nature' (B112);[104] 'All people have a chance to know themselves and be moderate' (B116).[105] But the real answer is to find what has an eternal value and will never depend upon a transitory context for its appreciation. There is only one source of such value that Heraclitus recognizes, and that is the honour of virtue that achieves recognition in everlasting fame among mortals.

The best choose one thing rather than everything: everflowing

111

honour among mortals; but the common people satisfy
themselves like cattle.

(B29)[106]

Honour is the best thing to choose precisely because it escapes from
the context-dependence of other values, which are desirable only by
contrast with some painful alternative and are confined to the temporal
life of an individual with desires. Ordinary people, as Clement observes
in interpreting this saying, measure their happiness by food and sex,
the values of non-human animals. But virtue achieves a different kind
of reward, one that extends beyond human recognition: 'Gods and
humans honour the war-dead' (B24).[107]

Thus although Heraclitus certainly does not regard the values of
the multitude as worthy of pursuit, he will not easily find anyone who
is qualified to rule. Aristocracy, in place of democracy, will be the rule
of the 'best', but the best are defined by their choice of honour or
virtue as the only lasting value worthy of pursuit. 'It is customary to
respect the advice of one' (B33);[108] 'One is ten thousand if he is the
best' (B49).[109]

Honour transcends context and the limitations of a single human
life. What is morally right, on the other hand, seems at first to be
defined by contrast with wrongdoing; Heraclitus observes that we use
the term of approval ('right') in a context where we imply a contrast
with some alternative:

They would not have known the term 'right', if there were no
such things as these.

(B23)[110]

'These' are, we presume (following the suggestions offered by Clement
when he quotes the text), examples of wrongdoing or misdeeds. But
Heraclitus is not content to leave morality in the same position as the
utilitarian values of health, food and rest. Mortals may in practice define
their notion of what is morally right by contrasting right with wrong,
but in some sense this is an error. We can notice the reference to
'they' again, which generally accompanies a disparaging remark on the
confusion of ordinary mortals. Perhaps, then, what is morally right
does have absolute value that is not dependent upon a respite from an
alternative range of evils, but mortals only learn to see it as the notion
abstracted from the absence of certain identifiable wrongs. Yet there
would, presumably, be a meaning for the word 'right' even were
there no wrongs in the world at all. That seems to be so for god,
because there are no such things as wrong for him. 'Everything for
god is noble and good and right, but humans have taken some to be
wrong and some right' (B102).[111] Indeed this fragment suggests that

112

our perception of evils as evils is observer-related: they are evils for us; and we confine the word 'good' to what is good for us. But that is to make goodness a merely human value. That mortal usage of right and wrong is out of line with the absolute value perceived from the god's eye view. So whereas it may seem to us that we could not appreciate the value of goodness in itself without the presence of evil, that is not how things appear to one who correctly perceives what the absolute value of morality is. Like honour, then, what is absolutely right escapes from the context of temporal values, and has significance independently of any human observer.[112]

❧ HERACLITUS' STYLE AND THE ❧ SIGNIFICANCE OF LANGUAGE

Heraclitus' message is conveyed not only by what his words say but also how they say it. To hear the *logos* the listener must attend to the structure of language and social practice, and not just to what Heraclitus or others may choose to say about them. Heraclitus' own use of language seems to be consciously designed to draw attention to the features that illustrate his theme. Some of these have already emerged since they contribute to the significance of texts we have been discussing. Many others are lost in translating the texts, because they depend upon juxtaposition of opposing words in such a way as to emphasize the tension between opposites (a possibility in Greek, which is an inflected language, but less easy in English where the order of words in a sentence determines their role). It will, nevertheless, be worthwhile collecting a number that illustrate two aspects of Heraclitus' use of word-play: (a) play on words that suggests a link between two similar words; (b) playing with the grammatical structure and syntax of a sentence, or with ambiguous words, to elicit more than one meaning from a single text.

Connecting Words of Different Significance

Heraclitus links the notion of what is common (*xunos*) with the idea of speaking with intelligence (*xun nooi legontas*) in fragment B114; it seems that this theme extends through a number of other texts that pick up on the same kind of language: B113, in which he suggests that thinking is common (*xunon*) to all; B51, in which people are said not to understand (*ou xuniasin*); and B34 in which those who are out of touch (*axunetoi*) are like the deaf, to mention just a few. It is clear that what is common (*xunos*) is what people need to be in touch with, or to understand, if they are to be said to speak or act with intelligence. Heraclitus is clearly drawing out this point, not so much by saying so, as by using the implicit connections between words of similar form to make his message apparent.

A similar sequence can be detected in the emphasis on 'agreement' (*homologein*) which resonates with the word *logos*. Something that differs is said to agree (*homologeei*) in B51, while in B50 it is wise for someone to agree (*homologein*) that all are one, once one has heard the *logos*. Again Heraclitus does not actually say what the connection between recognizing the *logos* and agreeing is, but the language itself reveals the connection, just as it reveals the role of *logos* in ensuring that what differs is systematically connected in a tense structure like the bow or lyre.

In B5 the participants in the ritual purification do so because they are polluted (*miainomenoi*). That is what makes the ritual a sensible one to engage in. But to the uncomprehending observer they are mad (*mainesthai*). They appear mad because they are engaging in more of the same action that caused them to be polluted. The connection between madness and pollution that is implicit in Heraclitus' choice of language relates to the context-dependent nature of both judgements: whether one is mad, or polluted, cannot be decided without an understanding of the context in which one's actions are taking place.

Deriving More than One Significance from One and the Same Word

Language neatly illustrates Heraclitus' claim that context determines the significance of things. The word *bios* is one which he explicitly comments on (B48: The name of the bow is life, its function death) but there are others where the point simply emerges from the fact that we cannot tell which way to take a word. Some of these involve taking a word in more than one sense: one example was the use of the word *allōs* to mean either 'differently' or 'pointlessly' in B5;[113] Heraclitus also seems to pun on the word 'shameless' (*anaidestata*) in B15, taking it to mean 'un-Hades-like' as well.[114] Similarly in B57 Hesiod is said to be the teacher 'of many' (*pleistōn*) but the context suggests that we could take this either to refer to the many subjects that he taught, or the many people who were taught by him. Both ideas are found in the context, and both ways of reading the text make good sense.

Other examples depend upon a word carrying not two different senses, but playing two different roles in the syntax of the sentence. The most famous is the word 'ever' in fragment B1, which can be taken with 'is' ('with this *logos* which is for ever') or with 'human people are out of touch' ('human people are for ever out of touch'). Heraclitus places the word in such a way that it works equally well with either; and there is no doubt that he believes both claims to be true. There seems every reason to suppose that he wanted one and the same word to perform two different functions, and to enter both contexts, carrying a separate though related significance to each. We can find a very similar example in the fragment on pollution discussed above. In this text (B5) the word for 'with blood' (*haimati*) is placed between 'tainted' and 'they purify themselves' in such a way that it can function equally well with either. This draws attention to the fact that the people are purified with the very same stuff that they were first polluted with. Clearly it is important to Heraclitus' message that one and the same word belongs in both contexts: 'Tainted with blood, they purify themselves...' and 'Tainted, they purify themselves with blood...'[115]

Words and names can be significant, and clearly for Heraclitus their significance tells us a lot about the kind of non-material connections between things that make the world a place governed by a systematic rationale. But the significance of the words may still depend upon the surrounding context, just as the names for god can change with the ritual context we encounter him in. This is why Heraclitus can say that the name Zeus is both the right name and the wrong name: 'One, alone, the wise, likes and dislikes to be spoken of by the name of Zeus' (B32).[116]

Although the meaning of this saying is obscure, it implies that the name applied to the one, or the wise, does matter (it likes or dislikes certain names, presumably because they do or do not have the right significance), but there will not be one name that is consistently right. It would be an error to suppose that the god must only be Zeus and must always go by that name. In certain circumstances that may be the wrong name. Just as in the case of Dionysus the variety of appropriate ritual did not distinguish two separate gods, so the correct use of a name other than Zeus will not tell against a single sole being, the wise.

Heraclitus does not explicitly discuss how language acquires significance in context, in the way that a modern philosopher of language might be expected to. But his handling of the language, and the claims he makes about significance in the more general sphere of human practices and social custom, indicate his commitment to the idea that language does not have meaning independently of the particular context in which it is used; indeed the same words in the same context may carry a plurality of meanings when read in a number of different ways, or by different readers with different points of view. Meaning is not fixed by the individual words, but is nevertheless governed by a system or rationale which explains how it can be open to various or opposed meanings, yet not become a meaningless flux of indeterminate sense.

The lord who has the oracle at Delphi neither speaks, nor
conceals, but signifies.

(B93)[117]

The 'lord' in question is the god Apollo; his oracle was such that the
Pythia, a priestess in a state of ecstatic possession, conveyed the god's
response to the petitioner. The god did not speak directly to the appli-
cant, nor did he keep his answer wholly to himself or deliberately
mislead; but the response he gave by way of the Pythia was not always
easy to interpret. It might indicate the truth, but only if you could
grasp the significance. One of the stories Herodotus tells is of Croesus
who consulted the Delphic Oracle for advice on whether to pursue his
empire-building strategy.[118] 'If you cross the river Halys you will
destroy a great empire' was the response he got. The response is
ambiguous because the meaning of 'a great empire' is not fixed until
we find a context within which it makes unequivocal sense. The petitioner is likely to assume that the god's response functions in the same
context as the question that was asked. In a conversation, in shared
human language, we should gather the sense from the context within
which the words were uttered, but the god's response comes detached
from any context. Hence Croesus can disastrously misunderstand the
response by taking the empire in question to be not his own but that
of his opponent.

Why does Heraclitus tell us about the oracle? Plainly the polysemic language of the Pythian Oracle bears some resemblance to the
polysemic language of Heraclitus' own utterances, which play upon
the multiple significance available to different readers, and from different syntactical construal of the phrases. But perhaps the difficulty
of interpreting the oracle without a context to fix the sense, to make
it speak directly instead of hinting at a meaning that is unobtainable,
also tells us something about the way in which language is itself wholly
dependent upon context for its shared significance as part of what is
common; and thus the oracle alerts us to the way that language functions, and hence to the sources of unity and opposition to which
Heraclitus hopes to draw our attention, if we could but hear what he
has to say.

 NOTES

1 Heraclitus belonged to the city of Ephesus during a period when it was under
Persian domination. He was probably of an aristocratic family, and he is likely
to have lived in the latter part of the sixth century and early part of the fifth
century BC. From fr. 40 it is evident that he is working in a period after

Pythagoras, Xenophanes and Hecataeus. He shows no knowledge of Parmenides, but there might be grounds for thinking that Parmenides alludes to Heraclitus (compare Parmenides B6.7 with Heraclitus B51 for example).

2 This feature adds to the difficulty, since when poetry is involved the metrical constraints can sometimes provide a key to reconstructing a reliable text, or more particularly determining which words are quoted and which paraphrased. Heraclitus does have a characteristic style (see below, 'Heraclitus' style') which can sometimes be recognized in dubious quotations (e.g. the habit of placing a word so that it plays more than one role in the sentence, cf. B1), and some fragments retain the Ionic dialect forms, though the absence of these need not mean that a fragment is not authentic.

3 There is one relatively lengthy passage known as fragment B1, which appears to belong to the beginning of Heraclitus' work. This is quoted by more than one ancient author, and implies that Heraclitus' work circulated as a written prose treatise, though it is possible that the written version was not prepared by Heraclitus himself. Diogenes Laertius, whose life of Heraclitus is extremely unreliable, reports a story that Heraclitus deposited his book in the temple of Artemis in such a way that it would be inaccessible to the general public (Diogenes Laertius [3.12], IX.6). If there is any truth in this it implies that Heraclitus had charge of the written version of his own treatise.

4 See the excursus 'On reading Heraclitus' in Kahn [3.7], 87–95, and Osborne [3.31], 1–11, 23–4.

5 The standard Greek text of the fragments is that of DK [2.2]. In this collection the fragments thought to be genuine are listed in section 22B. The letter B prefixed to a fragment number indicates its presence in this collection. The order of fragments in DK is primarily determined by the alphabetical order of the quoting authorities, a procedure deliberately adopted by Diels to avoid imposing his own interpretation in assembling a sequence of texts. Robinson [3.9] retains DK's order. Kahn [3.7] rearranges the texts, but provides concordances to enable the reader to trace a particular fragment.

6 The Penguin Classics collection *Early Greek Philosophy* [2.6] translated by Jonathan Barnes carefully presents the fragments with some of the necessary material from the surrounding context, sufficient, in most cases, to enable the reader to get some sense of the basis for the writer's understanding of the text. On the absolute necessity for paying heed to this context in any serious work on Heraclitus see Osborne [3.31]. The two recent editions of Heraclitus (Kahn [3.7], Robinson [3.9]) are both seriously inadequate, in that they provide virtually nothing of the context for the fragments.

7 Thinkers condemned or criticized for impiety are usually revising the conventional theology rather than denying any place for divine beings. Anaxagoras (apparently condemned at Athens in c.430 BC) introduced a divine 'mind' as the governing cause of the way the world is. Socrates was accused of introducing new gods. His divine sign was perceived as a deity exclusive to himself, and hence constituted a kind of private religion that appeared as a threat to the community in a Greek polis.

8 Religion is mentioned as the last topic in Heraclitus' book by Diogenes Laertius [3.12] (*Lives* IX.5) but it is unlikely that the edition he knew was Heraclitus' own. I deal with it first, partly to emphasize its place in his

thinking, partly because the sayings on the subject are classic examples of his style of thought, and raise important issues of a general nature.

9 See below 'The Unity of Opposites'.

10 On the rituals for homicide involving purification with blood see Parker [3.20], app. 6, 370–4.

11 Reading *allōs* with the manuscript and Kahn [3.7], Robinson [3.9], Marcovich [3.2], rather than *allōi* (with *further* blood) which was an emendation suggested by Fränkel and adopted by Kranz in DK (5th edn and later).

12 The text is preserved entire in the *Theosophia*, an anonymous Christian collection of pagan material from *c.*500 AD; it is also paraphrased in some other texts, assembled by Marcovich [3.2], 455–8. The second part (quoted below) is also recorded by Celsus (apud Origen); see n. 16.

13 Kahn [3.7], 266; Robinson [3.9], 78; Burkert [3.19], 309; Parker [3.20], 371–2, for example.

14 See below 'Heraclitus' style'.

15 Heraclitus seems to use the word 'human' to contrast with god, whose method of purifying is the sacred one. In what follows I shall sometimes use 'religious' or 'sacred' and 'secular' which is our normal terminology for the distinction he is making, sometimes 'divine' and 'human' which is Heraclitus' terminology, e.g. in B78 and B119.

16 This second part of B5 is quoted not only in the *Theosophia* (see n. 12) but also by Celsus (preserved in Origen's *Against Celsus*) and is discussed at some length by Origen. Celsus takes the fragment to be a comment on the correct use of religious images and its dependence on the believer's proper understanding of the gods. Origen responds by hijacking the fragment for his own ends.

17 See below, 'The Unity of Opposites'.

18 B61. The text is preserved by Hippolytus of Rome [3.13], a Christian bishop of the early third century AD, in the *Refutation of all Heresies* IX.10. This section of the *Refutation* tries to demonstrate that the heretic Noetus, like Heraclitus, confuses things of opposed significance. See Osborne [3.31], ch. 4.

19 B60. The text is preserved by Hippolytus [3.13] *Refutation* IX.10. See below, 'The Unity of Opposites'.

20 B58. The text is preserved by Hippolytus [3.13] *Refutation* IX.10.

21 Preserved by Stobaeus *Anthology* IV.40.23, Plutarch *Quaestiones Platonicae* 999, and Alexander of Aphrodisias *On Fate* 6. The fragment is peculiarly difficult to interpret; the interpretation offered by Alexander appears to cohere with that offered here, which, however, brings out a quite different sense from that normally put upon the text by recent scholars ('a person's character is his fate (divinity)', Robinson [3.9], 69), but makes the most of the typically Heraclitean style with its ambiguous placing of *anthrōpoi*. The alternative readings with a genitive (*anthrōpou* or *anthrōpōn*), given by Plutarch and Alexander respectively (the former adopted by Bollack-Wismann [3.5]) retain the same sense.

22 From a summary of the quotations given by Celsus from Heraclitus on the subject of the difference between divine and human wisdom, included by Origen, *Against Celsus*, 6.12.

23 See below 'The Logos'.

24 See below 'Custom and Shared Practice'.

25 Both parts of B15 (see further below) are quoted in close connection by Clement of Alexandria *Protrepticus* II.34.5.

26 This quotation is listed as the second part of B15. The Lenaia was a particular festival of Dionysus associated with ritual madness on the part of women. See Seaford [3.22], 239, 322. Heraclitus uses a rare verb ('to Lenaia-ize') to speak of the performance of these ritual activities.

27 See below 'The Unity of Opposites'.

28 B60; see n. 19.

29 B57, 'Hesiod is the teacher of a great many; they understand that he knew a great many things, though he did not recognize day and night. For they are one.' The text is preserved by Hippolytus [3.13], *Refutation* IX.10 (see n. 18).

30 B103. The text is preserved by Porphyry *Quaestiones Homericae ad Iliadem* XIV.200.

31 Heraclitus probably thought the earth was flat, though the evidence is unclear (Diogenes Laertius [3.12], *Lives* IX.11) but he may have been aware that the length of day varies from north to south, and he recognized that the hours of day and night are not absolute but determined by the presence or absence of the sun (B99 and cf. B57).

32 See below 'Harmony and the Recognition of What is Obscure'.

33 *anaidestata*, 'un-Hades-like' as well as 'shameless' if we adopt the widespread view that there is significant word-play here (Kahn [3.7], 336 n. 390 with further references). See below 'Heraclitus' Style'.

34 The identification of Hades and Dionysus does not seem to be a peculiar doctrine of Heraclitus, nor does it commit him to monotheism. The evidence for a cult connection between the two is quite extensive, particularly in south Italy, and the dionysiac mysteries are associated with death rituals. See Seaford [3.22], 319–26; C. Sourvinou Inwood 'Persephone and Aphrodite at Locri: a model for personality definitions in Greek Religion', *Journal of Hellenic Studies* 98 (1978): 101–21, 109, repr. in Sourvinou Inwood *'Reading' Greek Culture*, Oxford, 1991; Rohde [3.21], 159, 184 n. 7; Marcovich [3.2], 254; J. C. Carter 'Sanctuaries in the *chora* of Metaponto', in S. E. Alcock and R. G. Osborne (eds) *Placing the Gods*, Oxford, Clarendon Press, 1994: 161–98.

35 B56, B57. See below 'The Errors of Other People'.

36 Something similar to this conclusion was suggested by Guthrie [3.24], 476 on the basis of fragment B68.

37 B71–3. See below 'The Errors of Other People' and 'Custom and Shared Practice'.

38 B89. See below 'Custom and Shared Practice'.

39 This section of the chapter is based on a paper delivered to a conference of the University of Wales Institute of Classics and Ancient History and due to appear in a forthcoming volume of proceedings.

40 The text appears in a list of sayings from Heraclitus quoted without context by John Stobaeus, *Anthology* III.1.179. Stobaeus wrote in the fifth century AD.

41 The text is quoted shortly after B1, (on which see below, 'The Logos') by Sextus Empiricus *Adversus Mathematicos* VII.133, who says that Heraclitus adds this claim after a few intervening things. The opening words show that it concludes an argument that established the role of what is 'common' in

determining the correct wisdom, conceivably B114. The text I translate, the one usually adopted by editors, follows a suggestion of Bekker since what Sextus Empiricus says is slightly garbled. The explanation of the term *xunos* is presumably by Sextus himself (a writer in the Sceptical (Pyrrhonist) school) for the benefit of his second century AD readers. He is discussing Heraclitus' views on the criterion of truth and knowledge.

42 See below 'The *Logos*'.

43 'The people should fight for their custom as if for a wall.' (B44) The text is quoted by Diogenes Laertius [3.12] (third century AD), *Lives* IX.2. He offers no interpretation. The word for 'custom' (*nomos*) can refer to formal legal provisions or to local established practice.

44 See above 'Ritual and the Gods', The text does not supply the word *nomos* after 'divine', but it is natural to understand it from the mention of human customs. An alternative translation would be 'all human customs are nourished by the one divine thing'.

45 The 'divine law' mentioned in B114 is identified with the laws of nature by some interpreters, notably Robinson [3.44], 483–4. This restricts the divine law to the laws of behaviour of physical or material bodies; it makes Heraclitus a materialist, whereas the stress on human social practices and language suggests his interests lie much more in the non-material connections between things that have no physical link.

46 The text is preserved by Hippolytus [3.13] *Refutation* IX.10 (see above n. 18). The word 'something' is missing in the text (unless there was no word there and 'god' is said to change); various suggestions have been made as to what is said to change when mixed with spices, the most popular being 'fire' (Diels's suggestion). The point is clear in any case: an admixture of spices will alter the effect and the name of something itself unchanged. It is probably best to avoid a term such as 'fire' that carries theoretical significance.

47 Reported by Plutarch (AD c.45–120) *De Superstitione* 166C.

48 The text is known from two relatively reliable sources: Sextus Empiricus *Adversus Mathematicos* VII.132, in the same context as fr. 2 (see above), and Hippolytus of Rome [3.13] in his ch. on Noetus *Refutation* IX.9. The opening sentence is also discussed for its grammatical structure (in which 'for ever' can be taken either with what follows or what precedes) by Aristotle *Rhetoric* 1407b11. Both Aristotle and Sextus say that the text occurred at the beginning of Heraclitus' book.

49 The text is preserved by Clement of Alexandria (AD 150–215) in his *Miscellanies* (V.115.3), which is a work comparing Greek thought with Christian thought. He takes this text to express the same idea as 'he that hath ears to hear let him hear'. Nussbaum ([3.37], 12) suggests that 'the saying' refers to what they say: their way of talking shows that they do not understand. See below 'The Errors of Other People'.

50 The text is preserved by Hippolytus ([3.13] *Refutation* IX.9), who appears to find in it an emphasis on the unity and agreement of opposite features. Robinson ([3.44], 481–3), in a characteristically physicalist move, reads the *logos* here as a kind of law of nature; see also Patricia Kenig Curd 'Knowledge and unity in Heraclitus', *Monist* 74 (1991): 531–49, at pp. 532–5.

51 The fragment (B50) can also be reads as alerting us to the objective truth of

Heraclitus' claims: it is not because it is *his* version but because it is independently true that it leads to assent.

52 *Cratylus* 402a, and cf. 401d and 411b.

53 *Theaetetus* [3.14], 152d and 179d–180a.

54 Plutarch *On the E at Delphi* 392B. The text is not necessarily wholly Heraclitus' own words. Plutarch associates the text with the issue of personal identity.

55 Eusebius, *Praeparatio Evangelica* XV.20.2, quoting Arius Didymus, quoting Cleanthes, quoting Zeno the Stoic to compare him with Heraclitus. The passage is concerned with the origins of souls, and takes Heraclitus to be referring to a constant flowing out of the soul (breath?) like a river that is always new and never runs dry.

56 Heraclitus Homericus (first century AD), *Homeric Questions* 24, who implies that he takes the text to be an allegory, but does not explain in what way.

57 Tzetzes *Notes on the Iliad* 126H; his main observation is that Heraclitus' remarks are obscure.

58 Marcus Aurelius *Meditations* IV.46, incorporating texts known as B76, B71, B72, B73.

59 'Fire lives the death of earth . . .' in Maximus of Tyre's version of B76; 'The death of fire is birth for air . . .' in Plutarch's version; 'The death of earth is to be born as (or become) water . . .' in Marcus Aurelius' version.

60 Clement of Alexandria *Miscellanies* V.14.104. Clement is developing an account of Heraclitus' notion that everything is periodically consumed by fire (*ecpyrosis*). This was a standard Stoic reading of Heraclitus, but is often disputed in recent scholarship. It has been recently reaffirmed by Kahn, see his Excursus I ([3.7], 147–53). This fragment implies that the system functions like a bonfire, in which any part might catch light at any time.

61 This text belongs later in the same passage of Clement *Miscellanies* V.14.104.5. He takes 'sea' to represent creation, which is then dissolved into fire periodically according to a regular system.

62 Quoted by Plutarch *On the E at Delphi* 388D-E. McKirahan's alternative translation ('as money for gold and gold for money', [3.11], 124) makes little sense and will not support the interpretation he offers on p. 140, since *chremata* (things) can mean money in the sense of property, but not coinage. There is, therefore, no way that this fragment can be taken to imply material persistence.

63 *Pace* Wiggins [3.45], 16.

64 Quoted by Hippolytus [3.13], *Refutation* IX.10 (see above n. 19). In Diogenes Laertius [3.12] (Lives IX 9. 8–9) the road up and down is associated with two directions of change through the elements in the cycle of natural change.

65 We think of a month as winter or summer depending on what activities we can perform or how the land yields its fruit. Thus Heraclitus need not know of the antipodes to identify summer and winter as observer-related; the first month of summer for the arable farmer may still see the sheep in winter pastures for the hill-farming shepherd.

66 Quoted by Hippolytus [3.13] *Refutation* IX.9, in the same context.

67 Quoted or summarized by Hippolytus [3.13] *Refutation* IX.10 (the same context). The text is somewhat uncertain.

68 Aristotle *Nicomachean Ethics* 1176a5–8.

69 Columella *On Agriculture* VIII.4.4.

70 Albert the Great *On Vegetables* VI.2.14 (the saying is paraphrased in Latin).

71 B96, from Plutarch *Quaestiones Conviviaes* 669A, and other sources.

72 [Plutarch] *Consolation to Apollonius* 106E, who suggests that the implication is that death is always present. The text is difficult to make sense of as it stands, and the word for 'inside' may be corrupt.

73 Eusebius explaining B12; see n. 55.

74 See Nussbaum ([3.37], 158–62) on the notion of immortality without any material continuity. For her the implied answer to B27 (see below) is 'nothing', but since no significance for us depends upon material identity I do not see the need for this conclusion. See also Hussey ([3.41], 526–7).

75 Clement *Miscellanies* IV.144.3, who compares Heraclitus' view with that expressed by Socrates in the *Phaedo*.

76 Quoted to illustrate the meaning of the word *bios* by the *Etymologicum Magnum* s.v. *bios*.

77 Aristotle *Metaphysics* 1005b23–6.

78 Sextus Empiricus [3.15] *Outlines of Pyrrhonism* I. 210–12.

79 Barnes ([3.23], 69–74) is, I think, alone among recent scholars in taking Heraclitus to be seriously guilty of contradiction.

80 See above 'The Logos'.

81 It is not clear what 'it' is. The context in Hippolytus, who quotes this after B50 mentioned above, implies that the two quotations are about the same thing. The neuter ('it differs') in B51 suggests that the subject is not the *logos* or the cosmos (both masculine), but other neuter subjects are available (the wise, B32; fire, B66; ethos, B78; unnamed neuter subject, B84a). The bow and lyre can be seen to belong together as attributes of the god Apollo, whose tendency to reveal and conceal illustrates the tension of opposites inherent in language, B93 (see below).

82 Hippolytus [3.13] *Refutation* IX.9; the link with the mention of harmony in B51 is made by Hippolytus who had just repeated the second part of B51.

83 Compare also B8 (reported by Aristotle *Nicomachean Ethics* 1155b4): 'Heraclitus says that opposition is convenient and that the finest harmony derives from things that differ.'

84 Clement *Miscellanies* II.2.4.2.

85 Diogenes Laertius *Lives* IX.7.

86 'Nature likes to hide' (B123), recorded by Themistius *Orations* 5.69b who links it with the notion of a divine harmony that is not available to human knowledge.

87 Clement *Miscellanies* II.4.17.8.

88 Sextus Empiricus *Adversus Mathematicos* VII. 126, who suggests that a foreign soul is one who trusts in non-rational perceptions. Modern interpretations also take 'foreign' as metaphorical, but vary on exactly how. The view presented here is that the soul fails to understand the message of the senses; the alternative (which coheres with the stress I have placed on language as a shared practice) is that it fails to understand the significance of its own language (not, of course, that it is literally not a Greek-speaker); see Nussbaum [3.37], 9–12.

89 Hippolytus [3.13] *Refutation* IX.9. My interpretation here differs in some details from [3.31], 162–3. See also Rethy [3.36].

90 See n. 49.

91 See above 'Custom and Shared Practice'.

92 Hippolytus ([3.13] *Refutation* IX.10), whose interest is in the unity of day and night. See further below 'Heraclitus' Style'.

93 Diogenes Laertius [3.12] *Lives* IX.1 who quotes the saying as evidence of Heraclitus' arrogant contempt.

94 Diogenes Laertius [3.12] *Lives* VIII.6, part of his account of Pythagoras' written work.

95 Clement *Miscellanies* V.140.5. Clement takes this to be a positive assertion of the need for knowledge in the search for the good.

96 Plutarch *Against Colotes* 1118C, who compares the text with the Delphic maxim 'Know thyself'.

97 Stobaeus *Anthology* III.1.174.

98 B39, cited by Diogenes Laertius [3.12] in his life of Bias (*Lives* I.88). 'His *logos* is greater' may mean his theory is better, his reputation is greater, or his written work is more extensive.

99 Diogenes Laertius [3.12] *Lives* IX.1. The text is uncertain and extremely difficult to translate. The opening words are identical to the first words of B32 (see below 'Heraclitus' Style').

100 Diogenes Laertius [3.12] *Lives* IX.2.

101 Proclus *Commentary on the First Alcibiades* 256.1–6. Proclus comments that Timon called Heraclitus 'reviler of the mob'.

102 Stobaeus *Anthology* III.1.177.

103 Stobaeus *Anthology* III.1.176.

104 Stobaeus *Anthology* III.1.178.

105 Stobaeus *Anthology* III.5.6.

106 Clement *Miscellanies* V.9.59.4–5, quoted after a summary of B104.

107 Clement *Miscellanies* IV.4.16.1.

108 Clement *Miscellanies* V.155.2.

109 Paraphrased by Theodorus Prodromos as part of a compliment to his correspondent.

110 Clement *Miscellanies* IV.9.7. I do not see any reason to agree with Kahn that there is a reference to a deity ('justice') in this text (Kahn [3.7], 201). Nor can he be right ([3.7], 185) that the term *dike* has a primary connection with penal correction; it is evident that its earliest meaning is for fitting and morally upright action. Morality is what is at issue.

111 Porphyry *Quaestiones Homericae ad Iliadem* IV.4. Porphyry is discussing how the gods can approve of war and battle, and affirms that god sees to it that all things are in fact in accordance with goodness and what is right.

112 It would probably be anachronistic to complain that Heraclitus' god fails to condemn moral evil. The point is probably more concerned with the partiality of human perceptions of evil, rather than the claim that nothing is offensive to god, however bad. It also accords with the sense that there is a measured plan to the whole system, which cannot go wrong in any way that ultimately matters.

113 See above 'Ritual and the Gods'.

114 Compare also the use of *logos* in B39 (see n. 98).

115 See also B119 (n. 22) and B84b: 'To toil for, and to be ruled by, the same

people is tiresome', or 'It is tiresome for the same people to toil and to be
ruled'. (There are other ways of reading this fragment. See Kahn [3.7], 169–70.)

116 The text is preserved by Clement of Alexandria in the same context as B34
(see n. 49) and B33 (n. 108). His interest is in links with Christian ideas, here
perhaps in implied monotheism and the acceptance of names other than Zeus
for the supreme divinity.

117 Known from Plutarch *De Pythiae oraculis* 404D and Stobaeus III.199. Plutarch
compares the god's use of the Pythia to convey the response with the sun's
use of the moon to transmit its light.

118 Herodotus I.53.

 BIBLIOGRAPHY

Fragments are mentioned in the text by their number in DK [2.2], vol. I, section
22; the letter B indicates the fragments listed as authentic quotations in part B of
that section. Part A contains testimonia (accounts of Heraclitus' life and doctrine
from ancient authors); I have cited such texts by the authors concerned, and not
according to the DK collection. Translations are my own, and differ, usually in
minor ways but occasionally radically, from those found in other collections. Where
the variant translation makes an important difference I have tried to indicate the
reasons in the text or notes.

Original Language and Bilingual Editions

3.1 DK [2.2].

3.2 Marcovich, M. *Heraclitus, editio maior*, Merida, Venezuela, Los Andes University Press, 1967. Full critical Greek text with textual commentary; also
includes English translation of those fragments considered genuine by Marcovich.

3.3 Wright [2.5].

3.4 Kirk, G. S. *Heraclitus: The Cosmic Fragments*, Cambridge, Cambridge University Press, 1954. Greek text (selected) with commentary and English
translation.

Bilingual Editions with Full Philosophical Commentary

3.5 Bollack, J. and Wismann, H. *Héraclite ou la séparation*, Paris, Les Éditions
de minuit, 1972. Greek and French.

3.6 Conche, M. *Héraclite: Fragments*, texte établi, traduit, commenté par M.
Conche, Paris, Presses Universitaires de France, 1986. Greek and French.

3.7 Kahn, C. H. *The Art and Thought of Heraclitus*, Cambridge, Cambridge
University Press, 1979. Greek and English.

3.8 KRS [1.6]. Includes selected texts in Greek and English.

3.9 Robinson, T. M. *Heraclitus: Fragments*, a text and translation with a commentary, (*Phoenix* suppl. vol. 2), Toronto, University of Toronto Press, 1987. Greek and English.

Editions in English Only

3.10 Barnes [2.6]. English translation.
3.11 McKirahan [2.7]. English translation with commentary.

Ancient Discussions

3.12 Diogenes Laertius, *Lives of Eminent Philosophers*, vol. 2 of 2 vols, with an English translation by R. D. Hicks (Loeb Classical Library), Cambridge, Mass., Harvard University Press, 1925.
3.13 Hippolytus of Rome *Refutation of All Heresies*, Greek text and English translation in C. Osborne, *Rethinking Early Greek Philosophy*, London, Duckworth, 1987 [3.31].
3.14 Plato *Theaetetus*. Greek text in *Plato*, vol. 1 (Oxford Classical Texts). English translation by M. J. Levett, rev. M. F. Burnyeat in M. F. Burnyeat, *The Theaetetus of Plato*, Indianapolis, Ind., Hackett, 1990.
3.15 Sextus Empiricus *Outlines of Pyrrhonism*, Vol. 1, *Sextus Empiricus*, in 4 vols, with an English translation by R. G. Bury (Loeb Classical Library), Cambridge, Mass., Harvard University Press, 1933.

Modern Reception

3.16 Heidegger, M. *Vorträge und Aufsätze*, Pfullingen, Verlag Gunther Neske, 1954.
3.17 Heidegger, M. and Fink, E. *Heraclitus Seminar*, trans. C. H. Seibert, Alabama, University of Alabama Press, 1979; repr. Evanston, Ill., Northwestern University Press, 1993.

Bibliography

3.18 Roussos, E. N. *Heraklit-bibliographie*, Darmstadt, Wissenschaftliche Buchgesellschaft, 1971.

Background

3.19 Burkert [1.43].

3.20 Parker, R. *Miasma: Pollution and Purification in Early Greek Religion*, Oxford, Clarendon Press, 1983.

3.21 Rohde, E. *Psyche: The Cult of Souls and Belief in Immortality among the Greeks*, London, Kegan Paul, 1925.

3.22 Seaford, R. *Reciprocity and Ritual*, Oxford, Clarendon Press, 1994.

General Discussions of Heraclitus' Thought

3.23 Barnes [2.8], ch. 4.

3.24 Guthrie [2.13] I, ch. 7.

3.25 Hussey [2.14], ch. 3.

3.26 Ramnoux, C., *Héraclite ou l'homme entre les choses et les mots*, 2nd edn., Paris, Les Belles Lettres, 1968.

Studies of Particular Aspects of Heraclitus' Thought

Issues of interpretation, evidence and ancient reception

3.27 Barnes, J. 'Robinson's *Heraclitus*', *Apeiron* 21 (1988): 97–104.

3.28 Cherniss [2.26].

3.29 Mansfeld, J. *Heresiography in Context: Hippolytus'* Elenchus *as a Source for Greek Philosophy*, Leiden, Brill, 1992.

3.30 O'Daly, G. 'Heraklit' in *Reallexicon für Antike und Christentum*, vol. XIV (1988): cols. 583–62.

3.31 Osborne, C. *Rethinking Early Greek Philosophy: Hippolytus of Rome and the Presocratics*, London, Duckworth, 1987.

Modern reception

3.32 Stern, D. G. 'Heraclitus and Wittgenstein's river images: stepping twice into the same river', *Monist* 74 (1991): 579–604.

3.33 Waugh, J. 'Heraclitus the postmodern Presocratic?', *Monist* 74 (1991): 605–23.

Perception and knowledge

3.34 Hussey, E. 'Epistemology and meaning in Heraclitus', in M. Schofield and M. Nussbaum (eds) *Language and Logos: Studies in Ancient Greek Philosophy Presented to G. E. L. Owen*, Cambridge, Cambridge University Press, 1982: 33–59.

3.35 Lesher, T. H. 'Heraclitus' epistemological vocabulary', *Hermes* 111 (1983): 155–70.

3.36 Rethy, R. 'Heraclitus fragment 56: the deceptiveness of the apparent', *Ancient Philosophy* 7 (1987): 1–7.

Psychology

3.37 Nussbaum, M. C. 'ψυχή in Heraclitus', *Phronesis* 17 (1972): 1–16, 153–70.
3.38 Robinson, T. M. 'Heraclitus on soul', *Monist* 69 (1986): 305–14.
3.39 Schofield, M. 'Heraclitus' theory of the soul and its antecedents in psychology', in S. Everson (ed.) *Companions to Ancient Thought 2: Psychology,* Cambridge, Cambridge University Press, 1991: 13–34.

Other topics

3.40 Emlyn-Jones, C. J. 'Heraclitus and the identity of opposites', *Phronesis* 21 (1976): 89–114.
3.41 Hussey, E. 'Heraclitus on living and dying', *Monist* 74 (1991): 517–30.
3.42 Mackenzie, M. M. 'Heraclitus and the art of paradox', *Oxford Studies in Ancient Philosophy* 6 (1988): 1–37.
3.43 Mourelatos, A. P. D. 'Heraclitus, Parmenides and the naive metaphysics of things', in E. N. Lee, A. P. D. Mourelatos and R. M. Rorty (eds) *Exegesis and Argument: Studies in Greek Philosophy presented to Gregory Vlastos* (*Phronesis* suppl. vol. 1), Assen, Van Gorcum, 1973: 16–48.
3.44 Robinson, T. M. 'Heraclitus and Plato on the language of the real', *Monist* 74 (1991): 481–90.
3.45 Wiggins, D. 'Heraclitus' conceptions of flux, fire and material persistence', in Schofield and Nussbaum (see [3.34]): 1–32.

CHAPTER 4

Pythagoreans and Eleatics
Edward Hussey

❦

❧ PYTHAGORAS AND THE EARLY ❧
PYTHAGOREANS

Pythagoras, a native of Samos, emigrated to southern Italy around 520, and seems to have established himself in the city of Croton. There he founded a society of people sharing his beliefs and way of life. This spread through the Greek cities of southern Italy and Sicily, acquiring political as well as intellectual influence. Some time after his death, the original society broke up and its continuity was lost; yet groups of self-styled 'Pythagoreans' appeared repeatedly thereafter.

Palpably reliable evidence about early Pythagorean activities is so scanty that some initial scepticism is in order about Pythagoras as a philosopher, or as a 'natural philosopher' in Ionian style.[1] Sporadic early reports depict Pythagoras as primarily a magician and miracle-worker; and, on the theoretical side, a collector and expositor in dogmatic style, rather than a creator or investigator. It is clear that some doctrines later seen as 'Pythagorean' were already current, around the same time, in the theological and cosmological poems attributed to Orpheus. Plato barely mentions Pythagoras by name; but incorporates into some of his myths material which is likely to be genuinely Pythagorean. After Plato, philosophically-inspired reconstructions of Pythagoras begin to appear, in which he is represented as the head of a regular school, promoting research into philosophy and the mathematical sciences; or as an enlightened statesman and instructor for political life.[2] At best, even when based on good sources, these fourth-century accounts (which themselves survive only in later reports) are more or less anachronistic idealizations. Still less reliance can be placed in the great mass of later statements about Pythagoras and his followers.

Indirectly, the fact that certain later fifth-century thinkers were called 'Pythagoreans' (see below) gives some indication of what theor-

etical interests were then attributed to Pythagoras. The cosmology of
Parmenides (see below) and the poems of Empedocles have a sub-
stratum of ideas that may be suspected to be Pythagorean in inspiration.
All in all, there is a body of general ideas, appearing by the mid fifth
century and reasonably firmly associated with Pythagoras, which was
to be influential in a programmatic way throughout the century, and
on Plato, above all, in the fourth. These ideas may be grouped under
the headings of 'metempsychosis' and 'mathematics'.

'Metempsychosis' and the Self

'Metempsychosis' was the doctrine of the repeated incarnations of an
immortal 'soul' or self, in human or animal or plant bodies. Centred
on that doctrine, and more or less closely tied to it were various ideas,
not necessarily clearly distinguished by Pythagoras himself.

(1) One was the radical redefinition of the *self* which the doctrine
involved: a new belief about what we human beings really are. The
implication is that we are not, as in traditional Greek belief, mortal
beings, with at best a shadowy afterlife in Hades, but that we are truly
immortal, perhaps fallen gods. Our real selves have always existed and
will always exist. And the heritage which they have lost, but may
recover, is a divine, paradise-like existence.

(2) Connected with that is the belief that we are *not at home* in the
body, in fact that this life and all incarnations are really punishments,
or at best periods of rehabilitation. It follows that we are not here
primarily to enjoy ourselves. It does *not* necessarily follow that the
body is intrinsically evil, or that the ordinary kinds of enjoyment are
bad in themselves. That extreme puritanical conclusion may have been
drawn by some, but probably not by Pythagoras himself.

(3) Pythagoras saw the world as sharply and systematically polarized
between good and evil. The real role of the self is to be a moral agent,
to participate in the moral struggle; and it is rewarded and punished
accordingly. A systematic cosmological dualism, associating all aspects
of the world with the good – evil polarity, seems also to have been
characteristically Pythagorean. It may be this dualism which accounts
(psychologically at least) for the doctrine of the cyclical recurrence of
events. Given a systematic dualism of good and evil, good must
triumph, but evil cannot be abolished. The simplest solution is to
suppose that there are cosmic cycles: at the end of each cycle, all beings
have been 'saved', and good triumphs; but then the moral fall starts all
over again.

(4) Yet another aspect is the kinship of all living things. What pre-

cepts, if any, Pythagoras deduced from this about human behaviour to other animals, is obscure.[3]

Mathematics and the Importance of Abstract Structure

Another leading idea of Pythagoras was that of the key importance of *mathematical structures* in the universe.

Pythagoras himself was no creative mathematician; there is no reliable evidence that he proved any mathematical theorems at all (not even 'Pythagoras' theorem'). The evidence suggests rather that the Pythagoreans' focus was on a speculative numerology applied to the cosmos. (For example, the dualism of good and evil was paralleled, and perhaps meant to be explained, by the dualism of odd and even numbers; and so on.) But from here the thought emerges, first, that mathematics is not just a useful practical device; that it reveals an abstract structure in things; and secondly that this abstract structure may be the key to the essential nature of things. It is through these ideas that Pythagoras became the midwife of pure mathematics, which began to develop from now on; and indeed the founder of the whole mathematical side of scientific theory.

❧ PARMENIDES ❧

The Poem of Parmenides

Parmenides was a citizen of the Greek city of Elea in southern Italy. His philosophical activity belongs to the first half of the fifth century. He expounded his thoughts in a poem, using Homeric hexameter verses. Verse for public recitation was then still a natural medium for diffusing ideas; yet the 'natural philosophers' of the sixth century had chosen prose, to show their rejection of the authority of the poets, and their closeness to ordinary experience. Parmenides' choice of hexameter verse may imply in its turn a rejection of the natural philosophers.

The poem begins with a first-person narrative of a journey. Accompanied by the daughters of the Sun, the narrator rides in a chariot into remote regions, to reach 'the gate of the paths of night and day'. Passing through, he is welcomed by a goddess, who promises that he is to 'find out everything'. She goes on to fulfil the promise, in an exposition which constitutes the whole of the rest of the poem.

Over one hundred verses of the poem survive, including all of the introductory narration and probably almost all of the first and fundamental part of the goddess's exposition. Together with comments of Plato, Aristotle and others, this is a fine corpus of first-rate evidence, the survival of which is due principally to Simplicius, the sixth-century Neoplatonist commentator on Aristotle.[4]

Yet controversy dogs almost every part of Parmenides' thinking, for a conjunction of reasons. First, there are gaps in our information at certain crucial points. Next, Parmenides' language is often obscure, in spite of his evident striving for maximal clarity. The constraints imposed, by the metre and vocabulary of epic verse, on the exposition of a subject-matter for which they were never designed, are bad enough. Then there is the problem of supplying whatever, in the course of his exposition, Parmenides left to be understood. Finally, his thought is itself novel and complex.

Any translation, therefore, and any overall reconstruction of Parmenides, including the one now to be outlined, cannot but be highly controversial at many points.[5]

The Promise of the Goddess

Central to the understanding of Parmenides is the promise made by the goddess:

> It is necessary that you find out everything: both the unmoving heart of well-rounded reality [*alētheiē*], and the opinions of mortals, in which there is no real guarantee of truth – but still, these things too you shall learn, how [*or:* since] it had to be that opinions should reputably be, all of them going through everything.
>
> (DK 28 B 1.28–32)

The division of the objects of discovery into two determines the structure of the rest of the poem. It rests on the distinction (explicit since Xenophanes at least) between what can and what cannot be certainly known. The first part, concerned with *alētheiē*, will contain only certainties. The second part, of which the truth cannot be guaranteed, will contain 'opinions of mortals'. As with Xenophanes, there are better and worse opinions: those to be revealed are not any old opinions, but ones which enjoy the status of being 'reputable', and which form a complete system.[6]

If we leave on one side, for the moment, the 'opinions' and what is here said about them,[7] the next fundamental question is the meaning of the word *alētheiē*. In English, it is usually translated by 'truth', to which it seems to correspond in the spread of its early usage. The adjective *alēthēs*, from which it is formed, has much the same spread as 'true' (covering the areas indicated by the words 'truthful', 'accurate', 'real', and 'genuine'; though not that of 'faithful'). But in Parmenides the translation 'reality' for Parmenides' *alētheiē* must be insisted on, in order to bring out the essential point: what is referred to here is not anything (words, speech, thoughts) that is or makes a true statement; it is what the true statement is *about*, and is guaranteed by: the underlying actual state of things, the reality. So, later on, the goddess marks the end of the first part by saying, 'At this point I end for you my trusty tale and thought concerning *alētheiē*.'[8]

While 'reality' may be taken as the closest word to the intended primary meaning here, it is also true that *alētheiē*, as in Homer, carries implications about the *certainty* of what is said, and of the *correctness* and *accuracy* of the method by which it is found. Parmenides wants to insist on these points too; which he does, here and elsewhere, primarily by words indicating trustworthiness and its guarantees (*pistos, pistis, peithō*). The goddess promises not only insight into some reality, but a guarantee of the truth of the insight.

This reality is 'well-rounded', presumably because it forms a satisfactorily coherent and closed system; and it has an 'unmoving heart', presumably because at least in essentials it is not subject to change. Both of these thoughts reappear significantly later.

The Choice of Ways

The narrator's 'finding out' of reality is represented as a matter of simply listening to the goddess. Yet there are hints that his was an active pursuit of the truth; it was his own desire that started him off. The metaphor of travel, and the implication of active pursuit in 'finding out', are now carried further. There is talk of 'ways of enquiry'; the listener is warned off from two of these 'ways', and told of 'signs' that appear in the course of the third. The exposition envisages an active rethinking, by the listener, of the course of Parmenides' thinking.

Why the *active* participation of the listener is needed becomes clear from what follows. The exposition concerning reality is in the form of a deductive argument, which one cannot properly follow and grasp, without recreating it in the movement of one's own mind. The 'ways of enquiry' are 'lines' (as we say) of argument, each following deductively from its own initial premiss, by the mention of which it is, naturally enough, identified in the exposition. Rigorous deductive arguments were possibly already in use in mathematics; but they must have been novel to most of Parmenides' contemporaries. Hence the efforts Parmenides makes, using the metaphor of the 'ways', to keep the course of the arguments, their interrelation and their overall effect, absolutely clear.

Come then, I will tell you (and you, listen and take in the story!),
which ways of enquiry alone are to be thought: the one, that it
is and cannot not be, is the path of conviction, for it follows
along after reality; the other, that it is not and that it is necessary
that it is not – *this* track, I tell you, is utterly unconvincing . . .

(DK 28 B 2.1–6)

This presents, as a starting-point, a choice between two such ways,
which are mutually exclusive. Clearly, though, they are not jointly
exhaustive, since there might also be ways involving unrealized possibilities ('it is, but might possibly not be', 'it is not, but might possibly
be'). In fact, in the sequel, Parmenides will present only one more way,
the 'way of mortals', which, as stated, is evidently self-contradictory.
The two named here are apparently the only ones that 'are to be
thought'; and, of these, one is to be rejected as false.

What is going on here seems to be as follows. Parmenides holds
(on what grounds, remains to be examined) that to speak of unrealized
possibilities involves a contradiction. Hence, taking 'is it?' as the basic
question at issue, there can be only two premisses to be considered:
'necessarily, it is', and 'necessarily, it is not'. The 'way of mortals',
which says that 'it is and it is not', is self-evidently contradictory; it is
therefore not 'to be considered'. None the less, it is mentioned later,
and the reader is expressly cautioned against it, because it is a
popular and appealing way. Of the two ways worth consideration, the
second, which says 'necessarily, it is not', also turns out to involve a
contradiction, but this is not evident at the start; it has to be shown
by argument. Once that has been done, the way that says 'necessarily,
it is' is the only remaining possibility. Accordingly, it is accepted as
true by elimination, and its consequences examined.

What then is meant here by 'it is' and 'it is not'? First, what is
'it'? In the Greek, the verb *esti* stands alone, as Greek verbs can,
without even a pronoun to function as the grammatical subject. But
unless Parmenides is making some radical and improbable departure
from ordinary practice, an intended subject of discourse, of which 'is'
and 'is not' are here said, must have been meant to be readily supplied
from the context. Unfortunately for us, the original context is now
partly missing. Between the promise of the goddess and the statement
of the two ways, some now lost stretch of text, probably not long,
once stood. None the less, what remains is sufficient for near-certainty
as to the intended subject.

The ways are 'ways of enquiry'. An enquiry, then, is presupposed
as being already afoot. What that enquiry is concerned with, is likely
to be what the first part of the goddess's promise is concerned with:
reality. It is true that the word *alētheiē* nowhere appears subsequently

in the subject place attached to the verb *esti*. In the exploration of the true way that says 'it is', the subject of 'is' appears sometimes, cloaked in the unspecific designation (*to*) *eon*, 'that which is'. This phrase, though, can be taken without artificiality as another, and metrically more convenient, way of referring to *alētheiē*. (So taken, it involves a metaphysical pun: see below on the meanings of the verb *einai*.)

This conclusion, that *alētheiē*, in the sense of 'reality', is the intended subject, is central to the interpretation of Parmenides to be presented here.[9] It has been reached by a simple yet powerful argument. It has yet to be subjected, though, to a series of severe tests. A reconstruction of Parmenides deserves acceptance only if it makes convincing sense of the *whole* of the surviving evidence.

The first test arises immediately. Can one make sense of an initial choice between 'necessarily, reality is' and 'necessarily, reality is not'? At this point, we must also ask about the possible meanings of the verb *einai* ('be').

In general, it seems to make sense, whatever *x* may be, if one is making an enquiry into *x*, to start by asking 'is there any such thing as *x* or not?' The normal usage of the verb *einai* easily covers such a sense of 'is'. In launching an enquiry into *alētheiē*, understood in extension from Homeric usage in a 'summed sense', as what would be jointly indicated by all true statements, Parmenides is in effect asking, sceptically, 'why do we have to suppose that there is any such thing in the first place?'

Since this entirely normal and familiar use of *einai* fits the context so well, there is no need at the outset to look for more exotic possibilities.[10] Later, though, when the subject of discourse is referred to as 'that which is' (*to eon*), a different use of the verb bears the logical weight. Another common use of *einai* is that in which it means (said of possible states of affairs) 'obtain, be the case'. If *alētheiē* is thought of as a 'summed state of affairs', then to say that there actually exists such a thing is just the same as to say that it is the case.

Parmenides' philosophical starting-point looks, in this light, rather like that of Descartes. Both start with a philosophical enquirer, an apparently isolated mind, trying to establish what it can know with absolute certainty. Parmenides approaches the problem via the concept of *alētheiē*, the reality that would have to underwrite any knowledge. What is next to be examined is his argument to establish that there must be such a reality. It is here that his further initial presuppositions, if any, are to be found. This is the argument that rejects the way that says 'it is not'.

The Rejection of 'it is not'

The passage in which Parmenides justifies the rejection of the second way is probably not preserved entire. There survive, in fact, only the beginning ((A) below) and the end, plus a single sentence presumably belonging closely with it ((B) below).

(A) ... *this* track, I tell you, is utterly unconvincing [*or*: undiscoverable]; for you would not recognize [*or*: become aware of] what is not (for that cannot be done), nor would you point it out.

(DK 28 B 2.6–8)

The claim is that the way 'it is not' must be rejected. The verbs on which the argumentative weight is thrown, are, in the aorist forms used here, common Homeric words for 'recognize' and 'point out'; they are cognitive 'success verbs'. Their objects can be either ordinary individuals or 'that'-clauses. So it is necessarily true that (1) 'you would not recognize [to be the case: i.e. get knowledge of], or point out [as being the case: i.e. show, demonstrate], what is not'.

The natural way to expand (1) into a relevant argument is as follows. If there is no such thing as reality, then no-one can recognize it, nor point it out. In that case there can be no knowledge (if knowledge requires recognition of reality) and no communication of knowledge.

This will suffice to reject 'it is not', provided two further premisses are available: (2) that knowledge involves or consists in awareness of reality, and communication of knowledge involves or consists in the pointing-out of reality; (3) that knowledge and its communication are possible.[11]

Did Parmenides supply any support for (2) and (3)? As to (2), there is no way of telling; maybe it was taken as following immediately from the meaning of *alētheiē*, as that which truths are *about*, and knowledge is *of*. As to (3), first of all some evidence of Aristotle comes in here opportunely. Aristotle identifies, as an underlying thesis of the Eleatics, that 'some knowledge or understanding (*phronēsis*) is possible' (Aristotle, *On the Heavens* III.1, 298b14–24). This supports the reconstruction; but does not tell what grounds if any were given for (3). It cannot be that this assumption is embodied in the initial acceptance of the 'enquiry', as something actually on foot, unless there was an argument to show that enquiry is always successful. It will now be suggested that in fact the remaining pieces of text, dealing with the rejection of 'it is not', give the supporting argument for (3).

(B) For the same thing is for thinking and for being.

(DK 28 B 3)

It must be that what is for saying and for thinking, is; for it is for being, but what is not is not [for being] . . .

(DK 28 B 6.1–2)

These passages are part of the conclusion of the rejection of 'it is not'. But they should be treated, at least initially, as (part of) a separate argument from the one reconstructed above. Once again, Homeric usage is an important guide. 'It is for being/thinking/saying' represents an idiom familiar in Homer: 'A is for x-ing' means either 'there is A available to do some x-ing' or 'there is A available to be x-ed'.

Much depends here on what sort of thing might be said to be 'available for saying and thinking'. In Homeric usage, the object of the verbs 'say' and 'think' is usually expressed by a 'that'-clause. What the clause describes is the state of affairs, in virtue of which the saying or thinking is true or not.

An interpretation is possible within these linguistic constraints. Parmenides is arguing for the thesis that what can be said and thought, must actually be the case; i.e. that one can say and think only 'things that are', these being thought of not as true statements but as actual states of affairs.

The argument has a very close affinity with one which troubled Plato in various places, notably in the *Sophist* (but he did not accept it as correct, in the *Sophist* or elsewhere).[12] The 'Platonic problem' (as it may be called for convenience) starts from the premiss (4), that saying and thinking must have, as objects, a state of affairs, actual or not; i.e. a genuine case of saying or thinking must be a case of saying or thinking that such and such is the case. But then, (5) if saying or thinking actually and not merely apparently occurs, its object must exist. Now, (6) for a state of affairs, to exist is just to be actual. Hence (7) only actual states of affairs are thought and said, i.e. all thinking and saying is true.

In what is left of Parmenides' text there appears, not quite this argument, but a far-reaching modal variation of it. What can be thought and said, must by (4) be at least a possible state of affairs ('it is for being'). But (8) there can be no unrealized, 'bare' possibilities. The argument to this effect is brought out effectively by the idiomatic 'is for being'. What 'is for thinking', also 'is for being', and therefore necessarily is. There can be nothing more to 'being for being', than just being. Anything that is not, cannot be in any sense, and so cannot even 'be for being'. Hence every possible state of affairs is actual, and so it must be that (7) what can be thought and said is true.

We must, then, disentangle here the result (7), that there is no false thinking or saying, from the strong modal principle (8), that there are no unrealized possibilities. They are, of course, akin; in both (7) and (8), there is a refusal to have any philosophical truck whatever with any non-existent state of affairs. It is principle (8) that also supplies what is obviously needed: an explanation of Parmenides' hitherto unjustified ruling-out of the ways 'it is but might not be' and 'it is not but might be'.

Both principles, (7) and (8), are important for the rest of the poem as well.[13] In the deduction of consequences from 'it is', principle (8) will have a central role. Moreover, error, by principle (7), doesn't consist in any 'saying' or 'thinking' but in the constructing of fictions of some sort, *apparent* statements. The effect of (7) is to force a new analysis of apparent falsehood, as will be seen later.

These two partial reconstructions may now be put together to make an overall reconstruction of the rejection of 'it is not'. The overall effect of the rejection of the way 'it is not' is to establish that since there must be true thinking and saying, there must be some objective reality. The first piece of text ((A) above) is a sketch of this overall argument, using premisses (1) (2) (3). In reply to this argument, a sceptic might question premiss (3): granted that thinking and saying occur, why should it be that some thinking and saying must be *true*?[14] So Parmenides engages with this objection in the further argument which terminates in the second piece of text ((B) above). This argues that (7) there is no such thing as false thinking and saying, and (8) there are no unrealized possibilities either.

On this reading, if Parmenides' starting-point is like that of Descartes, and his first task is to show that knowledge is possible, his next problem, having shown that, is of a Kantian kind: given that knowledge and correct thought *must* be possible, what if anything follows about the nature of things? With the premisses (1), (2) and (3), he is able to show for a start that there must be such a thing as reality. There must be something for the knowledge to be *about*, and *of*, which by being so guarantees it.[15]

The 'Way of Mortals'

After rejecting the way that says 'it is not', the goddess mentions, as unacceptable, yet another way, not previously mentioned:

Then again [I shut you out] from this [way], which ignorant
mortals wander along [or: construct], two-headed (for it is
helplessness that steers the wandering mind in their breasts); they
drift along, deaf and blind, in a daze, confused tribes: they accept

as their convention that to be and not to be is the same and not
the same [*or*: that the same thing and not the same thing both
is and is not]; the path of all of them is back-turning.

(DK 28 B 6.4–9)

For surely it will never be forced that things that are not should
be ...

(DK 28 B 7.1)

There is no problem in understanding the rejection of a way that is
clearly self-contradictory. But why does Parmenides identify this way
as the way of 'mortals'; and are all human beings meant, or only some
particular group?

From the text, the 'mortals' seems to be 'people' generally,
humanity in the mass. The 'confused tribes' can hardly be just a particular group of theorists.[16] Besides, the goddess associates this way
with an unthinking interpretation of the evidence of the senses, which
is due to 'habit of much experience' and therefore presumably almost
universal among adults:

do not let the habit of much experience drive you along this way,
exercising an unexamining eye, and a hearing and a tongue full
of noise; but judge by reason the controversial test which I have
stated.

(DK 28 B 7.3–6)

It seems to be, not sense perception itself which is at fault here, but
people's lazy habits in selecting and interpreting the information given
by sense perception. The distinction had already been made by Heraclitus, who remarked: 'Bad witnesses to people are eyes and ears, if
[those people] have uncomprehending souls' (DK 22 B 107). It is reason
that must dictate how sense perception is to be understood, and not
the other way round.

On what grounds Parmenides took ordinary people to be enme-
shed in contradiction about reality, is not yet clear. The reference to
'the controversial test which I have stated' must include the rejection
of 'it is not'. Parmenides may see people as accepting both 'it is' and
'it is not', because, while they see the need to assume some kind of
reality, they at once contradict that assumption, as Parmenides believes,
by allowing reality to contain features which are excluded by the test.
For example, the existence of unrealized possibilities, and other things
which are yet to be expressly excluded. The 'controversial test' probably
includes also the negative implications of what is yet to come: the
examination of the way that says 'it is'.

Consequences of 'it is'

The other ways having been shown false, only the way that says 'it is' remains, so that this must be true.

> Only one story of a way is still left: that it is. On this [way] are very many signs: that what is cannot come-to-be nor cease-to-be; [that it is] whole, unique, unmoving and complete – nor was it ever nor will it be, since it is all together now – one, coherent.
>
> (DK 28 B 8.1–6)

The 'signs' are best taken as the proofs, to follow, of the properties announced here as belonging to 'what is' (*eon*), i.e. reality. Evidently the deduction of the consequences of 'it is' constitutes, as expected, the journey along the way.

(a) Reality cannot come-to-be nor cease-to-be (B 8.6–21)

> For, what origin will you seek for it? How and from where did it grow? Nor will I let you say or think that [it did so] out of what is not, for it is not sayable or thinkable that it is not. Besides, what necessity would have driven it on to come-to-be, later or sooner, starting from what is not?
>
> (DK 28 B 8.6–10)

The first section of proof reveals the techniques of argument characteristic of this part. For convenience, the subject ('what is' or 'reality') will be denoted by E. Suppose that E does at some time come-to-be. Then Parmenides asks: *out of what* does it come-to-be? The implied premiss is: (10) whatever comes-to-be, comes-to-be out of something. Parmenides seems to have taken (10) as self-evidently true; it is plausible to connect it with other places in this argument where he seems to have some variety of the Principle of Sufficient Reason in mind.

So, if E comes-to-be, it comes-to-be out of F (say). Then for F, in turn, there are the two possibilities: F is, or F is not. Parmenides considers the second possibility, but not, apparently, the first one. This is a first problem.

There is an extra twist to it. So far, we have considered Parmenides' reasonings about 'it is' and 'it is not' without taking account of the ambiguities of the present tense. The rejection of the way 'it is not' does not call for these to be considered. But the Greek present tense is ambiguous in the same ways as the English one; and where, as here, possible past and future events are being discussed, it becomes necessary to distinguish the various uses. 'It is' and 'it is not' may be timeless, or refer to the time of the coming-to-be, or to the time of utterance,

139

if that is different. Parmenides gives us no help at all on this point; but it is plausible to assume that he means the question 'is F or is it not?' to be understood as specialized (in line with ordinary usage) to the time of coming-to-be. This results, as will now be shown, in an intelligible argument.

The question is then: E comes-to-be out of F; is F, or is it not, at the time of E's coming-to-be? First, if F is, at that time, then at that time it is part of E, since E (on the interpretation followed here) is the whole of reality. But nothing can come-to-be out of a part of itself, since that does not count as coming-to-be at all. This point will account for Parmenides' failure to examine the supposition 'F is'.

Second, suppose then that F, at the time of E's coming-to-be, is not. This is the case which Parmenides examines. He gives two arguments.

One argument is: 'It is not sayable or thinkable that it [F] is not'. This invokes the results of the rejection of the way that says 'it is not'. By principle (7), 'F is not' is not sayable or thinkable, because it is not true.

But why is 'F is not' not true? By principle (1), if it were true, then F would not be capable of being recognized or pointed out; so it could not figure intelligibly in any sentence; so no sentence including it could be true, a contradiction. Parmenides in what follows will repeatedly appeal to the same consequence of (1): namely (11), *no* sentence of the form 'X is not' can be true.

It might be objected that this principle (11) (so far as has been shown) applies only to what is not *at the time when the utterance is made*; in other words that here too there is a crucial ambiguity in the present tense. What if F is not, at the time of coming-to-be, but is, at the time of speaking? In that case, it would seem to be possible to recognize and point out F, and say of it intelligibly that it was not, at some earlier time. Again, Parmenides seems unaware of this objection. Is there a hole in his proof? It is more charitable, and perhaps more plausible, to suppose that Parmenides tacitly applies a principle of tense-logic such as this: (12) for any time t, and any statement S, if it is true now that S was (will be) true at t, then it was (will be) true at t that S is true then. By this means, Parmenides can transfer the force of principle (1) to the time of the supposed coming-to-be. 'F is not' cannot be (have been, be going to be) true at *any* time, because, if so, it would be true at the relevant time that 'F is not'; but, by principle (11), the truth of 'F is not' (at any time) would involve a contradiction.

The powerful general moral to be drawn, which will find further applications, is that, in assigning the properties of what is, none may be assigned which involves reference to things that supposedly *at any time* are not.

The other argument begins: 'Besides, what necessity would have driven it on to come-to-be, later or sooner, starting from what is not?'

The demand for a 'necessity', to explain what would have happened, implies, again, some variety of the Principle of Sufficient Reason. In an initial state in which there is nothing that is, there could hardly be any way of grounding the necessity. Even if there were, why did it operate 'later or sooner': at one particular time rather than at another?

The rest of section (a) is occupied, on this interpretation, only with recapitulation and summing up. Only the case of coming-to-be has been discussed; there is no parallel treatment of ceasing-to-be, presumably because the arguments are intended to be exactly analogous.

(b) Reality is undivided, coherent, one (B 8.22–25)

Nor is it divided, since it is all in like manner, nor is it in any respect more in any one place (which would obstruct it from holding together) nor in any respect less: all is full of what is. Hence it is all coherent, for what is comes close to what is.

(DK 28 B 8.22–5)

The underlying strategy here is parallel to that of section (a). Suppose that reality (E) is divided. What that implies is that something divides E. What could that be?

By the fact that E is 'summed', comprising all that is, anything other than E has to be something that is not. By the same argument as before, it can never be true to say that E is divided by something that is not. Hence E is not divided by anything other than itself. This limb of the argument, though suppressed here as obvious, appears in the parallel passage at 8.44–8.

What is here explored is the other possibility: that E is divided by itself, i.e. by its own internal variations. The possibility of internal qualitative variations is not mentioned; presumably they would not count as creating divisions. What is mentioned is the possibility of variations of 'more' and 'less', i.e. in 'quantity' or 'intensity' of being. These are rejected, by the observation that 'it is all in like manner'. Being admits of no degrees; anything either is or is not.

(c) Reality is complete, unique, unchanging (B 8.26–33)

The same, staying in the same, by itself it lies, and thus it stays fixed there; for strong necessity holds it in the fetters of the limit, which fences it about; since it is not right that what is should be incomplete, for it is not lacking – if it were, it would lack everything.

(DK 28 B 8.29–33)

141

This is a train of argument in which exposition runs the opposite way to deduction. It must be read backwards from the end. The starting-point is that reality (E) is complete or 'not lacking'. Once again the strategy is the same, that of *reductio ad absurdum*. Suppose E is lacking; then E must lack something. What is this something? It cannot be part of E, for then it would not be lacking from E. Therefore it is not part of E, and hence is not; but it is not true that it is not, by the now familiar argument.

Given that E is not lacking, it is complete, and has a 'limit'. The word used here has no close English equivalent: Homer's usage applies it to anything that marks or achieves any kind of completion. Here, the 'limit' functions as a constraint on reality: the need for completeness is a (logical) constraint. Completeness rules out, in particular, all change and movement, and enforces uniqueness: reality is 'by itself' or 'on its own'. Why?

Completeness has these consequences because it embodies the principle that E contains everything that is. This now enables Parmenides to get some grip on the problem of the past and the future. If past (or future) realities are still (or already) real, then they form part of reality; if not, not. The further question about the reality of the past (or future), does not here have to be decided. Either way, there can be no such thing as change or movement of reality: for those would imply the previous existence and present non-existence of some part of reality. Either past (future) and present coexist but differ, and then change is unreal; or the past (future) does not exist and then change is impossible.

For similar reasons it must be 'by itself', that is, unique, and not existing in relation to anything else. For 'anything else' that could be taken into account could not fail to be part of it.

(d) Reality is spherically symmetrical (B 8.42–9)

The grand finale of the way 'it is' combines points made earlier in a striking image:

> But since there is an outermost limit, it is perfect from every
> direction, like the mass of a well-rounded ball, in equipoise
> every way from the middle. For it must not be that it is any
> more or any less, here or there. For neither is there what is not,
> which would obstruct it from holding together, nor is there any
> way in which what is would be here more and here less than
> what is; for it is all immune from harm. For, equal to itself from
> every direction, it meets its limits uniformly.
>
> (DK 28 B 8.42–9)

What is new in this section is spherical symmetry. From its 'being all

142

alike' (the uniformity of its manner of being) and its perfection, is deduced its symmetry about a centre. What is surprising is not the symmetry, since that could be seen as a form of perfection, but the 'middle', a privileged central location, introduced without explanation (on this see the next section).

The Nature of Reality

Having followed the proofs of the properties of reality, one may still be uncertain just what those properties are. How strong, for instance, is the claim that reality is 'one and coherent' meant to be? Does 'completion' include spatial and temporal boundedness, and in general does reality have any spatial or temporal properties at all? How, if at all, is it related to the world apparently given in ordinary experience?

Is reality spatial or temporal or both?

First, the question of spatial and temporal properties. Parmenides shows no hesitation in applying to reality words which would normally imply spatial and temporal properties. It is 'staying in the same thing' and it 'stays fixed there'; and 'what is comes close to what is'. The word 'limit' (*peiras*) by itself implies nothing about space or time; but it is also said that this limit 'fences it about' and is 'outermost'. The simile of the ball might not be meant spatially, but what of the statement that reality is 'in equipoise every way from the middle'?

Recall that reality has been interpreted to be a state of affairs. Such a thing, though it may persist or not through time, can hardly itself have a spatial location or extension. This point chimes with another: if one supposes that reality is spatially extended, its spherical symmetry is problematic. The 'limit' cannot possibly be meant as a spatial boundary, since for reality to be bounded in space would be for it to be incomplete. It must be right, then, to take the spatial terms metaphorically. They must be aids to grasping how reality inhabits a kind of 'logical space'. This works out smoothly. The 'spherical symmetry' must express metaphorically the point that reality is exactly the same, however it is viewed by the mind: it presents no different 'aspects'. The 'middle', about which it is symmetrical, can be identified with the 'heart of well-rounded reality' mentioned earlier; and be some kind of logical core (more on this later). Likewise the undividedness and coherence of reality mean that it is unified, not logically plural, not self-contradictory. 'What is lies close to what is', in the sense that any internal variation between parts does not constitute an essential difference. 'Staying the same in the same and by itself' makes the point that reality does not exist in relation to anything other than itself, and so not in relation to any external temporal or spatial framework; it is unique, and provides its own frame of reference. The metaphorical understanding of these terms is supported, above all, by the nature of the proofs. As has been seen, these make no appeal at all to properties of the space and time of experience.

With respect to time, though, the situation is different. It is at least possible to conceive of a state of affairs as being in, and lasting through, time. Parmenides argues against any *change* in reality; but this is still consistent with the view that reality is something which persists, without change, *through* time. Did he wish to go further? There are good reasons for thinking so.

First, the point made in connection with space, that reality exists 'by itself', without relation to anything other than itself, means that, if reality exists in and through time, time must itself be seen as an aspect of reality. The basic temporal phenomenon must be the temporal extension of reality. This already goes some way beyond the simple notion of a persisting reality.

Second, the argument (section (c) above) to the conclusion that reality is changeless and 'by itself' seems powerful enough to rule out, not merely change, but even mere time-lapse in relation to reality.

Third, the initial list of conclusions states: 'nor was it ever, nor will it be, since it is all together now.' If one cannot even say that 'it was' and 'it will be', then one cannot say that it persists. Nor is it necessary to understand 'now' as a 'now' which implies a 'time when'. It is much more plausibly a metaphorical 'now', indicating a single timeless state, in which there is no longer any distinction of before and after, and therefore no meaning in tensed statements.

The metaphorical interpretation of these spatial and temporal terms, as applied to reality, does not, of course, imply that for Parmenides the spatial and temporal properties of ordinary objects are *illusory*. It still remains to be seen (in the next section) how Parmenides deals with the world of ordinary experience.[17]

In what sense is reality one?

There is no doubt that Parmenides was a monist of some kind; the comments of Plato and Aristotle alone would prove it, even if the fragments were lacking.[18] The relevant proofs are those given under (b) and (c) in the previous section. While argument (b) shows that reality is internally one ('not divided'), argument (c) shows *inter alia* that there is nothing other than reality (it is 'unique' or 'by itself'). Together these yield a monistic thesis: reality is both unified and unique, so there is but one thing.

Just what this monism amounts to, may be seen by seeing what it excludes. The minimum that it must exclude is the error made by mortals when (in a passage to be discussed below) they decide to 'name two forms, one of which ought not [to be named]; this is where they have gone astray' (B 8.53–4). The fundamental error of the 'mortals' of the cosmology is to allow there to be two different subjects of (apparent) discourse, rather than just one.

Parmenides is then committed at least to a logical monism: there is one and only one subject about which anything is true. This seems also to be the maximum that needs to be claimed, and the maximum that is imputed by Aristotle's remark that '[Parmenides] seems to be getting at that which is one in definition' (*Metaphysics* I.5, 986b18–19). The argument for unity (section (b)) demands nothing more. In particular it does not exclude internal variation, nor does it impose qualitative homogeneity. Reality consists of a set of facts true of itself. It is not excluded that reality might be constituted by more than one such fact; and after all many statements about reality are made by the goddess herself in the course of the argument; it would be absurd to suppose that they are meant to be seen as identical. Even though one may talk (as even the goddess sometimes does) in a misleading conventional way, this 'plurality' of facts must not be understood as a genuine plurality: what we are really dealing with here is different aspects of reality. Even when different parts of reality are distinguished, the correct formulation does not admit them as subjects in their own right, but speaks only of 'what is': 'what is comes close to what is'; 'what is cannot be here more or here less than what is'.

So when the goddess distinguishes 'the unmoving heart', and the 'middle', of reality, implying that there is also a peripheral part, she must be understood as speaking, in a conventional way, about a situation which could be described more correctly. What she means by it, has now to be considered.

The Errors of 'Mortals' and the Place of Ordinary Experience

It remains to ask how this reality is supposed to be related to the world of ordinary experience.

In Parmenides' rejection of the 'way of mortals', it was seen that sense-experience in itself did not seem to be blamed for their mistakes. It was mortals' habitual misinterpretation of sense experience which caused them to fall into self-contradiction.

After the exploration of the nature of reality, it is possible to specify the fundamental mistake of 'mortals' more clearly, and Parmenides does so:

145

The same thing is for thinking and [is] the thought that it is; for you will not find thinking apart from what is, in which it is made explicit. For nothing other is or will be outside what is, since that has been bound by fate to be whole and unchanging. Hence it will all be [just] name, all the things that mortals have laid down, trusting them to be real, as coming-into-being and perishing, being and not being, changing place and altering bright colour.

(DK 28 B 8.34–41)

'Mortals', here too, includes all who accept a world of real plurality and real change. Such people are committed to the reality of what are in fact conventional fictions or 'names', taken as putative objects of thinking and saying. The passage starts with a reaffirmation of the principle derived from the 'Platonic problem' (see above): 'what can be thought is just the thought that it is', since this is (with its various consequences) the only true thought. Because there is no saying and thinking something false, apparent false thought must be 'mere names'. So too at the beginning of the cosmology (see next section), where we shall see that even 'mere names' (like other conventions, so long as intelligently made and properly observed) can have their uses.

It is the subjects of ordinary discourse, the things that we normally identify as the plural changing contents of the world, that are here denounced as just 'name', conventional noises and nothing more. Since statements about them cannot be true, they are not capable of being genuinely spoken and thought about.

The self-contradictory 'way of mortals' is now explained. 'Mortals' recognize the existence of an objective reality, and therefore say 'it is'. But they also have to say 'it is not', because they take reality to be something truly plural and changing.[19]

The denunciation of 'mortals' does *not* exclude the substantial reality of the ordinary world of experience – provided a construction is put upon that world which is radically different from the usual one, on the two key points of plurality and change. The temporal dimension may be kept, so long as it is in effect spatialized, with becoming and change ruled out as an illusion. The multiplicity of things in both spatial and temporal dimensions may be kept, so long as it is seen as non-essential qualitative variation within a single logical subject.

Finally, if this is right, it yields a satisfactory sense for the mentions of the 'unmoving heart' of reality and of its 'middle', a core implying a periphery. The 'heart' or 'middle' is constituted by the necessary truths discovered by reasoning, which alone are objects of knowledge. The outside is 'what meets the eye': the contingent snippets of reality as perceived by the senses. Sense-perception, even when in fact veridical, presumably does not yield knowledge because of the possibility of deception.[20] What it reveals, not being part of the core of reality, is non-essential and not demonstrable by reasoning.

The Nature and Structure of Empirical Science: Cosmology as 'Opinions of Mortals'

Parmenides' stringently exclusive conception of knowledge does not entail the uselessness of all other cognitive states. Far from it. He recognizes both the possibility and the practical value of 'opinions' about the cosmos, when organized into a plausible and reliable system. Here, building on the ideas of Xenophanes, he turns out to be the first recognizable philosopher of science.[21]

This is why the conclusion of the investigation of reality does not mark the end of the poem. There still remains the second half of the promise of the goddess, which must now be recalled:

> It is necessary that you find out everything: both the unmoving heart of well-rounded reality [*alētheiē*], and the opinions of mortals, in which there is no real guarantee of truth – but still, these things too you shall learn, how [*or:* since] it had to be that opinions should reputably be, all of them going through everything.
>
> (DK 28 B 1.28–32)

This promise of an exposition of 'mortal opinions' is taken up at the end of the exploration of reality:

> At this point I cease for you my trusty tale and thought concerning reality; from now on, learn the opinions of mortals, hearing the deceptive ordering of my words ... This world-ordering I reveal to you, plausible in all its parts, so that surely no judgement of mortals shall ever overtake you.
>
> (DK 28 B 8.50–1 and 60–1)

What Parmenides says about his system of 'opinions' confirms the conclusion already reached, that for him sense-perception cannot give knowledge. For he is at pains to emphasize that such a system has no 'proper guarantee of truth'; and that it is 'deceptive' (it purports to give knowledge, but does not). It appeals to empirical evidence for support, not to reason. So it lacks any claim to be an object of knowledge. The deeper reason why it cannot be supported by appeal to pure reason is presumably that it is concerned with 'peripheral', contingent aspects of reality.

But there is still a problem. If conducted in the usual way, a cosmology must also necessarily be not so much false as meaningless verbiage, since it takes seriously the illusions of plurality and change, speaks as though they were real, and offers explanations of such changes in terms of physical necessities. Parmenides' 'Opinions' is such a cosmology. Why does he deliberately offer a system of which he himself thinks, and indeed implicitly says (in calling it 'deceptive', and basing it on an 'error'), that it is not merely not certain, but, taken literally, meaningless all through?

One possible answer is that Parmenides thought that his convenient, but literally meaningless, statements could be at need translated back into the correct but cumbersome language of timelessness and logical monism. Unfortunately, there is no indication in the text that it is merely a question of words.

He does at least seem to reassure us that, meaningless or not, these statements are *practically* useful. In some way they correspond to the way the world presents itself to us. The fictitious entities they mention correspond to the fictions we create on the basis of our misread ordinary experience. That experience shows they may be usefully manipulated to give a practically workable understanding of the phenomenal world.[22] (Cosmology so conceived is like science as seen by 'operationalist' philosophers of science; and like divination and natural magic – a thought perhaps taken further by Empedocles.[23])

Within such limits, cosmology may none the less be required to satisfy certain formal demands.[24] Parmenides sets out these demands explicitly, for the first time. The original promise of the goddess stresses that the cosmology to be told is (1) reliable; (2) comprehensive. Both of these points are echoed in the later passage. (1) Reliability is echoed by 'deceptive' and 'plausible'. The demands on the cosmology are further that it be a 'world-ordering', not only (2) comprehensive but also (3) coherent and formally pleasing; and (4) the best possible of its kind. These last two points may also include economy or beauty of explanation. The Principle of Sufficient Reason, which is closely related to the demand for economy, appears, as in the exploration of reality, so again in the cosmology, to yield a symmetry between the two cosmic components.

In fact, Parmenides devises an elegant and economical basis for cosmology by following a hint given by the 'way of mortals'. Any conventional cosmology has to tread that false way, and to say both 'it is' and 'it is not'. The simplest way to commit this error is to suppose initially not one logical subject but two: one which is, and one which is not.[25] The physical properties of the two subjects are then a kind of cosmic parody or allegory of the logical properties of what is and what is not.

Now, they have fixed their judgements to name two forms, one of which should not [be named]; this is where they have gone astray. They have separated their bodies as opposites, and laid down their signs apart from one another: for the one form, heavenly flaming *Fire*, gentle-minded, very light, the same as itself in every direction, but different from the other one; but that [other] one too by itself [they have laid down] as opposite, unknowing *Night*, a dense and weighty body.

(DK 28 B 8.53–9)

Fire and Night are the physical embodiments of the two opposed principles. The cosmology is dualistic, and there is reason to suspect that, as with the Pythagoreans from which it may borrow, the dualism was a moral (and an epistemic) as well as a physical one. The two opposed 'forms' are associated from the outset with knowledge and ignorance; perhaps also with good and evil. Traces of morally charged struggles and loves of 'gods' within the cosmos remain in the testimony.[26] A cycle of cosmic changes is the most likely explanation of a detached remark (DK B 5) about circular exposition.

Not only is the basis economical, but there are overall formal demands on the two forms. They must jointly exhaust the contents of the cosmos; and there must be cosmic symmetry as between them (DK B 9).[27]

Conclusion: the Trouble with Thinking

This account of Parmenides must end with questions on which certainty seems to be out of reach.

The overarching question is this: is Parmenides' 'framework', in which his theory of reality is embedded, itself meant to be grounded in that theory of reality? By the 'framework' is meant roughly the following: the original assumption about the actual existence of thinking and certain knowledge; the distinction between knowledge and opinion; the application of logic in the discovery of the nature of reality; and the assertion of the practical, empirical effectiveness of systematized 'opinions'.

Even if this question cannot ultimately be given any confident answer, it usefully focuses attention on one sub-problem, which has so far been kept to one side. This is the problem about the relation between thinking and reality. We have seen that thinking, for Parmenides, can only be of truths, indeed of necessary truths, about reality. Is it a necessary truth that thinking occurs? If so, that truth itself is of course a necessary truth about reality; and whatever it is that thinks must be (part of) reality. If so, one would think that it ought to be

149

deducible from the nature of reality that it thinks about itself. No such deduction appears in the text, though; and the thesis that true thinking occurs seems to be (as Aristotle took it) an initial assumption which is taken as unquestionable, but not formally proved.

On this point, there are two parts of the poem which might serve as some kind of a guide. One is the introductory narrative of the journey to the goddess. Another is the outline of 'physical psychology', a general theory of perception and thought, which is attested as part of the cosmology.

The journey to the goddess

The chariot-ride of the narrator in the introduction (preserved in DK B 1) has usually been taken as an allegory of Parmenides' own intellectual odyssey, and of the framework with which he starts.[28] Its chronology and geography are elusive and dreamlike. The individual beings mentioned, even the narrator and the goddess herself, are but shadowy outlines. Only certain *technological objects* – the chariot wheels and axle, the gate and its key – stand out in relief. Is Parmenides here proclaiming his advances in the technology of thinking, as the motive power in, and the key and gateway to, all that follows? The 'paths of Night and Day' would then be the ways of 'it is' and 'it is not'. The chariot, the horses, the daughters of the Sun who act as guides, and Parmenides' own ambition, would correspond to everything Parmenides needs to get him as far as the choice of ways, – that is, to the 'framework'. All too much, though, must be left uncertain, even if such an approach looks plausible in general.

The empirical psychology

The psychology or 'theory of mental functioning' which was outlined in Parmenides' cosmology is, equally, not much more than a tantalizing hint. Theophrastus says that for Parmenides as for several others 'sense perception is by what is similar', and goes on:

> 'As for Parmenides, he goes into no detail at all, but just [says] that, there being two elements, cognition [*gnōsis*] is according to what predominates. For, as the hot or the cold predominates, the intellect [*dianoia*] alters, but that [intellect] which is [determined] by the hot is in a better and purer state, though even that kind needs a kind of proportioning. He says:
>
> > According as the compounding of the wandering limbs is in each case, in such a way is mind present in people; for it is

the same thing in each and in all that the nature of the limbs has in mind: the more is the thought.

For he talks of sense perception and mental apprehension as being the same; which is why [he says that] memory and forgetting occur from these [constituents] by the [change of] compounding. But whether, if they are in equal quantities in the mixture, there will be mental apprehension or not, and what state this is, he does not go on to make clear. That he also makes sense perception [occur] for the other element [[(the cold)]] in itself, is clear from the passage where he says that the corpse does not perceive light and hot and noise, because of the lack of fire, but does perceive cold and silence and the opposite things. And in general [he says that] everything that is has some kind of cognition. Thus it seems he tries to cut short, by his dogmatic statement, the difficulties that arise from his theory.

(Theophrastus *On the Senses* 3–4, citing DK 28 B 16)

This would seem to be at least a two-tier theory. The lower tier is basic sense perception, available to everything that exists, and 'by the similar'; i.e. what is fire can perceive fire, what is night can perceive night, and what is a mixture can perceive both. The higher tier is that of mind and thought, somehow due to a 'proportionate compounding' in human (and other?) bodies.[29]

Any inferences from these indications can be but tentative. Briefly, the general shape of Parmenides' theory of reality shows that any real thinking must be (part of) reality thinking about itself.[30] The account of Parmenides' intellectual journey may be taken as acknowledging the need for starting-points for thinking – for a 'framework'. The theory of mental activity in the cosmology is of course infected with the fictitiousness of the whole cosmology; yet it is probably meant to correspond, somehow, to the truth about thinking. If one element ('fire') in the cosmology corresponds to reality, then the fact that it is fire that cognizes fire reflects the truth that it is reality that thinks of reality. It is a pity we can know no more of what Parmenides thought about thought.

ZENO

Introduction

Zeno of Elea, fellow citizen and disciple of Parmenides, became famous as the author of a series of destructive arguments. There is no good evidence that he put forward any positive doctrines. Plato and Aristotle were deeply impressed by the originality and power of the arguments; such knowledge of Zeno as survives is due principally to them and to the Neoplatonist scholar Simplicius.[31]

The Arguments against Plurality

(a) Plato on Zeno's book and the structure of the arguments

Plato's dialogue *Parmenides* describes a supposed meeting in Athens, around 450 BC, of the young Socrates and others with two visitors from Elea, Parmenides and Zeno. Plato's fictional narrator gives some biographical data about the two Eleatics, and recounts a conversation between 'Socrates' and 'Zeno' which tells (127d6–128e4) of the genesis of Zeno's arguments against plurality, their structure and their aim. Even if based solely on Plato's own reading of Zeno's book, this has to be taken seriously as testimony.[32]

According to this testimony, there was a book by Zeno which consisted entirely of arguments directed against the thesis 'there are many things'. Each argument began by assuming the truth of this thesis, and proceeded to deduce a pair of mutually contradictory conclusions from it, in order to make a *reductio ad absurdum* of the original thesis. In support of this account, Simplicius the Neoplatonist gives verbatim quotations from two of the arguments, which can be seen to exemplify the pattern; Plato's narrator himself gives the outline of another.

(b) The aim of the arguments

This account of the structure of Zeno's arguments leads 'Socrates' in the dialogue to the view that Zeno's aim was simply to refute the thesis of pluralism ('that there are many things'), in any sense incompatible with Parmenides' theory, and thereby to establish Parmenidean monism. However, this conclusion of 'Socrates' is not completely accepted by 'Zeno', who denies that the book was a 'serious' attempt to establish Parmenidean monism, and goes on:

> actually this [book] is a way of coming to the aid of Parmenides' theory, by attacking those who try to make fun of it [on the grounds] that, if there is one thing, then many ridiculous and self-contradictory consequences follow for the theory. Well, this book is a counter-attack against the pluralists; it pays them back in the same coin, and more; its aim is to show that their thesis, that there are many things, would have even more ridiculous

152

consequences than the thesis that there is one thing, if one were to go into it sufficiently.

(*Parmenides* 128c6–d6)

The natural way to read this is as saying that the arguments had an *ad hominem* element. 'Zeno' cannot be saying that Parmenides' thesis really had ridiculous consequences; 'even more ridiculous consequences' points to the employment by Zeno of assumptions made by Parmenides' opponents, but not accepted by Zeno himself.

Yet 'Socrates', a little earlier, has said that the arguments give 'very many, very strong grounds for belief' (128b1–3) that pluralism, of any variety incompatible with Parmenides, is false. In Plato's opinion the arguments, however they originated, were usable against all varieties of anti-Parmenidean pluralism. Therefore Plato's testimony on Zeno cannot be fully understood unless we know how he interpreted Parmenides, which cannot be investigated in this chapter.

Provisionally, it is enough to note that there is no danger of contradiction in Plato's testimony, provided we may assume that Zeno's original opponents made, and Zeno himself used against them, only such assumptions as were either inconsistent with Parmenides; or plausibly seen as articulations of common-sense.[33] The question can be finally decided, if at all, only by analysis of the arguments themselves.

One further piece of information is given at 135d7–e7: the arguments were about 'visible things', i.e. they addressed themselves to the question of pluralism in the ordinary world, using assumptions derived from experience.[34]

(c) The argument by 'like' and 'unlike'

According to Plato (*Parmenides* 127d6–e5), the argument (the first one in the book) purported to show that 'if there are many things, they must be both like and unlike'. Nothing further is known.

(d) The argument by 'finitely many' and 'infinitely many'

Simplicius preserves the entire text of this argument. The compressed, austere style is reminiscent of Parmenides.

> If there are many things, it must be that they are just as many as they are and neither more of them nor less. But if they are as many as they are, they would be finite.
>
> If there are many things, the things that are are infinite. For there are always other things between those that are, and again others between those; and thus the things that are are infinite.

(DK 29 B 3, Simplicius *Physics* 140.27–34)

The first limb insists on the implications of countability. If it is true to say 'there are many things' and to deny that 'there is one thing', that implies that (a) there is one correct way of counting things; (b) that that way of counting the things that are leads to a definite result. But a definite result implies finitely many things: if there were infinitely many, counting them would lead to no result at all.

The second limb invokes the relation 'between' (*metaxu*). Any two distinct things are spatially separate (the converse of Parmenides' argument for the oneness of reality from its undividedness). But what separates them must itself be something that is, and distinct from either. From this principle, an infinite progression of new entities is constructed.

Though this involves an appeal to spatial properties, it might easily be rephrased in terms of logical ones. The principle would be: for any two distinct things, there must be some third thing different from either which distinguishes them from one another; and so on.

(e) The argument by 'sizeless' and 'of infinite size'

Again Simplicius is our source. He quotes two chunks of the text, and enough information to recover the rest in outline.

The first limb claimed that 'if there are many things, they are so small as to have no size'. The argument proceeded, according to Simplicius, 'from the fact that each of the many things is the same as itself and one' (*Physics* 139, 18–19). It is not difficult to make a plausible reconstruction here. First, to speak of a 'many' implies, as in (d), a correct way of counting. The many must be made up of securely unified ones. Then consider each of these units. The line may have been (compare Melissus DK B 9): what has size has parts; what has parts is not one. Hence each of the units must be without size.

The second limb contradicted this in successively stronger ways. First, it claimed to show that, in a plurality, what is must have size. Suppose something does not have size, then it cannot be:

> For if it were added to another thing that is, it would make it no larger: for if something is no size, and is added, it is not possible that there should be any increase in size. This already shows that what is added would be nothing. But if when it is taken away the other thing will be no smaller, and again when it is added [the other thing] will not increase, it is clear that what was added was nothing, and so was what was taken away.
>
> (DK 29 B 2, Simplicius *Physics* 139.11–15)

This argument in terms of adding and taking away obviously makes essential use of the assumption 'there are many things'; it could not, therefore, have been turned against Parmenides. It also needs some principle such as 'to be is to be (something having) a quantity': not a 'commonsense' axiom, but one likely to be held by most mathematizing theorists of the time.[35]

The next and final step proceeds from size to infinite size:

> But if each [of the many things] is, then it is necessary that it has some size and bulk, and that one part of it is at a distance from another. The same account applies to the part in front: for that too will have size and a part of it will be in front. Now, it is alike to say this once and to keep saying it all the time: for no such part of it will be the endmost, nor will it be that [any such part] is not one part next to another. Thus if there are many things, it must be that they are both small and large: so small as to have no size, so large as to be infinite.
>
> (DK 29 B 1, Simplicius *Physics* 141.2–8)

One axiom used is that anything having size contains at least two parts themselves having size. This clearly generates an unending series of parts having size. Less clear is the final step from 'having infinitely many parts with size' to 'infinite (in size)', which apparently was taken with no further argument. There is some analogy with the 'Stadium' and 'Achilles' (see (c) below): just as the runner's supposedly finite track turns out to contain an infinite series of substretches, each of positive length, so here the object with supposedly finite size turns out to contain an infinite series of parts, each having size. If we try to recompose the original thing out of the parts, we shall never finish, but always be adding to its size; and this, Zeno might plausibly claim, is just what is meant when we say something is infinite in size.[36]

(f) Methods and assumptions

In the light of the arguments themselves as preserved, the question of their aims and methods can be taken up again.

It is evident that some of the assumptions used by Zeno in these arguments are not due to simple 'common sense'. Common sense does not make postulates about the divisibility *ad infinitum* of things having size; nor suppose that 'to be is to be something having a quantity'; nor insist on a single correct way of counting things. Hence Zeno's arguments are not directed against unreflecting 'common sense'. In fact, these are the kind of assumptions that are naturally and plausibly made, when one sets about theorizing, in an abstract and mathematical spirit, about the physical world.

The methods and the style of proof are also mathematical. Noteworthy are the constructions of progressions *ad infinitum*, and the remark when one is constructed: 'it is alike to say this once and to keep saying it all the time'. However many times the operation is repeated, that is, it will always turn out possible to make precisely the same step yet again.[37]

The Arguments about Motion

(a) Aristotle's evidence

There is only one certain primary source for the content of Zeno's arguments about motion: Aristotle, who states and discusses them in *Physics* VI and VIII (VI 2, 233a21–30; VI 9, 239b5–240a18; VIII 8, 263a4–b9). Aristotle's source is not known; no book of Zeno that might have contained them is recorded. It is perfectly possible that they reached Aristotle by oral tradition. In any case, while there is no reason to doubt that they are substantially authentic, there is also no reason to suppose that Zeno's own formulations have been faithfully preserved. (A source possibly independent of Aristotle is mentioned in (c) below.)

The four individual arguments, as Aristotle reports them, derive contradictions from the supposition that something moves. Three of them purport to show that what moves, does not move. They are 'dramatized', in so far as they introduce particular supposed moving things: a runner; two runners; an arrow; three moving and stationary masses. Aristotle presents the arguments as designed to be mutually independent.[38]

(b) The 'Stadium' and the 'Achilles'

Suppose a runner is to run along a running-track. The stretch to be traversed (call it S) may be considered as divided up into substretches in various ways. Given the starting and finishing points we understand what is meant by 'the first half of S', 'the third quarter of S' and so on. It seems that however short a substretch is specified in this way, it will always have positive length and may be thought of as divided into two halves.[39]

Going on in this way we can specify a division of S into substretches which will be such that the runner runs through a well-ordered but infinite series of substretches. First the runner traverses the first half, then half of what remains, then half of what remains, and so on. In this way, for any positive integer n, at the end of the nth substretch the runner has covered

$\dfrac{(2^n - 1)}{2^n}$ of S, and the nth substretch is $1/2^n$

of the whole length of the track. However large a finite number n becomes, the fraction is never equal to 1; there are infinitely many substretches.

With such a division, the series of substretches is well-ordered, and the runner who traverses S has been through *all* of the substretches in order: for every finite number N, the runner has traversed the Nth substretch. Hence the runner has traversed an infinite series of substretches, in a finite time; but this is impossible.

This is an expansion of Aristotle's formulations (*Physics* VI 2, 233a21–23; VI 9, 239b11–14) of the 'Stadium' argument.[40] The 'Achilles' (*Physics* VI 9, 239b14–29) makes the same point more dramatically, pitting a very fast runner against a very slow one. The slow runner is given a start. The stretch covered by the faster runner is divided up in such a way that it appears the faster can never catch the slower within any finite time. This drives home the point that speed is irrelevant. No limit of speed is prescribed or needed by the argument; the speed of the fast runner could increase without limit without removing the problem.

(c) The 'Arrow'

Another way of looking at things supposedly in motion throughout a time-stretch is to select any one moment during that stretch. Say an arrow is in flight.

1 At any one moment the arrow must be 'in one place'. No part of it can be in two places at once; so it must occupy 'a space equal to itself' (i.e. of the same shape and size).
2 The arrow must be at rest at this moment. There is no distance through which it moves, *in* a moment; hence it does not move *at* a moment, so it must be at rest at that moment.
3 But the moment chosen was an arbitrary moment during the flight of the arrow. It follows that the arrow must be at rest at *all* moments during its flight.
4 Hence, since the arrow during its flight is never not at a moment of its flight, the arrow is always at rest during its flight; so it never moves during its flight.

The above argument cannot claim to be more than a plausible filling-out of Aristotle's abbreviated report (*Physics* VI 9, 239b5–9 and 30–3).[41] Aristotle himself is interested only in step (4), where he thinks to find the fallacy; he gives the only briefest sketch of (1), (2) and (3).[42]

(d) The 'Moving Rows'

Aristotle (*Physics* VI 9, 239b33–240a18) reports this argument in terms of unspecified 'masses' on a racecourse; to make it easier for a modern reader, the masses may be thought of as railway trains.[43]

Consider three railway trains of the same length, on three parallel tracks. One of the trains is moving in the 'up' direction, another is moving at the same speed in the 'down' direction, and the third is stationary. As may be easily verified, either of the moving trains takes twice as long to pass the stationary train as it does to pass the other moving train.

Just how Zeno derived a contradiction from this fact, is uncertain. According to Aristotle, Zeno simply assumed that the passing-times must be equal, since the speeds are equal and the two masses passed are equal in length. Then it follows that the time is equal to twice itself. The assumption, though, has often been thought too obviously false to be Zeno's. It may simply be Aristotle's attempt to fill a gap in the argument as it reached him.[44] Yet Aristotle himself thought it not obviously fallacious, and worthy of detailed refutation.

(e) Method and purpose of the four arguments

As Aristotle describes them, these four arguments are simply 'the arguments of Zeno about motion which cause difficulties to those who try to solve them': no suggestion that they were *all* of Zeno's arguments on the subject. Aristotle presents them as mutually independent, and in an order which is not dictated by his own concerns, presumably that of his source.

Once again, as with the arguments against plurality, some of the assumptions are manifestly theorists' initial assumptions, rather than those of simple 'common sense'; but they are close to common sense.[45] If one starts trying to think systematically in an abstract way, analogous to mathematics, about the phenomena of motion and its relation to time and space, these are assumptions that it is natural to start with. It is natural to assume that both the time-stretch and the track of the moving thing may be treated for theoretical purposes as geometrical lines obeying Euclidean geometry. This means that they are divisible *ad infinitum*, and that points along them exist 'anywhere': i.e. at all places corresponding to lengths constructible by Euclidean procedures. There was no theory equivalent to that of the real numbers available in Zeno's time, but such assumptions correspond to elementary theorems and constructions of plane geometry as it was beginning to be developed.

The way of thinking about physical phenomena embedded in

Zeno's assumptions is therefore an abstracting, mathematizing physicist's way. Zeno's original opponents are likely to have been natural philosophers, very likely from the loose group of 'Pythagoreans' (see below), who were then taking the first steps towards a mathematized theory of the natural world.[46]

Just because Zeno's assumptions are natural ones for any mathematising theorist to make, his arguments still arouse heated discussion among philosophers. The suggestion, still sometimes made, that Zeno's arguments have been made obsolete by developments in modern mathematics (particularly differential calculus and the theory of infinite series), misses the point. The value and interest of all Zeno's arguments is just that they are challenges to the foundations of any mathematics and any physics that uses infinites and indivisibles of any kind and applies them to the physical world.[47]

Other Arguments

Reports of yet other arguments by Zeno survive.

Aristotle records a problem about place: 'if everything that is is in a place, clearly there will be a place of the place too, and so *ad infinitum*' (*Physics* IV 1, 209a23–5). Elsewhere he gives the problem in the form: 'if a place is something, in what will it be?' (*Physics* IV 3, 210b22–24). If this was originally one argument, it constructed an infinite series out of the common assumption that everything that is, is in a place, which is something other than itself: applying the assumption to places themselves, we shall have places of places, places of places of places, and so on. Such a series could have figured in one of the arguments against plurality. In any case, it would be a good parry to any attack on Parmenides' monism which sought to show that his 'One' must occupy a place other than itself.

Also from Aristotle (*Physics* VII 5, 250a19–22): Zeno argued that, if a heap of grain makes a noise when it falls, then a single grain and any fractional part of it must make a noise too. One may conjecture that Zeno's dilemma was: either it makes a proportionately small noise, or none at all. If the latter, a natural and fundamental assumption of mathematizing physics is undermined: the assumption that the magnitudes of effects are in direct proportion to the magnitudes of their causes. But if the former, then why do we not hear the proportionately small noise? If it fails to affect our senses, the assumption of proportionality breaks down somewhere else. Such an argument would obviously fit Zeno's programme of attack on any possible mathematical physics.

Conclusion

Examination of the evidence for Zeno's arguments leads to satisfyingly consistent results, and bears out the testimony of Plato.

First, Zeno attacked principally certain commonly-held views involving the reality of plurality and change, but did not confine himself to those targets. This fits well with Parmenides, who saw the twin beliefs in the reality of essential plurality and of change as the two marks of deluded 'mortals'.[48]

Second, Zeno's argumentative assumptions are taken from his opponents. They may be characterized as those of theoretical physics in its infancy, of 'mathematicized common sense'.

❧ PHILOLAUS AND 'THE PEOPLE ❧ CALLED PYTHAGOREANS'

In the mid to late fifth century, there were various people and groups claiming to be 'Pythagorean'; they were found principally in the west of the Greek world (Sicily and southern Italy). Aristotle, our most reliable source, tells of certain 'Italians' or 'people called Pythagoreans' who had a programme of reducing everything to mathematics (*Metaphysics* I.5, 985b23–986b8 and 987a9–27).[49] The only individual one, about whom something of tangible philosophical interest can be known, is Philolaus of Croton.[50]

Five fragments which may be reasonably taken as genuine reveal a theory of underlying structure in the universe which is heavily influenced by the development of mathematics as an abstract study.[51] This theory is propounded, it seems, on the basis of an analysis of ordinary human knowledge and its presuppositions.

Philolaus' starting-point is *gnōsis*, the everyday activity of cognitive 'grasping' (individuation, identification, reidentification, reference) of ordinary individual things. This 'cognizing' implies that its objects 'have number', i.e. are in some sense measurable or countable. Quite generally, any cognizable object must be marked off from everything else by a sharp, definite boundary. Whether this boundary be spatial or temporal, the object within it will have some measurable quantity (volume, time-duration). Also, a cognizable collection of objects must have a number; indeed even a single object must be recognizable as a single object and not a plurality, which implies a definite and practically applicable method of counting. These points are recognizably related to some arguments of Parmenides and Zeno. Zeno (see above, pp. 153–4) argues that a 'many' implies a definite number; but also that it implies definite, distinct units and hence boundaries round these units. That what is must be a unit and have a boundary is also argued in Parmenides (see above, p. 41).

The concept of a 'boundary' is central here. Philolaus' analysis of the presuppositions of cognition leads him to a logical separation of the contents of the universe into 'things which bound' and 'things unbounded'. Everything in the cosmos, and that cosmos itself, is claimed manifestly to exhibit a structure 'fitted together' from the two kinds of thing. This dualism is obviously closely related to views which Aristotle attributes to 'the people called Pythagoreans'. He reports that some of them set up two 'columns of correlated opposites', which featured such items as limit/unlimited, odd/even, one/plurality, right/left, male/female, etc. (*Metaphysics* I.5, 986a22–6).

Philolaus' careful attempt to build up a general ontology on the basis of an analysis of ordinary cognition, guided by mathematics, leads him naturally in the direction of Aristotelian 'form' and 'matter'. Whatever stuff an individual is thought of as being 'made of', is in itself not 'bounded'; for it might be present in any quantity. But for there to be an individual, there must be also a 'bound'.

Further explication of just what is involved in this 'fitting together' is not found, and it seems that Philolaus thought this question beyond the reach of human knowledge. That conclusion is in conformity with his method. The 'everlasting being' of things, or 'nature itself', is the subject of 'divine cognition' only. The 'fitting together' is achieved 'in some way or other'. Mathematics, clearly, cannot help; for it too exemplifies, rather than explains, the dualistic structure. All that we can say is that even humble human cognition presupposes such a structure of things in particular and in general; the first example, it has been suggested, of a Kantian transcendental argument.[52]

❦ MELISSUS ❦

Melissus of Samos (active around the mid fifth century) is best grouped with the philosophers of Elea, to whom he obviously owes much. In spite of the preservation of ten fragments (plus a paraphrase of other arguments) by Simplicius, and a reasonable amount of supporting testimony (the most useful from Aristotle), Melissus' intentions are not obvious. Many of his arguments seem obviously weaker and cruder than those of Parmenides; on these grounds he was dismissed with contempt by Aristotle.[53]

Foundations of Monism

As found in the quotations by Simplicius, Melissus starts by considering 'whatever was' (DK B 1). The emphatic use of the *past* tense already signals a departure from Parmenides. It may have been justified by an initial argument to the effect that thinking and speaking require the existence of something thought or spoken about; it is impossible to think or speak 'about nothing'.[54] By the time we reflect on our own thinking and speaking, they are in the past, so what is guaranteed by the argument is that something *was*.

'Whatever was' is also apparently more non-committal than 'reality'. As quickly becomes clear, however, this entity is conceived of by Melissus as extended in space and in time. It is 'the universe' rather than 'reality'. Various things are proved about it. First (B 1), it cannot have come into being, because it would have to have done so out of nothing, which is impossible. Next (B 2), it always was and always will be; Melissus here assumes that ceasing-to-be is just as impossible as coming-to-be.

Next (B 3), an obscure argument to show that the universe is spatially unbounded, perhaps intended to parallel the argument for no coming-to-be and no ceasing-to-be. The thought seems to be that a 'beginning' or 'end' in space is just as inconceivable as one in time; in either case we should have to suppose that there was nothing beyond. But that is unacceptable, apparently. Why? Possibly again for the reason that a statement ostensibly 'about nothing' (i.e. where 'nothing' appears to refer to what the statement is about) is not a statement at all.

Finally, an argument for the unity of the universe: 'If it were two, they could not be unbounded, but would have bounds with each other'. Why should internal boundary lines be ruled out? Perhaps (cf. Parmenides and Zeno) because even internal boundary lines involve what is not; they cannot be part of either of the components they separate, so are either themselves components, and need further boundaries, or are 'nothing', which is again impossible. So there cannot be two or more distinct components in the universe.

A further vital point, proved we know not how, was that the universe is homogeneous. It also has no 'bulk' or 'body', on the grounds that that would mean that it would have physical parts, and not be a unity (B 10).

Arguments against Change, Void and Motion

Melissus' arguments against the possibility of any kind of change proceed briskly but none too convincingly. First, qualitative change would imply lack of internal homogeneity in the universe, since it would have to be qualitatively different at different times. Next comes 'change of *kosmos*'; apparently some more essential type of change (change of internal structure?). The argument is that such a change necessarily involves what has already been ruled out: e.g. increase or partial perishing or qualitative change.

There follows the at first sight bizarre corollary that the universe does not experience pain or mental distress; since pain and distress imply change or inhomogeneity in various ways. To deny that would be pointless, unless the universe were at least possibly a sentient being. If Melissus, like Parmenides, began with the assumption that some mental activity occurred, that would for him have the consequence that the universe has mental activity and so is sentient.

Next, there can be no such thing as void, which would be 'nothing' and therefore does not exist. Hence there must be a plenum, which cannot admit anything from outside into itself, and so there can be no movement, since nothing can budge to make room for the moving thing. Two corollaries: first, no actual dividing of the undivided universe is possible, since that implies movement. Second, there can be no inner variation in respect of density, since 'less dense' can be understood only as meaning 'having more void'.

The Relation to Ordinary Experience and the Attack on Sense Perception

Where does Melissus' monism leave common sense and sense perception? The messages of sense perception cannot be true. Melissus bases his attack on the fact that sense perception tells us that change occurs. The argument is: if something is really so rather than so, it cannot cease to be true that this is so. Hence, if our senses tell us that, e.g. this water is cold, and then that this water has heated up, they would be contradicting themselves. So either our senses do not really tell us anything; or there is no change, when again our senses have misled us.

The aim is clear: it is to undermine any common-sense objections to the positive doctrine about the universe. It therefore has to be an independent argument. The central idea of this independent argument against change is that nothing that is true can cease to be true, 'for there is nothing stronger than what is really so'. We need a conception of truth as unchanging; but then the deliverances of sense perception need to be at least reinterpreted, for they give us only time-bound truths. So we need to revise the common-sense notion that sense perceptions are straightforwardly true.

163

❧ CONCLUSION ❧

This chapter began with Pythagoras, as the presumed source of some persistently influential thoughts. His influence on philosophy was diffuse and non-specific. His questioning of 'what we really are', and his insistence that we are moral agents in a morally polarized world, prepared for the creation of moral philosophy by Socrates and Plato.[55]

Above all, Pythagoras' insistence on the relevance of mathematics and importance of abstract structure links him to the Eleatics. For what seems to be common to both Pythagoreans and Eleatics is that they take seriously the ideal of mathematically exact knowledge, the constraining force of mathematically rigorous argument, and the cardinal role of abstract structure in the nature of things. (Pythagoras' other main concerns – the nature and destiny of the self, and the dualism of good and evil – surface in the Eleatics, if at all, only in Parmenides' cosmology.)

The Eleatic philosophers, likewise, had an influence which reached far beyond their few actual followers, and is still active today. Higher standards of precision in statement and rigour of argument are noticeable everywhere in the later fifth century. Metaphysical argument in the Eleatic style appears: in Melissus, and as an intellectual exercise or for sceptical purposes, as in the sophist Gorgias. More significantly, Socrates' step-by-step, mostly destructive argumentation is Eleatic in spirit; it developed into the philosophical method of Plato and Aristotle, both of whom pay tribute to 'father Parmenides'.

In the philosophy of scientific theorizing, it was Zeno's dazzling attacks on incipient mathematizing physics that, for a long time, stole the show. Their effect was not wholly negative: they stimulated further investigations into the foundations of mathematics, and its relation to the physical world, which culminated in the work of Aristotle. The more constructive thinking of Parmenides and Philolaus about scientific theorizing has only very recently begun to be understood and appreciated.

 NOTES

1 The classic study of Walter Burkert (Burkert [2.25]) supersedes all previous discussions of the evidence. It may go too far in the direction of scepticism about Pythagoras as theoretician: see Kahn [4.2]. The (pre-Burkert) catalogue of sources in Guthrie [2.13] Vol I: 157–71 is still serviceable.

2 Those of Aristoxenus, Dicaearchus and Heraclides Ponticus were the earliest and most influential: see Burkert [2.25], 53–109.

3 Certain animal foods were taboo, but a comprehensive ban on the slaughter

and eating of animals is improbable and poorly attested for Pythagoras himself. Some under Pythagorean or Orphic influence, such as Empedocles, did observe such a ban. On the whole subject of the taboo-prescriptions and mystical maxims (*akousmata*, *sumbola*) of the early Pythagoreans, see Burkert [2.25], 166–92.

4 The fragments of Parmenides have been edited many times. DK is the standard edition for reference purposes; the most reliable and informed recent edition, on matters of Greek linguistic usage and of textual history, is that of Coxon [4.8], which also gives much the fullest collection of secondary ancient evidence. Among minor sources are some other Neoplatonists (Plotinus, Iamblichus, Proclus), and Sextus Empiricus the Sceptic.

5 The scholarly literature is extensive. A small selection is given in the bibliography; the monograph of Mourelatos [4.24] can be particularly recommended for clarity, fullness of information and breadth of approach. The footnotes below offer very brief indications of the spread of opinion on cardinal points; they do not try to outline the arguments needed to justify the reading given in the text.

6 On Xenophanes and his relevance here, Hussey [2.35], 17–32.

7 On the 'opinions of mortals' see below pp. 147–9.

8 On *alētheiē* and related words in early Greek, scholarly discussion has been too often darkened by philosophical prejudice. See the useful study of Heitsch [4.29]; also Mourelatos [4.24], 63–7 and references there.

Alētheiē in Parmenides is taken as 'reality' by Verdenius [4.30], Mourelatos [4.24], 63–7, Coxon [4.8], 168. Others understand it as 'truth' or 'manifest or necessary truth'.

9 So Verdenius [4.30]. Allied to this view are those who take the intended subject to be 'what is' in the sense of 'what is the case' (e.g. Mourelatos [4.24]). Other leading candidates for the role of subject of discourse: 'that which is' (so e.g. Cornford [4.19], Verdenius [4.27], Hölscher [4.22], O'Brien [4.12]); 'what can be spoken and thought of' (Owen [4.46]), 'whatever may be the object of enquiry' (Barnes [2.8]). That a wholly indefinite subject ('something') or no specific subject at all is intended, at least initially, is suggested in different ways by e.g. Calogero [4.18], Coxon [4.8].

10 On the verb *einai* 'be' in early Greek, see items [4.31] to [4.34] in the Bibliography. The entirely straightforward Homeric usage ('*X* is' = 'there is such a thing as *X*') is the obvious first hypothesis for the *esti* and *ouk esti* paths. Some, though, have put the so-called 'veridical' uses ('be' = 'be true' or 'be' = 'be so', 'be the case') in the forefront (e.g. Jantzen [4.23], Kahn [4.42]); others make the use of *einai* in predication central (e.g. Mourelatos [4.24]); yet others (Calogero [4.18], Furth [4.41]) have suggested that in Parmenides this verb is a 'fusion' of two or more of the normal uses.

11 In fact premiss (2), even without (1) and (3), gives a reason to reject the way that says 'it is not'. For this way says, about reality generally, that it doesn't exist or obtain. So by its own account it can't state any truth, since truth presupposes reality. But there is nothing to show that Parmenides took this short cut.

12 Plato *Theaetetus* 188c9–189b6, *Sophist* 237b7–e7. On the versions of this argument in Plato, see e.g. items [4.49] to [4.51] in the Bibliography.

13 It is true that in places the words 'say' (*legein, phasthai*), 'think' (*noein*) and their derivatives are used in ways that seem inconsistent with principle (7). (a) The goddess describes (at least) two ways as those 'which alone are to be thought' (B 2.2), including (at least) one false one. (b) She warns Parmenides against a false way: 'fence off your thought from this way of enquiry' (B 7.2), as though it were possible to think its falsities. (c) She speaks of '[my] trusty account ("saying") and thought about reality' (B 8.50–1), as though it were possible to have *un*-trusty thought. Of these passages, though, (b) and (c) are rhetorical flourishes, in no way essential to the argument; while (a), which occurs before principle (7) has been introduced, need only mean that *at most* those two ways can be thought.

14 Xenophanes, for instance, would have questioned the ambition of establishing the truth, rather than mapping out by enquiry *coherent possibilities for well-based opinion.*

15 Whether this reality is *objective* or not, is not here at issue. On this question, see 'Conclusion; the Trouble with Thinking'.

16 Though verbal echoes suggest that Parmenides (not surprisingly) had Heraclitus, with his aggressive use of (?apparent) contradictions, particularly in mind.

17 Some have taken the spatial and temporal ways of speaking literally. Literal sphericity and centre: e.g. Cornford [4.19], Barnes [2.8]; against this, e.g. Owen [4.46], 61–8. Persistence through time: e.g. Fränkel [4.20], sect 6; Schofield [4.48]; against this, Owen [4.47] The tense-logical principle ascribed to Parmenides at p. 140 above would not commit him to the reality of time in any sense.

18 For example, Plato *Sophist* 242d4–6; *Parmenides* 128a4–b3; Aristotle *Metaphysics* I.5, 986b10–19. Recent views on just what the monism amounts to, and of the reliability of Plato's testimony, have differed widely; Barnes [4.39] maintains that Parmenides is not a monist at all.

19 The contemptuous term 'mortals' may itself hint at their double mistake, by itself presupposing that mistake: it is plural, and it implies the reality of death. By their very error, they condemn themselves to appear to themselves as plural and ephemeral. Interesting parallels for this in early Brahmanical monism, e.g. in the Katha Upanishad:

> ... Herein there's no diversity at all.
> Death beyond death is all the lot
> Of him who sees in this what seems to be diverse.

(R. C. Zaehner, *Hindu Scriptures* (Everyman's Library: London and New York, Dent/Dutton, 1966): 178)

20 That the bare possibility of deception suffices to destroy a claim to knowledge had been pointed out by Xenophanes (DK 21 B 34).

21 On Xenophanes see the section 'The Promise of the Goddess'.

22 But what it is (if anything), in the nature of reality, that underwrites this practical usefulness, is not clear. There is a hint ('it *had to be* that opinions should reputably be', B1.32) that Parmenides did envisage such a guarantee; and see below on the cosmology as formally parallel to the section dealing with *alētheiē.*

Scholarly opinion has been much divided on the status and purpose of the section concerned with the 'opinions of mortals'. They have been taken, for example, as a 'dialectical' refutation by analysis of the presuppositions of ordinary mortals (Owen [4.46]), a 'history of the genesis of illusion' (Hölscher [4.22]), a 'case-study in self-deception' (Mourelatos [4.24]); or as reportage of the latest (Pythagorean) fashion in cosmology (Cornford [4.19]). Or, as here, they have been taken to be meant seriously as empirical science (and philosophy of science); so e.g. Calogero [4.18], Verdenius [4.27], Fränkel [4.20].

23 Empedocles promises magical powers to the disciple who meditates on his cosmology: Empedocles DK B 110 and 111.

24 On the internal structure of the 'opinions', and the parallelism with Alētheiē, see Mourelatos [4.24], 222–63.

25 This reading is supported by Aristotle's testimony (Metaphysics I.5, 986b31–987b2).

26 'Love' as a power: DK B 13, cf. Aristotle Metaphysics I.3, 984b20–31; struggles of gods: Plato Symposium 195c, Cicero On the Nature of the Gods I.II.28 (DK 28 A 37). There is no need to be puzzled by the appearance of Hesiodic divinities here, if Parmenides, as suggested, is taking an 'operationalist' view of what he is doing.

27 On details of the cosmology not discussed here (except for the theory of mental functioning, on which see pp. 150–1; see Guthrie [2.13] II: 57–70.

28 But there is much disagreement about the details. An extended ancient allegorization is found in Sextus Empiricus (Adversus Mathematicos VII.111–14). For the important parallels in Homer, Hesiod and Orphic writings, see Burkert [4.28].

29 On the theory of mental functioning, Fränkel [4.20], sect. 3; Laks [4.54]. Both text and meaning of the lines of Parmenides here quoted by Theophrastus are, unfortunately, uncertain at vital points.

30 Of course it does not follow from this that reality's thinking is what alone constitutes reality, nor that reality is just what thinks itself. (It does follow that reality is not ultimately 'mind-independent', in that it is necessarily thought by itself. In this rather special sense, Parmenides is an idealist, but not provably in any wider sense.)

31 Zeno was 'the Eleatic Palamedes' (Plato Phaedrus 261d6), the 'inventor of dialectic' (Diogenes Laertius Lives VIII.57; W. D. Ross Aristotelis Fragmenta Selecta, Oxford, 1955: 15).

32 Plato's evidence has not gone unchallenged. Zeno has sometimes been read as attacking Parmenides as well as his opponents, particularly by those who question whether Parmenides was a monist. The attempt of Solmsen [4.72] to undermine Plato's testimony was countered by Vlastos [4.73]; but even Vlastos doubts Plato's testimony that all the arguments in the book were directed against plurality.

33 Closeness to common sense is also suggested by the knockabout flavour of 'making fun' (kōmōidein). (The phrase 'as against all the things that are said' (127d9–10) is too vague to be of use.) But mere unreflecting common sense would not have tried to make fun of Parmenides by arguments, as Zeno implies his opponents did.

34 This fits the earlier suggestions of ad hominem argumentation by Zeno. It does not imply that, in Plato's opinion, Parmenides' monism was a monism about the ordinary world.

35 So Aristotle, *Metaphysics* III 4, 1001b7–16, who calls the argument 'crude' because of this assumption.

36 Vlastos ([4.64], 371) points out that the step made here was taken as valid by many later ancient writers.

37 Other possible arguments of Zeno against plurality appear at: Aristotle *On Generation and Conception* 1.2, 316a14–317a12 (not attributed, and introduced in the context of Democritus' atomism); and Simplicius *Physics* 139.24–140, 26, Themistius *Physics* 12.1–3, Philoponus *Physics* 80.23–81.7 (attributed to Parmenides or Zeno). On these as possibly Zeno's: see Vlastos [4.64], 371–2 and Makin [4.66].

38 On their possible interdependence, see section (e).

39 Compare the assumption needed in (e) above, that anything having size can be divided into two things each having size.

40 Sometimes known as the 'Dichotomy'. Aristotle's own solution is at *Physics* VIII 8, 263a4–b9.

41 Aristotle's phrase corresponding to 'at a moment' is 'in the now', i.e. 'in the present understood as an indivisible instant'. This excludes periods of time, even supposedly indivisible ones. It is possible that Zeno's argument somehow depended crucially on the instant's being taken as *present* (as suggested by Lear [4.67]).

42 Diogenes Laertius (*Lives* IX.72, DK 29 B 4), using a source independent of Aristotle, gives a summary of an argument which may possibly descend from Zeno's formulation of step (2): 'that which moves does not move either in the place in which it is, or in the place in which it is not'.

43 The long illustrative example (240a4–17), implying a lettered diagram, is given as Aristotle's own contribution; there is no reason to attribute it to Zeno.

44 Attempts to reconstruct a more satisfactory argument include those of Furley [4.63] and Owen [4.68].

45 In some interpretations, the arguments have been seen as systematically exhausting the theoretical possibilities for pluralism. The idea goes back to the nineteenth century; notable in this connection is the theory of Owen [4.68]. On such a view, time and the track of the moving thing are considered in the 'Stadium' and the 'Achilles' as divisible *ad infinitum*; but in the 'Arrow' and the 'Moving Rows' as 'atomized', i.e. as consisting ultimately of indivisible units of extension.

46 On the indications connecting Zeno's arguments with 'Pythagoreans' see Caveing [4.62], 163–80.

47 This is not to deny that modern mathematics enables us to give sharper formulations both of the arguments and of the possibilities for meeting them: see especially Grünbaum [4.75].

48 See above pp. 145–7.

49 On Aristotle's description and criticism of this programme, see Huffman [4.78], 57–64; and Kahn [4.2].

50 The surviving fragments attributed to Philolaus are due to various late sources (Diogenes Laertius, some Neoplatonists, and the anthology of Stobaeus). Their authenticity is controversial; on this question, see Burkert [2.25], 238–68; [4.78], 17–35.

The reading of Philolaus given here is indebted to Burkert [2.25] and particularly to Nussbaum [4.79],

51 See DK 44 B 1, 2, 4, 5, 6.
52 Nussbaum [4.79], 102.
53 Aristotle *Metaphysics* I.5, 986b25–7 ('rather crude'); *Physics* I 2, 185a10–11 ('low-grade'). One purported source, the pseudo-Aristotelian essay *On Melissus Xenophanes Gorgias* (*MXG*), is an exercise in 'philosophical reconstruction', from which it is not possible to disentangle with confidence any further information about Melissus. *MXG* is not drawn on here. The most noteworthy modern attempt to rehabilitate Melissus as a philosopher is that of Barnes [2.8], chs. 10, 11, 14.
54 This is a conjectural interpretation of Simplicius' paraphrase, *Physics* 103.15: 'if nothing is, what would one say about it as though it were something?'
55 It is not safe, though, to read back the mind–body dualism of Plato's middle period into Pythagoras.

BIBLIOGRAPHY

Pythagoras and the Early Pythagoreans

Texts

No authentic writings survive. Collections of early Pythagorean *akousmata* and *sumbola*, and other later testimony about Pythagoras and the early Pythagoreans, are in DK [2.2]: I, 446–80. On the surviving fragments of 'Orphic' writings, see West [4.5].

General studies

4.1 Burkert [2.25].
4.2 Kahn, C. H. 'Pythagorean philosophy before Plato', in Mourelatos [2.19]: 161–85.

'Orphism' and sixth- and fifth-century religion

4.3 Burkert [1.43], 290–304.
4.4 Dodds [2.28], ch. 5.
4.5 West, M. L. *The Orphic Poems*, Oxford, Oxford University Press, 1983.
4.6 Parker, R. 'Early Orphism', in A. Powell (see [2.36]): 483–510.

Early Greek mathematics and science

4.7 Lloyd [1.7]. See also [2.27], [2.34], [2.38], [2.41].

Parmenides

Texts with translation and commentary

4.8 Coxon, A. H. *The Fragments of Parmenides*, Assen/Maastricht, Van Gorcum, 1986.

4.9 Gallop, D. *Parmenides of Elea, Phoenix* suppl. vol. 18, Toronto/Buffalo/London, University of Toronto Press, 1984.

4.10 Heitsch, E. *Parmenides: Die Fragmente*, 2nd edn, Munich/Zürich, Artemis Verlag, 1991.

4.11 Hölscher, U. *Parmenides: Vom Wesen des Seienden*, Frankfurt, Suhrkamp Verlag, 1969.

4.12 O'Brien, D. and Frère, J. in P. Aubenque (ed.) *Études sur Parménide*, vol. I: *Le Poème de Parménide*, Paris, J. Vrin, 1986.

4.13 Tarán. L. *Parmenides*, Princeton, NJ, Princeton University Press, 1965.

4.14 Untersteiner, M. *Parmenide: testimonianze e frammenti*, Florence, La Nuova Italia Editrice, 1967.

General studies and collections of essays

4.15 Aubenque, P. (ed.) *Études sur Parménide*, vol. II: *Problèmes d'interprétation*, Paris, J. Vrin, 1986.

4.16 Austin, S. *Parmenides: Being, Bounds, and Logic*, New Haven and London, Yale University Press, 1986.

4.17 Bormann, K. *Parmenides: Untersuchungen zu den Fragmenten*, Hamburg, Felix Meiner Verlag, 1971.

4.18 Calogero, G. *Studi sull'eleatismo*, new edn, Florence, La Nuova Italia Editrice, 1977.

4.19 Cornford, F. M. *Plato and Parmenides*, London, Kegan Paul, 1939.

4.20 Fränkel, H. 'Studies in Parmenides', in Allen and Furley [2.15], vol. 2: 1–47.

4.21 Heidegger, M. *Parmenides*, Bloomington and Indianapolis, Indiana University Press, 1992.

4.22 Hölscher, U. *Anfängliches Fragen*, Göttingen, Vandenhoeck and Ruprecht, 1968.

4.23 Jantzen, J. *Parmenides zum Verhältnis von Sprache und Wirklichkeit*, Munich, C. H. Beck, 1976.

4.24 Mourelatos, A. P. D. *The Route of Parmenides*, New Haven and London, Yale University Press, 1970.

4.25 Owens, J. (ed.) *Parmenides Studies Today, Monist* 62/1, 1979.

4.26 Reinhardt, K. *Parmenides und die Geschichte der griechischen Philosophie*, 2nd edn, Vittorio Klostermann, Frankfurt, 1959.

4.27 Verdenius, W. J. *Parmenides: Some Comments on his Poem*, Groningen, J. B. Walters, 1942.

The proem

4.28 Burkert, W. 'Das Proömium des Parmenides und die Katabasis des Pythagoras', *Phronesis* 14 (1969): 1–30.

Alētheiē in early Greek and in Parmenides:

4.29 Heitsch, E. 'Die nicht-philosophische *alētheia*', *Hermes* 90 (1962): 24–33.
4.30 Verdenius, W. J. 'Parmenides B 2, 3', *Mnemosyne* ser. 4, 15 (1962): 237.

The verb *einai* ('be') and the concept of *being* in early Greek and in Parmenides:

4.31 Hölscher, U. *Der Sinn vom Sein in der älteren griechischen Philosophie*, Sitzungsberichte der Heidelberger Akademie der Wissenschaften, philosophisch-historische Klasse, Jahrgang 1976, 3. Abhandlung, Heidelberg, Carl Winter Universitätsverlag, 1976.
4.32 Kahn, C. H. *The Verb 'Be' in Ancient Greek*, Foundations of Language, suppl. series 16, Dordrecht and Boston, Reidel, 1973.
4.33 —— 'Why existence does not emerge as a distinct concept in Greek philosophy', *Archiv für Geschichte der Philosophie* 58 (1976): 323–34.
4.34 Matthen, M. 'Greek ontology and the "Is" of truth', *Phronesis* 28 (1983): 113–35.

Methods of argument, and the nature of thinking

4.35 Lesher, J. 'Parmenides' critique of thinking: the *poludéris elenchos* of Fragment 7', *Oxford Studies in Ancient Philosophy* 2 (1984): 1–30.
4.36 Mourelatos, A. P. D. 'Mind's commitment to the real: Parmenides B 8.34–41', in Anton and Kustas [2.16]: 59–80.

The choice of ways and the rejection of 'is not'

4.37 Finkelberg, A. 'Parmenides' foundation of the way of Truth', *Oxford Studies in Ancient Philosophy* 6 (1988): 39–67.
4.38 Hintikka, J. 'Parmenides' *Cogito* argument', *Ancient Philosophy* 1 (1980): 5–16.

The nature of what is

4.39 Barnes, J. 'Parmenides and the Eleatic One', *Archiv für Geschichte der Philosophie* 61 (1979): 1–21.
4.40 Finkelberg, A. 'Parmenides between material and logical monism', *Archiv für Geschichte der Philosophie* 70 (1988): 1–14.
4.41 Furth, M. 'Elements of Eleatic ontology', in Mourelatos [2.19]: 241–70.
4.42 Kahn, C. H. 'The thesis of Parmenides', *Review of Metaphysics* 22 (1969): 700–24.

4.43 —— 'More on Parmenides', *Review of Metaphysics* 23 (1969): 333–40.

4.44 Ketchum, R. J. 'Parmenides on what there is', *Canadian Journal of Philosophy* 20 (1990): 167–90.

4.45 Malcolm, J. 'On avoiding the void', *Oxford Studies in Ancient Philosophy* 9 (1991): 75–94.

4.46 Owen, G. E. L. 'Eleatic questions', *Classical Quarterly* NS 10 (1960): 84–102; repr. in Allen and Furley [2.15], vol. 2; 48–81, and in M. Nussbaum (ed.) *Logic, Science and Dialectic: Collected Papers in Greek Philosophy*, London, Duckworth, 1986: 3–26.

4.47 —— 'Plato and Parmenides on the timeless present', *Monist* 50 (1966): 317–40; repr. in Mourelatos [2.19]; 271–92, and in Nussbaum. (see [4.46]): 27–44.

4.48 Schofield, M. 'Did Parmenides discover eternity?', *Archiv für Geschichte der Philosophie* 52 (1970): 113–35.

The 'Platonic problem' of not-being

4.49 Denyer, N. *Language, Thought and Falsehood in Ancient Greek Philosophy*, London and New York, Routledge, 1991.

4.50 Pelletier, F. J. *Parmenides, Plato and the Semantics of Not-Being*, Chicago and London, University of Chicago Press, 1990.

4.51 Wiggins, D. 'Sentence meaning, negation and Plato's problem of non-being', in G. Vlastos (ed.) *Plato: A Collection of Critical Essays*, I: *Metaphysics and Epistemology*, Garden City, NY, Doubleday, 1971: 268–303.

Cosmology (including psychology)

4.52 Curd, P. K. 'Deception and belief in Parmenides' *Doxa*', *Apeiron* 25 (1992): 109–33.

4.53 Finkelberg, A. 'The cosmology of Parmenides', *American Journal of Philology* 107 (1986): 303–17.

4.54 Laks, A. 'The More' and 'The Full': on the reconstruction of Parmenides' theory of sensation in Theophrastus *De Sensibus* 3–4', *Oxford Studies in Ancient Philosophy* 8 (1990): 1–18.

4.55 Long, A. A. 'The principles of Parmenides' cosmology', *Phronesis* 8 (1963): 90–107, reprinted in Allen and Furley [2.15], vol. 2: 82–101.

4.56 Schwabl, H. 'Sein und Doxa bei Parmenides', in H.–G. Gadamer (ed.) *Um die Begriffswelt der Vorsokratiker*, Darmstadt, Wissenschaftliche Buchgesellschaft, 1968: 391–422.

Miscellaneous

4.57 Furley, D. J. 'Notes on Parmenides', in Lee, Mourelatos and Rorty (see [3.43]): 1–15.

4.58 Gadamer, H.-G. 'Zur Vorgeschichte der Metaphysik', in Gadamer (see [4.56]): 364–90.

Zeno

Texts with translation and commentary

4.59 Lee, H. D. P. *Zeno of Elea*, Cambridge, Cambridge University Press, 1936.
4.60 Untersteiner, M. *Zenone: testimonianze e frammenti*, Florence, La Nuova Italia Editrice, 1963.

Translations of the relevant parts of Plato *Parmenides* can be found in Cornford [4.19]. The testimony of Aristotle in the *Physics* is translated in:
4.61 Barnes, J. (ed.) *The Complete Works of Aristotle*, Princeton, NJ, Princeton University Press, 1984.

General studies

4.62 Caveing, M. *Zénon d'Élée: prolégomènes aux doctrines du continu*, Paris, J. Vrin, 1982.
4.63 Furley, D. J. *Two Studies in the Greek Atomists*, Princeton, NJ, Princeton University Press, 1967: 63–78.
4.64 Vlastos, G. 'Zeno of Elea', in P. Edwards (ed.) *The Encyclopedia of Philosophy*, vol. 8, New York, The Macmillan Company and The Free Press, 1967: 369–79. Reprinted in Vlastos *Studies in Greek Philosophy*, ed. D. W. Graham, vol. 1, Princeton, NJ, Princeton University Press, 1995: 241–63.

The arguments against plurality

4.65 Fränkel, H. 'Zeno of Elea's attacks on plurality', in Allen and Furley [2.15], vol. 2: 102–42.
4.66 Makin, S. 'Zeno on plurality', *Phronesis* 27 (1982): 223–38.

The arguments about motion

4.67 Lear, J. 'A note on Zeno's arrow', *Phronesis* 26 (1981): 91–104.
4.68 Owen, G. E. L. 'Zeno and the mathematicians', *Proceedings of the Aristotelian Society* 58 (1957/8): 199–222; repr. in Allen and Furley [2.15], vol. 2: 143–65; in Salmon [4.76]: 139–63 and in Nussbaum (see [4.46]): 45–61.
4.69 Pickering, F. R. 'Aristotle on Zeno and the Now', *Phronesis* 23 (1978): 253–7.
4.70 Vlastos, G. 'A note on Zeno's arrow', *Phronesis* 11 (1966): 3–18; repr. in Allen and Furley [2.15], vol. 2: 184–200, and in Vlastos (ed. Graham) (see [4.64]); vol. 1: 205–18.
4.71 —— 'Zeno's racecourse', *Journal of the History of Philosophy* 4 (1966): 95–108; repr. in Allen and Furley [2.15], vol. 2: 201–20, and in Vlastos, ed. Graham (see [4.64]), vol. 1: 189–204.

Plato's testimony on Zeno

4.72 Solmsen, F. 'The tradition about Zeno of Elea re-examined', *Phronesis* 16 (1971): 116–41; repr. in Mourelatos [2.19]: 368–93.

4.73 Vlastos, G. 'Plato's testimony concerning Zeno of Elea', *Journal of Hellenic Studies* 95 (1975): 136–62, repr. in Vlastos, ed. Graham (see [4.64]); vol. 1: 264–300.

Zeno, Aristotle and modern philosophy

4.74 Bostock, D. 'Aristotle, Zeno and the potential infinite', *Proceedings of the Aristotelian Society* 73 (1972/3): 37–51.

4.75 Grünbaum, A. *Modern Science and Zeno's Paradoxes*, London, Allen and Unwin, 1968.

4.76 Salmon, W. C. (ed.) *Zeno's Paradoxes*, Indianapolis and New York, Bobbs-Merrill, 1970.

4.77 Sorabji, R. *Time, Creation and the Continuum*, London, Duckworth, 1983.

Philolaus and 'The People Called Pythagoreans'

Text with commentary

4.78 Huffman, C. A. *Philolaus of Croton: Pythagorean and Presocratic*, Cambridge, Cambridge University Press, 1993.

Studies

4.79 Nussbaum, M. C. 'Eleatic conventionalism and Philolaus on the conditions of thought', *Harvard Studies in Classical Philology* 83 (1979): 63–108.
See also [4.1] and [4.2].

Melissus

Text with translation and commentary

4.80 Reale, G. *Melisso: testimonianze e frammenti*, Florence, La Nuova Italia Editrice, 1970.

CHAPTER 5

Empedocles

M. R. Wright

❧◦❖◦❧

❧❧ INTRODUCTION ❧❧

Empedocles was a native of Acragas (Agrigento) in Sicily, a Doric colony founded on the south coast of the island in the sixth century BC, which soon grew to rival Syracuse in its prosperity. A line of temples, many of which are still standing, attested to its wealth and public piety; behind the city rose the dramatic volcano of Etna, and the plains further into the hinterland were held sacred to Demeter and her daughter Persephone, and their associated mysteries and cults.

Empedocles' lifetime spanned the greater part of the fifth century, probably from 494 to 434 BC. His family was aristocratic, but more inclined to democracy than oligarchy. There are various anecdotes supporting his own pro-democratic outlook, and his part in overthrowing a tyrannical regime in the city. He had a reputation as an experienced orator, and taught, or at least influenced, the great Sicilian rhetorician Gorgias. He is also credited with giving practical help in various emergencies, and his work shows a detailed interest in anatomy, embryology and physiology, as well as in more general biological and botanical themes. He claims to have travelled extensively, and to have been both well-known and popular:

> Whenever I enter prosperous towns I am honoured by both men and women. They follow me in countless numbers, to ask what is best for them, some seeking prophecies, others, long pierced by harsh pains, ask to hear the word of healing for all kinds of illnesses.
>
> (fr. 112.7–12)

As a result of such claims, and of the confidence in his understanding of natural science, he acquired a reputation as a wonder-worker. There was however no sound basis for this, or for the legend, preserved in the same context, of his suicide leap into the volcano at Etna. Despite their romantic appeal, a life-style as a magician and this dramatic death are both firmly rejected as fabrications by the early local historian Timaeus. As was often the case such biographical details probably arose from particular interpretations of the philosopher's own words in different contexts. Because of his known political sympathies Empedocles is more likely to have ended his years in exile in south Italy or mainland Greece; he is reported to have been barred from Sicily when the descendants of his political enemies opposed his return.

Empedocles' travels through the towns of south Italy, for which there is evidence independent of his own words, would have brought him into contact with the philosophical activity there. He is likely to have known of the Pythagorean communities around Croton and the pan-Hellenic foundation of Thurii in 443 BC, which involved the sophist Protagoras and later attracted the historian Herodotus. He was certainly influenced by Parmenides in Elea and was a contemporary of Zeno there. His place in the history of pre-Socratic thought is further confirmed by the notice in the first book of Aristotle's *Metaphysics* that he was younger than Anaxagoras but his philosophy came earlier.

Like Parmenides, Empedocles wrote in verse, in the epic hexameters and style of Homer's *Iliad* and *Odyssey*. It is reported from Timaeus that part of his work was recited at the Olympic games as one of the display pieces, and his talent as a poet later earned praise from Aristotle. Although he is credited with various writings in the *Life of Empedocles* by Diogenes Laertius – a *Hymn to Apollo*, an essay on Xerxes' invasion of Greece, a medical treatise, political works, tragedies and epigrams – there is reliable evidence for just two poems, known as *Physics* (or *On Nature*) and *Katharmoi* (*Methods of Purification*). These titles were probably assigned later, and have since been understood by some as alternatives for one comprehensive work. All in all there are over 450 lines extant from the Empedoclean corpus, more than from any other pre-Socratic, in over 130 fragments, some in continuous blocks and others as individual verses or phrases. From various surviving summaries and doxographical evidence it appears that these form a nucleus of the original which allows for a reasonably confident reconstruction of the main topics of his philosophy and his treatment of them.

There are two main themes: one deals with scientific and cosmological principles, set out in the fragments traditionally assigned to the *Physics*, and is addressed to the student Pausanias; the second, the subject of the *Katharmoi*, has the form of a public proclamation to the citizens of Acragas, and is concerned more with psychology, purification and related ritual. The fragments may be attached to one or other of these themes according to explicit citations from ancient authors, the use of the second person singular or plural for the addressee and other criteria, but the placing of many is dubious. Recently there have been attempts to relocate some important fragments from the *Katharmoi* to a *Proem* of the *Physics*, and so significantly reduce the content and subject-matter of the public poem, or to take them all as from a single work. In whatever way the fragments are arranged (and the case for two separate works is still the stronger) scholarship on Empedocles has always been much concerned with the problem of reconciling a complex scientific philosophy explained to a particular individual with public exhortations to a moral and religious life-style that appears to be incompatible with it. In Empedocles' case the problems of compatibility and consistency are increased by the the fact that he expounded his ideas in the form of epic poetry rather than through the medium of prose, which had first been developed by the Ionians in the sixth century BC as a medium more appropriate than verse for philosophical exposition. The exotic vocabulary and complex style that characterize Empedocles' talent often make his work ambiguous and obscure, especially when contrasted with the simpler language and more direct argument of Parmenides' poem, but they also add to its fascination.

As with later figures in the history of ideas, it is not necessary to assume a 'conversion' from science to religion or a disillusioned rejection of religious principles in favour of the rigours of science, since obviously a common issue may be approached from different points of view, appropriate to the immediate context and level of understanding assumed. Nor is it as obvious now as formerly appeared that there is such a great divide between science and theology that the two cannot be expected to engage the same mind at the same time. Few ancient Greek philosophers would have recognized such a division, and now once more the distinctions are blurring. The last sentence of *God and the New Physics* (Harmondsworth, Penguin, 1984), for example, by the contemporary cosmologist Paul Davies shows an innate sympathy with the comprehensive approach found two thousand years earlier in Empedocles:

> It is my deep conviction that only by understanding the world
> in its many aspects – reductionist and holistic, mathematical and
> poetical, through forces, fields and particles as well as through
> good and evil – that we will come to understand ourselves and
> the meaning behind this universe.

(Davies, 1984: 229)

In some recent developments which are likely to dominate scientific studies into the next millennium it is possible to view Empedocles as a distant precursor. First the combined study of physics, chemistry and biology is apparently unlocking the secret of life itself as the mapping of the sequences of the DNA molecule progresses. These rest on the myriad variations of a genetic alphabet of just the four letters A, T, G and C (the initials of adenine, thymine, guanine and cytosine), the basic building blocks of protein being in principle something like Empedocles' four 'roots'. As with Empedocles the results cover the whole spectrum of life, from the simplest plant forms to humans, and show large areas of overlap in genetic material between what were thought to be widely differing species. It is expected that there will be great rewards in improved understanding of disease, in new cures and in the manipulation of the limits of life in birth and death; those who work in these areas are given Nobel prizes, the modern equivalent of being 'crowned with ribbons and garlands, honoured by all'. Then the latest theories in cosmology also have great popular appeal, and books on the subject become best-sellers. A particular interest here which is relevant to the student of the pre-Socratics and especially of Empedocles is the search for a unified theory which will explain the complexity of phenomena from the immensely large to the most minute as a seamless manifestation of basic principles.

A third focus of modern science comes in new research into the old mind–body problem, where the study of the brain, and advances in parallel neural computing, might well engender a more sympathetic attitude to the reductionism of the early thinkers as well as providing a context in which it is still worthwhile to discuss the working of individual sense-organs in something akin to Empedoclean terms. Finally it becomes necessary to find a way of life for humans in the light of the latest discoveries, to deal with individual emotions (especially the polarities of erotic attraction and aggressive hostility) and to direct decision-making towards the development of viable relationships and societies that do not conflict with other living creatures and the natural environment. It is in these four main areas, in the theories of elements, of cosmology, of perception and cognition, and of the unity of life, that Empedocles' position in the history of philosophy is assured.

THE THEORY OF ELEMENTS

Empedocles started from a basic principle that was his most influential discovery in the history of science: the understanding of the nature of an element, and the reduction of all apparent generation, alteration and destruction, along with the particular and changing characteristics of what is perceived, to a limited number of persisting and unchanging basic entities. Empedocles had assented to the conclusion from the 'Way of Truth' of his predecessor Parmenides that there could be no absolute birth or death, since these entail temporal non-existence, which was found to be logically unacceptable; his wording here follows the Eleatic argument closely:

> It is impossible for there to be a coming into existence from what
> is not, and for what exists to be completely destroyed cannot
> be fulfilled, nor is to be heard of.
>
> (fr. 12)

Parmenides had likewise denied the corresponding spatial non-existence; Empedocles identified this as void (what is empty or *kenon*) and then, on similar logical grounds, refused its admittance as a divider between the continuity and homogeneity of being, for 'there is no part of the whole that is empty' (fr. 13). This also meant that there could be no addition to or subtraction from the total sum, for, as he says elsewhere, 'What could increase the whole? And where would it come from?' (fr. 17.32). The common acceptance of additions and subtractions as births and deaths should consequently be understood as merely 'names' mistakenly used in human speech:

> When there has been a mixture in the shape of a man which
> comes to the air, or the shape of the species of wild animals, or
> of plants, or of birds, then people say that this is to be born, and
> when they separate they call this again ill-fated death; these
> terms are not right, but I follow the custom and use them myself.
>
> (fr. 9)

Empedocles then developed from the hint of the two forms of light and night in Parmenides' 'Way of Opinion' the concept of a minimum number of elements, with permanent and unalterable characteristics, which could account for a world of plurality and variety according to their proportion and arrangement in compounds.

Like Parmenides, Empedocles was also a poet wrestling with a new vocabulary, and for his opening move, instead of saying in a straightforward manner that the number of elements was four, and that they correspond to fire, air, earth and water, his words translate as:

> Hear first the four roots of all things: bright Zeus, life-bringing
> Hera, Aidoneus and Nestis, whose tears are the source of mortal
> streams.
>
> (fr. 6)

The botanical term 'roots' (*rizōmata*) indicated the vitality of the substructures, their unseen depths and the potential for growths from them, while the divine names were an indication of their potency and sempiternity. Why were these four chosen? Perhaps Empedocles had in mind the Homeric division of the world which allotted the sky to Zeus, the sea to Poseidon, the underworld to Hades, and left the earth common to all, and then adapted this division to apply to two pairs of male and female principles, one higher (Zeus the fire above, and Hera the air), and one lower (Aidoneus for earth, and Nestis as water). Four was the economical minimum number, reinforced by the importance of the opposites of hot and cold, dry and wet for the earlier Milesians, and by the adoption of different basic principles: – of air (by Anaximenes), of fire (by Heraclitus), of water (attributed to Thales) and the general tradition of earth as the mother of all. A group of four (the first square number and associated with justice for the Pythagoreans) also allowed for mutual activity within a structure of balance and equilibrium. Most obviously the four comprised the natural masses visible in a coastal town of Sicily: – the earth below, the sea at its edge, the air above and fire visible in the bright sun and also in the lava pouring from the volcanoes.

This is confirmed by one fragment of Empedocles which states that an understanding of the true nature of things can come simply from looking around:

> since all these – sun and earth and sky and sea – are one with the parts of themselves that have been separated off and born in mortal things.
>
> (fr. 22)

At their first appearance the four were given divine names, since they had now taken the place of the traditional gods as the true immortals, but Empedocles' vocabulary was not consistent. As well as the names of gods and goddesses, he also listed them by the common terms of fire, air, earth and water, or by their most obvious manifestations as sun, sky, earth (*chthōn* as well as *gaia*), and sea or rain. He posited just these four, no more and no less, eternally existing, ever the same, equal in privilege and power, but capable, as they mingle, separate and reassemble, of producing a variety of phenomena. The evidence for their individual characteristics, as for their very existence, was to be found in their appearance as conglomerates in the natural world:

> sun with its radiant appearance and pervading warmth, heavenly bodies bathed in heat and shining light, rain everywhere dark and chill, and earth the basis of firmly rooted solids.
>
> (fr. 21.3–6)

Such qualitative differences as hot and cold, wet and dry, light and dark, remain whether the four are separated out in perceived stretches of bright sky, mist, land and sea, or brought together in compounds, in which the characteristics of the predominating elements may be apparent, but others imperceptible because of the smallness of the component particles.

Empedocles therefore considered the four roots or elements to be basic and permanent corporeal entities, forming temporary arrangements as their parts were brought into compounds of different shapes, although they themselves were not subject to alteration of any kind. He constantly rammed the point home:

> these are the only real things, but as they run through each other they become different objects at different times, yet they are throughout forever the same.
>
> (fr. 17.34–5 and cf. 21.13–4, 26.3–4)

Birth and death, generation and destruction have to be accepted as illusory, the consequence merely of the mingling and separating of parts of the elements in various proportions, which give to the different structures their apparent individuality. The context in fragment 21 explains further:

> From them (the four 'roots') comes all that was and is and will be hereafter – trees have sprung from them, and men and women, and animals and birds and water-nourished fish, and long-lived gods too, highest in honour. For these are the only real things, and as they run through each other they assume different shapes, for the mixing interchanges them.
>
> (fr. 21.9–14)

To illustrate the possibility of the wide diversity of phenomena generated from just four elements Empedocles used the simile of a painting, which can show in two dimensions a variety of plant, animal and human life, although it consists basically of pigments of a few primary colours in a particular arrangement:

> As painters, men well taught by wisdom in the practice of their art, decorate temple offerings when they take in their hands pigments of various colours, and after fitting them in close combination – more of some and less of others – they produce from them shapes resembling all things, creating trees and men and women, animals and birds and water-nourished fish, and long-lived gods too, highest in honour; so do not let error convince you that there is any other source for the countless perishables that are seen . . .
>
> (fr. 23.1–10)

This fragment also throws light on how parts of elements are placed together in a compound. Empedocles is not speaking of a complete fusion, like blue and yellow blending to form green, but, according to the common practice in Greek painting, of the juxtaposition of pigments or washes (usually black, white, red and yellow) to produce the effect of figures and objects. The parts of elements involved in a compound may be very small, as when for example they form the alternating channels of fire and water in the eye, or are compared to metals ground down to fine powders, but even so they are not reducible to absolute minima. In positing elements in Aristotle's phrase (*On the Heavens* 305a4) that are 'divisible but never going to be divided', Empedocles' philosophy here contrasts on the one hand with the complete infinite divisibility of compounds in Anaxagoras' theory and on the other with Democritean atomism.

Empedocles' far-reaching conclusion that despite appearances to the contrary all animate and inanimate forms should be understood as particular arrangements in different proportions of a small number of unchanging, qualitatively distinct elements immediately became standard, and was taken into account by philosophers, cosmologists, natural scientists and medical writers throughout antiquity, and into the Middle Ages and beyond. As a basic principle it foreshadows contemporary assumptions in a number of areas, for example that the main ingredients of living things are the elements of carbon, hydrogen and oxygen, that language, literature and mathematics can be expressed as encoded variations of the binary numbers zero and one, and that the genetic range of species is reducible to an arrangement of the four basic letters of the DNA strings.

Some further motive force however was required in Empedocles' scheme to explain how the four elements come into compounds and separate into their own masses. For this role he posited opposed principles of attraction and repulsion which, in his vivid vocabulary, he called *philia* ('love', 'friendship') and *neikos* ('strife', 'hate'). As the visible masses of earth, sea, sun and sky had provided evidence for the four elements and their characteristics in the composition of individual constructs, so a further inference was drawn from the power which these two basic drives have in human experience and action to their involvement in the widespread generation and destruction of forms of life. Empedocles attributed the continual grouping, separating and regrouping of elements in temporary compounds to the beneficient or destructive effects of these forces:

> For all these – sun and earth and sky and sea – are one with the parts that have been separated off and born in mortal things. In the same way, those that are more ready to combine are made similar by love and feel mutual affection. But such as are more different from each other in birth and mixture and the moulding of their forms are most hostile, inexperienced in union, and grieving at their generation in strife.

(fr. 22)

The same patterns of constructive unity and corruptive separating could also be found on a larger scale, in the different kinds of life found in the distinctive elemental masses:

> This is well known in the mass of mortal limbs: at one time, in the maturity of a vigorous life, all the limbs that are the body's portion come into one under love; at another time again, torn asunder by evil strifes, they stray on the borderline of life. So it is for plants, and for fish that live in the water, and for wild animals who have their lairs in the hills, and for the wing-sped gulls.
>
> (fr. 20)

From such quotations it is clear that Empedocles' arguments for the existence of universal principles of attraction and repulsion were derived from empirical observations in the natural world of the processes of birth and growth being countered inevitably by decline and disintegration, and from consideration of the powerful stimuli to action engendered by love and hate in human experience. In addition a crucial significance had been given to love (as *erōs*) in Hesiod's *Theogony* which Parmenides had adapted for his cosmology, and Anaximander and Heraclitus had used the political terminology of aggression and war for the tensions and oppositions necessary to the maintenance of the present world order.

Love and strife in this theory are, like the elements, ungenerated, unchanging and indestructible, and Empedocles presented them as set against each other in eternal rivalry for universal government. They are not however material, as fire, air, earth and water are, or like them visually recognizable on a large scale; instead the student is told to, 'contemplate love with the mind':

> She is acknowledged to be inborn in human bodies, and because of her their thoughts are friendly and they work together, giving her the name Joy, as well as Aphrodite. No mortal has perceived her as she moves among them, but pay attention to my line of argument, which will not mislead you.
>
> (fr. 17.21–6)

The existence of the opposed stimuli is to be *inferred* from an understanding of how the elements act and react to each other, and any apparent personification is a question of allegory or poetic licence.

Empedocles described his principles of attraction and repulsion in terms of equal balance and power. They are able to extend over the elements and act on them, with expanding and contracting areas of application as the four are brought together or held further apart. Love 'increases' and takes up more place in the sense that more and more elemental particles may be brought together to mingle, and the converse holds 'when Strife rises to its honours as the time is completed' (fr. 30), and the elements move out of their combinations to group with their own kind. The two principles are manifest in the patterns of attraction and separation of the elements, and are contained within the same limits as them. In Empedocles' theory the consequences of this wide-ranging polar opposition are to be found at different levels: in the repeated patterns of movements and arrangements of the elements within the cosmos, in the genesis and destruction of successive generations of mortal life, and for individuals in their friendships and enmities.

❧ COSMOLOGY ❧

Empedocles' four-element cosmos was a spherical everlasting *plenum*. Parmenides had previously argued that it is peculiarly self-contradictory to assert the existence of 'what is not' (*mē on*). Applied temporally this meant that there could be no generation or destruction (which would entail earlier or later non-existence), and in spatial terms there had to be continuity, balance and homogeneity 'as in the bulk of a well-rounded sphere'. Empedocles took this as the literal shape of the cosmos, and, as has been shown, further adapted the Eleatic argument by equating the non-existent with *kenon* (empty space), and then denying its existence: 'there is no part of the whole that is empty or overfull' (fr. 13).

The atomists later agreed with this identification of non-being with empty space, but then reinstated it as an existing void. In Empedocles' theory, however, the elements are contained within the cosmos with no spaces between them, nor did he allow the possibility of variation in consistency; this possibility had been adopted by the Ionian Anaximenes previously, to account for differences between solid, liquid and gaseous substances by assuming a process of rarefaction and condensation of primary matter. For Empedocles, earth, air, fire and water assimilate and separate in the *plenum*, shifting together and moving apart in continually changing arrangements and rearrangements, while each keeps its character inviolate.

The evidence on the whole suggests that the activity of the elements under the principles of attraction and repulsion follows certain patterns in recurring cycles. There is an unceasing alternation of all the elements at one time coming into a unity through Love (where their particles are so completely and finely mingled that no part can be distinguished from any other) and then at another of separating into their respective masses under the influence of Strife. At this stage they are probably to be envisaged in the traditional form of concentric spheres, with earth at the centre, surrounded by water and air, and the fiery sky (the *ouranos*) enclosing the whole. The processes of elemental movement from one extreme to the other and back again result in a generation of mortal things, as is explained in part of one of the longest fragments:

> A twofold tale I shall tell: at one time it grew to be one only from many, and at another again it divided to be many from one. There is a double birth of the mortal, and a double passing-away; for the uniting of all things brings one generation into being and destroys it, and the other is reared and scattered as they again divide. And these things never cease their continual exchange of position, at one time all coming together through love, at another again being borne away by strife's repulsion. So in so far as one is accustomed to arise from many and many are produced from one as it is again being divided, to this extent they are born and have no abiding life; but in so far as they never cease their continual exchange, so far they are forever unaltered in the cycle.
>
> (fr. 17.1–13)

Empedocles took the description of the elements as logically prior ('hear first the roots of all things . . .'), and, although there can be no chronological beginning to eternal recurrence, for the purposes of the narrative he apparently started with an account of the elements in separation, indicating how in such a state earth, water, air and fire would cling to their own kind, shunning association with each other, in a sterile and unharmonious lack of order (*akosmia*). When, however, the power of Strife began to wane, the principle of attraction gradually pulled the separated parts together until eventually their individual characteristics (as earth, air, sea and sun) were no longer manifest, but they became completely united, taking the form of a unique cosmic divinity:

> held fast in the close covering of harmony . . . two branches do not spring from his back, there are no feet, no swift knees, no organs of generation, but he is equal to himself in every direction, the same all over, a rounded sphere, rejoicing in encircling stillness.
>
> (frs. 28–9)

Empedocles said however that inevitably, at a time ascribed somewhat enigmatically to a 'broad oath', Strife would enter and begin to cause the disintegration of the divine harmony. In the resulting movements, as the elements 'run through each other', the present world order would be generated, with its teeming variety of plant, animal and human life.

During this time Love should be envisaged initially as the more powerful force, and, on the analogy of a craftsman, as engendering well-constructed forms of life in sympathy with each other. But Strife, with increasing power and ferocity, is preparing to tear them apart, and eventually to bring down the cosmic edifice in the return once more to *akosmia*. The limits of the powers of both attraction and separation are presumed to be held, like the elements which they control, within the circumference of the sphere, the *kuklos*, that persists throughout; beyond these lies what is described in the doxography without further explanation as 'idle matter' (*argē hulē* is the term at Aetius I.5.2).

Some of the details of the process are controversial, and even the basic idea of cosmic phases being repeated has been challenged, and, given the fragmentary nature of the primary sources, there can be no certainty. But the consensus of opinion, supported by such testimony as we do have from the primary and secondary sources, suggests a reconstruction along the following lines, with Empedocles' poetic skill giving a vivid character to his descriptions of elements reacting to contrary forces. At one time the four ('fire and water and earth and measureless height of air') were completely separate under Strife, and Love lay inactive at the circumference; then came the increase of her power, initiated (in the metaphor of the invasion of foreign territory) by a move to the centre, and the consolidation of her position as Strife was pushed back. This alternation was manifest in the elements consequently 'running through' each other, and so causing the rise of a generation of mortal beings. Some monsters and strange shapes emerged at first, even separate limbs and 'heads without necks', but these were short-lived, whereas those that were well formed and fitted for survival became a viable generation of living creatures. Love was eventual victor in the cosmic battle, bringing all the elements into one, and so generating the blessed god (*theos eudaimonestatos*), in which Strife had no part. But the ideal state came to an end, and, when the time was completed, Strife struck as Love had done by rushing to claim the centre. This caused a mighty disturbance as 'one by one all the parts of the god began to tremble' (fr. 31).

Empedocles saw the emergence of the present world as a consequence of this upheaval. In the succeeding phase of his cosmogony, as Strife began the process of separation, he introduced the important concept of a rotation (a vortex or *dinē*) starting in the centre, which was the immediate cause of the separating of the closely mingled parts of the different elements. First it seems that air was drawn out and flowed round in a circle, followed by fire, which solidified some of the air into the *ouranos* as *aithēr* and brought down the heavier particles as atmospheric mist. The force of the rotation also compressed parts of the earth into the centre, and water consequently exuded from it to form the sea ('sea is the sweat of earth' as Empedocles expressed it in a typical homology, fr. 55). Such fire as was still in the earth warmed some of the remaining water to produce hot springs, and hardened lumps of earth into rocks; as it moved upwards to join its counterparts it also created the conditions of warm, moist clay which would be capable of engendering life, first in the form of trees and plants, and then of animals and humans.

This imaginative narrative, pieced together from direct quotations and indirect report, was in the tradition of the early pre-Socratics, but treated with much more acumen and sophistication. The use of a swirl in the original mixture to start the separation, the outward movement of the lighter air and fire, and what looks something like an early theory of gravity, when the bulk of earth at the centre drew parts of earth elsewhere towards itself, show a remarkable mind at work.

Further evidence of Empedocles' achievements comes in the wealth of insight preserved on many of the individual aspects of the subsequent phenomena. Starting with the initial formation of the elemental masses – 'earth and swelling sea, moist air and Titan sky' (fr. 38.4) – Empedocles included explanations for the spherical shape of the earth, volcanoes beneath the earth's surface and the salinity of the sea. Of particular interest in this section was the recognition that the moon is a satellite of earth reflecting the sun's brightness ('a circle of borrowed light moves swiftly round the earth', fr. 45), and that solar eclipses are caused by the moon coming directly between sun and earth; and when Empedocles says that 'earth causes night by coming under the sun's rays' (fr. 42) it is tempting to assume that he realized that this meant that night on the upper surface of a spherical earth would be complemented by day in the antipodes.

THE NATURAL WORLD

At some time into the present era, once the main bulk of the elements were separated out into the distinct masses of earth, sea and air, with fire visible in the sky as sun and stars and as volcanoes erupting from the earth, then living creatures began to emerge. Empedocles described this genesis, in a typical blend of poetry and science, as derived from amorphous lumps which bubble up from the earth's surface during the separating process:

And now hear this – how fire, as it was being separated, brought up by night the growths of men and pitiable women, for the account is to the point and well-informed. First whole-nature forms, having a share of both water and heat, emerged from the

187

earth; fire as it tended to reach its like, kept sending them up,
when they did not yet show the lovely shape of limbs, or voice,
or language native to men.

(fr. 62)

With the passage of time the forms were further articulated until they
become recognizable as the human race, able then to reproduce sexually
and communicate by language.

In a world antithetical to the present one Empedocles found a
place for the bi-form monsters of myth in a kind of genetic nightmare:

Many creatures with a face and breasts on both sides were
produced, human-faced bulls and again bull-headed humans,
others with male and female nature combined.

(fr. 61)

Some of these were put together from different parts – heads without
necks, arms without shoulders – but, despite the bizarre nature of the
concept, a more serious point was being made. As Aristotle reports:

Wherever all the parts came together as though for a purpose,
the creatures survived, being organized spontaneously in an
appropriate way. Those that did not then died out (and continue
to do so), as Empedocles said of his 'human-faced bulls'.

(*Physics* 198b29–32)

It would be an exaggeration to read into the reports of Empedocles'
views here a precursor of a Darwinian theory of the survival of the
fittest, but he does seem to have been prepared to recognize that for
survival a species or 'animal-kind' must be able to reproduce itself, and
have organs that are mutually supportive in nutrition and growth: teeth
to masticate food, a stomach with which to digest it, and a liver to
transform it into blood and tissue. In any case the unsuccessful hybrids
were shunted into a different era, complementary to the present one,
when the cosmos was coming out of a state of disorder into one in
which unity would eventually prevail.

The world which the human race now inhabits is by contrast to
be understood as coming from a better past into a more turbulent
future. In Empedocles' terms Love has not yet relinquished her hold
on the elements, and in the battle against the forces of dissolution she
has considerable if temporary success in the formation of harmonious
wholes. These depend on the formula of elements in the compound,
again a crucial scientific point lurking behind Empedocles' loose poetic
language:

And the kindly earth received into its broad hollows of the eight
parts two of the brightness of Nestis and four of Hephaestus;

and these came to be white bones, marvellously held together by
the gluing of harmony.

(fr. 96)

Aristotle quoted these lines in a compliment to Empedocles for realizing
that it was not so much the elements of which something is made
which give it its character but the *logos* or ratio of their combination;
it was rare to find among the pre-Socratics a foreshadowing of what
later came to be known as Aristotle's 'formal cause'. The particular
ratio here of four parts fire: two earth: two water (or on an alternative
version one each of water and air) is a simple one, but the achievement
is in the understanding of the principle of proportion in the formation
of organisms rather than any sophistication in its development.

The last line of the quotation – 'marvellously held together by
the gluing of harmony' – shows the 'bonding' of the elements, not as
an additional ingredient, but inherent in their attraction when they
come together in the right formula. Another way for the poet to express
this is was to envisage the artisan-goddess fashioning living forms as
artefacts:

When Kypris was busily producing forms, she moistened earth
in water and gave it to swift fire to harden.

(fr. 73)

In other fragments she acted as a baker or sculptor, and sometimes as
a carpenter, joining the organic parts together. More conventionally,
she personified the sexual urge, the mutual desire that brings male and
female together, and ensures the continuation of the species. The theme
continued in a section devoted to embryology, which included an'
account of sex differentiation within the womb. This was a subject
which interested many pre-Socratics, and Empedocles' medical experience may have sharpened his concerns in this area. On one occasion,
when he maintained that both the male and female contribute to the
embryo's substance, matching like the two parts of a tally, he was closer
to the truth of the shared parental donation of chromosomes than was
Aristotle with his preference for the domination of the male.

In his account of life now on earth Empedocles had explanations
for a wide variety of phenomena, from the structure of trees, plants
and fruits through to a broad range of animal species. He comments
for example on the normal combination of hard bone surrounded by
soft flesh as an instance of a chance compound developing a formal
structure, represented as the artisan at work:

bones within and flesh as an outer covering, a kind of flaccidity
chanced on at the hands of Kypris

(fr. 75)

but in some creatures the hard and soft tissues are reversed:

> In those with heavy backs who live in the sea . . . you will notice
> that earth is on the top surface of the flesh of sea-snails and
> stony-skinned turtles.

(fr. 76)

Here the collecting and hardening of earth 'on top' is a means of
protection for the organism, and this prevails over the tendency of earth
to come to the centre.

But the carapace is also the sea-turtle's bone structure. In this and
in many other fragments Empedocles shows a remarkable first awareness of biological analogy and homology in similarities found between
plant and animal structures. The elements themselves are first called
rizōmata or root clumps, and this type of language is extended
throughout the natural world in a variety of contexts. Empedocles
regarded humans as plants that grow from 'shoots', he called the auricle
of the ear a 'sprig of flesh', he had a common word for the bark of a
tree and for the skin of a grape and apple peel, olive trees were said to
bear 'eggs', and *amnion* was the term used both for the skin of an egg
and the caul of an embryo. Processes similarly correlate, and it seems
to be a similar change in the liquid, a *sēpsis*, which makes wine of
water, yoghurt of milk and colostrum of blood. Connections between
primitive and more advanced species were drawn when horses' manes
were seen as analogous to the spines of hedgehogs, and a famous
fragment took this further:

> Hair, leaves, the close-packed feathers of birds and scales on
> strong limbs – as the same they grow.

(fr. 82)

The shared function here of covering and protection crosses the forms
of life and the different elements to link humans and plants in land,
birds in the air, and fish in water.

PERCEPTION AND COGNITION

Another advance in the history of science came when Empedocles
originated the concept of pores and effluences to explain the workings
of the organs of senses in animals and humans, a theory which also
extended the range of homology through the various species. The
medical philosopher Alcmaeon had previously suggested that channel-
like pores led from the eye to the brain, but Empedocles set up a
universal theory of perception, according to which all bodies have pores
close packed on their surfaces, and effluences like films 'from everything

in existence' are capable of entering the opening of these pores where there is symmetry between them. According to his method Empedocles gave some common examples of the theory at work before arguing for its extension over a wider range. He cited the way in which water can mix with wine but not oil as evidence for symmetry and asymmetry of the pores and 'thick parts' of the liquids. Another example was when saffron dye became firmly fixed into a piece of linen, and the magnet could be explained by effluences dragging the iron until it closes with the pores in the stone. Something like this also happens in nutrition and growth, where nourishment is broken up in the organism and distributed to appropriate parts of the body according to their fit, for like substances are attracted to their like, and unite with them:

> So sweet seized on sweet, bitter rushed to bitter, sharp came to sharp, and hot coupled with hot.
>
> (fr. 90)

The application of the theory could then proceed to cover the range of human and animal perception, which also occurs in the context of the attraction of likes, as given in the Empedoclean lines most widely quoted in antiquity:

> With earth we perceive earth, with water water, with air divine air, with fire destructive fire, with love love, and strife with baneful strife.
>
> (fr. 109)

In more straightforward terms this means that the element within a sense-organ draws to itself the corresponding elemental part of an external object and assimilates it in the act of perception. As we perceive fire outside ourselves, for example, by means of fire within, then the fire in the constitution is increased, and so with earth, air and water. Further, we have control to some extent over our perceptions, with the implication on the moral plane that the inner strength of love or strife can be increased by concentrating on its like in the external world, with consequent profit or loss in general well-being or disharmony. In the extension to human relations such compatibility between likes produces unity and friendship, whereas those who are most different from each other 'in birth and mixture and the moulding of their form' wander alone, hostile and in deep grief (fr. 22).

A good example of Empedocles combining scientific theory with poetry – here in a Homeric-type simile – comes in his account of vision:

> As when a man who intends to make a journey prepares a light for himself, a flame of fire burning through a wintry night; he

fits linen screens against all the winds which break the blast of
the winds as they blow, but the light that is more diffuse leaps
through, and shines across the threshold with unfailing beams.
In the same way the elemental fire, wrapped in membranes and
delicate tissues, was then concealed in the round pupil – these
keep back the surrounding deep waters, but let through the more
diffuse light.

(fr. 84)

This and some related fragments show that Empedocles' account of the
structure of the eye is remarkably accurate. He explains how the fiery
part of the eye, i.e. the lens, is concealed behind the dark opening of
the pupil and protected by membranes and tissues composed of earth
and air. Surrounding the membranes, and prevented by them from
quenching the fire, is water. There are pores in this fire and water, and
vision occurs when effluences from objects fit into these pores, dark
colours being seen when they fit into the pores of water, and light
colours in the pores of fire. Eyes that have less fire (i.e. a smaller pupil
and lens) see better by day, and those with more by night. The particular point of the lantern simile is to show the function of the
membranes, which keep the water in the eye from the fire, but allow
the fire to penetrate through it.

In his explanation of the sense of hearing Empedocles supposed
that external sounds, which are emanations of air particles, enter the
channel of the outer ear (which he called a 'sprig of flesh', again linking
plant and animal organs); if they fit the pores there they then rever-
berate within as 'in a trumpet bell'. Empedocles accounted for smell in
a similarly modern way as the entry of odorant particles into receptive
sockets on the surface of the organ – of the nostrils in the higher
animals, but extending over the whole body in lower forms of life. All
skin surfaces may be sensitive to odours, and so 'all are apportioned
breathing and smelling' (fr. 102).

The theory extended beyond that of simple perception, according
to the lines which probably followed on fragment 109, quoted above:

all things are fitted together and constructed out of these (the
elements), and by means of them they think and feel pleasure
and pain.

(fr. 107)

Pleasure might occur as a result of the appropriate conjuncture of
elemental compounds within the body's physical structure, but also as
a response to external stimuli that harmonize with this structure, or
from the replenishment of a deficiency by a complementary mixture
of similar proportions. Conversely pain was thought to be caused by

ill-adjusted coalitions, the clash of contraries or excessive replenishment. Examples of such painful experiences could be found in nutrition when the food absorbed could not be assimilated to the body, and in harmful perceptual encounters such as with a bright light or loud noise where the intake overwhelms the organ. Asymmetry of pores in the sense-organ and the effluences from the external object were also able to provide an explanation for organs being unable to distinguish each other's objects, for the eye sees colours but not sounds, whereas sounds as effluences or 'waves' from a distant object are symmetrical with the pores of the ear, and odours enter and fit with the nostrils.

Empedocles recognized that pores through the surface of the body in simpler animal forms could be aware of and assimilate odours from distant objects in a way analogous to humans taking them in through the nostrils, or hunting-dogs sniffing spoors in the form of odorous effluences left by their prey, which enable them to follow a trail. Skin and nostrils are not only the organs of smell, but are also involved in respiration; this again is widespread, so that Empedocles was ready to claim that 'all things are apportioned breathing and smelling' (fr. 102) in a way similar or analogous to human respiration. One of the longest fragments deals with this topic, and, as with the quotation on the eye, uses an engaging simile:

> This is the way in which all things breathe in and out: they all
> have channels of flesh which the blood leaves, stretched over
> the surface of the body, and at the mouth of these the outside
> of the skin is pierced right through with close-set holes, so that
> blood is contained, but a passage is cut for the air to pass through
> freely. Then, when the smooth blood rushes away from the
> surface, a wild surge of blustering air rushes through, and when
> the blood leaps up, the air is breathed out again. It is like a girl
> playing with a clepsydra . . .
>
> (fr. 100.1–9)

The clepsydra was a common household utensil for transferring liquid from one container to another, and for measuring. It had a narrow opening at the top, which could be plugged by hand, and a perforated base. Empedocles compared the movement of air into and out of the body through skin pores (and in human and higher animals through the two large pores that are the nostrils) to that of water into and out of the perforated base of the clepsydra. He used the clepsydra as a model (comparable to Harvey's use of a pump as a model for the heart), rather than as a specific experimental device.

For the first time in extant Greek physiological theory respiration was here connected with the movement of the blood. Empedocles recognized that the blood is in continuous motion as air is breathed in and exhaled, not yet understanding that the movement involves a circulation but taking it as oscillatory, from the heart to and from the body's surface in small-scale channels. Taking the perforations in the clepsydra to correspond to these channels or pores, Empedocles explained inhalation as blood moving inwards followed by air entering the pores, and exhalation (comparable to the child unplugging the clepsydra) as the blood returning to the surface as the air is expelled again into the atmosphere. No void is involved, but, as is obvious, the heart and chest area expands with the intake of air and returns to normal as the air goes back out through the channels. The comparison is not exact in every detail for the blood obviously does not pour out of the body into an external container, but Empedocles did not claim an exact correlation. The model works admirably in showing a mutual movement of air and blood in respiration, the corresponding oscillation of the blood within the body, and the way in which it can be held in the capillaries at the extremities by the pressure of the air outside.

Empedocles took these discoveries further in suggesting that the blood acts as a kind of neural system between the individual sense organs (which in touch and smell can include the whole of the body surface) and the centre of the cognitive system which, like most Greek philosophers apart from Plato, he located in the heart:

> In seas of blood coursing to and fro, there above all is what men call thought, because for humans blood around the heart is thought [noēma].

> (fr. 105)

The basis for this apparently strange statement is not only that blood travels incessantly to and from the organs to the heart and so acts as a conduit (the 'broadest path of persuasion' goes from the eyes and hands to the cognitive centre according to fragment 133), but also because of its physical construction. It contains all the elements, and in a ratio closer to equal amounts of each than in any other part of the body; and Empedocles attributed the sophistication of this compound to the powerful principle of attraction (here personified as the goddess of love):

> And earth, anchored in the perfect harbours of Aphrodite,
> chanced to come together with them in almost equal quantities,
> with Hephaestus and rain and all-shining air, either a little more,
> or less where there was more. From these came blood and the
> different forms of flesh.

> (fr. 98)

Earth here is a crucial ingredient in the formation of the tissues: with less of this element there is blood, and with more there would be flesh.

Aristotle's pupil Theophrastus wrote a history of early theories of perception and in it interpreted Empedocles' theory as it would be when stripped of its poetic vocabulary:

> We think chiefly with the heart-blood, for there the elements are more fully mingled than in any other part of the body. Those who have an equal or almost equal mingling of these elements are the most intelligent and have the keenest sense perceptions, but those whose condition is the reverse are the most stupid.
>
> (Theophrastus *On the Senses* 10–11)

The proportion of ingredients (as in any chemical formula) is crucial for the performance of the compound; here the best intelligence comes from the mixture most approaching equality as, in other examples cited by Theophrastus, the orator has a good mixture in his tongue and the craftsman in his hands.

On the mind-body problem all the pre-Socratics were in principle reductionists, since in Aristotle's terminology they recognized only 'material cause'. In Empedocles' theory the centre of cognition was explained as constituted of the same elements as everything else, i.e. of earth, air, fire and water, but the quality of thought is dependent on their increase and decrease, and consequent proportion relative to each other. This means, as he says, that

> Human wisdom grows according to what is present.
>
> (fr. 106)

and it is also the case that

> As one's constitution changes, so the present thoughts are always changing.
>
> (fr. 108)

The continual modifications here of incoming and outgoing thoughts are taken to correspond both to fluctuations in the outside world and to alterations in the inner condition.

The less intelligent (including in particular those who infer erroneous general conclusions too quickly from inadequate evidence) quite literally have inadequate means of 'grasping' the truth, whereas a wealth of appropriate thoughts results in proper understanding (frs 2, 3, 132). Although the medical terminology of heart and lungs (*phrenes*), midriff (*prapides*) and intestines (*splangchna*) even in the Homeric poems was losing its literal meaning, Empedocles' constant use of it points to a consistent theory of a physical basis for rational activity. In this way he can envisage a struggle in the *phrēn* between deceit and persuasion (fr. 23), introduce evidence to strengthen feeble conviction (fr. 35), speak of thoughts entering the *phrontis* of the Muse (fr. 131), and describe a wise man, perhaps Pythagoras, stretching his *prapides* when he remembers generations that are past and makes prophecies for the future (fr. 129).

Similarly Empedocles sees the instruction of his student as a literal transfer via speech from one to the other. This is shown when he asks that a 'pure stream' of thoughts in the form of the words that express them might pass from his lips to his pupil (fr. 3), and he advises Pausanias to ensure that his sense-organs are in their different ways receptive to the transfer of truth:

> do not keep back trust from seeing, hearing, taste or any other
> channel for thinking, but think each thing in the way in which
> it is clear.
>
> (fr. 3)

When Pausanias has taken in the account the argument is to be divided into its component parts and almost literally digested like food in the stomach area (fr. 4.3). And Empedocles gives a final exhortation:

> If you put the words I say firmly into your crowded thoughts,
> and contemplate them with clear and constant attention,
> assuredly they will all be with you through life, and you will
> gain much else from them, for of themselves they will cause
> each [new thought] to grow into your character, according to its
> nature. But if you should reach out for things of a different
> kind, for the countless trivialities that dull human meditation,
> straightaway they will leave you as the time comes round . . .
>
> (fr. 110.1–8)

The meaning here would seem to be that the mixture of the bodily components reflects or represents whatever is thought about in the external world, while the continual physical changes in the structure of the body alter that mixture, with corresponding shifts in the nature and range of the thinking. The resulting thoughts may be further confused or dulled according to the intention or effort of the thinker, or correspondingly made purer.

There is further a great confidence, an optimism that the consequent scientific knowledge of the processes of nature will bring with it the power to control them. Empedocles suggests to his student that the understanding of the elements of earth, air, fire and water alone and in combination, in virtue of one's own thoughts being akin to them and made up of like parts, will allow their manipulation. In this way it might be possible for the internal elements that make up the intelligent mind to control their like in the external masses; the chance would most obviously come in the vagaries of the weather:

You will check the force of tireless winds, which sweep over land and destroy fields with their blasts; and again if you wish you will restore compensating breezes. After black rain you will bring dry weather in season for people, and too bring tree-nourishing showers after summer dryness.

(fr. 111.3–8)

The knowledge of the working of elements within the body's structure could also form the basis of medical skill, allowing the avoidance and curing of illness and the postponement of old age. The climax would be a restoration to life:

You will lead from Hades the life-force of someone who has died.

(fr. 111.9)

Whether the story is true or based on this line, the biographers report that Empedocles did resuscitate a women who had been in a coma; it would be consistent with Empedocles' interest in respiration that an understanding of its mechanism would enable one to restart the heart and so renew the life of a patient.

THE UNITY OF ALL THINGS

The series of fragments in the *Physics* has shown an original, sharply observant and analytical mind suggesting solutions to a comprehensive range of problems in the realm of natural science. Empedocles' second poem *Katharmoi* (*Methods of Purification*), which a minority have taken to be another part of the same poem, is superficially quite different in tone and content from what has been discussed so far. The *Physics* had been in the form of instruction to a single student, but the *Katharmoi* opened with an address in the plural, to Empedocles' fellow-citizens of Acragas, and went on to celebrate the high esteem in which the philosopher was held. He travelled he says 'as an immortal god, mortal no longer', on his journey through prosperous towns, and people flocked to him for prophecies and cures.

The most important fragment, which needs to be quoted in full, gives an explanation of his position:

There is a decree of necessity, ratified long ago by gods, eternal, and sealed by broad oaths, that whenever one in error, from fear, [defiles] his own limbs – daimons to whom life long-lasting is apportioned – having by his error made false the oath he swore, he wanders from the blessed ones for three times ten thousand years, being born throughout the time as all kinds of mortal forms,

197

exchanging one hard way of life for another. For the force of air pursues him into sea, and sea spits him out on to earth's surface, earth casts him into the rays of blazing sun, and sun into the eddies of air; one takes him from another and all abhor him. I too am now one of these, an exile from the gods and a wanderer, trusting in raging strife.

(fr. 115)

After this comes the statement:

before now I have been at some time boy and girl, bush, bird, and a mute fish in the sea.

(fr. 117)

Empedocles then went on to describe a journey to an unfamiliar place, a cave, peopled by pairs of personified opposites, including 'Earth and Sun, Discord and Harmony, Beauty and Ugliness, lovely Truth and blind Uncertainty', as well as 'Birth and Death, Sleep and Wakefulness, Movement and Rest'. This is followed by an account of a time in the past that was an adaptation of the 'golden age' under Kronos in traditional mythology, when there was no war, all creatures were tame and friendly, and the ruling power was Kypris, another name for Aphrodite, goddess of love.

A universal law, extending 'through wide-ruling air and measureless sunlight', was then said to bring about a change which was a degeneration from this ideal state. Empedocles in his own person expresses regret for a crime he committed, described as 'the cruel deed of eating flesh', and, in verses which recall Agamemnon killing his daughter Iphigenia at the altar of Artemis, the standard pious ritual of the sacrifice of an animal is shown to be comparable to the impious slaying of kin. Furthermore, the traditional meal of the meat of the sacrificed animal enjoyed by the community becomes a re-enactment of the tragedy of a Thyestes, who unwittingly consumed his own children:

The father will lift up his dear son in a changed form, and, blind fool, as he prays he will slay him, and those who take part in the sacrifice bring [the victim] as he pleads. But the father, deaf to his cries, slays him in his house and prepares an evil feast. In the same way son seizes father, and children their mother, and having deprived them of life devour the flesh of those they love.

(fr. 137)

The citizens of Acragas are urged to give up such practices, which further the work of strife, and instead to honour the power of love, personified as Kypris, in the old way:

with holy images and painted animal figures, with perfumes of
subtle fragrance ... and libations of golden honey.

(fr. 128.5–7)

Empedocles apparently extended the injury to the common bond of
life displayed in animal sacrifice even to plants, for Plutarch, in the
context of fragment 140: 'keep completely from leaves of laurel', reports
a prohibition against tearing off leaves because of the injury to the
parent tree. He also links the themes once more in another fragment,
which gives a ranking of the highest types of plants and animals in a
scale of an exchange of lives:

> Among animals they are born as lions that make their lair in the
> hills and bed on the ground, and among fair-leafed trees as
> laurels.

(fr. 127)

And finally the highest human lives are listed, as the last stage before
becoming a god:

> And at the end as prophets, minstrels, healers and princes they
> come among men on earth; and from these they arise as gods,
> highest in honour.

(fr. 128)

The ways in which the subject-matter of these fragments bears on those
already discussed as from the *Physics* may now be explored. Any
interpretation should be based on the direct quotations as far as possible, for there is very little reliable external evidence, and the comments
of ancient authors, even when giving a quotation, have to be used with
caution, and stripped as far as possible of their own particular bias.

It is appropriate to start with the four elements. A *daimōn* is the
term given in the *Katharmoi* to an individual divinity, the enhanced
form of life that is superior to a human but still a temporary compound
of the true immortals, the four elements. When, in fragment 115 quoted
above, it is said that the air drives the *daimōn* into sea, sea casts him
on to earth, earth into sun, and sun back to the swirling air, these areas
of banishment refer explicitly to the masses of the four elements
described and explained in the *Physics*. The language of 'a changing of
the paths' for the combining of living creatures from elemental parts, the
separating of them at death and their subsequent rearrangement into
other forms is common to both poems. The boy, girl, bush, bird and
fish of fragment 117 are obvious examples of the types of mortal life
that the *daimōn* assumes as he goes from one hard way of life to
another, and they are lives in different elements. Empedocles has
explained that, according to necessity and universal law, coming under

Strife results in so-called birth as *thnēton*, 'a mortal thing'; so, finding himself as prophet, leader, minstrel and healer at the highest stage of mortal life he would suppose that the law had run its course in his case. Since this involves lives in different elements, he might well consider that he has himself been born in some way as a bird in the air, fish in the sea and plant on earth. This need not imply that he *remembers* being in these states; it is an inference from the law that the *daimōn* of necessity takes on a variety of forms.

Like the four roots, Love and Strife have their place in the *Katharmoi*; the terminology is similar, and it is the account of their nature and function in the *Physics* that helps in the understanding of their role in this second context. The principle of Philia throughout is responsible for universal friendship, unity and the good of the cosmos; Strife, 'raging' and 'destructive', is the cause of hatred, enmity and separation. In the *Physics* bodies were said to grieve at their birth in hatred and anger, and to be 'torn apart by evil strifes' (frs. 20 and 22); the theme is repeated in the representation of this world in the *Katharmoi* as 'a joyless place' and 'the field of blind delusion' (fr. 121).

The traditional mythology of anthropomorphic gods was rejected by Empedocles, and instead he gave the elements the names of Olympian gods – Zeus, Hera and Hephaestus – to signify immortality and universal power. He also replaced the former age of the Titan Kronos, the time of 'the golden race of mortals' in Hesiod's poem, with the past sovereignty of Love as Kypris, and this in turn reflected the description of the cosmic sphere under Love as an ideal and blessed state of harmony, with strife absent. A place was found however for the more conventional 'long-lived gods, highest in honour' as the original *daimones* 'who have a share of blessed life', and as divinities in the final stage of a series of lives that include plants, animals and humans (fr. 128, quoted above). These are all temporary arrangements of elements, in which the combinations that are gods are distinguished merely because they last longer before their inevitable dissolution than the other forms of life, as he explains:

> trees sprang from [the elements], and men and women, animals
> and birds and water-nourished fish, and long-lived gods too,
> highest in honour.
>
> (fr. 21)

This erasing of the dividing line between men and gods, which in the epic tradition was fixed and except in rare cases impassable, has two effects. One is to reduce the level of these gods by showing them superior only in having a longer and happier existence than other forms; the second is to raise the status of plants, animals and humans by recognizing in them a nature akin to that of honoured gods, but with a shorter and less fortunate term of existence as particular arrangements of elements. Empedocles, as has been shown in the famous example of the comparability of hair, leaves, feathers and fish-scales, demonstrated that the functions of the different structures were similar in different life forms and also that they all in some analogous way were 'apportioned breathing and a sense of smell' (fr. 102). But he went further to say:

As chance wills, all things have the power of thought.

(fr. 103)

and later reiterated the point:

All things have intelligence and a share of thought.

(fr. 110.10)

The inadequacy that Aristotle's successor Theophrastus complained of in all the pre-Socratics – that they failed to distinguish perception and thought – becomes an advantage here for Empedocles. In his universal ascription of the power of thought (*phronēsis*) he was able to show a seamless stretch of activity from the simplest awareness of a part of one element for another of its kind and an attraction towards it, through a range of more sophisticated perceptions in animal life to human ratiocination. So the physical and biological theory, which removes the traditional distinctions between life as god, man, animal, bird, fish and plant and sets them along the one spectrum, makes the suggestion of a transition from one form of life to another less startling.

The accepted frontiers of birth and death were also broken down. Empedocles thought that humans generally have a narrow outlook:

After observing a small part of life in their lifetime ... they are convinced only of that which each has experienced, yet all boast of finding the whole.

(fr. 2.3–6)

Instead of rash generalizations based on limited experience people should realize that their life does not begin with birth and end with death but is part of a broader scheme. And this conclusion is supported with the arguments from Parmenides that nothing comes from nothing, and that what is cannot cease to be. Birth and death in Empedocles' theory are merely names, to be understood in reality as the mingling and separating of eternally existing elements, which are subject on the cosmic and the human scale to the alternating control of Love and Strife. Since, therefore, birth is not to be considered as generation from what was not there before, nor death the annihilation of that which now is, it is no surprise to learn that there is some kind of existence before and after this present life:

Someone who is wise in such matters would not surmise in his mind that people are, and meet with good and ill, for as long as they live, for a lifetime as they call it, and that before they were formed, and after they have disintegrated, they do not exist at all.

(fr. 15)

One more connecting topic that is present in the two aspects of Empedocles' work deals with the elemental structure of blood, and its significance for life and intelligence. In fragment 105 Empedocles said that, 'For humans, blood around the heart is thought [*noēma*].' This is explained by Theophrastus, in his history of previous views on sensation, as meaning that the elements in the structure of the blood and tissues of the heart are mingled in a better proportion (that is, closer to the ratio of one to one of the minimal parts) than elsewhere in the body. Here therefore is the cognitive principle; it is analogous in its composition to the physical structure of the sphere under Love, in the state that was described as 'holy mind' and 'most happy god'. The combination of elements that comes nearest in this world of increasing Strife to such an optimum condition is said to be found in the blood around the heart, so the controversial prohibition against bloodshed can be seen to have a place in the overall scheme. There are three reasons: first, the shedding of blood is given as a cause of the exile of the *daimōn* from a happier state; second the earlier age of Kypris/ Aphrodite was characterized by the absence of animal sacrifice; and third the continuing shedding of blood in war, and in the name of religion, is given as grounds for the continuing misery of human life.

The themes of *Physics* and *Katharmoi* are not therefore diametrically opposed, but connect on several issues. The theory of four elements helps to explain the exchange of lives of the *daimōn* in earth, sea, air and sun, and the account of the cosmic activity of Love and Strife is necessary to show how one can come under these powers, and the inevitable consequences. The frontiers of birth and death no longer hold, and traditional theology has to be revised. Plants, animals, men and gods have a common origin and nature, and there are no fixed boundaries marking off the kinds of life. And the principle of thought, based on a materialistic structure, has features common to the individual and the cosmos as a whole.

Throughout Empedocles' work there is emphasis on an alternation between god and human, mortal and immortal. The elements united under Love are a cosmic god; when held apart by Strife they are separate but still immortal; and in the intervening times they take on mortal forms. The god-like *daimones* are born as mortals, and in turn 'many-times dying men' become immortal gods. But in the *Katharmoi* the alternation of the states 'mortal' and 'immortal' takes on a vividly personal tone. Notions of wrongdoing, banishment and return to happiness give individual histories to gods and mortals, which at first sight appears incompatible with a theory that explains particular forms of life as a temporary arrangement of elemental parts.

A solution to this difficulty can be found in an appreciation of the different contexts in which the underlying ideas are set. Before the present state of the world all things were said to have been united under Love; this was an ideal state, and the present one a degeneration from it. In physical terms the elements were exactly mixed and held fast in harmony, with Neikos, the principle of enmity and separation, having no control. The interpretation of this for publication to the people of Acragas was in terms of a previous 'golden age' comparable to the era of general happiness and universal friendship traditionally ascribed to Kronos in the Isles of the Blessed. Then, at a fixed time, there came an end to the ideal state. Strife entered the cosmic sphere, causing tremors that resulted in elements separating out from the mixture; it was as a consequence of this further disturbance that the conditions arose that were appropriate for the emergence of varied forms of life. In the language of the *Katharmoi* Strife gained control of some of the *daimones* and separated them from their fellows, causing them to take on 'an unfamiliar garment' of skin and tissues (fr. 126); that is, the substance is reconstituted as forms of lives in different elements. That this is the same process viewed in two ways is confirmed by the mention of the oath at the appropriate moment in each case: the time for the end of the state of harmony, for the rise of Strife and the consequent generation of mortal lives, is held secure by the 'broad oath of necessity', a striking way of indicating the inevitability of universal law.

Empedocles sees himself involved in these cosmic events. The elements of which each individual is composed have, in this present phase of the cosmic cycle, been pulled apart from their original unity and plunged into rounds of so-called births and deaths. Life on earth is therefore to be viewed as an exile from an earlier true home. In terms of human law exile is the standard penalty for blood-shedding and perjury, and so these are given as the acts committed by the *daimōn*, who consequently takes on a series of mortal forms, and lives in one element after another. Although the *daimōn* has come under the power of Strife and so is said to have acted 'wrongly', this does not imply wrong intention or opportunity for choice on the part of the *daimōn*, for it was 'according to necessity' that Strife would gain control. And when Empedocles says that he has been born as boy, girl, plant, bird and fish, no personal remembrance of such states is involved, but it is an inference from the universal law ordaining that the *daimōns* be born in different elements as different kinds of mortal life.

There would however seem to be some constant factor to justify Empedocles' use of *egō* ('I' as first person) at each stage of his history, which would be incompatible with the theory of the complete dispersal at death of the elemental parts that make up the individual. Now in the *Physics*, as has been shown, the elements, eternal and unchanging, are called gods, which, when the time comes round, adopt the form of mortal things. The supreme cosmic god (*theos eudaimonestatos*, where the adjective has connotations of a good and happy daimonic status) is the union of the whole under Love, resulting in holy mind (*phrēn hierē*), until attacked and broken into separated parts by Strife. The *daimones* of the *Katharmoi* similarly were united under Love, then forced to separate by Strife, but will again return, after being prophets, minstrels, doctors or leaders, as 'gods highest in honour'. It is said that they will share 'hearths and tables', but this is to be taken as a standard adaptation of the ancient tradition of privileged people winning admittance to the banquets of the gods, and implies no more than achieving some kind of divine status.

It is the wisdom shown in the most advanced types of humanity which would be enhanced when the mortal life returns to the divine; in this condition it would approach and perhaps even be expected to share in the supreme 'holy mind' (*phrēn hierē*). In this context comes Empedocles' own advice to his student cited earlier (p. 196)

> If you put the words I say firmly into your crowded thoughts,
> and contemplate them with clear and constant attention,
> assuredly they will all be with you through life, and you will
> gain much else from them, for of themselves they will cause
> each [new thought] to grow into your character, according to its
> nature. But if you should reach out for things of a different
> kind, for the countless trivialities that dull human meditation,
> straightaway they will leave you as the time comes round ...
>
> (fr. 110. 1–8)

If the thinking, the *phronēsis* in which all things partake, becomes most perfect, in physical terms the combination of elements in the structure becomes completely integrated, and in *Katharmoi* language the wise man is about to return to daimonic status.

In the complete blending of elements which provides the structure for the perfected *phronēsis* the individual qualities of the elements would so balance each other that their individual characteristics would no longer be apparent. This state would be similar to the characterless and unvarying composition of 'the most blessed god', which, as has been shown, described the condition of the cosmos in the harmony of

Love, before the intrusion of Strife and the emergence of mortal life. Other pre-Socratic philosophers had made use of a similar principle (or *archē*) which had no perceptible features. Anaximander, for example, had posited a neutral source of becoming in the *apeiron*, and Anaximenes had generated a cosmos from characterless air, which he regarded as a mean between the rarer and the more compact; Anaxagoras, soon after Empedocles, spoke of an initial state of affairs as 'all things together', where no colour or other distinguishing feature could be picked out. Empedocles adapted such notions to link the nature of the individual daimonic thought to that of the original cosmos, and our present cognitive powers to what survives of that original now at the circumference of the sphere. In this he also foreshadows the Aristotelian theory of a fifth element (the *quinta essentia*) eternally encircling the cosmos, to which the human *psuchē* is related.

The historian of Greek philosophy, W. K. C. Guthrie, said in the introduction to his chapter on Empedocles that 'in the union of rational thought with mystical exaltation, he sums up and personifies the spirit of his age and race' ([2.13] II: 125–6). But it would be more appropriate to see Empedocles in the light of recent developments in modern science as the search is renewed for 'a theory of everything'. In investigations that range from the study of the very smallest atomic structures to the vastness of the cosmos, and in the latest attempts to bridge the gulf between life on earth and activity in outer space, a fresh sympathy might be found for an original thinker from the ancient world, sometimes dismissed as an engaging eccentric, who found ways in which the familiar earth and the forms of life it contains were involved in the history of the whole. Enriched by the poetic style, and the exotic and often archaic language in which they were expressed, Empedocles' ideas still hold interest. His achievements are especially to be found in the comprehensive theory of elements subject to opposed forces, in the reduction of all life forms to greater or less sophistication on a single scale, in the perceptive insights into human origins and behaviour, and general biological structures and functions, and in the first attempts to link these themes to the cycles of regeneration at the outer limits of cosmic space.[1]

 NOTE

1 General interest in the philosophy of Empedocles has recently been increased by the discovery of nearly forty scraps of papyrus fragments in the archives of the University of Strasbourg, first reported in *The Times* for 16 April 1994. The scraps, which range from a single letter to a portion of some contiguous verses, come from an early Greek papyrus found in a burial site in upper Egypt. They

have been identified as Empedoclean, connected with citations from the cycle of birth and death in the contexts both of natural science and 'purifications'. The publication with commentary by Professor Alain Martin of Brussels is eagerly awaited.

 BIBLIOGRAPHY

Texts and Translations

5.1 Bollack, J. *Empédocle*, vol. 1, *Introduction à l'ancienne physique*; vol. 2, *Les Origines: édition et traduction des fragments et des témoignages*; vol. 3, parts 1 and 2, *Les Origines: commentaire*, Paris, Les Éditions de Minuit, 1965–9.

5.2 Dumont, J.-P. *Les écoles présocratiques*, 2nd edn, La Flèche (Sarthe), Gallimard, 1991.

5.4 Gavalotti, C. *Empedocle: Poema fisico e lustrale*, Milan, Mondadori, 1975.

5.5 Inwood, B. *The Poem of Empedocles*, – a text and translation with an introduction, (*Phoenix* suppl. vol. 29), Toronto, University of Toronto Press, 1992.

5.6 Wright, M. R. *Empedocles: The Extant Fragments*, New Haven and London, Yale University Press, 1981; rev. ed. (with additional bibliography and 'Afterword'), London, Duckworth (Bristol Classical Press), and Indianapolis, Ind., Hackett, 1995.

5.7 Zafiropoulo, J. *Empédocle d'Agrigente*, Paris, Budé, 1953.

Commentaries and Interpretations

5.8 Barnes, H. E., 'Unity in the thought of Empedocles', *Classical Journal* 63 (1967): 18–23.

5.9 Brown, G. 'The cosmological theory of Empedocles', *Apeiron* 18 (1974): 97–101.

5.10 Darcus, S. M. 'Daimon parallels the Holy Phren in Empedocles', *Phronesis* 22 (1977): 175–90.

5.11 Graham, D. W. 'Symmetry in the Empedoclean cycle', *Classical Quarterly* NS 38 (1988): 297–312.

5.12 Hershbell, J. P. 'Empedocles' oral style', *Classical Journal* 63 (1968): 352–7.

5.13 —— 'Hesiod and Empedocles', *Classical Journal* 65 (1970): 145–61.

5.14 Imbraguglia, G. *et al.*, *Index Empedocleus*, 2 vols, Genoa, Erga, 1991; vol. I, text, commentary and essays, Vol. II, index.

5.15 Johnston, H. W. *Empedocles: Fragments*, Bryn Mawr, Bryn Mawr College, 1985. Basic commentary.

5.16 Kahn, C. H. 'Religion and natural philosophy in Empedocles' doctrine of the soul', *Archiv für Geschichte der Philosophie* 42 (1960): 3–35, repr. in Anton and Kustas [2.16] and Mourelatos [2.19].

5.17 Lambridis, H. *Empedocles: A Philosophical Investigation*, Alabama, University of Alabama Press, 1976.

5.18 Long, A. A. 'Thinking and sense-perception in Empedocles: mysticism or materialism?', *Classical Quarterly* NS 16 (1966): 256–76.

5.19 —— 'Empedocles' cosmic cycle in the sixties', in Mourelatos [2.19].

5.20 Longrigg, J. 'The "Roots of all things"', *Isis* 67 (1976): 420–38.

5.21 Millerd, C. E. *On the Interpretation of Empedocles*, Chicago, University of Chicago Press, 1908.

5.22 O'Brien, D. *Empedocles' Cosmic Cycle*, Cambridge, Cambridge University Press, 1969.

5.23 —— *Pour interpréter Empédocle* (*Philosophia antiqua* 38), Leiden, Brill, 1981.

5.24 Osborne, C. 'Empedocles recycled', *Classical Quarterly* NS 37 (1987): 24–50.

5.25 Reiche, H. *Empedocles' Mixture. Eudoxan Astronomy and Aristotle's 'Connate Pneuma'*, Amsterdam, A. Hakkert, 1960.

5.26 Rostagni, A. 'Il poema sacro di Empedocle', *Rivista di Filologia* 1 (1923): 7–39.

5.27 Rudberg, G. 'Empedokles und Evolution', *Eranos* 50 (1952): 23–30.

5.28 Sedley, D. 'The proems of Empedocles and Lucretius', *Greek, Roman and Byzantine Studies* 30 (1989); 269–96.

5.29 —— 'Empedocles' theory of vision and Theophrastus' *De Sensibus*', in W. W. Fortenbaugh and D. Gutas (eds.) *Theophrastus: His Psychological, Doxographical and Scientific Writings*, Rutgers University Studies in Classical Humanities, New Brunswick, NJ, Rutgers University Press, 1992: 10–31.

5.30 Solmsen, F. 'Love and strife in Empedocles' cosmogony', *Phronesis* 10 (1965): 109–48.

5.31 —— 'Eternal and temporal beings in Empedocles' physical poem', *Archiv für Geschichte der Philosophie* 57 (1975): 123–45.

5.32 van der Ben, N. *The Proem of Empedocles' Peri Physeos*, Amsterdam, B. R. Grüner, 1975.

5.33 van Groningen B. A. 'Empédocle, poète', *Mnemosyne* 9 (1971): 169–88.

5.34 Wellmann, E. 'Empedokles (3)', in Pauly-Wissowa (ed.) *Realencyclopädie*, vol. V, cols 2507–12, Stuttgart, J. B. Metzler, 1905.

5.35 Wilford, P. A. 'Embryological analogies in Empedocles' cosmology', *Phronesis* 13 (1968): 10–18.

5.36 Zuntz, G. *Persephone* Book 2: *Empedokles' Katharmoi*, Oxford, Clarendon Press, 1971.

CHAPTER 6

Anaxagoras and the atomists

C. C. W. Taylor

❦

➤ ANAXAGORAS ➤

In the course of the fifth century BC the political and cultural pre-eminence of Athens attracted to the city a considerable number of intellectuals of various kinds from all over the Greek world. This phenomenon, the so-called 'Sophistic Movement', is fully described in the next chapter; here it suffices to point out that, in addition to the discussions of moral and theological questions for which the sophists are more widely known, the activities of many of them included popularization and extension to new areas, such as the study of the origins of civilization, of the Ionian tradition of general speculative enquiry into the natural world (see Chapter 2). Anaxagoras stands out from his sophistic contemporaries as a truly original thinker, who sought not merely to transmit the Ionian tradition, but to transform it radically in a number of ways, and in so doing to enable it to meet the challenge of Eleatic logic, which had threatened the coherence of the cosmological enterprise.

An Ionian from Clazomenae on the central coast of Asia Minor, Anaxagoras was a contemporary of Protagoras and Empedocles. Aristotle says (*Metaphysics* 984a11–12: DK 59 A 43) that he was older than the latter, and (probably) that his writings are later than those of Empedocles (the interpretation of the crucial sentence is disputed). It is reliably attested that he spent thirty years in Athens and that he was closely associated with Pericles, though there is some dispute among scholars on when the thirty years began and ended, and whether they were a single continuous period or discontinuous. Socrates in the *Phaedo* (97b–98c: DK 59 A 47) describes reading Anaxagoras' book as (probably) quite a young man, but implies that he was not personally acquainted with him; some have taken this as evidence that Anaxagoras had already left Athens for good by about the middle of the century,

208

but the evidence is weak. It is clear that, in common with other intellectuals, his rationalistic views on matters touching on religion (in his case, his materialistic accounts of the nature of the sun and other heavenly bodies) made him unpopular in certain circles, and there is a tradition (questioned by Dover [6.6]) that he had to flee from Athens (with the assistance of Pericles) to escape prosecution. He is said to have died at the age of 72, probably in the early 420s.

He appears to have written, as did Anaximander, a single comprehensive prose treatise, referred to by later writers, such as Simplicius, by the traditional title *On Nature*. In the *Apology* (26d, DK 59 A 35) Socrates states that it was on sale for a drachma, about half a day's wage for a skilled craftsman, which indicates that it could be copied in well under a day. The surviving quotations from it (almost all preserved by Simplicius), totalling about 1,000 words, therefore probably represent quite a substantial proportion of it. In what follows I shall be concerned with two central topics of this work, the nature of the physical world and the nature and cosmic role of mind.

The Physical World

For all post-Parmenidean thinkers the central challenge was to show how natural objects, including the world order itself, could come to be, change and cease to be without violating the Eleatic axiom that what is not cannot be. Parmenides had argued that that axiom excluded coming to be (for what comes to be comes from what is not), change (for what changes changes into what it is not) and ceasing to be (for what has ceased to be is not). Anaxagoras' contemporary Empedocles met this challenge by redescribing change (including coming and ceasing to be) as reorganization of the four elements, earth, air, fire and water. Those elements satisfy the Parmenidean requirement in its full rigour, since they are eternal and changeless. What we observe and call change, coming to be and destruction is in reality nothing but reorganization of these elemental components; hence neither organic substances, such as animals and plants, nor their components, bones, hair, blood, leaf tissue, etc., *strictly speaking* ever come into being or cease to be. Put anachronistically, coming into being reduces to elemental rearrangement, and what is reduced is thereby eliminated from a strict or scientific account of the world.

Anaxagoras agreed with Empedocles that what is conventionally regarded as coming to be and destruction is in fact reorganization of basic items. He asserts this fundamental thesis in fragment 17:

The Greeks are not correct in their opinions about coming to be and destruction; for nothing comes to be or is destroyed, but they are mixed together and separated out from things which are in being. And so they would be correct to call coming to be mixing together and destruction separation.

The language is strikingly reminiscent of Empedocles' fragment 9:

Now when they [i.e. the elements] are mixed and come to light in a man or a wild animal or a plant or a bird, then they say it has come to be, and when they separate, then they call that dismal destruction; they do not call it as they ought, but I too assent to their usage.

But there is a crucial difference, in that Anaxagoras rejected Empedocles' core belief in the primacy of the four elements. Even if we accept (as I shall assume) that Anaxagoras' book was written later than Empedocles' poem on nature, it must be a matter for conjecture how far Anaxagoras arrived at his view of what was physically basic through conscious opposition to the views of Empedocles. What is, however, indisputable, is that Anaxagoras' view of the physically basic constituted a radical departure from that of Empedocles (and *a fortiori* from that of his Ionian predecessors); that divergence, moreover, marked a fundamental innovation in the conception of physical reality and of the relation between reality and appearance.

For Anaxagoras' account of what is physically basic we may begin with fragments 1 and 4. Fragment 1, according to Simplicius the opening sentence of Anaxagoras' book, describes the original state of the universe, in which everything that there is was so mixed up together that nothing was distinguishable from anything else. What these things were fragment 4 tells us; they were 'the wet and the dry and the hot and the cold and the bright and the dark and a lot of earth in with them and an infinite number of seeds, all unlike one another'. In this list we see: first a list of the traditional opposite qualities, as in Anaximander for example; second, earth, one of Empedocles' four elements; and third, an infinite number of seeds. 'Seeds' is a biological term, denoting roughly what we would call the genetic constituents of organisms; the seed of a kind of plant or animal is what develops into a new instance of that plant or animal type, and, as Vlastos [6.19] points out, the process was ordinarily conceived as one in which the seed, seen as 'a compound of all the essential constituents of the parent body from which it comes and of the new organism into which it will grow' (p. 464), develops by assimilating more of the same kinds of constituent supplied by the environment. That these constituents were identified by Anaxagoras with the organic stuffs, flesh, blood, fibre, etc., which compose organisms of different kinds, is suggested by fragment 10:

'How could hair come to be from what is not hair, and flesh from what is not flesh?' For the naked embryo to develop into the hirsute adult, the seed must have contained hair, the presumably minute quantity of which was supplemented by the amounts of hair contained in the nourishment which the growing animal assimilated.

In Anaxagoras' primeval mixture, then, we find qualities, namely the opposites, and stuffs mingled together without any categorial distinction. The stuffs include the four Empedoclean elements; earth is mentioned in fragment 4, and air and *aithēr*, the bright upper atmosphere, (traditionally conceived as a form of fire) in fragment 1, while the principle of fragment 10 ('*F* cannot come to be from what is not *F*') implies that water is a constituent in the mixture too. But the elements have no special status relative to other stuffs; earth is no more primitive than bone or flesh (contrast Empedocles frs 96 and 98). In fact the central and most novel feature of Anaxagoras' world-picture is that it contains no elemental stuffs. Relative to substances such as trees or fish, and to their parts, such as leaves and fins, all stuffs are elemental, since substances come to be through rearrangment of stuffs. But relative to other stuffs, no stuffs are elemental, since every stuff is a component of every stuff; 'so everything is in everything, nor is it possible for them to be apart, but everything has a share in everything' (fr. 6), 'in everything there is a share of everything, except mind' (fr. 11).

Some interpreters (Cornford [6.5], Vlastos [6.19]), finding a literal reading of these statements intolerably uneconomical, have urged a restricted reference for the second occurrence of 'everything', interpreting 'in everything there is a share of everything' as 'in every substance there is a share of every opposite'. On this view the basic items of Anaxagoras' ontology are the opposites, stuffs such as flesh and earth being 'reduced' to clusters of (opposite) qualities as in Berkeley and Hume. (Schofield even describes stuffs as 'logical constructions' of opposites ([6.17], 133).) The texts in which these statements occur contain no hint of any such programme. They give no justification for restricting the reference of 'everything' more narrowly than to the 'all things' which were together in the original mixture, which undoubtedly include the stuffs air and *aithēr* (fr. 1) and on the most natural reading earth and an infinite number of seeds (fr. 4). Moreover, the idea that qualities are ontologically more basic than stuffs also lacks support from the fragments. Those, to repeat, present the picture of the original state of things as a mixture of constituents of all kinds, every one of which is equally a constituent, not only of the mixture, but of every other constituent. Further, they attest that the 'everything in everything' principle holds in the present world order as much as it did in the original state (fr. 6). Can sense be made of these claims on the generous interpretation of 'everything' which is here adopted?

Before proceeding to that question we should consider another restriction on the generality of 'everything' proposed by Cornford [6.5]. Observing correctly that the concept of seed is a biological one and that the biological processes of nutrition and development are particularly prominent in the fragments and testimonia, Cornford restricts the 'everything in everything' principle to organic substances, interpreting it as 'in every organic substance there are seeds of every organic substance'. While the indefinite variety of observable biological transformations provides grounds for accepting that every organic substance can come from every other, and must therefore (by the principle that F cannot come from what is not F) be a constituent of every other, there is no ground to extend this to non-organic substances. To use his example ([2.15], 280), since we never observe acorns turn into emeralds, there is no reason why Anaxagoras should have believed that acorns contain portions of emerald. On the other hand, Aristotle reports (*Physics* 203a23–4, DK 59 A 45) that Anaxagoras held that every part is a mixture in the same way as the whole (i.e. the universe) because he saw that anything comes to be from anything, and Lucretius cites the coming to be of gold, earth and other non-organic stuffs along with, and explained by the same process as, organic generation (I.830–42, DK 59 A 44). The comprehensive character of traditional Ionian explanation makes it plausible that Anaxagoras should have accepted the universal thesis. Xenophanes had already noticed the transformation of animals and plants into stone by fossilization (DK 21 A 33), and the transformations of stone into earth and earth into water by erosion, of water to wine, wine to animal tissue, etc. were matters of common observation (see Simplicius' commentary on the passage from the *Physics* cited above (DK 59 A 45)). It is therefore highly plausible that Anaxagoras should have held that we can have no reason to say of any two things that they cannot be transformed into one another by some chain of causation, however long. We know that the atomists, following Parmenides, appealed to the Principle of Sufficient Reason, arguing, for example, that since there was no more reason for atoms to have one shape rather than another, and since they obviously had some shapes, therefore they must have all possible shapes (Simplicius, *Physics* 28.9–10). Similarly, Anaxagoras may have reasoned that since some transformations are observed to occur, and there is no reason for one transformation to occur rather than another, all transformations must be assumed to occur.

I shall take it, then (1) that Anaxagoras drew no systematic distinction between stuffs and qualities and (2) that he believed that every amount or bit of any stuff (or quality) contains quantities or bits of every other stuff (or quality). On the assumption that if a given amount of a given stuff (amount A of stuff S) contains amounts B, C, D ... of stuffs X, Y, Z ... then A is larger than B, and larger than C and larger than D etc., ... it immediately follows that there is no smallest quantity of any stuff. For any quantity of any stuff, however small, contains smaller quantities of every stuff, and so on *ad infinitum*. Anaxagoras asserted this conclusion explicitly: 'for there is no smallest part of what is small, but always a smaller' (fr. 3), and according to Simplicius deduced it from the premiss that everything is in everything and is separated out from everything.

But if there is a portion of every stuff in every stuff, what distinguishes one stuff from another? Anaxagoras' answer is given at the end of fragment 12; 'Nothing is like anything else, but each single thing most clearly is and was that of which it contains most'. This dark saying is explained by Aristotle in *Physics* 187b1–7 (not in DK):

> Therefore they say that everything is mixed in everything, because they saw everything coming into being from everything. And they appeared different and were called by different names from one another on account of the quantitatively predominant component in the mixture of infinitely many components; for there is nothing which is as a whole pure white or black or sweet or flesh or bone, but the component each thing has most of, that is what the nature of the thing appears to be.

That is to say, every stuff contains amounts of every stuff, but in different proportions, and in each stuff the component of which there is the largest amount gives its character and name to the whole. Thus a lump of earth contains, in addition to earth, 'seeds' of every other stuff and quality, but it contains more earth than any of the others (the other 'seeds' may be thought of as impurities in the sample of earth). So any sample of earth is not *pure* earth, but *predominantly* earth; in general, to be a sample of S is to be *predominantly* S. (The texts leave it indeterminate whether something predominantly S must contain more S than all other components put together, or merely more S than any other component; I shall assume that the weaker condition is sufficient.)

This doctrine may seem to threaten Anaxagoras with a dilemma. Either it commits him to the existence of samples of pure S, which is inconsistent with the doctrine that everything contains a bit of everything, or it is empty. Taking the first horn, it is clear what it means to say that a sample of S is predominantly S. Analyse the original sample, by whatever physical process is available, into its components S, A, B, C ... Continue the analysis until you reach pure samples of each component. Then you will discover that the amount of pure S is larger than the amount of pure A, larger than the amount of pure B, etc. But now it is false that everything contains a bit of everything; analysis will have succeeded in doing what Anaxagoras explicitly says (fr. 8) it is impossible to do, namely separate from one another the things in the cosmos 'and chop them off with an axe'.

Prima facie Anaxagoras should prefer the other horn. According to this there are no pure samples of any stuff; every sample of every stuff, however small, will contain as impurities amounts of every other stuff. But now what does it mean to say that gold contains more gold than hot, sweet, blood, vegetable fibre...? It can't mean that it contains more pure gold than pure hot... since there are no such pure stuffs. It means that it contains more gold than hot etc., i.e. more stuff that contains more gold than hot etc., and the stuff that that stuff contains more of is the stuff that contains more gold etc., and so on for ever. That is to say, we can never give a complete specification of what it is that gold contains most of; gold just is what contains more *gold* than anything else, and so on for ever. In semantic terms, we have no account of what F means if all we can say is ' "A is F" means "A is predominantly F" '.

But in order to understand the name of a stuff it is not necessary that it should be possible, even in principle, to isolate pure samples of that stuff. As Kripke[1] has shown, the names of stuffs are proper names whose reference is fixed by those observable properties which typically, though contingently, characterize that stuff. Thus gold is that stuff, whatever it is, which is yellow, shiny, malleable, etc. The specification of what stuff it is which has those properties is the task of the best available theory, in modern terms the theory of elements, which identifies gold as the element with atomic number 79. The only resource available to Anaxagoras to identify stuffs is via their constitution; thus gold just is that stuff which when analysed yields more samples of yellow, shiny, malleable stuff than red, warm, sticky, liquid stuff (and so on for every stuff-description). Analysis goes on for ever, in principle at least; even when the technical limit is reached of whatever process of physical separation has been employed, we know a priori that every sample of yellow, shiny, malleable stuff contains infinitely many samples of every kind of stuff, but always more of yellow, shiny, malleable stuff than of any other.

An objection to the attribution of this theory to Anaxagoras is that it seems flatly to contradict Aristotle's evidence (DK 59 A 43, 45, 46) that in Anaxagoras' system the elements were 'the homoeomerous things'. In Aristotelian terminology a homoeomerous substance is one whose parts are of the same nature as the whole, e.g. every part of a piece of flesh is a piece of flesh, as opposed for example to a plant, whose parts are leaves, roots etc., not plants. In general, stuffs, which we have seen to be among Anaxagoras' basic things, are in Aristotelian

214

terms homoeomerous. Hence Anaxagoras is committed to holding that every part of a piece of gold is a piece of gold, which contradicts the account given above, according to which a piece of gold contains, in addition to pieces of gold, portions of every other substance and quality. (This contradiction is the basis of Cornford's interpretation of 'everything in everything' as 'every opposite in every substance'.) This difficulty seems to me illusory. One possibility (adopted by McKirahan [2.7], 208, n. 38) is that in identifying Anaxagoras' basic substances as 'the homoeomerous things' Aristotle means merely to identify them as stuffs, i.e. the things which *in Aristotle's theory* are homoeomerous, without attributing to Anaxagoras the thesis that those stuffs are in fact homoeomerous. This may well be right. It is, however, possible that Anaxagoras may have maintained (the texts are silent) that stuffs and qualities are indeed homoeomerous, despite containing portions of every stuff and quality. He could do so consistently if by 'homoeomerous' he meant 'having every part of the same kind as the whole', and if by part he understood what is produced by division. He *might* then have maintained that however minutely one divided up a lump of gold, what would be produced would be fragments of gold, the other stuffs and qualities being separable, if at all, not by division, but by other processes such as smelting. That would be, in effect, to distinguish parts, separable by division, from portions, separable, if at all, otherwise than by division. (It is not necessary for this hypothesis to suppose that Anaxagoras marked that distinction by any explicit distinction of terminology.) I emphasize that this suggestion is offered merely as a possibility, and that I am not maintaining that it has positive textual support. The crucial point is that the interpretation of the 'everything in everything' doctrine which I have defended above is not *inconsistent* with Aristotle's statements that Anaxagoras' basic things were homoeomerous.

That doctrine is neither empty nor viciously regressive; it is an ingenious construction which allows Anaxagoras to maintain consistently two of his fundamental theses: (1) there is a portion of every stuff in every stuff, (2) each stuff is characterized by the character of its predominant portion. Its crucial flaw is its lack of explanatory force; the character of a stuff is 'explained' by its principal component's having precisely that character, which is in turn 'explained' by its principal component's having precisely that character, and so on *ad infinitum*. A central element in explanation, the simplification of a wide range of diverse phenomena via laws connecting those phenomena with a small range of basic properties, is absent. Nor is this an oversight, since the effect of the principle 'What is *F* cannot come from what is not *F*' is precisely to exclude the possibility that the 'explanation' of something's having a property should not contain that very property in the explanans. The slogan 'Appearances are the sight of what is non-apparent' (fr. 21a) thus proves to state a central, and quite startling, Anaxagorean doctrine. At first sight it appears to state the empiricist axiom that theories about what is unobserved must be based on observation, and it was presumably in that sense that Democritus is said by Simplicius to have approved it. But in fact Anaxagoras' claim is much stronger; he is asserting that the observable phenomena literally do give us sight of what is unobserved, in that the very properties which we observe characterize the world through and through. (This was presumably the point of the remark of Anaxagoras to his associates recorded by Aristotle (*Metaphysics* 1009b26–8, DK 59 A 28), that they would find that things are just as they supposed.) This does not contradict fragment 21, where Anaxagoras is reported by Sextus as declaring that the weakness of the senses prevents us from judging the truth, and as supporting this claim by citing the imperceptibility of the change produced by pouring a pigment drop by drop into a pigment of a different colour. Rather, the two fragments complement one another. The senses are unable to discern the infinite variety of components in any observable thing, and hence to detect in them the microscopic rearrangements whose accumulation eventually produces an observable change (fr. 21); yet the nature of those components has to be what is revealed by observation at the macroscopic level (fr. 21a).

Just as there are in Anaxagoras' theory no elements, i.e. basic stuffs, so there are no basic properties. It cannot, therefore, be the task of theory to devise an account of the world sufficient to explain the phenomena, since the phenomena must ultimately be self-explanatory. Theory has, however, the more limited task of explaining how the observed world has come to be in the state in which it is; this brings us to another central Anaxagorean concept, that of Mind.

Mind

In the famous passage of the *Phaedo* cited above, in which Socrates describes his intellectual progress, he states that he was dissatisfied by the absence of teleological explanation from the theories of the early philosophers. Anaxagoras promised to make good this deficiency, since he claimed that the world is organized by Mind. Socrates, assuming that this organization by a cosmic intelligence must aim at the best possible state of things, eagerly perused Anaxagoras' book for an account of that state and how it was attained, and was all the more disappointed to discover that in his cosmology Anaxagoras made no use of teleology, remaining content, like his predecessors, with purely mechanistic explanations.

The evidence of the fragments of Anaxagoras' views on Mind is consistent with this passage. The most important piece of evidence is fragment 12, which contains a number of theses about the nature and activity of Mind, as follows:

Nature	Mind is	(a) unlimited
		(b) self-directing
		(c) separate from everything else
		(d) the finest and purest of all things
		(e) all alike, the greater and the less

Activity	Mind	(f) takes thought for everything and has the greatest power
		(g) controls everything which has a soul
		(h) directed the entire cosmic rotation, initiating it and continuing it
		(i) knew all the mixtures and separations of everything
		(j) organized whatever was, is and will be.

The first problem is, what is the reference of Anaxagoras' term *Nous*? Is it mind in general, instanced in different individual minds (as in 'the concept of mind'), or a single cosmic mind? The answer is that it is probably both. The specification of mind given by (a)–(e) seems to be an attempt to differentiate mind as a constituent of the universe from all other constituents. Mind is the finest and purest of all things, it is self-directing (as opposed to other things, which (according to (f), (g) and (j) are directed by mind), and it (alone) is separate from everything else, whereas everything else contains a portion of everything else. (Compare fr. 11, 'In everything there is a portion of everything except mind, but there are also some things which contain mind.') But the account of mind's activity, most especially (h), strongly suggests the activity of a single supreme mind, which organizes the cosmos as a whole. It is clear, too, that that is how Plato represents Socrates as understanding Anaxagoras, especially *Phaedo* 97c: 'Mind is what organizes and is the cause of everything ... the mind which organizes everything will organize and arrange each thing as is best'. The characteristics listed in (a)–(e) are characteristics of all minds, both 'the greater and the less' (i.e. presumably the supreme cosmic mind and subordinate minds, including but not necessarily restricted to human minds), which are explicitly stated in (e) all to be alike. The activities listed in (f)–(j) are activities of the cosmic mind, though (g) may also perhaps refer to an individual mind directing each ensouled thing, doubtless under the overall direction of the cosmic mind. (Aristotle says (*On the Soul* 404b2–4, DK 59 A 100) that Anaxagoras sometimes identified soul with mind and attributed the latter to all animals, but appears unsure of what precisely he meant, while the pseudo-Aristotelian work *On Plants* reports that he regarded plants as a kind of animals and attributed consciousness and thought to them (815a15ff., DK 59 A 117).) Assuming that the fragments refer both to the cosmic mind and to individual minds, they are inexplicit as to the relation between the former and the latter. The minds of humans and of other animals are clearly subordinate to the cosmic mind, but it is unclear what the model of subordination is, i.e. whether particular human and other minds are parts of the cosmic mind, or agents operating under its direction.

The only assertion which Anaxagoras supports by any argument is (c): mind cannot be a constituent of any stuff, for if it were it would (by the 'everything in everything' principle) be a constituent of every stuff. Why should it not be? Empedocles had maintained that 'everything has intelligence and a share in thought' (fr. 110); why should Anaxagoras have demurred? The reason which he gives in fragment 12 is that if mind were a constituent of anything, the other constituents would prevent it from exercising its directive function. Mind has to be external to what it controls, as the rider has to be external to the horse. It is hard to see any force in this argument. We think of organisms as self-directing, and assume that some part of the organism functions as a control mechanism. Why should the mind of a human or animal not be a built-in control mechanism for the animal, or the cosmic mind such a mechanism for the cosmos as a whole?

It is problematic precisely because of what is implied by the description of mind as unlimited. All stuffs exist eternally (fragment 17), and are therefore temporally boundless, and are unlimited in amount (fragments 1 and 3). Perhaps (a) is simply to be read as making the same claims for mind, but the opening of the fragment appears to contrast mind with the other things, and it is at least tempting to look for a sense of 'unlimited' (*apeiron*) in which mind alone is unlimited. Such a sense may be suggested by fragment 14, which states that mind is where all the other things are. Mind is not, as we have seen, a constituent of anything else, but it knows and controls everything, and is here said to be where everything else is. The picture seems to be of mind as everywhere, pervading everything without being part of anything. This would differentiate mind from the other stuffs, for though every stuff is contained in every stuff, there are some places where it is not, namely those places which are occupied by other stuffs. Mind, on the other hand, if this suggestion is right, is not excluded from any place by the presence of any stuff in that place. This, together with the description of mind as the finest and purest of all things, may suggest that Anaxagoras was groping towards the conception of mind as immaterial, but it would be anachronistic to suggest that that conception is clearly articulated in the fragments.

The fragments provide scant information on how the cosmic mind directs and organizes the cosmos. Fragment 12, supplemented by some secondary sources (DK 59 A 12 (Plutarch), 42 (Hippolytus) and 71 (Aetius)), indicates that a cosmic rotation separated out the original undifferentiated mass by centrifugal force into the main elemental masses, and also attests that the original rotation is continuing and will continue to a greater and greater extent. But what the connection is between the rotation and other kinds of natural change, e.g. the generation and development of plants and animals, and how mind is supposed to organize the latter, remains obscure. In particular, our extant evidence, consistently with Socrates' complaint in the *Phaedo* (see above) says nothing about how natural change, of whatever kind, is directed towards the best.

It is none the less likely that Anaxagoras held the cosmic mind to be divine. The explicit statements to this effect in ps.-Plutarch's *Epitome* and in Stobaeus (DK 59 A 48) are not confirmed by similar assertions in the fragments. However, the description of its activity in fragment 12, as 'taking thought for everything and having the greatest power', 'controlling' (*kratein*) everything ensouled and the whole cosmic rotation, 'knowing everything that is mixed together and separated out' and 'organizing' (*diakosmein*) everything is irresistibly suggestive not only of traditional divinities such as Zeus but also of the cosmic divinities of Anaxagoras' philosophical predecessors, the divine mind of Xenophanes which 'without labour controls all things by the thought of its mind' (DK 21 B 25, cf. 26) and the holy mind of Empedocles 'darting through the whole cosmos with swift thoughts' (DK 31 B 134).[2]

In this respect, as in many of the details of his astronomy and cosmology, Anaxagoras preserves some of the features of earlier Ionian thought. The conventional picture of him as a child of the fifth-century enlightenment is to that extent one-sided, yet it is not altogether inaccurate. In fact the two aspects are complementary; Anaxagoras represents in a striking way the vitality of the Ionian tradition, specifically its adaptability to the rigour of Eleatic thought and to the critical spirit of the later fifth century. That feature is, if anything, even more pronounced in the thought of the atomists, especially that of Anaxagoras' younger contemporary Democritus.

❦ THE ATOMISTS ❦

Atomism was the creation of two thinkers, Leucippus and Democritus. The former, attested by Aristotle, our primary source, as the founder of the theory, was a shadowy figure even in antiquity, being over-shadowed by his more celebrated successor Democritus to such an extent that the theory came to be generally regarded as the work of the latter, while Epicurus, who developed and popularized atomism in the third century BC, went so far as to deny that Leucippus ever existed. Nothing is known of his life. Even his birthplace was disputed, some sources associating him with one or other of the two main centres of early Greek philosophy, Miletus and Elea, others with Abdera, the birthplace of Democritus. Of his dates all that can be said is that since he was certainly older than Democritus he lived during the fifth century. No lists of his works survive, and only a single quotation is ascribed to him by a single ancient source (Stobaeus).

Only a little more is known about Democritus. He came from Abdera, on the north coast of the Aegean (also the birthplace of Protagoras), and is reported as having described himself as young in the old age of Anaxagoras, i.e. probably in the 430s. He is traditionally said to have lived to a very great age (over 100 years on some accounts), and may therefore be supposed to have lived from about the middle of the fifth till well into the fourth century (though some scholars dispute the accounts of his longevity). He is quoted as saying that he visited Athens (where no one knew him), and is said to have had some slight acquaintance with Socrates. Of his works, which according to the list preserved in Diogenes Laertius' *Life* were many and encyc-lopaedic in scope, including a complete account of the physical universe and works on subjects including astronomy, mathematics, literature, epistemology and ethics, none survive. Ancient sources preserve almost 300 purported quotations, the great majority on ethics (see below), but also including some important fragments on epistemology preserved by Sextus. Our knowledge of the metaphysical foundations and physical doctrines of atomism relies on the doxographical tradition originating from Aristotle, who discusses atomism extensively. The precise relation between Leucippus and Democritus is unclear. Aristotle and his fol-lowers treat Leucippus as the founder of the theory, but also assign its basic principles to both Leucippus and Democritus; later sources tend to treat the theory as the work of Democritus alone. While it is clear that the theory originated with Leucippus it is possible that the two collaborated to some extent, and almost certain that Democritus developed the theory into a universal system.

Physical Principles

According to Aristotle, the atomists, like Anaxagoras, attempted to reconcile the observable data of plurality, motion and change with the Eleatic denial of the possibility of coming to be or ceasing to be. Again like him, they postulated unchangeable primary things, and explained apparent generation and corruption by the coming together and separation of those things. But their conceptions of the primary things and processes differed radically from those of Anaxagoras. For the latter the primary things were observable stuffs and properties, and the primary processes mixing and separation of those 'elements'. For the atomists, by contrast, the primary things were not properties and stuffs but physical individuals, and the primary processes not mixing and separation but the formation and dissolution of aggregates of those individuals. Again, the basic individuals were unobservable, in contrast with the observable stuffs of Anaxagoras; consequently their properties could not be observed, but had to be assigned to those individuals by theory.

Since the theory had to account for an assumed infinity of phenomena, it assumed an infinite number of primary substances, while postulating the minimum range of explanatory properties, specifically shape, size, spatial ordering and orientation within a given ordering. All observable bodies are aggregates of basic substances, which must therefore be too small to be perceived. These corpuscles are physically indivisible (*atomon*, literally 'uncuttable'), not merely in fact but in principle; Aristotle reports an (unsound) atomistic argument, which has some affinities with one of Zeno's arguments against plurality, that if, (as for example Anaxagoras maintained) it were theoretically possible to divide a material thing *ad infinitum*, the division must reduce the thing to nothing. This Zenonian argument was supported by another for the same conclusion; atoms are theoretically indivisible because they contain no void. On this conception bodies split along their interstices; hence where there are no interstices, as in an atom, no splitting is possible. (The same principle accounts for the immunity of the atoms to other kinds of change, such as reshaping, compression and expansion; all require displacement of matter within an atom, which is impossible without any gaps to receive the displaced matter.) It is tempting to connect the assumption that bodies split only along their interstices with the Principle of Sufficient Reason, which the atomists appealed to as a fundamental principle of explanation (arguing for example that the number of atomic shapes must be infinite, because there is no more reason for an atom to have one shape than another (Simplicius, *Physics* 28.9–10, DK 67 A 8)). Given the total uniformity of an atom, they may have thought, there could be no reason why it should split at any point, or in any direction, rather than any other. Hence by the Principle of Sufficient Reason, it could not split at all.

Atoms are in a state of eternal motion in empty space; the motion is not the product of design, but is determined by an infinite series of prior atomic interactions (whence two of Aristotle's principle criticisms of Democritus, that he eliminated final causation and made all atomic motion 'unnatural'). Empty space was postulated as required for motion, but was characterized as 'what is not', thus violating the Eleatic principle that what is not cannot be. We have no evidence of how the atomists met the accusation of outright self-contradiction. As well as explaining the possibility of motion, the void was postulated to account for the observed plurality of things, since the atomists followed Parmenides (fragment 8, 22–5) in maintaining that there could not be many things if there were no void to separate them. The theoretical role of the void in accounting for the separation of atoms from one another has an interesting implication, recorded by Philoponus (*Physics* 494.19–25 (not in DK), *On Generation and Corruption* 158.26–159.7, DK 67 A 7). Since atoms are separated from one another by the void, they can never strictly speaking come into contact with one another. For if they did, even momentarily, there would be nothing separating them from one another. But then they would be as inseparable from one another as the inseparable parts of a single atom, whose indivisibility is attributed to the lack of void in it (see above); indeed, the two former atoms would now be parts of a single larger atom. But, the atomists held, it is impossible that two things should become one. Holding atomic fusion to be theoretically impossible, and taking it that any case of contact between atoms would be a case of fusion (since only the intervening void prevents fusion), they perhaps drew the conclusion that contact itself is theoretically impossible. Hence what appears to be impact is in fact action at an extremely short distance; rather than actually banging into one another, atoms have to be conceived as repelling one another by some sort of force transmitted through the void. Again, though no source directly attests this, the interlocking of atoms which is the fundamental principle of the formation of aggregates is not strictly speaking interlocking, since the principle of no contact between atoms forbids interlocking as much as impact. Just as impact has to be reconstrued as something like magnetic repulsion, so interlocking has to be reconstrued as quasi-magnetic attraction. If this suggestion is correct (and it is fair to point out that no ancient source other than Philoponus supports it) it is a striking fact that, whereas the post-Renaissance corpuscular philosophy which developed from Greek atomism tended to take the impossibility of action at a distance as an axiom, the original form of the theory contained the a priori thesis that all action is action at a distance; consequently that impact, so far from giving us our most fundamental conception of physical interaction, is itself a mere appearance which disappears from the world when the description of reality is pursued with full rigour.

Chance and Necessity

While the broad outlines of the views of the atomists on these topics can be fairly readily reconstructed, there is much obscurity about the details. The atomists' universe is purposeless, mechanistic and deterministic; every event has a cause, and causes necessitate their effects. Broadly speaking the process is mechanical; ultimately, everything in the world happens as a result of atomic interaction. The process of atomic interaction has neither beginning nor end, and any particular stage of that process is causally necessitated by a preceding stage. But exactly how the atomists saw the process as operating is obscure. This obscurity is largely attributable to the fragmentary nature of the evidence which we possess, but it may be that the statement of the theory itself was not altogether free from obscurity.

The fundamental text is the single fragment of Leucippus (DK 67 B 1): 'Nothing happens at random, but everything from reason and by necessity.' The denial that anything happens 'at random' (*matēn*) might well be taken in isolation to amount to an assertion that all natural events are purposive, since the adverb and its cognates frequently have the sense 'in vain' (i.e. not in accordance with one's purpose) or 'pointlessly'. If that were the sense of 'not *matēn*' then 'from reason' (*ek logou*) would most naturally be understood as 'for a purpose'. These renderings are, however, very unlikely. The majority of the sources follow Aristotle (*On the Generation of Animals* 789b 2–3, DK 68 A 66) in asserting that Democritus denied purposiveness in the natural world, explaining everything by mechanistic 'necessity'.[3] A reading of Leucippus which has him assert, not merely (*contra* Democritus) that some, but that all natural events are purposive, posits a dislocation between the fundamental world-views of the two of such magnitude that we should expect it to have left some trace in the tradition. Moreover, the attribution of all events to necessity, a central feature of the mechanistic Democritean world-view, is itself attested in the fragment of Leucippus. We ought, then, to look for an interpretation of the fragment which allows it to be consistent with Democritus' denial of final causation.

Such an interpretation is available without forcing the texts. Sometimes (e.g. Herodotus VII.103.2, Plato *Theaetetus* 189d) *matēn* is to be rendered not 'without purpose' but 'without reason' ('in vain' and 'empty' have similar ranges of application). Given that construal of *matēn*, 'from reason' is to be construed as 'for a reason', where the conception of reason is linked to that of rational explanation. The first part of the fragment ('Nothing happens at random, but everything from reason') thus asserts, not universal purposiveness in nature, but a principle which we have already seen to be pervasive in atomism, the Principle of Sufficient Reason. Instead of a radical discontinuity between Leucippus and Democritus, the fragment, thus construed, attests commitment to a principle basic to atomism. The second half ('and by necessity') makes a stronger claim, which links the notion of rational explanation to the notions of necessity and of cause. The stronger claim is that whatever happens has to be happen, cannot but happen. This amounts to a specification of the reason whose existence is asserted in the first half of the sentence; nothing happens without a reason, and, in the case of everything which happens, the reason for which it happened was that it had to happen. But the claim that whatever happens happens 'by necessity' is not just the claim that whatever happens has to happen, though the former implies the latter. For the concept of necessity is not a purely modal concept requiring elucidation via its connection with other such concepts, such as possibility and impossibility. Rather, necessity is conceived as an irresistible force bringing it about that things have to happen. This is indicated both by the causal force of the preposition *hypo* (rendered 'by' in the expression 'by necessity'), and also by the fact that Democritus is reported as *identifying* necessity with impact and motion ((Aetius I.26.2, DK 68 A 66) on the interpretation of this see below). Impact and motion, then, take over the determining role traditionally assigned to Necessity, when the latter is conceived (as in Parmenides and Empedocles) as an ineluctable, divine cosmic force (cf. Plato, *Protagoras* 345d5 'Against necessity not even the gods fight').

Nothing, then, just happens; every event occurs because it had to occur, i.e. because it was made to occur by prior impact (namely, of atoms on one another) and prior motion (namely, of atoms). So there can be no chance events, i.e. no events which simply happen. On the other hand, we have evidence that the atomists assigned some role to chance in the causation of events, though precisely what role is not easy to determine. Aristotle (*Physics* 196a24–8, DK 68 A 69), Simplicius (*Physics* 327.24–6, DK 68 A 67; 330.14–20, DK 68 A 68) and Themistius (*Physics* 49.13–16 (not in DK)) all say that Democritus attributed the formation of every primal cosmic swirl to chance (indeed Aristotle finds a special absurdity in the theory that while events in a cosmos occur in regular causal sequences, the cosmos itself comes into being purely by chance). Cicero (*On the Nature of the Gods* I.24.66, DK 67 A 11) says that heaven and earth come into existence 'without any compulsion of nature, but by their [i.e. the atoms'] chance concurrence', while Lactantius (*Divine Institutions* I.2.1–2, DK 68 A 70) baldly attributes to Democritus and Epicurus the view that 'everything happens or comes about fortuitously'. Aetius I.29.7: 'Democritus and the Stoics say that it [i.e. chance] is a cause which is unclear to human reason' may be read either as asserting or as denying that Democritus believed that there are genuinely chance events. Read in the latter way it attributes to Democritus the view that we explain an event as due to chance when its real cause is unknown; on the former reading the view attributed to Democritus is that chance is itself a real cause of events, but an unfathomable one (the position mentioned by Aristotle without attribution at *Physics* 196b5–7). A passage from Epicurus' *On Nature* (fr. 34.30 in Arrighetti), which one might hope to be our most authoritative source, is similarly ambiguous. There Epicurus describes the atomists as 'making necessity and chance responsible for everything', a formulation which is ambiguous between two positions; (1) 'necessity' and 'chance' are two names for a single universal cause, (2) necessity and chance are distinct but jointly exhaustive causes of everything.[4]

The passage of Lactantius is of little weight; he states that the fundamental question is whether the world is governed by providence or whether everything happens by chance, and says that Epicurus and Democritus held the latter view. It is plausible that he took their denial of providence to commit them to that view, since he himself took those alternatives to be exhaustive. This passage, then, gives no independent ground for the attribution to either philosopher of the thesis that literally everything happens by chance.

We are still, however, left with those passages attesting Democritus' belief that every cosmic swirl, and therefore every cosmos, come into being by chance. That might be thought to be confirmed by the statement in Diogenes Laertius' summary of Democritus' cosmology that he identified the cosmic swirl itself with necessity (IX.45, DK 68 A 1). On this interpretation the statement that everything happens by necessity is confined to events within a cosmos, and states that all such events are determined by the atomic motions constituting the swirl. The swirl itself, however, is not determined by itself, nor by anything; it just happens. Eusebius (*Praeparatio Evangelica* XIV.23.2, DK 68 A 43) also reports Democritus as ascribing the formation of worlds to chance, and goes further by reporting him as holding that the pre-cosmic motion of the atoms was also random ('these atoms travel in the void *hōs etuchen* (literally "as it chanced"). On this view necessity governs, but is local to, a world order, which itself arises by chance from a pre-cosmic state where there is no necessity.

The recognition of pure chance is, however, inconsistent with the Principle of Sufficient Reason, which we know the atomists accepted. It therefore seems preferable to look for some interpretation of the evidence which is consistent with that principle. That interpretation is provided by the first reading of the Aetius passage cited above, namely that the ascription of events to chance is a confession of ignorance of their causes, not a denial that they have causes. Some features of the evidence support this suggestion. Diogenes' summary of the cosmology of Leucippus (IX.30–3, DK 67 A 1) concludes with the sentence, 'Just like the coming into being of worlds, so do their growth, decay, and destruction occur according to a certain necessity, the nature of which he does not explain.' In line with his famous dictum, then, Leucippus held that all events including the formation of worlds happen according to necessity, but was unable to say what it is that necessitates cosmic events. It is then plausible that either he himself or Democritus said that such events may *be said* to occur by chance, in the sense that we are (whether merely in fact or in principle is indeterminate) ignorant of their causes. Simplicius' evidence suggests just that; in *Physics* 327.24–6 his attribution to Democritus of the view that the cosmic swirl arises by chance is avowedly his own inference from the fact that Democritus did *not* say how or why that occurs. In *Physics* 330.14–20 he says that although Democritus appeared (*edokei*) to have made use of chance in his account of the formation of worlds, in his more detailed discussions (*en tois merikōterois*) he says that chance is not the cause of anything. That suggests that he merely seemed to ascribe cosmogony to chance (perhaps by speaking of it as a chance occurrence in the sense of an occurrence whose cause is unknown). Explanations of specific kinds of events and of particular events were governed by the principle that there are no chance events, but no attempt was made to offer explanations of the fundamental cosmic processes themselves. That need not imply that they are literally uncaused, but that they might as well be treated as such, since their actual causes are of a degree of complexity outstripping the powers of the human mind to discover.

For the atomists, then, everything happens of necessity; the identification of necessity with the mechanical forces of impact and motion may have been due to Democritus. But what exactly was his view on this? Aetius (I.26.2, DK 68 A 66) reports him as identifying necessity with 'impact and motion and a blow of matter'. Are impact and motion given equal status in this identification, or is it taken for granted that motion is always caused by prior impact? On the former construal some motion may be either uncaused, or attributable to a cause other than impact. In favour of the first alternative is Aristotle's evidence (*Physics* 252a32–b2, DK 68 A 65) that Democritus held that one should not ask for a cause of what is always the case. He might then have said that the atoms are simply always in motion. But while that principle allows him to exclude the question, 'What causes the atoms to be in motion?', the Principle of Sufficient Reason requires that the question, 'Why is any particular atom moving with any particular motion?' should have an answer, and it might appear inevitable that that answer should refer to a prior atomic collision. We have, however, to recall the evidence from Philoponus that atoms never actually collide or come into contact, with its implication that the basic physical forces are attraction and repulsion. Attraction, as we saw, explains, not atomic motion, but the immobility of atoms relative to one another, since the relative stability of atoms in an aggregate has to be explained, not by their literal interlocking, but by their being held together *as if* interlocked by an attractive force operating over the tiny gaps between the atoms in the aggregate. In addition, some form of attraction may also have explained some atomic motions; Sextus cites Democritus (*Adversus Mathematicos* VII.116–8, DK 68 B 164) as holding that things of the same kind tend to congregate together, and as illustrating that phenomenon by examples of the behaviour of animate (birds flocking together) and inanimate things (grains of different sorts being separated out by the action of a sieve, pebbles of different shapes being sorted together by the action of waves on a beach). That this principle was applied to the atoms appears from Diogenes' account of the cosmogony of Leucippus, where atoms of all shapes form a swirling mass from which they are then separated out 'like to like'. The separation out of atoms of different *sizes* could adequately be accounted for by the stronger centripetal tendency of the larger, itself a function of their greater mass. But the context in Diogenes, where the atoms have just been described as of all shapes, with no mention so far of size, suggests that 'like to like' is here to be understood as 'like to like in shape'. Aetius' report of Democritus' account of sound (IV.19.3, DK 68 A 128) asserts that atoms of like shape congregate together, and contains the same illustrative examples as the Sextus passage; it is plausible, though not explicitly asserted, that this same principle accounts for the formation of aggregates of spherical atoms, for example flames.

We have, then, evidence that Democritus' dynamics postulated three fundamental forces: a repulsive force which plays the role of impact in a conventional corpuscular theory, and two kinds of attractive force, one of which draws together atoms of the same shape and another which holds together atoms of different shapes in an atomic aggregate. It is plausible that he applied the term 'necessity' to all three, regarding them alike as irresistible. It must, however, be acknowledged first that the evidence for this theory is fragmentary and also that even if it is accepted we have no idea whether or how Democritus attempted to unify these forces into a unified theory. Stated thus baldly, the theory has obvious difficulties; for example, if two atoms of the same shape collide, do they rebound or stick together? If all atoms have both attractive and repulsive force there must be some yet more basic principles determining what force or combination of forces determines their motion. Our sources give no hint of whether Democritus had so much as considered such questions.

Epistemology and Psychology

While we have no evidence to suggest that Leucippus was concerned with epistemological questions, there is abundant evidence of their importance for Democritus. It is quite likely that the latter's epistemological interests were stimulated at least in part by his fellow citizen and elder contemporary Protagoras (see below). Our evidence is highly problematic, in that it provides support for the attribution to Democritus of two diametrically opposed positions on the reliability of the senses. On the one hand, we have a number of passages, including some direct quotations, in which he is seen as rejecting the senses as totally unreliable; on the other, a number of passages ascribe to him the doctrine that all appearances are true, which aligns him with Protagorean subjectivism, a position which he is, however, reported as having explicitly rejected. The former interpretation is supported mainly by evidence from Sextus, and the latter mainly by evidence from Aristotle and his commentators, but we cannot resolve the question by simply setting aside one body of evidence in favour of the other. The reasons are that: (1) in the course of a few lines (*Metaphysics* 1009b7–17, DK 68 A 112) Aristotle says both that Democritus says that either nothing is true, or it is unclear to us, and that he asserts that what appears in perception is necessarily true; (2) in *Adversus Mathematicos* (VII.136, DK 68 B 6) Sextus ascribes some of Democritus' condemnation of the senses to a work in which 'he had undertaken to give the senses control over belief'. Prima facie, then, the evidence suggests that both interpretations reflect aspects of Democritus' thought. Was that thought, then, totally inconsistent? Or can the appearance of systematic contradiction be eliminated or at least mitigated?

The former interpretation is based on the atomists' account of the secondary qualities, whose observer-dependence Democritus seems to have been the first philosopher to recognize. Our senses present the world to us as consisting of things characterized by colour, sound, taste, smell, etc., but in reality the world consists of atoms moving in the void, and neither atoms nor the void are characterized by any secondary quality. We thus have a dichotomy between how things seem to us and how they are in reality, expressed in the celebrated slogan (fr. 9) 'By convention sweet and by convention bitter, by convention hot, by convention cold, by convention colour, but in reality atoms and the void.' Further, the distinction between the reality of things and the appearances which that reality presents has to be supplemented by an account of the causal processes via which we receive those appearances. Atomic aggregates affect us by emitting from their surfaces continuous streams of films of atoms which impinge on our sense organs, and the resulting perceptual states are a function of the interaction between those films and the atomic structure of the organs. For example, for an object to be red is for it constantly to emit films of atoms of such a nature that, when those films collide with an appropriately situated perceiver, the object will look red to that perceiver.

Hence we are doubly distanced from reality; not only phenomenologically, in that things appear differently from how they are, but also causally, in that we perceive atomic aggregates via the physical intervention of other aggregates (namely the atomic films) and the action of those latter on our sense organs. A number of fragments stress the cognitive gulf which separates us from reality: (fr. 6) 'By this principle man must know that he is removed from reality'; (fr. 8) 'Yet it will be clear that to know how each thing is in reality is impossible'; (fr. 10) 'That in reality we do not how each thing is or is not has been shown many times' and (fr. 117) 'In reality we know nothing, for truth is in the depths.'

This evidence immediately presents a major problem of interpretation. On the one hand fragment 9 and associated reports stress the gulf between appearance and reality, claiming that the senses are unreliable in that they misrepresent reality. That dogmatic claim presupposes that we have some form of access to reality, which enables us to find the sensory picture unfaithful to how things are in fact. On the other hand, fragments 6, 8, 10 and 117 make the much more radical claim that reality is totally inaccessible, thereby undercutting the thesis that there is a gulf between appearance and reality. Fragment 7, 'This argument too shows that in reality we know nothing about anything, but each person's opinion is something which flows in' and the second half of fragment 9, 'In fact we know nothing firm, but what changes according to the condition of our body and of the things that enter it and come up against it' attempt uneasily to straddle the two positions, since they draw the radically sceptical conclusion from a premiss about the mechanism of perception which presupposes access to the truth about that mechanism. We might conclude that Democritus simply failed to distinguish the dogmatic claim that the senses misrepresent reality from the sceptical claim that we can know nothing whatever about reality. An alternative strategy is to look for a way of interpreting the evidence which will tend to bring the two claims nearer to consonance with one another.

We can bring the two claims closer to one another if the 'sceptical' fragments are interpreted as referring, not to cognitive states generally, but specifically to states of sensory cognition. These fragments will then simply reiterate the thesis that we know nothing about the nature of reality *through the senses*, a thesis which is consistent with the slogan stated in the first half of fragment 9 and which dissolves the apparent tension internal to fragment 7 and the second half of fragment 9. Support for that suggestion comes from consideration of the context in which Sextus quotes fragments 6–10, namely that of Democritus' critique of the senses; of this Sextus observes, 'In these passages he more or less abolishes every kind of apprehension, even if the senses are the only ones which he attacks specifically.' It thus appears that Sextus understands Democritus as referring in these fragments to the senses only, though in his (i.e. Sextus') view the critique there directed against the senses in fact applies to all forms of apprehension. This is confirmed by the distinction which Sextus immediately (*Adversus Mathematicos* VII.135–9) attributes to Democritus between the 'bastard' knowledge provided by the senses and the 'genuine' knowledge provided by the intellect (fr. 11). The latter is specifically said to be concerned with things which fall below the limits of sensory discrimination, and we must therefore suppose that the atomic theory itself is to be ascribed to this form of knowledge. This is supported by those passages (*ibid.* VIII.6–7, 56) in which Sextus associates the position of Democritus with that of Plato, in that both reject the senses as sources of knowledge and maintain that only intelligible things are real; for Plato, of course, the intelligible things are the Forms, whereas for Democritus they are the atoms, which are inaccessible to perception and, consequently, such that their properties are determinable only by theory.

Thus far the prospects for a unified interpretation of Democritus' epistemology look promising. The position expressed in the fragments cited by Sextus is not general scepticism, but what we might term theoretical realism. The character of the physical world is neither revealed by perception nor inaccessible to us; it is revealed by a theory which, starting from perceptual data, explains those data as appearances generated by the interaction between a world of imperceptible physical atoms and sensory mechanisms also composed of atoms. But now, as Sextus points out (*ibid.* VIII.56 (not in DK)) and Democritus himself recognized (in the famous 'complaint of the senses' (fr. 125)) scepticism threatens once again; for the theory has to take perceptual data as its starting-point, so if the senses are altogether unreliable, there are no reliable data on which to base the theory. So, as the senses say to the mind in fragment 125, 'Our overthrow is a fall for you.'

Commentators who (like Barnes [2.8]) read fragment 125 as expressing commitment to scepticism (despairing or exultant, according to taste) on the part of Democritus, naturally reject the unitary interpretation proffered above. On this view fragments 117 and 6–10 are not restricted to sensory cognition, but express a full-blooded rejection of any form of knowledge, which must be seen as superseding the distinction between appearance and reality of fragments 9 (first part) and 11 and the claim to 'genuine knowledge' in the latter. Yet Sextus presents 6–11 in a single context (*Adversus Mathematicos* VII.135–40) without any suggestion of a conflict within the collection. Moreover, in *Outlines of Pyrrhonism* I.213–4 (not in DK) he points out that, though the Sceptics resemble Democritus in appealing to phenomena of conflicting appearances, such as the honey which tastes sweet to the healthy and bitter to the sick, in fact Democritus uses those phenomena to support, not the sceptical position that it is impossible to tell how the honey is in fact, but the dogmatic position that the honey is itself neither sweet nor bitter. (I interpret the latter as the assertion that sweetness and bitterness are not intrinsic attributes of the structure of atoms which is the honey (see above).) Sextus, in short, sees Democritus not as a sceptic, but as a dogmatist. Indeed, Sextus does not cite fragment 125, and it is possible that he did not know the text from which it comes; VIII.56 shows that he was aware of the problem which is dramatized in the fragment, but he clearly saw it as a difficulty for Democritus, rather than as signalling Democritus' rejection of the basis of his own theory.

At this point we should consider in what sense the theory of atomism takes the data of the senses as its starting-point, and whether that role is in fact threatened by the appearance–reality gap insisted on in fragment 9. According to Aristotle (*On Generation and Corruption* 315b6–15, DK 67 A 9; 325b24–6, DK 67 A 7) the theory started from sensory data in the sense that its role was to save the appearances, i.e. to explain all sensory data as appearances of an objective world. Both Aristotle (*On Generation and Corruption*) and Philoponus (his commentary, 23.1–16 (not in DK)) mention conflicting appearances as among the data to be saved; the theory has to explain both the honey's tasting sweet to the healthy and its tasting bitter to the sick, and neither appearance has any pretensions to represent more faithfully than the other how things are in reality. All appearances make an equal contribution to the theory. That is a position which atomism shares with Protagoras, but the latter assures the equal status of appearances by abandoning objectivity; in the Protagorean world there is nothing more to reality than the totality of equipollent appearances. For Democritus, by contrast, the reconciliation of the equipollence of appearances with the objectivity of the physical world requires the gap between appearance and reality. Without the gap a world of equipollent appearances is inconsistent, and hence not objective. But there is no ground for denying equipollence; *qua* appearance, every appearance is as good as every other. Hence the task of theory is to arrive at the best description of an objective world which will satisfy the requirement of showing how all the conflicting appearances come about.

So far from threatening the foundations of the theory, then, the appearance–reality gap is essential to the theory. But in that case what is the point of the complaint of the senses in fragment 125? Surely that text provides conclusive evidence that Democritus believed that the gap threatened the theory, and hence (assuming that he understood his own theory) conclusive evidence against the interpretation which I am advancing. I do not think that the text does provide such evidence, for the simple reason that we lack the context from which the quotation comes. The point of the complaint need not (and given the nature of Democritus' theory certainly should not) be the admission that the theory is self-refuting. It is at least as likely to be a warning against misunderstanding the account of the appearance–reality gap as requiring the abandonment of sensory evidence. We may imagine an anti-empiricist opponent (Plato, say) appealing to the gap to support the claim that the senses are altogether unreliable, and should therefore be abandoned (as is perhaps indicated by *Phaedo* 65–6). In reply Democritus points out that the attack on the senses itself relies on sensory evidence. Sextus does indeed align Democritus with Plato in this regard (*Adversus Mathematicos* VIII.56). It is my contention, however, that when we put the Aristotelian evidence of the atomists' acceptance of the appearances as the starting-point of their theory together with all the other evidence, including the fragments, we have to conclude that the picture of Democritus as a failed Platonist is a misunderstanding. The atomists' distinction between appearance and reality does not involve 'doing away with sensible things'; on the contrary, appearances are fundamental to the theory, first as providing the data which the theory has to explain and second as providing the primary application for the observationally-based terminology which is used to describe the nature and behaviour of the entities posited by the theory (cf. [6.46]).

A final objection, however, comes from Aristotle himself, who describes Democritus as concluding from conflicting appearances 'that either nothing is true, or it is unclear to us' (*Metaphysics* 1009b11–12). This is a very puzzling passage, for a number of reasons. Aristotle is explaining why some people go along with Protagoras in believing that whatever seems to be the case is so, and in the immediate context (1009a38ff.) cites the phenomena of conflicting appearances and the lack of a decisive criterion for choosing between them as conducing to that belief. But at 1009b9 he shifts from the thought that conflicting appearances lead to the view that all appearances are true to the sceptical account of those phenomena, namely that it is unclear which of the appearances is true or false, 'for this is no more true than that, but they are alike'. This, he says (i.e. the belief that none of the appearances is truer than any other) is why Democritus said that either nothing is true, or it is unclear to us. So Democritus is represented as posing a choice of adopting either the dogmatic stance that none of the appearances is true, or the sceptical stance that it is unclear (which is true). Yet in the next sentence Aristotle says that because he and others assimilate thought to perception they hold that what appears in perception is necessarily true, the position which we have already seen him attribute to Democritus in a number of places. So unless Aristotle is radically confused, the disjunction 'either none of the appearances is true, or it is unclear to us' must be consistent with the thesis that all perceptions are true. If 'it is unclear to us' is read as 'it is unclear to us which is true', then the claims are inconsistent. I suggest, however, that what Democritus said was to the effect that 'either nothing is true, or it (i.e. the truth) is unclear'. The first alternative he plainly rejected, so he maintained the second. And that is precisely what he maintains in fragment 117: the truth (about the atoms and the void) is in the depths, i.e. it is not apparent in perception, i.e. it is unclear (adēlon) in the sense that it is not plain to see. That he used the term adēlon to apply to atoms and the void is attested by Sextus (Adversus Mathematicos VII.140, DK 68 A 111), who cites Diotimus as evidence for Democritus' holding that the appearances are the criterion for the things that are unclear and approving Anaxagoras' slogan 'the appearances are the sight of the things that are unclear' (opsis tōn adēlōn ta phainomena). The truth, then, i.e. the real nature of things, is unclear (i.e. non-evident), but all perceptions are true in that all are equipollent and indispensable to theory.

If that is what Democritus held, then it may reasonably be said that 'true' is the wrong word to characterize the role of appearances in his theory. 'All appearances are equipollent' is equally compatible with 'All appearances are false', and in view of his insistence on the non-evident character of the truth it would surely have been less misleading for him to say the latter. Though there are some difficult issues here, I shall not argue the point, since I am not concerned to defend Democritus' thesis that all appearances are true. I do, however, accept that he actually maintained that thesis and have sought to explain why he did and how he held it together with (1) his rejection of Protagorean subjectivism and (2) the views expressed in the fragments cited by Sextus.[5]

In conclusion, it should be observed that the persuasiveness or otherwise of the atomists' account of the secondary qualities cannot be separated from that of the whole theory of perception of which it is part, and that in turn from the theory of human nature, and ultimately of the natural world as a whole. As presented by the atomists, the theory is entirely speculative, since it posits as explanatory entities microscopic structures of whose existence and nature there could be no experimental confirmation. Modern developments in sciences such as neurophysiology have revised our conceptions of the structures underlying perceptual phenomena to such an extent that modern accounts would have been unrecognizable to Leucippus or Democritus; but the basic intuitions of ancient atomism, that appearances are to be explained at the level of the internal structure of the perceiver and of the perceived object, and that the ideal of science is to incorporate the description of those structures within the scope of a unified and quantitatively precise theory of the nature of matter in general, have stood the test of time.

Democritus' uncompromising materialism extended to his psychology. Though there is some conflict in the sources, the best evidence is that he drew no distinction between the rational soul or mind and the non-rational soul or life principle, giving a single account of both as a physical structure of spherical atoms permeating the entire body. This theory of the identity of soul and mind extended beyond identity of physical structure to identity of function, in that Democritus explained thought, the activity of the rational soul, by the same process as that by which he explained perception, one of the activities of the sensitive or non-rational soul. Both are produced by the impact on the soul of extremely fine, fast-moving films of atoms (*eidōla*) constantly emitted in continuous streams by the surfaces of everything around us. This theory combines a causal account of both perception and thought with a crude pictorial view of thought. The paradigm case of perception is vision; seeing something and thinking of something alike consist in picturing the thing seen or thought of, and picturing consists in having a series of actual physical pictures of the thing impinge on one's soul. While this assimilation of thought to experience has some affinities with classical empiricism, it differs in this crucial respect, that whereas the basic doctrine of empiricism is that thought derives from experience, for Democritus thought is a form of experience, or, more precisely, the categories of thought and experience are insufficiently differentiated to allow one to be characterized as more fundamental than the other. Among other difficulties, this theory faces the problem of accounting for the distinction, central to Democritus' epistemology, between perception of the observable properties of atomic aggregates and thought of the unobservable structure of those aggregates. We have no knowledge of how, if at all, Democritus attempted to deal with this problem.

Theology

Another disputed question is whether Democritus' materialistic account of the universe left any room for the divine. According to most of the ancient sources, he believed that there are gods, which are living, intelligent, material beings (of a peculiar sort), playing a significant role in human affairs. They are atomic compounds, and like all such compounds they come to be and perish. They did not create the physical world (of which they are part), nor, though they are intelligent, do they organize or control it. They are as firmly part of the natural order as any other living beings. Specifically, Democritus believed the gods to be living *eidōla*, probably of gigantic size, possessing intelligence, moral character and interest in human affairs. While some sources suggest that these *eidōla* emanate from actual divine beings, the majority of sources agree that they are themselves the only divine beings which Democritus recognized. Some modern scholars (e.g. Barnes [2.8], ch. 21 (c)) interpret this as amounting to atheism, taking Democritus to have held that the gods are nothing more than the contents of human fantasy. But for Democritus *eidōla* are not intrinsically psychological; they are not contents of subjective states, but part of the objective world, causing psychological states through their impact on physical minds. In that case the theory must explain their source and their properties, notably their being alive. Since they are of human form, it is plausible to suggest that their source is actual humans, possibly giants living in the remote past. They are themselves alive in that, flowing from beings permeated with soul-atoms, they contain soul-atoms themselves. Consistently with this naturalistic theology Democritus gave a naturalistic account of the origin of religion, identifying two types of phenomena as having given rise to religious belief, first the occurrence of *eidōla* themselves, presumably in dreams and ecstatic states, and second celestial phenomena such as thunder, lightning and eclipses.

Democritus' theology thus contrives to incorporate some of the most characteristic features of the gods of traditional belief, notably their anthropomorphism, power, longevity (though not, crucially, immortality) personal interaction with humans and interest (for good or ill) in human affairs, within the framework of a naturalistic and materialistic theory. It is thus, despite the bold originality of its account of the divine nature, notably more conservative than some of its predecessors (especially the non-anthropomorphic theology of Xenophanes) and than its Epicurean successor, whose main concern is to exclude the gods from all concern with human affairs.

Ethics and Politics

The evidence for Democritus' ethical views differs radically from that for the areas discussed above, since while the ethical doxography is meagre, our sources preserve a large body of purported quotations on ethical topics, the great majority from two collections, that of Stobaeus (fifth century AD) and a collection entitled 'The sayings of Democrates'. While the bulk of this material is probably Democritean in origin, the existing quotations represent a long process of excerpting and paraphrase, making it difficult to determine how close any particular saying is to Democritus' own words. Various features of style and content suggest that Stobaeus' collection of maxims contains a greater proportion of authentically Democritean material than does the collection which passes under the name of 'Democrates'.

Subject to the limitations imposed by the nature of this material, we can draw some tentative conclusions about Democritus' ethical views. He was engaged with the wide-ranging contemporary debates on individual and social ethics of which we have evidence from Plato and other sources. On what Socrates presents as the fundamental question in ethics, 'How should one live?' (Plato, *Gorgias* 500c, *Republic* 352d), Democritus is the earliest thinker reported as having explicitly posited a supreme good or goal, which he called 'cheerfulness' (*euthumia*) or 'well-being' (*euestō*), and which he appears to have identified with the untroubled enjoyment of life. It is reasonable to suppose that he shared the presumption of the primacy of self-interest which is common both to the Platonic Socrates and to his immoralist opponents, Callicles and Thrasymachus. Having identified the ultimate human interest with 'cheerfulness', the evidence of the testimonia and the fragments is that he thought that it was to be achieved by moderation, including moderation in the pursuit of pleasures, by discrimination of useful from harmful pleasures and by conformity to conventional morality. The upshot is a recommendation to a life of moderate, enlightened hedonism, which has some affinities with the life recommended by Socrates (whether in his own person or as representing ordinary enlightened views is disputed) in Plato's *Protagoras*, and, more obviously, with the Epicurean ideal of which it was the forerunner.

An interesting feature of the fragments is the frequent stress on individual conscience. Some fragments stress the pleasures of a good conscience and the torments of a bad one (frs 174, 215) while others recommend that one should be motivated by one's internal sense of shame rather than by concern for the opinion of others (frs 244, 264, Democrates 84). This theme may well reflect the interest, discernible in contemporary debates, in what later came to be known as the question of the sanctions of morality. A recurrent theme in criticisms of conventional morality was that, since the enforcement of morality rests on conventions, someone who can escape conventional sanctions, e.g. by doing wrong in secret, has no reason to comply with moral demands (see Antiphon fr. 44 DK, Critias fr. 25 DK and Glaucon's tale of Gyges' ring in Plato's *Republic*, 359b–360d). A defender of conventional morality who, like Democritus and Plato, accepts the primacy of self-interest therefore faces the challenge of showing, in one way or another, that self-interest is best promoted by the observance of conventional moral precepts.

The appeal to divine sanctions, cynically described in Critias fragment 25, represents one way of doing this, and there are some traces of the same response in Democritus. While his theory of the atomic, and hence mortal, nature of the soul admits no possibility of post-mortem rewards and punishments, the theory allows for divine rewards and punishments in this life. Fragment 175 suggests a complication: the gods bestow benefits on humans, but humans bring harm on themselves through their own folly. Is the thought that the gods do not inflict punishment arbitrarily, but that humans bring it on themselves? Or is it rather that the form which divine punishments take is that of natural calamities, which humans fail to avoid through their own folly? The latter alternative would make the pangs of conscience one of the forms of divine punishment, while the former would see it as a further sanction. Either way (and the question is surely unanswerable) we have some evidence that Democritus was the earliest thinker to make the appeal to 'internal sanctions' central to his attempt to derive morality from self-interest, thus opening up a path followed by others including Butler and J. S. Mill.

The attempt, however pursued, to ground morality in self-interest involves the rejection of the antithesis between law or convention (*nomos*) and nature (*phusis*) which underlies much criticism of morality in the fifth and fourth centuries. For Antiphon, Callicles, Thrasymachus and Glaucon, nature prompts one to seek one's own interest while law and convention seek, more or less successfully, to inhibit one from doing so. But if one's long-term interest is the attainment of a pleasant life, and if the natural consequences of wrongdoing, including ill-health, insecurity and the pangs of conscience, give one an unpleasant life, while the natural consequences of right-doing give one a contrastingly pleasant life, then nature and convention point in the same direction, not in opposite directions as the critics of morality had alleged. (We have no evidence whether Democritus had considered the objections that conscience is a product of convention, and that exhorting people to develop their conscience assumes that it must be.) Though the texts contain no express mention of the *nomos–phusis* contrast itself, several of them refer to law in such a way as to suggest rejection of the antithesis. Fragment 248 asserts that the aim of law is to benefit people, thus contradicting Glaucon's claim (*Republic* 359c) that law constrains people contrary to their natural bent. Fragment 248 is supplemented and explained by fragment 245; laws interfere with people's living as they please only to stop them from harming one another, to which they are prompted by envy. So law frees people from the aggression of others, thus benefiting them by giving them the opportunity to follow the promptings of nature towards their own advantage. The strongest expression of the integration of *nomos* and *phusis* is found in fragment 252: the city's being well run is the greatest good, and if it is preserved everything is preserved, while if it is destroyed everything is destroyed. A stable community, that is to say, is necessary for the attainment of that well-being which is nature's goal for us. This quotation encapsulates the central point in the defence of *nomos* (emphasized in Protagoras' myth (Plato, *Protagoras* 322a–323a)) that law and civilization are not contrary to nature, but required for human nature to flourish, a point also central to the Epicurean account of the development of civilization (see especially Lucretius V).

I conclude with a brief discussion of the vexed question of the connections (or lack of them) between Democritus' ethics and his physical theory. In an earlier discussion ([6.46]), I argued against Vlastos's claim [6.47] to find significant connections between the content of the two areas of Democritus' thought. Vlastos's position has found some recent defenders (and my views some critics), including Sassi [6.43]; these discussions seem to me to call for some re-examination of the question.

It is, I take it, common ground that in composing his ethical writings Democritus had not abandoned his physical theory, and therefore that, at the very least, he would have sought to include nothing in the former which was inconsistent with the latter. I shall make the stronger assumption that he took for granted in the ethical writings the atomistic view of the soul as a physical substance pervading the body. I remain, however, unconvinced of any closer connection between physics and ethics. In particular, I see no indication that any ethical conclusions (e.g. that the good is 'cheerfulness') were supposed to be derived from the physical theory, or that the physical theory provided any characterizations of the nature of any ethically significant psychological state. Put in modern terms, I see no evidence that Democritus believed in type–type identities between ethical states such as cheerfulness and physical states such as having one's soul-atoms in 'dynamic equilibrium' (Vlastos, in [4.64], 334). My earlier criticisms of this kind of view seem to me to stand.

There is, however, one particular point on which I now think that I took scepticism too far. This was in my rejection of Vlastos's interpretation of fragment 33, that teaching creates a new nature by altering the configuration of the soul-atoms. My reason was that *ruthmos* was an atomistic technical term for the shape of an individual atom, not for the configuration of an atomic aggregate, for which their term was *diathigē*. Hence *metaruthmizei* (or *metarusmoi*) in the fragment could not mean 'reshape' in the sense 'produce a new configuration'. But, as Vlastos had already pointed out, the catalogue of Democritean titles includes *Peri ameipsirusmiōn* 'On changes of shape' (Diogenes Laertius IX.47), which cannot refer to changes in the shapes of individual atoms (since they are unchangeable in respect of shape), and must therefore refer to changes in the shape of atomic aggregates. Further, Hesychius glosses *ameipsirusmein* as 'change the constitution (*sungkrisin*) or be transformed', and though he does not attribute the word to any author it is at least likely to have been used in that sense by Democritus, since neither the verb nor its cognates are attested to anyone else. It therefore now seems to me that Vlastos's reading of the fragment is probably right. Teaching, like thought and perception, is for Democritus a physical process involving the impact of *eidōla* on the soul, with consequent rearrangement of the soul-aggregate. (Cf. fr. 197, 'The unwise are shaped (*rusmountai*) by the gifts of fortune...') Acceptance of that causal picture does not, of course, commit one to endorsing type–type psychophysical identities.

Psycho-physical identity having been set aside, some looser connections between Democritus' ethics and other areas of his thought may perhaps be discerned. I argued [6.46] for a structural parallel between ethics and epistemology, a suggestion which still seems to me plausible. Another vague connection is with cosmology. It is not unreasonable to suppose that Democritus saw at least an analogy between the formation of worlds (*kosmoi*) from the primitive atomic chaos by the aggregation of atoms under the force of necessity and the formation of communities (also termed *kosmoi*, frs 258–9) by individuals driven by necessity to combine in order to survive, and it may be that the aggregation of like individuals to like, which is attested as operating in the formation of worlds (DK 67 A 1 (31)), had some counterpart in the social sphere.

Conclusion

Atomism can thus be seen as a multi-faceted phenomenon, linked in a variety of ways to various doctrines, both preceding, contemporary and subsequent. Atomistic physics is one of a number of attempts to accommodate the Ionian tradition of comprehensive natural philosophy to the demands of Eleatic logic. Atomistic epistemology takes up the challenge of Protagorean subjectivism, breaks new ground in its treatment of the relation of appearance to reality and constitutes a pioneering attempt to grapple with the challenge of scepticism. Atomistic ethics moves us into the world of the sophists and of early Plato in its treatment of the themes of the goal of life, and of the relations between self-interest and morality and between *nomos* and *physis*. Chapters in subsequent volumes attest the enduring influence of the atomism of Leucippus and Democritus throughout the centuries, whether as a challenge to be faced, most notably by Aristotle, or as a forerunner to Epicureanism in all its aspects, and thereby to the revival of atomistic physics in the corpuscular philosophy of the sixteenth and seventeenth centuries.[6]

NOTES

1 S. Kripke, *Naming and Necessity*, 2nd edn., Oxford, Blackwell, 1980.

2 For fuller discussion see Lesher [6.14].

3 An apparent exception is Aetius I.25.3 (DK 28 A 32, from ps. – Plutarch and Stobaeus). After ascribing to Democritus (and Parmenides) the doctrine that everything is according to necessity, the citation continues 'and the same is fate and justice and providence and the creator'. The reference of 'the same' (*tēn autēn*) is presumably the feminine noun *anangkē*; Democritus is therefore said to have identified necessity with fate, justice, providence and the creator. Apart from the authority of this testimony, its meaning is problematic. It might be taken (in opposition to all the other evidence), as ascribing purpose and moral content to necessity, but could as well be taken as explaining justice and providence away as nothing more than necessity, i.e. as saying 'necessity is what (so-called) fate, justice and cosmic providence really are'. Since in the next section ps. – Plutarch cites Democritus' mechanistic account of necessity as impact (I.26.2, DK 68 A 66) consistency is better preserved by the latter reading.

4 In Epicurus' own theory, chance and necessity are distinct causes (*Letter to Menseceus* 133, Diogenes Laertius *Lives X*, sections 122–35), so if he is assuming that the atomists share his view, the position he ascribes to them is (2). But that assumption is not required by the text, which leaves open the possibility that the view ascribed is (1).

5 Richard McKim argues [6.39] that Democritus held all appearances to be true in a robuster sense of 'true' than that for which I argue here, namely that 'they are all true in the sense that they are true to the *eidōla* or atomic films which cause them by streaming off the surfaces of sensible objects and striking our sense organs' (p. 286). Though McKim does not discusss what it is for appearances to be true to the *eidōla*, I take it that he is attributing to Democritus the account of the truth of appearances which Epicurus is held by some writers to have maintained, namely that sense impressions faithfully register the physical characteristics of the *eidōla* which impinge on the sense organs. (See G. Striker 'Epicurus on the truth of sense-impressions', *Archiv für Geschichte der Philoso-*

phie 59 (1977): 125–42 and C. C. W. Taylor 'All impressions are true', in M. Schofield, M. Burnyeat and J. Barnes (eds) *Doubt and Dogmatism*, Oxford, Clarendon Press, 1980: 105–24.) While I am in total sympathy with McKim's account of Democritus' overall epistemological strategy, I am unwilling to follow him in attribution of the Epicurean theory to Democritus, since none of our evidence gives any support to the suggestion that Democritus gave that or any particular account of the truth of appearances. I agree that he probably held that, for the reason dramatized in the complaint of the senses, all appearances had to be in some sense or other true if there was to be any knowledge at all. But against McKim I hold that we have insufficient evidence to attribute to Democritus any account of the sense in which appearances are true, beyond the implicit claim that all appearances are equipollent. It is plausible to suppose that Epicurus' account was devised in attempt to make good that deficiency. See also Furley [6.33].

6 I am grateful to Gail Fine, David Furley and Robin Osborne for their comments on earlier drafts.

 BIBLIOGRAPHY

Anaxagoras

Texts

6.1 DK [2.2] II, sect. 59.
6.2 Mansfield [2.4]
6.3 Sider, D. *The Fragments of Anaxagoras*, Beiträge zur klassischen Philologie 118, Meisenheim am Glan, Anton Hain, 1981. Greek text of fragments with English translation and notes.

Studies

6.4 Barnes [2.8], chs 16, 19(*c*).
6.5 Cornford, F. M. 'Anaxagoras' theory of matter', *Classical Quarterly* 24 (1930): 14–30 and 83–95, repr. in Allen and Furley [2.15] II: 275–322 (page refs to [2.15]).
6.6 Dover, K. J. 'The freedom of the intellectual in Greek society', *Talanta* 7 (1976): 24–54, repr. in Dover, *The Greeks and Their Legacy*, (*Collected Papers*, vol. II), Oxford, Blackwell, 1988: 135–58.
6.7 Furley, D. J. 'Anaxagoras in response to Parmenides', in Anton and Preus [2.17]: 70–92.
6.8 —— [2.31], ch. 6
6.9 Furth, M. 'A "philosophical hero"?: Anaxagoras and the Eleatics', *Oxford Studies in Ancient Philosophy* 9 (1991): 95–129.
6.10 Graham, D. W. 'The postulates of Anaxagoras', *Apeiron* 27 (1994): 77–121.
6.11 Guthrie [2.13] II, ch. 4.

6.12 Inwood, B. 'Anaxagoras and infinite divisibility', *Illinois Classical Studies* 11 (1986): 17–33.

6.13 Kerferd, G. B. 'Anaxagoras and the concept of matter before Aristotle', *Bulletin of the John Rylands Library* 52 (1969): 129–43, repr. in Mourelatos [2.19]: 489–503.

6.14 Lesher, J. H. 'Mind's knowledge and powers of control in Anaxagoras DK B12', *Phronesis* 40 (1995): 125–42.

6.15 McKirahan [2.7], ch. 13.

6.16 Mann, W. E. 'Anaxagoras and the *homoiomerē*', *Phronesis* 25 (1980): 228–49.

6.17 Schofield, M. *An Essay on Anaxagoras*, Cambridge, Cambridge University Press, 1980.

6.18 Strang, C. 'The physical theory of Anaxagoras', *Archiv für Geschichte der Philosophie* 45 (1963): 101–18, repr. in Allen and Furley [2.15] II: 361–80.

6.19 Vlastos, G. 'The physical theory of Anaxagoras', *Philosophical Review* 59 (1950): 31–57, repr. in Allen and Furley [2.15] II: 323–53, in Mourelatos [2.19]: 459–88 and in Vlastos, ed. Graham (see [4.64]) I: 303–27 (page refs to [2.19]).

The Atomists

Texts

6.20 DK [2.2] II, sect. 67 (Leucippus), 68 (Democritus).

6.21 Luria, S. *Democritea*, Leningrad, Soviet Academy of Sciences, 1970. Original texts of fragments and testimonia with Russian translation and commentary.

Collections of articles

6.22 Benakis, L. (ed.) *Proceedings of the First International Conference on Democritus*, Xanthi, International Democritean Federation, 1984.

6.23 Romano, F. (ed.) *Democrito e l'atomismo antico. Atti del convegno internazionale*, (*Siculorum Gymnasium* 33.1), Catania, University of Catania, 1980.

Studies

6.24 Barnes [2.8], ch. 17, 19(*b*), 20, 21(*c*), 23(*d*), 24(*e*).

6.25 —— 'Reason and necessity in Leucippus', in Benakis [6.22] I: 141–58.

6.26 Bicknell, P. 'The seat of the mind in Democritus', *Eranos* 66 (1968): 10–23.

6.27 —— 'Democritus on precognition', *Revue des Études Grecques* 82 (1969): 318–26.

6.28 Burkert, W. 'Air-imprints or *eidōla*: Democritus' aetiology of vision', *Illinois Classical Studies* 2 (1977): 97–109.

6.29 Furley [4.63] Study 1 'Indivisible magnitudes'; ch. 6 'The atomists' reply to the Eleatics', repr. with emendations in Mourelatos [2.19]: 504–26.

6.30 —— 'Aristotle and the atomists on infinity', in I. Düring (ed.) *Naturphilosophie bei Aristoteles und Theophrast*, Proceedings of the Fourth Symposium Aristotelicum, Heidelberg, Lothar Stiehm Verlag, 1969: 85–96, repr. in Furley [2.32]: 103–14.

6.31 —— 'Aristotle and the atomists on motion in a void', in P. K. Machamer and J. Turnbull (eds) *Motion and Time, Space and Matter*, Columbus, Ohio, Ohio State University Press, 1976; 83–100, repr. in Furley [2.32]: 77–90.

6.32 —— [2.31], ch. 9–11.

6.33 —— 'Democritus and Epicurus on sensible qualities', in J. Brunschwig and M. C. Nussbaum (eds) *Passions and Perceptions*, Proceedings of the Fifth Symposium Hellenisticum, Cambridge, Cambridge University Press, 1993: 72–94.

6.34 Guthrie [2.13] II, ch. 8.

6.35 Hussey, E. 'Thucididean history and Democritean theory', in P. Cartledge and F. Harvey (eds) *Crux, Essays in Greek History presented to G. E. M. de Ste. Croix*, London, Duckworth, 1985: 118–38.

6.36 Kahn, C. H. 'Democritus and the origins of moral psychology', *American Journal of Philology* 106 (1985); 1–31.

6.37 Kline, A. D. and Matheson, C. A. 'The logical impossibility of collision', *Philosophy* 62 (1987): 509–15. Discussion by R. Godfrey 'Democritus and the impossibility of collision', *Philosophy* 65 (1990): 212–17.

6.38 Luria, S. 'Die Infinitesimallehre der antiken Atomisten', *Quellen und Studien zur Geschichte der Mathematik* B 2, 1933; 106–85.

6.39 McKim, R. 'Democritus against scepticism: All sense-impressions are true', in Benakis [6.22] I: 281–90.

6.40 Makin [2.52].

6.41 O'Brien, D. *Theories of Weight in the Ancient World*, vol. I, *Democritus: Weight and Size*, Paris, Les Belles Lettres, and Leiden, E. J. Brill, 1981. Reviewed by D. J. Furley 'Weight and motion in Democritus' theory', *Oxford Studies in Ancient Philosophy* 1 (1983): 193–209, repr. in Furley [2.32]; 91–102.

6.42 Procopé, J. F. 'Democritus on politics and the care of the soul', *Classical Quarterly* NS 39 (1989): 307–31; 40 (1990); 21–45.

6.43 Sassi, M. M. *Le teorie della percezione in Democrito*, Florence, La Nuova Italia, 1978.

6.44 Sedley, D. 'Two conceptions of vacuum', *Phronesis* 27 (1982): 175–93.

6.45 —— 'Sextus Empiricus and the atomist criteria of truth', *Elenchos* 13 (1992): 19–56.

6.46 Taylor, C. C. W. 'Pleasure, knowledge and sensation in Democritus', *Phronesis* 12 (1967): 6–27.

6.47 Vlastos, G. 'Ethics and physics in Democritus', *Philosophical Review* 54 (1945): 578–92; 55 (1946): 53–64, repr. in Allen and Furley [2.15] II; 381–408 and in Vlastos, ed. Graham (see [4.64]), I: 328–50.

CHAPTER 7

The sophists

G. B. Kerferd

In the fifth century BC the term *sophistēs* was used in Greece as a name
to designate a particular profession, that of certain travelling teachers
who went from city to city giving lectures and providing instruction
in a variety of subjects in return for fees. One of the implications of
the name *sophistēs* was 'making people wise or skilled' and it is probable
that at an earlier stage the term was used to mean simply a wise man
or a man skilled in a particular activity, such as poetry, music, the
arts or a diviner or seer or the possessor of certain other kinds of
mysterious knowledge. It is surely no accident that professional sophists
of the fifth century BC liked to emphasize their affinity with such
earlier sophists and wise men generally. While such a view was one
which it was natural enough for the sophists to adopt, it failed to do
justice to the actual form of the word *sophistēs*; in modern terms it
implies that what is being referred to is someone who does something,
nomen agentis, but what the sophist did was to attempt to make other
people proficient in the practice of wisdom. In other words it was the
function of the *sophistēs* to act as a teacher.

The fifth-century sophists were, then, above all else teachers. This
raises immediately two questions: what things did they teach and what
were the methods used in their teaching? But the answers to these
questions must depend to a considerable extent on an understanding
of the way in which the sophists functioned in Greek societies in the
fifth century, and above all on what their function was at Athens.
Plutarch, in his *Life of Cimon* (chapter 15), claimed that by the middle
of the fifth century the multitude at Athens had come to be released,
and had overthrown all the ancient laws and customs that had hitherto
been observed. The result was a full and unmixed democracy promoted
and supported by Pericles. But, as I have written elsewhere[1] in fact it
is clear from the carefully phrased statement of Thucydides (II.37.1) that

244

Periclean democracy rested on two fundamental principles; Thucydides' words were:

> it is called a democracy because the conduct of affairs is entrusted not to a few but to the many, but while there is equality for all in civil affairs established by law, we allow full play to individual worth in public affairs.

From this it may be seen that the two principles may be stated as follows: while power should be in the hands of the people as a whole and not with a small section of the citizen body, high offices carrying the right to advise and act for the people should be entrusted to those best fitted and most able to carry out these functions.

It should be clear that if a society was to be based on both of the above two principles, this favoured the development of certain more or less specialized skills, above all the ability to speak and argue in public. When it is remembered that ordinary school education for male citizens at Athens was completed by the age of 14 it should be clear that the competition for success in the newly developed Periclean democracy created a real need for a type of further education such as that supplied by the sophists. But it would be a mistake to suppose that this need was something confined to Athens. Individual sophists came from many parts of the Greek world and travelled extensively, teaching and lecturing everywhere that they went. Thus Gorgias taught pupils in Argos and at another period was apparently settled in Thessaly, and Antiphon, who was himself an Athenian, was said to have set up a kind of citizen's advice bureau offering some sort of psychiatric service to those who needed it, in Corinth of all unlikely places. Virtually every other sophist of whom we have knowledge is stated to have spent much of his time travelling. What all this suggests is that throughout the Greek world there was an emergent demand for the provision of secondary education in the fifth century BC and that this demand was satisfied at least in part by the development of the Sophistic Movement as a whole.

What I have found it convenient to call the Sophistic Movement, a term which might be greeted with some criticism as suggesting that the movement as a whole was somehow organized, was essentially a pattern or kind of thinking in the period from about 460 to 380 BC, and it was the product above all of individual sophists. We have the names of some twenty-six such individuals, and ideally the history of philosophy should involve a consideration of each of these separately, together with a discussion of how each reacted or responded to the thought of his predecessors and contemporaries. But in the absence of surviving works by individual sophists we simply do not have the evidence for the reconstruction of their several views on an individual basis. Secondly, when we do have evidence for the views of an individual sophist it is in many cases clear that these views were held in common between several or indeed all of the sophists in the period in question. Consequently it seems appropriate to begin with an attempt to state what were at an early stage recognized as the distinctive doctrines and methods of teaching and argument characterizing the movement as a whole.

What may be called generically the sophistic method of argument requires an understanding of three key technical terms: dialectic, anti-logic and eristic. First for the term 'dialectic': in its most general sense this meant in Greek 'discussion' involving two or more persons, and its most obvious application is to be found in the written dialogues of Plato, although this was not exactly the way in which Plato wished to understand the term. At a quite early stage in the fifth century its use was already more precise and this more specialized sense was attributed by Aristotle (*Sophistical Refutatins* 10, 170b19, DK 29 A 14) to Zeno the Eleatic who wrote before the middle of the fifth century BC. This more specialized sense involved a method of refutation which consisted in opposing two contradictory statements in order to proceed to the acceptance of one of the two statements as truer or more appropriate. Dialectical discussions in this sense of the term flourished above all on the basis of questions and answers, or more generally, on brief statements made by either party to a debate, or even by a single person only. This was to become a marked feature of what is known as the Socratic *Elenchos*, which is especially associated with the practice followed by Socrates in the early dialogues of Plato. There Socrates reduces opponents to confusion in argument by persuading them to give their agreement to two contradictory views on a given question, either because the initial view is seen to imply its own contradiction or because it is matched by an independently established second proposition which is found to contradict it. In the period after the classical sophists the term 'dialectic' came also to be used as a name for Plato's own preferred method of reasoning. This was a method of escape from the contradictions on Plato's view inherent in phenomenal experience, leading to the ascent to the world of Forms, which alone for Plato were free from internal contradictions.

The method of arguing by opposing contradictory arguments is best known to us from Protagoras, who seems to have held that two opposed arguments or propositions are to be found concerning everything whatsoever, and to have developed a method of argument based on this supposed fact. In their simplest form two propositions are found to be opposed to one another when one is the negative of the other, as for example in the statements that the wind is hot and the wind is not hot. Protagoras' method of argument based on this doctrine is referred to by Plato (*Republic* 454a) as the 'art of antilogic'. Protagoras' aim was to teach his pupils how to make one proposition stronger than its opposed argument, whether this involves arguing for the positive or the negative of the two opposed propositions. Plato's objection to this method, which he attributes not only to Protagoras but to other sophists as well, is that the attempt to establish one statement as true about the phenomenal world in opposition to its opposite is mistaken; truth is not to be found in phenomena but only in the world of the Forms. What is worse than this, he maintains, is that anyone who attempts to establish one such argument in opposition to another is not really seeking truth at all since truth is not to be found in this way. It follows that anyone proceeding in this way cannot be seeking the truth but is simply trying to secure victory in an argument. This Plato calls the art of Eristic (*Sophist* 231e and frequently). I have argued elsewhere[2] that the meaning of 'Eristic' for Plato is always distinct from the meaning of 'Antilogic' though he is prepared freely to apply the same two terms to the same people and to the same procedures. Antilogic is the opposition of one proposition to another which contradicts it, and this is in fact a respected and necessary part of the Socratic *Elenchos* and the process of dialectic. Eristic on the other hand is what occurs when people are concerned to secure apparent victory in argument without any concern for what is in fact the truth. Plato's charge against the sophists is that they developed the method of antilogic simply for eristic purposes, and his concealed criticism is that this was because they failed to use it in order to ascend by dialectic to an understanding of the Forms.

The opposition of one argument to another has a clear practical application, namely the process of public debate whether political or philosophic. It consequently provided an effective basis for sophistic teaching on rhetoric and some have supposed that the teaching of rhetoric was not only an essential element in the Sophistic Movement but constituted the whole of their intellectual activity.[3] On this view the sophists were teachers of rhetoric and this is all that needs to be said about them. They would then, it is argued, have no claims to a place in this history of Greek philosophy.

Such a judgement raises conceptual issues of considerable importance. In modern discussions it has long been a matter of convention to oppose rhetoric to philosophy. Rhetoric is regarded as the art of persuasive or impressive speaking or writing, or the use of language to persuade or impress often with the implication of insincerity or exaggeration. Philosophy on the other hand is seen as the love of wisdom or knowledge, especially that which deals with ultimate reality or with the most general causes and principles of things. But it is probable that no such opposition was to be found in the earliest Greek uses of the expression 'the art of rhetoric'; this was understood simply to refer to the best and most correct use of language. Thus in Plato's *Gorgias* (449e1ff.), when Socrates asks the sophist Gorgias 'what is rhetoric about?' he receives the answer that it is the art which makes men good at speaking and also makes them good at thinking about the subjects on which it teaches them to speak. This raises the possibility that on Gorgias' view the most correct use of language will be that which best expresses the nature and structure of reality or the way things are. This is in no way inconsistent with the *use* of rhetoric as a means of persuasion, and Socrates proceeds in what follows in the *Gorgias* to secure admissions from Gorgias that persuasion was a major feature of rhetoric. But for Gorgias, persuasion, at least when properly used, is based on the communication of truth. For most or all of the sophists, however, truth is based on a phenomenalistic view of reality, and this is something which Plato rejected. So in Plato's eyes the sophists were to be condemned because when they were concerned with the art of persuasion they were not concerned with the communication of non-phenomenalistic truth.

❧ PROTAGORAS ❧

Protagoras was the most famous of all the sophists and Plato seems to have believed that he was the first to adopt the name of sophist and to charge fees for the instruction which he offered (*Protagoras* 349a2–4). He was born in Abdera, an Ionian colony on the coast of Thrace, probably not later than 490 BC, and he probably died after 421 BC. According to one tradition he was educated as a boy under Persian religious teachers at his house in Thrace. He probably first visited Athens well before 443 BC, as in that year he was asked by Pericles to frame a constitution for the new pan-Hellenic colony of Thurii in southern Italy. It is clear that throughout his life Protagoras was able to rely on the support of Pericles. He was said to have died by drowning on a sea-voyage, when he had to leave Athens after he had been tried and convicted of impiety. As a result of his trial it was recorded that his books were burnt in the agora after they had been called in from those who possessed them, by a herald's proclamation. The immediate basis for the charge of impiety seems to have been his work *On the Gods*, of which the opening words were:

> concerning the gods, I cannot know either that [or perhaps 'how']
> they exist or do not exist or what they are like in appearance,
> for there are many things which prevent one's knowing: the
> obscurity of the subject and the shortness of human life.
>
> (DK 80 B4)

As a result Protagoras came to be included in later lists of alleged atheists from the sophistic period, alongside Prodicus, Critias, Euripides, Anaxagoras and Phidias. It seems more probable however that Protagoras' position was actually one of agnosticism rather than outright atheism.

Diogenes Laertius, who wrote probably in the third century AD, lists twelve works as written by Protagoras and from other later writers we can add a further six titles. The tradition of the discussion and interpretation of Protagoras' most important doctrines begins with Plato, above all in the dialogues *Protagoras* and *Theaetetus*. But all we have by way of actual fragments of Protagoras' writings is a handful of brief statements and single sentences, and it is not possible to form any certain idea of the arrangement and order of the arguments in his writings. What must be done is to attempt a reconstruction of his doctrines on the basis of the doxographic tradition, and we have good reason to suppose that the doxographic tradition as a whole was ultimately rooted in what Protagoras had actually written.

By far the most famous of his doctrines is that known by the catch-phrase as the *homo mensura* or man the measure theory. This was stated in the first sentence of a work entitled *On Truth*, perhaps with a subtitle *Overthrowing Arguments*. The fragment reads, 'Of all things man is the measure, of things that are that [or perhaps "how"] they are and of things that are not that [or "how"] they are not (DK 80 B1).' Every feature of this famous sentence has been the subject of vigorous controversies, and there is no agreement among scholars as to its precise meaning. In what follows I attempt to state the main matters of controversy and to suggest what seem to me to be the most likely interpretations. In the nineteenth century quite a number of scholars took the word 'man' in the quotation to mean not the individual human being but mankind as a whole, and on this view things are presented to us according to the structure and arrangement of what is to be known as human nature, thus bringing Protagoras' doctrine into line with the idealism of Immanuel Kant. But against this view it seems clear that Democritus, Plato, Aristotle and Sextus Empiricus all took 'man' in Protagoras' quotation as referring to each individual man. On this view each individual man is the measure for himself of what he experiences. Next, what is meant by 'that' or 'how', which is simply a rendering of the single Greek word *hōs*? Once again scholars are divided. If the meaning is to be taken as 'that', then the doctrine as a whole is to be interpreted as meaning 'Man is the measure of the existence of things that exist and the non-existence of things that are not.' So for an example, if we as individuals or collectively believe that the gods exist then for us they do exist, and if we believe that they do not exist then for us there are no gods. But if the meaning of *hōs* is to be taken as 'how' then 'Man' for Protagoras is the measure not merely of whether things exist or not, but of the way in which they exist, in other words of all their phenomenal qualities. It is clear from Plato's *Theaetetus* that Plato supposed that Protagoras' doctrine certainly included phenomenal qualities. This can clearly be seen when he gives as an example the case of a wind and explains that for Protagoras sometimes when the same wind is blowing it feels cold to one person and to another person not cold. On the everyday view the wind itself is either cold or not cold, and one of the percipients is mistaken in supposing that the wind is as it seems to him and the other percipient is right. This seems clearly to be the view that Plato is concerned with in his discussion of Protagoras' doctrine. But there are at least three ways of understanding what Protagoras may have supposed to be the case: (1) there is no one wind at all but only two private winds, my wind which is cold and your wind which is not. (2) There is a public wind but it is neither cold nor warm; the apparent coldness of the wind only exists privately for me when I have the feeling that it is cold. The wind itself exists independently of my perceiving it but its coldness does not. This view, however, does not exclude the possibility that while the wind itself is neither hot nor cold it may still contain causal elements which produce in me the sensation of cold. (3) The wind is itself both cold and warm; the two qualities can and do coexist in the same physical object and I perceive one of the qualities while you perceive the other.

Each of these three interpretations has been vigorously defended by groups of modern scholars and there is no agreement as to which is correct.[4] Here I can only say that I believe that both the evidence of Plato and of the later doxographic tradition definitely supports the third of the above views, namely that all perceived qualities are in fact objectively present in the perceived object. From this it follows that all perceptions that actually occur are true and perception as such is infallible; it would not occur if the basis for what is experienced were not actually *there*, and as it were waiting to be perceived.

Clearly the man–measure doctrine is of considerable interest as a doctrine of *perception*. But its importance is even wider than this, since Plato in the *Theaetetus* makes it clear that it was applied by Protagoras not only to qualities which we would say are perceived by the senses, but also to values such as good and bad, advantageous and disadvantageous and so on. It is not clear, though it is entirely possible, that Protagoras regarded these attributes as similar to beautiful and ugly and so as themselves in some sense rooted in external reality. But the doctrine that whatever seems right and admirable to any one individual is necessarily and infallibly right for that individual has clear echoes in present-day thinking about values. Its importance for political arguments and discussions cannot easily be exaggerated, and it was a major contribution to the analysis of the processes of democracy so recently developing at Athens.

Protagoras' views about the nature of men in society and the process of political activity can be inferred in some detail from what Plato says in the *Protagoras* and which he most probably derived from some of Protagoras' own writings. According to Plato, Protagoras set himself up as a teacher of *Aretē* (human virtue or human excellence). This will involve Protagoras training a man in the habit of good judgement about his own affairs, showing him how best to order his own household, and in the affairs of his city showing how he may have the most influence on public affairs both in speech and action (*Protagoras* 318e–319a). Protagoras is thus committed to the doctrine that virtue is something which may be taught, as opposed to the view that it is simply inherited or acquired from essentially aristocratic groupings within larger human societies. Plato proceeds to expound the doctrines of Protagoras in two stages, first through a myth and then through a more analytic and rationalized account (a *Logos*) intended to convey the same doctrines. Protagoras, as Plato and Aristotle do after him, begins his analysis with an account of the development of human societies. First men lived scattered and dispersed and there were no cities at all. But even then they had already developed the ability to provide themselves with dwelling places, clothes, shoes and bedding, and had learnt to talk and to worship the gods. In addition they gradually acquired and so came to possess sufficient skills with their hands to provide themselves with food. They thus possessed a certain technical wisdom which enabled them to develop some of the material elements of civilization. But they were in the process of being destroyed by wild animals which were stronger than they were. This led them to join together and found cities primarily aimed at securing their self-defence. But as they lacked the art required for living together in cities they began to commit injustices against one another and so began to scatter again and to be destroyed. Zeus, in order to preserve mankind, sent Hermes to give them the two qualities needed for them to live together, namely the qualities of respect for what is right (*Aidōs*) and a feeling for Justice (*Dikē*) between individuals. These qualities are given to all men and all men are to share in them, with the exception that those incapable of sharing in them are to be killed as being a plague to the city. But while all men after this action by Zeus do share in these qualities they do not do so equally; some have larger shares than others. So much in mythical terms. In the rational explanation that Protagoras gives after the myth a number of points are made clear. The universal share in *Aidōs* and *Dikē* that results from the gift of Zeus is not innate, nor is it in fact acquired automatically; it is the product of a process of education, which starts in infancy. The fact that the individual's share in these two essential qualities is acquired and then developed by teaching provides a justification for the profession of the sophist, who is able to regard himself as an exceptionally able teacher. The whole approach provides a theory of justification – the first known to history – for participatory democracy. All citizens have a claim to participation in the political processes of the city since all share in the qualities needed for the city to function. But they do not share equally in these qualities, and it is accordingly appropriate that within a democracy leadership should be exercised by those who are exceptionally able. Many other aspects of normal political activity at Athens and elsewhere in Greece were probably discussed in Protagoras' political writings – we have brief notes to the effect that he discussed a theory of punishment as something to be accepted both as a deterrent and also as a form of education leading to reform of the errant individual. Finally mention may be made of the intriguing and puzzling statement, found in Diogenes Laertius (III.57, DK 80 B 5), that the whole of the content of Plato's *Republic* was to be found in the work by Protagoras entitled *Contradictory Arguments* (*Antilogikoi Logoi*). While this in itself is clearly not credible, that it could even be said to be the case is perhaps evidence of the extremely wide-ranging nature of Protagoras' writings on politics. More precisely, it may have been possible for an enthusiastic supporter of what Protagoras had written to discern structural similarities with the *Republic*, in which Plato is concerned with the development of rational societies from earlier organizations that had not yet grasped the need for a rational understanding of and a just respect for the functions of other citizens.

It is possible that the unifying basis of Protagoras' numerous theories was always his distinctive method of arguing. The tradition preserved by Diogenes Laertius (IX.51) tells us that Protagoras was the first to declare that in the case of every question there are two arguments opposed to each other, and that he used this supposed fact as a method of debate. We can expand this statement from other sources somewhat as follows: of the two arguments one will be positive, stating that something is the case, and the other will be negative, stating that something is not the case. In the light of the man–measure doctrine both of the opposing arguments will be true in virtue of their position in the world of appearances. But one view will, at least on certain occasions, be better than the other in that it promotes more desirable results. When one of the two contrary arguments is proposed, one that does not promote desirable effects, such an argument may seem to the ill-informed person to be the stronger of the two arguments. It is then the task of the wise man to make the weaker argument stronger so that it will prevail in competition with what then becomes the weaker argument. To do this is the function of the orator in a developed political society. It is also the function of the sophist as teacher to make the weaker argument stronger and to show others how to do this. An interesting application of this approach may perhaps be seen in Protagoras' detailed consideration of the nature of language. This, perhaps rather surprisingly, included a doctrine of the correct forms of linguistic expression. He seems to have made an analysis of sentences into narrative, questions, answers, commands, reported narrative, wishes and summonses. Aristotle tells us that he set out to correct ordinary Greek genders to bring usage into accord with the supposed 'real' gender of things and concepts. One may conjecture that this could be justified, while still keeping the basis of Protagoras' relativism, which was that it is better and more expedient for the genders of words to express the perceived genders of things around us. The whole question of the relation between words and things was of fundamental importance for all of the sophists, as far as we know, and it gives us the key to an understanding of the next figure to be considered here, namely Gorgias.

⚫ GORGIAS ⚫

Gorgias came from Leontinoi (modern Lentini), an Ionian colony in Sicily. He was born probably between 490 and 485 BC and he outlived Socrates, who died in 399 BC. The most famous single event in his life was his visit to Athens in 427 BC when he came as leader of a group of envoys from his native city in order to seek Athenian support for Leontinoi in its war with Syracuse. The requested alliance was secured after Gorgias had amazed the Athenian assembly by his rhetorical skill (DK 82 A 4). He also, perhaps after his Athenian visit, travelled extensively throughout the Greek world; he is recorded as speaking at Olympia, Argos, Delphi, and in Thessaly and Boeotia. But above all he taught pupils at Athens, for which teaching he received considerable sums of money. After his death he was honoured by the setting up of a golden statue of himself both at Delphi and at Olympia, for the latter of which it may be that the base survives to the present day.

In Sicily Gorgias had been a disciple of Empedocles, and his own doctrine of perception was clearly derived from that to be found in his master's poem. Plato devoted a whole dialogue, the *Gorgias*, to a discussion of his views on rhetoric, and Aristotle is recorded as having written an attack on Gorgias' doctrines, unfortunately no longer extant. We have the titles of some eleven writings attributed to Gorgias. Two speeches survive, apparently complete, and we have two detailed summaries of his treatise *On Nature*. It is on this work that his claims to a significant place in the history of philosophy must depend. One summary of it is preserved in some four (printed) pages of Greek in Sextus Empiricus, *Adversus Mathematicos* (VII.65–87). A second summary, with some significant differences from Sextus, is found in the third section of a piece of writing wrongly attributed to Aristotle, and so included in the Aristotelian corpus, under the title *On Melissus, Xenophanes and Gorgias* (*MXG* for short). Both the reconstruction of the argument in Gorgias' treatise and its interpretation are difficult and controversial. Scholarly discussion has essentially passed through three stages. First and for a very long period it was held that the work was simply not meant to be taken seriously. On this view Gorgias had written an extended parody or joke against philosophers. If it had any serious purpose it was to be seen as a purely rhetorical exercise in a method of argument which philosophers were supposed to have used and which simply made them ridiculous.[5] A second stage in the interpretation of Gorgias' treatise was reached by those who *were* prepared to take it seriously, and who took it as an elaborate attack on the philosophic doctrines of the Eleatics, and to a lesser extent the doctrines of certain physical philosophers among the pre-Socratics.[6] On this view the verb 'to be' in Gorgias' treatise has the meaning 'to exist'. The treatise itself is divided into three parts. The first part maintains that nothing exists, and this is established by arguing that 'not-being' does not exist, nor does 'being' exist. This is directed against the contention of Parmenides that only being exists. Gorgias by his arguments thus achieves a position of philosophic nihilism. Parmenides had destroyed the manifold world of appearances, but he kept the unitary world of true being. Gorgias completed the negative process begun by Parmenides by denying also the world of being, so that we are left simply with nothing.

This second stage in the interpretation of Gorgias' treatise had at least one advantage; it took the treatise seriously and did assign to Gorgias a place in the history of philosophy, albeit one that was negative and destructive. The second part of Gorgias' treatise on this view tried to ram home the argument by contending that even if something does exist it cannot be known by human beings. In the third part it is argued that even if something exists and is knowable, no knowledge or understanding of it can be communicated to another person.

But if this second approach is an improvement over the first, it now begins to seem that perhaps it does not go far enough. What is happening is that we are now beginning to have a certain reassessment of the uses of the verb 'to be' in ancient Greek in the light of certain modern doctrines. It is now common to make a clear distinction between 'is' as a copula followed by a predicate, as in '*X* is *Y*', and an existential sense where the verb has the meaning 'exists' as in '*X* exists'. But we can understand the claim that anything which exists must necessarily be *something*. From this it could follow that the existential use of the verb 'to be' is always to be understood as implying one or more predicates. This in turn has the effect of reducing the existential use to a special case of its use as a copula, namely one in which predicates are necessarily involved, but are not actually expressed. We are now also familiar with the view that in order to understand the function of language it is necessary to pay attention to two distinguishable things, namely what is the meaning of words and phrases, and to what if anything they refer. It is now beginning to seem to be the case that Gorgias may have been attempting to make use of just this distinction. On this view it is the relation between words and things with which he is concerned.[7] This, it can be argued, emerges in the second and third parts of his treatise, where he is arguing that it is not possible for a *thing* to be known by human beings because we are only indirectly in contact with objective things, either by perception or by the use of words to describe them. Likewise no knowledge or understanding of things can be conveyed from one person to another, since the only means we have of attempting to do this is by means of words. Words transfer only themselves and not the things to which they refer. I believe that much further work is needed before we can hope to arrive at an adequate interpretation of Gorgias' treatise. It does not matter if the account just outlined above is dismissed as simplistic. What would be of the greatest importance would be that Gorgias in his treatise was perhaps the first thinker to grapple directly with the problem with which we have come to be familiar for rather more than a hundred years, namely the distinction made by Frege between meaning and reference.

Plato in the *Meno* (76c–e) is quite explicit that Gorgias had a precise theory of perception based on Empedocles' doctrine of effluences from physical objects. Perception takes place when one or more effluences from a physical object fit exactly into pores or passages in the human body, and for them to do this they must be neither too large nor too small. It is such shapes or effluences which provide us, for example, with our perception of colours. Gorgias followed Empedocles in his contention that no one sense can perceive the objects of any other sense. We do not have precise details as to how Gorgias developed his theory of perception, but there is every reason to suppose that it was a matter of great importance to him.

The gulf between words and things was apparently also exploited by Gorgias in his teachings on rhetoric, both in theory and in the practice to be followed by speakers if they were to hope to be successful. At the practical level he stressed the importance of being able to speak briefly as well as at length according to the needs of the situation, and also the importance of appeals to the emotions as a means of persuasion. In addition he recommended an elaborate series of stylistic devices, listed by later writers under technical names such as antithesis, isokolon (two or more clauses with the same number of syllables), parison (parallelism of structure between clauses), and homoeoteleuton (a series of two or more clauses ending with the same words or with words that rhyme). At the more theoretical level he developed a doctrine of attention to the right time and situation, in Greek the *kairos*. Secondly he stressed the need to devote attention to things that are probable, and thirdly to arguments which are 'suitable' or appropriate. Finally he gave expression to a doctrine of 'justified deception'. This he used to give a theoretic basis for literature, above all for tragedy, and he seems to have applied this also to the practice of making speeches, contending that the man who indulges in this practice is acting with more right on his side in his use of myths and appeals to emotions than is the person who is not acting as a deceiver. But the end result is that the person who is deceived in this way is the wiser because a man who is not without experience in the reading of literature will let himself be won over by the pleasure of spoken words. Clearly the doctrine involved was highly technical, but the implication was probably that a man's view of the world around him is improved by the study of literature and the teaching he receives from the sophists.[8]

Gorgias' influence among his contemporaries was so extensive that he came close to establishing a school for those who came after him, not in the sense of a particular organization, but rather in that a number of thinkers and teachers continued to express ideas and doctrines clearly derived from him. These included Alcidamas of Elaia, Isocrates the orator, Licymnios of Chios, Meno of Larisa, Polus of Acragas who is an important character in Plato's *Gorgias*, and Protarchus of Athens, who is a key speaker in Plato's *Philebus*. Of special interest is the sophist Lycophron who was said to have been an associate of Gorgias. In addition to certain social and political doctrines concerning nobility of birth and its lack of any real basis in nature he is reported to have argued that the Greek verb for 'is' should be confined to existential cases, such as 'Socrates exists', and should not be extended to its use with a predicate, as in 'Socrates is white' or 'Socrates is two cubits in height' as this would have the effect of making the same thing both one (Socrates) and many (the various predicates) at the same time.

◆► PRODICUS ◄◆

Prodicus came from the island of Ceos in the Cyclades, where he was probably born before 460 BC, and he was still alive at the time of the death of Socrates. He came frequently to Athens, sometimes on official business for Ceos. On one occasion he gained a high reputation for a speech before the Council, and at other times he was involved in the teaching of young men, for which he received large sums of money. Plato records that Socrates had sent pupils to him for instruction before they were ready to come to Socrates himself (*Theaetetus* 152b). Like Gorgias he gave public display lectures for which the technical name was *Epideixeis*, and one of these, *On the Choice of Herakles*, was summarized by Xenophon, who puts it in the mouth of Socrates (*Memorabilia* II.1.21–34). It seems to have come from a work entitled *Hours* (*Hōrai*) which included encomia on other persons or characters as well as Herakles. He also wrote a treatise *On the Nature of Man*, and another on *The Correctness of Names*. In a separate work *On Nature* he called the four elements, earth, air, fire and water, all gods as well as the sun and moon, on the ground that they were the source of life for all things. But what made Prodicus famous among all the sophists was his treatment of language. For this we have no record of any actual written version, but it must at the very least have featured prominently in his lectures and in his teaching. Our fullest information about Prodicus' views on language comes to us from Plato's *Protagoras*, in which Prodicus figures as one of the sophists taking part in the discussion that resulted from the visit of Protagoras to the house of Callias. We have further information from other dialogues of Plato. It is clear that he developed a very precise doctrine about the need for an extremely accurate use of words. This involved distinguishing sharply between words that might seem to have similar meanings. The theoretical basis for these distinctions between words was made clearer to us by the discovery in 1941 of a papyrus commentary on *Ecclesiastes* which attributes to Prodicus the doctrine that it is not possible to contradict. The reason for this paradoxical contention is stated to be because only the person who speaks the truth makes a meaningful statement. The person who appears to contradict him is not in fact saying anything at all, and so in effect is not actually speaking. What this implies is that meaningful statements necessarily refer to something which is the case, while statements which appear to contradict such meaningful statements by denying that they are true, are themselves without meaning since they have nothing to which they can refer. This should probably be related to the doctrine ascribed to Prodicus by Alexander of Aphrodisias (DK 84 A 19), that in proper linguistic usage each word or phrase should be related to one thing only and to no other. In modern terms this amounts to the attribution to Prodicus of a referential theory of meaning.

Prodicus was famous also for his rationalizing account of the origins of religious beliefs. The details of exactly how he did this are unfortunately not clear, but he seems to have supposed that human beings began by personifying physical objects that were of use to them, so bread becomes Demeter and wine becomes Dionysus. Finally it may be stated that the pseudo-Platonic dialogue *Eryxias* credits Prodicus with a doctrine of the relativism of values, which I have argued else-where[9] may in fact be true for the historical Prodicus.

❧ HIPPIAS ❧

Hippias of Elis was a younger contemporary of Protagoras and he is depicted by Plato in the *Protagoras* as present along with other sophists at the house of Callias. The dramatic date for this is about 433 BC. He was apparently still alive at the death of Socrates in 399 BC. He travelled extensively as a professional sophist, making a famous visit to Sicily, and made a great deal of money. He claimed to be at home in all the learning of his day, and was credited with a large number of writings, both in prose and in verse in the forms of epics, dithyrambs and tragedies. His polymathy was no doubt aided by certain exceptional powers of memory. It appears that these were developed by special techniques which he also taught to others, and he was said to have been able to remember fifty names after a single hearing. In addition to his epideictic displays he was known to have been ready to teach astronomy, mathematics and geometry, genealogy, mythology and history, painting and sculpture, the functions of letters, syllables, rhythms and musical scales. Of particular importance for the history of Greek thought must have been his *synagōgē* which, it appears, was a collection of passages, stories and pieces of information from earlier writers both Greek and non-Greek. It thus stands at the beginnings of the doxographic approach to Greek thought, above all to the pre-Socratics, and it probably underlay to some extent both Plato's and Aristotle's schematized views of their predecessors. Another work of great importance was his list of victors at the Olympic games based on local written records, which provided a foundation for subsequent Greek historical chronology. The collection of Plato's writings includes two dialogues directly concerned with Hippias, the *Hippias Major* and the *Hippias Minor*. The authenticity of each of these dialogues has been questioned by modern scholars, probably wrongly at least in the case of the *Hippias Major*. But in either case, they provide evidence which there is good reason for us to accept. Hippias is presented throughout as incapable of standing up to the questioning of Socrates. It has been suggested that Hippias came close to personifying the type Plato most abhorred as a generic sophist. None the less his intellectual versatility is clearly represented, even though it is always dismissed as accompanied by superficiality.

When we turn to consider the philosophic doctrines associated with Hippias we are confronted with an initial difficulty. We do not know for certain whether Hippias held any overall or unifying basis for his polymathy. But there *is* some evidence for an overall philosophical position given in the *Hippias Major* (301b–e) where reference is made to a 'continuous theory of being'. This is apparently based on the view that there is something continuous that is carried through classes as well as through the physical bodies of things without interruption, and this is wrongly divided or cut up by the use of words. The implication here is that language cannot represent the true nature of the external world.

That he did have a doctrine of some kind about nature is supported by what we are told about him in Plato's *Protagoras*, where he contrasted law and nature; he favoured nature against law, which acts as a tyrant and compels human beings to do or submit to many things which are contrary to nature. He further argued that like is akin to like by nature, and called for men to draw the logical consequences from this. One of these consequences is that some or even all men are alike by nature, and as a result we should recognize as friends and kinsmen those men who are alike by nature. Unfortunately the context in Plato (*Protagoras* 337d–e) does not make it clear exactly what he supposed was the range of the likeness to be found in men. If, as is possible, he held the view that it is all men who are alike by nature he would then be seen as an advocate of the doctrine of the unity of mankind. But other scholars have supposed that he may have been confining his remarks to Greeks only, and so to have been preaching simply pan-Hellenism. An even more restricted interpretation is possible. What, according to Plato, Hippias is actually saying is that he considers those whom he is addressing, namely 'you', as kinsmen and intimates and fellow citizens by nature, not by law, on the basis that like is akin to like by nature. We who are the wisest of the Greeks, no doubt meaning by this sophists, should accordingly refrain from quarrelling with each other like the basest of men. This suggests that he is advocating a recognition of the unity of wise men or scholars, as distinct from ordinary people. The people to whom he is speaking are those who 'know the nature of things' and are the wisest people among the Greeks. In that case what he is advocating is the unity of Greek scholars rather than the unity of mankind as a whole, or perhaps even only the unity of sophists within the Sophistic Movement.

However that may be, the actual contributions made by Hippias to Greek scholarship were by no means inconsiderable. In mathematics he is credited with a history of Greek geometry after Thales. When

Proclus came to write his history of geometry he drew on a work by Eudemus of Rhodes, not now extant, and he makes it clear that at least some of Eudemus' information about the period before Plato was derived from Hippias. In addition Hippias was credited with his own attempted solution to the problem of the squaring of the circle. This consisted in the invention of the curve later known as the quadratrix, the name for which may have been derived from Hippias' own expression, which we know from Proclus' commentary on Euclid (DK 86 B 21)[10] was *grammē tetragōnizousa*.

There was also a practical side to Hippias' activities, based on his doctrine of the ideal of self-sufficiency in the individual. This ideal he put into practice for himself; he appeared at Olympia on one occasion when all his own clothing and equipment had been made by himself. In particular, according to the author of the *Hippias Minor* (368b–c), he had manufactured for himself his own engraved finger ring and another seal as well, then a strigil, an oil flask, his own sandals, cloak, tunic and Persian-style girdle.

❧ ANTIPHON ❧

The expression 'Antiphon the sophist' is currently used by many scholars as a means of identifying the author of three works, namely *On Concord*, *On Truth* and a *Politikos*, to which is sometimes added a work *On the Interpretation of Dreams*. But in the manuscripts that have come down to us under the general title of the Attic Orators we have a set of speeches attributed to an Athenian, Antiphon of Rhamnous, who is often referred to as Antiphon the orator. This Antiphon was condemned to death and executed in 411 BC, after the overthrow at Athens of the oligarchy of the Four Hundred, of which he was a member (Thucydides VIII.68). We are confronted with a major and as yet unresolved question, namely whether Antiphon the sophist is to be identified with Antiphon the orator or not. The evidence is conflicting and uncertain. But according to one tradition an Antiphon who was a writer of tragedies was put to death at the court of Dionysius I of Syracuse some time between 405 and 367 BC (Philostratus *Lives of the Sophists*, I.15.3). If this was Antiphon the sophist, then clearly he was not the same as Antiphon the orator. But he just may have been a third Antiphon, to be added to the other two in the historical tradition.

From the point of view of the history of philosophy it is probably allowable for us to sidestep this question; it is the four works of the supposed Antiphon the sophist which alone are of real interest from a philosophic point of view. These indeed were not regarded as important

before 1915, when his reputation was transformed by the publication
in the collection of the Oxyrhynchus Papyri of two quite large fragments of the work *On Truth*. A further fragment was added in 1922.
Then in 1984 a small further fragment of fewer than 200 scattered
letters was published with a dramatic result since it shows that the
standard supplements of the fragments known previously, made by
Wilamowitz and included in the standard edition of the fragments in
Diels–Kranz (87 B 44) are in fact incorrect. They were based on an
overall view of Antiphon's position which can now in all probability
be seen to involve at least an element of distortion.

The first surviving section of *On Truth* begins

> Justice then consists in not transgressing the laws and customs of
> the city in which one is a citizen. So a man would employ
> justice best in his own interests if he were to regard the laws as
> important when witnesses are present, and when they are not
> he were to regard the demands of nature as of greater importance.

The opposition between law and the requirements of human nature as
sources of values was widely discussed throughout the sophistic period,
and some have argued that it can be taken as a typical or even as a
defining doctrine for the movement as a whole. But Antiphon's preference for nature over law involves a further concept, that of benefit or
advantage to each individual man, and this leaves open the question
whether exceptionally some laws may actually be of benefit to our
natures. In that case nature could become a norm for laws. Support
for this interpretation may be drawn from the surviving fragments
which we have from the second treatise of Antiphon, namely *On
Concord*, which seems clearly enough to be arguing for the value of
harmony or concord both in society and within the personality of an
individual man. This raises the question of how, if at all, it is possible
to reconcile the doctrine of *On Truth* with that of *On Concord*. The
simplest answer is also the most likely to be correct, namely that an
attack on traditional justice and on traditional societies is perfectly
compatible with the promulgation of the ideal of a better and radically
different society based on 'true' values and (true) justice. Such arguments could be used to support the position of an oligarch at Athens,
and would be understandable if Antiphon the sophist was in fact the
same person as Antiphon the orator. But they need not imply any
oligarchical political stance, as they are also compatible with the view
that it is the function of a democracy so to revise the laws of a
city that they are brought into accord with nature.

Two further works are possibly relevant here. *On the Interpretation of Dreams* seems to have argued that dreams cannot be used
directly to foretell the future, but require rational interpretation first,

though they *can* be used for predictive purposes. Finally mention must be made of the work with the intriguing title *The Art of Avoiding Distress*. In the later doxographic tradition this is attributed to Antiphon the orator, but it would seem rather to have affinities with what we know of the psychological interests of Antiphon the sophist, assuming always that there were two Antiphons and not simply one. This piece of writing outlined an extension of the treatment provided by doctors for those who are ill. Antiphon was said to have set up a kind of clinic functioning as a citizen's advice bureau or modern style Samaritan Service in a dwelling-place near the market in Corinth. In a notice in front of the building he claimed that help could be provided to those in distress by discussing matters with them, and, through talking to them, finding out the causes of their illness (DK 87 A 6). If this tradition is sound it seems more likely to be true of the sophist rather than the orator, since the latter is less likely to have functioned away from Athens. A further statement of psychiatric interest is that preserved by Stobaeus (DK 87 B 57), namely that 'illness is a holiday for those who are cowards, for such people do not go out into the world to undertake activities'.

Among other aspects of Antiphon's interests should be mentioned the brief references, which are all that survive, to discussions about the nature of time, the functioning of the sun and the moon, the bitterness of the sea and the formation of the surface of the earth, the behaviour of bile and other physiological processes, and an attempt to solve the problem of the squaring of the circle by continually doubling the number of sides in an inscribed regular polygon (DK 87 B 26–8, 29–32 and 13).

❧ LESSER SOPHISTS ❧

Thrasymachus of Chalcedon in Bithynia was well known as a sophist who travelled from city to city and claimed fees for his teaching. A number of writings are attributed to him, but we know virtually nothing of their contents. He appeared as a character in a lost play by Aristophanes, the *Daitaleis* performed in 427 BC. But his fame springs for us from his confrontation with Socrates in the first book of Plato's *Republic*. There he puts forward the view that justice is the interest of the stronger, and he infers from this that justice accordingly is normally to be understood as consisting in seeking the interest of some one or more persons other than oneself. Accordingly justice is folly, the only reasonable course being always to pursue one's own interest. Clearly Plato regarded this as an important if wrong-headed sophistic contention, and in a sense the whole of the rest of the *Republic* after the first book is concerned to give us Plato's refutation of Thrasymachus.

Three further characters who appear in Plato's dialogues are Callicles in the *Gorgias*, and Euthydemus and Dionysodorus in the *Euthydemus*. According to Plato, Callicles came from the deme of Acharnae in Attica, and it is at his house in Athens that his friend Gorgias is staying at the opening of the *Gorgias*. Like Thrasymachus Callicles is presented as approving actions which the world calls unjust, and he approves of them because they express for him a higher justice, the justice of nature. Such justice he goes so far as to call the law of nature, in what is apparently the first occurrence of the phrase which was to become of such importance in the history of European thought. The importance of what Callicles has to say in the dialogue can hardly be questioned. But it should be mentioned that modern scholars have expressed doubts both as to whether he was a real person and if so as to whether he should be classed as a sophist.[11]

Euthydemus and Dionysodorus were brothers and came originally from Chios. In Plato's *Euthydemus* they are addressed as sophists (271 CI) and are said to have had many pupils. Euthydemus' most distinctive doctrine is perhaps that referred to in Plato's *Cratylus* (386d), namely that all things belong equally to all things at the same time and always. The most likely explanation of this statement is that which takes it as meaning that all things possess all attributes together and all the time. If this is what he is saying, then it would seem to provide an underlying basis for Protagoras' man–measure doctrine. All perceived qualities are in fact always present in perceived objects, and this is shown by the fact that the verbal attribution of any quality to any thing is always possible. Words only have meaning because they refer to what is actually the case. This would explain the doctrine attributed to Dionysodorus (*Euthydemus* 284c5) according to which no one says things that are false: all statements that anyone can make are true because all attributes are necessarily actually present in the things to which reference is being made. Consequently it is not possible to make genuinely contradictory statements, since contradiction would be asserting that one statement is true and the other which conflicts with it is false.

Three names in addition to the above may be mentioned in passing. Critias, who was a first cousin of Plato's mother, was one of the Thirty Tyrants who held power at Athens at the end of the Peloponnesian war. He was classed as a sophist by Philostratus, and has regularly been listed among the sophists ever since, down to the present day. He wrote tragedies, in at least one of which he included a rationalizing account of belief in the gods. But he is not known to have been a teacher, and he should accordingly in all probability be excluded from the list of sophists. The opposite is the case with the thinker Antisthenes of Athens who came to be regarded as the founder of the Cynic sect. As a result he has usually been discussed by modern writers under the general heading of the Cynic movement. But his claims to have been the founder of this movement are subject to serious doubt, and there is fairly convincing evidence that he should rather be classed as a sophist.[12] He lived a long life, from the middle of the fifth century long into the fourth century BC. We know from Aristotle (*Metaphysics* 1024b26) that he held the two distinctive sophistic doctrines that we have already mentioned several times, namely that it is not possible to contradict and that it is not possible to say what is false.

The final name to be mentioned here is that of Socrates. Although presented by Plato as the arch-enemy of the sophists and all they stood for, it is none the less true that Socrates can only be understood if he is seen as a member of the world in which he lived. Socrates had a great influence on the young men who became his disciples, even though he did not accept any payment from them for his teaching. Two things at least emerge clearly from what Plato has to tell us: Socrates had begun early in his life with a critical interest in the problems of physical science (*Phaedo* 96a–99d), and he also deployed a distinctive method of argument which involved the refutation of unacceptable propositions and the promotion of acceptable answers to the question 'What is the correct account to be given as to what is x?' above all when x is a moral or political concept. This became famous as the Socratic method of *Elenchos*, and this alone would be sufficient to justify us in considering him as an active member of the Sophistic Movement, in fact as an unpaid sophist.

In addition to named sophists it is necessary to discuss a number of anonymous sophistic writings, of which several survive, at least in summary form. The first of these is known as the *Dissoi Logoi*, the title being taken from the first two words of the opening paragraph, which are repeated in the next three chapters. The text is found at the end of the main manuscripts of Sextus Empiricus, and it is written in a dialect which is a form of literary Doric. This has suggested to some that it may have originated in Sicily or southern Italy, but there is no other positive evidence for this. It has commonly been supposed that it was composed soon after 400 BC on the basis of the reference in I.8–10 (DK 90) where the victory which the Spartans won over the Athenians and their allies is spoken as a most recent event. But this dating is quite uncertain and others have argued for a much later date.

The pattern of arguments followed throughout the treatise is established in the first chapter where we are told that 'some say that good is one thing and bad is another thing, while others say that they are the same, and that for the same person it is on one occasion good and on another occasion bad.' This formulation is potentially ambiguous. On one view to say that good and bad are the same thing might be taken to say that the two terms are identical in meaning, or it might mean that any one thing will be both good and bad either simultaneously or at different times and in different relationships. It is however the second interpretation which should be preferred: the meanings of the two terms are always different and it is the way in which they are to be applied as attributes to particular things or situations which varies. What we are explicitly told is that as the name or term used differs so does the thing. This is repeated three times in subsequent sections, in one of which (II.1) 'thing' is expressed by *sōma* or physical body. There seems no doubt that what we are being confronted with is the familiar sophistic problem of varying predicates attached to physical objects in the external world. The whole approach of the *Dissoi Logoi* amounts to an application of the sophistic doctrine of relativism. After good and bad in the first section the same treatment is applied to the terms for beautiful and ugly, then to just and unjust, the truth and falsehood of propositions, and the question of the teachability or otherwise of wisdom and virtue. After the discussion of these terms the treatise concludes with arguments that election by lot is a bad method of election in democracies, that the art of the man who is skilled in argument (and so has been trained by a sophist) is the same as the art of the statesman, and that a developed use of memory is essential for intellectual wisdom and its application in the conduct of human affairs.

A second anonymous treatise is known as the *Anonymus Iamblichi*. This was identified in 1889 when Friedrich Blass showed that some ten pages of printed Greek text in the *Protrepticus* of Iamblichus were taken apparently virtually unaltered from an otherwise unknown piece of writing of the fifth or fourth centuries BC. Attempts to assign it to one of the known sophists of the period are now generally regarded as unsuccessful. But the sophistic origin of the material is not in question. It provides a manual of how to succeed in life. This is dependent on the achievement of *aretē* or virtue, which requires both natural qualities and efforts maintained over a period of years. When achieved, human *aretē* is found to have involved acting in accordance with law and justice in order to benefit as many persons as possible. Respect for law brings with it good government, which benefits all greatly, and removes the danger of tyranny. The treatise thus provides a kind of complementary antithesis to the perhaps more famous sophistic doctrine which would place the claims of nature above those of human laws. In fact, according to the *Anonymus* it is not the man who scorns vulgar justice who is going to succeed, it is rather the man who exercises control over himself and co-operates with the society in which he lives.

By way of conclusion mention may be made of a further series of anonymous works which various modern scholars have supposed should be attributed to sophistic writers, but for the *content* of which we have only rather slight information. These may be listed as *On Music* published from a Hibeh papyrus in 1906; a work entitled *Nomima Barbarika* concerned with the contrasting customs of different peoples; *On Laws*, consisting of materials extracted in 1924 from Demosthenes, *Oratio* XXV; *On Citizenship* which actually survives among the works attributed to Herodes Atticus in the second century AD, and a supposed treatise *On Magnificence* (as a quality of persons), which may have some relationship with the *Dissoi Logoi*. Sophistic doctrines and materials are to be found in many places in the Hippocratic corpus, particularly in the treatises *On Art*, *On Ancient Medicine*, *On Breathing* and *De Locis in Homine*. To these may be added the pseudo-Xenophontine *Constitution of the Athenians*, which cannot have been written by Xenophon, and seems to have been put together partly under the influence of the doctrine of opposing arguments developed by Protagoras.

 NOTES

1 Kerferd [7.15], 16.
2 Kerferd [7.15], ch. 6.
3 For this view of the sophists see the description by H. Sidgwick, *Journal of Philology* 4 (1872); 289.
4 For view (1) see A. E. Taylor, *Plato, The Man and his Work*, 4th edn, 1937: 326. For (2) see most recently Guthrie [2.13] III: 184, and for (3) F. Cornford, *Plato's Theory of Knowledge*, London, 1935, and most recently K. von Fritz, in Pauly-Wissowa [see 5.34], s.v. Protagoras, 916f.
5 So, for example, Gomperz [7.13], 1–38.
6 So G. Grote, *History of Greece* VIII, (London, John Murray, 1883), pp. 172–4.
7 See [7.28].
8 For fuller discussion see W. J. Verdenius, in [7.9], 116–28.
9 Kerferd [7.31].
10 272.3 in Proclus, *In Primum Euclidis Elementorum Librum Commentarii*, ed. G. Friedlein, Leipzig, Teubner, 1871 p.272–3.
11 For discussion, see Dodds [7.24], 12–15.
12 So by Guthrie [2.13] III: 304ff.

BIBLIOGRAPHY

Original Language Editions

7.1 DK [2.2], vol. II, C. *Ältere Sophistik*, sections 79–90. (Cited as DK with section number, e.g. DK 80 for Protagoras.)

7.2 Untersteiner, M. *Sofisti, testimonianze et frammenti*, fasc. I–IV, Florence, La Nuova Italia, 1949–62, Fasc. I–III 2nd edn 1962–7. With Italian translation.

Translations

7.3 Dumont, J. P. *Les sophistes, fragments et témoignages*, Paris, Presses Universitaires, 1969. French.

7.4 Sprague, R. K. *The Older Sophists: A Complete Translation*, Columbia, SC, University of South Carolina Press, 1972, repr. 1990. English.

Bibliographies

7.5 Classen, C. J. (ed.) *Sophistik* (Wege der Forschung 187), Darmstadt, Wissenschaftliche Buchgesellschaft, 1976, Bibliographie 641–70. New edition 'Bibliographie der Sophistik', in *Elenchos* 6 (1985): 75–140 (down to 1985).

7.6 —— 'Die greichische Sophistik in der Forschung der letzten dreissig Jahre', *Lampas, Tijdschrift von nederlandse classici* 8 (1975): 344–63.

Collections of articles

7.7. Boudouris, K. (ed.) *The Sophistic Movement*, Athens, Athenian Library of Philosophy, 1984.

7.8 Classen [7.5].

7.9 Kerferd, G. B. (ed.) *The Sophists and their Legacy* (*Hermes* Einzelschriften 44), Wiesbaden, Steiner, 1981.

Discussions of the Sophistic Movement as a Whole

7.10 Bett, R. 'The sophists and relativism', *Phronesis* 34 (1989): 139–69.

7.11 de Romilly, J. *Les Grands Sophistes dans l'Athènes de Périclès*, Paris, de Fallois, 1988. English translation, Oxford, Clarendon Press, 1992.

7.12 Dupréel, E. *Les sophistes, Protagoras, Gorgias, Prodicus, Hippias*, Neuchatel, Du Griffon, 1948, repr. 1978.

7.13 Gomperz, H. *Sophistik und Rhetorik, das Bildungsideal des eu legein*, Leipzig, Teubner, 1912, repr. Stuttgart, Teubner, 1965.

7.14 Guthrie [2.13], vol. III, part 1. Published separately as *The Sophists*, Cambridge, Cambridge University Press, 1971. French translation, Paris, 1976.

7.15 Kerferd, G. B. *The Sophistic Movement*, Cambridge, Cambridge University Press, 1981. Italian translation, Bologna, Il Mulino, 1987.

7.16 Levi, A. *Storia della sofistica*, Naples, 1966.

7.17 Untersteiner, M. *I sofisti*, Turin, Einaudi, 1949, 2nd edn, Milan, Lanpugnani Sigri, 2 vols, 1967. English translation, Oxford, Blackwell, 1954. French translation, Paris, Vrin, 2 vols, 1993.

Individual Sophists

Protagoras

7.18 Burnyeat, M. F., 'Conflicting appearances', *Proceedings of the British Academy* 65 (1975): 69–111.

7.19 —— 'Protagoras and self-refutation in later Greek philosophy', *Philosophical Review* 85 (1976): 312–26.

7.20 Kerferd, G. B. 'Plato's account of the relativism of Protagoras', *Durham University Journal* 42 (1949): 20–6.

7.21 —— 'Protagoras' doctrine of justice and virtue in the *Protagoras* of Plato', *Journal of Hellenic Studies* 73 (1953): 42–5.

7.22 Taylor, C. C. W. *Plato*, Protagoras, trans. with notes, Oxford, Clarendon Press, 1976, 2nd (rev.) edn, 1991.

Gorgias

7.23 Cassin [2.61].

7.24 Dodds, E. R. *Plato* Gorgias, a revised text with introduction and commentary, Oxford, Clarendon Press, 1959.

7.25 Howiger, R. J. *Untersuchungen zu Gorgias' Schrift über das Nichtseiende*, Berlin, Heiner, 1973.

7.26 Kahn [4.32].

7.27 Kerferd, G. B. 'Gorgias on nature or that which is not', *Phronesis* 1 (1955–6): 3–25.

7.28 —— 'Meaning and reference: Gorgias on the relation between language and reality', in Boudouris [7.7]: 215–22.

7.29 Morgan, K. A. 'Socrates and Gorgias at Delphi and Olympia', *Classical Quarterly* NS 44 (1994): 375–86.

Prodicus

7.30 Binder, G. and Liesenborghs, L. 'Eine Zuweisung der Sentenz *ouk estin antilegein* an Prodikos von Keos', *Museum Helveticum* 23 (1966): 37–43.

7.31 Kerferd, G. B. 'The relativism of Prodicus', *Bulletin of the John Rylands Library* 37 (1954): 249–56.

7.32 Rankin, H. D. 'Ouk estin antilegein', in Kerferd [7.9]: 25–37.

Hippias

7.33 Snell [2.57].
7.34 Patzer, B. *Der Sophist Hippias als Philosophiehistoriker*, Freiburg, Alber, 1986.
7.35 Woodruff, P. *Plato* Hippias Major, ed. with commentary, Oxford, Blackwell, 1982.

Antiphon

Text
7.36 *Oxyrhynchus Papyri*, London, Egypt Exploration Society, vol. XI (1915), nr. 1364, vol. XV (1922), nr. 1797, vol. LI (1984), nr. 3647. Latter discussed by J. Barnes 'New light on Antiphon', *Polis* 7 (1987): 2–5.
7.37 *Corpus dei papiri filosofici greci e latini*, Florence, Casa Editrice Leo S. Olschki, vol. I.1, 1989, Autori noti nr. 17, Antipho.
Studies
7.38 Bignone, E. *Studi sul pensiero antico*, Naples, Loffredo, 1938: 1–226.
7.39 Kerferd, G. B. 'The moral and political doctrines of Antiphon the sophist', *Proceedings of the Cambridge Philological Society* 184 (1956): 26–32.
7.40 Morrison, J. S. 'Antiphon', *Proceedings of the Cambridge Philological Society* 187 (1961): 49–58.

Thrasymachus

7.41 Kerferd, G. B. 'The doctrines of Thrasymachus in Plato's *Republic*', *Durham University Journal* 40 (1947): 19–27; repr. in Classen [7.5]: 545–63.
7.42 Maguire, J. P. 'Thrasymachus – or Plato?', *Phronesis* 16 (1971): 142–63; repr. in Classen [7.5]: 564–88.

Callicles

7.43 Dodds [7.24], appendix 'Socrates, Callicles and Nietzsche', 387–91.

Euthydemus and Dionysodorus

Text (in translation)
Sprague [7.4]: 294–301.
Studies
7.44 Chance, T. H. *Plato's Euthydemus – Analysis of What is and is not Philosophy*, Berkeley, Calif., and London, University of California Press, 1992.
7.45 Hawtrey, R. S. W. *Commentary on Plato's Euthydemus*, Philadelphia, Pa., American Philological Society, 1981.
7.46 Sprague, R. K. *Plato's Use of Fallacy, A Study of the* Euthydemus *and Some Other Dialogues*, London, Routledge, 1962: 1–11.

Antisthenes

7.47 Brancacci, A. OIKEIOS LOGOS, *la filosofia di Antistene*, Naples, Bibliopolis, 1990.

7.48 Guthrie [2.13], vol. III: 304–11.

7.49 Rankin, H. D. *Sophists, Socratics and Cynics*, London, Croom Helm: 219–28.

Dissoi Logoi

7.50 Boot, F. 'The philosophical position of the author of the Dissoi Logoi', *Philosophical Inquiry* 4 (1982): 118–23.

7.51 Conley, T. M. 'Dating the so-called Dissoi Logoi, a cautionary note', *Ancient Philosophy* 5 (1985): 59–65.

7.52 Robinson, T. M. *Contrasting Arguments* – an edition of the Dissoi Logoi, New York, Arno Press, 1979. Reviewed by C. J. Classen, *Phoenix* 36 (1982): 83–7.

The Anonymus Iamblichi

7.53 Cole, A. T. 'The Anonymus Iamblichi and his place in Greek political thought', *Harvard Studies in Classical Philology* 65 (1961): 127–63.

7.54 Levi [7.16], ch. 6, first published under the name D. Viale 'L'anonimo di Giamblicho', *Sophia* 9 (1941): 321–30. German translation by C. J. Classen, in Classen [7.5]: 612–26.

CHAPTER 8

Greek arithmetic, geometry and harmonics: Thales to Plato

Ian Mueller

❧❖❧

❧ INTRODUCTION: PROCLUS' ❧ HISTORY OF GEOMETRY

In a famous passage in Book VII of the *Republic* starting at 521c, Socrates proposes to inquire about the studies (*mathēmata*) needed to train the young people who will become leaders of the ideal *polis* he is describing, that is, the subjects that will draw their souls away from the sensible world of becoming to the intelligible world of being and the dialectical study of the Forms. Socrates goes on to discuss five such studies: arithmetic, plane geometry, solid geometry, astronomy and harmonics. The purpose of this chapter is to discuss some important aspects of the development of these mathematical sciences other than astronomy in the Greek world down to the later fourth century.

As will become clear, discussion of this topic involves a wide range of interrelated historical, philosophical, and philological questions on many of which opinion still remains sharply divided. My goal here is more to explain what the questions are than to offer answers to them. As a framework for my discussion I shall use a passage from Proclus' commentary on Book I of Euclid's *Elements* ([8.74], 64.7ff.), which is sometimes referred to as the Eudemian summary, on the assumption that its ultimate source is Eudemus' history of geometry written *c.*300.[1] I shall simply call it Proclus' history. Proclus begins by mentioning the origin of geometry in Egyptian land-surveying and the origin of arithmetic in Phoenician commercial activity. He then turns to the accomplishments of the Greeks, beginning with the proverbial Thales, standardly supposed to have flourished *c.*585, of whom he says:

271

Thales, who had traveled to Egypt, was the first to introduce geometry into Greece. He made many discoveries himself and taught his successors the principles for many other discoveries, treating some things in a more universal way, others more in terms of perception.

([8.74], 65.7–11)

After a perplexing reference to an otherwise unknown brother of the poet Stesichorus, Proclus turns to Pythagoras, standardly supposed to have been born sometime between c.570 and c.550:

Pythagoras transformed the philosophy of geometry into the form of a liberal education, searching in an upward direction for its principles and investigating its theorems immaterially and intellectually. He discovered the doctrine of the irrationals and the construction of the cosmic figures. After him Anaxagoras of Clazomenae applied himself to many questions in geometry, and so did Oinopides of Chios, who was a little younger than Anaxagoras. Both these men are mentioned by Plato in the *Lovers* [132a5–b3] as having got a reputation in mathematics. Following them, Hippocrates of Chios, who discovered how to square lunes, and Theodorus of Cyrene became eminent in geometry. For Hippocrates wrote a book of elements, the first of those of whom we have any record who did so.

([8.74], 65.7–66.8)

At this point Proclus turns to the age of Plato, so that the material just described represents his whole history of sixth- and fifth-century geometry. Anaxagoras is thought to have flourished c.450. Our main source for Theodorus is Plato's *Theaetetus*, in which he is represented as an approximate contemporary of Socrates. We should then assign Oinopides and Hippocrates to the last half of the fifth century. I will discuss fifth- and sixth-century mathematical science in the second part of this chapter. As Proclus' history suggests, we have a clearer idea of specifically scientific work for the late fifth century than we do for the earlier period, for much of which we depend on reports on the quasi-legendary Thales and Pythagoras.

Proclus' history is much more detailed for the fourth century. He focuses on Plato and his associates. A natural inference from what he says would be that all mathematical work in the fourth century was ultimately inspired by Plato. I quote only the material from Proclus which mentions the three figures whom I will be discussing in Part One of this chapter: Archytas, Theaetetus and Eudoxus:

After these people Plato made a great advance in geometry and the other mathematical sciences because of his concern for

them. . . . At this time . . . Archytas of Tarentum and Theaetetus
of Athens also lived; these people increased the number of
theorems and gave them a more scientific organization . . .
Eudoxus of Cnidus, who was . . . one of those in Plato's circle,
was the first to increase the number of general theorems; he
added another three proportionals to the three [already in use];
and, applying the method of analysis, he increased the number
of propositions concerning the section, which Plato had first
investigated.

([8.74], 66.8–67.8)

The last associate of Plato mentioned by Proclus is a Philip of Mende,
standardly assumed to be Philip of Opus.[2] Proclus concludes his history
when he introduces Euclid:

Those who have written histories bring the development of the
science up to this point. Euclid is not much younger than these
people; he brought the elements together, and he gave an order
to many propositions of Eudoxus and perfected many of
Theaetetus's; moreover, he gave irrefutable proofs to propositions
which had been demonstrated rather loosely by his predecessors.

([8.74], 66.8–68.10)

The chronology of Archytas, Theaetetus and Eudoxus is very obscure,
but a certain consensus has emerged, based importantly on assumptions
about the relationships among their mathematical achievements. Theaetetus is thought to have died in 369 before he was fifty. Eudoxus is said
to have lived 53 years; his death year is now generally put around the
time of Plato's (348–7) or shortly thereafter. Archytas is thought to be
an approximate contemporary of Plato, and so born in the 420s. The
important issue is not the exact dates, but the assumed intellectual
ordering: Archytas, Theaetetus, Eudoxus.

◄◄ PART ONE: THE FOURTH CENTURY ►►

(1) The Contents of Euclid's Elements

The oldest Greek scientific text relevant to arithmetic, geometry, and
solid geometry is Euclid's *Elements*. I give a brief description of its
contents. Although the proofs of Books I and II make use of the
possibility of drawing a circle with a given radius, the propositions are
all concerned with straight lines and rectilineal angles and figures. The
focus of Book III is the circle and its properties, and in Book IV Euclid
treats rectilineal figures inscribed in or circumscribed about circles. In

Books I–IV no use is made of the concept of proportionality (x:y :: z:w) and in consequence none – or virtually none – is made of similarity. It seems clear that Euclid chose to postpone the introduction of proportion, even at the cost of making proofs more complicated than they need to have been. Indeed, he sometimes proves essentially equivalent propositions, first independently of the concept of proportion and then – after he has introduced the concept – using it. Moreover, sometimes the proportion-free proof looks like a reworked version of the proof using proportion.[3]

Book V is a logical *tour de force* in which Euclid gives a highly abstract definition of proportionality for what he calls magnitudes (*megethē*) and represents by straight lines. The essential content of the definition may be paraphrased as follows:

> V, def. 5. x:y :: z:w if and only if whenever a multiple m·x is greater than (equal to or less than) a multiple n·y, m·z is greater than (equal to or less than) n·w, and (V, def. 7) x:y > z:w if for some m and n m·x > n·y and m·z ⩽ n·w.

Euclid proceeds to prove a number of important laws of proportionality, e.g., alternation (V.16: if x:y :: z:w, then x:z :: y:w) using a strictly formal reduction to the definition and to basic properties of multiplication and size comparison. In Book VI Euclid applies these laws to plane geometric objects.

Geometry disappears at the end of Book VI when Euclid turns to arithmetic, the subject of VII–IX. Logically these three books are completely independent of the first six. In them Euclid uses a notion of proportionality specific to numbers, i.e., positive integers, and proves for numbers laws of proportionality already proven for magnitudes in Book V.

In Book X there is a kind of unification of arithmetic and geometry. Euclid distinguishes between commensurable and incommensurable magnitudes, again represented by straight lines, and proves:

> X.5–8. Two magnitudes are commensurable if and only if they have the ratio of a number to a number.

I shall briefly discuss the proof of these propositions at the end of section 5, but in the immediate discussion I shall treat this equivalence as something which can be taken for granted as well known to Greek mathematicians of the fourth and perhaps even fifth century. The bulk of Book X is given over to an elaborate classification of certain 'irrational' (*alogos*) straight lines.[4] Euclid proves the 'irrationality' of a number of straight lines, the most important being:

the medial, the side of a square equal to a rectangle with incommensurable 'rational' sides;

the binomial, the sum of two incommensurable 'rational' straight lines;

the apotome, the difference of two incommensurable 'rational' straight lines.

Book XI covers a great deal of elementary solid geometry quite rapidly; by contrast with his procedure in Books I – IV and VI, Euclid appears willing to use proportionality whenever he thinks it simplifies his argumentation. Book XII is characterized by the method used in establishing its principal results, the so-called method of exhaustion. The method of exhaustion is, in fact, a rigorous technique of indefinitely closer approximations to a given magnitude. It depends on what is traditionally called the axiom of Archimedes or Archimedean condition. Euclid purports to prove a form of the 'axiom' in:

X.1. Two unequal magnitudes being set out, if from the greater there be subtracted a magnitude greater than its half, and from that which is left a magnitude greater than its half, and if this process be repeated continually, there will be left some magnitude which will be less than the lesser magnitude set out.

Most of the results proved in Book XII concern solids, but the first and simplest, XII.2, establishes that circles C, C' are to one another as the squares $sq(d)$ and $sq(d')$ on their diameters d and d' (XII.2). To prove this Euclid first shows (XII.1) that if P and P' are similar polygons inscribed in C and C', then P:P' :: $sq(d):sq(d')$. He then argues indirectly by assuming that C is not to C' as $sq(d)$ is to $sq(d')$, but that for some plane figure C* which is, say, smaller than C', C:C* :: $sq(d):sq(d')$. He inscribes in C' successively larger polygons P_1', P_2', ... (see Figure 8.1) until a P_n' of greater area than C* is reached, and then inscribes a similar polygon P_n in C. By XII.1, $P_n:P_n'$ :: $sq(d):sq(d^1)$, so that C:C* :: $P_n:P_n'$, and C:P_n :: C*:P_n'. But this is impossible since C is greater than P_n and C* is less than P_n'.

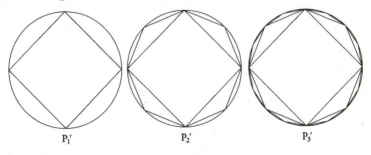

P_1' $\qquad\qquad$ P_2' $\qquad\qquad$ P_3'

Figure 8.1

275

In book XIII Euclid shows in XIII.13 – 17 how to construct each of the five 'cosmic figures' or regular solids, the triangular pyramid contained by four equilateral triangles, the octahedron contained by eight such triangles, the icosahedron contained by twenty, the cube contained by six squares, and the dodecahedron contained by twelve regular pentagons. In XIII.13 – 17 Euclid also characterizes the relationship between the edge e of the solid and the diameter d of the circumscribed sphere. For triangular pyramid, cube, and octahedron the results are simply stated; for example, for the triangular pyramid the square on d is $1\frac{1}{2}$ times the square on e. However for the other two solids Euclid uses materials from Book X, taking the diameter d to be a 'rational' straight line, and showing that the edge of the dodecahedron is an apotome, and that the icosahedron is a line which he calls minor and defines in X.76. These characterizations of the edges of the regular solids apparently provide the main motivation for the elaborate classification undertaken in Book X.

(2) Eudoxus and Books V and XII of Euclid's Elements

Two scholia associate Book V with Eudoxus. The more interesting one says:

> This book is said to belong to Eudoxus of Cnidus, the mathematician who lived at the time of Plato, but it is nevertheless ascribed to Euclid and not wrongly. For why shouldn't a thing be assigned to one person as far as its discovery is concerned, even though it is agreed by everyone that it is Euclid's as far as the arrangement of things with respect to elementhood and with respect to the relations of implication with other things of what has been arranged?
>
> ([8.30] 5: 282.13–20)

It is difficult to make any precise determination of the roles assigned to Eudoxus and Euclid by this scholium, but it would seem that at least some equivalent of the Book V definition of proportionality and an indication of its viability should be ascribed to Eudoxus, and some non-trivial reorganization to Euclid.

Book XII is also closely connected with Eudoxus. For in the preface to *On Sphere and Cylinder* I ([8.22] 1:4.2–13) Archimedes ascribes to him proofs of equivalents of two propositions from Book XII, and in the prefatory letter to *The Method* ([8.22] 2: 430.1–9) he contrasts Eudoxus being the first person to prove these propositions with Democritus being the first to assert one or both of them without proof[5]. Moreover, in the preface to the *Metrica* Heron ([8.45] 3: 2.13–18) credits Eudoxus with the first proofs of one of these propositions and of XII.2. In the prefatory letter to *Quadrature of the Parabola* ([8.22] 2: 264.5–25) Archimedes connects the proof of the equivalents of several propositions in Book XII with what he there calls a lemma and is more or less equivalent to X. 1. It seems clear that Eudoxus was responsible for some considerable part of the contents of Book XII, although again we have no way of knowing how much Euclid contributed to its formulation. Since the treatment of proportion in Book V and the use of exhaustion in Book XII can be said to represent the outstanding logical and conceptual achievements of the *Elements*, there is good reason to compare Eudoxus' accomplishments with foundational work of the nineteenth century by people such as Weierstrass, Cantor, Dedekind, and Frege.[6]

(3) *Theaetetus and Book XIII of the* Elements

The *Suda* ([8.87] 2: 689.6–8) says that a Theaetetus of Athens 'was the first to describe the so-called five solids.' The connection of Theaetetus with the regular solids is confirmed by a scholion on Book XIII:

> In this book, the thirteenth, the five figures called Platonic are described. However, they are not Plato's. Three of the five are Pythagorean, the cube, the pyramid, and the dodecahedron; the octahedron and the icosahedron belong to Theaetetus. They are called Platonic because Plato mentions them in the *Timaeus*. Euclid put his name also on this book because he extended the elemental ordering to this element as well.
>
> ([8.30] 5: 654.1–10)

We have seen in the introduction that Proclus credits Pythagoras with discovering the construction of the five solids, but his statement is unlikely to be reliable. The most plausible understanding of ancient testimonia about the regular solids has been provided by Waterhouse [8.10], and it confirms both the *Suda* claim that Theaetetus was the first to describe the five solids and the scholiast's distinction between the solids of the Pythagoreans and those of Theaetetus. Waterhouse suggests that there was an early recognition of the cube, pyramid, and dodecahedron,[7] but that Theaetetus tried to produce a completely general account of the regular solids and brought into geometry both the simple octahedron and the complex icosahedron. As we have seen in section 1, the characterization of the edges of the dodecahedron and icosahedron in Book XIII seems to provide the whole rationale for Book X. And we find Theaetetus connected with Book X as well.

(4) Theaetetus and Book X of the Elements: the Three Means and Harmonics

In his commentary on Book X of the *Elements* Pappus of Alexandria describes a relationship between Theaetetus and Book X analogous to the relation between Eudoxus and Book V described by the scholium quoted above:

> It was Theaetetus who distinguished the powers which are commensurable in length from those which are incommensurable, and who divided the more generally known irrational lines according to the different means, assigning the medial line to geometry, the binomial to arithmetic, and the apotome to harmony, as is stated by Eudemus the Peripatetic. Euclid's object on the other hand was the attainment of irrefragable principles, which he established for commensurability and incommensurability in general. For rationals and irrationals he formulated definitions and differentiae, determined also many orders of the irrationals, and brought to light whatever of definiteness is to be found in them.
>
> ([8.60], I.1)

Later Pappus writes:

> Those who have written concerning these things declare that the Athenian Theaetetus assumed two lines commensurable in square [only] and proved that if he took between them a line in ratio according to geometric proportion, then the line named the medial was produced, but that if he took the line according to arithmetic proportion, then the binomial was produced, and if he took the line according to harmonic proportion, then the apotome was produced.
>
> ([8.60], II.17)

These assertions require some explication. I begin with the notions of geometric, arithmetic and harmonic proportion, and with a fragment of Archytas' *On Music*:

> There are three musical means, the first arithmetic, the second geometric, the third subcontrary (*hupenantios*), which is also called harmonic. There is an arithmetic mean when there are three terms in proportion with respect to the same excess: the second term exceeds the third term by as much as the first does the second. . . . There is a geometric mean when the second term is to the third as the first is to the second . . . There is a subcontrary

278

mean (which we call harmonic) when the first term exceeds the second by the same part of the first as the middle exceeds the third by a part of the third.

(Porphyry [8.73], 93.6–15, DK 47 B 2)

Here Archytas speaks of three types of means rather than three types of proportions, although the vocabulary of proportions also slips into what he says. In the present context I shall speak of the three types of mean and use the word 'proportion' only for expressions of the form 'x:y :: z:w'. The geometric mean is, of course, the middle of three terms standing in a standard proportion. The arithmetic mean is simply the arithmetic average of two terms x and z, that is $\frac{1}{2}$ (x + z). The harmonic mean is usually given a more general definition which we find in Nicomachus ([8.55], II.25.1; cf. Theon of Smyrna [8.92], 114.14–17), according to which:

y is the harmonic mean between x and z if and only if

$$(x - y) : (y - z) :: x : z \text{ (so that y is } \frac{2xz}{x + z})$$

It is generally believed that the arithmetic and harmonic means were introduced in connection with harmonics, and with the realization that the fundamental concords of Greek music are expressible by elementary ratios:

fourth (doh–fa)	4:3
fifth (doh–sol or fa–doh')	3:2
octave (doh–doh')	2:1

The simplest representation of all three of these relations together is:

doh fa sol doh'
12   9   8   6

where 9 is the arithmetic and 8 the harmonic mean between 12 and 6. I shall consider the discovery of these relations in section 2 of Part Two. The important point for now is that harmonics forms part of the background of Theaetetus's handling of the three 'generally known' irrationals.[8]

The Greek word standing behind 'power' in the translation from Pappus is *dunamis*, which Euclid uses only in the dative: straight lines are said to be commensurable *dunamei* (in square) when the squares with them as sides are commensurable.[9] Pappus' vocabulary presumably reflects the passage at the beginning of Plato's *Theaetetus* (147d–148b) to which he refers. In the passage Theaetetus says that Theodorus was teaching something about *dunameis*, showing that the three-foot *dunamis* and the five-foot *dunamis* are not commensurable in length with the one-foot *dunamis*, doing each case separately up to the seven-teen-foot *dunamis*, where he stopped. Theaetetus and his companion took it that there were infinitely many *dunameis* and produced a general characterization of them. Making a comparison between numbers and figures, they divided all *number* into what we would call square and non-square, and made a parallel division among lines which square (*tetragōnizein*) the numbers, calling the set which square the square numbers lengths and those which square the non-squares *duna-meis*, 'as not being commensurable in length with the lengths, but only in the planes which they produce as squares'.

It does not seem possible to assign a uniform precise meaning to the word *dunamis* in the *Theaetetus* passage. Ultimately Theaetetus defines *dunameis* as the straight lines which square a non-square number, so that all *dunameis* are incommensurable with the one-foot length. But in the description of Theodorus's lesson Theaetetus refers to the one-foot *dunamis*, which is certainly commensurable with a one-foot length. So it seems likely that the general meaning of *dunamis* in the description of the lesson is simply 'side of a square' or 'side of a square representing an integer'. When Pappus says that Theaetetus 'distinguished the *dunameis* which are commensurable in length from those which are not commensurable', it seems likely that he means something like this by *dunamis* and that he ascribes to Theaetetus a distinction between the straight lines commensurable in length with the one-foot *dunamis* – or, equivalently, with a line set out – as 'rational' from those which are not.

The comparison between numbers and figures to which Plato's Theaetetus refers is quite clear in much Greek arithmetic vocabulary, of which 'square' and 'cube' are perhaps the most common modern survivors. But we do not find in Euclid anything genuinely like the representation of a unit as a straight line u with a corresponding unit square $sq(u)$, and other numbers represented both as multiples of u and as rectangles contained by such multiples (cf. Figure 8.2). But this seems

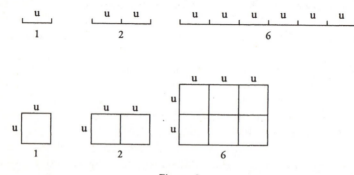

Figure 8.2

to be what lies behind the discussion in the *Theaetetus*. That is to say, it looks as though Theodorus was using a unit length u and proving what we would call the irrationality of $\sqrt{n}$ for certain n by showing that the side s_n of a square corresponding to n was incommensurable in length with u. Theaetetus made a generalization of what he was shown by Theodorus by assuming or proving that:

(i) n is a perfect square if and only if s_n is commensurable with u.

It should be clear that there is a big difference between assuming and proving (i). And although the proof of implication from left to right is quite straightforward, the proof of right-left implication is far from it. In fact, it is just the proposition we would assert by saying that the square root of any non-square positive integer is irrational. There is no extant ancient proof of such an assertion.

We may gain more insight by formulating the question raised by Theaetetus in the *Theaetetus* and his answer to it as:

Question: If y is the geometric mean between m·u and n·u (i.e. if the square on y is equal to the rectangle on m·u and n·u), under what conditions is y commensurable with u?

Answer: If y is the geometric mean between m·u and n·u, then y is commensurable with u (if and) only if y ≈ k·u, for some k.

Phrased this way, Theaetetus' problem is equivalent to looking at the geometric mean y between two commensurable straight lines x and z, and asking whether it is commensurable with the lines. One correct answer to this problem is the following:

(ii) If y is the geometric mean between straight lines x and z, y is commensurable with x if and only if x has to z the ratio of a square number to a square number.

(ii) is equivalent to *Elements* X.9, which a scholiast ascribes to Theaetetus:

This theorem is the discovery of Theaetetus, and Plato recalls it in the *Theaetetus*, but there it is set out in a more particular way, here universally. For there squares which are measured by square numbers are said to also have their sides commensurable. But that assertion is particularized, since it doesn't include in its scope all the commensurable areas of which the sides are commensurable.

([8.30] 5: 450.16–21)

If Theaetetus was interested in the commensurability of the geometric mean between commensurable straight lines with the straight lines, it does not seem unreasonable to suppose that he would also have considered the arithmetic and harmonic means between commensurable straight lines and seen right away that these are commensurable with the original lines.[10]

So we can imagine that Theaetetus showed that the arithmetic or harmonic mean between two commensurable straight lines is commensurable with the original lines, but that this holds for the geometric mean only in the case where the original lines are related as a square number to a square number; if they are not so related, he could only say that the geometric mean is commensurable in square with the original straight lines. He might now wonder whether, if we insert a mean x between lines y, z which are commensurable in square only, x is commensurable (at least in square) with y (and z). In fact this can be shown to hold for none of the means, and so we might imagine Theaetetus having proved:

> (iii) The insertion of any of the three means between incommensurable 'rational' lines produces an 'irrational' line.

We might imagine him pushing on to further 'irrational' lines by inserting further means (cf. *Elements* X.115), but I suspect that, if Theaetetus were looking to the notion of commensurability in square as a kind of limit on incommensurability, the recognition that any of the means between lines commensurable in square only goes beyond that limit might have given him pause. He would then have had a 'theory' summarized by (iii). This theory only gets us to the medial, not to the binomial and apotome. To explain the introduction of the binomial and medial we need only recall that the motivation for the whole theory of 'irrational' lines seems to be provided by the treatment of the regular solids in Book XIII.[11]

There remains the question of what exactly Theaetetus did and how it is related to Books X and XIII of the *Elements*. Pappus' statement that Euclid formulated definitions for rationals and irrationals 'and differentiae, determined also many orders of the irrationals, and brought to light whatever of definiteness is to be found in them' suggests that quite a bit of book X is due to him. On the other hand, if one assumes, as it seems necessary to do, that Theaetetus' interest in apotomes grew out of his study of the regular solids, then it seems plausible to assume that he established the characterizations of the edges of dodecahedron and icosahedron which we find in the *Elements*. But once we make that assumption it seems hard to deny that essentially all of X and XIII is due to Theaetetus,[12] and that Euclid's changes were more formal than substantive. However, we have no way of drawing an exact boundary between the work of the two men.

(5) Theaetetus and the Theory of Proportion

I have already alluded in section 1 to the major peculiarity involved in the treatment of proportionality in the *Elements*. Euclid gives one definition of proportionality for 'magnitudes' in Book V and another for numbers in Book VII. Then in X.5–8, with no indication that there is any problem, he introduces proportions involving both numbers and magnitudes. Understandably those who view the *Elements* as a loosely strung together compilation of independent treatises have focused considerable attention on this juncture in the text. A standard position is that (a) the ultimate sources of Book VII are chronologically earlier than the work of Eudoxus incorporated in Book V; (b) since Book X deals with incommensurable magnitudes, it obviously cannot be based on the theory of proportion of Book VII; and (c) since Book V has nothing to say about numerical ratios, Book X cannot be based on Eudoxus's theory. What, then, could it be based on? This alleged gap in our knowledge was filled by Becker [8.96], starting with a remark on definitions in Aristotle's *Topics* (VIII.3.158b24–35):

> Many theses are not easy to argue about or tackle because the definition has not been correctly rendered, e.g., whether one thing has one contrary or many. . . . It seems that it is also the case in mathematics that some things are difficult to prove because of a deficiency in a definition. An example is that a line which cuts a plane [i.e. parallelogram] parallel to a side, divides the line and the area similarly. For the assertion is immediately evident when the definition is stated. For the areas and the lines have the same *antanairesis*. And this is the definition of the same ratio.

Commenting on this passage, Alexander of Aphrodisias says ([8.20], 545.15–17) that Aristotle calls *anthuphairesis antanairesis* and that early mathematicians called magnitudes proportional if they have the same *anthuphairesis*. In terms of Figure 8.3 Aristotle's example of a proposition difficult to prove presumably says something like:

Parallelogram ABED is to parallelogram BCFE as AB is to BC.

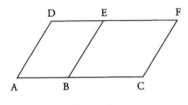

Figure 8.3

283

In the *Elements* Euclid proves a similar result as VI.1. using the Book V definition of proportionality.

Neither *anthuphairesis* nor *antanairesis* occurs with a mathematical sense in an ancient text outside the *Topics* passage and Alexander's comment on it, but the verb *anthuphairesthai* is used by Euclid in the *Elements*, where Heath [8.32] translates it 'be continually subtracted' or 'be continually subtracted in turn'. Two propositions in which this verb occurs are:

> VII.1. Two unequal numbers being set out and the less being continually subtracted in turn from the greater, if the number which is left never measures the one before it until a unit is left, the original numbers will be prime to one another.

> X.2. If, when the lesser of two unequal magnitudes is continually subtracted in turn from the greater, that which is left never measures the one before it, the magnitudes will be incommensurable.

And the verb turns up in the proof of VII.2, which shows how to find the greatest common measure of two numbers, and in that of X.3, which shows how to find the greatest common measure of two commensurable magnitudes. The method used to find a common measure is what Alexander means by *anthuphairesis*. I illustrate its use to find the greatest common measure or divisor, 2, of 58 and 18:

$$
\begin{array}{lll}
1 & 58 - 18 = 40 & \\
2 & 40 - 18 = 22 & \\
3 & 22 - 18 = 4 < 18 & 58 = (3{\cdot}18) + 4 \; (4 < 18) \\
4 & 18 - 4 = 14 & \\
5 & 14 - 4 = 10 & \\
6 & 10 - 4 = 6 & \\
7 & 6 - 4 = 2 < 4 & 18 = (4{\cdot}4) + 2 \; (2 < 4) \\
8 & 4 - 2 = 2 & \\
9 & 2 - 2 = 0 & 4 = (2{\cdot}2)
\end{array}
$$

I now give a general representation of the procedure for magnitudes x_1 and x_2 with $x_1 > x_2$:

$$
\begin{array}{ll}
1 & x_1 = m_1{\cdot}x_2 + x_3 \text{ with } x_3 < x_2 \\
2 & x_2 = m_2{\cdot}x_3 + x_4 \text{ with } x_4 < x_3 \\
3 & x_3 = m_3{\cdot}x_4 + x_5 \text{ with } x_5 < x_4
\end{array}
$$

This procedure either stops with

n. $x_n = m_n{\cdot}x_{n+1}$, for some n,

or proceeds forever with

i. $x_i = m_i x_{i+1} + x_{i+2}$, for every i.

Euclid takes for granted that, if we are dealing with numbers, the procedure will stop because eventually we will get 1 (the unit) as a remainder; we might say that in this case 1 is the greatest common measure, but Euclid normally distinguishes between 1 and a number. The argument that if the procedure stops at step n, x_{n+1} is the greatest common measure relies only on ideas about measuring, adding and subtracting, as does the argument that, if the procedure doesn't stop, there is no common measure.[13]

The *anthuphairesis* of two quantities x_1 and x_2 is completely represented by the series of multipliers m_1, m_2 . . . produced by the process of alternate subtraction. So presumably the definition of proportionality referred to by Aristotle says that two pairs of magnitudes are in proportion if the series produced by applying *anthuphairesis* to the first pair is the same as the series produced for the second. This definition obviously does apply to both numbers and to magnitudes. Since Aristotle refers to Eudoxus in several passages and the proportionality definition of Book V is ascribed to Eudoxus, there is reason to think that Aristotle is referring to a definition of the 'early' mathematicians, i.e. earlier than Eudoxus. Given other assumptions which we have already mentioned, it is a short step to ascribing the anthuphairetic definition of proportionality to Theaetetus and to supposing that the original of Book X was based on this definition. A crucial assumption for this view is the idea that there is a serious gap in the proofs of X.5–8. This claim is hard to evaluate because there are serious logical difficulties in Euclid's treatment of proportionality in arithmetic itself.[14] But if, as is generally done, those difficulties are ignored, and we assume that at least by the time of Book X Euclid includes numbers among magnitudes, then the only law which Euclid has not proved in Book V and which he needs to justify X.5–8 is trivial.[15] The assumption that Euclid left the proof of this law to his readers or students does not seem to me implausible. However, even if this is true, Aristotle's remark in the *Topics* makes it very likely that at some point before his and Eudoxus' time an anthuphairetic theory of ratios was developed to apply to commensurable and incommensurable magnitudes.[16] Whether we should ascribe this theory to Theaetetus seems to me moot.

(6) Archytas, Harmonics and Arithmetic

In section 4 I described the representation of the fundamental concords fourth, fifth and octave in terms of the ratios 4:3, 3:2, 2:1. In a fragment from *On Mathematics* (Porphyry [8.73], 56.5–57.27, DK 47 B 1), Archytas correlates high pitches with fast movements and low pitches with slow ones in a piece of physical acoustics.[17] We find an analogue of this correlation in the prologue of Euclid's *Sectio Canonis*, our earliest text in mathematical harmonics. The prologue concludes with an argument that it is 'reasonable' that:

> SC Assumption 1. The concordant intervals are ratios of the form n + 1 : n or n : 1, i.e. they are either 'epimorics' or multiples.

It seems possible that Archytas put forward an argument of the same kind, although only Euclid makes an explicit correlation between pitch and frequency.[18] Euclid's argument for SC Assumption 1 relies only on an analogy between the idea that concordant notes make a single sound and the fact that ratios of the two forms are expressed by a single name in Greek: double is *diplasios*, triple *triplasios*, etc., and 3:2 is *hēmiolios*, 4:3 *epitritos*, 5:4 *epitetartos*, etc. There is no question that the argument is a *post hoc* attempt to justify previously established correlations; and it fails rather badly as a foundation for the programme of the *Sectio*, which is:

1 to establish the numerical representation of the fundamental concords;
2 to use mathematics to disprove apparent musical facts, such as the existence of a half-tone;
3 to construct a diatonic 'scale'.

In the treatise Euclid tacitly takes for granted that addition of intervals is represented by what we would call multiplication of ratios, subtraction of intervals by what we would call division. To divide an interval represented by m:n in half is, then, to find i, j, k such that i:k :: m:n, and i:j :: j:k. In addition to SC Assumption 1 Euclid also relies on the following empirical 'facts':

> SC Assumption 2. fourth + fifth = octave.
> SC Assumption 3. fifth – fourth = tone.
> SC Assumption 4. The concords are in order fourth, fifth, octave, octave + fifth, and double octave.
> SC Assumption 5. Certain other intervals, in particular the double fourth and double fifth, are discordant and neither multiple nor epimoric.

SC Assumption 5 brings out a kind of duplicity in the *Sectio*. In a (for him) ideal world Euclid would be able to say that all and only the concordant intervals are epimoric or multiple. To say that they all are would conflict with the fact that the octave + fourth (represented by 8:3) is concordant; Euclid passes over this interval in silence. To say that only they are would conflict with the fact that the tone (represented by 9:8 the 'difference' between 3:2 and 4:3) and the interval represented by 5:1 are discordant. Clearly Euclid picks and chooses his 'facts' as he needs them.

Although the foundation of the *Sectio* is very nebulous and hardly what we would call scientific, and although SC Assumption 5 is used in a very arbitrary way, the core of the argumentation depends on quite sophisticated number theory. I shall not discuss the argumentation in detail,[19] but do wish to mention three propositions of pure mathematics proved in the *Sectio*:

> SC Propositions 1, 2. If $d_1:d_2 :: d_2:d_3$, then d_2 is a multiple of d_1 if and only if d_3 is.
> SC Proposition 3. If $d_1:d_2 :: d_2:d_3 :: \ldots :: d_{n-1}:d_n$, then $d_1:d_n$ is not epimoric.

SC Proposition 2 enables one to establish the result that Plato ascribes to Theaetetus ((i) in section 4 above). In his proof of SC Proposition 2 Euclid justifies the crucial step by saying, 'But we have learned that if there are as many numbers as we please in proportion and the first measures the last, it will also measure those in between.' Euclid's formulation here varies slightly from the formulation of the equivalent assertion as *Elements* VIII.7, a proposition which Euclid derives by *reductio* from its equivalent VIII.6: 'If there are as many numbers as we please in continuous proportion and the first does not measure the second, none of the other numbers will measure any other.'

SC Proposition 3 is of special interest for fourth-century mathematics because Boethius ([8.28] III.11, DK 47 A 19) ascribes a similar proof to Archytas. To facilitate comparison of the two proofs I first give a simplified version of the *Sectio* proof:

> Suppose $d_1:d_n$ is epimoric, and (i) let $d + 1$ and d be the least numbers in the ratio of d_1 and d_n. (ii) No mean proportionals fall between $d + 1$ and d, since no numbers fall between them at all. (iii) Therefore, there are no d_i such that $d_1:d_2 :: d_2:d_3 :: \ldots$ $d_{n-1}:d_n$.

To justify this last step Euclid invokes the equivalent of *Elements* VIII.8 when he says, 'However many means fall proportionally between the least numbers, so many will also fall proportionally between numbers having the same ratio.'

In Euclid's actual argument step (i) is replaced by something like the following argument:

> (i') Let d and d' be the least numbers such that $d':d :: d_1:d_n$. Then d' and d have only the unit as common measure. Now

consider d' – d; by the definition of 'epimoric' d' – d is a part of d and a part of d'; therefore it is the unit.

In asserting that d' and d have only the unit as common measure Euclid is apparently relying on the equivalent of VII.22 ('The least numbers of those having the same ratio with one another are relatively prime') and the definition of relatively prime numbers as those having only the unit as common measure (VII, def. 12).

The proof ascribed to Archytas by Boethius is even messier. In place of (i') it has:

(i") Let $d + d^*$ and d be the least numbers such that $(d + d^*:d) :: d_1:d_n$, so that, by the definition of 'epimoric', d^* is a part of d. I assert that d^* is a unit. For suppose it is greater than 1. Then, since d^* is a part of d, d^* divides d and also $d + d^*$, but this is impossible. 'For numbers which are the least in the same proportion as other numbers are prime to one another and only differ by a unit.' Therefore d^* is a unit, and $d + d^*$ exceeds d by a unit.

After inferring (ii") that no mean proportional falls between $d + d^*$ and d, Boethius concludes, presumably by reference to something like VIII.8:

(iii") Consequently, a mean proportional between the two original numbers d_1 and d_n cannot exist, since they are in the same ratio as $d + d^*$ and d.

In the quoted lines in (i") the equivalent of VII.22 is again cited, but, as Boethius points out, the words 'only differ by a unit' are not correctly applied to arbitrary ratios in least terms but only to epimoric ones.[20]

It seems reasonable to suppose that Archytas was responsible for something like the proof ascribed to him by Boethius, and that Euclid improved it in the *Sectio*, perhaps relying on the *Elements* as an arithmetical foundation. It even seems reasonable to suppose that Archytas composed some kind of Ur-*Sectio*, on which our *Sectio* was somehow based. However, it seems to me unlikely that our *Sectio* is simply an improved version of a work of Archytas. For Euclid's diatonic scale is the standard one used by Plato in the *Timaeus* (35b–36a) for the division of the world soul into parts, whereas we know from Ptolemy ([8.77], 30.9–31.18, DK 47 A 16) that Archytas's diatonic was quite different.[21]

The question whether Archytas' tuning is mathematical manipulation without musical significance must be considered moot. Barker ([8.14], 46–52) has argued that musical practice may have played a much more significant role in Archytas' theorizing than is usually allowed, but he leaves no doubt that a kind of mathematical a priorism, particularly the faith in the consonance of epimorics, played a central role in Archytas' musical thought. Moreover, a passage in Porphyry ([8.73], 107.15–108.21, DK 47 A 17) suggests that Archytas used very arbitrary numerical manipulations to determine the relative concordance of octave, fifth, and fourth, subtracting 1 from each term of the corresponding ratios, adding the results for each interval and taking lower sums to mean greater concord; since $(2 - 1) + (1 - 1) < (3 - 1) + (2 - 1) < (4 - 1) + (3 - 1)$, he declared the octave to be more concordant than the fifth, which, in turn is more concordant than the fourth.

This mixture of mathematical reasoning and mathematical mystification makes it difficult for us to classify the musical work of Archytas (and even of Euclid) as either science or numerology.[22] It is difficult to believe that Archytas did not know the truth of VIII.7 and 8, at least for the case of one mean proportional. But it is hard to see how he could even begin to think about such results without a well-developed idea of arithmetical reasoning and proof.[23]

❧ PART TWO: THE SIXTH AND FIFTH ❧ CENTURIES

(1) Thales and Early Greek Geometry

In addition to his general remarks about Thales quoted in the introduction Proclus ([8.74]) records four of Thales' mathematical achievements, twice citing Eudemus as authority. I quote the passages:

(a) The famous Thales is said to have been the first to prove that the circle is bisected by the diameter. (157.10–11)

(b) We are indebted to the ancient Thales for the discovery of this theorem [asserting the equality of the base angles of an isosceles triangle] and many others. For he, it is said, was the first to recognize and assert that the angles at the base of any isosceles triangle are equal, although he expressed himself more archaically and called the equal angles similar. (250.20–251.2)

(c) According to Eudemus, this theorem [asserting the equality of the non-adjacent angles made by two intersecting straight lines] . . . was first discovered by Thales. (299.1–4)

(d) In his history of geometry Eudemus attributes to Thales this theorem [asserting the congruence of triangles with two sides and one angle equal]. He says that the method by which Thales is said to have determined the distance of ships at sea requires the use of this theorem. (352.14–18, all four passages in DK 11 A 20)

Other passages[24] credit Thales with a method for determining the height of a pyramid by measuring its shadow and call him 'the first to describe the right triangle of a circle', whatever that may mean. However, the crucial passages are the four I have quoted. Dicks ([8.88], 302–3) seizes on the last to argue that Eudemus' attributions to Thales are reconstructions which presuppose that Thales demonstrated in a basically Euclidean way geometrical theorems implicit in his more practical accomplishments. Even if one accepts the plausibility of this approach to ancient doxographical reports, two features of these particular ones may cause one to hesitate: the detailed point in (b) about Thales' archaic vocabulary, and the fact that in (a) Thales is said to have proved something which is (illegitimately) made a matter of definition in Euclid's *Elements* (I, def. 17).

It is also striking that all four of the propositions ascribed to Thales can be 'proved' either by superimposing one figure on another (d) or by 'folding' a configuration at a point of symmetry. It seems possible that Thales' proofs were what we might call convincing pictures involving no explicit deductive structure. But once one ascribes even this much of a conception of justification to Thales, one is faced with what would seem to be serious questions. How did it come about that Thales would formulate, say, the claim that a diameter bisects a circle? If he was just interested in the truth 'for its own sake', then we already have the idea of pure geometrical knowledge. But if, as seems more plausible, he was interested in the claim as a means to justifying some other less obvious one, then we seem to have the concept of mathematical deduction, from which the evolution of the concept of mathematical proof is not hard to envisage. We need not, of course, suppose that Thales was a rigorous reasoner by Euclidean standards; merely saying that he explicitly asserted and tried to justify mathematical propositions of a rather elementary kind is enough to give us a primitive form of mathematics.

Of course, we would like to know something about the historical background of Thales' interests. Proclus and other ancient sources give credit to the Egyptians, but modern scholars tend to be sceptical about these claims.[25] Van der Waerden and others have invoked the Babylonians to fill the gap. I quote from his discussion of Thales ([8.13], 89), which shows that he also credits Thales with a high standard of mathematical argumentation.

We have to abandon the traditional belief that the oldest Greek mathematicians discovered geometry entirely by themselves and that they owed hardly anything to older cultures, a belief which

was tenable only as long as nothing was known about
Babylonian mathematics. This in no way diminishes the stature
of Thales; on the contrary, his genius receives only now the honor
that is due it, the honor of having developed a logical structure
for geometry, of having introduced proof into geometry. Indeed,
what is characteristic and absolutely new in Greek mathematics
is the advance by means of demonstration from theorem to
theorem. Evidently, Greek geometry has had this character from
the beginning, and it is Thales to whom it is due.

(2) Harmonics in the Sixth and Fifth Centuries

In his commentary on Ptolemy's *Harmonics* ([8.73], 30.1–9), Porphyry
says:

> And Heraclides writes these things about this subject in his
> *Introduction to Music*:
>   As Xenocrates says, Pythagoras also discovered that musical
> intervals do not come to be apart from number; for they are a
> comparison of quantity with quantity. He therefore investigated
> under what conditions there result concordant or discordant
> intervals and everything harmonious or inharmonious. And
> turning to the generation of sound, he said that if from an
> equality a concordance is to be heard, it is necessary that there
> be some motion; but motion does not occur without number,
> and neither does number without quantity.

The passage continues by developing an even more elaborate theory of
the relationship between movements and sound than the ones I mentioned earlier in section 6. Scholars who are doubtful that Pythagoras
was any kind of scientist are happy to deny that Heraclides is Heraclides of Pontus, the student of Plato, and to restrict the extent of the
citation of Xenocrates to the first sentence.[26] Even this sentence implies
that Pythagoras discovered something about numbers and concords,
and I think everyone would agree that, if he discovered any such thing,
it was the association of the fundamental concords with the ratios 4:3,
3:2 and 2:1. It is commonly thought that this association must have
been known by people familiar with musical instruments quite independently of theoretical proclamations, but that 'Pythagoras invested the
applicability of these ratios to musical intervals with enormous theoretical significance' [KRS p.235]. Burkert ([8.79], 374–5) has pointed out
how difficult it is to identify an early instrument which would facilitate
recognizing the correlation of pitch relations with numerical ratios.
    The traditional story of Pythagoras' discovery of the ratios – for

which our earliest source is Nicomachus ([8.57], 6) – depends upon false assumptions about the causal relation between pitches produced and the weights of hammers striking a forge or weights suspended from plucked strings. However we find a perfectly credible experiment, involving otherwise equal bronze discs with thicknesses in the required ratios, associated with the early Pythagorean Hippasus of Metapontum (Scholium on *Phaedo* 108d [8.64], 15, DK 18.12).[27] Hippasus is thought to have flourished in the earlier fifth century. In an important sense he is our only clear example of a Pythagorean mathematical scientist before Archytas. But the stories about his relations to the Pythagoreans and the division of the school into *akousmatikoi* and *mathēmatikoi* surround him in a mysterious fog which is not fully penetrable.[28]

In section 4 I described the close relation of the doctrine of means with harmonics, and quoted the passage in which Archytas describes the three basic means. Proclus ([8.74], 67.5–6) indicates that Eudoxus added other means to the basic three. Nicomachus ([8.55], II.21) says that all the ancients, Pythagoras, Plato and Aristotle, agreed on the arithmetic, geometric and harmonic means. Iamblichus ([8.54], 100.22–4) says that Hippasus and Archytas introduced the name 'harmonic' in place of 'subcontrary', and in two passages ([8.54], 113.16–17, 116.1–4) he associates the introduction of additional means with Hippasus and Archytas. Whether or not the additional means can be ascribed to Hippasus, it seems plausible to suppose that he did work with ratios and at least the first three means in the earlier fifth century. His doing so certainly implies some level of mathematical abstraction and manipulation, but presumably the level might be fairly low.

We do not gain much clarification in this matter when we turn to the other main allegedly fifth-century treatment of mathematical harmonics, which is ascribed to Philolaus. In the second part of DK 44 B 6 (put together from two versions, Stobaeus ([8.86] I.21.7d) and Nicomachus ([8.57], 9)), Philolaus constructs an octave with seven tones, the first four of which quite clearly form a tetrachord in the standard diatonic system (see note 21). In his own vocabulary he mentions the ratios for the three fundamental concordant intervals, and asserts the following:

fifth–fourth = 9:8;
octave = five 9:8 intervals + two 'dieses';
fifth = three 9:8 intervals + one 'diesis';
fourth = two 9:8 intervals + one 'diesis'.

Boethius ([8.28] III.8, DK 44 B 6) tells us that for Philolaus the 'diesis' or smaller semitone is the interval by which 4:3 is greater than two tones, so that there is no reason to doubt that Philolaus has the mathematics of the standard diatonic scale. However Boethius goes on to say that the 'comma' is the interval by which 9:8 is greater than two 'dieses', and that the 'schisma' is half of a 'comma', and the 'diaschisma' half of a 'diesis'. The 'diesis' should be 256:243 and the 'comma' 531441:524288. Neither of these intervals can be divided in half in the sense of the *Sectio Canonis*. Since Philolaus seems clearly to recognize that the tone cannot be divided in half, it is rather surprising that he apparently takes for granted – what is false in terms of the *Sectio* – that there are half 'dieses' and half 'commas'.

But the situation becomes even more problematic when one takes into account III.5 of *De Institutione Musica* (DK 44 A 26). For there Philolaus garbles together the combining and disjoining of ratios with the adding and subtracting of numbers. He also moves without comment from taking an interval as a ratio between two numbers m and n and as their difference m – n. He begins by taking 27 as the cube of the first odd number, and then expresses the tone (9:8) as 27:24. He says that this is divisible into a larger and smaller part, the 'apotome' and the 'diesis', the difference between them being a 'comma'.[29] Taking the standard value for the 'diesis', 256:243, he treats it as if it were 13 (= 256 – 243), pointing out that 13 is the sum of 1 ('the point'), 3 ('the first odd line') and 9 ('the first square'). To find the 'apotome' he uses the value 243:216 (9:8) for the tone and says that 27 (= 243 – 216) is the tone. The value of the 'apotome' is then 14 (= 27 – 13) and the value of the 'comma' is 1 (= 14 – 13). This discussion is, of course, pure nonsense. For Burkert the nonsense is genuine late fifth-century Pythagoreanism, which 'shows a truly remarkable mixture of calculation and numerical symbolism in which 'sense' is more important than accuracy' ([8.79], 400). For Huffman ([8.61], 364–80), whose Philolaus and fifth-century Pythagoreanism are much more scientific than Burkert's, just the description of the seven-note scale with the diatonic tetrachord is genuine Philolaus. I remark only that everywhere in what we might call the Pythagorean tradition of Greek music, including Archytas, Plato, Euclid and Ptolemy, the sense of the cosmic power of pure numbers and the willingness to indulge in meaningless numerical manipulation is always present. What distinguishes Philolaus, from Euclid and Ptolemy certainly, and for the most part from Archytas as well, is the apparent confusion between numerical relations or ratios and absolute numbers. Even if we waive the question of authenticity, I do not think there is sufficient evidence to decide whether Philolaus represents the sort of thing one would expect of any fifth-century Pythagorean. But there is little doubt that it can be expected of some.

(3) Arithmetic in the Sixth and Fifth Centuries

It is customary to associate the representation of the fundamental concords as ratios with an important concept of Pythagorean lore, the *tetraktus*, the first four numbers represented by the triangle of Figure 8.4 and summing to 10, the perfect number encapsulating all of nature's truth.[30]

Figure 8.4

In II.8 of his *Introduction to Arithmetic* Nicomachus introduces the notion of a triangular number, that is a number which can be represented in triangular form, as in Figure 8.5.

Figure 8.5

It is clear that the triangular numbers form an infinite sequence and that the nth triangular number is the sum of the first n numbers.[31] I shall call these arrays of dots figurate numbers. In succeeding chapters Nicomachus describes square numbers, pentagonal numbers, and so on up to octagonals. In his commentary on Nicomachus's presentation of triangular numbers Iamblichus says ([8.54], 58.19–25; cf. Aristotle, *Categories* 14.15a29–33) that the number added to the mth n-agonal number to get the m + 1th is called the gnomon, the thing which preserves the shape of a thing when added to it. He explains that the term was taken from geometry, where it was applied to the excess by which one square exceeds another. Figure 8.6 shows what he means and how the gnomon functions in the generation of square numbers.[32] It makes quite clear that the nth square number is the sum of the first n odd numbers, one example of the way in which relatively simple

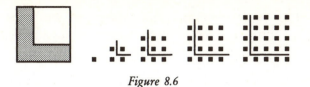

Figure 8.6

manipulation of figurate numbers can establish mathematically interesting results independently of anything resembling a stylized Euclidean deduction.

But the difference between such deduction with its definitions, technical vocabulary, diagrams and formalistic descriptions, on the one hand, and informal manipulation designed to bring out general truths about numbers or rules for producing them is not great. Nor are the moves from the sacred *tetraktus* to triangular numbers to generalizations about them and other polygonal numbers. Our evidence for figurate numbers is late, Theon of Smyrna, Nicomachus, and Iamblichus being the principal sources. There is no trace of figurate numbers in Euclid. Nevertheless, most scholars take the material in Theon, Nicomachus and Iamblichus to be early. In his *History* Heath discusses this material under the rubric 'Pythagorean arithmetic' before he discusses Thales. I do not wish to suggest that his doing so is illegitimate, but only to insist that once one admits an interest, even a numero-mystico-theological interest, in accumulating general numerical laws and rules on the basis of the manipulation of configurations of dots, one has the fundamentals of a scientific arithmetic, although not, of course, an arithmetic in which one advances 'by means of demonstration from theorem to theorem', to use van der Waerden's description of the geometry of Thales.[33]

As an example of the power of the manipulation of figurate numbers, I want to consider the so-called Pythagorean theorem (*Elements* I.47). It is now a commonplace of mathematical history that the theorem is not the discovery of Pythagoras,[34] but was known by the Babylonians centuries before he was born. One need not, however, suppose that Greek knowledge of the theorem came ultimately from Babylonia. The primary Greek account of Pythagoras's discovery of the theorem[35] caused even his later admirers difficulty because in it the allegedly vegetarian Pythagoras was said to have celebrated his discovery by sacrificing an ox. For example, Proclus ([8.74], 426.5–9) says:

> If we listen to those who like to give an account of old things, one will find them attributing this theorem to Pythagoras and saying that he sacrificed an ox on its discovery.

Proclus then immediately turns to praise for Euclid for generalizing the theorem from squares to similar figures (*Elements* VI.31). Proclus also attributes to Pythagoras a procedure for generating numbers satisfying the theorem;[36] the procedure starts with an odd number m and takes $\dfrac{m^2 - 1}{2}$ and $\dfrac{m^2 - 1}{2} + 1$. Heath ([8.7]: 80) shows how this rule could be related to the generation of the square numbers through the addition of gnomons. It is clear from Figure 8.6 that the square number $(n + 1)^2$ is generated from a square number n^2 by the addition of the gnomon $2n + 1$; but if $2n + 1 = m^2$, $n = \dfrac{m^2 - 1}{2}$ and $n + 1 = \dfrac{m^2 - 1}{2} + 1$.

Becker [895] pointed out an odd feature of the last sixteen propositions (IX.21–36) of the arithmetic books of the *Elements*. In IX.20 Euclid proves one of the old chestnuts of arithmetic, the infinity of the prime numbers. In IX.21 Euclid proves on the basis of definitions only that the sum of any number of even numbers is even; and there follows a string of other relatively elementary propositions. However, the string culminates in another old chestnut of arithmetic (IX.36), that if $p = 2^0 + 2^1 + 2^2 \ldots + 2^n$ and is prime, $p \cdot 2^n$ is perfect, i.e. equal to the sum of its factors other than itself.[37] Euclid's proof of this result uses propositions proved before IX.21 and none from IX.21–34. IX.21–34 are, with the exception of 32, a self-contained deductive sequence dependent only on definitions. Becker argued that the propositions in the sequence could all be proved on the basis of figurate numbers if one understood the product of two numbers to be a rectangle with the numbers as 'sides' (see Figure 8.7, which represents the product of 3.5), and understood even and odd in the way they are defined in the *Elements*, where an even number is said to be one which is divisible into two equal parts and an odd to be one which is not even or which differs from an even number by 1 (VII, defs 6 and 7). Becker also showed that 36 could be incorporated into the sequence and proved on the same basis, eliminating the need for IX.35, which Euclid proves as a lemma for 36. Becker's claim that he had reconstructed a piece of early Pythagorean deductive arithmetic has won considerable, although not universal, acceptance among historians of Greek mathematics.

Subsequently Becker ([8.1], 41, [8.2], 51–2) offered a proof of the same kind for what he called the irrationality of $\sqrt{2}$, but which we can think of as the claim that there is no square number which added to itself produces a square number. Clearly if a Pythagorean was

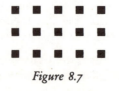

Figure 8.7

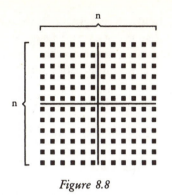

Figure 8.8

interested in finding numbers satisfying the Pythagorean theorem in general, he might have been interested in finding numbers satisfying it in the particular case of isosceles right triangles. Like the justification of Pythagoras' rule for finding numbers satisfying the Pythagorean theorem, the proof begins by imagining what things would be like if such numbers were found. It is easy to see (Figure 8.8) that the square of an even number is even and, in fact, divisible into 4 equal square numbers. But if $n^2 = 2m^2$, then n^2 is even by definition and the left and right halves of the figure are equal to m^2, which itself is divisible into two square numbers, each equal to $(\frac{n}{2})^2$. Clearly then m^2 is a smaller number than n^2 and is twice a square number, which is twice a smaller square number m_1^2, which obviously will be twice a smaller square number m_2^2, and so on *ad infinitum*. But such an infinite sequence of smaller numbers is impossible.

Becker's reconstruction is a reconstruction. There is no evidence to support the claim that there ever were arguments of the kind that he presents, let alone that they were given by early Pythagoreans. Burkert ([8.79], 434–7) raises a number of objections to the reconstruction, of which I mention two.[38] The first is that the reconstructed theory has a deductive structure, but the Pythagoreans 'did not deduce one proposition from the other'. The second is that the Pythagoreans, being 'simpler souls' would be satisfied with seeing inductively that there are no configurations satisfying the equation $n^2 = 2m^2$ and could not proceed by imagining a configuration satisfying it. Both of these assertions seem to me to beg important questions. It may well be a mistake to assign Euclidean formality to the early fifth century, but there doesn't seem to me anything conceptually or psychologically difficult in imagining that Pythagoreans who showed that, say, the sum of two even numbers is even by using figurate numbers might show that an even plus odd number is odd by pointing out that an even plus an odd number is an even number plus an even number plus 1. Nor does it seem to me difficult to imagine a Pythagorean simple soul who has seen 'inductively' that no n^2 is $2m^2$ using a picture like Figure 8.8 to demonstrate the fact, while ignoring the point that the figure 'really' shows only that $12^2 = 72 + 72$ and does not represent 72 as a square number.

(4) Geometry in the Sixth and Fifth Centuries

Application of areas

Proclus's general description of Pythagoras' contributions to geometry has a blatantly Neoplatonic sound. Burkert ([8.79], 409–12) has invoked a partial similarity to a sentence of Iamblichus ([8.51], 70.1–7) to argue that Proclus' entire description of Pythagoras with the ascription to him of the study of irrationals and the construction of the regular solids – for Proclus the goal of the *Elements* as a whole – is unreliable. In section 3 of part one I pointed out that Theaetetus probably was the first person to treat the five regular solids in a roughly systematic way. Before discussing irrationality I want to mention a passage in which Proclus cites Eudemus for an ascription, not to Pythagoras, but to the 'ancient' Pythagoreans.[39]

In *Elements* I.44 Euclid shows how, given a straight line AB, a triangle b, and an angle EFG, to construct a parallelogram ABCD equal to b and with angle DAB equal to angle EFG (See Figure 8.9).

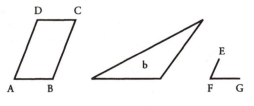

Figure 8.9

At the beginning of his discussion of this proposition Proclus ([8.74], 419. 15–18) writes:

> Those around Eudemus say that the following things are ancient and discoveries of the muse of the Pythagoreans: the application [*parabolē*] of areas and their excess [*hyperbolē*] and their deficiency [*elleipsis*].

In I.44 the given area b is 'applied' to the straight line AB. In VI.28 (VI.29) Euclid shows how, given a rectilineal figure b (b') and a parallelogram EFGH, to apply to a straight line AB a parallelogram AB′C′D

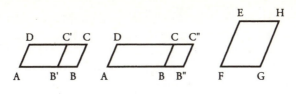

Figure 8.10

(AB″C″D) which is equal to b (b′) and 'deficient' ('excessive') by a parallelogram BB′C′C (BB″C″C) similar to EFGH (See Figure 8.10).[40]

In his headnote to Book II of the *Elements* Heath ([8.32] 1:372) writes:

> We have already seen how the Pythagoreans and later Greek mathematicians exhibited different kinds of numbers as forming different geometrical figures. Thus, says Theon of Smyrna (p. 36, 6–11), 'plane numbers, triangular, square and solid numbers, and the rest are not so called independently ... but in virtue of their similarity to the areas which they measure; for 4, since it measures a square area, is called square by adaptation from it, and 6 is called oblong for the same reason'. A 'plane number' is similarly described as a number obtained by multiplying the two numbers together, which two numbers are sometimes spoken of as 'sides', sometimes as the 'length' and 'breadth' respectively of the number which is their product.
>
> The *product* of two numbers was thus represented geometrically by the *rectangle* contained by the straight lines representing the two numbers respectively. It needed only the discovery of incommensurable or irrational straight lines in order to represent geometrically by a rectangle the product of any two quantities whatever, rational or irrational; and it was possible to advance from a geometrical arithmetic to a geometrical *algebra*, which indeed by Euclid's time (and probably long before) had reached such a stage of development that it could solve the same problems as our algebra so far as they do not involve the manipulation of expressions of a degree higher than the second.
>
> (Cf. van der Waerden [8.13], 124)

Heath here presents what I will call the algebraic interpretation of Greek mathematics, an interpretation he takes over from Tannery and Zeuthen.[41] We can get a good enough sense of what he has in mind by considering the propositions I used to illustrate application of areas. These propositions are given their 'algebraic' sense when, as Heath's remarks suggest, the angle EFG is taken to be right, the parallelogram

EFGH to be a square, and the other parallelograms to be rectangles. For then the area b represents a known quantity b and the straight line AB represents a known quantity a. In I.44 AD represents the value x which solves the equation 'ax = b'.[42] And in VI.28 (VI.29) the straight line BB' (BB'') represents the solution of the equation '$(a - x)x = ax - x^2 = b$' ('$(a + x)x = ax + x^2 = b$'). Similarly, to construct a square equal to a given rectilineal figure (II.14) is to solve '$x^2 = b$'.

It is important to see that the algebraic interpretation of an important part of Greek mathematics involves treating its geometric form as mere form. The qualitative geometric character of Greek mathematics becomes a mask for a quantitative and calculational notion of 'what's really going on'. It is in large part because of this picture that Heath moves Pythagorean arithmetic to the front of his *History*, preceding it by a chapter on 'Greek numerical notation and arithmetical operations', a chapter which likewise relies entirely on late Greek sources.

Tannery, Zeuthen and Heath all did their work before the decipherment of Babylonian materials. These materials provided the basis for an interpretation of Babylonian mathematics as an algebra which solves numerical problems. With this discovery people were in a position to argue that the geometrical clothing which the Greeks allegedly put on their 'algebra' was sewn out of Babylonian cloth to clothe a Babylonian body.[43] And the answer to why the Greeks bothered with all the fancy tailoring was found in their deductive rigour and the discovery of incommensurability. I quote van der Waerden ([8.13], 125–6):

> In the domain of numbers the equation $x^2 = 2$ cannot be solved, not even in that of ratios of numbers. But it is solvable in the domain of segments; indeed the diagonal of the unit square is a solution. Consequently, in order to obtain exact solutions of quadratic equations, we have to pass from the domain of numbers to that of geometric magnitudes. Geometrical algebra is valid also for irrational segments and is nevertheless an exact science. It is therefore logical necessity . . . which compelled the Pythagoreans to transmute their algebra into a geometric form.[44]

Thus we have a complicated story of (a) Greek borrowing of Babylonian computational mathematics, (b) discovering incommensurability, and (c) developing a rigorous geometric disguise for carrying on with Babylonian computation. If we assume that when Eudemus says that the discovery of application of areas was ancient and Pythagorean, he intends to refer to what we call early Pythagoreans, the whole history has to be moved back at least to the early fifth century. The way Burkert ([8.79], 465) avoids this difficulty is to leave the word 'ancient' out of account and argue that the discovery of incommensurability is 'not far from Theodorus of Cyrene',[45] and hence to make (c) apply to 'late' Pythagoreans. My preference is to give up the whole idea that Greek mathematics is essentially computational and hence the idea that it rests on Babylonian achievements. With this point of view the question of the discovery of incommensurability becomes independent of positions on the nature and origins of Greek mathematics and can be approached on its own. I wish I could say that approaching the question this way made one answer or another probable, but, if we abandon Proclus' statement about Pythagoras, the evidence for dating is unsatisfactory. The *terminus ante quem* is provided by references to irrationality in Plato; and if we believe that the mathematics lesson of the *Theaetetus* gives an indication of the state of mathematical knowledge in the 410s, we will be struck by the fact that Theodorus starts his case-by-case treatment with 3, and not 2; we might, then, take 410 as the *terminus*.

The discovery of incommensurability: Hippasus of Metapontum

The version of the Becker proof of the irrationality of $\sqrt{2}$ which I presented in section 2 of this part is just a reformulation of the argument to which Aristotle refers (*Prior Analytics* I.23.41a26–7) when he illustrates *reductio ad absurdum* by referring to the proof that 'the diagonal of the square is incommensurable because odd numbers become equal to evens if it is supposed commensurable'. A version of this proof occurs in our manuscripts as the last proposition of *Elements* X, but is printed in an appendix by Heiberg ([8.30] 3: 408.1ff.). That version differs from the proof I gave in avoiding direct reference to the impossibility of an infinitely descending sequence of numbers by assuming that n and m are the least numbers such that $n^2 = 2m^2$ and inferring that, since n is even, m must be odd; but then the argument shows that m must be even. It is frequently assumed that some such proof was the first proof of incommensurability, partly because of the passage in Aristotle and partly because side and diagonal of a square are the standard Greek example of incommensurability. In its Euclidean form the proof presupposes a fairly sophisticated understanding of how to deal with ratios in least terms – an important subject of *Elements* VII, which is dependent on *anthuphairesis*. There are various ways of minimizing this presupposition, but in general those who believe that the Euclidean proof is a version of the original proof have used its relative sophistication to argue either that the proof must be late or that Greek mathematics must have been sophisticated relatively early.

Von Fritz [8.46] ascribed the discovery of incommensurability to the Pythagorean Hippasus of Metapontum on the basis of two texts of Iamblichus printed under DK 18.4. The first says:

> About Hippasus they say that he died at sea for impiety because he published and described the sphere composed of twelve pentagons [i.e the dodecahedron] and allowed himself to be credited with the discovery, but all these things were the discoveries of 'that man' (for this is the way they refer to Pythagoras and not by his name). Mathematics advanced because of these things, and two people were most of all considered the first mathematicians of the time, Theodorus of Cyrene and Hippocrates of Chios.
>
> (Iamblichus [8.53] 78.27–36)

In the other text Iamblichus ([8.51] 132.11–23) does not mention Hippasus, but says that the divine destroyed at sea the person who revealed the construction of the dodecahedron. Iamblichus adds that 'some people say it was the person who spoke out about irrationality and incommensurability who suffered this'. Von Fritz claimed that Hippasus discovered irrationality in connection with the regular pentagon (the face of the dodecahedron) and the star or pentagram, a Pythagorean symbol formed by connecting alternating vertices of the pentagon. I sketch, with reference to Figure 8.11, the reasoning von Fritz ascribed to Hippasus.

Suppose one tries to find the greatest common measure of the side AE and the diagonal AD. It is clear that AE ≈ AE', so that AD − AE ≈ E'D. But E'D < AE and E'D ≈ AA'. Hence when E'D measures AE' it leaves A'E' as a remainder. But now E'D ≈ D'D ≈

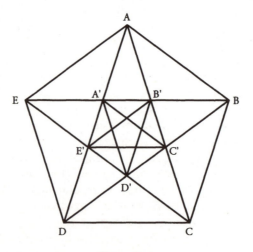

Figure 8.11

A'D', so performing *anthuphairesis* on A'E' and E'D is the same as performing it on A'E' and A'D', i.e. on the side and diagonal of the regular pentagon A'B'C'D'E'. Clearly, the initial situation repeats itself and will repeat itself infinitely often as *anthuphairesis* is continued. Hence diagonal and side have no common measure.

A Euclidean version of this argument would, of course, require justifications of the equalities and inequalities educed. One might assume that Hippasus could and would give such justifications. But, like Becker's arguments with the number configurations, Hippasus's alleged argument could be a verbalization of something which is 'seen' to be true from the figure. However, the Hippasus argument, like the proof using the expression of ratios in least terms, presupposes the use of *anthuphairesis* to find a common measure,[46] and hence – using the correlation between commensurability and having the ratio of a number to a number – the desire to express quantitative relations numerically. This desire is a primary mathematical component of numerous scholarly representations according to which the early Pythagoreans were committed to a view that 'everything is number', sought to find numerical expressions for all kinds of relationships, and were thrown into a crisis by the discovery of incommensurability.[47] The metaphysical component of these representations of early Pythagoreanism has, I think, been largely discredited, as have the attempts to connect Zeno's paradoxes with the issue of incommensurability.[48] And so perhaps has the idea that the discovery of incommensurability caused some kind of crisis (as opposed to a difficulty requiring a solution) in mathematics itself. But, as we have seen, the view that Greek mathematics was importantly numerical and calculational and that the discovery of incommensurabilty 'forced' it to become geometricized remains an anchor of many contemporary presentations of Greek mathematics. However, the information which we have is more than merely compatible with the view that the Greeks pursued arithmetic and geometric investigations, including the application of areas, at a reasonably early time and that they continued to do so after the discovery of incommensurability. The question of how rigorous early Greek mathematics was seems to me quite unanswerable. If we accept the reports on Thales' geometric accomplishments at more or less face value, we are presumably committed to saying that some idea of proof was functioning in Greek mathematics at a very early stage. If we do not, we are in no position to make any definite statement about its emergence, except that it did emerge. There are analogues of mathematical argument in Parmenides' deduction and in Zeno's dialectical argumentation. But the direction of influence seems to me quite indeterminable. I make no more than my guess in saying that I don't believe that mathematical argument was influenced by either one of them[49] and that, whereas Parmenides' argumentation looks to be autonomous and satisfactorily explained without invoking mathematical precedent, Zeno's considerations of infinite divisions seem likely to reflect mathematical preoccupations.

The later fifth century: the quadrature of the circle

In his history Proclus moves directly from Pythagoras to Anaxagoras, Oinopides of Chios, Hippocrates of Chios, and Theodorus of Cyrene. After his brief remark on the advancement of mathematics because of Hippasus' mathematical revelations, Iamblichus mentions only the last two of these people ([8.53], 78.27–36, quoted in the previous section). We know essentially nothing about the mathematical accomplishments of Anaxagoras,[50] although Plutarch (*On Exile* 607F, DK 59 A 38) tells us that he managed to square the circle while in prison. From passages in Aristotle and comments on them we learn of other apparent attempts to square the circle by Antiphon (late fifth century), Bryson (fourth century), and Hippocrates of Chios.[51] Antiphon apparently argued that one of the successively larger inscribed polygons of a sequence like the one indicated in Figure 8.1 would coincide with the circumscribing circle, and Bryson that, since there is a square larger than a given circle and a square smaller than it, there is one equal to it. From the point of view underlying Eudoxus' method of exhaustion Antiphon's argument would seem to ignore the difference between arbitrarily close approximation and coincidence. Bryson's argument is not a fallacy, but establishes (on the basis of some intuition about continuity) only the existence of a square equal to a given circle without showing how to construct it.

Hippocrates and Oinopides

Hippocrates' reasoning has been the subject of considerable discussion because Simplicius' presentation of his argument, based on the account of Eudemus, is our fullest representation of a piece of fifth-century mathematics. In the *Physics* (I.2.185a14–17) Aristotle refers to a quadrature by means of segments as if it made an incorrect inference from true geometrical principles. In the *Sophistical Refutations* (11.171b13–18) he refers to a false proof of Hippocrates in a context in which he also mentions Bryson's quadrature and a quadrature by means of lunes, that is, plane figures contained by two circle arcs such as the darkened areas in Figure 8.12. Subsequently (171b38–172a7) Aristotle characterizes the quadrature by means of lunes in much the way that he characterized the quadrature by means of segments in the *Physics*. The ancient commentators on the *Physics* passage, starting with Alexander, all take the quadrature by means of segments to be the quadrature by means of

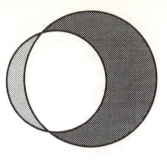

Figure 8.12

lunes and to be the work of Hippocrates. In his comment on the *Physics* passage ([8.84], 60.27–30) Simplicius invokes Eudemus:

> I will set out precisely what Eudemus says, but for the sake of clarity I will add a few things taken from Euclid's *Elements*, because Eudemus comments in the old-fashioned way and sets out explanations in abbreviated form.

Obviously our perception of Hippocrates' reasoning is mediated by both Simplicius and Eudemus. We might suppose that, once the quotations from Euclid have been subtracted, the remainder of the material which follows is by Eudemus, but that still leaves us with the question of distinguishing Eudemian from Hippocratic material, a question which does not seem to be capable of being settled.[52] Simplicius' extract from Eudemus begins as follows:

> In the second book of his history of geometry Eudemus says the following. The quadratures of lunes, which are not considered as superficial constructions (*diagrammata*) because of their connection with the circle, were first described by Hippocrates in a way which was considered to be in order. Let us therefore touch on this subject in more detail and go through it. He made himself a starting-point and set out as the first of the things useful for the quadratures, the proposition that:
> (i) similar segments of circles have to one another the same ratio as their bases have in square.
> He showed this on the basis of having shown that:
> (ii) diameters [of circles] have the same ratios in square as the circles do, a proposition which Euclid puts second in Book XII of the *Elements*, where the proposition says 'Circles are to one another as the squares on their diameters'. For as the circles are to one another, so are their similar segments, since:
> (iii) similar segments are those which are the same part of a

circle, for example, a semicircle is similar to a semicircle, a third of a circle to a third of a circle. Therefore,

(iv) similar segments admit equal angles, at least the angles of all semicircles are right, and the angles of segments greater than semicircles are less than right angles and as much less as the segments are greater than semicircles, and the angles of segments less than semicircles are greater than right angles and as much greater as the segments are less than semicircles.

([8.84], 60.30–61.18, my numbers inserted)

Proposition (ii) is, as Simplicius says, equivalent to *Elements* XII.2, which is proved by the method of exhaustion (see section 1 of part one). Simplicius says that Hippocrates 'showed' (*deiknumi*) (ii), but scholars are reluctant to admit that he could have proved it in a rigorous fashion. Euclid takes (iv) as the definition of similar segments (III, def. 11), but he himself makes very little use of them. Hippocrates apparently defined two segments to be similar if they are the same 'part' of the circles of which they are segments. In Euclid a part of something is one nth of it, which would mean that Hippocrates picked out very few of the similar segments, indeed, none greater than a semicircle, and certainly none of the incommensurable ones. The way in which Hippocrates gets from (iii) to (iv) suggests that he wasn't using much of a notion of proportionality at all, and just arguing in some sort of loose way. Obviously this looseness bears on the question whether or not Hippocrates knew about incommensurability. Again we are faced with standard kinds of choice: blame Simplicius or Eudemus for misunderstanding; assume that Hippocrates' argumentation was not entirely rigorous; assume that incommensurability was discovered after Hippocrates squared his lunes or at least not long before. Finally, the move from (ii) to (i) seems to require some proposition about the relationship between the base of a segment of a circle and the diameter of the circle, perhaps that the segment is to the semicircle as the square on its base is to the square on the diameter. But we are not told how Hippocrates might have proved this.

Hippocrates squared in succession three particular lunes, one with a semicircle as outer circumference, one with an outer circumference greater than a semicircle, and one with an outer circumference less than a semicircle, and then a circle plus a particular lune. Simplicius' report does not make it seem as though Hippocrates claimed to have shown how to square the circle because he had shown how to square a circle plus a lune and how to square lunes with an outer circumference of 'any size'. Perhaps he did, but it seems equally likely that the investigations described by Simplicius were an attempt at quadrature which somehow was interpreted to involve a claim to success.

It is not possible for me to describe here Hippocrates' four quadratures.[53] I shall, however, mention one construction described by Simplicius. In the left configuration in Figure 8.13, EG is parallel to KB, EK $\approx$ KB $\approx$ BG, EF $\approx$ FG, and the circle segments on EF, FG, EK, KB and BG are all similar.

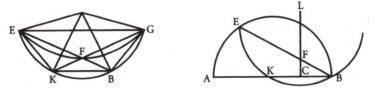

Figure 8.13

It should be clear that the lune EKBGF will be squarable if:

$$3 \cdot sq(KB) \approx sq(EK) + sq(KB) + sq(BG) \approx sq(EF) + sq(FG) \approx 2 \cdot sq(EF)$$

since then the circle segments on EK, KB and BG are together equal to the circle segments on EF and FG and the lune EKBGF is equal to the rectilineal figure EKBGF.

The right configuration in Figure 8.13 shows how Hippocrates manages to produce this result. He starts from a semicircle AKCBE with centre K, and lets CL be the perpendicular bisector of KB. He then finds F on CL such that the continuation of BF intersects the semicircle at E with $2 \cdot sq(EF) \approx 3 \cdot sq(KB)$. It is then a simple matter to carry out the rest of the construction. What our text doesn't tell us is how Hippocrates proposed to find F. This could be done by a so-called verging argument (*neusis*). There is no problem in constructing a straight line E'F' satisfying $2.sq(E'F') \approx 3 \cdot sq(KB)$. One might think of the verging argument as a matter of marking E'F' on a line (or ruler) and then moving the line around until a position is found in which E' lies on the circumference, F' on CL, and the line passes through point B. However, the problem can also be solved by a fairly complicated application of areas.

It seems reasonable to suppose that the original Hippocratean material from which Simplicius' report ultimately derives represented a high standard of geometric argumentation. Since Proclus tells us that Hippocrates was the first person said to have written elements, it also seems reasonable to suppose that at least parts of Hippocrates' geometric work were built up in something like the Euclidean way. Hippocrates' interest in mathematical methodology is borne out by another of his accomplishments, his reduction of the problem of constructing a cube twice the size of a given one to the finding of two mean proportionals between two given straight lines x and y, that is finding z and w such that x:z :: z:w :: w:y (Eutocius [8.44], 88.17–23, DK 42.4). According to Proclus ([8.74], 212.24–213.11), Hippocrates was the first person to 'reduce' outstanding geometric questions to other propositions.

That by Hippocrates' time there had been a fair amount of reduction of problems to quite elementary geometric materials is borne out by what little we know of the geometric work of his fellow countryman Oinopides. According to Proclus ([8.74], 283.7–10, DK 41.13) Oinopides investigated the problem of erecting a perpendicular to a given straight line 'because he believed it was useful for astronomy'.[54] Oinopides' interest in what is a quite elementary geometric construction is often connected with another passage in Proclus ([8.74], 333.5–9, DK 41.14) in which, on the authority of Eudemus, Oinopides is said to have discovered how to construct an angle equal to a given one (*Elements* I.23). It seems almost certain that Oinopides could not have been concerned with the practical carrying out of these constructions by any means whatsoever, but with justifying them on the basis of simpler constructions. But these constructions are themselves so simple that it is hard to see how this could have been Oinopides' concern if he was not working on the basis of something like the ruler-and-compass foundation of the *Elements*. That is to say, it looks as though by the later fifth century Greek geometry has moved close to what became a permanent foundation. It seems to me most plausible to imagine this concern with the equivalent of foundations as the outcome of a rather lengthy history of geometric demonstration.

Of course, the problems involving Hippocrates' use of the theory of proportion, his *neusis* construction, and his 'showing' of the equivalent of *Elements* XII.2 remain unsolved. My suggestions on these questions are made with no great confidence. I see no way to make good sense of the passage on similar segments which follows Simplicius' citation of XII.2, and prefer to treat it as Simplicius' unsatisfactory attempt to provide a derivation of (i) from (ii) using (iii), and then to connect (iii) with Euclid's definition of similar segments. If this is correct, then Simplicius had no more information on these questions than what he says before he cites Euclid. In general I accept the standard view that only in the fourth century did the Greeks develop techniques for dealing with proportions involving incommensurables. But I am also inclined to put the date of the discovery of incommensurability back to the time of Hippasus of Metapontum, whether Hippasus himself discovered it in connection with the pentagon or it was discovered in something like the way Becker has suggested. I infer that the Greeks worked for more than half a century using laws of proportion which they were not able to prove in a rigorous way. Hence

I also infer that the interest in providing a rigorous foundation for the treatment of proportionality is a fourth-century interest. If this is correct, then we need not suppose that Hippocrates' 'elements' included any explicit theory of proportion.

Similarly, in the case of XII.2, I think we should assume that Hippocrates could not have proved this in the Euclidean way, and that, if he did, indeed, 'show' it, he did so in some intuitive way. The *neusis* construction offers us the alternative of assigning to Hippocrates either a full development of the method of application of areas or the use of an intuitively based construction which cannot in general be done with unmarked ruler and compass alone. Simplicius' silence on Hippocrates' technique makes it seem to me likely that he did not know which alternative Hippocrates adopted, and that Eudemus did not say. My inclination is to assume that Hippocrates used the intuitive construction. Of course, to say that Hippocrates used a *neusis* construction in his quadrature is not to say that he did or did not do the same kind of thing in his 'elements'. And even if he did use such constructions there, he may also have been interested in carrying out as many constructions as possible using some kind of compass and straight edge. In any case, it seems clear from Hippocrates' quadratures that he knew a good deal of the elementary geometry in Euclid's *Elements*, and had put it into some kind of reasonably rigorous order.

Hippias of Elis and the teaching of the mathematical sciences

There is one other fifth-century figure to be mentioned in connection with quadrature, the sophist Hippias of Elis, who described a curve known as the quadratix (*hē tetragōnizousa grammē*) because of its use in squaring the circle. It seems probable that Hippias used it only for the trisection of angles.[55] The quadratix is defined as follows (see Figure 8.14). Let ABCD be a square, ABED the quadrant of a circle with radius AB. Let AB make a uniform sweeping motion through the

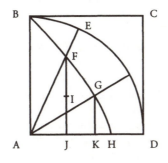

Figure 8.14

quadrant in the same time in which BC falls uniformly to coincide with AD. The quadratix is the curve BFGH described by the intersection of the two moving straight lines.

The quadratix enables one to divide an angle in any given ratio, since it is easy to prove that if the given ratio is IJ:FJ and GK is made equal and parallel to IJ, then angle GAD:angle FAD :: IJ:FJ. The quadrature of the circle is more difficult. One first establishes the length of circumference of the circle by showing that:

arc BED:AB :: AB:AH[56]

and then uses a result, associated with Archimedes[57] and proved by the method of exhaustion:

A circle has the same area as a right triangle with one leg equal to its radius and the other equal to its circumference.

Hippias of Elis is known to us from Plato's dialogues, where he is represented as an intellectual jack-of-all trades, who has a prodigious memory, performs numerical calculations at a speed which amazes his audience, and teaches the 'quadrivium', calculation (*logismos*), astronomy, geometry and music (*Protagoras* 318e). In the *Theaetetus* (145a) Plato represent's Theatetus' instructor Theodorus, the remaining fifth-century mathematician mentioned in Proclus' history, as knowledgeable in the subjects of the quadrivium. Unfortunately, we know no more about Theodorus' accomplishments than we are told in the *Theaetetus*; that is to say, the only thing about which we can be reasonably certain is that Theodorus taught something about incommensurability. For my purposes the important point is that Hippias and Theodorus show us that already in the fifth century the core of Plato's scientific curriculum was being taught in Greece.[58] In this chapter I have not discussed astronomy, but I hope I have made clear that if the other mathematical sciences of the curriculum had reached a high level of development by Plato's time, the groundwork for that achievement had been firmly laid by the end of the fifth century.

 NOTES

1 Dates are BCE (before Common Era) unless there is an indication to the contrary. For scepticism about the Eudemian provenance of this history see Lan [8.76].
2 Materials on the people other than Eudoxus and Archytas, who are mentioned by Proclus in the second part of his history, are collected in Lasserre [8.65].
3 See Mueller [8.38], 161–2, 192–4 and, for a historically oriented discussion of the avoidance of proportion in Books I–IV, Artmann [8.94].
4 I put 'rational' and 'irrational' in quotation marks to make clear that the

irrationality defined in Book X (definitions 3 and 4) is importantly different from the standard modern conception. Given an arbitrary straight line r taken as 'rational' (*rhētos*), Euclid calls a straight line x 'rational' if and only if x and r are commensurable 'in square' (*dunamei*), i.e. if and only if the square with x as side is commensurable with the square with r as side. And a rectilineal area is called 'rational' or 'irrational' depending on whether or not the side of a square equal to the area is 'rational'. If we think of r as of length 1, then the straight line corresponding to $\sqrt{2}$ is 'rational' because the square on it is twice as large as the square on r.

5 For a discussion of Democritus as a mathematician see Heath [8.7] 1: 176–81.

6 For discussion of Eudoxus' equally impressive achievements in geometrical astronomy see, e.g. Dicks [8.16], 151–89 or Neugebauer [8.18], 675–89.

7 The dodecahedron is very complicated mathematically, but it occurs naturally as a crystal, and there are quite early fabricated versions of it. Neither of these two things is true of the complicated icosahedron.

8 I here omit the argument establishing the correlation between these means and the irrationals which underlies Pappus' description of Theaetetus's accomplishment.

9 Euclid also describes a straight line as *dunamenos* an area when it is equal to the side of a square equal to the area. For this use cf. Plato, *Theaetetus* 148b2.

10 This is obviously the case for the arithmetic mean. A proof in Greek style for the harmonic mean is elaborate; the core idea is that the harmonic mean between integers m and n $\frac{2mn}{m+n}$.

11 See section 1 above. Book XIII only makes use of apotomes and lines related to them, not binomials. But the symmetry between binomials and apotomes would seem to provide a satisfactory explanation of the development of a theory of both.

12 Van der Waerden adopts an extreme version of this position. For him Book XIII itself was written by Theaetetus and incorporated in the *Elements* without revision. Book X, which was also written by Theaetetus, was changed in its very early parts for reasons which we will discuss in the next section, but the body of the book, 'which is concerned with the 13 kinds of 'irrational' lines, was left practically unchanged by Euclid, except that he and his followers added a number of less important propositions and remarks, intended to clarify the very difficult subject' (van der Waerden [8.13], 179).

13 In this case Euclid's argument requires the 'axiom of Archimedes' (see section 1 above).

14 See Mueller [8.38] 58–72

15 Namely, x: (m·x) :: y: (m·y). Cf. Heath [8.32] 3: 25 and 2: 126–9.

16 The idea of a pre-Eudoxian anthuphairetic conception of proportionality is most fully developed by Fowler [8.68].

17 The same kind of view is ascribed to 'those around Archytas and Eudoxus' by Theon of Smyrna ([8.92], 61.11–17, DK 47 A 19ᵃ).

18 'Movements which are thicker produce higher notes, thinner ones lower' ([8.30] 8: 158.8–9).

19 There is a quite full discussion in Barker [8.14], 190–208.

20 In IV.2 ([8.28], 303.19–304.6) Boethius reproduces the proof from the *Sectio*.

21 For discussion see Barker [8.14], 56–75. To explain the difference I first remark

that it is customary to give a scale for two octaves, each divided into two fourths or tetrachords separated by a tone; each tetrachord is divided in the same way into three intervals. The standard diatonic tuning is represented by:

9.8   tone

9.8   tone

256:243   'leimma' (note that $\frac{4}{3} = \frac{9}{8} \times \frac{9}{8} \times \frac{256}{243}$)

whereas Archytas' is:

9:8

8:7

28:27.

22 One could say much the same thing about the question of the basic attitude underlying Plato's attitude toward mathematical science. Much that he says suggests to us a quite scientific outlook, but passages like the division of the world soul in the *Timaeus* (35a–36b) or the description of the marriage number in the *Republic* (546b–c) make it difficult to feel confident about his general stance or about the many passages which are vague enough to sustain both a scientific and a mystifying reading.

23 For a discussion of Archytas' construction of a cube twice the size of a given one, which is a *tour de force* of the spatial imagination, see, e.g., Heath [8.7] 1: 246–9.

24 See Heath [8.7] 1: 128–37.

25 See, e.g., van der Waerden [8.13], 35–6. Cf. Neugebauer's remark ([8.10], 91) about astronomy: 'Ancient science was the product of a very few men; and these few happened not to be Egyptians.'

26 See Burkert [8.79], 380–2. For a defense of Heraclides of Pontus as Porphyry's source see Düring [8.78], 154–7.

27 Burkert ([8.79] 378–9), wishing to stress non-Pythagorean interest in music theory, fastens on a corrupt text (Theon of Smyrna [8.92], 59.4–21, DK 18 A 13) in which a physically impossible experiment involving the striking of vessels filled to various heights with liquid, *may* be ascribed to Lasus of Hermione, a person from the last half of the sixth century, who, according to the *Suda* ([8.87] 3:236.23–7), was the first to write a book (*logos*) on music, to introduce dithyrambs into competition, and to introduce eristic arguments (!)

28 See Burkert [8.79], 192–207.

29 Philolaus' two accounts of the comma are equivalent since:
tone – two *dieses* = (tone – *diesis*) – *diesis* = *apotome* – *diesis*.

30 On the *tetraktus* see Delatte [8.80], 249–68.

31 I here ignore difficulties involved in treating 1 as a number. For Nicomachus ([8.55], II.8.3) 1 is 'potentially' a triangular number.

32 On Euclid's definition of 'gnomon' (*Elements* II, def. 2) and the origin of the word itself, see Heath, [8.32] 1: 370–2.

33 Burkert ([8.79], 433–4) accepts the figurate number material as early and admits that 'even a game may be regarded legitimately as a kind of mathematics'. But he insists on the deductive character of even Thales' geometry, in the context of which 'Pythagorean arithmetic is an intrusive quasi-primitive element'.

34 Even contemporary defenders of the idea of an early Pythagorean mathematics are usually willing to concede that attributions of scientific achievements to Pythagoras are always subject to question and will settle for an attribution to the 'early Pythagoreans', a somewhat vague locution which I take to refer to the period before 450. In this essay I stress ancient attributions to Pythagoras because they offer the greatest challenge to sceptics. I am, however, only interested in early Pythagorean science, not in the science of Pythagoras.

35 For the sources see Heath [8.7] 1: 144–5.

36 [8.74], 428.10–21. In the continuation Proclus attributes a parallel method to Plato.

37 For example, $2^0 + 2^1 + 2^2 = 7$, $7.2^2 = 28$, and $28 = 2^0 + 2^1 + 2^2 + 7 + 14$.

38 Burkert also objects that Becker's proof of IX.36 'requires an abundant use of modern algebraic notation'. Here I think he points to a problem which cannot be avoided in writing out an argument which turns on perceived spatial relations. The argument I have given uses the fact there are no infinitely descending sequences of integers, which is a form of what we know as the principle of mathematical induction, but which is immediately obvious from the figurate representation of numbers. On the other hand, Burkert is right to question whether the notion of perfection involved in IX.36 could have coexisted with the notion of perfection involved in calling 10, the sum of 1, 2, 3 and 4, perfect. But such a consideration does not seem to me decisive.

39 I signal, but do not discuss, another passage ([8.74], 379.2–5) in which Proclus says that Eudemus ascribed to the Pythagoreans the discovery and proof of the proposition that the sum of the angles of a triangle is equal to two right angles (*Elements* I.32). Burkert ([8.79], 451, n. 21) apparently takes these to be 'late' Pythagoreans.

40 Being able to carry out VI.28 depends on a condition on b which I here ignore.

41 See, e.g., Tannery [8.107] and ch. 1 of Zeuthen [8.111]. For criticism of the algebraic interpretation with other references see Unguru [8.108].

42 In I.45 Euclid generalizes I.44 by making b an arbitrary rectilineal figure. In [8.32] Heath gives the algebraic interpretation of I.44–5 on p. 374 of vol. 1 and that of VI.28–9 on pp. 258–67 of vol. 2. He gives a similar and even more elaborate account of Book X on pp. 4–10 of vol. 3. For a purely geometric reading of Book X see Taisbak [8.39].

43 See, e.g., van der Waerden [8.13], 124.

44 Cf. Neugebauer [8.10], 146–52, Burkert [8.79], 454, neither of whom share van der Waerden's enthusiasm for the Pythagoreans.

45 But possibly made earlier by Hippasus of Metapontum as early as c.450.

46 Von Fritz [8.46], 403 refers to this technique as 'an old one, known by craftsmen as a rule of thumb many centuries before the beginning of Greek philosophy and science'. However, he gives no evidence for this characterization.

47 As an example of this view see Raven [8.105], and for criticism the review by Vlastos (*Gnomon* 25 (1953): 29–35).

48 For one attempt see Hasse and Scholz [8.100], and for criticism van der Waerden [8.109].

49 The view that Parmenides' argumentation was the source of Greek mathematical rigour was put forward most fully in Szabó [8.100]. It is endorsed by Burkert

[8.79], 424–6. For criticism see Knorr [8.102] and the review of Szabó by Bowen (*Historia Mathematica* 11 (1982); 335–45).

50 See Heath [8.7] 1: 172–4.

51 For discussion see Heath [8.7] 1: 183–200, 220–5 and Mueller [8.103].

52 Compare the different analyses of Rudio [8.85] and Heath [8.7] 1: 183–91.

53 There are quite full discussions in Heath [8.7] 1: 191–200 and Bulmer-Thomas [8.49].

54 For a discussion of Oinopides' work in astronomy see Bulmer-Thomas [8.59].

55 For the relevant texts see Heath [8.7] 1: 225–6, who, however, reaches a different conclusion about Hippias and quadrature.

56 Of course, since H results when AB and BC coincide, H can only be determined as the limit of a sequence of points produced before they coincide.

57 *Measurement of a Circle*, prop. 1.

58 At the beginning of the fragment (DK 47 B 1) from *On Mathematics* referred to at the beginning of section 6 part one, Archytas also mentions the four mathematical sciences as brothers. Burkert ([8.79], 380, n. 46) questions the authenticity of the remarks, but one part of his objection rests on the text printed in DK, which combines a passage in Porphyry in which astronomy is described but not named with a passage in Nicomachus in which astronomy is called spherics, but is not described.

❧ BIBLIOGRAPHY ❧

General Works

8.1 Becker, O. *Grundlagen der Mathematik in geschichtlicher Entwicklung*, Freiburg and Munich, Verlag Karl Alber, 1954.

8.2 —— *Das mathematische Denken der Antike*, Göttingen, Vandenhoeck und Ruprecht, 1957.

8.3 —— (ed.) *Zur Geschichte der griechischen Mathematik*, Darmstadt, Wissenschaftliche Buchgesellschaft, 1965.

8.4 Bowen, A. C. (ed.) *Science and Philosophy in Classical Greece*, New York and London, Garland Publishing, 1991.

8.5 DK [2.2].

8.6 Gillespie, C. C. (ed.) *Dictionary of Scientific Biography*, 16 vols, New York, Charles Scribner's Sons, 1970–90. Cited as *DSB*.

8.7 Heath [2.34].

8.8 Knorr, W. R. *The Ancient Tradition of Geometric Problems* Boston, Basel and Stuttgart, Birkhäuser, 1986.

8.9 Mueller, I. (ed.) *ΠΕΡΙ ΤΩΝ ΜΑΘΗΜΑΤΩΝ*. Essays on Greek Mathematics and its Later Development (*Apeiron* 14.4), South Edmonton, Academic Printing and Publishing, 1991.

8.10 Neugebauer, O. *The Exact Sciences in Antiquity*, 2nd edn. Providence, Brown University Press, 1957.

8.11 Sprague [7.4].

8.12 Thomas, I. (ed. and trans.) *Selections Illustrating the History of Greek Mathematics*, 2 vols, Cambridge, Mass. Harvard University Press, 1939.

8.13 van der Waerden, B. L. *Science Awakening*, (trans. Arnold Dresden), New York, John Wiley and Sons, 1963.

Music Theory

8.14 Barker, A. (ed.) *Greek Musical Writings*, vol. 2, Cambridge, Cambridge University Press, 1989.

8.15 —— 'Three approaches to canonic division', in Mueller [8.9], pp. 49–83.

Astronomy

8.16 Dicks, [2.27].

8.17 Heath [2.33].

8.18 Neugebauer, O. *A History of Ancient Mathematical Astronomy*, 3 vols, New York, Heidelberg, Berlin, Springer-Verlag, 1975.

8.19 van der Waerden, B. L. *Die Astronomie der Griechen: Eine Einführung*, Darmstadt, Wissenschaftliche Buchgesellschaft, 1988.

Ancient Authors Cited

For each author works are cited in the following order: (1) original text, (2) translation, (3) secondary works in alphabetical order.

Alexander of Aphrodisias

8.20 Wallies, M. (ed.) *Alexandri Aphrodisiensis in Aristotelis Topicorum Libros Octo Commentaria* (Commentaria in Aristotelem Graeca II.2), Berlin, George Reimer, 1891.

Antiphon (DK 80)

8.21 Morrison, J. S. (trans.) 'Antiphon', in Sprague [7.4], pp. 106–240. English translation.

Archimedes

8.22 Heiberg, J. L. (ed.) *Archimedis Opera Omnia cum Commentariis Eutocii*, 2nd edn, vols 1 and 2, Leipzig, B. G. Teubner, 1910, 1913.

8.23 Heath, T. L. *The Works of Archimedes*, 2nd edn, Cambridge, Cambridge University Press, 1912.

Aristotle

8.24 Bekker, I. (ed.) *Aristoteles Graece*, Berlin, George Reimer, 1831.
8.25 Barnes, J. (ed.) *The Complete Works of Aristotle*, Princeton, NJ, Princeton University Press, 1984. English translation.
8.26 Heath, T. *Mathematics in Aristotle*, Oxford, Clarendon Press, 1949.

Archytas (DK 47)

8.27 Bowen, A. C. 'The foundation of early Pythagorean harmonic science: Archytas, fragment 1', *Ancient Philosophy* 2 (1982): 79–94.

Boethius

8.28 Friedlein, G. (ed.) *Boetii De Institutione Arithmetica. De Institutione Musica*, Leipzig, B. G. Teubner, 1867.
8.29 Bower, C. M. (trans.) *Anicius Manlius Severinus Boethius, Fundamentals of Music*, New Haven and London, Yale University Press, 1989. English translation.

Euclid

8.30 Heiberg, J. L. and Menge, H. (eds) *Euclidis Opera Omnia*, 9 vols, Leipzig, B. G. Teubner, 1883–1916. (Vols 1–4 contain the *Elements*, and vol. 5 the scholia on the *Elements*; the *Sectio Canonis* is printed in vol. 8.)
8.31 Stamatis, E. S. (ed.) *Euclidis Elementa*, 4 vols, Leipzig, B. G. Teubner, 1969–73 (a second edition of the first four volumes of Heiberg and Menge [8.30]).
8.32 Heath, T. L. *The Thirteen Books of Euclid's* Elements, 2nd edn, 3 vols, Cambridge, Cambridge University Press, 1926. The *Sectio Canonis* is translated in Barker [8.14], pp. 190–208. English translation.
8.33 Artmann, B., 'Euclid's *Elements* and its prehistory', in Mueller [8.9], 1–47.
8.34 Barker, A., 'Methods and aims in the Euclidean "Sectio Canonis"', *Journal of Hellenic Studies* 101 (1981): 1–16.
8.35 Bowen, A. C. 'Euclid's *Sectio Canonis* and the history of Pythagoreanism', in Bowen [8.4], pp. 164–87.
8.36 Bulmer-Thomas, I. 'Euclid', in *DSB* [8.6], 4: 414–37.
8.37 Knorr, W. R. *The Evolution of the Euclidean Elements*, Dordrecht and Boston, D. Reidel, 1975.
8.38 Mueller, I. *Philosophy of Mathematics and Deductive Structure in Euclid's* Elements, Cambridge, Mass, MIT Press, 1981.
8.39 Taisbak, C. M. *Coloured Quadrangles: A Guide to the Tenth Book of Euclid's* Elements, Copenhagen, Museum Tusculanum Press, 1982.

Eudemus

8.40 Wehrli, F. (ed.) *Eudemos von Rhodos* (= Die Schule des Aristoteles 8), Basel, Benno Schwabe, 1955.

Eudoxus

8.41 Lasserre, F. *Die Fragmente des Eudoxos von Knidos*, Berlin, Walter de Gruyter, 1966.

8.42 Huxley, G. 'Studies in the Greek astronomers I. Eudoxian topics', *Greek, Roman, and Byzantine Studies* 4 (1963): 83–96.

8.43 Stein, H. 'Eudoxos and Dedekind, on the ancient Greek theory of ratios and its relation to modern mathematics', *Synthese* 84 (1990): 163–211.

Eutocius

8.44 Heiberg, J. L. (ed.) *Archimedis Opera Omnia cum Commentariis Eutocii*, 2nd edn, vol. 3, Leipzig, B. G. Teubner, 1915.

Heron

8.45 Schmidt, W. Nix, L., Schöne, H. and Heiberg, J. L. (eds and trans) *Heronis Alexandrini Opera quae Supersunt Omnia*, 5 vols, Leipzig, B. G. Teubner, 1899–1914.

Hippasus of Metapontum (DK 18)

8.46 von Fritz, K. 'The discovery of incommensurability by Hippasus of Metapontum', *Annals of Mathematics* 46 (1945), repr. in and cited after Allen and Furley [2.15] I: 282–412.

Hippias of Elis (DK 86)

8.48 Gallop, D. (trans.) 'Hippias', in Sprague [7.47], pp. 94–105. English translation.

8.47 Bulmer-Thomas, I. 'Hippias of Elis', in *DSB* [8.6] 6: 405–10.

Hippocrates of Chios (DK 42)

8.49 Bulmer-Thomas, I. 'Hippocrates of Chios', in *DSB* [8.6] 6: 410–18.

8.50 Lloyd, G. 'The alleged fallacy of Hippocrates of Chios', *Apeiron* 20 (1987): 103–28.

Iamblichus

8.51 Deubner, L. and Klein, U. (eds) *Iamblichi de Vita Pythagorica Liber*, Stuttgart, B. G. Teubner, 1975.

8.52 Guthrie, K. S. (ed., and trans.) *The Pythagorean Sourcebook and Library*, Grand Rapids, Mich., Phanes Press, 1987, pp. 57–122. English translation.

8.53 Festa, N. and Klein, U. (eds) *Iamblichi de Communi Mathematica Scientia Liber*, Stuttgart, B. G. Teubner, 1975.

8.54 Pistelli, H. and Klein, U. (eds) *Iamblichi in Nicomachi Arithmeticam Introductionem Liber*, Stuttgart, B. G. Teubner, 1975.

Nicomachus

8.55 Hoche, R. (ed.) *Nicomachi Geraseni Pythagorei Introductionis Arithmeticae Libri II*, Leipzig, B. G. Teubner, 1866.

8.56 D'Ooge, M. L. (trans.) *Nicomachus of Gerasa, Introduction to Arithmetic*, New York, The Macmillan Co., 1926. English translation.

8.57 von Jan, K. (ed.) *ΝΙΚΟΜΑΧΟΥ ΓΕΡΑΣΗΝΟΥ ΑΡΜΟΝΙΚΟΝ ΕΓΧΕΙΡΙ-ΔΙΟΝ* in von Jan, K. (ed.) *Musici Scriptores Graeci*, Leipzig, B. G. Teubner, 1895, 237–65.

8.58 Barker [8.14], 245–69. English translation.

Oinopides (DK 41)

8.59 Bulmer-Thomas, I. 'Oenopides', in *DSB* [8.6] 10: 179–182.

Pappus

8.60 Thomson, W. (ed. and trans.) *The Commentary of Pappus on Book X of Euclid's* Elements (Harvard Semitic Series 8), Cambridge, Mass. Harvard University Press, 1930.

Philolaus (DK 44)

8.61 Huffman, [4.78].

Plato and the Academy

8.62 Burnet, J. (ed.) *Platonis Opera*, 5 vols, Oxford, Clarendon Press, 1900–7.

8.63 Hamilton, E. and Cairns, H. (eds) *The Collected Dialogues of Plato*, Princeton, NJ, Princeton University Press, 1971. English translation.

8.64 Greene, W. C. (ed.) *Scholia Platonica* (American Philological Association Monographs 8), Haverford, Pa., American Philological Society, 1938.

8.65 Lasserre, F. (ed.) *De Léodamas de Thasos à Philipe d'Oponte*, Naples, Bibliopolis, 1987.

8.66 Anton, J. (ed.) *Science and the Sciences in Plato*, Albany, NY, Eidos Press, 1980.
8.67 Cherniss, H. 'Plato as mathematician', *Review of Metaphysics* 4 (1951): 395–405, repr. in *Selected Papers*, ed. L. Tarán, Leiden, E. J. Brill, 1977, pp. 222–52.
8.68 Fowler, D. H. *The Mathematics of Plato's Academy*, Oxford, Oxford University Press; paperback edn with addenda, 1991.
8.69 Frajese, A. (ed.) *Platone e la matematica nel mondo antico*, Rome, Editrice Studium, 1963.
8.70 Mueller, I. 'Mathematics and education, notes on the Platonist program', in Mueller [8.9], pp. 85–104.
8.71 —— 'Mathematical method and philosophical truth', in R. Kraut (ed.) *The Cambridge Companion to Plato*, Cambridge, Cambridge University Press, 1992, pp. 170–99.

Plutarch

8.72 *Plutarch's Moralia*, 15 vols, Cambridge, Mass. Harvard University Press, 1927–69.

Porphyry

8.73 Düring, I. (ed.) *Porphyrios Kommentar zur Harmonielehre des Ptolemaios*, Göteborg, Elanders Boktryckeri Aktiebolag, 1932.

Proclus

8.74 Friedlein, G. (ed.) *Procli Diadochi in Primum Euclidis Elementorum Librum Commentarii*, Leipzig, B. G. Teubner, 1873.
8.75 Morrow, G. R. (trans.) *Proclus, A Commentary on the First Book of Euclid's Elements*, Princeton, NJ, Princeton University Press, 1992. English translation.
8.76 Lan, C. E. 'Eudemo y el "catalogo de géometras" de Proclo', *Emerita* 53 (1985): 127–57.

Ptolemy

8.77 Düring, I. (ed.) *Die Harmonielehre des Klaudios Ptolemaios*, Göteborg, Elanders Boktryckeri Aktiebolag, 1930.
8.78 —— (trans.) *Ptolemaios und Porphyrios über die Musik*, Göteborg, Elanders Boktryckeri Aktiebolag, 1934.

Pythagoras and the Pythagoreans (DK 14–20, 58)

8.79 Burkert, [2.25].

8.80 Delatte, A. *Études sur la Littérature Pythagoricienne*, Paris, Librairie Ancienne Honoré Champion, 1915.

8.81 van der Waerden, B. L. *Die Pythagoreer*, Zürich and Munich, Artemis Verlag, 1979.

8.82 Zhmud, L. ' "All is number"?', *Phronesis* 34 (1989): 270–92.

8.83 —— 'Pythagoras as mathematician', *Historia Mathematica* 16 (1989): 249–68.

Simplicius

8.84 Diels, H. (ed.) *Simplicii in Aristotelis Physicorum Libros Quattuor Priores Commentaria* (Commentaria in Aristotelem Graeca IX), Berlin, George Reimer, 1882.

8.85 Rudio, F. (ed. and trans.) *Der Bericht des Simplicius über die Quadraturen des Antiphons und des Hippokrates*, Leipzig, B. G. Teubner, 1907.

Stobaeus, Joannes

8.86 Wachsmuth, C. and Hense, O. (eds) *Ioannis Stobaei Anthologium*, 5 vols, Berlin, Weidmann, 1884–1912.

Suda

8.87 Adler, A. (ed.) *Suidae Lexicon*, 4 vols, Leipzig, B. G. Teubner, 1928–35.

Thales (DK 11)

8.88 Dicks, D. R. 'Thales', *Classical Quarterly* NS 9 (1959): 294–309.

Theaetetus (Lasserre [8.65] 3)

8.89 Bulmer-Thomas, I. 'Theaetetus', in *DSB* [8.6] 13: 301–7.

8.90 Thesleff, H. 'Theaitetos and Theodoros', *Arctos* 24 (1990): 147–59.

Theodorus of Cyrene

8.91 Bulmer-Thomas, I. 'Theodorus of Cyrene', in *DSB* [8.6] 13: 314–19.

Theon of Smyrna

8.92 Hiller, E. (ed.) *Theonis Smyrnaei Philosophi Platonici Expositio Rerum Mathematicarum ad Legendum Platonem Utilium*, Lepizig, B. G. Teubner, 1878.

8.93 Lawlor, R. and D. (trans.) *Theon of Smyrna, Mathematics Useful for Understanding Plato*, San Diego, Calif., Wizards Bookshelf, 1979. English translation.

Other Secondary Sources

8.94 Artmann, B. 'Über voreuklidische "Elemente", deren Autor Proportionen vermied', *Archive for History of Exact Sciences* 33 (1985): 292–306.

8.95 Becker, O. 'Die Lehre von Geraden und Ungeraden im neunten Buch der euklidischen Elemente', *Quellen und Studien zur Geschichte der Mathematik, Astronomie und Physik*, Abteilung B. 3 (1936): 533–53; reprinted in Becker [8.3], pp. 125–45.

8.96 —— 'Eine voreudoxische Proportionenlehre und ihre Spuren bei Aristoteles und Euklid', *Quellen und Studien zur Geschichte der Mathematik, Astronomie und Physik*, Abteilung B. 2 (1933): 311–33.

8.97 von Fritz, K. 'Die APXAI in der griechischen Mathematik', *Archiv für Begriffsgeschichte* 1 (1955): 13–103; repr. in von Fritz [8.99], pp. 335–429.

8.98 —— 'Gleichheit, Kongruenz und Ähnlichkeit in der antiken Mathematik bis auf Euklid', *Archiv für Begriffsgeschichte* 4 (1959): 7–81; repr. in von Fritz [8.99], 430–508.

8.99 —— *Grundprobleme der Geschichte der Antiken Wissenschaft*, Berlin and New York, Walter de Gruyter, 1971.

8.100 Hasse, H. and Scholz, H., *Die Grundlagenkrisis der griechischen Mathematik*, Charlottenburg, Pan-Verlag Kurt Metzner, 1928.

8.101 Knorr, W. R. 'On the early history of axiomatics, the interaction of mathematics and philosophy in Greek antiquity', in J. Hintikka, D. Gruender and E. Agazzi (eds) *Theory Change, Ancient Axiomatics, and Galileo's Methodology* (Proceedings of the 1978 Pisa Conference on the History and Philosophy of Science, vol. 1), Dordrecht, D. Reidel, 1981.

8.102 KRS [1.6].

8.103 Mueller, I. 'Aristotle and the quadrature of the circle', in N. Kretzmann (ed.) *Infinity and Continuity in Ancient and Medieval Thought*, Ithaca, NY, Cornell University Press, 1982, pp. 146–64.

8.104 —— 'On the notion of a mathematical starting-point in Plato, Aristotle, and Euclid', in Bowen [8.4], pp. 59–97.

8.105 Raven, J. E. *Pythagoreans and Eleatics*, Cambridge, Cambridge University Press, 1948.

8.106 Szabó, A. *The Beginnings of Greek Mathematics*, trans. A. M. Ungar, Dordrecht, D. Reidel, 1978.

8.107 Tannery, P. 'De la solution géométrique des problèmes du second degré avant Euclide', *Mémoires de la Société des Sciences Physiques et Naturelles de Bordeaux*, 2e série, 4 (1882): 395–416; repr. in P. Tannery *Mémoires Scientifiques*, 17 vols, Toulouse, Edouard Privat and Paris, Gauthier-Villars, 1912–50, vol. 1, pp. 254–80.

8.108 Unguru, S. 'History of ancient mathematics: some reflections on the state of the art', *Isis* 70 (1979): 555–65.

8.109 van der Waerden, B. L. 'Zenon und die Grundlagenkrise der griechischen Mathematik', *Mathematische Annalen* 117 (1940): 141–61.

8.110 Waterhouse, W. C. 'The discovery of the regular solids', *Archive for History of Exact Sciences* 9 (1972–3): 212–21.

8.111 Zeuthen, H. G. *Die Lehre von den Kegelschnitten im Altertum*, trans. R. V. Fischer-Benzon, Copenhagen, Verlag von Andr. Fred. Høst & Søhn, 1886.

CHAPTER 9

Socrates and the beginnings of moral philosophy
Hugh H. Benson

↬ INTRODUCTION ↫

Cicero in *Tusculan Disputations* famously tells us that

> Socrates first called philosophy down from the sky, set it in cities
> and even introduced it into homes, and compelled it to consider
> life and morals, good and evil.
>
> (V.4.10)[1]

Again in the *Academica* he attributes to Varro the following view:

> It is my view, and it is universally agreed, that Socrates was the
> first person who summoned philosophy away from mysteries
> veiled in concealment by nature herself, upon which all
> philosophers before him had been engaged, and led it to the
> subject of ordinary life, in order to investigate the virtues and
> vices, and good and evil generally, and to realize that heavenly
> matters are either remote from our knowledge or else, however
> fully known, have nothing to do with the good life.
>
> (I.5.15, trans. Rackham)

Here we have two of the clearest statements of a tradition that stretches
from perhaps as early as Aristotle[2] to the present day:[3] moral philosophy begins with Socrates.

Nevertheless, this tradition should strike us as odd. In this very
volume we have seen instances of moral philosophy – or at least a
reasonable facsimile of it – predating Socrates. The Pythagoreans appear
to be committed to something like a moral philosophy, while many of
the so-called 'natural philosophers' appear to have moral commitments
as only a quick glance at their fragments makes clear. Moreover, a

323

number of philosophers flourishing virtually contemporaneously with Socrates would seem to have an equal claim to fathering moral philosophy. The sophists – Protagoras, Gorgias, *et al* – certainly seem to have moral views that rival Socrates', while the fragments of Democritus exhibit a moral theory.

Of course, part of the difficulty here is that the notion of having or practising a moral philosophy is quite vague. Does it suffice merely to entertain moral propositions? If so, then moral philosophy began long before Socrates. On the other hand, if it requires something else, what else? Answering this question is both difficult and perhaps uninteresting. But even if we were to answer it, we would still be a long way from confirming or disconfirming the Ciceronian tradition. To do this we would need to rehearse the entire history of philosophy up to Socrates focusing on whether any of Socrates' predecessors or contemporaries had or practised a moral philosophy so defined. Such a task is obviously well beyond anything that can be accomplished in an essay of this sort. Consequently, I will not attempt it. Instead, I propose to focus on a characteristic feature of Socratic moral philosophy, a feature that may have motivated the Ciceronian tradition. For morality, according to Socrates, is a knowledge or expertise to be practised and studied just like any other knowledge or expertise. What distinguishes it from other instances of knowledge and expertise is its object: roughly, the good. This is the message at the core of Socratic philosophy, a message Socrates believed he was called upon to spread. Whether such a message is new to the intellectual scene of fifth century Greece, or if so, whether that justifies crediting Socrates with the origins of moral philosophy, I leave for others to decide. My goal here is to come to grips with the substance of Socratic moral philosophy, whatever its intellectual ancestors and contemporaries may have been.

❧ THE SOCRATIC PROBLEM ❧

Before beginning this task we must address an issue that all discussions of Socratic philosophy must face: Whom am I referring to when I use the name 'Socrates'? The question arises because the historical individual that goes by this name (and who was the mentor of Plato, an associate of Xenophon, Alcibiades and Chaerephon, and general pest on the streets of Athens in the latter part of the fifth century BC) apparently wrote nothing. Our knowledge of the philosophical views of this individual derives primarily from four distinct sources: Aristophanes, who wrote a comedy entitled the *Clouds* in which Socrates is a major figure;[4] Xenophon, who wrote a variety of Socratic works, perhaps the most important of which is the *Memorabilia* which purports to be a record of a number of Socratic conversations[5]; Plato, who wrote twenty dialogues in which Socrates is the primary speaker[6]; and Aristotle, who refers to Socrates over forty times throughout his corpus.[7] This alone would pose no problem; we think we know quite a bit about Themistocles or Pericles and yet we possess none of their writings either. The problem arises because the portraits of Socrates painted by our first three sources are so different.[8] According to Aristophanes, Socrates is a sophistic natural philosopher who was willing to teach anyone who would pay for it how to make the weaker argument the stronger and who denied the existence of the gods of common opinion. According to Xenophon, Socrates was an unexciting didactician, who was quick to give advice concerning the most common matters and who was a paragon of common morality and religious practice. And according to Plato, Socrates was a non-dogmatic, perhaps even sceptical, moral philosopher, who examined and exposed others' pretenses to wisdom, denied that he taught anything, and espoused such non-traditional, in some cases even paradoxical, theses as 'no one ever does wrong willingly', 'it is wrong to harm one's enemies', and 'knowledge is necessary and sufficient for virtue'. The problem, then, is to decide which of these three portraits accurately represents the actual historical Socrates who walked the streets and frequented the gymnasia of fifth-century Athens.

Perhaps the clearest and currently most widely accepted solution to this problem[9] can be found in Gregory Vlastos's last book *Socrates: Ironist and Moral Philosopher* [9.93].[10] According to Vlastos, our three principal sources are Plato, Xenophon and Aristotle. He dismisses the Aristophanes portrait as the comic caricature that it is,[11] and then goes on to maintain that the Platonic portrait is more equivocal than I have let on. Vlastos argues that there are at least two distinct portraits of Socrates in the Platonic dialogues: one to be found in the early dialogues and another to be found in the middle and late dialogues.[12] The argument proceeds by detailing ten theses each consisting of two parts. One part contains a feature or view attributable to Socrates in the early dialogues; the other part contains a feature or view at odds with that of the first part and attributable to Socrates in the middle dialogues. For example, according to Vlastos, the Socrates of Plato's early dialogues is exclusively a moral philosopher, while the Socrates of Plato's middle dialogues is a 'moral philosopher and metaphysician and epistemologist and philosopher of science and philosopher of language and philosopher of religion and philosopher of education and philosopher of art'.[13] Vlastos concludes from this that in the Platonic dialogues Socrates maintains two philosophical views 'so different that they could not have been depicted as cohabiting the same brain throughout unless it had been the brain of a schizophrenic. They are so diverse in content and method that they contrast as sharply with one another as with any third philosophy you care to mention.'[14] Next, Vlastos argues on the basis of the testimony of our other two sources – Aristotle and Xenophon – that the philosophical view maintained by Socrates in the early dialogues is the philosophical view of the historical Socrates. For example, Vlastos argues that the Socrates of the middle dialogues advances a theory of separated Forms, while the Socrates of the early dialogues does not, and then points to *Metaphysics* 1078b30–2 where Aristotle distinguishes between Plato and Socrates precisely on the grounds that the former did, while the latter did not, separate the Forms.[15] Finally, Vlastos maintains that Plato's overriding concern in composing his dialogues – the early ones as well as the middle and late ones – is always philosophy. Consequently, 'in any given dialogue Plato allows the persona of Socrates only what he (Plato) considers true'.[16]

The conclusion of Vlastos's argument results in an interpretation of the Platonic portrait of Socrates that can be summed up in the following three theses:

1   The philosophical views advanced by Socrates in the early dialogues are distinct from the philosophical views advanced by that character in the middle dialogues (interpretation derived from Vlastos's ten theses).
2   The philosophical views advanced by Socrates in the early dialogues represent the philosophical views of the historical Socrates (thesis based on the independent testimony of Aristotle and Xenophon).
3   The philosophical views advanced by Socrates in the early dialogues represent the philosophical views of Plato before he adopted the classical Platonism of the middle dialogues (thesis based on Vlastos's grand methodological hypothesis).

I believe that this interpretation of the Platonic Socrates is generally correct.[17] Consequently, my answer to the question with which this section began is as follows. When I use the name 'Socrates' in the course of this essay I am referring to the actual historical individual who goes by that name, was the mentor of Plato, an associate of Xenophon, Alcibiades and Chaerephon, and a general pest on the streets and in the gymnasia of fifth-century Athens. I take as my primary source of evidence for the philosophical views of this individual the early dialogues of Plato, but I also take these views to be confirmed in part by the portraits of Aristotle and Xenophon.[18] This is the Socrates of this essay.

❧ FOLK MORALITY ❧

We can now turn to the task with which this essay began: coming to grips with Socratic moral philosophy. Since according to the Ciceronian tradition Socrates is doing something very unusual in advancing a moral philosophy, we can begin by turning to those views with which Socrates contrasts his own: common or folk morality and sophistic morality. Let me begin with folk morality and a passage in the *Protagoras* (319b3–319d7).

The main conversation in the *Protagoras* begins when Socrates asks Protagoras what he professes to teach. When Protagoras answers that he professes to teach virtue (*aretē*), Socrates expresses surprise.[19] He had always believed that virtue could not be taught – or so he says – and one of his arguments for this is that the Athenians are wise, but they don't think that virtue can be taught.[20] Evidence that the Athenians don't believe that virtue can be taught is derived from their behaviour in the Assembly. When they are faced with a decision regarding the building of temples, the building of ships, or any other technical matter (*en technēi*), they are unwilling to listen to the advice of anyone other than the relevant experts: temple-builders, shipwrights, etc. But when they are faced with a decision regarding the management of the city they are willing to consider the advice of anyone, 'be he carpenter, smith or cobbler, merchant or ship-owner, rich or poor, noble or low-born' (319d2–4, [9.82]).

If this is supposed to provide evidence that the Athenians fail to believe that virtue can be taught the idea must be something like this. The Athenians distinguish between those decisions that require virtue and those that do not. In the case of those that do not, the Athenians permit only the experts to be heard. In the case of those that do, the Athenians permit any and everyone to be heard. Thus, the Athenians do not regard virtue as an expertise, and so do not believe it can be taught. When Protagoras responds to this first Socratic argument, he does not deny that everyone – or at least everyone in a political community – possesses virtue sufficient for giving advice about such matters. Instead, Protagoras denies that virtue – so understood – fails to be an expertise.[21] Protagoras maintains that the Athenians believe that virtue is an expertise possessed by all the citizens to some degree or other. This, however, is apparently not how Socrates understands their view.

Here then we have Socrates' conception of common Athenian morality. According to Socrates, the common or folk view is that virtue is not an expertise – at least, if by expertise one has in mind some sort of special or unique ability. Instead virtue is something possessed to one degree or another by everyone; it is easily or automatically

327

acquired; and everyone is a competent adviser concerning it. Thus, if Socrates contrasts his own moral view with this folk view, he must believe that virtue is an expertise like temple-building, ship-building, and the rest; not something possessed by everyone; nor easily acquired. For Socrates, decisions that require virtue require the advice of an expert. But why should we think that Socrates contrasts his own moral view with this folk view? Doesn't Socrates put this view forward not only as the common view, but also as his own in contrast to Protagoras? Yes he does, but there are a number of reasons to doubt that Socrates is genuinely committed to the view he attributes to the Athenians in this passage.[22]

First, at the end of the *Protagoras* (361a5–c2) Socrates expresses his dismay that he and Protagoras appear to be arguing for the opposite of what they had maintained at the beginning. Immediately prior to this passage they had been discussing the relationship between courage (*andreia*) and wisdom (*sophia*). Protagoras maintained that the two are altogether different on the grounds that many men are ignorant yet courageous. Socrates argued on the contrary that courage is wisdom (*sophia*) about what is to be feared and what isn't (360d4–5), and so those who are ignorant cannot be courageous. Socrates concludes by noting that while he had earlier maintained – presumably at 319b3–d7 – that virtue is not knowledge (*epistēmē*) and so cannot be taught, he is now arguing that it is knowledge, on the basis of the claim that all the virtues – courage, justice, temperance and piety – are nothing other than knowledge. Protagoras on the other hand had maintained that virtue was knowledge and so could be taught and now he is arguing that it is not knowledge.[23] Exactly how to take Socrates' position here at the end of the *Protagoras* is a difficult question,[24] but however else we take it we can no longer rest secure in the thought that Socrates accepts the view he attributes to the many at 319b–d.

Second, outside the *Protagoras* there are other passages in which Socrates testifies to his rejection of the folk view. In the dialogue named for him, Crito urges Socrates to escape from prison in part on the grounds that the many apparently believe that it is the proper thing to do. Socrates responds by asking whether one should pay attention to the views of everyone or rather only to the views of the wise (*tōn phronimōn*). For example, Socrates asks, in the case of physical training should one pay attention to the views of anyone and everyone or to the views of the expert – the doctor (*iatros*) or the physical trainer (*paidotribēs*) – the instructor and one who knows (*tōi epistatēi kai epaionti*)? When Crito replies that it is the advice of the expert that ought to be heeded in this case, just as the Athenians in the *Protagoras* would maintain, Socrates continues that the same point holds in other cases, but especially in the case of matters concerning justice or injustice, the shameful and the fine, the good and the bad, that is, matters of the sort they are presently considering (47a–d). According to Socrates in this passage in the *Crito*, it is not the advice and opinion of the many that ought to be heeded in facing the decision whether to escape, but rather the advice and opinion of the one – if there is one – who knows. Thus, while Socrates does not explicitly say that when faced with decisions concerning (and so requiring) virtue, one should not consider the views of just anyone, but only the views of the expert, he does say that in these circumstances one should only pay attention to the one who knows and the analogy with the doctor and physical trainer suggests that the knowledge involved is expertise.[25]

In another passage Socrates' rejection of the folk view that virtue is not an expertise is more explicit. The *Laches* begins with two fathers soliciting the advice of two Athenian generals – Laches and Nicias – concerning the proper education of their sons. In particular, they want to know whether they should enrol their sons in a particular form of military training. When the two generals offer incompatible advice, Laches recommending against the training, Nicias recommending in its favour, one of the fathers turns to Socrates for his vote to decide the issue. Socrates responds that this is no way to reach a decision. Again he points to the example of physical training and maintains that in this case we would not heed the advice of the majority, but rather the advice of the one who had been trained under a good physical trainer (*paidotribēi*) – again, just as the Athenians in the *Protagoras* would maintain. As Socrates puts it, 'for I think that it is necessary to judge by knowledge but not by number if one intends to judge well' (*Laches* 184e8–9). Thus, Socrates continues, the proper way to decide the issue that faces the fathers is to heed the advice of the expert (*technikos*) concerning that thing about which they are currently seeking advice. After determining that the thing concerning which they are now seeking advice is the proper care of the soul, Socrates concludes that in order to decide whose advice ought to be heeded – Socrates', Laches', or Nicias' – they must determine which of the three is an expert concerning the care of the soul (185e1–6). When Socrates forswears his own expertise concerning this matter, Laches and Nicias permit their expertise to be tested. Rather than asking the generals whom they have made better or who their teachers have been (189d5–e3), Socrates indicates that another way to test their expertise concerning this matter is to determine if they know what virtue is (190b7–c2). Since this may be too large a task, Socrates narrows the question to whether they know what a part of virtue is – that is, whether they know what courage is (190c8–e3). This is the question that occupies the remainder of the *Laches*. Thus, Socrates here explicitly maintains that when faced with a decision that the Athenians would acknowledge requires virtue we should not heed the advice of everyone. Rather it is only the advice of the expert that should be heeded. Socrates here identifies the virtue required to give such advice with some form of expertise and the expertise itself appears to amount to, or at least require knowledge of the nature of virtue.

Finally, this passage in the *Laches* points us to a further consideration in favour of Socrates' rejection of folk morality: Socrates' elenctic mission. In testing the expertise of Laches and Nicias, Socrates is engaging in his elenctic mission, a mission he claims in the *Apology* derives from Chaerephon's trip to the Delphic Oracle. According to Socrates, Chaerephon once asked the oracle at Delphi whether anyone was wiser (*sophōteros*) than Socrates, to which the oracle responded that no one was. When Chaerephon reported this episode to Socrates, he was at loss as to what the oracle could mean. On the one hand, Socrates 'knew that he was wise concerning nothing great or small' (*Apology* 21b4–5),[26] and yet on the other hand, the oracle could not lie. Socrates, thereupon, set out to test the oracle by trying to uncover someone wiser than he. First, he went to the politicians, all of whom believed themselves to be wise but were shown not to be (*Apology* 21c3–e2). Next, he went to the poets. Not only did the poets think themselves wise concerning their poetry, but were not, but the poets also took themselves to be wise about other matters, concerning which they were not (*Apology* 22a8–c8). Finally, Socrates turned to the manual experts (*cheirotechnas*).[27] These, he discovered, did indeed know many of the fine things they were reputed to know, but unfortunately this knowledge of theirs encouraged them to believe that they were wise concerning other very great things (*ta megista*) when they were not (*Apology* 22c9–e5). Socrates concludes from this investigation of the oracle that,

> the god is wise and that his oracular response meant that human wisdom is worth little or nothing, and that when he says this man, Socrates, he is using my name as an example, as if he said: 'This man among you, mortals, is wisest who, like Socrates, understands that his wisdom is worthless.' So even now I continue this investigation as the god bade me – and go around seeking out anyone, citizen or stranger, whom I think wise. Then if I do not think he is, I come to the assistance of the god and show him that he is not wise.
>
> (*Apology* 23a5–b7; trans. Grube.)

Here then Socrates once again contrasts his own view with that of the average Athenian citizen. The average Athenian citizen – be he a politician, a poet, a manual expert, or anyone else – thinks himself wise about the great things, but is not. Such wisdom or expertise is not as easy to come by as they suppose. Socrates lacks this wisdom as well, but he also lacks the false conceit that he has it. Herein lies Socratic wisdom: recognition of his ignorance concerning the great things – recognition, that is, of his lack of moral knowledge or expertise.[28] Unlike the average Athenian, Socrates does not take himself to be in the position to give advice concerning decisions that require virtue. This is the role of a moral expert, something that Socrates, unlike the average Athenian, realizes he is not.

But this is not the end of the story. Socrates has found in his investigation of the oracle a mission[29] – the elenctic mission I referred to above.[30] Socrates does not merely test an individual's claim to moral wisdom and when he finds it lacking abandon him. Rather, as the passage quoted above indicates, when Socrates discovers that the individual lacks the knowledge he thinks he has, Socrates attempts to show him that he lacks it. But why? Socrates assumes that such moral knowledge is desirable. All of us – average Athenian and everyone – desire to possess it. Indeed, Socrates believes that such expertise is so desirable, that to encourage us to possess it, all Socrates needs to do is show us that we lack it. Consider how Socrates redescribes his elenctic mission following the jury's hypothetical order to cease philosophizing:

> Gentlemen of the jury, I am grateful and I am your friend, but I will obey the god rather than you, and as long as I draw breath and am able, I shall not cease to practice philosophy, to exhort you and in my usual way to point out to any one of you whom I happen to meet: 'Good Sir, you are an Athenian, a citizen of the greatest city with the greatest reputation for both wisdom and power; are you not ashamed of your eagerness to possess as much wealth, reputation and honours as possible, while you do not care for (*epimelēi*) nor give thought to wisdom or truth, or the best possible state of your soul (*phronēseōs de kai aletheias kai tēs psuchēs hopōs hōs beltistē*)?' Then, if one of you disputes this and says he does care (*epimeleisthai*), I shall not let him go at once or leave him, but I shall question him, examine him and test him, and if I do not think that he has attained the goodness (*aretēn*) that he says he has, I shall reproach him because he attaches little importance to the most important things and greater importance to the inferior things. I shall treat in this way anyone I happen to meet, young or old, citizen or stranger, and more so the citizens because you are more kindred to me. Be sure that this is what the god orders me to do, and I think there is no greater blessing for the city than my service to the god. For I go around doing nothing but persuading both young and old among you not to care for (*epimeleisthai*) your body or your

wealth in preference to or as strongly as for the best possible
state of your soul (*hōs tēs psuchēs hopōs aristē estai*).

(*Apology* 29d2–30b2; trans. Grube).

Here then we have the first moral philosophy or moral perspective
against which Socrates contrasts his own – the common or folk view.
According to folk morality, virtue is something everyone – or nearly
everyone[31] – already possesses. It is not an expertise – at least if by
expertise one has in mind some sort of special or unique ability. Consequently, it is fairly easy to come by[32] and everyone is in a position to
give advice concerning those affairs that require virtue. For Socrates,
however, things are otherwise. Virtue is an expertise, like physical
training, temple-building, and the rest. It is not easy to come by[33] and
few – if any – people possess it or are in a position to give advice on
matters that require it. But it is valuable, and we should all make it
our business to obtain it.

❧ SOPHISTIC MORALITY ❧

For Socrates virtue appears to be an expertise. But how, then, does
Socratic morality differ from the moral perspective of the sophists?
Don't the sophists – in so far as we can characterize their view generally
– believe that virtue is an expertise possessed by relatively few individuals? Indeed, don't they profess to be able to teach this expertise to
anyone willing to pay for it? And aren't many apparently willing to do
so[34] because of the sophists' claim that those who possess this expertise
will become eminently more successful in public affairs – that is, at
being virtuous – than those who do not possess it? Whether or not
this accurately characterizes the sophistic position,[35] it is clear that this
is how Socrates would characterize it. Moreover, it is equally clear that
he rejects it.

Recall that in the *Protagoras* Socrates characterizes Protagoras'
position as the claim to teach 'political expertise' (*tēn politikēn technēn*)
and to make men better citizens (*politas*)[36] which he later characterizes
as the claim to teach virtue (*aretē*).[37] Moreover, Protagoras does not
deny it. Rather he only denies – somewhat unsatisfactorily – that every
member of the political community fails to already possess what he
teaches.[38] Again in the *Hippias Major*, Socrates describes Hippias'
wisdom (*sophia*) – the expertise of the sophists (*tēn tōn sophistōn
technēn*)[39] – as 'the sort that makes those who study and learn it
stronger in virtue (*aretēn*)' (*Hippias Major* 283c3–4; Woodruff trans.). In
the *Gorgias*, Socrates sums up Gorgias' position on rhetoric – Gorgias'
expertise – as the view that the rhetor will not give advice in the

Assembly on matters relating to health, ship-building, wall-building or the military. On these matters, the rhetor will accede to the advice of the relevant expert. Rather, it will only be on matters concerning the just and the unjust that the rhetors will give expert advice.[40] When Gorgias objects that the rhetor will be best able to persuade concerning all matters that face the Assembly, – not merely the just and the unjust, but ship-building, wall-building and the rest, he is forced to concede that it is only on matters concerning the just and the unjust that the rhetor genuinely gives expert advice – a concession that ultimately leads to Gorgias' downfall. Finally, in the *Euthydemus*, the two eristic experts – the brothers, Euthydemus and Dionysodorus – claim to be the best teachers of virtue alive.[41] But in the *Euthydemus*, especially, there can be no doubt that Socrates rejects this claim.

Nevertheless, in rejecting the sophistic moral perspective Socrates need not be rejecting the sophistic view that virtue is an expertise. He may instead reject the view that virtue is the particular expertise that the sophists proclaim it is. And indeed, this is precisely what he does, as the *Euthydemus* makes clear.[42] Following the eristic brothers' claim to teach virtue, Socrates asks them to display their expertise at persuading the young Cleinias to pursue the love of wisdom (*philosophian*) and the care for virtue (*aretēs epimeleian*).[43] The next portion of the dialogue consists of two pairs of displays: first the eristic brothers' display (275c–277c), then Socrates' example of what he had in mind (277d–282e), another eristic display (282e–286b), and then again another Socratic example picking up where the first left off (288b–292e). The two Socratic displays are frequently referred to as the first and second protreptics.

In the first protreptic Socrates maintains that everyone seeks happiness or to fare well (278e3–279a1)[44] and that in order to be happy or fare well one must possess goods (279a1–4). Next, Socrates argues that the only genuine good is knowledge or wisdom, all other prima facie goods are good only in so far as they are guided by knowledge (279a4–281e5).[45] Consequently, Socrates concludes that everyone should seek to become as wise as possible (282a5–6). Socrates asks whether one should 'acquire every sort of knowledge (*epistēmē*) or whether there is one sort of knowledge which it is necessary for the one who is happy and a good man to possess, and if so what it is' but the question is not pursued until the beginning of the second protreptic.

In the second protreptic Socrates argues that not just any knowledge or expertise is the one necessary for happiness or faring well. The relevant knowledge or expertise is one which combines 'making something and knowing how to use what it makes' (289b5–6). This eliminates lyre-making (*luropoiikē*) and pipe-making (*aulopoiikē*), since these expertises fail to know how to use what they make. But it also eliminates perhaps more plausible candidates: the speech-making expertise (*logopoiikēn technēn*), the military expertise (*strategikē*) and the political expertise or the expertise of a king (*hē politikē kai hē basilikē technē*). The first two are eliminated because they fail to know how to use what they make;[46] the last is rejected because what it makes is too difficult to determine. In each case, Socrates rejects an expertise as the one required to make us happy – that is, he rejects an expertise as virtue – but it is not because it is an expertise, but because it is an expertise of the wrong sort. What sort of expertise is required can, however, be gleaned from elsewhere.

Consider first the *Laches*. When Laches proposes wise endurance as the proper definition of courage (192d10–12), Socrates enquires whether he thinks that those who endure the relevant dangers with the expertise of horsemen, or the expertise of the sling, or the expertise of the bow, or the expertise of well-divers, or any other expertise of this sort are more or less courageous than those who endure without the relevant expertise (193b9–c8). Laches answers that they are less courageous, and so abandons his definition. The suggestion is that whatever the proper definition of courage may be, it appears not to be wise endurance when wisdom is understood as these sorts of expertise.[47] Moreover, when Socrates turns to Nicias' definition that courage is knowledge of fearful and daring things, he asks Nicias whether knowledge of fearful and daring things is anything other than knowledge of future goods and evils. Nicias responds that it is not. Next, Socrates asks whether it belongs to the same knowledge to know future, past and present things. When Nicias answers that it does, Socrates points out that it follows on Nicias' view that courage is knowledge of all goods and evils, which is the whole of virtue and not its part, contrary to Nicias' initial claim that courage is part of virtue. Again, whatever we take Socrates' view to be concerning the proper definition of courage, the suggestion here seems to be that in so far as courage is defined as knowledge of the good and the bad it will be identical to virtue, not a part of it.[48] Virtue, according to Socrates in the *Laches*, appears to be knowledge of the good and the bad. Here, then, we have a hint of Socrates' answer to the question with which we were left at the end of the second protreptic of the *Euthydemus*. The knowledge or expertise that is virtue – that is necessary to make us happy and fare well – is not a knowledge or expertise like horsemanship or well-diving, but the knowledge or expertise of the good and the bad.

Finally, we can turn to the *Charmides*. The last half of this dialogue consists of a long, complicated, and often tortuous discussion of Critias' definition that temperance is knowledge of oneself (164d3–5). By 173a this definition has been modified to mean that temperance is knowledge of what one knows and does not know (172c9), and as

Socrates conceded earlier, life in accordance with that knowledge would be free from error (171d6–172a3). Now Socrates relates a dream in which temperance – understood as knowledge of what one knows and does not know – rules (*archoi hē sōphrosunē*). He grants that in such a situation one would live according to knowledge and so be free from error, but he wonders whether one would fare well and be happy (*eu an prattoimen kai eudaimonoimen*). Ultimately, Socrates and Critias agree that one would not. After denying that it is the knowledge of draught-playing (*petteutikon*), calculation (*logistikon*), or health – presumably medicine – that makes one fare well or be happy, Critias asserts that it is knowledge of the good and the bad (174b10). This leads Socrates to ask whether the doctor is any less successful in producing health or the shoemaker is any less successful at making shoes when knowledge of the good and the bad is lacking. Critias responds that they are not and Socrates concludes that it is the production of these things 'well and beneficially' that is removed when the knowledge of the good and bad is lacking (174c9–d1). This contrast recalls a similar contrast in the *Euthydemus* between making and using.[49] Once again, Socrates distinguishes between those expertises that do not make one happy and fare well, and the one expertise that does: the ruling expertise he was searching for in the second protreptic of the *Euthydemus*. Indeed, as in the *Laches*, Socrates suggests what it is: the knowledge or expertise of the good and the bad.[50]

Much of this is necessarily speculative. We have at best hints, suggestions, indications that Socrates takes the knowledge or expertise that makes us happy and fare well as the knowledge or expertise of the good and the bad. But what is not speculative is that Socrates takes the knowledge or expertise that makes us happy and fare well to be virtue, nor is it speculative that that knowledge or expertise is not the expertise the sophists claim to teach. It is not the eristic brothers' expertise in fighting with words, Gorgias' expertise of persuasion, Hippias' diverse expertises, nor whatever Protagoras' expertise is supposed to be. For Socrates, virtue is an expertise – contrary to folk morality – but it is not the expertise of the sophists.

A SKETCH OF SOCRATIC EXPERTISE

If, then, for Socrates virtue is an expertise, the obvious question that arises is, What is an expertise for Socrates? Fortunately a considerable amount of energy has already been devoted to this topic. Brickhouse and Smith, for example, list the following conditions which an expertise must meet: rationality or regularity, teachability or learnability, explicability, inerrancy, uniqueness, distinctness of subject-matter, and knowledge or wisdom.[51] Rather than merely rehearsing this work, I propose to address this question from a slightly different angle. I propose to ask what sort of thing an expertise is according to Socrates.

To begin an expertise appears to be a power or capacity (*dunamis*).[52] Early on in the *Euthydemus*, Socrates explains that all those present asked the two eristic brothers to 'demonstrate the power (*dunamis*) of their wisdom' (274c6–d3). Similarly, at the beginning of the *Gorgias*, Socrates beseeches Gorgias to teach him 'what the power (*dunamis*) of his expertise is and what it is he advertises and teaches' (447c1–3). In both passages the point is the same: in professing to possess expertise, Gorgias and the eristic brothers are professing to have a power or capacity, and Socrates wants to know what power or capacity they are professing to possess. Socrates assumes that if a person possesses knowledge, wisdom or expertise, that person possesses a power or capacity.[53]

That knowledge is understood as a kind of power or capacity is reinforced by the Prometheus story in the *Protagoras*. As Protagoras tells the story, the gods charged Epimetheus and Prometheus with distributing powers or capacities to each of the mortal creatures as was fitting. Unfortunately, Epimetheus (who was given the task of making this assignment, while Prometheus agreed to inspect it) used up all the powers available to him (e.g. strength, speed, winged flight, size, tough skin, thick hair) on the irrational creatures, leaving humans quite unprovided for (321b6–c1). Prometheus, thereupon, stole the practical wisdom (*sophian*) of Hephaestus and Athena – Hephaetus' expertise (*technēn*) in working with fire and Athena's other expertise[54] – and gave them to humanity. In this way, according to the story, humans acquired their practical wisdom, but not yet their political expertise (*politikēn*). This latter was reserved for Zeus to supply, who seeing that humans were able to obtain food and shelter, but were unable to fight against the beasts and to come together in cities, sent Hermes to distribute to all of humanity conscience and justice (*aidō te kai dikēn*) – the political expertise (*tēn politikēn technēn*). According to this story, then, once Epimetheus had doled out to the irrational creatures all of the powers fitting and necessary for survival,[55] other powers or capacities had to be obtained for humans. Thus, Prometheus gave to them the power of practical wisdom, while Zeus gave to them the power of political wisdom. In both cases, wisdom or expertise is presumed to be a power or capacity.

Indeed, the idea that political wisdom or expertise, i.e. the virtues, is a power or capacity is further supported by the question with which the remainder of the *Protagoras* is preoccupied: whether or not the virtues are one. Following Protagoras' Great Speech, of which the Prometheus story is a part, Socrates asks the question which will resolve the one 'small' remaining difficulty: are justice, temperance, wisdom, piety and courage distinct parts of virtue or are they all different names for one and the same thing (*Protagoras* 329c6–d1)? Protagoras responds that this is an easy question to answer: virtue is one thing and justice, temperance, piety, etc. are its parts. Socrates appeals to the analogies of the parts of gold and the parts of a face (*Protagoras* 329d4–8) and asks his question again.

> And does each of them [i.e. the parts of virtue] have its own
> separate power [*dunamin*]? When we consider the face, the eye
> is not like the ear, nor is its power [*dunamis*] the same, nor any
> other part like another in power [*dunamin*] or in other ways.
> Is it the same with the parts of virtue, that none is like any other,
> either in itself or in its power [*dunamis*]? Surely, it must be, if
> it corresponds to our example.
>
> (*Protagoras* 330a4–b2; adapted from Taylor [7.22])[56]

Socrates' question, then, is – at least in part – whether, according to Protagoras, political expertise is one power or more.

It may be objected, however, that this last passage especially indicates not that virtue or political expertise is a power or capacity but that it is that in virtue of which one has a power or capacity.[57] The suggestion is that an eye stands to its power just as courage – one of the virtues and so an expertise – stands to its power. An eye is not the power to see. Rather, it is that in virtue of which an individual has the power to see. The eye and its power are ontologically distinct. If we take the analogy to the virtues and expertise strictly, then, we must take the expertise to be ontologically distinct from its power. It is not a power; it is what confers a power on its possessor.

While I cannot fully argue the point here, I believe that this is to take the analogy with the parts of the face too strictly. Recall that the point of the analogies is to get clear about what Protagoras is maintaining when he claims that the virtues are distinct. Is he maintaining that they all are (or have) the same kind of power but differ in some other way, or is he maintaining that their powers differ as well? It is at least open to Socrates to maintain contrary to Protagoras that they are (or have) the same kind of power, and so that they do not differ in any essential way.[58] Moreover, there is simply no organ analogous to the eye in the case of expertise or the virtues. Surely, the possession of fully functioning vocal chords does not suffice for the possession of the expertise of rhetoric, for example. But to postulate some entity between the vocal chords and the power to persuade that is rhetoric is simply to add an unnecessary ontological layer. Indeed, it is to add an ontological layer that is not demanded by the text. None of the passages that I have cited are incompatible with understanding expertise as a kind of power in the way that knowledge – on a justified true belief model – is a kind of belief. Perhaps most important, there are various passages in which Socrates appears to use the word for power and the words for knowledge or expertise interchangeably.[59] At the very least these passages indicate that the ontological distinction that the present objection presupposes is of little moment for Socrates. For all these reasons, as well as others,[60] I conclude that for Socrates an expertise is some sort of power or capacity.

Saying this, however, only raises a further question: what according to Socrates is a power or capacity? Surprisingly little attention has been devoted to this question, but there are a few preliminary things we can say. First, a Socratic power or capacity is typically associated with particular types of activities or behaviours.[61] For example, in the *Laches* Socrates defines quickness as 'the power *to do* many things in a short time concerning speech and running and all other things' (*Laches* 192b1–3). In the *Hippias Minor* he describes the one who has power (the *dunatos*) as the one '*who does* what he wants when he wants' (*Hippias Minor* 366b7–c1). And finally in the *Ion*, Socrates says,

> What *moves* you [Ion] is a divine power [*dunamis*], like the power [*dunamis*] in the stone which Euripides dubbed the 'Magnesian', but which most people call the 'Heraclean'. This stone, you see, not only attracts iron rings on their own, but also confers on them a power [*dunamin*] *by which they do* the same thing that the stone does.
>
> (*Ion* 533d3–31; adapted from Saunders trans.)

But as many commentators have pointed out, for Socrates, a thing does not have a power simply in virtue of the fact that it acts or behaves in certain ways. It does not have a power simply in virtue of what it does. Rather, for Socrates, a thing has a power in virtue of some state of the thing that occasions it in the appropriate circumstances to do what it does. A power for Socrates is not the mere tendency to perform a certain sort of activity, but rather the state of a thing that results in such activity.[62] Thus, for Socrates, the power is ontologically prior to the activity the power is associated with. The activities are defined in virtue of the power that produces them, not vice versa.[63]

Second, a power or capacity for Socrates is to be identified by its peculiar object. For example, in the *Charmides*, after indicating that since temperance is knowledge of knowledge it must be a power (*dunamis*), Socrates infers that it must be 'of something' (*tinos einai*), citing as examples that the greater has the power (*dunamin*) to be of the lesser (168b5–8) and the double the power (*dunamis*) to be of the half. Thus, according to Socrates, if there is a double of itself, then the double will be both double and half of itself. In general, he maintains that 'the very thing which has its own power (*dunamin*) applied to itself will have to have that nature towards which the power (*dunamis*) was directed' (*Charmides* 168c10–d3; adapted from Sprague trans.). He explains this with the following examples: since hearing is of sound, hearing would have to be a sound if it were to be of itself, and since sight is of colour, sight would have to be coloured if it were of itself. While the details of these passages may be difficult to sort out, the general idea appears clear enough. Associated with every power is an object, property, nature or being (*ousian*). Thus, the powers of the greater, the double, hearing and sight have as their respective objects the lesser, the half, sound, and colour. Moreover, the power must always be of this object; if it were of a different object, it would be a different power. It is only on this assumption that Socrates can draw his conclusions that if the greater is of itself, then it must be lesser (as well as greater), if the double is of itself, it must be half (as well as double)[64], if hearing is of itself, it must be a sound, and if sight is of itself, it must be coloured.[65]

Thus, since virtue is an expertise, it is a power. As a power it must be associated with a particular sort of activity and have a specific object. The activity is evidently virtuous activity[66], while the object appears to be the good (and the bad) in light of our earlier discussion. But in saying this we have left out the cognitive aspect of expertise. For expertise is not just a power; it is a cognitive power. This cognitive aspect of expertise is manifested in Socrates' view that expertise is infallible, inerrant or luck-independent.

Consider, for example, Socrates' claim in the first protreptic of the *Euthydemus* that having included wisdom in his list of goods necessary for happiness it would be superfluous to add good luck; for 'when wisdom is present no good luck is lacking to the one for whom it is present' (*Euthydemus* 280b2–3). The idea here is that the person with wisdom or knowledge will invariably make decisions or choices conducive to his or her happiness. Just as the expert ship pilot invariably makes decisions or choices conducive to getting to the port safely, given the circumstances she is in, so the wise or knowledgeable individual will invariably make decisions or choices conducive to attaining happiness, given her circumstances. Many scholars believe that Socrates takes these choices to be sufficient for happiness;[67] others maintain that Socrates takes other goods in addition to be necessary for happiness.[68] But most would agree that wisdom or knowledge is sufficient for 'getting things right'. It is in this sense that good luck is not necessary for the wise individual. Just as the wise ship pilot does not need to rely on lucky guesses in getting to the port safely (although she may need to rely on luck in obtaining calm seas, which may or may not be necessary for arriving at the port safely), so the wise individual need not rely on lucky guesses in attaining happiness (although she may need to rely on luck in obtaining other goods which may or may not be necessary for attaining happiness).[69]

Again, in so far as Socrates is inclined to identify wisdom or expertise with definitional knowledge,[70] Socrates' request at *Euthyphro* 6e3–6 to be taught what piety is 'so that looking to it and using it as a paradigm, I can say that that which is such as it, whether done by you or anyone else, is pious and that which is not such as it, is impious' is making a similar point: the individual with definitional knowledge of piety will not make mistakes concerning which things are pious and which are not. She will always 'get things right'. Wisdom, expertise, or definitional knowledge regarding piety somehow guarantees correct judgements regarding piety.[71]

In fact, in the *Gorgias* Socrates apparently distinguishes between expertise and knack with this very point in mind. At 464e2–465a7 and 500e3–501b1 this distinction is drawn almost entirely on the basis of the fact that the former possesses a *logos* of its object, while the latter does not.[72] It is in virtue of the possession of this *logos*[73] that an expertise can reach correct judgements concerning which things are good, for example, and so can say why each of the good things are good. A knack on the other hand, lacking this *logos* must merely guess at which things are pleasant, for example, and why they are. It is the definitional knowledge of the object of the expertise that accounts for the expertise's infallibility with respect to its object.

While I have only just brushed up against the many issues surrounding these passages, they all point in the same general direction: the cognitive aspect of an expertise can be found in its infallibility for reaching correct judgements concerning its object. An expert temple-builder always makes correct judgements concerning temple-building.[74] It is, indeed, for this reason that her advice is heeded when considering temple-building. Thus, the characteristic Socratic view that virtue is an expertise[75] amounts to the view that virtue is a power associated with a specific activity and a specific object. As a cognitive power, virtue also infallibly produces correct judgements regarding its object. We have seen some reason to suppose that for Socrates the object of the expertise that is virtue is the good. Thus, virtue is an expertise that enables its possessor infallibly to reach correct judgements regarding the good – whether, for example, escaping from prison or setting out to defeat the Sicilians is good. To learn more about the specific activities associated with virtue so understood, we must turn to Socrates' account of the good.

❧ THE GOOD ❧

A complete account of Socrates' moral perspective must address the question of virtuous behaviour or activity. Thus far our examination of the characteristic feature of Socrates' moral philosophy has focused almost entirely on the nature of a virtuous person. I have been concerned to exhibit the cognitive power that such a person possesses. Such a focus, however, might be thought to obscure another way in which Socrates' moral perspective is to be contrasted with that of the sophists. For it is often thought that Socrates is a defender in some sense of traditional moral behaviour against the supposed immoralism of the sophists.[76] If such a view is correct we should expect it to emerge out of Socrates' account of the expertise of virtue, since, as I indicated above, the activities associated with a power or capacity are defined in virtue of the power associated with them and not vice versa. To some extent our expectations will not be disappointed. But to see this we must turn to Socrates' account of the good.

In the *Gorgias*, Socrates indicates that the good is the rational end of all our actions. It is for the sake of it that we do everything we do, and we do not do it for the sake of anything else.[77] In the *Euthydemus*, we saw that Socrates maintains that happiness or faring well is the object of everyone's rational desires.[78] It is reasonable to infer, then, that for Socrates the good is happiness or faring well.[79] Let us call this eudaimonism.[80] Given eudaimonism, then, it would appear that no one ever intentionally acts contrary to his or her own good.[81] Since everyone rationally desires his or her own good, it is only mistaken beliefs about what contributes to one's good that could explain one's acting contrary to one's good. Knowledge of which activities benefit one is sufficient for performing those activities.[82] This is not because Socrates fails to recognize the necessity of desire for motivating action, but because for Socrates everyone rationally desires his or her own good. Consequently, since for Socrates virtue is the cognitive power whose object is the good and which infallibly produces correct judgements about the good, the virtuous person will never act contrary to his or her own good. Such a person will know which activities benefit him or her, and given his or her rational desire, he or she will perform them. Such actions will by definition be virtuous actions, – since actions are defined in virtue of the power they result from. Thus, for Socrates, knowledge of the good is sufficient for virtuous activity as well. No one ever acts viciously except out of ignorance of the good.[83]

Thus the characteristic feature of Socratic morality, the view that virtue is the expertise of the good – what we might call Socratic intellectualism – does have the consequence that virtuous activities benefit the agent who performs the activities. But as a defence of traditional moral behaviour it appears to be a failure. For nothing in the account of Socratic virtue as I have described it indicates that the moral expert will recognize those activities associated with traditional morality as good or beneficial. If Socratic morality is not to be the primarily amoral thesis that virtue is simply the cognitive power whose object is the agent's own good and that is associated with those activities that promote the agent's own good, whatever they happen to be, Socrates must believe that some or most of those activities typically associated with traditional morality promote the agent's good.[84] But where is the defence of this view?

There are various passages in which Socrates compares the good of the body to the good of the soul and maintains that virtuous actions promote the health of the soul and vicious actions make it sick.[85] But as a defence of traditional morality these passages are rather slight. Either Socrates is not referring necessarily to traditionally virtuous behaviour or if he is the passages appear to be merely stipulative. For while a defence of the position maintained in these passages can be derived from the account of Socratic virtue I have been proposing no part of that defence requires that the actions that promote the health of the soul are traditionally virtuous activities. On the other hand, there appears to be no independent defence in these passages for the claim that traditionally virtuous activities promote the health of the soul.

Perhaps a more plausible defence can be derived from the longer passages in which Socrates is arguing against the immoralism of Callicles in the *Gorgias* and of Thrasymachus in the first book of the *Republic*. Certainly the argument against Callicles, for example, purports to defend the claim that virtuous actions are always more beneficial for the agent than vicious actions against Callicles' claim that unbridled pleasure-seeking is most beneficial for the agent. Whatever else Socrates is attempting to do in this passage he appears to be arguing that at least one sort of traditionally vicious behaviour harms the soul. While both of these arguments against immoralism deserve serious further study, there remains something unsatisfactory about them, a lack of satisfaction that Plato explicitly notes at the beginning of the second book of the *Republic*.[86] But it is in these passages, if anywhere, that Socrates' defence of traditional morality is to be found.

❧ CONCLUSION ❧

Let us return briefly to the Ciceronian tradition with which this essay began. According to this tradition moral philosophy in some sense begins with Socrates. We have seen a sense in which such a tradition is justified. Socrates is unique, at least among the average Athenian citizen and the sophists, in maintaining that morality or virtue is a knowledge or expertise of the good. Against the folk view, he maintains that morality or virtue is an expertise that is not possessed by everyone, but which everyone should make it their business to obtain. It is not easily obtainable, but it is obtainable none the less, and few of us are in the position to give advice concerning it. Against the sophists, Socrates maintains that it is not an expertise reducible to others. It is not rhetoric or antilogic or even polymathy. It is its own unique branch of knowledge. It is knowledge or expertise of the good.[87] Nevertheless, in saying this Socrates has really only supplied what might be called the formal features of morality or virtue. Socrates' own claim to lack the expertise that is virtue[88] prohibits him from supplying a more substantive moral theory. Perhaps this is yet another way in which Socrates stands at the beginning of moral philosophy. Many, if not all, of the subsequent Greek moral philosophers may be seen as completing the work that Socrates could only begin.

 NOTES

1 From Guthrie [9.33]. Other translations are my own unless otherwise noted.

2 See Aristotle *The Parts of Animals* 642a28 and *Metaphysics* 987b1–4 and 1078b17.

3 See the title of the present essay. See also Guthrie [9.33], 97–105. Indeed, much of what I have to say here in the introductory section regarding this tradition and the puzzle it raises follows Guthrie's remarks. My response to this puzzle, however, diverges significantly from Guthrie's.

4 Socrates is also mentioned in the *Frogs* and the *Birds*.

5 His other Socratic works are the *Apology*, *Symposium* and the *Oeconomicus*.

6 Not counting those dialogues which are generally considered spurious. The *Alcibiades* I and the *Cleitophon* have recently garnered some supporters; for the former see Annas [9.1] and for the latter see Roochnik [9.75]. If they are genuinely Platonic, then 22 of the dialogues feature Socrates as a primary speaker.

7 Not counting the occasions in which he uses Socrates as an example in various arguments.

8 Aristotle's portrait agrees in most essentials with the Platonic portrait.

9 I am hedging here because I am well aware that there are many first-rate Socratic scholars who do not accept Vlastos's solution. See, esp. Kahn [9.40], [9.41], [9.42], [9.43], [9.44], [9.45], [9.46], and [9.47]. Moreover, even among those scholars who accept the substance of Vlastos's approach, few would accept it in all of its detail. Nevertheless, Vlastos's well-deserved scholarly reputation, the plausibility of the approach, and the characteristic clarity and force of his argument will likely make his approach the paradigm for years to come. In any case, I believe the basic outline of the approach to be correct.

10 Vlastos [9.94] was published posthumously under the editorship of Myles Burnyeat.

11 Actually, Vlastos's dismissal of Aristophanes is made explicitly only in Vlastos [9.91]. I am somewhat more sympathetic to Aristophanes' portrait than is Vlastos.

12 The Platonic dialogues have traditionally been divided into three groups, corresponding to their supposed order of composition: the early dialogues (in alphabetical order): *Apology, Charmides, Crito, Euthydemus, Euthyphro, Gorgias, Hippias Major, Hippias Minor, Ion, Laches, Lysis, Menexenus, Protagoras, Republic* I; the middle dialogues (in alphabetical order): *Cratylus, Parmenides, Phaedo, Phaedrus, Republic* II–X, *Symposium* and *Theaetetus*; the late dialogues (in alphabetical order): *Critias, Laws, Philebus, Politicus, Sophist, Timaeus*. (I have excluded the *Meno* from these three groups, because it is commonly taken to be transitional between the early and middle periods, containing elements of both.) While more fine-grained orderings have been proposed, they have never received the general support that this coarse-grained ordering has. Nevertheless, I should not be taken to suggest that everyone would agree with this method of dividing up the dialogues. Kahn (see earlier note) argues for a different division among the dialogues, while unitarians of various sorts have long argued against the utility of reading the dialogues with reference to their supposed order of composition. See most recently, Nails [9.59].

13 Vlastos [9.93], 48. The other nine theses that Vlastos lists are roughly: (2) Socrates$_m$ (henceforth the Socrates of the middle dialogues) has an elaborate theory of separated Forms; Socrates$_e$ (henceforth the Socrates of the early dialogues) does not; (3) Socrates$_e$ seeks knowledge elenctically and denies that he has any; Socrates$_m$ seeks demonstrative knowledge and claims to have it; (4) Socrates$_m$ has a tripartite model of the soul; Socrates$_e$ does not; (5) Socrates$_m$ is a mathematical expert; Socrates$_e$ is not; (6) Socrates$_e$ is a populist; Socrates$_m$ is an elitist; (7) Socrates$_m$ has an elaborate political theory; Socrates$_e$ does not; (8) Socrates$_m$ has a metaphysical grounding for his homoerotic attachments; Socrates$_e$ does not; (9) For Socrates$_e$ religion is practical and realized in action; for Socrates$_m$ religion is mystical and realized in contemplation; (10) Socrates$_e$ has an adversative philosophical method, Socrates$_m$ a didactic one.

14 Vlastos [9.93] 46.

15 The other theses Vlastos considers in this regard are (3) and (4).

16 Vlastos [9.93], 117 and n. 50. See also [9.93], 49–53. Vlastos labels this his 'grand methodological hypothesis'.

17 Each of these theses has had its detractors. Graham [9.29] has recently objected to the third thesis. Kahn [9.46], Nehamas [9.65], and Beversluis [9.11] have all objected to the second thesis, primarily because of their scepticism about the reliability of the Aristotelian testimony. Finally, two different sorts of objections have been raised to the first thesis. Kahn [9.46] and Nails [9.60] have objected to seeing any significant difference between the views advanced in the early dialogues and those advanced in the middle dialogues. Kraut [9.52], Irwin [9.37], Taylor [9.83] and others have objected to seeing the difference to be as radical as Vlastos sees it. I find only this last objection to be persuasive, and so would modify Vlastos' approach along the lines advocated by Kraut, Irwin and Taylor.

18 Indeed, to some extent by Aristophanes as well. The moral philosophy that can be found advanced by Socrates in Plato's early dialogues – as we will see – can easily be confused with the moral philosophy (if that is the correct name for it) advanced by the sophists, at least as Socrates/Plato understood the sophists.

19 I am here running roughshod over a number of subtleties of the text that I believe are peripheral to my present concern. Socrates does not actually ask Protagoras what he professes to teach, but rather how Hippocrates would be improved or benefited if he became Protagoras' pupil. Nor does Protagoras actually answer that he teaches virtue. Rather Protagoras says that if Hippocrates becomes his pupil, every day he will go away being better at political expertise (*tēn politikēn technēn*) or at being a citizen (*politēs*); see Socrates' summation of Protagoras' answer and Protagoras' approval. Nevertheless, Socrates clearly takes Protagoras to be professing to teach virtue. See *Protagoras* 320b4–c1.

20 The other argument is that those who possess virtue are unable to pass it on; *Protagoras* 319d7–320b3. Another version of this argument can be found at *Meno* 93a5–94e2.

21 See 322b5–c3, where Protagoras appears to identify the political expertise (*politikēn technēn*) with conscience and justice (*aidō te kai dikēn*) which Zeus distributes among all the members of the community.

22 See Seeskin ([9.79], 121) who takes this passage as evidence that for Socrates virtue is not an expertise.

23 Note the apparent interchangeability of expertise (*technē*), wisdom (*sophia*), and knowledge (*epistēmē*) in these passages. At 319b3–328d2, Socrates had indicated that virtue was not an expertise (*technē*), while Protagoras had indicated that it was. At 361a5–c2, however, Socrates describes his earlier view as the view that virtue is not knowledge (*epistēmē*), and Protagoras' as the view that virtue is knowledge (*epistēmē*). Again, the argument from 349d2–360e5 has the conclusion that courage is wisdom (*sophia*), which Socrates describes at 361a5–c2 as leading to the view that virtue is knowledge (*epistēmē*). Protagoras uses knowledge and expertise interchangeably at 360e–351a and Socrates uses them interchangeably at 357b.

24 Taylor ([7.22], 213–14) and Vlastos ([9.93], 124) apparently take the expression of inconsistency to be insincere or illusory. The argument that has intervened between 319 and 360 is taken to suffice to reject the folk view. Brickhouse and Smith ([9.17], 99), however, apparently take this to be an expression of a genuine failure or inconsistency in Socrates' position. Seeskin ([9.79], 143) and Guthrie ([9.33], 114 n. 1) would seem to agree. See also Irwin [9.39] and Santas [9.78].

25 Note also that in the *Protagoras*, at least, Socrates was unconcerned to distinguish knowledge and expertise. See n. 23.

26 For the debate concerning the translation of this passage see Vlastos ([9.93], 237), Annas ([9.2], 44) and Woodruff ([9.96], 62 n. 3).

27 Socrates has in mind here not simply experts in general – *technikoi* – but experts in various manual pursuits: sculptors, painters, cobblers, etc. A more natural translation of *cheirotechnas* would be 'craftsmen' or 'artisans', but that conceals the distinction between *technikos* and *cheirotechnas*.

28 For the connection between knowledge or wisdom of the great things and

moral wisdom or expertise see Brickhouse and Smith [9.17], 34. For a similar interpretation of Socratic wisdom see Irwin [9.39], 27–8.

29 On how Socrates derives a mission from this oracular pronouncement see Reeve [9.73], 24–28 and Brickhouse and Smith [9.12] and [19.15], 87–100.

30 The method that Socrates practices in carrying out this mission is the *elenchos* (which can be roughly translated as 'refutation', 'test', or 'cross-examination'). Its general form is the following: First, Socrates gets the interlocutor (the individual whose claim to knowledge or expertise is being tested) to express some belief, p, usually, but not always, concerning the definition of some moral concept. Next, Socrates gets the interlocutor to express some other beliefs, q, r and s. Third, Socrates goes on to show that these premises entail the negation of the original belief, i.e. the apparent refutand, p. Thus, the conjunction p and q and r and s is false. Considerable debate, sparked in part by Vlastos' classic 'The Socratic Elenchus', concerns what Socrates concludes from such elenctic episodes. Some take Socrates to conclude that p or one of the other premises is false; see Gulley [9.31], Nakhnikian [9.61], Vlastos [9.88], Kraut [9.50], Polansky [9.72], and McPherran [9.55]. Others take Socrates merely to conclude that the interlocutor's beliefs are inconsistent; see Stokes [9.81], Benson [9.3] and [9.8], and perhaps Brickhouse and Smith [9.16] and [9.17], 3–29. For the difference between the Socratic *elenchos* and the method of the sophists see Benson [9.4] and Nehamas [9.64].

31 This depends on whether we accept Protagoras' account of folk morality. If we do, then according to Protagoras, the Athenians do not maintain that everyone possesses virtue, but only those abiding within a political community.

32 In maintaining that virtue is fairly easy to come by they need not maintain that the process is automatic or simple. The point is simply that it does not require any special training – but just the sort of training the typical Athenian 'gentleman' provides his 'sons'. See Anytus in the *Meno* at 92e–93a.

33 Although Socrates need not think that it can be taught in the way that the average Athenian thinks that ship-building is taught. Indeed, Socrates may not believe that it is an expertise that can be taught at all.

34 See, for example, Hippias' boast concerning the riches he has made in this way at *Hippias Major* 282d6–e8.

35 See the previous chapter.

36 *Protagoras* 319a3–5.

37 *Protagoras* 320b4–c1.

38 Indeed, this would seem to be Protagoras' greatest challenge: to make coherent his profession to teach virtue and his acceptance of folk morality. See the conclusion of the *Protagoras* as well as *Theaetetus* 177e–179b.

39 *Hippias Major* 281d5. Note the interchangeability of expertise and wisdom throughout this passage.

40 *Gorgias* 455a8–d5.

41 *Euthydemus* 273d8–9; see also 274e5, 285a2–b5, and 287a9–b1.

42 Socrates' distinction between knacks (*empeiriai*) and expertises (*technai*) at *Gorgias* 463a–465d indicates that Socrates would also reject that what the sophists practice is an expertise. But even if it were an expertise, like the expertises of medicine and physical training, it would still not be virtue. Not because

virtue fails to be an expertise, but because virtue fails to be that particular expertise.

43 Note the interchangeability of wisdom and virtue here and at *Euthydemus* 278d2–3. See also the *Apology* 29d2–30b2 quoted above.

44 See Irwin [9.36], Chance [9.18] and Brickhouse and Smith [9.17] for the interchangeability of happiness (*eudaimonia*) and to fare well (*eu prattein*) at *Euthydemus* 278e–282d.

45 See Brickhouse and Smith [9.17], 103–12 for an excellent discussion of the various subtleties surrounding this passage. See also *Meno* 87d–89a for a similar argument.

46 Actually the military expertise does not make anything either. Rather it captures or discovers things. But Socrates does not reject it on these grounds, but on the grounds that it fails to know how to use what it captures or discovers.

47 In indicating that this is the suggestion of this passage I do not mean to be claiming that Socrates takes the *elenchos* in which these points are made to constitute a proof that Laches' definition is false. I have argued elsewhere that Socrates understands his individual elenctic arguments as establishing no more than the inconsistency of the interlocutor's beliefs. See Benson [9.3] and [9.8]. My point here is simply that Socrates' views can be gleaned from this passage – in part because they are repeated in other early dialogues – not that Socrates takes (nor should we take) what he believes to be relevant to the results of this particular *elenchos*.

48 Again, I do not intend here to suggest that this is the conclusion Socrates thinks he has established by means of his *elenchos* with Nicias at the end of the *Laches*. See previous note.

49 To see how Socrates may have taken these two contrasts to be the same consider Socrates' example of the miner who produces gold. This expert can produce gold successfully lacking knowledge of the good and the bad. But he can't produce it beneficially – that is, produce it in a way that will benefit him – if he lacks the knowledge of how to use it, that is, if he lacks the knowledge of the good and the bad. If we are to take these two contrasts to be essentially the same and we are to take the knowledge or expertise of the good and the bad as the knowledge or expertise that makes us happy and fare well – that is, virtue – then what is the product of this knowledge? The good. In taking virtue to be an expertise we may or may not need to view it as essentially productive. For important discussions surrounding this issue see Irwin [9.34] and Roochnik [9.76].

50 Again, however, I hasten to point out that I do not take this to be the 'hidden meaning' of the *Charmides* or the conclusion Socrates takes his *elenchoi* in the *Charmides* to establish. See previous notes on the *Laches*.

51 Brickhouse and Smith [9.17], 6–7. Note that they prefer to translate *technē* as 'craft' rather than 'expertise'. See also Reeve [9.73], 37–53, Woodruff [9.96], 68–81, and Irwin [9.34], 73–7.

52 See Brickhouse and Smith [9.17], 37, Penner [9.69], 197, Penner [9.68], 321–2, Ferejohn [9.24], 383 n. 18, Ferejohn [9.23], 15 and Irwin [9.34], 296 n. 28.

53 See also *Republic* 346a1–3 and *Charmides* 168b2–4.

54 Taylor [9.82], 84 glosses this as perhaps spinning, weaving, pottery and cultivation of the olive.

55 See *Protagoras* 320e2–3.

56 See also *Protagoras* 331d1–e4, 333a1–b6, 349b1–c5, and 359a2–b2.

57 I owe the clear expression of this objection to C. C. W. Taylor.

58 On Socrates' position as contrasted with Protagoras' here see the debate concerning the Socratic doctrine of the unity of virtues: Vlastos [9.87], 221–70 and 418–23, Penner [9.67] and [9.71], Taylor [7.22], Irwin [9.39], 31–52 and 78–94, Devereux [9.20] and [9.21], Ferejohn [9.23] and [9.24], and Brickhouse and Smith [9.17], 60–72 and 103–36.

59 *Hippias Minor* 365d6–366a4, *Gorgias* 509d2–e1, and *Hippias Major* 296a4–6. See also the Prometheus story mentioned above in which Protagoras sometimes has Epimetheus doling out the powers, for example strength and speed, and sometimes the things in virtue of which the creature has a particular power, for example thick hair.

60 See, for example, *Republic* 477d7–e1 where Plato – as opposed to the Socrates of the early dialogues – explicitly identifies knowledge (*epistēmē*) and belief (*doxa*) as powers or capacities.

61 I say 'typically' because it is difficult to say what activities are associated with the powers of the greater, the double, the heavier, the lighter, the older, and the younger in the *Charmides* (168b–d), for example.

62 See Irwin's A-powers ('x and y have the same A-power when each of them does F (where F is some kind of behaviour); each of them has the power to F') versus B-powers ('x and y have the same B-power when each of them is in the same state, G, which causes their behaviour') ([9.34], 44–46); Socratic powers are Irwin's B-powers. See also Penner's tendencies and motive forces or states of the soul ([9.67]); Taylor's dispositional quality versus permanent state ([7.22], 110); Ferejohn's P1: 'A has the power to do X if A intended to do X, and there were an occasion for A to do X, A would do X' versus P2: 'A has the power to do x if there is some unique (simple or complex) occurrent property P such that (i) A has P, and (ii) anyone with P who intended to do X, and who had the occasion to do X, would do X' ([9.23], 18; [9.24], 382–83 and n. 18); and Vlastos's tendencies versus dispositions ([9.87], 434).

63 The issue here is complicated somewhat by the fact that Socrates appears to allow that the same activity can be associated with different powers – for example, in the *Laches* Socrates appears to allow that the activity of fleeing the enemy in the face of danger which typically is associated with cowardice, can also be associated with the power of courage – while at the same time indicating in the *Republic* that wage-earning activities can only be associated with the wage-earning power or expertise. The resolution of this issue is to be found in recognizing that activities are susceptible to differing descriptions. For Socrates, a perspicuously described activity is properly associated with only one power. The perspicuity of the description is tied to the power that produced the activity. But all of this goes considerably beyond the issues with which I am currently concerned.

64 Socrates apparently takes these to be absurd or impossible consequences; see *Charmides* 168e3–7.

65 One of the complications involved in this passage is the apparently equivocal use of the genitive. On the one hand, the genitive is used to pick out the special object associated with each power; on the other hand, it is used to pick out the

power itself when it is 'of' itself. Perhaps the best way to understand this is to distinguish between the object of the power and what it can be directed toward. Thus, sight and hearing can both be directed toward this bell since the bell both is coloured and makes a sound. The idea might be put as follows: a power can be directed toward a particular object just in case that object has the property associated with that power. Thus, sight can be directed towards itself just in case sight is coloured. Another passage that indicates that a power is to be identified by its object is *Gorgias* 447c1–456a6; see Penner [9.68], 320–322. Unfortunately, there are a few passages that suggest that distinct powers can have the same object; see *Gorgias* 451a–c and 464a–465d. This tension, however, can be resolved in a longer discussion of this topic.

66 To some extent this is as uninformative and potentially problematic as we might expect in light of the complication noted in n 63 above.

67 See, for example, Vlastos [9.93] and Irwin [9.36].

68 See Brickhouse and Smith [9.17] and [9.14].

69 For a discussion of the argument on behalf of the luck-independence of wisdom in the *Euthydemus* see Chance [9.18], 60–62 and Irwin [9.36], 92–6. See also Brickhouse and Smith [9.17], 119 n 31 for a similar account of the underlying idea of this passage. The same point is made concerning knowledge at *Charmides* 171d6–172a3 and concerning expertise at *Republic* 340d8–341a4. In the *Euthydemus*, while the first protreptic begins with frequent and consistent appeals to wisdom (*sophia*), by the end wisdom (*sophia*) and knowledge (*epistēmē* and *phronēsis*) are being used interchangeably.

70 I here forego the argument for such an identification, although *Laches* 184e–190c discussed above establishes that definitional knowledge is at least a necessary condition of expertise. Dubbing this sort of knowledge 'definitional knowledge' is potentially misleading because if what I am arguing is correct, knowledge of what F–ness is is definitely not merely something like justified true belief of a definitional proposition, although it may very well entail such a thing. Nevertheless answers to Socratic 'What is F-ness?' questions have been for so long associated with definitions, it is difficult not to understand the knowledge that such an answer manifests as definitional knowledge. For more on Socratic 'What is F-ness?' questions, see Robinson [9.74], Nakhnikian [9.61], Beversluis [9.9], Nehamas [9.62], Irwin [9.34] and [9.39], Benson [9.5], Kidd [9.49] and Taylor [9.84]. See also Aristotle (*Metaphysics* 1078b17–19) who apparently sees a connection between Socrates' innovation regarding moral philosophy and his interest in definitions.

71 See also *Protagoras* 360e8–361a3. This raises a number of issues concerning the relationship between definitional knowledge of virtue, for example, and knowledge that someone is virtuous or that virtue is teachable. For more on the controversies surrounding these issues see Geach [9.25], Irwin [9.34] and [9.39], Vlastos [9.90] and [9.92], Nehamas [9.63], Beversluis [9.10], Woodruff [9.95], Benson [9.6], Penner [9.70] and [9.71], and Brickhouse and Smith [9.17].

72 Dodds [9.22], 226 explains that the distinction between *technai* and *empeiriai* is drawn in two ways: 'by their aim, which is merely pleasure, and by their empirical character, which means that they cannot give any rational account of their procedure. . . .' He goes on to explain the connection between the two ways as follows (228–229): 'A *technē* differs from an *empeiria* in that it is based

on a rational principle (*logos*), and can thus explain the reasons for its procedure in every case. This difference is connected with the one just mentioned [i.e. between pleasure and the good]; for in Plato's view *to beltiston* is in each case rationally determinable, whereas *to hēdu* is not. Thus in matters of diet a doctor can predict on general principles what will be *beltiston*, and give a reason for his prediction, if he knows enough about the chemistry of nutrition; but the patient's likes and dislikes are not predictable.' (Irwin [9.35] 209–10 appears to give a similar account.) In both Irwin and Dodds the suggestion seems to be that it is the rationality of *technai* that is basic. In aiming at pleasure rhetoric cannot be rational and so cannot be a *technē*.

73 For the identification of definitional knowledge with the possession of the *logos*, see Woodruff [9.96], 74–75 and Reeve [9.73] 42–43.

74 See *Republic* 340d8–341a4.

75 This, then, is how I understand one of the so-called Socratic paradoxes that knowledge is (necessary and sufficient for) virtue. See, for example, Penner [9.71], 5, who writes 'as if we needed evidence for the claim that 'Virtue is knowledge' is Socratic!' Penner here is objecting to Devereux [9.20] (see also Devereux [9.21]), but even Devereux does not deny that the doctrine can be found in some of the Socratic dialogues, e.g. the *Protagoras*. See also Kraut [9.51], 286: 'The credentials of (B) [Virtue is knowledge] as a genuine Socratic principle are impeccable. He endorses it not only in the *Protagoras* (361b1–2), but in the *Meno* (87c11–89a4) and the *Laches* (194d1–3) as well; in the *Charmides* (165c4–6) and the *Euthyphro* (14c5–6), the search for temperance and piety eventually leads to the idea that these qualities are forms of knowledge; and if we wish to look outside the early dialogues, we can find Aristotle (*Nicomachean Ethics* 1144b28–30) and Xenophon (*Memorabilia* III.9.5–6) attributing (B) to Socrates.' Even Brickhouse and Smith [9.17], ch 4 agree that for Socrates knowledge or wisdom is necessary and sufficient for virtue. Indeed, it is because they accept Socrates' commitment to this doctrine that they are forced to distinguish between virtue – which knowledge of the good is sufficient and necessary for – and virtuous actions – which knowledge of the good is neither necessary nor sufficient for. See also Guthrie [9.33], 130–39, and Taylor [9.84], 137, among others.

76 See Xenophon's portrait of Socrates mentioned above. One way this issue is sometimes put is that Socrates collapses the convention (*nomos*)/nature (*phusis*) distinction that the sophists made so much of. (For the sophists' view of this distinction see, for example, Kerferd [9.48], 111–131, de Romilly [9.19], 113–116, and Guthrie [9.32], 55–131.) The idea here is that Socrates is supposed to have believed that activities enjoined by conventional or traditional morality are essentially the same as those enjoined by nature.

77 See *Gorgias* 499e7–500a1. See also 467c5–468c1. See Irwin [9.35], 208 who correctly points out that *Gorgias* 499e 7–500a1 really claims that the good is what we *should* aim at, but what Polus and Socrates had agreed to earlier was that the good is what we *do* aim at. I follow Irwin's first reading of the latter passage.

78 See *Euthydemus* 278e3–279a1. The happiness involved here, like the good referred to in the *Gorgias*, is the agent's own. See Vlastos [9.93], 203 n.14, for

example. For the translation of *eudaimonia* as happiness see Vlastos [9.93], 200–3.

79 See Vlastos [9.93], 204 n 20, for example, who maintains that the identity of happiness and the good is so obvious to Plato and Socrates that neither of them feels compelled to argue for it. Vlastos cites their apparent interchangeability in Socrates' statement of Callicles' position at *Gorgias* 494e–495b. See Irwin [9.36], 92 n. 12 for some reason to worry about this identity.

80 A number of different theses have been delineated under this general title. See, for example, Vlastos [9.93], 203–9, Brickhouse and Smith [9.17], 103–4 and Irwin [9.39], 52–3.

81 This is Santas' prudential paradox; [9.78], 183–89. He cites on behalf of Socrates' commitment to this principle *Meno* 77b–78b, *Protagoras* 358c and *Gorgias* 468c5–7. To get the prudential paradox from Socratic eudaimonism we may also need the claim that there are no non-rational desires or that non-rational desires always succumb to rational desires.

82 I here sidestep the issues surrounding Brickhouse and Smith's [9.17] denial that virtue and so knowledge of the good is sufficient for happiness. Whichever side of this dispute we favour, someone who acts contrary to his or her own good does so unintentionally. It is either because the individual fails to know which action benefits him or her or the individual through some misfortune or lack of non-moral good is unable to perform the action. Henceforth, I will take Socrates' position to be the sufficiency thesis in order to simplify the explication.

83 This is Santas' moral paradox: that 'all who do injustice or wrong do so involuntarily'; ([9.78], 183). He cites the following passages: *Gorgias* 460b–d, 509e5–7, *Protagoras* 345c and 360d3.

84 See Santas ([9.78], 190) and Taylor ([9.84], 149), who maintain that in order for Socrates to get from the prudential paradox to the moral paradox Socrates must contend that virtuous behaviour benefits the agent and vicious behavior harms the agent.

85 See, for example, *Crito* 47d–e and *Gorgias* 477b–480a. For the identification of the individual with the soul see Brickhouse and Smith [9.17], 101 n. 41.

86 See Irwin ([9.35], 193) who writes concerning the argument in the *Gorgias*, 'Perhaps Plato believes that someone who rejects *nomos* and its conception of justice as a whole can justify himself only by advocating the complete self-indulgence supported by Callicles. Plato does not show that Callicles' ground is the only reasonable ground for a general criticism of *nomos*.'

87 Note that for Socrates the study of moral philosophy promotes one's virtue.

88 See, for example, *Apology* 20b9–c3, 20d7–e3, 21b4–5, 23b2–4, *Charmides* 165b4–c2, *Laches* 200c2–5, *Hippias Major* 304d4–e3, *Gorgias* 509a4–7.

Translations cited in this chapter, but not included in the bibliography, are:

Cicero *De Natura Deorum* and *Academica*, trans. H. Rackham, Cambridge, Mass., Harvard University Press, 1979.

Plato *Five Dialogues: Euthyphro, Apology, Crito, Meno, Phaedo*, trans. G. M. A. Grube, Indianapolis, Ind., Hackett, 1982.

Plato *Hippias Major*, ed. and trans. P. Woodruff, Indianapolis, Ind., Hackett, 1982.

Plato *Ion*, trans. T. Saunders, in T. Saunders (ed.) *Plato: Early Socratic Dialogues*, Harmondsworth, Penguin, 1987.

Plato *Laches* and *Charmides*, trans. R. K. Sprague, Indianapolis, Ind., Bobbs Merrill, 1973.

BIBLIOGRAPHY

9.1 Annas, J. 'Self-knowledge in early Plato', in D. J. O'Meara (ed.) *Platonic Investigations*, Washington, DC, Catholic University of America Press, 1985, pp. 111–38.

9.2 —— 'Plato the Sceptic', *Oxford Studies in Ancient Philosophy* suppl. (1992): 43–72.

9.3 Benson, H. H. 'The problem of the elenchus reconsidered', *Ancient Philosophy* 7 (1987): 67–85.

9.4 —— 'A note on eristic and the Socratic elenchus', *Journal of the History of Philosophy* 27 (1989): 591–99.

9.5 —— 'Misunderstanding the "What is F-ness?" question', *Archiv für Geschichte der Philosophie* 72 (1990): 125–42.

9.6 —— 'The priority of definition and the Socratic *elenchos*', *Oxford Studies in Ancient Philosophy* 8 (1990): 19–65.

9.7 —— (ed.) *Essays on the Philosophy of Socrates*, New York: Oxford University Press, 1992.

9.8 —— 'The dissolution of the problem of the elenchus', *Oxford Studies in Ancient Philosophy* 13 (1995): 45–112.

9.9 Beversluis, J. 'Socratic definition', *American Philosophical Quarterly* 11 (1974): 331–6.

9.10 —— 'Does Socrates commit the Socratic fallacy?', *American Philosophical Quarterly* 24 (1987): 211–23; repr. in Benson [9.7].

9.11 —— 'Vlastos' quest for the historical Socrates', *Ancient Philosophy* 13 (1993): 293–313.

9.12 Brickhouse, T. C., and Smith, N. D. 'The origin of Socrates' mission', *Journal of the History of Ideas* 44 (1983): 657–66.

9.13 —— 'Vlastos on the elenchus', *Oxford Studies in Ancient Philosophy* 2 (1984): 185–96.

9.14 —— 'Socrates on goods, virtue, and happiness', *Oxford Studies in Ancient Philosophy* 5 (1987): 1–27.

9.15 —— *Socrates on Trial*, Princeton, NJ, Princeton University Press, 1989.

9.16 —— 'Socrates' elenctic mission', *Oxford Studies in Ancient Philosophy* 9 (1991): 131–60.

9.17 —— *Plato's Socrates*, New York, Oxford University Press, 1994.

9.18 Chance [7.44].

9.19 de Romilly [7.11].

9.20 Devereux, D. T. 'Courage and wisdom in Plato's *Laches*', *Journal of the History of Philosophy* 15 (1977): 129–41.

9.21 —— 'The unity of the virtues in Plato's *Protagoras* and *Laches*', *Philosophical Review* 101 (1992): 765–90.

9.22 Dodds [7.24].

9.23 Ferejohn, M. T. 'The unity of virtue and the objects of Socratic enquiry', *Journal of the History of Philosophy* 20 (1982): 1–21.

9.24 —— 'Socratic virtue as the parts of itself', *Philosophy and Phenomenological Research* 44 (1984): 377–88.

9.25 Geach, P. T. 'Plato's *Euthyphro*: an analysis and commentary', *Monist* 50 (1966): 369–82; repr. in Geach, *Logic Matters*, Oxford, Blackwell, 1972.

9.26 Gomez-Lobo, A. *The Foundations of Socratic Ethics*, Indianapolis, Ind., Hackett, 1994.

9.27 Gould, J. *The Development of Plato's Ethics*, Cambridge, Cambridge University Press, 1955.

9.28 Gower, B. S. and Stokes, M. C. (eds) *Socratic Questions: New Essays on the Philosophy of Socrates and Its Significance*, London, Routledge, 1992.

9.29 Graham, D. W. 'Socrates and Plato', *Phronesis* 37 (1992): 141–65.

9.30 Grote, G. *Plato and the Other Companions of Sokrates*, London, John Murray, 1875.

9.31 Gulley, N. *The Philosophy of Socrates*, London, Macmillan, 1968.

9.32 Guthrie [7.14].

9.33 —— *Socrates*, Cambridge, Cambridge University Press, 1971 (Vol. III, part 2 of Guthrie [2.13]).

9.34 Irwin, T. H. *Plato's Moral Theory: The Early and Middle Dialogues*, Oxford, Clarendon Press, 1977.

9.35 —— *Plato: Gorgias*, Clarendon Plato Series, Oxford, Clarendon Press, 1979.

9.36 —— 'Socrates the Epicurean', *Illinois Classical Studies* 11 (1986): 85–112; repr. in Benson [9.7].

9.37 —— 'Socratic puzzles: a review of Gregory Vlastos, *Socrates: Ironist and Moral Philosopher*', *Oxford Studies in Ancient Philosophy* 10 (1992): 241–66.

9.38 —— 'Say what you believe', in T. Irwin and M. C. Nussbaum (eds) *Virtue, Love and Form: Essays in Memory of Gregory Vlastos*, Apeiron 26, 3 and 4 (1993): 1–16.

9.39 —— *Plato's Ethics*, Oxford, Oxford University Press, 1995.

9.40 Kahn, C. H. 'Did Plato write Socratic dialogues?', *Classical Quarterly* NS 31 (1981): 305–20; repr. in Benson [9.7].

9.41 —— 'Drama and dialectic in Plato's *Gorgias*', *Oxford Studies in Ancient Philosophy* 1 (1983): 75–122.

9.42 —— 'Plato's methodology in the *Laches*', *Revue Internationale de Philosophie* 40 (1986): 7–21.

9.43 —— 'On the relative date of the *Gorgias* and the *Protagoras*', *Oxford Studies in Ancient Philosophy* 6 (1988): 69–102.

9.44 —— 'Plato's *Charmides* and the proleptic reading of Socratic dialogues', *Journal of Philosophy* 85 (1988): 541–9.

9.45 —— 'Plato and Socrates in the *Protagoras*', *Methexis* 1 (1988): 33–52.

9.46 —— 'Vlastos' Socrates', *Phronesis* 37 (1992): 233–58. (Review of [9.93].)

9.47 —— 'Proleptic composition in the *Republic*, or why Book I was never a separate dialogue', *Classical Quarterly* NS 43 (1993): 131–42.

9.48 Kerferd [7.15].

9.49 Kidd, I. 'Socratic Questions', in Gower and Stokes [9.28], pp. 82–92.

9.50 Kraut, R. 'Comments on Vlastos', *Oxford Studies in Ancient Philosophy* 1 (1983): 59–70.

9.51 —— *Socrates and the State*, Princeton, NJ, Princeton University Press, 1984.

9.52 —— 'Review of Gregory Vlastos *Socrates, Ironist and Moral Philosopher*', *Philosophical Review* 101 (1992): 353–8.

9.53 Lesher, J. H. 'Socrates' disavowal of knowledge', *Journal of the History of Philosophy* 25 (1987): 275–88.

9.54 Lesses, G. 'Crafts and craft-knowledge in Plato's early dialogues', *Southwest Philosophical Studies* 13 (1982): 93–100.

9.55 McPherran, M. L. 'Socrates and the duty to philosophize', *Southern Journal of Philosophy* 24 (1986): 541–60.

9.56 —— 'Comments on Charles Kahn, "The relative date of the *Gorgias* and the *Protagoras*"', *Oxford Studies in Ancient Philosophy* 8 (1990): 211–36.

9.57 —— 'Socratic reason and Socratic revelation', *Journal of the History of Philosophy* 29 (1991): 345–73.

9.58 Moline, J. *Plato's Theory of Understanding*, Madison, Wis., University of Wisconsin Press, 1981.

9.59 Nails, D. 'Platonic chronology reconsidered', *Bryn Mawr Classical Review* 3 (1992): 314–27.

9.60 —— 'Problems with Vlastos' Platonic developmentalism', *Ancient Philosophy* 13 (1993): 273–92.

9.61 Nakhnikian, G. 'Elenctic definitions', in Vlastos [9.86]: 125–57.

9.62 Nehamas, A. 'Confusing universals and particulars in Plato's early dialogues', *The Review of Metaphysics* 29 (1975): 287–306.

9.63 —— 'Socratic intellectualism', *Proceedings of the Boston Area Colloquium in Ancient Philosophy* 2 (1986): 275–316.

9.64 —— 'Eristic, antilogic, sophistic, dialectic: Plato's demarcation of philosophy from sophistry', *History of Philosophy Quarterly* 7 (1990): 3–16.

9.65 —— 'Voices of silence: on Gregory Vlastos' Socrates', *Arion* 2 (1992): 157–86. (Review of [9.93].)

9.66 Nussbaum, M. C. 'Aristotle and Socrates on learning practical wisdom', *Yale Classical Studies* 26 (1980): 43–97.

9.67 Penner, T. 'The unity of virtue', *Philosophical Review* 82 (1973): 35–68; repr. in Benson [9.7].

9.68 —— 'Socrates on the impossibility of belief-relative sciences', *Proceedings of the Boston Area Colloquium in Ancient Philosophy* 3 (1987): 263–325.

9.69 —— 'Desire and power in Socrates: the argument of *Gorgias* 466a–468e that orators and tyrants have no power in the city', *Apeiron* 24 (1991): 147–202.

9.70 —— 'Socrates and the early dialogues', in R. Krant (ed.) *The Cambridge Companion to Plato*, Cambridge, Cambridge University Press, 1992, pp. 121–69.

9.71 —— 'What Laches and Nicias miss – and whether Socrates thinks courage is merely a part of virtue', *Ancient Philosophy* 12 (1992): 1–27.

9.72 Polansky, R. 'Professor Vlastos's analysis of Socratic elenchus', *Oxford Studies in Ancient Philosophy* 3 (1985): 247–60.

9.73 Reeve, C. D. C. *Socrates in the Apology: An Essay on Plato's Apology of Socrates*, Indianapolis, Ind., Hackett, 1989.

9.74 Robinson, R. *Plato's Earlier Dialectic*, 2nd edn, Oxford, Oxford University Press, 1953.

9.75 Roochnik, D. L. 'The riddle of the *Cleitophon*', *Ancient Philosophy* 4 (1984): 132–45.

9.76 —— 'Socrates' use of the techne-analogy', *Journal of the History of Philosophy* 24 (1986): 295–310; repr. in Benson [9.7].

9.77 —— 'Socratic ignorance as complex irony: a critique of Gregory Vlastos', *Arethusa* 28 (1995): 39–51.

9.78 Santas, G. X. *Socrates: Philosophy in Plato's Early Dialogues*, Boston, Mass., Routledge and Kegan Paul, 1979.

9.79 Seeskin, K. *Dialogue and Discovery: A Study in Socratic Method*, Albany, NY, State University of New York Press, 1987.

9.80 —— 'Vlastos on elenchus and mathematics', *Ancient Philosophy* 13 (1993): 37–54.

9.81 Stokes, M. C. *Plato's Socratic Conversations, Drama and Dialectic in Three Dialogues*, Baltimore, Md., Johns Hopkins University Press, 1986.

9.82 Taylor, C. C. W. [7.22].

9.83 —— 'Critical notice: *Socrates: Ironist and Moral Philosopher*', *Philosophical Quarterly* 42 (1992): 228–34.

9.84 —— 'Socratic ethics', in Gower and Stokes [9.28], pp. 137–52.

9.85 Teloh, H. *Socratic Education in Plato's Early Dialogues*, Notre Dame, Ind., University of Notre Dame Press, 1986.

9.86 Vlastos, G. (ed.) *The Philosophy of Socrates: A Collection of Critical Essays*, Garden City, NY, Doubleday, 1971.

9.87 —— *Platonic Studies*, 2nd edn, Princeton, NJ, Princeton University Press, 1981.

9.88 —— 'The Socratic elenchus', *Oxford Studies in Ancient Philosophy* 1 (1983): 27–58; repr. in Vlastos [9.94].

9.89 —— 'Afterthoughts', *Oxford Studies in Ancient Philosophy* 1 (1983): 71–4; repr. in Vlastos [9.94].

9.90 —— 'Socrates' disavowal of knowledge', *Philosohical Quarterly* 35 (1985): 1–31; repr. in Vlastos [9.94].

9.91 —— 'Socrates', *Proceedings of the British Academy* 74 (1988): 87–109.

9.92 —— 'Is the "Socratic fallacy" Socratic?' *Ancient Philosophy* 10 (1990): 1–16; repr. in Vlastos [9.94].

9.93 —— *Socrates: Ironist and Moral Philosopher*, Ithaca, NY, Cornell University Press, 1991.

9.94 —— *Socratic Studies*, ed. M. Burnyeat, Cambridge, Cambridge University Press, 1994.

9.95 Woodruff, P. 'Expert knowledge in the *Apology* and *Laches*: what a general needs to know', *Proceedings of the Boston Area Colloquium in Ancient Philosophy* 3 (1987): 79–115.

9.96 —— 'Plato's early theory of knowledge', in Everson (see [2.35]), pp. 60–84; repr. in Benson [9.7].

9.97 Zeller, E. *Socrates and the Socratic Schools*, trans. O. Reichel, 3rd edn, London, Longmans, Green and Co. 1885.

CHAPTER 10

Plato: metaphysics and epistemology

Robert Heinaman

❧❖❧

❧ METAPHYSICS ❧

The Theory of Forms

Generality is the problematic feature of the world that led to the development of Plato's Theory of Forms and the epistemological views associated with it.[1] This pervasive fact of generality appears in several guises. (1) Normally, *one* characteristic is exhibited by *many* individuals. Redness, for example, characterizes many objects. (2) General terms such as 'is red' are correctly applied to many objects, and abstract singular terms such as 'triangularity' appear to name something without naming any individual. (3) We can *think* of general characteristics such as redness and of general facts such as that 'the triangle is a three-sided plane figure', where what is thought cannot be identified with a red individual or a fact about an individual triangle. (4) I can not merely think of but *know* general notions such as triangularity and general truths about them. Plato was the first western philosopher to focus attention on these facts, and his Theory of Forms attempts to explain their existence.

Although the first philosopher to draw attention to the problem of universals, Plato himself did not use any word that could be translated by 'universal'. The Greek terms normally used in the middle dialogues' 'classical' Theory of Forms are *eidos* and *idea*, which mean shape or form.

These terms already appear without their later metaphysical weight in early dialogues, where they signify moral characteristics which Socrates wants to define. In a famous passage of the *Metaphysics* (987a32–b8) Aristotle wrote,

356

Having in his youth first become familiar with Cratylus and with the Heraclitean doctrines (that all sensible things are ever in a state of flux and there is no knowledge about them), these views he held even in later years. Socrates, however, was busying himself about ethical matters and neglecting the world of nature as a whole but seeking the universal in these ethical matters, and fixed thought for the first time on definition. Plato accepted his teaching, but held that the problem applied not to sensible things but to entities of another kind – for this reason, that the common definition could not be a definition of any sensible thing, as they were always changing. Things of this other sort, then, he called Ideas . . .

This fits what we find in early dialogues where, in asking questions of the form 'What is X?' Socrates[2] is seeking a general definition stating what X *is*, not merely what X is *like*. The correct definition of X should not only be coextensive with X but illuminate the nature of X: the *being* or *reality* or *essence* (*ousia*) of X.

While taking over Socrates' interest in general definitions, Plato went further by raising the question of 'what the problem applied to': *what* do we define when we truly state, for example, that

(1) Virtue is knowledge of good and evil?

Further, Plato had a deep interest in mathematics, seeing it as a paradigm of knowledge, and the same question arises for mathematical truths such as

(2) The triangle is a three-sided plane figure.

Precisely *what* is the subject-matter of such a statement?

I believe the following sort of reasoning lay behind Plato's answer to this question: Whatever such truths are about, their being about *that* must explain why they are *eternally* and *changelessly* true. By contrast, truths about sensible objects such as (3) Socrates is sitting inevitably become false. The explanation for this feature of (3) seems straightforward: (3) is about Socrates, a changeable object, and it is because Socrates changes that the statement about him changes from true to false.

Since (3)'s changeable subject-matter explains its change in truth value, it appears plausible to suppose that what explains the fact that (2) is eternally and changelessly true is that it is about an eternal and changeless subject (cf. *Timaeus* 29b).

If so, with what could such a subject be identified? Apart from one brusquely dismissed proposal to be mentioned shortly, Plato believed that the only alternative to Forms which needs to be ruled out consists in sensible objects. Now, as Aristotle informs us, Plato was influenced by a student of Heraclitus named Cratylus who said that the world is in constant flux, and he himself held a similar view of the sensible world. Whatever the exact meaning of Plato's claim, it certainly entailed that the instability of sensible objects excludes them as the subject-matter of eternal truths.

Even if sensible objects sustain the same features for some time, they eventually perish and so could not be what *eternal* truths are about. If the triangle is a three-sided plane figure even after a particular sensible triangle perishes, the general truth cannot be reporting any fact about it. After its demise, no state of affairs involving the particular triangle exists, so no such state of affairs can be the reality represented by the general truth.

So, I take Plato to have reasoned, (2) is about a Form, an eternal and changeless entity, and that is why (2) is an eternal and changeless truth. Similarly, there will be a Form of Virtue underlying a true definition such as (1), thereby justifying Plato's belief in an objective moral reality which is as independent of human capacities and interests as mathematical reality.

A related and absolutely fundamental point for understanding why Plato believed in the Forms lies in their role as objects of thought. Its importance is stressed at the end of the criticism of the Theory of Forms in the *Parmenides* when, in face of all the alleged problems for the theory, Plato comes down to one bedrock argument that furnishes unanswerable proof for the existence of Forms:

> If one does not allow Forms of things in view of all the present difficulties and others like them, and does not distinguish some single Form in each case, *one will have nothing on which to fix one's thought*, since one is not allowing that in each case there is an Idea that is always the same, and so one will utterly remove the possibility of discourse.

> (135b–c)

Plato sees thought as involving an awareness of entities external to the thinker where these entities furnish the contents of the thought. For, first of all, when I think of triangularity I am thinking about something, my thought has a content. So, Plato (fallaciously) reasons, what I am thinking of exists. Therefore triangularity is a being that I am aware of when thinking of triangularity. And second, to think of triangularity is not to be aware of some thought inside my own mind. Thought is directed toward a content other than itself – a Form (*Parmenides* 132b–c).

So thought, like perception, mentally connects us with a reality outside ourselves, and Plato regularly speaks of thinking as a kind of mental vision. By thinking of triangularity I stand in a relation to a being which is the content of the thought. And since I can think of triangularity when no particular triangles exist, particular triangles could not be the reality I am then related to and aware of in thinking of triangularity. For *what* is thought when I think of triangularity does not vary with the shifting population of particular triangles. So at no time could the object of thought be identified with sensible objects.[3]

For Plato, this shows not merely that the object of thought – the Form of triangularity – differs from particular triangles, it proves the Form's complete independence of them. Hence, Forms are not only eternal and changeless, they exist independently of what happens in the sensible world.

The reference to discourse at the end of the passage quoted from the *Parmenides* indicates that what holds for thought applies equally to language: general words have a meaning or content that must be identified with the Forms. Although Plato distinguishes between words and statements, he does not (yet) distinguish the ways in which they function. Both signify some objective reality which is identified with their content.[4]

Only Forms are objects of knowledge. To see why we must look more closely at Plato's view of the sensible world.

The eternity, changelessness and independence of the Forms are part of what Plato has in mind when, under the influence of Parmenides' conception of being as an eternal changeless reality, he says that the Forms are real or *are* in a strong sense to be contrasted with the *appearance* and *becoming* characteristic of sensible objects. *Being* also comprises truth – *really being* such and such – and when Plato says that knowledge is of *being* the notion of truth is fused with the idea that a subject S's *being* F involves S being F *in virtue of its own nature*, and therefore *being eternally and changelessly* F, and hence never being the opposite of F.

So the nature of S explains why S *really is* F. Only what is F in this way is a stable F, a pure F, a true, perfect and real F. A subject cannot be a real F, it cannot be its nature to be F, if it ever appears contrary to F, which Plato (at times) conflates with appearing to be *not* F.

We saw that in early dialogues Plato says that being or reality is displayed in a general definition. Such being or reality – where this now has all the connotations noted above – is found only among the Forms. Beauty, for example, is beautiful in virtue of its own nature, and hence is eternally and changelessly beautiful without any trace of its opposite, ugliness.

In contrast, sensibles are never beautiful in virtue of their own nature: they inevitably appear ugly in another respect, or in comparison to another thing, or at another time. If a beautiful object is not ugly at the same time, it will nevertheless eventually become ugly since it is undergoing continuous change. For example, sensible objects constantly change place, and if a beautiful object approaches a more beautiful object the first will be uglier than the second, and hence appear ugly as well as beautiful. Or one may move to a position from where the object appears ugly rather than beautiful. If, unavoidably, A will appear ugly as well as beautiful, then we cannot explain A's beautiful appearance by saying that it is A's nature to be beautiful. It *is* not beautiful *in itself*, it merely presents an appearance of beauty in virtue of 'participating' in a being outside of itself, the Form of Beauty. That is – this is the only content Plato ever gives to *participation* – the sensible resembles or imitates the nature of Beauty. We must look beyond the sensible object to explain its appearance. It is dependent on the Form which is, by contrast, entirely independent of it.

This situation of appearing F without *being* F applies to all features of sensible objects. There is nothing that they *really are*. We cannot say that this stuff before us really is snow because changes are constantly going on in the sensible world which will lead to the disappearance of snow. It is not snow in itself, it does not have the nature of snow, or *any* nature since all its features will eventually disappear or be joined by their contraries. So we must look beyond the snow itself to explain why it is cold. We can say that the stuff before us is cold because it participates in the Form of Cold, or, more interestingly, that it is cold because it participates in the Form of Snow, which always brings along Coldness. But we cannot explain why it is cold by saying that the stuff before us has the nature of Snow, and therefore is cold.

At times Plato goes further[5] and suggests that the constant change undergone by sensible objects leaves them bereft of any kind of identity between what we *call* different phases of the 'same' object. Plato believes in particular qualities which are peculiar to the object they are found in. Socrates' health, for example, is peculiar to him and differs from Aristotle's health. A sensible object is a bundle of such qualities and when the qualities change the numerical identity of the object changes as well, even if we call it the same because of the similarity[6] between the earlier and later objects. Not only can we not properly say that this object *is* healthy, we cannot say that it *is* Socrates, for that would impute a stability which it does not possess. For the same reason it is misleading to refer to sensible phenomena with the word 'this': it suggests permanence and stability that the sensible phenomena are too volatile to merit.[7]

The *Timaeus* identifies individual qualities with images of the

Forms which cannot be legitimately called this or that but should only be derivatively described in reference to their models – Forms – as, for example, 'such as' water. One point of this characterization is that the images and sensible objects composed of them are derivative from, dependent on and less real than the Forms they reflect, as images in mirrors or water are derivative from, dependent on and less real than their ordinary models. When shifting phenomena change from air to water to earth, etc., we can, during the second stage, say that the image is such as water since there is a fleeting resemblance to Water. (Similarly we could say that a mirror image of water is 'such as' water, imitates or resembles water, without really being water.) But the image's disappearance shows that we could not have pinned it down as 'this' or 'that': like mirror images, the phenomena lack any nature which they could be said to be.

The *Timaeus* further develops Plato's view of the sensible world by introducing the 'dim and difficult' notion of space as an entity needed besides Forms and images on the grounds that an image requires a medium or receptacle where it can exist. Space has no feature of its own since that would interfere with its imaging the contrary feature. But since its nature is stable and unchanging, it can properly be spoken of as 'this'. What we observe in the phenomenal world should be described by saying (e.g.): this (namely, space) is such as fire. An analogue would be the statement that gold is triangular: as an underlying medium gold receives and exhibits the feature without really being that feature and without its own nature being affected by the presence of the shape.

Knowledge exists, and its object must plainly be what *is*, reality. And here all the aspects of *being* noted above coalesce: truth, essence, eternity, changelessness, stability and intrinsic intelligibility. For Plato, a paradigm case of knowledge would be expressed in the definition of the being or nature of triangularity. Since in knowing that the triangle is a three-sided plane figure one has knowledge of reality, *what* reality precisely is it that is known? Not a sensible triangle for, as we saw, the changeable character of sensible objects exposes their lack of the being demanded of an object of knowledge: they *are* not anything but only appear to be and imitate reality. The nature and being of a triangle is not present in but beyond the sensible object and there is nothing there in the sensible to be known. Since sensibles have no natures to be known, the objects of knowledge must be different: the Forms.

Nevertheless, we do have mental states related to sensible objects. These, however, are perceptions and opinions or judgements (*doxai*) based on perception, not knowledge. Lacking any notion of a proposition or sense that could serve as the content of a cognitive mental state, Plato identifies this content with the being in the world that the mental state is about. Since judgement or opinion differs from knowledge – it can be correct or incorrect, it is not based on an account of its object – the entity that is its content, Plato argues, can no more be identical with the *being* grasped by knowledge (namely, the Forms) than a colour can be what we hear. Still, since opinion does have a content it cannot be directed toward sheer nothingness. So the objects of opinion fall between being and not being. Sensible objects, appearing both to be F and not to be F for many properties, must be the entities that furnish opinions with their content.[8]

Again, the Forms must be changeless and eternal, and as objects of knowledge they must *be* the natures expressed in definitions.

For Plato, even if there were (or are) eternal triangles in the sensible world, there would be a distinct Form of Triangularity because we could not otherwise explain why the triangles have something *in common*, share *one general* feature.

If it is by reference to the Form of Triangularity that we explain why particular triangles have something in common, then (*Republic* 597b–c; cf. *Timaeus* 31a) there must be only one Form of Triangularity. An individual's being F is explained by its participation in F. If, *per impossibile*, we had two Forms of triangularity, T_1 and T_2, then if object *a* were a triangle because it participated in T_1 and *b* were a triangle because it participated in T_2, we could not explain why *a* and *b* have something in common. To do that we must relate them both to one and the same entity, one and the same Form.

To explain how things have features in common, then, we must suppose that for each property there is one and *only* one Form.

We have, Plato believes, the ability to think of ideal standards such as perfect equality, for when we judge that sensible objects are equal we may judge at the same time that they fall short of perfect equality. So to judge is to compare the sensible objects with another entity. For to think about perfect equality – to have *that* as a content of thought – is for the mind to stand in a relation to a reality outside the mind. The question then arises of how to explain this awareness and our ability to think – from among all the entities that exist – of precisely *it*.

I could no more have become aware of this entity through examining the contents of my own mind than I could have by introspection become aware of Mount Everest. And Plato appears to believe that the explanation of my ability to think of perfect equality must be that at some time or other I experienced it. To perceive sensible equals is not to experience perfect Equality since none of them really *is* equal: they are inevitably also unequal, the opposite of equal. It is not, Plato thinks, by observing an object that is no more equal than unequal that I can acquire the notion of perfect equality. So it must be through acquaintance with the Form of Equality, which is perfectly equal, that I acquired the ability to think of perfect Equality.

So a Form of F-ness is a paradigm of F, it is perfectly F. This is part of a Form's *being* in a way that sensibles are not.

This idea that a Form of F is itself F has come to be known as 'self-predication'.[9] Already in the earliest dialogues, where the Theory of Forms is undeveloped, we observe thought and language that naturally evolved into the self-predication assumption. For example, proposed definitions were often expressed as in the following definition of justice:

(1) Doing one's own *is just*.[10]

If the definition is correct, since

(2) Doing one's own = justice

it follows that

(3) Justice is just.

In early dialogues such statements are taken to express self-evident truths.[11] A statement of this form is also implied by the assertion that if Beauty is correctly defined as X, then X must be more beautiful than anything else[12] and cannot be the opposite of beautiful;[13] and by an argument that X cannot be the definition of Beauty because it is not beautiful.[14]

Assertions of (3)'s form are entailed by Plato's belief that if an object b explains why an object a is F, b must itself be F[15] and somehow impart its own F-ness to a. Plato considers it self-evident that if a is F, F-ness is a *being*, and the presence of F-ness explains why a is F.[16] It follows that F-ness must itself be F.

This condition on explanation is important once the Theory of Forms is developed, for Plato uses it and related principles in the *Phaedo* to mount a rationalist attack on experience of the sensible world as a source of knowledge, and to argue that explanations of phenomena in terms of perceptible and mechanical processes lead to absurdity. Typically, Plato believes, if we use our senses to identify some sensible property, physical process or object X as the explanation of something – Y – in the sensible world, the following absurdities arise: (1) X is contrary to Y, or (2) in other cases the contrary of X appears to bring about Y, or (3) in other cases X appears to bring about the contrary of Y. To suppose that a contrary could be explained by its own contrary is like supposing that we could explain why snow is cold by appealing to the presence in it of something hot.

Plato's explanations of phenomena in terms of participation in Forms avoid these difficulties.[17] The 'safe and stupid' explanation of why a sensible object is cold, for example is that it participates in the Form of Coldness. The 'clever' explanation appeals to the fact that certain kinds of thing are necessarily associated with one opposite characteristic and exclude another; as Snow, for example, must, in virtue of its own nature, be characterized by Coldness and exclude Hotness. So the clever explanation of why a sensible object is cold could be that it participates in the Form of Snow.

Although clearly distinguished from *teleological* explanations, Plato gives no indication that his preferred explanations differ in kind from those he rejects. But while the latter include what Aristotle would label efficient causes, Plato's recommended explanations are more like 'formal causes'. A safe and stupid explanation states *what it is* for a sensible to be F. The clever explanation's account of why the snow is cold combines with the snow's participation in Snow the point that 'snow' entails 'cold', just as 'triangle' entails 'interior angles equal to 180 degrees'.

The important point for self-predication is that Plato's explanations avoid the alleged difficulties confronting physical, mechanical explanations. The items appealed to possess the characteristic explained and never possess the contrary. Thus, the Form of Snow is cold, and the Form of Coldness is cold. Self-predication is essential to Plato's idea of explanation.

It is also essential to his account of participation. A sensible object gives the *appearance* of Beauty, so although it cannot *be* beautiful, the appearance can only be accounted for if the sensible object 'participates' in the Beauty which it cannot be. And for the sensible to participate in Beauty is for it to resemble or imitate the nature of Beauty which it does not possess. If there is resemblance, then there is a shared characteristic.[18] And if this is not strictly true, that is not because the Form of Beauty is not really beautiful, but because the sensible is not really beautiful and only appears to be such as the Form truly is.

Resemblance and self-predication are also important for recollection since Plato thinks we are often reminded of and re-acquire knowledge of Forms by observing sensible objects that resemble them.

Again, self-predication alone makes sense of Plato's theory of love. Love is the desire to possess what is beautiful and the supreme object of love is the Form of Beauty. So the Form must be beautiful. How could the object of the most intense and most pleasurable eros *not* be a beautiful object?

As the goal of a passionate longing, the Forms are objects of desire, and to 'acquire' them by knowing them is a mystical experience of *divine*[19] beings. All people, most unconsciously, yearn to recapture the vision of the Forms which they enjoyed before birth. This alone did give them and would give them complete satisfaction and happiness.

All this makes some sense only if the Forms are perfect paradigms. Because of their greater reality 'possession' of the Forms gives true satisfaction in a way in which possession of sensibles does not. And part of that greater reality consists in the Forms being perfectly what sensible objects are only deficiently or in appearance.

Similarly, Forms are more real because of their greater 'cognitive visibility' in comparison with sensible objects.[20] If we want to learn what a property F is, the observation of a sensible F will typically prove of little use since the property will be bound up with its opposite, and so the observation will provide a confused idea of what F-ness is. However, if we could attain a clear view of the Form we would immediately know what F-ness is because it is a 'pure' and perfect example of F uncontaminated by its opposite (cf. *Philebus* 44d–45a). Here again, the greater reality of the Forms depends on their being paradigms.

Self-predication, then, is fundamental for Plato's philosophy. However, it is a mistake, arising, in part, from confusions that helped to make it seem entirely natural.

1 Plato does not distinguish different uses of 'to be.' His single Form of Being merges these different uses with the features of true being noted before. So the existential use is run together with the identifying use,[21] the existential use is conflated with the predicative use,[22] and the predicative use is confused with the identifying use.[23] Given the last confusion, since, plainly, Beauty is Beauty, it may also seem self-evident that Beauty is beautiful.

2 Pre-Socratic philosophers did not always properly distinguish between objects and properties. Thus, Anaxagoras spoke of 'the hot' and 'the cold' on a par with 'earth' as elements from which things come to be. If Plato too was not clear on this point, then it would have been natural for him to think of Beauty as a beautiful object.[24]

   The point is not that Plato did not distinguish attributes and objects but that he did not adequately distinguish the kinds of thing which they are.

3 Greek uses expressions formed from the definite article and an adjective such as 'the beautiful' to name properties. Occasionally Plato will even use the adjective on its own as the subject of a sentence to refer to a Form. Such expressions lend themselves to being understood as operating in the same manner in which they *do* operate when applied to sensible individuals, namely as *describing* the object named. And this danger is especially serious in Plato's case for (*Cratylus* 384d–385c) he does not adequately distinguish naming and describing. So he could easily understand terms design-

ating the Form of Beauty – 'the beautiful' and 'beautiful' – as describing and not merely naming the Form.

4   The definition

(D) The triangle is a three-sided plane figure

specifies the condition an individual must satisfy to be a triangle. But even if 'the triangle' in (D) names a universal, the rest of the sentence does not *describe* the universal. That is, (D) – however it should be construed – does not say that the universal *triangle* is a three-sided plane figure, is a triangle, in the way an individual triangle is. But that is just how Plato understands (D).

This connects with a failure to distinguish different types of general predication. Supposing there is a Form of Man we could say that

(a) Man is eternal, changeless, etc.

Here properties are attributed to the Form just as they are attributed to Socrates when I say he is white, henpecked, etc. Man is an entity that is an eternal thing, etc. But

(b) Man is an animal, mortal, etc.

makes a different sort of claim. Thus, whereas there may be some plausibility in proposing that (b) means

(c) Every man is an animal, mortal, etc.,

(a) certainly does not mean

(d) Every man is a universal, eternal, etc.

The predications in (a) are true because they are about a Form: all Forms have those properties. The predications in (b) are true because they are about the specific concept Man. If the two types of predication are not distinguished, one might understand the predications in (b) in the same way as those in (a). Then definitions such as

Man is a rational animal

may make it seem obvious that Man is a man, Triangularity is a triangle, etc.

Plato's metaphysics is built on the contrast between Forms and sensible objects. These contrasts make Forms *more real* than sensible objects. Forms are natures existing independently of sensibles: eternal, changeless, divine, immaterial, imperceptible, knowable and intelligible in virtue of their natures. Free of contrary attributes, they are perfectly beautiful, just, etc. and of the highest value. Sensible objects, by contrast, are dependent on Forms: material, perceptible, transient, in constant flux, of little or no value, or evil; lacking intrinsic natures, they *are* not really anything but bound up with opposites and unintelligible.

Being utterly contrary to what is found in the sensible world, Forms do not exist in but apart from the world around us.[25] While their images exist in us,[26] they exist 'in themselves', and this means that they do not exist in us or anywhere 'here on earth'[27] in the 'corporeal and visible place.'[28] They exist in 'another place,'[29] the 'intelligible place,'[30] 'the place in which the most blessed part of reality exists,'[31] a place 'untainted by evils'[32] – heaven[33] or a 'place beyond heaven.'[34]

The Parmenides

Parmenides 127d–136e presents the puzzling spectacle of Plato putting forward criticisms of his own Theory of Forms. Probably the prevalent view today is that the dialogue documents Plato's realization of the unacceptable consequences of self-predication, which he therefore abandons.

I disagree. Plato portrays a youthful, immature Socrates not yet in possession of the philosophical acumen that would enable him to answer the objections to his underdeveloped theory. But Plato himself, I believe, is not concerned about the objections because, in his view, they arise from confusion or an inadequate understanding of the Theory of Forms. I will only have space to discuss the first version of the Third Man Argument (132a–133a), the 'TMA'.[35]

The argument's validity rests on two assumptions not given in the text: Self-Predication,

(SP) A Form of F-ness is F

and 'Non-Identity',

(NI) If all members of a set of objects are F in virtue of participating in a Form of F-ness, no member of that set = that Form of F-ness.

The only assumption on the surface of the text is the 'One over Many Assumption,'

(OM) If several objects are F, there exists a Form of F-ness by virtue of participating in which they are F.

Whereas Plato maintains that only one Form exists for any attribute, he appears committed to infinitely many Forms for each attribute.

For suppose that sensibles

(1) a, b and c are large.

Then by (OM)

(2) there exists a Form of Largeness: $Largeness_1$.

By (SP) it follows that

(3) $Largeness_1$ is large.

So now we have a new set of large things:

(4) a, b, c and $Largeness_1$ are large.

By (OM), applied to this new set of large objects,

(5) there exists a Form of Largeness: $Largeness_2$.

And given (NI), $Largeness_2$ differs from $Largeness_1$: since $Largeness_1$ is large by virtue of participating in $Largeness_2$, it cannot be $Largeness_2$. When endlessly repeated, these steps produce an infinite number of Forms of Largeness.

Since Plato nowhere explains his attitude toward this argument, we will never know what he thought of it. The question must be addressed on the basis of indirect evidence.

Attention has focused on self-predication since that is in fact a mistake. As we saw, self-predication is essential to Plato's earlier Theory of Forms, so the TMA's presumption of self-predication does not render it irrelevant to Plato's position.[36]

The belief that the argument's point is to prove the unacceptability of self-predication runs into the problem that self-predication is present in what is now generally agreed to be a dialogue later than the *Parmenides*, namely the *Timaeus*.[37] There, despite *Parmenides* 133a's rejection of resemblance, sensibles participate in paradigmatic Forms by resembling and imitating them. Resemblance brings along self-predication.

That the target is not self-predication is also indicated by a peculiar argument separating the two versions of the Third Man Argument. Socrates proposes that Forms might be *thoughts*, to which Parmenides objects that then everything is a thought, and hence either everything thinks or else, while *being* a thought, does not think.

The argument assumes that *a thought* thinks. Further, we saw that one confusion behind self-predication is the failure to distinguish between predications such as

(i) Man is eternal

and

(ii) Man is mortal.

If Socrates participates in the Form of Man, then *only* (ii)'s predicate can be legitimately transferred to Socrates. But when from the proposal that Forms are thoughts Parmenides concludes that

(iii) Man is a thought,

the predication is of the type that occurs in (i). So one who was clear about the difference between (i) and (ii) would not take Socrates' participation in Man together with (iii) to imply that Socrates is a thought.

But such is Plato's inference. Now, Plato certainly rejects the idea that Forms are thoughts, so he is probably making what *he* considers a sound objection against it. If the point of the TMA were to expose and reject self-predication, why would Plato, in the midst of this demonstration, deliberately present a fallacious argument against a view he wants to refute, where the fallacy is of precisely the sort involved in the error of self-predication?

But if Plato did not abandon self-predication, how could he respond to the Third Man Argument? By restricting the One over Many Assumption, the only assumption expressly given in the text.[38] Platonists in the Academy regularly limited the inference from a set of Fs to a Form of F to cases where the members of the set do not stand in relations of priority and posteriority; and, according to Aristotle, Plato himself accepted this restriction.[39] Aristotle reports this view in the *Eudemian Ethics* (1218a1–8):

> There is not something common over and above and separate
> from things in which the prior and posterior exist. For what is
> common and separate is prior (*proteron*) since the first (*prōton*)
> is taken away when what is common is taken away. For example,
> if *double* is first of the multiples, *multiple*, which is predicated
> [of particular multiples, namely *double, triple*, etc.] in common,
> cannot be separate. For then there will be [a multiple] prior to
> *double*.

But *double* is the first multiple and cannot have a multiple prior to it. So there is no Form of *Multiple* over and above specific multiples. The rationale for this principle assumes self-predication: it is *because* the Form of Multiple would be *a* multiple that it would be, impossibly, a multiple prior to *double*.

Ontological priority is in question: if x's non-existence entails y's non-existence, but x can exist without y, then x is prior to y. Aristotle reports that Plato regularly used this notion of priority.[40]

One page before the quoted passage Aristotle points out that a Form of F is, in just that sense, prior to particular Fs: the Form of Good is the first and prior good because if taken away the other goods would be taken away. That is because for them to be good is for them to participate in, and thus depend on, the Form, while the Form is not similarly dependent on the particular goods: *being good* is its nature, so it is good in itself.

Likewise for any other Form. So at step (4) of the argument,

(4) a, b, c and Largeness₁ are large,

Plato can block reapplication of the One over Many Assumption and the inference to a new Form. One subject – the Form – is the first of 'the larges' and prior to the others.

Of course, if the reason given above was Plato's justification for thus restricting the One over Many Assumption, then the restriction is unacceptable since it rests on self-predication. In fact, then, but unknown to Plato, the Third Man Argument presents a serious problem for the theory of Forms.[41]

Many have detected revision of the Theory of Forms in a discussion of 'friends of the Forms' in the *Sophist* (248a–249d). Some believe Plato is allowing that the Forms can change, some believe that motion is allowed to be real, and some believe that the Forms have become 'powers' (*dunameis*) or potentialities for change – all contrary to what Plato previously believed.

Interpretation of the passage is made difficult by its aporetic character, and the entire discussion (236–51) ends in aporia. The Eleatic Stranger, who leads the *Sophist's* conversation, examines a dispute between 'giants' who define being in terms of matter, and 'gods' who explain that being consists of the immaterial and changeless grasped by reason independently of the senses. The latter are called 'friends of the Forms' and are often thought to include Plato himself. Hence, when their position is criticized it is thought that Plato is criticizing his own previous position.

Before discussing the friends of the Forms, the Stranger criticized the materialists and introduced the following definition of *being:* x is a being just in case x has a power to act on, or be acted on by, something else. The friends of the Forms might be expected to reject the definition because it admits material objects as beings, but the only explanation given for their rejection is their denial that Forms – the beings – possess a power to act or be acted on.

The Eleatic Stranger raises two objections against the friends of the Forms. (1) They allow that Forms are known. But *to know* is to act, and therefore *to be known* is to be acted on. Hence, in being known the Forms are acted on, and therefore changed. (2) He cannot accept that intelligence does not belong to 'what wholly is'. But if intelligence belongs to being, so must life, soul, and hence change, belong to being.

Now, to determine Plato's attitude to this criticism, we need to know: Does Plato accept the Eleatic Stranger's definition of being?

And to answer this we would need to answer the following question: Is the notion of *being* defined in terms of the capacity to act or be acted on *being* in the strong sense or the weaker notion applicable to material objects?

The *Sophist* itself fails to settle these questions. But if we look to later dialogues where the earlier contrast between being and becoming is reaffirmed,[42] and assume that the *Sophist* does not represent a temporary detour, then we can say the following: (1) If the *Sophist* defines being in the strong sense, then Plato cannot accept its definition since he later reaffirms that being cannot apply to the sensible world of becoming. (2) If the *Sophist* is defining being in the weaker sense, then Plato could accept it consistently with his contrast between a stronger notion of being and becoming. For the fact that x is acted on does not, as the Stranger falsely suggests (248e), entail that x is altered. One example of 'acting' and 'being acted on' was that if x possesses an attribute F, then F acts on x, and x is acted on by F. In this sense the Form of Figure 'acts' on the Form of Triangularity, and, according to the *Sophist's* doctrine of the communion of Forms, the Form of Being 'acts' on the Form of Difference. Obviously, this does not entail that Triangularity or Difference change, and the passage ends with the changelessness of the objects of knowledge reaffirmed (249b–c; cf. *Politicus* 269d).

If it is said that the vehemence with which the Stranger asserts that motion, life, mind and wisdom belong to 'the *wholly* real' shows that he is asserting their being in the strong sense, this is consistent with the earlier Theory of Forms.[43] It too asserted the existence of Forms of Soul and Life in the *Phaedo*.[44] The Form of Motion is casually referred to in Socrates' outline of his *immature* Theory of Forms in the *Parmenides* (129e), and the Form of Knowledge is mentioned later in the same dialogue (134a–e; cf. *Phaedrus* 247d–e).[45]

While there is no clear evidence for the suggested alterations in the Theory of Forms, the *Sophist* does undeniably contain one new development: for the first time Plato speaks of Forms participating in other Forms: the 'communion of Forms'. Hitherto, Plato was only concerned to give the ontological analysis of the fact behind a true statement that a subject S is F when S is an individual. But in many cases – and many cases of the sort that Plato would be particularly interested in – the subject of a statement asserting that S is F will name a Form. If the case where S is an individual demands explanation, it is obvious that the general case likewise demands an explanation. And this

Plato provides for the first time with his doctrine of the communion of Forms.

A central passage in the *Sophist* (251a–257a) presents a series of arguments to distinguish five 'greatest Kinds': Being, Sameness, Difference, Rest and Motion. Many have found more sophisticated theories here, but I believe that communion of Forms is the same relation as his earlier notion of participation – in the sense that for a Form S to participate in a Form F is for S to possess F as a property, just as for an individual S to participate in a Form F is for it to have F as a property.[46] Consequently, self-predication is a feature of the *Sophist's* Kinds[47] since the ontological analysis of the fact that *the Triangle is a figure* is: the Kind Triangularity participates in the Kind Figure, and hence *is a figure* in the same way as particular triangles are. Given that the Kinds are also 'divine' (254b), they must be the same Forms which we find in the middle period dialogues.

Divinity also characterizes the 'Henads' of the *Philebus* (62a), a very late dialogue mainly concerned with ethical problems but containing important and notoriously obscure passages on metaphysics with Pythagorean overtones absent from earlier works. The obscurity is probably due, in part, to the metaphysics of the *Philebus* being grounded in Plato's 'unwritten doctrines,'[48] about which our knowledge is very thin.

Plato divides 'all beings' into the categories of (1) Limit, (2) the Unlimited, (3) the mixture of Limit and the Unlimited, (4) the cause of this mixture. (4) is relatively clear, being identified with intellect, but the rest of the scheme resists interpretation because of the shifting usage of the notions of Limit and Unlimited, and the bizarre diversity of examples from the mixed class.

The Limit–Unlimited contrast is associated with the contrast between one 'Henad' with a specific number of species, and its indefinitely large range of generable and destructible instances (16c–d). But Limit is later explained in terms of the notion of a numerical ratio or measure (25a), and still later connected to the ideas of *moderation* and a *balanced* and *good* proportion (26a). Correspondingly, the Unlimited is not only associated with the idea of an indefinite range of particular instances but is explained in terms of scales of qualities referred to with pairs of comparative adjectives: hotter–colder, higher–lower, etc., which are generally characterized as admitting the more and the less, and as in themselves admitting no definite quantity. Further, the Unlimited also includes pleasure and the *life* of pleasure. The difficulties are further compounded by Plato's identification of these different notions of Limit and Unlimited (23c) and by the disparate nature of the examples from the mixed class: it includes a moderate amount of pleasure, the life which combines pleasure and intellect, the art of music, fair weather, health and virtue of character. As these last examples show, Plato's scheme cannot be interpreted in terms of Aristotle's notions of form (Limit), matter (Unlimited) and composite (mixture). Nevertheless, it appears that Plato is analysing entities into what can be loosely called 'formal' and 'material' elements.

How do the Forms fit into this classification? If the One of the One–Many problem raised at 13e–15c corresponds to a (perhaps 'mathematicized') Form from earlier dialogues, then since the One–Many problem arises for all items in classes (1)–(3) (23e, 24e, 26d), Forms do not fall under any one of these classes but rather there are Forms for all the beings in (1)–(3). So, for instance, the Unlimited will include both the Form of Pleasure and particular instances of pleasure.

As in the *Sophist*, Plato displays greater interest in the relations between Forms than he did before. The *Philebus* addresses the problem of reconciling the Form's unity with the fact that it not only has many individual instances but will often be divisible into further species which are themselves Forms. Perhaps 15d–17a proposes a solution to this problem, but if so it is, like much of the *Philebus*' metaphysics, steeped in obscurity.[49]

∾ EPISTEMOLOGY ∾

Recollection

The recollection theory is Plato's explanation of our ability to think of and acquire knowledge of general notions and general truths, where general notions are understood as Forms and general truths the facts about Forms.[50] The theory claims that in this life we can think of and know the Forms only because we experienced them before birth and thereby acquired knowledge of them. This 'active' knowledge is lost at birth but remains latent in the soul, and perception of sensibles that resemble the Forms, or teaching by another, or enquiry into the Forms by a dialectical conversation which (ideally) operates independently of the senses, may lead to full recovery of the latent, innate knowledge.

To understand why Plato adopted this extravagant theory we must recall his picture of thought as a relation to – as an *awareness of* – beings outside our minds. Suppose that yesterday you found yourself thinking of my cousin Ruth Collins in Lancaster County, Pennsylvania, a person you never heard of before. As you could not have simply pulled out of yourself the awareness of this person who is a real being existing independently of you, if it could be established that you have had no experience of her since birth, it might be plausible to suppose that you must have somehow experienced her before birth. And how else *could* we explain your ability to think of *her*?

Of course, we are unable to think about sensible objects we have not encountered since birth. Plato believes, however, that we *can* think of general notions and general truths which we have never experienced in our present life, and so the problem which does not exist for sensible objects does exist for general notions and general truths.

Thus, the *Phaedo* says we have the ability to think of Equality. Where could it come from? Not merely from perception of sensible equals, for they, unlike the Form, appear unequal as well as equal. This establishes that the Form is a different entity from the sensibles. So even if the sensible equals were perfectly similar to the Form of Equality, our awareness of them on its own could not have made us aware of and able to think of that entirely distinct entity, Equality itself.[51] No more than the perception of several people exactly like Ruth Collins could have given you the ability to think of her. But perception of the sensible equals may revive our latent knowledge, and once we are aware of Equality we may carry out a dialectical enquiry leading to complete knowledge of it.

In the *Meno*, recollection explains a slave boy's ability to think of a mathematical truth; call it 'p'. Plato reasons: the slave boy produces this thought that p so it must have already been *in* him. Since nothing the slave boy experienced since birth could have put it into him, he must have become aware of it before birth (cf. *Phaedo* 73a–b). What Plato finds puzzling, what requires explanation, is the slave boy's ability to *think* of the mathematical fact, and it is by explaining this that the recollection theory explains the slave boy's ability to make a judgement about and, later,[52] to know the mathematical fact. This is the more natural for Plato because his picture of thought as an active awareness of some being in the world makes it hard to distinguish thinking and knowing.

Now, the correct explanation of the slave boy's ability is, at one level, straightforward. The sentence asserting that p is composed of words the meaning of which the slave boy already knows. And it is simply a fact about human beings that they can construct new statements and know what they are saying as long as they know the meanings of the words in the statement and can follow the relevant linguistic rules.

Only in the *Sophist* will Plato begin to appreciate the importance of the difference between the ways in which words and statements function. In earlier dialogues, statements are understood to be assigned to beings in the same way as names.[53]

374

Related confusions can be found in Plato's failure adequately to discriminate (1) objects and facts; (2) knowledge of objects and knowledge of facts; (3) propositions and facts.

Plato nowhere distinguishes an ontological category of facts as distinct from objects; both are referred to indifferently as 'beings'. Stating a fact with a sentence or thinking a thought is seen by Plato as a reference to or an awareness of some reality external to the thinker which is, furthermore, identified with the *content* of the thought, namely the fact in question. *What is said* is quite naturally identified with the fact – the reality – reported.[54]

So Plato sees the slave boy as someone who has some general mathematical truth, *p*, as the content of his thought, where this is identified with the fact that *p* 'grasped' by the slave boy's mind. In thinking that *p* the slave boy is related to and aware of some part of reality outside himself, and just as I could not think of an object I had never experienced, so Plato believes the slave boy could not think of and be aware of the fact that is the content of his thought if he had never experienced *it* before. As he has not experienced it since birth, he must have done so before birth.

In the *Meno* the recollection theory is also relevant to the paradox of enquiry raised before Socrates' examination of the slave boy. The paradox is stated in two ways that are not equivalent:

1 I cannot enquire into something of which I am completely ignorant.
2 I could not know if I came across what I was enquiring into because I could not recognize it as what I was searching for.

The recollection theory can answer (2). The slave boy, for example, has latent knowledge of *p* which, when revived by Socrates' cross-examination, enables him to 'recognize' *p*.

But the recollection theory does not and is not meant to answer (1).[55] To set up X as an object of enquiry I must *actively* 'know' X, and latent knowledge cannot by itself explain such awareness of X. Once we distinguish between propositions and facts, the solution to (1) is straightforward: I can know what is said by 'p' without knowing whether it is the case that p. So I can enquire whether it is the case that p without knowing whether it is the case that p. But with this solution unavailable to him, Plato's responds to (1) not with an explanation of how enquiry is possible but by arguing that as a matter of fact enquiry can lead to knowledge and so we *ought* to persist in enquiring into things we do not know.

> For inasmuch as all nature is akin, and the soul has learned all
> things, when a man has recalled one piece of knowledge . . .

nothing prevents him from finding out all the other things.

(*Meno* 81c–d)

If I learn A, which is similar to B, then I may recollect B. And if B is similar to C then I may recall C, and so on. It is this sort of stepwise enquiry which Socrates conducts here (*Meno* 82e 12–13).[56]

Dialectic

That stepwise procedure of recollection is an example of Plato's dialectical method. This developed from the negative and destructive Socratic elenchus – the procedure of refutation portrayed in early dialogues – into a method for achieving positive knowledge. The *Phaedo* contrasts it with empirical investigation which leads to the difficulties mentioned previously, and emphasizes that enquiry should proceed by reason alone. The Forms can only be apprehended by reason, and it will be by thinking about *them*, by having *them* in our mental view, that we will acquire knowledge of them, not by turning to the sensibles that only confusingly reflect the natures we wish to know.

'Dialectic' is from *dialegesthai* ('to converse') and dialectic is a conversation proceeding by question and answer. The questioner leads the enquiry and begins by asking his interlocutor (possibly himself) a question, typically about how to define some concept. An initial hypothesis is proposed which the questioner attacks by getting his respondent to answer a further series of questions where the answers lead to some difficulty or absurdity. They then go back and, taking this result into account, another answer is proposed. And so on. In early dialogues this procedure produced negative results, but the *Phaedo* claims that it is the method to follow in order to acquire knowledge of the Forms. In successful enquiry the ability of a proposed definition p to withstand attempted refutations provides partial confirmation of its correctness. And for further confirmation we can select a plausible 'higher' hypothesis which would explain p, and deduce the original hypothesis from it.

This is not only the method for discovering the truth; the person with genuine knowledge must be able to successfully carry it out. Knowledge of X enables its possessor to 'give an account' of X, and, in standard cases, this involves the ability to state and explain the nature of X and to explain why that account is correct. It further involves the ability to defend the proposed definition against objections. These abilities demand expertise and understanding of an entire discipline.

A problem is that the method leads to a regress: after unsuccessfully attacking p we further confirm p by deducing it from q; then q must be challenged, and if it survives it must be further confirmed by deducing it from r; and so on. At each stage we are explaining a proposition by another which we do not know, and if we do not know the basis of our explanation we do not know or understand what we purport to explain in terms of that basis.

Unlike the *Phaedo*, the *Republic* shows some concern for this problem in the famous divided line analogy, where Plato criticizes mathematicians because they fail to scrutinize critically their assumptions, cannot explain why they are true, and hence do not know them; and therefore also do not know the conclusions derived from them. Dialecticians avoid this failing by critically examining assumptions which they can explain and defend. The backwards regress is said, vaguely, to end in apprehension of an unhypothesized beginning: the Form of the Good. Plato does not elaborate, but since the Good is the first principle, there must be nothing more basic in terms of which the Good can be explained or defined. Knowledge of it will have to consist in some sort of intuition.

This is probably related to the *Phaedo*'s best method of explanation, which was abandoned as too difficult in favour of the 'safe and stupid' and 'clever' forms of explanation mentioned above. Plato clearly believes that the proper explanation of a phenomenon is a teleological explanation of why it is *best* for things to be thus and so, and therefore a proper explanation presupposes some account of what the good is.

In the *Phaedo* teleological explanation is presented as an *alternative* explanation of a fact about the sensible world which can be less adequately explained by a clever or safe and stupid explanation in terms of participation in Forms. But in the *Republic*, where the concern is with Forms alone, it appears rather that, for example, a mathematical theorem q is explained in terms of the mathematician's starting-point p, which is in turn – eventually – explained in terms of the Good. The Good is also the ultimate explanation of q *via* its explanation of p. Similarly, in the *Republic* the *being* of other Forms, and not merely sensible phenomena, will ultimately be explained by reference to the Form of the Good (*Republic* 509b).

Later, the *Timaeus* identifies the contrast between teleological and mechanical explanations of features of the sensible world with a contrast between Reason and Necessity, and now some things are explained by one factor, some by the other, and some by both. Reason has priority over Necessity, acts to produce what is best and is solely responsible for anything that is intrinsically good such as order and proportion. At the cosmic level it is represented by the 'Demiurge,' the creator who looks to the Forms and tries to embody them in disorderly matter. Necessity is responsible for randomness, disorder and evil in the material world, but also acts in subordination to Reason to explain features which are necessary conditions for and concomitant causes of certain instrumental goods, much like Socrates' bones and sinews in the *Phaedo* (99a).[57]

In later dialogues[58] dialectic involves less argumentation and greater interest in classification. The *Republic*'s conception of a master science establishing the starting-points of subordinate disciplines disappears, and is apparently not required for understanding an area of enquiry. For all Plato explicitly says, distinct disciplines are now autonomous. The procedure called 'collection and division' does not provisionally posit a hypothesis and then subject it to critical scrutiny. Rather, it standardly begins when undefined species are unified under a defined genus. This genus is divided into species, which are in turn divided into subspecies, etc., until indivisible species are reached. Conjoining the divisions thus passed through yields definitions of the items at the end of the chains. Dichotomy – the division of a genus into two species – may be followed when the aim is to define a particular Form, since the remaining species will then be irrelevant. But when we want clarification of a genus the number of divisions made at any stage should match the natural, objective divisions in the subject-matter.

However, collection and division does not exhaust the content of Plato's later 'dialectic'. It comprises (*Sophist* 253b–d):

1 dividing things according to Kinds;
2 producing definitions of Forms;
3 not identifying distinct Forms or distinguishing identical Forms;
4 knowing what Forms can and cannot combine.

(1) often aims at (2), and the misidentification of distinct Forms (violating (3)) may result from failure to properly divide a genus (cf. *Politicus* 285a). But that is not how misidentification of the Greatest Kinds is avoided in the *Sophist* (254b–257a), nor is it obvious how (4) is connected with division. *Sophist* 254bf. aims for (3) and (4) but uses arguments characteristic of the earlier dialectical method, and makes no use of the sorts of divisions which occur at the beginning of the dialogue. Perhaps Plato thought that when, unlike with many of his own examples, philosophically important Forms were investigated, then the sort of argumentation found in the *Sophist* passage might be required.[59]

The Theaetetus *and the* Sophist

The *Theaetetus* represents Plato's most sustained investigation into the nature of knowledge. Structured around an attempt to define knowledge, it, like the early dialogues, ends in frustration. But scholars have been quick to find positive lessons which we are *meant* to draw from the discussion.[60]

The dialogue divides into three sections which consider proposals to define knowledge as (1) perception, (2) true judgement, and (3) true judgement with an account. (3) resembles contemporary definitions of knowledge in terms of justified true belief, but one difference is that all three suggestions define knowledge not as a disposition but as a mental *event*: perception or judgement, where judgement occurs when the soul *says* something to itself (180e–190a, *Sophist* 263e–264a).

(1) Because knowledge is infallible and of what is, if knowledge is perception then perception is infallible and of what is. Since x may (e.g.) appear warm to A and cold to B, (1) entails a Protagorean relativism validating both perceptions: what A perceives *is for* A and what B perceives *is for* B. The object is not warm or cold *in itself*: no objective reality independent of the perceptions exists that could falsify them.

Less straightforwardly, Plato connects (1) to a Heraclitean doctrine of constant flux. If what a sensible object x is for A is nothing more than how x appears to A, then x lacks an intrinsic nature – it is nothing in itself – and hence, in the strong sense of 'being', x *is* nothing. Given the connection between 'being' and permanence, x also lacks stability and constantly changes. For sensible objects are continuously changing place so as to present different appearances to different perceivers.

The refutation of (1) initially attacks the relativism and flux doctrines which it is said to imply. Of several objections raised against Protagoras, the main difficulty is that his position is self-refuting. Protagoras' 'Man is the measure' doctrine was not that it appears to Protagoras that what appears to any person A is for A, but that, absolutely, what appears to A is for A. But most people reject this, that is, for most people it appears that it is not the case that what appears to A is for A. So if what appears to them is for them, Protagoras' doctrine does not hold for them. Protagoras' absolute claim is false.

As for the flux doctrine, if everything continuously changes in every respect, no object can be accurately called anything since 'it is always slipping away while one is speaking'. So nothing we might call 'perception' is any more perception than not perception, and therefore, on the proposed definition of knowledge, nothing is any more knowledge than not knowledge.[61]

Finally, Plato attacks the definition directly by arguing that no perception can ever be an instance of knowledge. The argument has aroused much interest because Plato is often, mistakenly, taken to be marking an important contrast between the objects of perception and judgement.[62] He first distinguishes the subject of perception from the senses through which the subject – the soul – perceives colour, sound, etc. A single subject is aware of the different kinds of sense object and observes relations between them.

Further, anything perceived through one sense cannot be perceived through a different sense. For example, I cannot hear a colour. So if anything is *common* to different kinds of sensible object, the soul cannot 'grasp' it by perception.

Now, 'being' is a common notion applicable to different kinds of sensible object: both a sound and a colour *are*. So the soul grasps 'being' not through a sense but on its own.

But to know is to know the truth, and knowing the truth is grasping being, i.e., awareness of what *really exists* or *is the case*. Since perception cannot grasp being it cannot put us into contact with the truth, and therefore it can never be knowledge.

Plato's argument rests on an ambiguity in the notion of 'grasping being'. When the common notions are first introduced, to grasp being is to understand the meaning of 'being' or what being is: being *itself* (*not* an object like red or a fact that *has* being) is not an object of perception but an object of thought. However, when in the passage's final argument it is claimed that to attain truth one must grasp being, the claim has plausibility only if grasping being is equivalent to grasping an object that *really exists* or a fact that *is the case*. And perception's inability to grasp what being itself is provides no reason to believe that perception cannot make us aware of what really exists. On the contrary, Plato himself affirms shortly afterwards (188e–189a) that if one perceives x, then x exists.

(2) The definition of knowledge as true judgement is quickly dismissed: true judgement can turn out to be true by luck, and then it is not knowledge.

(3) The final definition meets this point by suggesting that knowledge is true judgement 'with an account'. But the notion of an account is unclear, and Socrates attempts to explain it in terms of a metaphysical theory he heard in a dream. The theory says there are simples and complexes. There is no account of the simples which can only be named and so are unknowable. Complexes are knowable and expressible in an account which is a weaving together of names.

Even at this abstract level the dream theory faces two objections. First, a complex either is or is not identical with its elements. If it is, then since its elements are unknowable, it is unknowable too. If it is not, then it does not have the elements as parts, and, since nothing else could be part of the complex, it must be simple and hence (according to the theory) unknowable. Second, if we consider simples and complexes such as syllables and their letters, the letters are knowable independently of any account of them.

Both arguments have plausibly been supposed to be meant to apply to the problem of knowledge of Forms. If a Form F is defined in terms of A, B and C, the knowledge of F expressed in the definition presupposes knowledge of A, B and C. And if A, B and C are known by knowing *their* definitions, the same problem recurs. Either there is an infinite regress and knowledge does not exist, or some kind of knowledge does not involve an account – a definition – of the thing known. This last seems to be the sort of knowledge needed of the *Republic*'s unhypothesized beginning, but Plato never clarifies what kind of knowledge it could be.

Although the final argument against the dream theory seems to show that knowledge does not need an account, Plato proceeds to consider different interpretations of 'account'. The serious suggestions – and it is important to bear in mind that the item known is an object – are that knowledge of X requires (1) the ability to analyse X into its elements or (2) the ability to give a mark distinguishing X from everything else.[63]

Against (1) Socrates objects that a person might correctly judge that the first syllable of 'Theodorus' contains 't' 'h' and 'e', but on another occasion, when writing the name of Theaetetus, incorrectly judge that that same syllable contains the elements 't' and 'e'. Then he did not know the syllable 't-h-e' the first time even though he correctly analysed it into its elements. Knowledge is infallible.

Against (2) Socrates objects that the ability to give a distinguishing mark of X is presupposed in having a true judgement about X: otherwise one would not have a true judgement about *X* to begin with. So (2) adds nothing to the idea of having a true judgement about X.[64]

With this the discussion comes to an end. One puzzle is the question of why Plato neglects the notion of giving an account which he himself uses in other dialogues when discussing knowledge. If being able to give an account includes the abilities to explain why something is so and to defend the claim in question, then some of the *Theaetetus'* difficulties are overcome.

Another problem arises from the dialogue's use of sensible objects as objects of knowledge. Does Plato now countenance knowledge of the sensible world, or is the negative conclusion of the dialogue rather meant to reinforce the lesson that we cannot explain the nature of knowledge when its objects are disregarded?

It seems the *Theaetetus* cannot be *intended* as a demonstration that an account of knowledge must fail if it does not bring in Forms as the object of knowledge, for if that were Plato's aim the neglect of his own interpretation of 'account' would only too obviously undermine his argument. And we've already seen that some objections against the proposal that knowledge be defined in terms of judgement apply equally well when its objects are taken to be Forms. For example, accounts of Forms are as vulnerable to the epistemological regress as accounts of anything else.[65]

None of the objections against proposed definitions of knowledge turn on the *objects* used in the examples not being of the right kind. The one firm conclusion of the dialogue is about the sort of state knowledge is, not the nature of its object: knowledge must be sought in *judgement* rather than perception (187a).

Despite this conclusion – which could be supposed to be undermined by the rest of the dialogue – one might still see the *Theaetetus* as reinforcing Plato's view that Forms are the sole objects of knowledge, where knowledge must be *contrasted* with judgement, not explained in terms of it. After all, it *is* clear that the *Theaetetus* cannot represent Plato's abandonment of his earlier view, given that later dialogues are still emphatically contrasting perception and judgement (*doxa*) with knowledge on the basis of a difference in their objects. Thus, the *Timaeus* (27d–28a, 51d–52a) asserts: Being (i.e. Forms) is grasped by intelligence (*noēsis*) with an account (or reason, *logos*), while becoming (the sensible world) is grasped by judgement (*doxa*) with perception. Yet, in direct contradiction of this, the *Theaetetus* considers definitions of knowledge that state that it is perception or a kind of judgement (*doxa*). So, perhaps, Plato takes the *Theaetetus*' failure as confirmation of the *Timaeus*' view on the objects of knowledge.

But this interpretation faces serious problems, the answers to which are far from clear. For example: why should the difficulties which afflict proposed definitions of knowledge in terms of *judgement (doxa)* disappear when knowledge is defined as a kind of *thought (noēsis)*?

Lacking the notions of proposition and sense, Plato can only identify the contents of thought with beings – facts or objects – in the world. Taking statements to name facts in the way that words name objects, Plato is inclined to construe stating or judging what is false as stating or judging where there is no content to be stated or judged. False judgement appears impossible.

Likewise, for Plato, if I think of X I am thereby related to a being in the world which is the content of the thought. And how could I think of X – that being which furnishes the content of my thought – if I was not aware of X, if I did not *know* X? And if I know Y as well as X, I would never say to myself that X is Y, i.e., I could not judge falsely that X=Y. While if Y is unknown to me it could never enter into any judgement I made, so again I could not falsely judge that X=Y.

These problems from the *Theaetetus* are attacked with the wax tablet and aviary models, which begin to make headway towards over-coming some of the obstacles to an account of false judgement in so far as they provide for the possibility of an object entering into thought via different routes. But it is the *Sophist* which presents Plato's sol-ution,[66] a solution which does not build on the *Theaetetus*.

The main philosophical section of the *Sophist* begins with the assertion that in order to show how false judgement is possible, Par-menides' assertion 'Never shall this be proved, that things that are not are' must be refuted. For a false statement says that what is not (= Not Being) is.

The main point needed to overcome Parmenides' dictum is that 'Not Being' or 'What is Not' does not signify *contrary* to being, i.e. non-existence, but *different* from being. Focusing on the 'greatest Kinds' – Being, Difference, Sameness, Rest and Motion – Plato, after explaining how some can participate in and hence *be* the others, points out that each is *different* from the others, and hence can be said to *not be* each of the others. So Not Being exists.

Next, we must be clear about the fact that a statement has two kinds of parts that function in different ways. The name signifies the being in the world that the statement is about, while the verb signifies what is said about the subject, namely the being in the world that is the attribute ascribed to the subject.

'Theaetetus is sitting' is true if *sitting* 'is with respect to Theaet-etus', i.e. if sitting = one of his attributes. And then 'Theaetetus flies' is false if *flying* 'is not with respect to Theaetetus', i.e. *is different from* every attribute that is with respect to Theaetetus. The fact that in this false statement *what is not* is said of Theaetetus does not mean that *nothing* is said about Theaetetus. For here *what is not* is not the *non-existent* or *non-existence*[67] but *flying* – a being.

Plato's solution marks a major advance when he clearly signals the difference between the ways in which words and statements func-tion. But with no clear notion of sense as distinct from reference, he still has nothing to say on the question of what could constitute the content of a false statement.

❦❦❦ NOTES ❦❦❦

1 My understanding of the Theory of Forms owes most to Ryle [10.43] and Frede [10.74]. See also Graeser [10.76], Ross [10.92]; Wedberg, 'The Theory of Ideas', in [10.97], 28–52; Bostock [10.67], 94–101, 194–201, 207–13. Crombie [10.36] can be consulted on all subjects covered by this chapter. I am very grateful to Christopher Taylor for his extensive and helpful comments on earlier drafts of this chapter.

Any discussion of the topics I discuss is bound to be controversial and some alternative interpretations can be found in works cited in the notes and bibliography. Limitations of space compel these references to be highly selective.

2 I assume the generally agreed view that the earliest dialogues closely reflect the methods and beliefs of the historical Socrates, but that in middle period dialogues the character of Socrates expresses views which go far beyond those of Plato's teacher.

3 Cf. the argument 'from things that are no more' from Aristotle's *On Ideas* in [10.63], 81–2. Note that the point in the text applies just as much to 'horse' and 'finger' as it does to 'beauty' and 'one'. Some believe *Republic* 523–5's distinction between concepts that do and do not give rise to thought shows that Forms are not needed for concepts such as 'horse' which, like the concept of 'finger', do not give rise to thought. But the passage only indicates that perception of particular fingers may suffice, epistemically, for recollection of the Form of Finger. The latter is an object of thought as distinct from perceptible fingers as the perceptible and 'oppositeless' squares and circles drawn in the sand are distinct from their corresponding Forms which are the objects of the mathematician's thought (*Republic* 510d–511a).

4 *Cratylus* 431b–c; cf. 432e, 385b–c. Similarly with the philosopher Parmenides: what is required for thought was not distinguished from what is required for speech.

5 *Symposium* 207d–208b: the relation between the different phases of 'one' life is the same as that between a parent and its offspring. See also *Cratylus* 439d; *Theaetetus* 154a, 159d–160a; *Timaeus* 49c–e. Contrast *Phaedo* 102e.

6 Even in this most extreme statement of the doctrine of flux, Plato allows that the later and earlier objects share many characteristics. Hence, he does not accept the *Theaetetus'* wild version of Heracliteanism which says that sensibles always change in every respect.

7 *Timaeus* 49d–e. For other views on flux, see Bolton [10.65], Irwin [10.80].

8 For a different interpretation, see Fine, 'Knowledge and Belief in *Republic* V–VII', in [10.101], 85–115.

9 This topic is thoroughly examined in Malcolm [10.85].

10 *Hippias Major* 289d, 291d, 292c–d, 297e, 304d; *Charmides* 161a–b; *Laches* 192c–d.

11 *Hippias Major* 292e; *Protagoras* 330c–e.

12 *Hippias Major* 291c.

13 *Hippias Major* 291d.

14 *Hippias Major* 296c–d.

15 *Lysis* 217c; *Charmides* 160e–161a, 169d–e; *Hippias Major* 291c; *Gorgias* 497e; *Meno* 87d–e; *Phaedo* 68d–e, 100e–101b; *Republic* 335d–e, 379a–c; *Parmenides* 131c–d; *Philebus* 65a.

16 *Hippias Major* 287c.

17 While Plato allows that physical conditions and phenomena are necessary conditions for the items he explains in other terms, the *Phaedo* (99a–b) denies them the title of 'explanations'. In the *Timaeus* (46c–d), however, he calls them secondary or co-operative causes or explanations.

18 *Parmenides* 139e, 148a.

19 See, for example, *Symposium* 211e, *Republic* 500c, *Phaedo* 84b, *Phaedrus* 250a, *Sophist* 254b, *Philebus* 62a.

20 See Vlastos [10.98], 58–75. For the ideas in the paragraph before last, see [10.98], 43–57.

21 *Timaeus* 38b.

22 *Republic* 478b12–c1 with 478d–479d.

23 *Phaedo* 74c1–2. Plato equates two questions: (1) Is Equality ever unequal? (2) Is Equality ever Inequality?

     Had he seen the difference, he should also have seen (2)'s irrelevance to his argument. He is trying to show that sensible equals differ from Equality because they possess a feature Equality lacks. But sensible equals no more appear to *be* Inequality than Equality does.

24 On this point see Frede [10.74], 51–2.

25 *Timaeus* 52a, c; *Symposium* 211a–b.

26 *Phaedo* 102d–e, 103b; *Republic* 501b; *Parmenides* 132d.

27 *Theaetetus* 177a.

28 *Republic* 532c–d.

29 *Phaedo* 80d.

30 *Republic* 508c, 509d, 517b.

31 *Republic* 526e.

32 *Theaetetus* 177a.

33 *Republic* 592b.

34 *Phaedrus* 247c–e.

35 Very briefly on the other objections: the first questions the range of Forms but does not present any positive objections. The second falsely assumes that Forms exist in sensible objects. The last objection mistakenly infers from the statements that (for example) the Form of Master is master of Slavery itself and not of any particular slave, and a particular master is a master of a particular slave and not of Slavery itself, that there can be *no* relations between individuals and Forms.

36 For another view, see Allen, 'Participation and predication in Plato's middle dialogues', in [10.64], 43–60, and in Vlastos [10.97], 167–83; H. F. Cherniss 'The relation of the *Timaeus* to Plato's later dialogues', in [10.64], 360–7; Nehamas [10.87].

37 In a famous paper ('The Place of the *Timaeus* in Plato's dialogues', in Allen [10.64], 313–38) G. E. L. Owen argued that the *Timaeus* should be dated prior to the *Parmenides*. This provoked H. F. Cherniss's response in the article cited in n. 36. Owen's thesis 'must be pronounced a failure' Vlastos [9.93], 264). See Brandwood [10.34], and, more briefly, 'Stylometry and chronology', in Kraut [10.41], 90–120.

38 The only author I have come across who notes the relevance of the following point to the Third Man Argument is Cherniss [10.71], 520.

39 [10.63], 84. Cf. *Philebus* 59c; Aristotle, *Nicomachean Ethics* 1096a17–19, ps.-Aristotle, *On Indivisible Lines* 968a9–14.

     This restriction on the One over Many Assumption was a commonplace among the Neoplatonists. See Proclus, *In Parmenidem*, V, 125, Cousin = 684, Stallbaum; Plotinus, *Enneads* VI, 1.1. Ammonius, *In Porphyrii Isagogen*, ed. A. Busse, Berlin, 1891, 28.10–12; 29.18–19; 82, 5–10; Olympiodorus, *In Categorias*, ed. A. Busse, Berlin, 1902, 58.35–7; Asclepius, *In Metaphysicorum Libros A–Z Commentaria*, ed. M. Hayduck, Berlin, 1888, 226. 21–2.

40 *Metaphysics* 1019a2–4.

41 For further discussion see Vlastos, 'The Third Man Argument in the *Parmenides*', in [10.64], 231–63; Strang, 'Plato and the Third Man', in [10.58] I, 184–200; Allen [10.19].

42 *Timaeus* 27d–28a, 51d–52a; *Philebus* 59a–c. Cf. *Politicus* 269d.

43 But possibly Plato is referring to the demiurge of the *Timaeus* or the world soul (cf. *Timaeus* 30b, *Philebus* 30c).

44 *Phaedo* 106d refers to the Form of Life. Keyt [10.81] convincingly argues the *Phaedo*'s commitment to Forms for substances such as Snow and the Soul.

45 *Sophist* 248a–249d is discussed in Keyt [10.82].

46 I defend this view in [10.78]. For other views see Ackrill 'ΣΥΜΠΛΟΚΗ ΕΙΔΩΝ', in [10.64], 199–206 (=[10.58]I, 201–9); and a sometimes inaccurate survey of alternative accounts in Pelletier [10.89].

47 I argue that the text of the *Sophist* bears this out in [10.77]. For other views, see, e.g. Vlastos, 'An Ambiguity in the *Sophist*', in [9.87], 270–308; Frede [10.73].

48 Aristotle, *Physics* 209b15. The unwritten doctrines are views attributed to Plato by Aristotle and ancient commentators which are, at least frequently, not clearly expressed in Plato's writings. The *Philebus*' notions of Limit and the Unlimited may be connected to Plato's generation of Forms from the One and the Great and the Small in his oral teachings (Aristotle, *Metaphysics* 987b18–21). On the unwritten doctrines, see, for example, Cherniss [10.70], Gaiser [10.75], Krämer [10.83], Robin [10.91], Vlastos, 'On Plato's oral doctrine', in [9.87], 379–403.

49 For discussion of the *Philebus*, see Hackforth [10.25]; Gosling [10.26]; Sayre [10.93], ch. 7; Striker [10.95].

50 At least this is so in the *Phaedo* where Forms and the recollection theory are said to stand and fall together (76e). Since we do not experience Forms in the world around us, the *Phaedo* in effect offers an explanation of a priori knowledge, where the knowledge is prior not to *all* of the soul's experience, but to its experience since birth in its present life. It is doubtful, however, that Plato is thinking of Forms in the earlier *Meno*, where they go unmentioned and we recollect things seen 'here' (81c6) in the present life. A related difference between the dialogues is that in the *Meno*, where knowledge is a kind of opinion (98a), both latent opinion and latent knowledge explain the slave boy's performance. While in the *Phaedo*, where Forms alone are recollected and are 'unopinable' (*adoxaston*, 84a), references to latent opinions disappear.

For general discussion of Plato's epistemology, see, for example, Gulley [10.102] and the papers on Plato in [10.101].

51 It doesn't matter whether x is or is not like y, or, in the first case, whether x does or does not (73a) fall short of y; the important point is that 'as long as while you are seeing *something else* (*allo*) from this vision you think of *something else* (*allo*)' (74c–d) it is recollection.

52 In the dialogue the slave boy does not recover active knowledge of p (85c–d), so what he *actually does* there which requires explanation in terms of recollection must be something else.

53 *Cratylus* 431b–c.

54 The confusion persisted into this century. 'Moore and Russell were constantly

perturbed by whether or not to identify true propositions with facts, which they took to be fully part of the real world, or merely to regard the one as corresponding to the other, whether to admit the existence of false propositions, and similar problems, and constantly changing their minds on these points' (M. Dummett, *Frege: Philosophy of Language*, London, Duckworth, 1973, p. 153).

55 There are good reasons to reject Gail Fine's suggestion that Plato answers (1) with the slave boy example by saying that, even though the enquirer lacks knowledge in any sense, he has true beliefs about the subject of enquiry ('Inquiry in the *Meno*' in [10.41], 200–26). First, the purpose of the slave boy example is to demonstrate the truth of the recollection theory (81e, *Phaedo* 72e–73b), not to solve the paradox of enquiry. Further, her attempt to explain away the references to the slave boy's knowledge as allusions to his past or future knowledge (n. 40) is refuted by the reference to 'the knowledge which he now has' at 85d9. Likewise *Phaedo* 73a is clearly saying that the slave boy could not have spoken the truth if *knowledge* had not been in him *then*. This is also the presumption of *Republic* 518b–d. There is no contradiction with *Meno* 85b–c's statement that the slave boy does not have knowledge since this denies that he has current, revived knowledge of p, not that he has latent knowledge of p.

56 For different views of the recollection theory, see the papers reprinted in [10.10].

57 This paragraph is based on Strange [10.94]. Some other works on the *Timaeus*: Cornford [10.23], Brisson [10.68], Mohr [10.86], Taylor [10.96]. For Plato's dialectical method in the middle dialogues the classic work is Robinson [10.105]. See also Sayre [10.106].

58 In particular, the *Phaedrus*, the *Sophist*, the *Politicus* and the *Philebus*.

59 For discussion of Plato's later dialectic, see Ackrill [10.99]; Sayre [10.106]; Stenzel [10.107].

60 Some works on the *Theaetetus*: Cornford [10.20]; McDowell [10.21]; Burnyeat [10.22]; Bostock [10.100].

61 One important issue of interpretation concerning the *Theaetetus* is the question of whether Plato revises his earlier views of the sensible world. For the famous debate between Owen and Cherniss (referred to in n. 37), see Allen [10.64], 332–5 and 349–60.

62 The standard view holds that Plato is saying that to know one must truly judge *that* something *is* the case (*grasping being* either is this judgement or is presupposed by it in virtue of 'is'), and that such an intentional content cannot be delivered by perception. But Plato uses singular terms and 'that' clauses indifferently to refer both to objects of judgement and objects of perception. (Judgement: 185c–d, 186a–d; 185a–b, 186b. Perception: 184b, 184d–185a; 185b–c.) Furthermore, on the standard view it is inexplicable that Plato blatantly ignores the point for the rest of the dialogue where many examples of objects of knowledge and judgement are individuals. Before, during and after 184–7 both things and facts are objects of the knowledge which the dialogue attempts to define, and this is one source of the difficulties troubling Plato's discussion.

63 Unlike present day epistemologists, Plato does not speak here of the justification of belief in a proposition.

64 This argument brings out Plato's inability to clearly distinguish *thinking* of X and *knowing* X: to think of X is already to know X.

65 Burnyeat in [10.22], 238.
66 For further discussion of the *Sophist's* solution, see McDowell [10.103] and Frede 'The *Sophist* on false statements,' in [10.41], 397–424.
67 Here I am assuming a view of Not-Being in the *Sophist* which not all will accept. This issue is discussed in Malcolm [10.84]; Frede [10.73] Owen 'Plato on Not-Being', in [10.58] I, 223–67; Heinaman [10.79]; Brown [10.69].

❧ GENERAL BIBLIOGRAPHY ❧
FOR CHAPTERS 10–12

Complete Greek Text

10.1 Burnet, J. *Platonis Opera*, 5 vols, Oxford, Clarendon Press (Oxford Classical Texts), 1900–7. A new text is in preparation; vol. I, ed. E. A. Duke *et al.*, appeared in 1995. A complete Greek text with English translation is published by the Loeb Classical Library (London and Cambridge, Mass., Harvard University Press). 12 vols (various editors).

Complete Translations

10.2 Cooper, J. (ed.) *Plato. Complete Works*, Indianapolis, Ind. and Cambridge, Hackett, 1995.
10.3 Hamilton, E. and Cairns, H. (eds) *The Collected Dialogues of Plato*, New York, Bollingen Foundation, 1961.
10.4 Jowett, B. *The Dialogues of Plato*, 4th edn, rev. D. J. Allan and H. E. Dale, 4 vols, Oxford, Clarendon Press, 1953.

Translations of Selected Works

10.5 Allen, R. E. *The Dialogues of Plato*, 2 vols, New Haven, Conn., Yale University Press, 1984 and 1991. (First 2 volumes of projected complete translation.)
10.6 Matthews, G. *Plato's Epistemology*, London, Faber and Faber, 1972. Contains translations of passages from *Meno, Phaedo, Republic, Parmenides, Theaetetus, Sophist*.
10.7 Saunders, T. J. (ed.) *Early Socratic Dialogues*, Harmondsworth, Penguin, 1987. Contains translations of *Ion, Laches, Lysis, Charmides, Hippias Major, Hippias Minor, Euthydemus*.

Translations of Separate Works (some with Greek text)
(Listed in probable order of composition by Plato)

10.8 Guthrie, W. K. C. *Plato:* Protagoras *and* Meno, Harmondsworth, Penguin, 1956.

10.9 Sharples, R. W. *Plato:* Meno, Warminster, Aris and Phillips, 1985. Greek text with facing translation and commentary.

10.10 Day, J. M. (ed.) *Plato's* Meno *in Focus*, London, Routledge, 1994. Contains a translation of the *Meno* with a collection of articles.

10.11 Hackforth, R. M. *Plato's* Phaedo, Cambridge, Cambridge University Press, 1955, repr. Indianapolis and New York, Bobbs-Merrill. Translation and commentary.

10.12 Gallop, D. *Plato*, Phaedo, Oxford, Clarendon Press, 1975. Translation with philosophical commentary. Revised version of translation with notes, Oxford and New York, Oxford University Press, 1993 (World's Classics).

10.13 Rowe, C. J. *Plato*: Phaedrus, Warminster, Aris and Phillips, 1986. Greek text with facing translation and commentary.

10.14 Grube, G. M. A. rev. C. D. C. Reeve *Plato*: Republic, Indianapolis, Ind., and Cambridge, Hackett, 1992. Translation with notes.

10.15 Waterfield, R. *Plato*, Republic, Oxford and New York, Oxford University Press, 1994. Translation with notes (World's Classics).

10.16 Halliwell, F. S. *Plato*: Republic V, Warminster, Aris and Phillips, 1993. Greek text with facing translation and commentary.

10.17 Halliwell, F. S. *Plato*: Republic X, Warminster, Aris and Phillips, 1988. Greek text with facing translation and commentary.

10.18 Cornford, F. M. *Plato and Parmenides*, London, Routledge and Kegan Paul, 1939. Contains a translation of *Parmenides* with commentary.

10.19 Allen, R. E. *Plato's* Parmenides, Oxford, Blackwell, 1983. Translation and analysis.

10.20 Cornford. F. M. *Plato's Theory of Knowledge*, London, Routledge and Kegan Paul, 1935. Contains translations of *Theaetetus* and *Sophist* with commentary.

10.21 McDowell, J. *Plato*, Theaetetus, Oxford, Clarendon Press, 1973. Translation with philosophical commentary.

10.22 Burnyeat, M. *The Theaetetus of Plato*, Indianapolis, Ind. and Cambridge, Hackett, 1990. Contains translation of *Theaetetus* by M. J. Levett, with introduction by M. Burnyeat.

10.23 Cornford, F. M. *Plato's Cosmology*, London, Routledge and Kegan Paul, 1937. Contains translation of *Timaeus* with commentary.

10.24 Rowe, C. J. *Plato*: Statesman, Warminster, Aris and Phillips, 1995, Greek text with facing translation and commentary.

10.25 Hackforth, R. *Plato's Examination of Pleasure*, Cambridge, Cambridge University Press, 1958. Contains translation of *Philebus* with commentary.

10.26 Gosling, J. C. B. *Plato*, Philebus, Oxford, Clarendon Press, 1975. Translation with philosophical commentary.

10.27 Saunders, T. J. *Plato*: The Laws, Harmondsworth, Penguin, 1970.

Other translations (of some of the above and of other dialogues) are published by

Hackett, Oxford University Press (Clarendon Plato Series and World's Classics), Penguin and (in French) Flammarion. Most contain notes or commentary.

Bibliographies

10.28 Cherniss, H. F. 'Plato, 1950–59', *Lustrum* 4 (1957): 5–308, and 5 (1960): 321–648.
10.29 Brisson, L. 'Platon, 1958–1975', *Lustrum* 20 (1977): 5–304.
10.30 Brisson, L. and Ioannidi, H. 'Platon, 1975–1980', *Lustrum* 25 (1983): 31–320 (corrections in vol. 26 (1984)).
10.31 Brisson, L. and Ioannidi, H. 'Platon, 1980–1985', *Lustrum* 30 (1988): 11–294 (corrections in vol. 31 (1989)).

Concordances

10.32 Ast. F. *Lexicon Platonicum*, 2 vols, Leipzig, Weidmann, 1835–6; repr. Bonn, Rudolf Habelt, 1956.
10.33 Brandwood, L. *A Word Index to Plato*, Leeds, W. S. Maney and Son, 1976.

Chronology

10.34 Brandwood, L. *The Chronology of Plato's Dialogues*, Cambridge, Cambridge University Press, 1990.
10.35 Ledger, G. R. *Re-Counting Plato*, Oxford, Clarendon Press, 1989.

General surveys of Plato

10.36 Crombie, I. M. *An Examination of Plato's Doctrines*, 2 vols, London, Routledge and Kegan Paul, 1962.
10.37 Friedländer, P. *Plato*, trans. H. Meyerhoff, 3 vols, London, Routledge and Kegan Paul, 1958–69. German original Berlin, de Gruyter, 1954–60.
10.38 Gosling, J. C. B. *Plato*, London and Boston, Routledge and Kegan Paul, 1973.
10.39 Grube, G. M. A. *Plato's Thought*, London, Methuen, 1935; repr. 1958; 2nd edn, London, Athlone Press, 1980, with new bibliography by D. J. Zeyl.
10.40 Guthrie, W. K. C. *A History of Greek Philosophy*, vols IV and V, Cambridge, Cambridge University Press, 1975 and 1978. See [2.13].
10.41 Kraut, R. (ed.) *The Cambridge Companion to Plato*, Cambridge, Cambridge University Press, 1992. Contains substantial bibliography.
10.42 Rowe, C. J. *Plato*, Brighton, Harvester, 1984.
10.43 Ryle, G. 'Plato', in P. Edwards (ed.) *The Encyclopedia of Philosophy*, New

York and London, Macmillan Inc. and The Free Press and Collier Macmillan, 1967, vol. VI, pp. 314–33.

Other Relevant Works

10.44 Adkins, A. W. H. *Merit and Responsibility*, Oxford, Clarendon Press, 1960.

10.45 Annas, J. *An Introduction to Plato's* Republic, Oxford, Clarendon Press, 1981.

10.46 Burkert [1.43].

10.47 Dodds [2.28].

10.48 Dover, K. J. *Greek Popular Morality in the Time of Plato and Aristotle*, Oxford, Blackwell, 1974.

10.49 —— *Greek Homosexuality*, London, Duckworth, 1978; 2nd edn, 1989.

10.50 Easterling, P. E. and Muir, J. V. (eds) *Greek Religion and Society*, Cambridge, Cambridge University Press, 1985.

10.51 Irwin, T. H. *Classical Thought*, Oxford, Oxford University Press, 1989.

10.52 Kahn [9.40].

10.53 Lloyd [2.37].

10.54 Mikalson, J. D. *Athenian Popular Religion*, Chapel Hill, NC, University of North Carolina Press, 1983.

10.55 Ober, J. *Mass and Elite in Democratic Athens*, Princeton, NJ, Princeton University Press, 1989.

10.56 Patterson, R. *Image and Reality in Plato's Metaphysics*, Indianapolis, Ind., Hackett, 1985.

10.57 Szlezák, T. A. *Platon und die Schriftlichkeit der Philosophie: Interpretationen zu den frühen und mittleren Dialogen*, Berlin, de Gruyter, 1985.

10.58 Vlastos G. (ed.) *Plato: A Collection of Critical Essays*, 2 vols., Garden City, NY, Doubleday, 1971.

10.59 —— [9.87].

10.60 —— [9.93].

10.61 —— [9.94].

10.62 Watson, G. *Plato's Unwritten Teaching*, Dublin, Talbot Press, 1973.

❧ BIBLIOGRAPHY ❧
FOR CHAPTER 10

Metaphysics

10.63 Alexander of Aphrodisias, *On Aristotle Metaphysics 1*, trans. W. Dooley, London, Duckworth, 1990.

10.64 Allen, R. E. (ed.) *Studies in Plato's Metaphysics*, London, Routledge and Kegan Paul, 1965.

10.65 Bolton, R. 'Plato's distinction between Being and Becoming', *Review of Metaphysics* 29 (1975): 66–95.

10.66 Bostock, D. 'Plato on "is not" (*Sophist* 254–9)', *Oxford Studies in Ancient Philosophy* 2 (1984): 89–119.

10.67 —— *Plato's* Phaedo, Oxford, Clarendon Press, 1986.

10.68 Brisson, L. *Le Même et l'Autre dans la structure ontologique du* Timée de Platon, Paris, Klincksieck, 1974.

10.69 Brown, L. 'Being in the *Sophist*: a syntactical enquiry', *Oxford Studies in Ancient Philosophy* 4 (1986): 49–70.

10.70 Cherniss, H. F. *The Riddle of the Early Academy*, Berkeley and Los Angeles, Calif., University of California Press, 1945.

10.71 —— *Aristotle's Criticism of Plato and the Academy*, Baltimore, Md., Johns Hopkins University Press, 1935; repr. New York, Octagon Books, 1964.

10.72 Fine, G. *On Ideas: Aristotle's Criticism of Plato's Theory of Forms*, Oxford, Clarendon Press, 1993.

10.73 Frede, M. *Prädikation und Existenzaussage*, Göttingen, Vandenhoeck and Rupprecht (*Hypomnemata* 18), 1967.

10.74 —— 'Being and Becoming in Plato', *Oxford Studies in Ancient Philosophy*, suppl. vol. (1988): 37–52.

10.75 Gaiser, K. *Platons Ungeschriebene Lehre*, Stuttgart, E. Klett, 1968.

10.76 Graeser, A. *Platons Ideenlehre*, Bern and Stuttgart, Paul Haupt, 1975.

10.77 Heinaman, R. 'Self-predication in the *Sophist*', *Phronesis* 26 (1981): 55–66.

10.78 —— 'Communion of Forms', *Proceedings of the Aristotelian Society* NS 83: (1982–3): 175–90.

10.79 —— 'Being in the *Sophist*', *Archiv für Geschichte der Philosophie* 65 (1983): 1–17.

10.80 Irwin, T. 'Plato's Heracliteanism', *Philosophical Quarterly* 27 (1977): 1–13.

10.81 Keyt, D. 'The fallacies in *Phaedo* 102a–107b', *Phronesis* 8 (1963): 167–72.

10.82 —— 'Plato's paradox that the immutable is unknowable', *Philosophical Quarterly* 19 (1969): 1–14.

10.83 Krämer, H. J. *Arete bei Platon und Aristoteles*, Heidelberg (Abh. d. Akad., Phil.-hist. Kl., 1959, 6), 1959.

10.84 Malcolm, J. 'Plato's analysis of τὸ ὄν and τὸ μὴ ὄν in the *Sophist*', *Phronesis* 12 (1967): 130–46.

10.85 —— *Plato on the Self-Predication of Forms*, Oxford, Clarendon Press, 1991.

10.86 Mohr, R. *The Platonic Cosmology*, Leiden, E. J. Brill, 1985.

10.87 Nehamas, A. 'Plato on the imperfection of the sensible world', *American Philosophical Quarterly* 12 (1975): 105–17.

10.88 —— 'Self-predication and Plato's Theory of Forms', *American Philosophical Quarterly* 16 (1979): 93–103.

10.89 Pelletier [4.50].

10.90 Penner, T. *The Ascent from Nominalism*, Dordrecht, D. Reidel, 1987.

10.91 Robin, L. *La Théorie platonicienne des Idées et des Nombres d'après Aristote*, Paris, Félix Alcan, 1908; repr. Hildesheim, Olms, 1963.

10.92 Ross, W. D. *Plato's Theory of Ideas*, Oxford, Clarendon Press, 1951.

10.93 Sayre, K. M. *Plato's Late Ontology*, Princeton, NJ, Princeton University Press, 1983.

10.94 Strange, S. 'The double explanation in the *Timaeus*', *Ancient Philosophy* 5 (1985): 25–40.

10.95 Striker, G. *Peras und Apeiron*, Göttingen, Vandenhoeck and Rupprecht (*Hypomnemata* 30), 1970.

10.96 Taylor, A. E. *A Commentary on Plato's* Timaeus, Oxford, Clarendon Press, 1928.

10.97 Vlastos [10.58], vol. 1.

10.98 —— [9.87].

Epistemology

10.99 Ackrill, J. L. 'In defence of Platonic division', in O. P. Wood and G. Pitcher (eds) *Ryle*, Garden City, NY, Doubleday, 1970, London, Macmillan, 1971, pp. 373–92.

10.100 Bostock, D. *Plato's* Theaetetus, Oxford, Clarendon Press, 1988.

10.101 Everson, S. (ed.) *Companions to Ancient Thought* 1: *Epistemology*, Cambridge, Cambridge University Press, 1990.

10.102 Gulley, N. *Plato's Theory of Knowledge*, London, Methuen, 1962.

10.103 McDowell, J. 'Falsehood and not-being in Plato's *Sophist*', in Schofield and Nussbaum [see 3.34], pp. 115–54.

10.104 Moravcsik, J. M. E. 'The anatomy of Plato's divisions', in Lee, Mourelatos and Rorty [see 3.43], pp. 324–48.

10.105 Robinson [9.74].

10.106 Sayre, K. M. *Plato's Analytic Method*, Chicago, University of Chicago Press, 1969.

10.107 Stenzel, J. *Plato's Method of Dialectic*, trans. D. J. Allan, Oxford, Clarendon Press, 1940.

10.108 Vlastos [9.93].

CHAPTER 11

Plato: ethics and politics

A. W. Price

<hr style="width:15%"/>

I

Plato followed his teacher Socrates into ethics by way of a question
that remained central in Greek thought: what is the relation between
the virtues or excellences (*aretai*) of character, and happiness
(*eudaimonia*)?[1] Both concepts were vague but inescapable, and inescap-
ably linked: happiness is the final end of action, and constitutes success
in life (cf. *Symposium* 205a2–3); so virtue, for which we commend
agents and actions, needed to be recommended by reference to happiness. The happiness that gives reason for action is primarily the agent's;
all Greek moralists hoped to grant the egocentricity without licensing
egoism. At least examples of moral virtues were generally agreed:
justice, piety, courage, temperance and the like. Happiness was more
elusive, and its paradigms more debatable. Herodotus has Croesus and
Solon disagree about whether the greatest happiness consists in enjoying
the greatest riches, or in living simply and dying well (I.30–2). The
demands of the virtues needed to be defined, and their status as virtues
justified by a conception of what it is for a human being to be happy.
Otherwise, there could be no telling whether it was pious of Euthyphro
to prosecute his own father for murder (*Euthyphro* 3e4–4e3), nor
whether Thrasymachus might be correct to claim injustice as a virtue
(*Republic* 1.348b8–e4). Plato's central treatment of these matters is in
the *Republic*, the masterpiece of his so-called 'middle' period. I shall
also pay attention to four works that consensus places as follows: the
Symposium, before the *Republic*; the *Phaedrus*, after the *Republic*;
the *Politicus* (or *Statesman*), after the *Phaedrus*; and finally (but
perfunctorily) the *Laws*, the long labour of his old age. An initial
question was properly abstract: what is the appropriate kind of way in
which to define a virtue? He poses this question in the *Republic* through
presenting variants on an approach that is not his own.

Perhaps moral virtue relates to action as follows: a virtue is a practice of acting, or a disposition to act, in a determinate way definable by a rule.[2] Thus, in the case of justice, Socrates – who, in tribute to the historical Socrates, appears as protagonist in most of the dialogues I shall be considering, but as a quasi-historical figure whose relations to the real Socrates, and to Plato himself, are intentionally undefined – asks Cephalus whether justice *is* telling the truth and returning what one has borrowed (331c1–3); justice as a quality of persons would then be a disposition to act so. Why, next, is justice, so understood, a virtue? This is initially contested by Thrasymachus. He offers no definition of justice, and it is uncertain whether he has a coherent conception of it. If we take him to be implicitly distinguishing legal from natural justice, the legally just is what accords with the laws and thus, in fact, serves the interests of the lawgivers (338e1–4). The naturally just extends more widely: it is what serves another's good – and so, within the perspective of the subject *qua* subject, broadly coincides with legal justice (343c3–4). Thrasymachus interprets interests as material, taking it for granted that it is in one's interest to pay less tax and take more in return (d6–e1). Now material goods are limited and transferable, so that their allocation is often a field of competition. Assessing justice and injustice instrumentally, as qualities of practices and dispositions that determine the distribution of losses and gains, he takes justice to be a tendency towards loss and injustice to be a tendency towards gain. If one's virtue must serve one's happiness, it follows that justice is not a virtue. Plato supplies in response a pastiche of Socratic ethics that at once puts Thrasymachus in his place, and marks his own point of departure.

Another member of the company, Glaucon, is not satisfied, and puts forward a different position, not as his own but as deserving a fairer run, to which Socrates' full reply will be no less than the remainder of the *Republic*. This is an imaginative variation upon Thrasymachus in which a class of rulers is replaced by a pair of agents, of which previously one was just and one unjust, whose power is ascribed on the model of the myth of Gyges to a magic ring bestowing invisibility. (We might introduce science fiction to the same effect.) Socrates had confronted Thrasymachus with contingencies: rulers can make mistakes, and command what is not in their interest (339c1–e8); even criminals need to co-operate, and must treat their accomplices justly (351c7–352d1). Gyges' ring now transports its possessors beyond human fallibility and individual impotence: both of them, just and unjust alike, will be unable now to refrain from breaking the rules of justice against adultery, murder and the like (II.360b3–c5). Ringless, we have reason to be just, but only as a second-best: able to do wrong but liable to be wronged, we make a social contract that both denies us the advantages and spares us the disadvantages of injustice (358e5–359a7).

What is the denotation of 'justice' within this aetiology? It is the class or characteristic of actions that are permitted by the law (358a3–4); its opposite is the legal category of forbidden wrongdoing or 'malum prohibitum'. However, there is a difficulty. We are told that it is naturally good to do wrong or act unjustly, and bad to be wronged or treated unjustly; the agreement is that that one should neither do nor suffer injustice (358e3–359a2). Thus it appears that justice is an artificial virtue (as Hume was to conceive it), while injustice is a natural and pre-contractual concept. This is coherent, if injustice was already recognized as a quality of actions, and the contract introduced justice as a practice. But how in a state of nature was justice to be understood, and its extension grasped as a unity? Perhaps Glaucon offers an implicit gloss that defines justice outside the law: to remain just is to abstain from what belongs to others (360b5–6). Socrates will not disagree: justice is neither having what belongs to others, nor being deprived of one's own (IV.433e6–11). Yet such remarks rather move within a moral circle than reduce the moral to the natural: it is equally apposite to say that what is my own is that of which it would be unjust to deprive me. We should rather suppose that it is retrospectively that the contract is motivated by fear of injustice *as such*: what existed before the contract was not resentment of injustice, but fear of a multitude of unwelcome actions some of which became unjust, or were deemed to be unjust, by being penalized – a selection presumably sensitive to practicalities. So the contract may be described after the event (as it is by Glaucon) as an escape from injustice, but it has to be explained as an escape from something else, or many other things; these will have included such cases of losing one's life or being deceived by one's partner as it was thought good to penalize, after the invention of law and morality, as murder or adultery.

This view is a positive transformation of Thrasymachus that takes laws not to be imposed by rulers on subjects, but to be adopted by free contractors. The structure of attack or apology remains the same: it is indirect and instrumental. Glaucon is recommending justice as the practice of acting in accordance with laws that human agents need to respect in order to reduce the risk of their being treated in ways to which they are by nature averse. For all its pretensions, morality is revealed as an under-servant of felicity.

Plato has two grounds for rejecting this approach. First, it does not work: the content of a virtue cannot be explicated by concrete rules of conduct. This is first intimated within the *Republic* when Socrates objects to Cephalus that it is wrong to identify being just with telling the truth and returning what one has borrowed, for these acts are not always just (as when a borrower is asked to return some weapons by a lender who has gone mad, I.331c1–d3). A more resilient participant than Cephalus might suppose that one has only to try again, but the objection falls within a pattern to which Socrates later alludes when he describes how the young can be corrupted by counter-examples to attempts to define the just or the fine by appeal to general laws or maxims (VII.538c6–e4). This pattern of objection was already familiar from early Platonic dialogues (cf. [11.5], 43–6): on the same ground, temperance cannot be identified with a quiet or gentle manner (*Charmides* 159b1–160d3), nor with shame (160e3–161b2), nor courage with endurance (*Laches* 192b9–d9). Unlike quietness, shame and endurance, a virtue is always good (*Charmides* 161a6–b2). We need to add that the endurance is wise, but how is wisdom to be defined (*Laches* 192d10–193a2)? One way out is by a special kind of vagueness: perhaps justice is giving all men their due (*Republic* I.331e1–4), and temperance is doing one's own (*Charmides* 161b3–6). But such paraphrases either invite the same objection, or move around the moral circle mentioned above: if giving all men their due does not reduce to returning what one has borrowed and the like, it may more vaguely be equated with giving them what is appropriate to them (*Republic* I.331e8–332c3), that is, giving them what they justly deserve. Glaucon's account fares better, but not well. That the just is that which the law prescribes or permits (II.359a3–4) is only plausible if the law uses terms (like 'murder' and 'adultery') whose descriptive connotations are debatable. Legislators properly find it difficult to define such terms precisely in advance, and are wiser to be content with the vagueness that invites casuistical debate about their application.

Secondly, Glaucon's framework provides virtue with the wrong kind of justification. To make clear what he would prefer, he offers Socrates an exhaustive trichotomy of goods: (1) goods that we welcome for their own sake and not for their consequences, such as enjoyment, and harmless pleasures that only bring enjoyment; (2) goods that we welcome both for their own sake and for their consequences, such as understanding, sight and health; (3) goods that we welcome only for their consequences, such as exercise, being healed, and doctoring or other money-making (357b4–d2). Socrates replies that he would place justice in class (2), which is the 'finest' category (358a1–3). We should view this not as a moralist's salesmanship, but in relation to a perennial conception: 'It is a requirement on moral action... that the action should not be merely instrumentally related to the intention: the end should be realized not merely through the action but in the action' ([11.21], 43).

Glaucon initially speaks of justice as a practice (358a5–6), but then as a state of soul (cf. n. 2): he wishes to hear what justice and injustice are, and what power (*dunamis*) each possesses in and of itself when it is present in the soul (b4–6, cf. 366e5–6). It becomes explicit that he is shifting his focus from its external to its internal operations when he asks how it acts upon its possessor (367b4, e3). The shift is motivated by his concern whether being just is a good thing to be. It suits Plato more particularly, both anticipating what is to come, and recalling the most pregnant passage of Book I: injustice occurring within an individual does not lose its power (the same word *dunamis*), but here too produces faction and enmity (I.351e6–352a3). Irrespective of whether the focus be internal or external, this talk of how a state acts upon a thing 'in and of itself' can seem a contradiction in terms, asking about consequences even as it excludes consequences, and has provoked much discussion.[3]

One suggestion has been that Glaucon wants to set aside not natural but artificial consequences, excluding rewards and penalties that are attached to the appearance (cf. II.367d4) but not psychological effects that attach to the reality; but this fails to fit, for strength and health are natural effects of taking exercise and receiving treatment, which are placed within category (3). We must rather suppose that injustice and enmity, justice and friendship, stand in an internal and necessary relation that helps to constitute what justice and injustice really *are* (in a manner in which strength does not define what it is to wrestle, nor health what it is to diet). Virtues and vices have real natures and not just verbal definitions; a proper understanding will reveal what it is for them to take effect within a soul. It may seem inconsistent of Glaucon to ask Socrates to praise justice in and of itself (358d1–2), to offer to praise injustice in the manner in which he wishes to hear the dispraise of injustice and the praise of justice (d3–6), and then to speak at length (within the fantasy of Gyges' ring) about the consequences of injustice, e.g. winning the opposite reputation, presumably through deception or other ploys that pile injustice on injustice (361a7–b3). However, he must mean not that it is appropriate to praise justice and injustice in the same way, but that he wishes them both to be praised appropriately: he will play at recommending injustice instrumentally as emancipation from a negative constraint, while Socrates must succeed in recommending justice intrinsically as a positive ideal. The unjust refuse to let justice stand between themselves and what they want; the just want to be just.

Glaucon intensifies the contrast: to exclude any ulterior motives, he proposes that they compare the intrinsic value of justice with the maximal instrumental benefits of injustice, imagining that the unjust agent receives all the rewards merited by justice, and the just agent all the penalties merited by injustice (360e1–362c8). In supposing that it is better to be just but impaled than unjust and respected, he implicitly makes a further requirement of the motivations of just agents: they must not only value justice for its own sake, but take its value to eclipse (or 'trump') all non-moral values. Otherwise the demands of justice would be bound to be outweighed on occasion, however rarely, by non-moral considerations. The attitude is Socratic (cf. [11.20], 209–11), but looks more heroic than rational unless injustice is its own worst punishment. In the *Crito*, an early and Socratic dialogue, Socrates compared a soul spoiled by acting unjustly to a body spoiled by living unhealthily (47d7–e7), but without any means to make out that injustice is more than analogous to ill health. When he equated living well with living 'finely and justly' (48b8–10), it was not clear whether that rested on good reasons, or on a refusal to make distinctions. Perhaps on both: if, as Socrates supposed, all desires are rational (though some may be erroneous), they can only aim at the right and good; there are no desires that, arising non-rationally, would be in fact be satisfied by what is bad and wrong; hence immorality is wholly a failure to achieve what one really wants (cf. *Gorgias* 467a8–468e5). The *Republic* will set out a different picture of the soul, which holds that reason is only one source of desire. This allows the soul a complexity like that of the body. When the *Gorgias*, a dialogue of transition which pioneers an anatomy of the soul, actually calls injustice a 'sickness' of the soul (480b1), the term is taking on an extended sense that is more than metaphorical. Plato must now provide more complex and less Socratic answers to the following questions: in what way are justice and injustice fundamentally inner states with decisive implications for the happiness of the individual? What is their relation to other virtues and vices that narrows our options to two: being virtuous and happy, or vicious and unhappy? And how do they connect with the moral action that we demand of one another?

II

Plato's line of answer proposes a paradox exactly tailored to the measure of the problem. On Glaucon's construction, justice is a social virtue that benefits society; this fits the view, later ascribed by Socrates not just to Thrasymachus but to unnamed poets and prose-writers, that it is the other person's good and one's own loss (*Republic* III.392a13–b4). Plato will reconceive it as social and personal at the same time: in its fundamental form, its field and profit are indeed within a society, but that society is oneself. Politics and psychology are mirrors of each other, so that the commonplace that justice is good for a society can be translated into a claim that it is good for the agent.

'My name is Legion: for we are many' (Mark 5: 9); Plato would have found these the words not of a madman, but of the best philosopher. Each of us contains a plurality of parts that are indeed not people, but may be pictured as interrelating rather as people do. What distinguishes the parts is the potentiality of conflict: this is revealed when we find someone not merely (as H. W. B. Joseph put it) 'similarly affected towards different objects', but 'contrarily affected towards the same' ([11.7], 53). Just as one man cannot simultaneously push and pull the same thing with a single part of his body (IV.439b8–11), so he cannot simultaneously accept and reject the same thing with a single part of his soul. Someone who thirsts for a drink, and yet refuses to drink, displays that his soul is multiple, containing contrasting sources of desire. If we specify that the thirst arises (like hunger) from physical depletion, but the refusal from rational calculation, we can distinguish his appetite from his reason (c2–e3). Further, we must separate his spirit from both: a man may be angry with his appetites, or his reason may condemn his anger (439e3–441c2). And this may only be a beginning, to be complicated by further investigation (435c9–d8, 443d7, cf. VI.504b1–c4). Such soul-parts are not distinct souls: they share a single consciousness, and lack their own sense perceptions. And yet they are not mere faculties either; indeed, they share certain faculties, such as those of believing and desiring. Rather, as clusters of beliefs and desires arising from different sources, and acting together or apart on bodily organs, they are agencies, and have some of the freedom that we ordinarily ascribe only to persons. Hence to talk of them in interpersonal terms can be apt, and only slightly metaphorical. When Socrates likens each soul to a trio of animals, a Cerberus, a lion and a man (IX.588c7–e1), he is graphically conveying how alien to one another are the repertories of the different parts. When he remarks that these can give commands (IV.439c6–7) or be obedient (441e6), and raise faction (442d1, 444b1) or be meddlesome (443d2, 444b2), he is using public imagery to capture private reality. Among the qualities of persons that are also literal qualities of parts, in Plato's view, are virtues and vices of character.

The easiest illustration of this is also its central application. Socrates feels and Plato plots a way to a definition of justice through a series of commonplaces. A principle of the specialization of labour is recommended as a sensible policy (II.370a7–b6, 374a3–e2, III.397d10–e9) before it returns as the essence of justice (IV.433a1–434d1). It is plausible to suppose that it must be more efficient if all agents concentrate on that single skill for which their nature and experience best suit them. It is truistic to say that it is unjust to take what belongs to others or lose what belongs to oneself (433e6–11).[4] Taken together, the two propositions suggest a less elementary thought about justice: if one agent does the job within the city that another agent could do better, the one is taking what is another's and the other is losing what is his own. The reasoning is doubly equivocal. It shifts from what *is* mine (my job or property) to what *ought to be* mine (the job or property of which I can make most). And it trades on the ambiguity of the notion of what I can do best between what I can do better than *anything* else, and what I can do better than *anyone* else. Unless talents are providentially distributed, these will not always coincide, so that what is best for me (which is doing the former), and what is best for my city (which is generally doing the latter), may come apart (cf. [11.5], 333 n. 34, 343 n. 28). The conclusion is a typically bold persuasive definition: playing an improper role within a city is theft. Plato's political application is well-known: there are to be three classes of citizen, guardians who theorize and govern, auxiliaries who police and defend, and artisans who marry and produce.

However, all this is provisional until we have seen whether the same characterization applies not only to each individual within the city, but within each individual (434d1–5). Of course, it is then claimed that it does (441d5–442b4), but the claim is not made carelessly. If there is no natural guarantee that reason will be better at resisting thirst than thirst at impelling drinking (cf. 439b3–5), what shows that it is proper for thirst to obey reason, and not for reason to capitulate to thirst? The answer lies in a fuller description of their aims and aptitudes. The social analogy, in which an agent's proper job is best both for the city and for himself, suggests that the proper function of a soul-part will at once benefit soul and part. Happily, these indeed go together: it is reason's task to govern the entire soul by knowledge of what is beneficial both to each part of the soul and to the community of its parts (441e4–442c8). It alone is capable of reflection and calculation (439d5), and so can take a wide and long view of the interests of the soul as a whole. An unruly appetite defeats its own ends also. What stimulates it is the prospect not merely of eating or drinking, but of doing so pleasurably (436a11); it identifies success not with indulgence itself, but with felt satisfaction. Hence it is not the case that the better it activates action, the better off it will be. A thirst that succumbs uncontrollably to any drink is not a thirst that makes the best of its opportunities: it will accept not only the water with which the dying Sidney scrupled to dispel his own discomfort, but also the gin that produces dehydration. The apprehension and application of practical truth can alone offer deliverance from 'fulfilment's desolate attic' (Larkin, 'Deceptions'). Given that reason is a wise altruist, and appetite a foolish egoist, it is true for *both* of them that it is just and best that reason rule and appetite obey. Thus, as demanded, justice admits the same account within city and soul.

What of the other virtues? The *Republic* originates the once famous doctrine of the four cardinal virtues in distinguishing three others that are also realized within both city and citizen. Within the soul, wisdom is primarily the quality of a reason that has firmly grasped theoretical and practical truth, courage of a spirit that holds fast to reason's guidance in the face of fear, and temperance of all the parts united in friendship and harmony (442b9–d1). A just soul must have these three virtues if it has the tripartite structure that Socrates describes. Even a quartet of virtues raises an old question. In earlier dialogues of Plato, such as the *Protagoras*, Socrates taught the unity of the virtues: to have one virtue is to have all virtues. That doctrine simplifies the defence of virtue, which can then be single; but can it survive the partition of the soul? The *Republic* is inexplicit, and interpreters disagree (cf. [11.5], 329–30, n. 26, [11.6], ch. 14). One ground for supposing that it cannot is the new possibility of *akrasia*. The *Protagoras* argued that to be wise is to be temperate, so that one cannot know that one ought to be resisting a pleasure to which one succumbs (352a8–357e8); but now appetite is permitted to defy reason, may one not have the wisdom to know that one should not drink even though one lacks the temperance or self-control to abstain? Such could have been true of the necrophilic Leontius when he rebuked his eyes for feasting on corpses even as he rushed forward for a closer gaze (*Republic* IV.439e7–440a3). This view may be right, but it is not required. If we may distinguish a wise reason from a wise person, we may say that a person as a whole only possesses wisdom – or, equivalently, wisdom only possesses a person as a whole – if his reason exercises effective rule (cf. 442c5–8; *Laws* III.689a1–c1). Thus we may suppose that a wise person must also be brave and temperate.

Among the questions that this leaves open is whether the brave and temperate must also be wise. If they must, then the virtues may indeed entail each other, but with the implication that only fully trained guardians can have any of them. Yet it cannot be Plato's intention that his Utopia should leave the great majority of its inhabitants in a vicious and therefore unhappy state. He needs to give wisdom a reach beyond the reason of the wise. He achieves this by anticipating a distinction that Aristotle was to make between two modes of 'possessing' reason, one displayed in reasoning, the other in listening to reasoning (*Nicomachean Ethics* I.7.1098a3–5). It is best to possess one's own understanding, and one can then safely enjoy freedom; otherwise, if one has the luck to live within Plato's Utopia, one may find the same governance through the subordination of one's reason, either for a time or for a lifetime, to the understanding of another (*Republic* IX.590c8–591a3). How is this governance to be effective when spirit or appetite is dominant? It is the art of the guardians to give the auxiliaries such a role that they can indulge their spiritedness, and the artisans such a role that they can indulge their appetitiveness, without acting unwisely or unreasonably. Auxiliaries are only contingently brave, and artisans only contingently temperate, in that they need guardians to contrive for them recurrent situations in which they can simultaneously serve spirit or appetite and observe reason. Within their souls, reason is not corrupt, for it would not command whatever spirit or appetite demanded. Yet it is weak, both in that it is directed by another's, and in that it can lead spirit or appetite only in a direction in which this is willing to go. Their courage or temperance is thus doubly parasitic: it depends upon a judgement which echoes another's wisdom, and which only prevails because that wisdom makes sure that it meets no resistance. Expulsion from Plato's paradise would be the fall of these men: in the terms of the rake's progress that he sketches in Books VIII and IX, auxiliaries would become timarchic men corrupted by honour, and artisans oligarchic, democratic or tyrannical men corrupted by pleasure. It is by moral luck that they attain to virtue of a kind. They are not fully brave or temperate but wholly unwise; rather, they are brave or temperate in a way through a wisdom that they can accept but not achieve. The unity of the virtues proper is reflected in a unity of popular virtue.

Thus the virtue of individuals is a unitary condition of their psychic parts. How is it needed to make them happy? The readiest answer to this question focuses upon temperance, which is defined within the soul as follows: 'We call a person temperate by reason of the friendship and harmony of these parts, that is, when the ruler and its two subjects agree that reason ought to rule, and do not raise raise faction against it' (IV.442c10–d1). Caring for all the parts alike, reason makes them 'friends' (IX.589b4–5); parts, like people, will be 'alike and friends' if they share the same governance (590d5–6). Socrates remarks again that vice is a sickness of the soul (IV.444e1), and can now explain. Eryximachus was giving fanciful expression to a Greek commonplace when he defined it as the task of medicine to produce 'love and concord' between the opposites (hot and cold, wet and dry, and so forth) that are the elements of the body (*Symposium* 186d6–e3). Mental health is the peace of mind that comes of parts of the soul that are friends and not factions. Without temperance, a man is prey to conflicting desires, perhaps subdued but not persuaded, which make him 'a kind of double individual' (*Republic* VIII.554d9–e1). There is a good and bad slavery: while reason is a benevolent master who educates desire, the appetites are a tyrannical one who frustrates it (IX.577d1–12). Reason can hope to rule with consent because of its altruism and intelligence. It was the soul's original nature (X.611d7–e3), and the origin of the mortal soul (*Timaeus* 42e7–8); so its attitude is paternalist, like that of a farmer tending his crops (*Republic* IX.589b2–3). In indulging necessary appetites (those we cannot divert, or whose satisfaction benefits us, VIII.558d9–e2), it keeps appetite content. Being a master of language, it can 'tame by *logos*', persuading and not compelling (554d2). As reason can grasp appetite's concept of the pleasant, while appetite cannot make out reason's concept of the good, reason can take appetite by the hand, whereas a recalcitrant appetite could only turn its back on reason.

So translated from the outer to the inner world, from society to soul, justice becomes not a demand but an overriding need. The story of Gyges' ring was a fable of external accidents; in its internal essence, there is no such thing as injustice with impunity. As Socrates will calculate with half-comical precision, the tyrant is 729 times unhappier than the philosopher-king (IX.587d12–e4).

III

Socrates elaborates his defence of justice with some felicity. And yet it raises two related questions:

(1) Is it coherent? Socrates is using two models to relate justice in society and soul (cf. [11.5], 331 n. 29). The first is of group-member dependency. Any quality of a city derives from the citizens who possess it (*Republic* IV.435e1–6) and from their displaying it within the city; thus guardians make it wise in exercising their wisdom on behalf of the city as a whole (428c11–d6), while auxiliaries make it brave in exercising their courage on its behalf (429b1–3). The other model is of macrocosm–microcosm: justice is identical in city and in citizen (II.368e2–369a3, IV.434d3–5). According to the first model the justice of a citizen is external, but according to the second it is internal: it is said explicitly that the justice of an individual consists in his doing his own business not externally, but within his soul and in respect of its parts (443c9–e2). So a just city is one whose citizens are just in exercising justice *within it*; yet just citizens are those who are just in exercising justice *within themselves*. Which seems not to cohere.

(2) Is it to the point (cf. [11.16])? When Thrasymachus and Glaucon questioned the value of justice, their starting-points were concrete and external: justice is not committing murder, or adultery. They were asking a general question about conduct of certain kinds. Socrates had already indicated a doubt as to whether justice can be defined in such terms, but he needs to connect his definition to their initial conceptions. Otherwise, he risks having quietly changed the subject from justice commonly conceived as respect for others to justice idiosyncratically reconceived as mental health. The analogy between soul and city may have confirmed that it is good for a city to be just, just as it is good

for a soul to be at peace. But the question was not that, but whether it benefits each citizen to be just *towards others*.

Both difficulties will be resolved if internal and external justice are related so closely that operating well within oneself is an exercise of the same disposition as acting justly towards others. Then internal justice will be an aspect of the same disposition or practice as external justice; to attempt to evaluate them separately would be false and artificial. This Socrates tries to make out. He confirms his own definition by applying a 'vulgar' test: the internally just man will be the last person to commit externally unjust acts such as theft and adultery (442d10–443b3). The connection also runs the other way: he evidently assumes that it will not alter the extension of the terms 'just' and 'unjust' if one calls that action just which 'preserves and helps to produce' internal justice, and that action unjust which tends to dissolve it (443e5–444a1). (The same reciprocity should apply within popular virtue, once this has been distinguished: the outer will manifest and maintain the inner, always within the contingency of an external governance that makes the popular virtues sufficient in context for good acts.) It suits Socrates to focus on unjust actions that overindulge appetite, and so 'feast' and 'strengthen' it (IX.588e5–6); and it extends the range of these actions that appetite takes on a love of money, initially as a means to its more basic satisfactions (580e5–581a1). Plato always views it with anxiety: in an earlier and memorable simile, unrestrained appetites are as insatiable as a leaking jar (*Gorgias* 493b1–3). Indulging appetite risks one's health, and it is only safe to satisfy necessary appetites. Every unjust action, strengthening tendencies that tend to take one over, is unsafe, and a proper object of concern to the agent who takes thought about the condition of his soul. If the action is *very* unjust, the concern can only be acute.[5]

Plato is seeking reasons for being just that are rooted in human nature, that is, in human psychology. A Martian's reasons for being moral would have to be very different if it were capable of an unconflicted contrariness of which we, in Plato's view, are not. The success of his ethics is here a function of his psychology. It depends upon taking spirit and appetite to be potentially rampant, and locating all criminal tendencies within them. (A pertinent objection is that the psychopath, for instance, may suffer not from passion but from boredom.)[6] Helpful, in a way, is that the parts are protean: spirit is given not only to anger but to pride (*Republic* VIII.553d4–6); appetite can even motivate a dilettantish taste for philosophy (561c6–d2). When Belloc's Mitilda told 'such dreadful lies' she may have been indulging spirit or appetite. Yet this variability is more convenient for saving the theory than for guiding our practice. In the absence of any determinate definition of the inclinations of the lower parts, and hence of any precise demarcation between the acts that discipline and the acts that indulge them, it becomes imperative to supplement a negative description of the costs of immorality by a positive account of the motivations natural to reason. It is also part of our nature, in Plato's view, that we possess a reason that is not just the slave of the passions (as Hume characterized it), but a pursuer of its own projects. We need to hear more about the appeal of acting justly in familiar ways, and how it is strong enough to captivate any soul in a state of healthy receptivity. Widening our focus around justice, we must ask what the charms are of treating others well that are irresistible to the intelligent soul.

IV

Platonism is marked by two metaphysical dualisms, of unchanging Forms and mutable participants, and of soul and body. The second dualism discourages a possible implication of the first: Platonists do not view the world of change with indifference, for it is another country within which souls operate, orienting themselves and others in colonial lives that realize the Forms under other skies.

In the *Phaedo*, we find Socrates teaching the way of death, urging his pupils to escape the cycle of reincarnation in order, as discarnate souls, to philosophize uninterruptedly. In the *Symposium*, composed at about the same time, he takes a more positive view of incarnate life. Within a body, even the life of the mind is an exercise in transience, but after a manner that creates a kind of permanence. 'Ways, habits, opinions, desires, pleasures, pains, fears' and even 'knowings' do not remain the same, but come and go in a cycle of loss and repair, each instance departing and being replaced by another, so that it appears to remain the same (207e2–208b2). This pattern within a life becomes the model for a pattern between lives that traverses not only the passage of time but the terminus of death. Poets, lawgivers and lovers so lead their mental lives as to pass on their best features to others. Thus, within a pederastic relationship, the man transmits his virtues to the boy, so that, as through physical children, but more nobly and more efficaciously, his life is reduplicated in a way that delivers it from his own death (209b5–c7). If the boy becomes a lover in turn, there is the chance of a chain of transmission that may achieve for the sequence of lovers a kind of immortality. The *Symposium* contains no developed psychology, but this prospect gains in point from the tripartition of the *Republic*. Tripartition comes with incarnation, and so, to the extent that human virtues are ways of making the best of a tripartite state, they are creatures of incarnate life. Philosophic lovers or lawgivers (poets are now distrusted) who value being *humanly* virtuous have reason to work not only for their own escape from reincarnation, but also for the continuation within other lives of the human virtues that they hope themselves to transcend.

Vicarious immortality is not explicitly adduced in the *Republic*, perhaps for the reason, as we shall see in Section VII, that there Socrates has tactical reason (despite Glaucon, but because of Thrasymachus) to play down the appeal of ruling. Yet he illustrates how it could be maximized in describing lawgivers who lay down the general plan of a Utopia where everything of importance is to be planned (e.g. V.458d9–e1), and there is no area of personal liberty within which their influence is not to intrude. It is a further goal of theirs that every life should connect with every other by a maximal mutual identification: 'In this city more than any other, when any individual fares well or badly, they would all speak in unison the word we mentioned just now, namely that *mine* is doing well, or that *mine* is faring badly' (463e3–5). Now 'this way of thinking and speaking' (464a1) can neither achieve anything in itself, nor have any magic to work in a vacuum: the language of pseudo-identity is not an Indian rope-trick. What is its substance?

Some have supposed that Plato takes an organic view of the state (*pro*, [11.13], 79–81; *contra*, [11.17]), a suggestion that may be both clarified and supported by a simile in which he compares the fully unified city to the body that feels pain as a whole when only a finger is wounded (462c10–d7). Just as it is the animal who feels pain, and not the finger, so it might be the city as a whole that feels at one with itself. In the face of the fact that a city is not a person, such a notion could only be mystical. Plato inclines rather to translate out talk about a city in terms of its citizens (as when he derives any quality of a city from its citizens, IV.435e1–6). In one respect, an organic view threatens to be at once opaque and sinister: it might imply that the happiness of persons can be sacrificed to the impersonal good of the state. Plato remains far from conceiving that even when he gets closest to it. In reply to a complaint by Adeimantus that he is denying his guardians the *dolce vita* that a ruling class expects, Socrates reminds him that their target was the happiness not of one class especially, but of the whole city; and he gives the simile of a statue whose eyes should be painted the colour that best suits the statue (420b5–d5). However, the point of the simile is that, just as we want eyes that look like eyes, so we want guardians who remain guardians, that is, who care for their fellow citizens. The contrast is between factional and general happiness, and not between the good of the citizens and the good of the city. When Socrates speaks of a myth that will make the citizens 'care more for the city and for each other' (III.415d3–4), the 'and' is exegetical and not conjunctive. His desire that the city remain 'one' (IV.423b9–10) expresses not a mystical or temperamental·love of unity, but a fear that rich and poor may form two cities hostile to one another (422e9–423a1). There is nothing sinister, either, in the claim that it is guardians who make the city count as wise, although they are by far the smallest class (428c11–e9), any more than when a company counts as innovative in virtue of the ingenuity of its design department. Even though he mocks a democratic and undiscriminating attitude to pleasures (VIII.561b7–c4), and argues that the truest pleasures are those of philosophy (IX.583b2–587b10), Plato never permits happiness to be the privilege of a few. Perhaps because he does not suppose that a choice has to be made (at least within his Utopia), he rather envisages that *all* citizens will achieve the happiness natural to them.

How then, if not within an organic state, is the term 'mine' to be used in unison? Since it is the guardians who guide the rest, it is their mentality that most needs moulding.[7] To preclude private interests that might conflict with public obligations, Socrates advocates the abolition, among guardians and auxiliaries, of marriage, family life and private property, and their replacement by eugenic couplings and common messes. Ignorance of one's parents risks the errors of an Oedipus, and it is ostensibly to prevent these that he proposes that those born as a result of some procreative festival will call whoever bred then 'mother' or 'father' (V.461d2–5). But when he adds a similar extension of 'sister' and 'brother' even though he is oddly unconcerned about coeval incest (d7–e3), it becomes clear that he sees a more positive value in the group family. Viewing each other as relations, the guardians will treat one another accordingly (463c3–d8). Thus they will live in perfect peace; and, if *they* don't quarrel, there will be no danger of rebellion or faction within the rest of the city (465b5–10). Plato's hope turns out to be that, so long as the guardians are perfectly united as an extended family, even the artisans will empathize with them and with one another. We may suspect that, even from his viewpoint, the latter would be subject to some tension of attitude: if they are spared the communism, this is plausibly because it would undermine the appetitive motivation which they represent, and which suits their productive role; and yet it is presumably because they possess a reason, if a debile and dependent one, that they are capable of an altruism within the city of which appetite is incapable within the soul. However, what counts as a 'necessary' appetite, deserving of satisfaction, must vary with natural disposition and civic role; a rational altruism can permit artisans a livelier appetitiveness than befits others. If so, they too may achieve Plato's personal and civic ideal of unity in becoming one man instead of many (IV.443e1), and yet identifying with everyone else.

Such is Plato's political ideal. His personal ideas shines forth in the defence of inspired madness that constitutes Socrates' second speech in the *Phaedrus*, though it is there enveloped in an aptly mythic glow that makes interpretation hazardous. Not only recollection of the Forms, but erotic companionship, are presented as recoveries of an earlier and happier state. Souls in heaven are pictured as following in the trains of the Olympian gods, and so forming more selective bonds of congeniality than are proper to civic relations. After the catastrophe of incarnation, followers of Zeus will look for someone to love who is by nature a philosopher and a leader, while followers of Hera will look for someone who is naturally regal, and so on (252e1–253b4). This fits well with the *Republic*'s acceptance of varied natural talents, but extends the varieties of personality. It does not only value the companionship of philosophers, but allows that spirited lovers, though less intellectual and less chaste, may eventually, in the ornithic imagery, regrow their plumage together and fly back to heaven (256b7–e2). (We may suppose that it is in order to relate even unphilosophical love to recollection that Socrates here exceptionally envisages tripartition even before incarnation.) Thus Plato seems willing to grant personal attachments a general power to facilitate and enhance whatever activities are their sphere. However, he finds them particularly apt to philosophy. One reason is the interpersonal nature of philosophizing. Most explicit here is the *Seventh Letter*: 'Only after long partnership in a common life devoted to this very thing does truth flash upon the soul, like a flame kindled by a leaping spark' (341c6–d1). Dialectic is essentially a kind of dialogue, a truth of which he keeps us in mind by the very genre of his writings. It is oral discussion, and not written communication, that can alone truly achieve the mental immortality described in the *Symposium*: living words sown in one soul contain a seed that can propagate them in others down an unending sequence (*Phaedrus* 276e4–277a4). The sphere of philosophy is friendship.

V

Plato calls his famous demand that philosophers be rulers and rulers philosophers 'the greatest wave' (*Republic* V.473c6–7). We must not forget that he was writing under a democracy, and one whose values, even within his parody (VIII.557a9–558c7), we too must find congenial. And yet he makes his conception of a class of guardians selected and trained for devotion to the city still more remarkable in its concrete elaboration.

Socrates assumes that aptitude for guardianship is genetically determined. He notoriously embodies this assumption in a 'noble fiction' that is to be instilled into all citizens (III.414b9–c2): everyone contains a trace of gold, silver, or iron and copper that marks him as a natural guardian, auxiliary, or artisan (415a4–7). Children commonly resemble their parents, but exceptions are to be demoted or promoted (a7–b3, cf. IV.423c6–d2). How and when the traces are to be detected is largely unspecified. Artisans will presumably receive some physical and mental training, in addition to the 'noble fiction', to prepare them for temperance; but it is not said what, nor whether it precedes or follows their assignment to that class. (In recent English educational terms, one might think of them as failing the eleven-plus.) Guardians and auxiliaries only divide in middle age when the former advance from mathematics and administration to philosophy and government. Relegation may occur at any time as occasion justifies: cowards in battle become artisans (V.468a5–7). Late promotion is more problematic, as it may be too late to catch up on education; parallel to demotion here is not promotion (as at III.415b2–3, IV.423d1–2), but public honour and private gratification (V.468b2–c4). Yet Plato's human stratification is a meritocracy, and not a caste-system.

In place of marriages, Socrates proposes the institution of eugenic matings (458d9–e4) arranged ostensibly by lot but actually with an eye to personal merit and stability of population (459d8–460b5).[8] This had better have the effect of creating better guardians *and* auxiliaries, and not a shortage of natural auxiliaries; it fits that courage, as well as intelligence, is a ground of selection (460b1–5, 468c5–8). He permits some freedom of sexual activity to those past the proper ages for breeding (461b9–c7), presumably because even they need some sexual satisfaction; but, likening 'erotic necessity' to geometric (458d5–7), he depersonalizes it. The only erotic attitudes that he allows to be discriminating in their objects depend upon culture (cf. III.403a7–c2), and are satisfied by kissing (V.468b12–c4). It may be wondered (as in [11.11], 159) whether their very selectivity must not make them out of place within Plato's all-embracing community.

In one respect Plato is millenia in advance of his time. He accepts that his principle of specialization applies also to women, but rejects an application that would justify the status quo.[9] Different natures should indeed have different functions within the city, but to infer that men and women should play different roles would be like permitting bald men to be cobblers but not men with hair, or vice versa; for most purposes it is irrelevant that the female bears and the male begets (453e2–454e4). Recent writers, tired of debating whether Plato avoids fascism, debate tirelessly whether he achieves feminism. Julia Annas has two complaints that rest, I think, rather upon prejudice than upon perception. First, she declares that Plato 'sees women merely as a huge untapped pool of resources', and that his 'only' objection to the subjection of women is that 'under ideal conditions it constitutes an irrational waste of resources' ([11.1], 183). She implies that, although concerned about 'production of the common good' ([11.1], 181), Plato views half the population exclusively as providers and not receivers, as means and not as ends. This should not easily be believed. Somewhat artificially, Socrates distinguishes the questions whether his proposals are feasible, and whether they are desirable (456c4–10, 457a3–4). His defence of their feasibility, sketched above, is explicitly about what is natural (b12–c2), and implicitly about what is just (though it uses his definition of justice and not the term 'just'). His defence of their desirability is simply that mental and physical education will produce the best possible men and women, which is the greatest good for a city (456e6–457a2). He says no more, doubtless because he simply has in mind that the best city is that whose citizens are best (cf. IV.435e1–6), a valuation that is intrinsic and not instrumental. Secondly, Annas complains that Plato retains a masculine stereotype of excellence in spending most of Book V 'claiming, irrelevantly and grotesquely, that women can engage in fighting and other "macho" pursuits nearly as well as men' ([11.1], 185).[10] It is true that Socrates pays special attention to women's new role as soldiers and athletes (V.452a7–e3); but this is because he feels that he has to confront the objection that, since physical exercise was taken naked, that would be indecent and ridiculous (cf. 457a6–b3). Otherwise, he gives no more emphasis to physical than to intellectual training (456b8–10, 456e9–457a1), and actually makes less mention of 'macho' pursuits such as athletics and soldiering (456a1–2, 457a6–7) than of medicine (454d2–6, 455e6), culture (e7), philosophy (456a4), and guardianship (a7–8, 457a8). Even when reflecting upon women, Plato is no philistine.

There are, however, two opposite regrets to qualify our admiration of his prescience. On the one hand, he distances himself too quickly from his own experience in denying women any distinctive qualities. The training and education of the guardians involve the reconciling of contrasted tendencies within the soul, the toughness of spirit and the tenderness of reason (III.410c8–e9), and facility and stability within reason itself (VI.503b7–d12). If he had presented this as a wedding of the masculine and the feminine (cf. *Laws* VII.802e8–11), he could have welcomed women more positively, not as monopolizers, but as icons, of tenderness and stability. On the other hand, he remains too slackly within the limits of his own experience when he has Glaucon remark that, broadly speaking, women are in everything 'far outdone' by men, and Socrates agree: 'In all occupations the woman is weaker than the man' (V.455d2–e2). Admittedly, the force of this is unclear, and has to be consistent with the reservation 'Many women are better than many men at many things' (d3–4, where the repetition of 'many' increases the rhetorical emphasis even as it reduces the logical content). It might imply a scarcity of female guardians, which would be inconvenient. It might just mean that men possess more energy and stamina in exercising the same abilities, which is one way of making sense of the summing-up: 'So man and woman have the same nature as guardians of the city, except that it is stronger in men and weaker in women' (456a10–11). But a passage that challenges prejudice should not take refuge in ambiguities. Plato has some, but not all, of the courage and imagination needed to flesh out his picture of a class of rulers unlike any rulers he knew.

VI

Though they can be allowed no monopoly on altruism, philosophers must be extraordinarily motivated to serve others if they are to merit the power that Plato would place in their hands. At the heart even of his social philosophy lies the theory of Forms. Within both personal and civic relations he expects these to be not distracting but inspiring.

In the *Phaedrus* Socrates makes an extraordinary linkage between Forms and faces. Of all the Forms, Beauty offers the clearest image of itself to our sight, so that 'it is the most apparent and the most loved' (250d3–e1). We then read that the lover would offer a sacrifice to the boy 'as to a statue and a god' (251a6–7), as if a boy, unlike a god, could be both. He is clearly in a state of deep confusion, and we should not be too quick to insist that what he really sees in the boy is the image and not Beauty itself. *In* (and not merely *while*) looking at him, he is 'carried back' to the Form (250e2–3): passionate seeing is infused by unconscious recollecting. When he turns his attention from body to soul, the same confusion recurs. He now recollects not a Form but a god, i.e., at least a mode of apprehending and realizing Forms. But gazing at the boy without grasping that he is remembering a god, he naturally credits the boy with the gifts that he in fact owes to the god and transmits to the boy; mistaking material for model, he supposes that he is imitating the boy even as he transmutes him (252e7–253b1). The confusion is salutary, for it inspires the generosity (b7–8) that does indeed make the lover godlike: it is through finding the boy 'equal to a god' (255a1) that he becomes himself 'possessed by a god' (b6). Appropriately within his defence of a higher madness, Socrates is allowing that the Forms can produce a moral revolution, replacing conventionality by authenticity (252a4–6), through metaphysical bewilderment.

The same transition from inspiration by a body to displacement of interest from body to soul was already an emphatic feature of the ladder of love in the *Symposium*. The omission there of any mention of recollection, a theme that Plato was developing about the same time in the *Phaedo*, can only be understood as a sacrifice for the sake of simplicity and unity of presentation. Alternately extending and raising his view, the lover shifts his interest from one body to all beautiful bodies, to one soul, to the practices and laws that mould all beautiful souls, to the branches of knowledge, and so to the most cognizable of all beauties, the Form of Beauty itself (210a4–e1). The Form is explicitly grasped only at the end, but must be supposed to have been exercising a subliminal influence from the beginning. The lovers of sights and sounds in *Republic* Book V, who not only lack but are incapable of knowledge of the Form, are fixated on a plurality of beauties (476b4–c4, 479e1–2). Though they doubtless use the general term 'beautiful', they are effectively nominalists and not realists about beauty, with no inkling that shifts of interest between individuals and even categories are intelligible as exercises of loyalty towards a single common property. They are aesthetes for whom every art-object is irreplaceable by any other. Those who make the ascent are different from early on: their hearts rapidly adjust to generalizations about beauty as a single property that comes in kinds and degrees. For Plato, this can only mean that, like homing pigeons, they are already potentially on target to retrieve the Form itself.

How will this effect their attitudes to persons? Their promiscuity will be unlike that of the indiscriminate lovers mentioned in the *Republic* who find a snub nose 'charming' and a Roman nose 'regal', a dark complexion 'virile' and a fair one 'divine' (474d7–e2). Inhabiting an erotic world of thick rather than thin concepts, of specificities and not abstractions, these find all adolescents attractive in different ways. The lovers of the *Symposium* realize that 'if one must pursue beauty of appearance, it is great folly not to consider the beauty of all bodies one and the same' (210b2–3). So the two promiscuities contrast, for the one depends on appreciating differences, the other on appreciating identity; the one values all individuals, while the other values nothing individual. Even at the second level of the ascent, where the objects of love are souls and mental qualities, there is no interest in varieties of personality. The right speeches are those 'that improve the young' (c2–3), with no suggestion of the theme in the *Phaedrus*, which is one of the links between its treatments of love and rhetoric, that different types of speech are appropriately directed at different temperaments (271b1–5, c10–d7). When the ascent is completed, the lover will look down at 'the wide sea of beauty' (*Symposium* 210d4) at a height from which individuals, and even kinds of individual, are no longer distinct.

We may then wonder whether the ladder of love is not an exit out of love in any ordinary sense. It is true that the summit of the ascent is not the end of the story. In a sexual metaphor, the lover will beget on Beauty 'not images of virtue but true virtue', and so become 'dear to the gods and, if any man can, immortal himself also' (212a3–7). Yet all this contrasts with the kind of immortality offered before (209c2–d1); there the lover begat on the boy virtues 'more beautiful and immortal' than physical children; here he begets virtue on Beauty itself so as to become, so far as is humanly possible, immortal in the manner of a god. The 'images of virtue' that the human lover generated in his beloved were perhaps no more real than those that poets generate in their audience (d1–4); the philosophical lover may generate 'true virtue' only in himself in the form of an intellectual state that relates him only to the gods. On this reading, a vicarious immortality dependent on the contingencies of personal relationships is transcended and replaced by a proprietary immortality that is no longer a child of chance. Gregory Vlastos concludes, 'What started as a pederastic idyl ends up in a transcendental marriage' ([10.59], 42).

If this egoistic intellectualism is the correct interpretation of the Platonic ascent, Forms provide not a new motivation towards morality, but a new problem for its justification. As Vlastos aptly comments, 'Were we free of mortal deficiency we would have no reason to love anyone or anything except the Idea: seen face to face, it would absorb all our love' ([10.59, 32–3). If so, Plato's erotics have problematic implications for his politics, for the Forms that distract lovers from loving should also distract philosopher-rulers from ruling. It is a famous problem in the *Republic* how to draw philosophers away from enjoying the truth into doing good, and this reading of the *Symposium* turns the screw. If Socrates' second speech in the *Phaedrus* seems very different, that might confirm that it has to be taken with caution. However, one may doubt whether it can be right to read the *Symposium* so inconveniently. It is clear from the *Phaedo* that 'true virtue' is not purely intellectual but rather consists of practical virtue 'together with wisdom' (69b3), here in the *Symposium* coming from apprehension of the Forms. Similarly procreative language to that of *Symposium* (212a2–5) serves in the *Republic* (VI.490b3–7) to describe the emergence of 'a sound and just character, which is accompanied by temperance' (c5–6). In the *Laws*, the effect of intercourse with divine virtue is to become outstandingly virtuous oneself (X.904c6–e3). The contrast in the *Phaedo* is with a slavish virtue that merely measures pleasures and pains; here in the *Symposium* it is with a pre-philosophical virtue that may be beautiful and immortal (209c6–7) but lacks understanding. There is no implication of any withdrawal from practical life.

More uncertain is whether there remains any intimate relationship with an individual. One might infer that there does not from a remark that 'slavery to the beauty of one' is 'base and mean-spirited' (210d1–3); but that complaint is actually more applicable if the lover is now developing his own virtue alone. We should rather distinguish the contemplation of beauty, which should be wide and individually non-discriminating, from the creation of beauty, which for most of us has to be personal and more selective. Better indicative is the context: personal love cannot cease to be Socrates' topic without a discontinuity of which one could expect a clearer warning. It is more likely that the 'true virtue' is generated both in the lover and in a beloved (unlike the 'images of virtue' which already existed in the lover and had only to be transmitted). If so, what the Forms provide is not a new egocentricity in the pursuit of virtue, but a new motivation for creating it as best one can – which for lovers is within a beloved, as for lawgivers it is within a community. Vicarious immortality was presented before the ascent-passage as the prolongation of a human good; a proprietary immortality is now the additional reward of a divine height of beneficence. So understood, this section of the *Symposium* is indeed an overture, and not an obstacle, to the wider and deeper concerns of the *Republic*.

The two works display a structural similarity: in both, a human explanation of caring for others is supplemented by a transcendental one that follows on introduction of the Forms. The *Symposium* first finds in vicarious immortality a human motive for creating virtue in another especially within an erotic relationship; the *Republic* first finds in communism among the guardians a human cause of identifying with others within a Utopia. But those capable of apprehending the Forms have an extra ground for doing good that also enables them to do more good. Plato's presentation in the *Republic* takes on a partly misleading emphasis from the dialectical context. In reaction to Thrasymachus' assertion that all rule is for the benefit of the rulers (I.338e1–339a4), Socrates claims that some 'compulsion and penalty' must be applied to the good if they are to be willing to rule; the greatest penalty is being ruled by someone worse (347b9–c5). Later he still accepts the principle, 'The city in which those who are to rule are least eager to do so must needs be the best and least divisively administered' (VII.520d2–4). It is only fair that philosopher-kings should be forbidden to linger among their own contemplations, and 'compelled' to rule, each in turn, in return for an education that, exceptionally, they owe to their city (a6–c3). This risks disappointing Glaucon, who wanted to hear justice praised for its own sake (II.358d1–2), for ruling reluctantly in payment of a debt might have no value in itself other than that, which is being questioned and cannot be presupposed, of justice itself; and even that value might be cancelled by the compulsion. However, the word 'compelled' carries no implication of the intrinsically unchoiceworthy: philosophers are also 'compelled' to gain a vision of the Form of the Good (VII.519c8–d1, 540a7–9). When Socrates remarks that philosopher-kings will practise ruling 'not as something fine but as something necessary' (b4–5), the thought must be that they will be obliged to rule, and not that they will get nothing out of it. Yet the emphasis is unhelpful: we have to look around for hints of what ruling offers rulers in itself that makes them willing though not enthusiastic. And we cannot extract an answer from sections II–III above: truant philosophizing, so long as it is pursued for the sake of truth and not for fun or out of one-upmanship, is hardly fattening the lion of spirit or the Cerberus of appetite. Philosophers, like Martians, escape the common costs of injustice.

We need to ask (as Vlastos possibly failed to) what it is to love a Form. To suppose that it is simply to enjoy contemplating it would be like supposing that a mother can only show her love for her child by looking at it. Loving the Forms is further to wish to fashion oneself after them in a just and orderly life (VI.500c2–d1). Once reason itself possesses wisdom, it desires that this possess the soul of which it is part, which requires that it rule wisely within the soul (IV.442c5–8). This already offers the agent a rich enough prize: becoming just and practising virtue likens a man to a god so far as is humanly possible (X.613a7–b1, cf. *Symposium* 212a5–7). Thus meeting an obligation can be a humble, if not the highest, part of the project of apotheosis. There is yet further point in moulding not just oneself but one's community: I love wisdom more if I wish it to characterize not only myself but my city, which demands that this be ruled by the wise; in a striking expression, it is a 'service' to justice to extend its domain in governing a city (VII.540e2–3). Moreover, to the extent that this attitude focuses on the Form itself, it will be impartial between cities as well as citizens. Identification with others previously replaced egoism by what has been called 'nostrism' (cf. [11.9], 72); devotion to Forms, and desire that things participate in them, now supplements egocentricity by impartiality. Here in the *Republic*, as not in the *Symposium*, we meet a passionate impersonality, inspired by the Forms, that values the existence of justice on earth as in heaven, with no special reference either to the agent or to his own circle or community. However high this valuation may be, it is compatible with a reluctance to rule. If I am a philosopher in Plato's Utopia, I shall consent to rule, for the sake both of being just myself and of making others just, when it is needed and because I am obliged; but I shall not compete to rule when justice would be equally achieved all round by another's ruling instead. I may value nothing above the rule of justice; but, to the extent that this is an end definable without even implicit reference to myself, I can be as keen as possible that it be achieved without being more than willing that it be achieved through me. It is thus that we may take Plato to be reconciling the rulers' reluctance with their devotion to the ruled.

VII

Forms have a further role to play, providing not only a special motivation to rule but a special competence in ruling. Dialectic, which leads through the world of the Forms, is also to provide a practical knowledge that entitles philosophers alone to lead their own lives and direct those of others. But how is it to do this? The *Republic* hardly faces up to the question. Karl Popper has a complaint that is for once not unfair: 'Plato's Idea of the Good is practically empty. It gives us no indication of what is good, in a moral sense, i.e. what we ought to do' ([11.13], 274 n. 32, cf. 145–6). The objection goes back to Aristotle (*Nicomachean Ethics* I.6.1096b35–1097a13), who had more to go by than the text of the dialogues. Yet in assessing it by the evidence we have, we need to remember some features of the *Republic* as a text that we inevitably neglect when we expound its content as a theory – as I have been doing. In a manner, the *Republic* deconstructs itself. It advances the thesis that it is dialectic alone, looking at the stars, that can guide the ship of state (to translate into metaphor an analogy spelled out at VI.488a7–489c7). The paradox is made vivid in the image of the philosopher's return from the light outside back into the Cave: one would expect him to be blinded by the darkness (VII.516e3–6), but are assured that he alone will see aright (520c3–6). The best guide is Johnny Head-in-Air. But who is presenting the case? A Socrates who remains Socratic in denying any pretensions to dialectic himself: he compares himself to a blind man on the right road (VI.506c8–9), and can only offer to speak in likenesses (e3–4). He is a pre-dialectical 'lawgiver' (V.458c6, VI.497d1) for a community that allows only dialecticians the right to rule.[11] His conclusions themselves imply that interpreters who take them as Platonic dogma must be making a mistake. His task is to present a persuasive case for dialectic without any ability reliably to anticipate its results. Consequently, we cannot expect more from him than gesture where we most want guidance, and need to be cautious even where he is communicative.

Socrates conceives of the goal of dialectic in two ways: it is apprehension of the nature of the Form of the Good (VII.532a5–b5), and of the interconnections between the branches of knowledge (531c9–d4, 537c1–7). Dialectic is thus foundational, evaluative and synoptic. Our world depends upon the world of Forms, which derives teleologically from the Good; unlike our world, which can only imperfectly marry the material with the ideal, the world of Forms is as it is because that is the best way anything can be. Apprehending the Forms would yield a grasp of the *is* and the *ought* of their world and of ours, but Socrates is unable to spell out how. One particular difficulty is this: our 'ought' is in part a moral 'ought', but how can morality, which is interpersonal, connect with the impersonal world of Forms? More technically, Plato is at least inclined to a doctrine of the self-predication of Forms; how then can there be a Form of Justice, when it is only persons, acts, intentions, and the like, that can be just? Consistently with his persona, Socrates supplies hints that are not answers. Quite deliberately, we may suppose, Plato has him twice take us by surprise. Justice has been defined in partite terms: a soul or city is just if its parts do their own thing. And yet it is by looking at the soul *before* partition that we shall best distinguish justice from injustice (X.611c4–5). Justice is personal. And yet it can be said that the Forms neither wrong nor are wronged by each other (VI.500c3–4). We should infer, I suggest, that the justice that Socrates has identified as one of the cardinal virtues is the human face of a vaguer reality. Specific talk of a Form of Justice is at home within a human perspective. Glimpsed outside that perspective, the opposite of injustice is no less than rational order (*kosmos* according to *logos*, c4–5). We may suppose that the four virtues, and indeed all virtues, are products of the refraction of that through the prism of mind and matter. (This would be the metaphysical ground of the unity of the virtues.) In patterning themselves and their society upon the Forms, philosophers make them 'as orderly and divine as is humanly possible' (c9–d1). Their goal is to make human activity a more faithful reflection of intelligible reality.

This is abstract, but not empty. There is an obvious analogy between the unity of the Forms (visible to the synoptic eye) and Plato's ideal – which we may well not share – of a wholly co-operative community. If we explain away his metaphysics as a projection from his ethics, that confirms the analogy. Yet the content of the *Republic* is generally less indefinite, and we need to reflect how the abstract and concrete connect. In a similar passage, we read that philosophers, forming a clear pattern in their minds through scrutiny of the truest truth, 'establish here norms concerning the fine, the just, and the good if they need establishing, and preserve those that are established' (484d1–3). This may express an ideal that contrasts both with Aristotle and with later Plato: dialectic might allow the deduction of moral principles, and civil laws and institutions, that are fixed and absolute. But the issue is debatable.[12] Little can safely be read out of the fact that much of the *Republic* is an imaginative exercise in lawgiving. We may view its laws less as attempts to anticipate the results of dialectic than as a mode of describing a city that does not exist. More recent Utopias (like Thomas More's) are commonly presented in the popular genre of travel-writing; Plato apes the more serious Greek genre of lawgiving for a colony (cf. the casualness of VII.534e1) – as he will do again, more fully and formally, in the *Laws*. Over some matters Socrates expresses a conservatism that is doubtless Plato's: innovation in music and gymnastics is especially discouraged (IV.424b5–c6). Yet the apparent fixity of Plato's ideal may owe more to the genre than to what Popper calls 'the rigidity of tribalism' ([11.13], 172). Certainly, to infer from Books VIII and IX (where Socrates sketches a decline from Utopia through a series of constitutions and characters terminating in the tyrannical) that Plato thought that all change is for the worse would be to misread systematic comparison as impossible history, for the primitive and pre-historical Golden Age was not an age of Platonists and philosopher-kings.

We may think of his Utopia as a thought-experiment that conveys concretely how a society could be informed by dialectic without consisting solely of dialecticians. In resting so much on the analogy between soul and city, while leaving open whether further investigation would multiply the parts of the soul, Socrates implicitly leaves open also whether there are precisely three classes of citizen. Indeed, his survey of the stages of advanced education in Book VII implies further subdivisions within guardians and auxiliaries. What then of the 'norms concerning the fine, the just and the good' (VI.484d2)? We must remember that Plato cannot be rigid about rules, either moral or legal, when he has rejected any attempt to define moral virtues in concrete behavioural terms (see section I above). It is true that courage was characterized as 'the preservation of the opinion that has arisen under the law through education concerning what things, and what kinds of thing, are to be feared' (IV.429c7–8). All but guardians need general opinions as guides for a reason raised in the *Politicus*: 'How could anyone be able to sit beside someone all his life and prescribe to him precisely what is fitting?' (295a9–b2). But no virtue can be captured by such rules, for the unity of the virtues applies in a manner even to acts: an act may be just without being brave, for its context may include no danger; but, as Cephalus learnt (*Republic* I.331cl–d3), an act is only just if it is best, and that is sensitive to circumstance. Despite some of the appearances, both moral and legal rigidities are out of place in the *Republic*.

VIII

I have suggested that we have to take a somewhat sceptical view of Socrates' quasi-legislation in the *Republic* if we keep in mind the theory on which it rests. This is uncertain, but has the effect of easing the transition to the later dialogues, the *Politicus* and *Laws*.

The *Politicus* essentially approves the institution of philosopher-kings: the Stranger confirms that the correct and real form of government is that in which the rulers are truly expert; whether they rule willing or unwilling subjects, with or without laws, is by the way (293c5–d2). The decisive questions are not concrete ('Do they kill and banish?', 'Do they import citizens or send out colonies?'), but abstract ('Are they applying knowledge and justice?', 'Are they improving the city?' (d4–e2)). This must be because there are no reliable generalizations linking the concrete and the abstract; absolute laws cannot do justice to the dissimilarities of men and situations (294a10–b6). A conception of precision (*t'akribes*, 284d2) can only be sketched imprecisely; expert statesmen, like all practical experts (c2), must be able to measure the greater and the lesser in relation not only to each other but to the 'mean', that is, 'the moderate, the fitting, the timely, the necessary, and all else that falls into the mean between extremes' (e5–8). Aristotle was to develop this more fully, but to very different effect: Plato aspires to the precision of an art of measurement, while he appeals to the perception of particular cases (*Nicomachean Ethics* II.9.1109b22–3). Within Plato, we must suspect, imprecision of description, and precision as an aspiration, are made for each other.

There are still roles for rules, either fixed or flexible. Even expert rulers will enact laws to guide action in their absence (*Statesman* 295a4–b2); but these are revisable by rulers, and overridable by subjects (c8–d7). More significant is the right role of laws within cities whose rulers are inexpert – that is, within all cities outside Utopia (meaning 'nowhere'). Here flexibility is dangerous. Where there is no knowledge, revision is likely to come of corrupt motives, whereas long experience, careful consideration and popular consent lie behind laws as they stand (300a1–b6). When rulers know what they are doing, consent does not matter (293c8–d2); when they do not, it does. It is if a doctor is expert that the patient's consent has no bearing on the desirability of the treatment (296b5–c2). However, as in medicine, political consent is at best an indication, and never a criterion, of getting things right. At least the primary *goal* of governing well must be to act justly oneself; but its *mark* is just action by the governed (c6–d4), which is a consequence and not a mode of procedure. Plato retains a counter-factual optimism: if a perfect ruler appeared, he would be welcome (301d4, cf. *Republic* VI.498d6–502a2); but, as it is, no such king is produced in our cities, and the best that we can do is follow in the track of the truest polity (301d8–e4). This causes Plato no enthusiasm. If a more practicable art, like medicine or navigation, were to proceed by rigid legislation, we should all find it absurd (298b6–299e9). Such government is an imitation of the true in a manner that makes it less a copy than a counterfeit (293e2–3, cf. 300c5–301a4): far from taking the ideal as a model, it despairs of achieving more than a simulacrum of success by means that are fit less to succeed than to avoid the worst causes of failure.

420

The *Laws* deepens and develops what is essentially the same conception, but with much more patience for the unideal. Its protagonist is an Athenian Stranger, who lacks at once the uncertainties and the aspirations of a Socrates. He distinguishes a 'first city and polity', which realizes the greatest possible unity, from one that is single to a secondary degree (V.739b8–e4). The ideal recalls the *Republic*: the means are communist (women, children, property held in common), the end unanimity in attitude and action; even things private by nature, eyes and ears and hands, must seem to operate in common. There is a new fluidity: the communism is to extend not only through a small class of guardians and auxiliaries, but 'so far as possible throughout the whole city' (c1–2). This corresponds to a more fluid psychology; the golden cord of reason has to contend with other cords that are hard and steely (I.644d7–645b1), but the field of conflict is not defined as tripartite (cf. [11.2]). However, reason was never immune to corruption, and the removal of the barriers that constituted partition fits a new anxiety that incarnation is always infection. It is not in human nature to acquire autocratic power without becoming full of insolence and injustice (IV.713c6–8, cf. XII.947e7–8). Our mortal nature inclines us to sacrifice public interest to private gain, 'creating a darkness within itself' (IX.875b6–c2). Only by the grace of God could a man be born with a character that would enable him safely to apply his intelligence and dispense with laws; as it is, true freedom is hardly to be found anywhere (c2–d3). The main obstacle to philosophical rule is nothing more contingent than our humanity.

Hence the second-best city is humanly the best. While still in fact evidently impracticable (cf. [11.3], 266–8, 311–12), it conveys more concretely what might be adequate to human needs if circumstances were different and consent obtainable. Though knowledge itself should never be enslaved to law (c7–d1), there is no security for any city in which the law is not master of the rulers (IV.715c6–d6). By a revision of Athenian practice, with an age-limit and an election instead of lot, officials are to be answerable to scrutiny by a board of auditors (XII.945e4–946e4); when autocracy is out of the question, even bureaucracy must be kept under control. Laws are to be prefaced by explanations and exhortations (IV.718b2–723d4). We may wonder whether these would not encourage jurors to apply the spirit rather than the letter of each law, but their intention seems simply to win comprehension and compliance (718c8–d7). It is illustrated profusely, almost compulsively, how minutely laws must define and differentiate the types of criminal offence. That some details of regulation must be left by the founding legislator to experiment and experience (e.g. VI.770b4–8) was also recognized in the less law-bound *Republic* (IV.427a2–7); here, even these are to become virtually immutable after ten years' trial (*Laws* VI.772b5–c7). Later revision must be excused by necessity, and will be inhibited by procedural obstacles (c7–d4). Where nature is weak, safety lies in a straitjacket.

Plato's morality is a melodrama, and the *Laws* denies it a happy ending. He always tends to dualisms, of Forms and world, soul and body, reason and unreason, unity and division, education and corruption. Social dramas are mirrored by conflicts within each soul. When he writes, 'There is a strange, wild, lawless kind of desire that is present even in those of us who seem most moderate' (*Republic* IX.572b4–6), the idealist is shaking hands with the cynic: Jacques Vergès, the French lawyer who defends the undefendable, has remarked, 'There is in the heart of the most honest man a cesspool filled with hideous reptiles.' A political Utopia that intends to make a heaven of earth has to make way for a second-best polity that is truer to man's fallen nature. We read Plato now not in order to share the consolations of hope or despair, but to be reminded of how it is part of our freedom to be able to enter imaginatively into a higher view of our potentialities, and a lower view of our actualities, than we can take quite seriously.

 NOTES

1 The traditional and inevitable translation of *eudaimonia* by 'happiness' is defended by Vlastos ([9.93], 201–3) with a qualification: he notes that *eudaimonia* has two features, 'a subjective (pleasurable contentment or satisfaction) and an objective one (attainment of good, well-being)', and concedes that the second looms larger within *eudaimonia* than within happiness.

2 As I shall use the terms, I am 'disposed' to act in a certain way in certain circumstances if I am such as to act so in those circumstances (if and when they arise), while I have a 'practice' of acting in a certain way in certain circumstances if I do act so in those circumstances (if and when they arise). Hence disposition and practice are logically equivalent, and both hypothetical in content. It is not an issue whether the disposition has intrinsic value, or only instrumental value derivative from the value of the practice. This usage fits the easy transitions in the *Republic* between state and activity (e.g. at *Republic* II.357d3–358b7, where Glaucon, proposing that justice be assigned intrinsic as well as instrumental value, first speaks of it as something to be practised, and then as an internal state of the soul).

3 E.g. Sachs ([11.16], 144–7 (=[10.58]II, 38–41)), Reeve ([11.15], 24–33), Irwin ([9.39], 189–91).

4 This thought suffices to show that it is indeed of justice, and not, more broadly, of righteousness or, indeed, being moral, that Plato is offering an account; cf. Vlastos ([11.18] sect. 1).

5 It may still be objected that Socrates is really assigning external justice only derivative value as a cause and a symptom of internal justice, and so disappointing Glaucon. I take his reply to be that internal and external are aspects

of the same disposition-*cum*-practice, of which the internal is naturally the focus of intrinsic value egocentrically conceived. One might compare dressing well, a single practice that involves both looking good to others, and looking good to oneself in the mirror. A better reply might be that, *pace Republic* IV.443c9–d1, psychic harmony is equally manifested in internal acts of mind and external actions. The just man treats others in ways that do not merely evidence and reinforce, but embody, his state of soul. He finds equal pleasure in internal and external activity, for it is in both that his psychic harmony becomes for him an object of experience.

6 I owe this example to Mark Rowe. It would need a speculative psychopathology to dissolve the objection on Plato's behalf.

7 The double process of externalization (from soul to society) and internalization (from society to soul) is illumined by Lear [11.10].

8 Whether in reaction to the frequent infelicity of Popper [11.13], or out of a distaste for moral commonplaces and a penchant for thought-experiments, modern writing on the *Republic* tends to be neutral or even sympathetic (e.g. Price [11.14], 179–93). But ominous parallels to Plato can readily be found in Kolnai [11.9], George Orwell's *1984*, and *Quotations from Chairman Mao Tse-Tung*. Thus Orwell nicely conveys the charmlessness of compulsory copulation: 'Even then he could have borne living with her if it had been agreed that they should remain celibate. But curiously enough it was Katharine who refused this. They must, she said, produce a child if they could ... She even used to remind him of it in the morning, as something which had to be done that evening and which must not be forgotten. She had two names for it. One was "making a baby", and the other was "our duty to the Party" ' (Harmondsworth, Penguin, 1989: 70).

9 The status quo was certainly repressive, though the orthodoxy of Annas [10.45], 181–2) needs some qualification in the light of Cohen ([11.4], ch. 6).

10 The complaint goes back to Rousseau: 'No longer knowing what to do with women, he found himself forced to turn them into men' (*Émile*, Book 5). It reappears, alas, in Price ([11.14], 170–1).

11 The case is not as simple as that of an amateur arguing for employing an architect, for two reasons: dialectic is needed to define ends as well as means; and Socrates indulges in plenty of designing himself.

12 Contrast Owen ([11.12], 89–94 (=[4.46], 77–82)), who finds the *Republic* rigid, with Klosko ([11.8], 167–72), who finds it flexible. The evidence is elusive, but, with or on behalf of Klosko, I would cite the following passages as qualifying the prevalent pretence to be legislating once and for all by acknowledging the proper limits of the law, the need to supplement its letter in the light of its spirit, and the possibility of moral development: *Republic* IV.424a4–b1, 425a3–e7, 426e4–427b2, V.458b9–c4, VI.497c7–d2.

BIBLIOGRAPHY

11.1   Annas [10.45].

11.2   'Bobonich, C. 'Akrasia and agency in Plato's *Laws* and *Republic*', *Archiv für Geschichte der Philosophie* 76 (1994): 3–36.

11.3 Brunt, P. A. *Studies in Greek History and Thought*, Oxford, Clarendon Press, 1993.

11.4 Cohen, D. *Law, Sexuality, and Society: The Enforcement of Morals in Classical Athens*, Cambridge, Cambridge University Press, 1991.

11.5 Irwin [9.34].

11.6 —— [9.39].

11.7 Joseph, H. W. B. *Essays in Ancient and Modern Philosophy*, Oxford, Clarendon Press, 1935.

11.8 Klosko, G. *The Development of Plato's Political Theory*, New York and London, Methuen, 1986.

11.9 Kolnai, A. *The War Against the West*, London, Victor Gollancz, 1938.

11.10 Lear, J. 'Plato's politics of narcissism', in T. Irwin and M. C. Nussbaum (eds) *Virtue, Love and Form: Essays in Memory of Gregory Vlastos* (see [9.38]), pp. 137–59.

11.11 Nussbaum, M. C. *The Fragility of Goodness: Luck and Ethics in Greek Tragedy and Philosophy*, Cambridge, Cambridge University Press, 1986.

11.12 Owen, G. E. L. 'The place of the *Timaeus* in Plato's dialogues', *Classical Quarterly* NS 3 (1953): 79–95; repr. in Allen [10.64] and in Owen, ed. Nussbaum [see 4.46].

11.13 Popper, K. R. *The Open Society and its Enemies, vol. I: The Spell of Plato*, 5th edn, London, Routledge and Kegan Paul, 1966.

11.14 Price, A. W. *Love and Friendship in Plato and Aristotle*, Oxford, Clarendon Press, 1989.

11.15 Reeve, C. D. C. *Philosopher-Kings: The Argument of Plato's Republic*, Princeton, NJ, Princeton University Press, 1988.

11.16 Sachs, D. 'A fallacy in Plato's *Republic*', *Philosophical Review* 72 (1963): 141–58, repr. in Vlastos [10.58]: II.

11.17 Taylor, C.C.W. 'Plato's totalitarianism', *Polis* 5.2 (1986): 4–29.

11.18 Vlastos, G. 'The theory of social justice in the *polis* in Plato's *Republic*', in H. North (ed.) *Interpretations of Plato*, Leiden, Brill, 1977: 1–40; repr. in Vlastos, ed. Graham, vol. II (see [4.64]).

11.19 —— 'The individual as object of love in Plato', in Vlastos [9.87], 3–42.

11.20 Vlastos [9.93].

11.21 Wollheim, R. 'The good self and the bad self', in Wollheim, *The Mind and its Depths*, Cambridge, Mass., Harvard University Press, 1993: 39–63.

CHAPTER 12

Plato: aesthetics and psychology

Christopher Rowe

◄◄◦❈◦►►

Plato's ideas about literature and art and about beauty (his 'aesthetics')
are heavily influenced and in part actually determined by his ideas
about the mind or soul (his 'psychology').[1] It is therefore appropriate
to deal with the two subjects in proximity to one another, and the
second before the first.

◄◄ THE SOUL ►►

Preliminaries

Giving an account of any aspect of Platonic philosophy is made
especially difficult by two facts about the way in which he wrote: that
he did all his writing, not in treatise form, but in the form of dialogues,
from which the direct authorial voice is absent (so that it is always in
principle an open question how much of what is contained in them he
might have wanted to endorse, and how firmly); and that each dialogue
– if we discount occasional cross-references – is in principle separate
from every other. It is nevertheless reasonable to suppose, especially
since there are some ideas which recur repeatedly, that we can gain a
fair idea from the Platonic corpus about how and what *Plato* thought,
and that the separateness of individual dialogues does not constitute an
absolute bar against using them jointly in an attempt to understand
that thought. But it remains a moot point how we are to treat apparent
differences between the ideas presented to us in different works:
whether perhaps as the response of a flexible mind to issues and problems, which nevertheless leaves untouched an underlying unity of

425

doctrine; or rather as changes of mind, which betray the author's philosophical development.

The issue is particularly important in relation to Plato's ideas about the *psuchē*, which appear to exhibit considerable variation between, and even within, individual dialogues, and to fit particularly well – at least in some respects – the hypothesis of a development in his thinking. In general, the developmental or evolutionary view of Plato has become almost standard among his interpreters (especially in the Anglo-Saxon world), partly because of an apparent coincidence between the results of investigations into the chronology of the dialogues and what has been seen as the gradual maturation of their ideas and arguments. A typical overview will describe the Platonic corpus as falling into three parts: early, middle, and late. The early period, on this account, broadly represents that of the 'Socratic' dialogues, when Plato was by and large occupied with representing and preserving the intuitions and arguments of his master Socrates; the middle period shows him constructing those positive ideas which we most closely associate with the name 'Plato' ('Forms', 'philosopher-kings', and so on); while in the late period, he moves into a more critical and reflective phase, perhaps rejecting or heavily modifying some of his earlier ideas. The pattern at first sight fits quite neatly and easily in the case of Platonic 'psychology'. In the *Apology*, which all are agreed belongs to a time early on in Plato's writing career, we find Socrates at his trial expressing an agnostic attitude towards the fate of an individual after death: *either* death is annihilation, *or* the soul is translated to another place, where it will encounter the wise men of the past (if, as he says, the stories are true). By contrast, in the *Phaedo* (assigned to the 'middle' period), Socrates spends his last hours arguing rationally but committedly for the immortality of the soul. It is in the *Phaedo*, too, that – on the account in question – we begin to see the formation of a detailed theory about the soul and its nature, which is developed further in the *Republic* (usually treated as the middle dialogue *par excellence*) and elsewhere. Finally, in the late dialogues, signs of a retreat have been detected from some aspects of the 'middle' theory, and there is a reduction in emphasis on the immortal nature of the soul, even if the idea itself is plainly not abandoned.

There are, however, a number of points on which a developmental interpretation of Plato's treatment of the soul looks vulnerable, or unhelpful. In the *Apology*, where Socrates is (fictionally) addressing a general audience of Athenian citizens, his description of the 'other place' to which the soul may be translated after death is formulated in mainly traditional terms, which may reflect more about what Plato considered appropriate to the dramatic audience than about either his own or Socrates' views.[2] Again, the fact that the *Symposium* manages to discuss immortality at length without once referring to the *soul* as immortal cannot reasonably be supposed to indicate that Plato has temporarily given up the idea, which is heavily canvassed in other dialogues apparently written at about the same time. This looks like a clear case of what we may only suspect in the case of the *Apology*, namely of Plato's deciding what to include and what to exclude by reference to a dramatic audience – in this case, a tragic playwright and his guests at a dinner-party.[3] In the *Phaedo*, he has Socrates carefully skirt round the question whether the soul has parts, which becomes central in other dialogues but in this context would impede the argument. This does not mean that we must adopt a strictly unitarian approach; what it does mean is that chronological arguments need to be used sparingly, and that there are likely to be other factors at work in determining the content of any particular dialogue.

Plato was probably the first Greek thinker to articulate a theory of the soul. Socrates had a concept of it, but not a fully-articulated theory; and the same is true of other pre-Platonic thinkers. Two of the main ideas on which Platonic thinking on the subject is predicated are, first, the traditional notion that the 'souls' of the dead are in Hades (so that *something* of us, however insubstantial, continues in existence), and second, the idea – found for example in the medical writers – of a fundamental contrast between 'soul', on the one hand, and body on the other.[4] Socrates' way of conceiving of the soul as the moral self can be seen as building on the second of these ideas, developing it into something like our familiar opposition between the bodily or carnal (as in 'carnal pleasures') and the spiritual; Plato combines this with the first, but in a version which owes much to both Pythagoreanism and mystery religion, and – for a selected, philosophical few – reverses the relationship between life and death: for those who have lived philosophically, it is death which is preferable to life, and which allows the true fulfilment of their goals.[5]

However it is probably as correct to talk of Plato's *appropriation* of Pythagorean and other religious ideas as of his being influenced by them. It is reasonably clear that he believes in the immortality of the soul (since he goes on returning to the question of how to prove it), and in the general proposition that the wise and the good[6] will enjoy a better existence after death than the ignorant and bad; and beliefs of this general type[7] were evidently quite widespread in the Greece of the late fifth and early fourth centuries BC. He also shows more than a passing interest in the distinctively Pythagorean notion of the 'trans-migration' of the soul, after a suitable interval, from one body to another (whether human or animal). But each of these beliefs seems to be rooted in a deeper one, about the primacy of goodness in the explanation of the world we inhabit, and about the possibility of squaring that with the evident corruptibility of human motivation. Moreover Plato usually himself raises questions about the way his descriptions of 'Hades' and of the fate of the human soul are to be taken, by casting them in the form of 'stories'. As he has Socrates say at the end of one of the most famous eschatological myths, in the *Phaedo*:

> to insist that these things are as I say is not fitting for a man of intelligence; but that either this or something like it is true about our souls and their habitations, if indeed the soul is evidently immortal – to risk thinking so, in my view, *is* fitting. (114d)

On such occasions, his use of the language of Pythagoreanism, or of initiatory religion, appears to hover tantalizingly between the literal and the metaphorical.

A large part of the problem here is that Plato's dialogues are no ordinary philosophical works, but – some of them – highly literary pieces, apparently written for a relatively wide reading public (at any rate one wider than his immediate circle or school), and designed above all to persuade the reader of the value of philosophy itself. This they attempt to do by a variety of means, but especially by portraying philosophy in action, and by showing it playing a large role in, or even taking over for itself, normally distinct spheres of activity. Thus the philosopher may be the ideal statesman, orator, poet, even lover; to see the truth is to join the divine feast, or to be initiated into the highest mysteries. And yet at the same time to do philosophy is to be involved in hard, often prosaic, argument. The common thread is a commitment to the importance of rationality: whatever is worth achieving in human life is for Plato achievable by the exercise of reason, and by the assertion of the rational over the irrational. Through this means the authentic Platonic philosopher would simultaneously realize his – or her[8] – full human potentialities, and begin to resemble the (rational, Platonic) gods. If Plato does indeed genuinely believe in the immortality of the soul, then there is no reason to think of this latter goal as a mere *façon de parler*. In some sense, the ultimate fate of the soul in a Platonic universe lies beyond its present temporary conjunction with a body. But there are clear signs that for human souls actually to become divine is either in principle or in practice impossible, and that as in Greek poetry and myth, to be god*like* is the most that we can attain.[9] It is probably this which is part of what the doctrine of transmigration is meant to express. Unlike the gods, we are ultimately bound into the cycle of birth and death[10] – and yet we share in their rationality.

If this is so, then we need to steer a middle course: neither should we assume that Plato takes literally all the many ideas that he develops through his characters in the dialogues (which would be dangerous on any account), nor should we attempt to eliminate altogether what may seem to us the more fantastic and apparently poetic elements among them. (Indeed, for some Neoplatonist and Renaissance interpreters the latter probably take us closer to the core of Platonism.) We must remain aware that Plato's philosophical writing is a complex matter, and that his motives as a writer may sometimes directly affect the content of that writing, as indeed may his chosen literary form. Thus, for instance, particular dialogues will often follow out a particular line of thought to the exclusion of others, which it is difficult to bring in within the fiction of a particular conversation (the treatment of immortality in the *Symposium* is one clear example; see above).

The Phaedo

The exercise of our reason matters for Plato because of what it can do for us. Reason enables us, most importantly, to recognize what is best for us, which is also what we desire; and this is one reason why even the driest discussion can be described in terms of passionate emotion; philosophers are *lovers* of the truth,[11] because truth is the only sure guide for the conduct of life, and a successful life is something that we all want. This kind of passionate attachment to reason is nowhere more evident than in the *Phaedo*,[12] in which Plato represents Socrates in his last hours justifying his optimism in the face of death. He claims that it is in death, if anywhere, that the philosopher will be able to achieve the wisdom he sought but was unable fully to achieve while alive. We cannot 'see' the truth in its purity when in our embodied state, because of the confusion created by the body and its desires; death is our – our souls' – final separation from body (if we have 'trained' ourselves to have as little traffic with the body as possible); it is therefore 'reasonable to suppose' that it is then that all will be revealed to us.[13] This informal argument is then followed by four more tightly constructed ones for the underlying assumption that the soul can be relied upon to survive death (and remains intelligent, unlike the witless shades of the Homeric Hades). The supreme importance of wisdom is thus illustrated on both the theoretical and the practical level: Socrates both argues, and shows by his behaviour, that it is something the philosopher desires to the exclusion of everything else. This is a hard and unattractive doctrine (and one that does not recur in quite the same form elsewhere in Plato); it is also somewhat para-doxical, in so far as the wisdom in question seemed originally to be valued – as it is at least in part, even according to the *Phaedo*[14] – for the sake of living a good life. On the other hand, if the soul *is* immortal, then Socrates' position is intelligible enough (even if no more attractive);

a single life in a body will have a vanishingly small importance, except in so far as it affects the quality of the soul's future existence. In any case, the general point is clear enough: that it is wisdom that counts, or wisdom with the virtue that flows from it.

This framing argument of the *Phaedo*, together with the four arguments for immortality, tells us a good deal about what Plato means, or can mean, by 'soul'.

> Does this not turn out to be purification [for the soul] . . .
> separating the soul as far as possible from the body, and
> habituating it to gather and assemble itself together from all
> quarters of the body, and to dwell so far as possible, both in
> the present and in the time to come, freed from the body as from
> fetters?
>
> (67c–d)

It is certainly a separate entity in itself, and itself invisible and 'bodiless' or incorporeal (as is confirmed later in the dialogue: cf. 85e); it is in its proper state, not when it is in the (or a) body, but when it is out of it – if the body is like a pair of leg-irons;[15] and it is essentially the rational, thinking element in us. But since what Socrates attempts to demonstrate, in the main part of the dialogue, is evidently *personal* immortality (the fear of death would hardly be assuaged by a rational assurance that something impersonal, something other than us, will survive), this immortal 'soul' must also represent our essential selves. If we put these last few points together, the result is that we are fundamentally rational (and incorporeal) beings, who become distorted or perverted by our association with the body, and are only fully ourselves when we are 'purified' of 'its'[16] desires, lusts and fears. Any irrational behaviour we may display is on this account simply a consequence of our enforced union with the body, though its effects will normally outlast our deaths – that is, unless we have 'purified' ourselves through philosophy, and 'practised dying and being dead' (64a).

Something like this view of the soul also emerges elsewhere in the corpus, but in competition with the essentially different view of it as partly rational and partly itself irrational, in the more or less literal sense of having irrational parts (as well as a rational one). As I have suggested, the *Phaedo* does not commit itself to saying either that the soul does or that it does not have parts;[17] and the coexistence of the two views in the *Republic* – which treats tripartition as (perhaps) a way of describing what the soul is like in consequence of its association of the body – shows that they are not wholly incompatible. But in the final analysis they represent two quite different conceptions of human nature, which in turn reflect Plato's ambivalence about the value of our life here on earth: one view emphasizing our (potential) kinship to the divine, the other our difference from it. In the context of the *Phaedo*, the unitary view is clearly more at home. Yet there are clear problems with it, and particularly about its compatibility with the demand for *individual* immortality. If any two souls were fully 'purified', then they would apparently be indistinguishable from each other, since they would both be purely rational and knowing beings, and what they knew – given the Platonic model of knowledge – would actually be the same. (Just so, at the end of Book II of the *Republic*, the argument seems to lead to the – admittedly unacknowledged – conclusion that there exists a multiplicity of identical, rational gods.) There are difficulties about identifying the individual with his or her soul, on any interpretation of 'soul', but these are at their greatest if our 'souls' are supposed to be coextensive with our rational faculties. Who would wish to be remembered as their ability to think, and nothing else – not even the content of their thought?)[18]

But soul also has at least one other role to play in the *Phaedo*. It is not only our true, rational self; it is also a *life-principle*, or as Socrates puts it in the last argument for immortality, what 'brings life' to the body (105c–d). The idea of soul as an originator of motion, indeed, as the only self-activating source of movement anywhere in the universe, is widespread in Plato. In the *Phaedrus* (245e), Socrates suggests that 'what is moved by itself' is the 'essence and definition' of soul; in the *Laws* (896a), usually agreed to be Plato's last work, it is 'that movement which is capable of moving itself by itself'. Now for someone, like Plato, who is apparently happy to think of the universe itself as fundamentally rational, i.e. both as ordered, and as actually a living and thinking being, the idea that the ultimate source of motion should be a rational entity makes a certain sense, on that macrocosmic level; but it makes rather less sense at the microcosmic level of human beings, compounds of soul and body, most of whose activities are necessarily irrational in nature. Functions like ingestion, digestion or excretion may be aspects of a rationally-designed system (or what resembles such a system), but it looks distinctly odd to put them under the control of the faculty of reason, when they are by their nature unthinking.

It seems obvious enough that the tripartite model of the soul will work better in this context, as it will in the previous one: if the soul which survives death retains its emotions and its irrational desires, it will have a considerably greater chance of standing in for the original person. In fact, this will turn out to be the case even in the *Phaedo* for all except the purified, philosophical soul. Whatever we suppose to be the non-mythical equivalent of the fates of non-philosophical souls which Socrates describes (living on the shores of lake Acheron, or being swept along in the appalling rivers of the underworld), there will be little point in punishing them unless they are recognizably the same souls, dominated by irrational impulses, which motivated the unsatisfactory behaviour for which they have been condemned; and indeed the *Phaedo* openly acknowledges the point, describing the unpurified soul as 'interspersed with what belongs to the category of the body', however it may be that something incorporeal can be 'interspersed' with anything (81c). To this extent the two models for understanding the soul, unitary and tripartite, will be practically indistinguishable.[19] But on either account virtually all individuality must be lost as soon as a soul enters another body. There will certainly be no memory of any previous bodily existence, and so even if it is the same soul-stuff that animates the new body, it might as well be a new soul; no one will recognize Socrates in his new existence, and he (if it is a he) will not even recognize himself.[20]

What he *will* have a memory of is of the Platonic Forms, though his memory will remain latent from birth unless and until he is able to 'recollect' it.[21] This is the Platonic doctrine of *anamnēsis*, which is brought in as the basis of the second argument for immortality in the *Phaedo*, and which claims that 'learning' in the important cases is really a matter of rediscovering knowledge of things we knew before we were born. We are nowhere told, except in a mythical context,[22] exactly when and how we came to know the Forms; we have simply had acquaintance with them in the past, and this is sufficient to guarantee our access, given the right conditions, to a collection of objects which are not themselves objects of direct experience in our bodily lives.[23] Once again, we are brought back to the essential unworldliness of the soul in Plato's thinking. His is an extreme form of dualism: the soul is not just a separate entity from the body, but one that, despite its function as originator of movement and change, seems to belong – by its essential nature – outside the body, and outside the world[24] in which that movement and change occur (though it still remains an open question whether any non-divine soul can remain *permanently* in a discarnate state). Only in the *Phaedo* is dualism allowed to be challenged, when one of Socrates' interlocutors brings forward the view that 'soul' is merely a kind of epiphenomenon of the mixture of physical constituents in a body (the 'harmony' theory of soul). But Socrates gives this rival account short shrift, dismissing it by means of arguments which with a little reformulation it might easily evade. Plato had evidently not seen the true strength of the competition to his own view.

The Soul in Other Dialogues

One question which is likely to occur to any reader of the *Phaedo* is why, if the soul's true place is outside the body, it is ever incarnated in the first place, and especially if everything in the world is for the best. An answer, which emerges from the *Phaedrus* and the *Timaeus*, is just that the scheme of things demands living things, and living things require souls to animate them.[25] In both dialogues, these souls have three parts: one higher and rational, and two irrational, respectively responsible for the higher and the lower emotions. In the *Timaeus*, the story of the creation represents the first and immortal part as being created by the divine craftsman out of the same stuff as the soul of the universe, while the other two are the products of lesser divinities, specifically to meet the requirements of bodily existence (to survive, we shall need, for example, an impulse to assert and defend ourselves, and a desire to take in food and drink).[26] In the *Phaedrus*, the three parts are compared to a charioteer and his two horses, one his natural ally, the other – the lusting, lecherous one – in permanent opposition to him; but unlike normal chariot teams, this one, including the charioteer, is a single whole, 'grown together'.[27] Out of the body, the most fortunate souls will be able to control their horses, and will join the gods, if only temporarily, to feast on reality and truth; in it, they will struggle against the lusts of the second horse to regain their memories of the feast.

This opposition between the highest and lowest parts is a fundamental feature of the tripartite model of the soul. It expresses what the *Phaedo* describes in terms of the opposition between soul and body, the 'lower' desires being precisely those which are there treated as belonging to the body itself. Plato's basic position is in a way bipartite rather than tripartite; that is, in so far as he sees the human soul as a battleground between the rational, on the one hand, and the irrational or 'bodily' on the other. The rational part is as it were the 'eye' of the soul, which will 'see' the truth, on two conditions: first, that it is itself fully developed; and second, that it is not prevented from doing so by the irrational in us.[28] This is the view which underlies the *Phaedo*, and it is also what we find in the *Laws*. But elsewhere we find the more complex tripartite model, which recognizes that some aspects of the irrational are not only necessary for our survival, but can contribute positively towards the good life. By splitting the irrational element into two parts, one of which is the natural 'ally' of reason, while the other tends to disrupt it, Plato is able to make this concession while still maintaining the sense of a basic opposition between rational and irrational.

However he also has independent grounds for this move. In Book IV of the *Republic*, he has Socrates argue at considerable length for the existence of three soul-parts. (In fact, Socrates introduces the term 'part' only with considerable hesitation: at first he prefers *eidos*, 'kind of thing', *ēthos*, 'character-type', or plain 'something', as in, for example, *triton ti*, 'a third something' (435bff.). But the *Phaedrus* and the *Timaeus* show no such reluctance, and the *Timaeus* actually locates the three parts in separate parts of the body.) Socrates has argued that the virtues of wisdom, courage, self-control and justice are attributable to a community or city in virtue of the qualities of, and relationships between, the groups who perform, respectively, the functions of rulers, soldiers, and producers; now he raises the question – since the ultimate aim in the context is to define the virtues (and especially justice) in the individual – whether the individual person has 'these same kinds of thing in his soul', so that the results on the larger scale can be carried over on to the smaller. Using the basic principle that 'the same thing will not be disposed to do or have done to it opposite things in the same respect and in relation to the same thing at the same time' (436b), he establishes to the satisfaction of his immediate audience, first, that we need to distinguish something in us in virtue of which we experience physical desires, e.g. the desire for drink, from something else which may on occasion cause us to resist a particular object of desire, e.g. this drink now, for a reason (it is contaminated, or poisonous); and second that we must equally separate 'spirit'[29] or the 'spirited part' from both of the other two. This part is naturally or ideally[30] the ally of reason, and never sides with the desiring part against reason, although we discover later that it may itself oppose reason.

The individual will possess justice and the other virtues when each of these three parts is performing its proper function, in harmony with the others. This means, above all, that both of the two lower parts are properly under the control of reason. If they are, then he will have only the right physical desires, and in the right measure, policed by the 'spirited' part;[31] if not, then either of the lower parts may dominate and distort the reasoning part and its judgements. This gives Plato a kind of theory of imperfect types, which offers a further explanation of the division of soul into three parts. The person who is dominated by the love of profit, on Plato's account, is 'oligarchic' man (oligarchic states being those run for the material benefit of the rulers); 'democratic' man is ruled by different sorts of desire in succession, and none in particular; and 'tyrannical' man, the tyrant himself, is controlled by a single, all-consuming master-lust. But there is also the person dominated by the love of honour, and the desire for self-assertion: the one Plato calls the 'timocratic' individual, the warrior of the *Iliad*, or the ambitious politician who is his counterpart in the democratic city-state.[32]

This picture of human nature as it should be, with reason ruling over unreason, may seem to be disturbed by some aspects of the *Phaedrus*, and in particular by Socrates' apparent readiness, in his central speech, to treat the philosopher as *mad* (244aff.). The beginning of the process of recollection of the Forms is described in terms of an encounter between lover and beloved: the beauty of a particular individual stirs the memory in the lover of Beauty Itself, and he is driven out of his wits by it, behaving in all the usual ways that lovers do – except that he manages to curb his lusts (in the shape of the black horse). The eventual outcome is a common life of philosophy, in which both older and younger partner recognize the real source of their original passion. Thus, paradoxically, a life of reason has its source in the opposite state, a kind of god-given madness which Socrates compares to that of the seer and prophet, of the religious initiate, and of the divinely inspired poet. But the paradox is clearly deliberate, and in fact the overtly crazy behaviour of the philosophical lover is restricted wholly to the first stage, when he first falls in love, as he supposes with the beloved himself; after that, he recovers himself, and only appears crazed to the outside world, for neglecting ordinary concerns.[33] Yet at the same time the context shows that we are supposed to imagine him still in an 'inspired' state, still 'in love', since his mind remains directed towards, among other objects, the one – Beauty – which originally stirred him to passion. In the *Symposium* we find what is recognizably a variant of this picture of the philosopher as lover. Having begun by falling in love with a particular beautiful individual, he will be led (by a mysterious guide)[34] ultimately to acknowledge the splendour of the Form from which that individual and all other beautiful things derive their beauty, and transfer his allegiance to that.

What emerges with particular clarity from the *Phaedrus* is that it is *reason itself* which longs for Beauty. What is stirred by the vision and the memory of beauty (and Beauty) is primarily the charioteer himself, though the second horse, from the philosophical point of view unfortunately, also responds in its own way. In fact, Plato consistently treats the reasoning part as having its own desires and its own pleasures. The lower parts of the soul cannot redirect themselves towards higher objects, since they just are those parts of the soul with which we desire respectively food, drink, etc., or honour. A horse cannot become a charioteer, nor can what we might call an instinct, unrefined by thought and reflection (a description which at least fits the 'appetitive' part), be turned into a rational wish, though both spirit and appetite may be trained to desire and enjoy those things in their respective spheres which reason determines to be right for them.[35] Of course, any time and energy spent on those things which are attractive to the lower elements mean less time and energy for higher things, and vice versa; and this makes it natural for Socrates to use the image of the diversion of a stream, as he does in the *Republic*: 'we recognize, I suppose, that if a person's desires incline vigorously towards one thing, they are by this degree weaker in other directions, like a stream which has been diverted into that other channel'.[36] But the desires themselves remain distinct. The desire for, and impulse towards, Beauty and the other Forms, the objects of reason and intellect, must therefore belong to the reasoning part itself.

In that case the opposition in Plato between rational and irrational is not a simple one between reason and desire, except in so far as 'desire' is identified with the lower or bodily desires. This point coincides with the consistent way in which (as we have seen) philosophy is described in the dialogues, as above all a *passionate* pursuit. If philosophy is not literally *erōs*, passionate sexual love, because that must be directed towards people, it is nevertheless like it, and – so Socrates claims, on Plato's behalf – it provides a degree of fulfilment far greater than what we can expect from ordinary *erōs*. The way in which the *Symposium* puts the philosopher's goal, as a kind of union with the forms, at first sight suggests the sublimation of sexual passion. But if that entails the desire for one thing, sexual union, being satisfied by another, 'being with' Beauty, such a scenario is – as I have already argued – incompatible with Platonic tripartition, and it is equally incompatible with any other conception of the soul which is represented in the dialogues (in the *Symposium* itself Socrates says nothing about what the soul is, or is like, just as he says nothing about its mortality or immortality). In terms of tripartition, the model for the soul adopted by that other dialogue on love, the *Phaedrus*, the 'ascent of love' would rather be a matter of the disguised substitution of the fulfilment of one sort of desire for the fulfilment of another.[37] But so remarkable will the experience of the philosopher's 'erotic' initiation be, on Socrates' account, that he will never miss what he once left behind.

The idea of reason as itself desiring and passionate also not only fits, but is demanded by, the sort of view of the soul which we found Plato favouring in the *Phaedo*, and to which he returns at the end of the *Republic*, even after having argued at length for tripartition.[38] If soul is in its essence rational and unitary, and capable of floating free through the universe, and perhaps especially if it activates and animates bodies, it cannot be pure rationality; thinking about things, even including doing them, by itself moves nothing. That is, without desire a unitary rational soul does not look like a remotely plausible candidate as a self-mover or source of movement for other things; it would, as we might put it, just lack a *motive* for doing anything.

Of course, the more reason appears like a separate agent, the greater the problems for the tripartite model. Similarly also in the case of the other parts: it will not be particularly helpful to analyse the soul, as a spring of action, into three more.[39] Perhaps that should encourage us to take seriously Plato's hint at the end of the *Republic*, and to suppose that he ultimately prefers a *Phaedo*-type view. But this is a less than completely satisfactory solution. The prominence of the idea of the tripartite soul, both in the *Republic* and elsewhere, reflects Plato's interest in the fact of internal conflict which it purports to explain, and makes it hard either for us or for him to set it aside. A better conclusion might be just that he finds the arguments for the two conceptions of soul equally balanced, and veers between the two as the context demands, just as he does between the different conceptions of humanity which they imply.

⚭ LITERATURE AND ART ⚭

Plato returns repeatedly to the subject of literature, particularly poetry, and his treatment of the poets is always hostile. One important passage which is often taken as an exception, and as marking a softening in his attitude, in fact includes some of the main themes of his attacks elsewhere. The passage is the one in the *Phaedrus* briefly referred to earlier, where Socrates is introducing the idea of erotic madness, and comparing it to other forms of madness. Third among these is 'possession and madness from the Muses', which issues in 'lyric and the rest of poetry', and 'by adorning countless achievements of past generations educates those who come after' (245a). Socrates contrasts this inspired poetry with poetry produced by someone not affected by the Muses' madness, who 'has been persuaded that after all skill will make him a good enough poet'; the poems of the mad leave those of the sane nowhere.

We should not be misled by the fact that Socrates here claims to be supporting the proposition that 'the greatest of good things come to us through madness, provided that it comes by the gift of the gods' (244a). There are clear signs of playfulness in the context as a whole, and the structure of the passage about the poets echoes the central argument of the little dialogue *Ion*, whose polemical intentions are not in doubt.[40] The poets claim to educate people, which implies that they have something to teach: they know something. But in fact – Socrates argues against Ion – those who are any good are out of their minds, and their poetry has its real source not in them, but in the Muses. In *Republic* X, Socrates reports an ancient quarrel between philosophy and poetry, on the basis (or so it seems) of what the poets have said about people who claim to be wiser than them (607b–c); in Plato's hands, philosophy gives as good as it gets.

The attack on the wisdom of the poets is carried out nowhere more extensively than in the *Republic* itself. Large parts of three of its ten books (II–III, and X itself) are written against poetry, arguing for the conclusion that the poets should be expelled from the ideal city as corrupting influences on the citizens, young or old. So the charge is even stronger: not only do they themselves lack wisdom, but so do their products. Now if these are the products of the Muses, then (since on Plato's view the gods are good and without jealousy or malice) we should expect them to contain the wisdom that the poets, according to the *Ion* and the *Phaedrus*, themselves lack. But in fact, it seems, the argument there is an opportunistic one, whose point is just about the poets' ignorance, and therefore their lack of qualification for a teaching role. 'If, as you say,[41] your poems are inspired,' Socrates asks, in effect, 'won't that mean that they come to you from outside?' To which they would presumably reply that they mean nothing of the sort, only that their poetry either is or seems to be a joint product of skill and something else which they cannot explain; in other words they would simply reject Socrates' simplistic assumption that 'inspiration' excludes human skill.

However there is a serious point behind the strategy of the *Ion*.[42] This is about the way in which poetry works on its audience, and, as it happens, on those who perform it: Ion is a 'rhapsode', a professional performer specializing in Homer, who also lectures about him. Socrates uses the image of a chain of iron rings suspended from a magnet. Each successive ring holds the next, and is held by the previous one, not through any contribution of its own, but in virtue of the force emanating from the original source. Similarly (Socrates claims) poet, performer and audience are simply carried away by the poetry of the Muses; it is in each case a passive process, and an irrational one, which none of them can therefore explain. What gives the simile much of its purchase is that Socrates and Ion agree that the experience, for performer and audience alike, depends on the emotions: the rhapsode feels sorrow and fear with and for the Homeric heroes, and is able to make his listeners do the same.[43]

It is this tendency for poetry to speak to the emotions, or to the irrational part in us, which Plato seems to want to identify as the underlying cause of its faults. The chief evidence for this is in the *Republic*. Socrates' criticisms of poetry – along with the other parts of 'music', in the Greek sense[44] – in Books II–III have to do with the capacity which it has for instilling beliefs and forming character-traits, i.e. those dispositions to behaviour which are referred to under the headings of the virtues and vices. The discussion is about the early education of future philosopher-rulers, and begins with the sorts of stories (*muthoi*, 'myths') which they should be told. The chief purveyors of stories, which are by definition 'untrue' or 'false' (*pseudeis*), either because simply fictional or because actually *lying*, are the poets, beginning with Homer and Hesiod, and many of their productions peddle seriously damaging 'untruths', particularly about the nature of the gods: that Kronos castrated his father Ouranos; that Zeus maltreated *his* father Kronos; that the gods fight and quarrel with one another. Gods must be represented to children as what they are, namely good, causes only of well-being (for our unhappiness, we are ourselves responsible), unchanging, telling only the truth. Only so will our future rulers grow up with the right attitudes towards gods and others who require their respect. Poetic descriptions of Hades constitute another category of untruth: to portray our fate after death as Homer does (and as Plato himself does, in his myths) is 'neither true . . . nor beneficial for those who are going to be good fighters'.[45] Descriptions of great men, and especially of gods, lamenting for the dead are also to be outlawed, on the grounds that if young people fail to laugh at them as they should, they'll be more likely to break into tears themselves; excessive laughter is to go too (in *Iliad* I, Homer has the gods bursting their sides with laughter as the lame Hephaestus bustles about: that won't do). Truthfulness, self-control, endurance – these are the qualities our poets should, and even occasionally do, encourage.

The last parts of Socrates' treatment of 'music' in this context turn out to offer a kind of bridge to his further, and crucial, defence of his position in Book X. The issue is first about how poets should address their audiences: through narrative, where the author speaks as it were for himself, or through *mimēsis*, which here seems to mean something like 'imaginative recreation' (the poet, and then the audience, take on the character being portrayed). The right mode, Socrates suggests, is combination of the two, but with a much greater proportion of straightforward narrative, because the only case where *mimēsis* will be acceptable is when the character involved is that of a good man, and one behaving as a good man should, failing in a few minor respects.[46] Finally, a choice is made about the modes of music which the young should hear, which turn out, unsurprisingly, to be the simpler ones, which contribute either towards the inculcation of warlike traits or towards a disciplined, harmonious, evenness of mind.[47] Both of these sections are essentially about the way in which literature ('music' in the wide sense) reaches into our souls, which is what will form the main plank of the argument in Book X. The allegation is, and will be, that the effects of poetry are insidious; that the poets, through the use of music and of *mimēsis*, sneak past our reasoning selves undetected.[48] The rulers of a good city will take advantage of this powerful instrument, and turn it to good. But this would involve a major reform of poetry. Existing poetry is powerful and *dangerous*.[49]

This explains the space which is devoted to the criticism of literature in the *Republic*, and specifically the way in which Socrates returns to it in the last part of this mammoth work: it is a subject of vital importance. Book X begins with a direct reference back to Books

II–III: 'we were absolutely correct in the way we proposed to found our city, and I say this not least with the subject of poetry in mind' (595a). More precisely, Socrates means 'our complete refusal to allow in all that part of it which is mimetic'. This is somewhat puzzling, since that was not what was proposed (some 'mimetic' elements were to be allowed), and it rapidly becomes clear that the target is going to be *all* existing poets. Thus a little later we find him saying 'So shall we lay it down that all poets [or "experts in the poetic art", *poiētikoi*], beginning from Homer, are *mimētai* of images of virtue and the other things they write about, and don't grasp the truth?'[50] This sentence, however, suggests a solution to the puzzle: Socrates is now attacking poets *in so far as* they are involved in 'imaginative recreation', but at the same time he is treating them as if that were the whole of poetry. The point that poetry could, ideally, contribute to the good life, or even sometimes actually does contribute to it, is now set aside, in favour of all-out attack. The attack in large takes its start from a negative reassessment of the whole idea of *mimēsis*: it is not now a neutral process, taking its colour from what is represented (or re-presented), but is itself something to be suspected and deplored. It is as if the stress had shifted from 'recreation' to 'imaginative'. At any rate, the *mimētai*, the poets, deal in *images* (*eidōla*), by which is clearly meant insubstantial and false images;[51] and these images, Socrates suggests, they present to one of the inferior elements in us.

That this is the basis of his argument in Book X receives confirmation from the continuation of the opening exchange, referred to above. We were absolutely correct in refusing to allow poetry into the city; 'and that we mustn't allow it in seems to me even more evident now that we have divided the soul into its categories'.[52] The complex argument that Socrates now mounts has the sole purpose of relating the effects of poetry to the lower part or parts of the soul, and marking them as bad for that reason.[53] (The usual view is that there are several different arguments involved; but the signs are that Socrates himself regards it as one long argument including a number of subsidiary ones.) We begin from the question about what *mimēsis* in general is. To find an answer to the question, Socrates takes the case of the painter, and contrasts his productions with those of the carpenter, and the Forms which (for the sake of the argument at least) are supposed to be in the carpenter's mind when he makes his bed or his table: the Bed Itself, the Table Itself. These are said to be 'in nature', and if anyone made them, it would have to be a god; by comparison with them, there is something counterfeit even about the carpenter's beds and tables, let alone those that the painter reproduces in his paintings.[54] By Greek counting, this puts the painter's products at third remove from the real thing, and the same will go for all other cases of *mimēsis*. Because *mimētai* (now including the poet) are not dealing with reality, or how things really are, they must inevitably relate to how things *appear* to be. People say that in order to write well, poets must know the truth, but in fact they do not. If they did, they would not be satisfied with recreating mere images (mere surface views of things), but would prefer to try to recreate the real thing: thus if Homer really knew about medicine, he would have been a doctor, and if he knew anything about virtue, he would have been a lawgiver rather than a poet.[55] This is the route by which we reach the conclusion about 'all poets', that they are '*mimētai* of images of virtue', without grasping the truth, for if they do in any way represent good men in their poetry, saying and doing 'virtuous' things, it cannot be because of their knowledge of virtue itself. But they have the techniques which enable them to convince anyone else who is ignorant[56] that they do know something.

Then, after another piece of persuasive description[57] to establish the poets' lack of knowledge, we reach the last stage of the argument. If *mimēsis* operates at third remove from the truth, Socrates asks, to which aspect of the human being does it direct itself? Things may appear to have different shapes and sizes from the ones they really have (so, for example, a stick will appear bent if seen through water); in such cases, reason tells us one thing, which is contradicted by appearances. If we use the principle we used before, in the case of the soul, that the same thing cannot act or be acted upon in opposite ways at the same time, then it follows that the part[58] of the soul which thinks things are other than they really are must be different from the one that 'relies on measure and calculation' (603a), which is of course the best, reasoning or calculating, part; it must therefore be one of the low-grade[59] parts. So any sort of art concerned with *mimēsis* (so, again, poetry too) will be a low-grade sort of mistress, consorting with the low-grade.

There are some problems here: it looks as if we shall need some subrational part which is nevertheless capable of having beliefs (e.g. that 'this stick is bent'), and neither the 'spirited' nor the appetitive part, from descriptions of them in other contexts, looks particularly well suited for having this capacity. In that case, we shall need an extra 'part' of the soul, which is different both from the part that is reasoning or calculating successfully, and from both of the other parts which were argued for in Book IV. In the event, when he comes to the question of which aspect of the mind[60] is affected by poetry, Socrates at first avoids identifying it with either of these original two lower parts, and again simply talks about something which is different from what is best, though it does also take on the features of an individual: 'as for the part which draws us towards recollections of our suffering and towards lamentations, and is insatiable for these – shan't we say that it is unreasoning, and lazy, and fond of cowardice?' (604d). Eventually, however, when he passes on to what he calls 'the greatest charge' against poetry (that it can corrupt even the best), he comes clean: 'And in relation to sex, too, and anger, and all those aspects of the soul which have to do with desire and pain and pleasure,[61] which we say accompany every action, it's the case that poetic *mimēsis* works similar effects [namely, carrying us away, so that we experience violent feelings of the kind that in ordinary life, outside the theatre, we forcibly repress]; for it nourishes these by watering them, when they ought to wither, and sets them in control of us when they themselves ought to be kept under control' (606d). We might fairly conclude that the problems which we saw affecting the original division of soul into 'parts' are back with a vengeance. Even if we allow the general point that poetry appeals to our feelings and emotions, Plato's own case – in Books II–III, but also as reinforced in the early part of Book X – is that it also instils *beliefs*; and in the sort of case which would parallel that of the straight stick which looks bent (while another part of us protests, ever more faintly, that it's straight), those beliefs will apparently have to be attributed to the irrational, unreasoning parts.[62] But the *Timaeus*, for example, located the appetitive part in the belly: can the belly have beliefs?

In the Greek context, that is not quite so absurd a suggestion as it might sound to us, for even Aristotle was prepared to take seriously the suggestion that the heart might be the organ of thought (and if Plato places reason in the head, it may be for peculiar reasons).[63] But on the whole Plato does not seem to want to locate beliefs in the 'irrational' parts; rather he prefers a model according to which our reasoning part is distorted and perverted, ceases to reason clearly, and so begins itself to harbour false notions. That, at any rate, appears to be what is entailed by the idea of the domination of the individual soul by the lower parts – which is precisely the idea which seems to re-emerge in the final stage of the argument ('sets them in control of us'). In terms of this model, poetry would work on, encourage, and 'water' the irrational parts, so that they came to shake the beliefs held by the reasoning part. In other words, it is not a case of contrary *beliefs* at all,[64] except in so far as poetry, in addressing the emotions and encouraging their expression, can be said to teach something ('that it is appropriate to give oneself over to violent emotions') which is contrary to what reason itself would teach. Whether that is, philosophically, a good position to adopt is another matter; what is clear is that it is the one Socrates finally reaches.

Plato's most prominent targets are usually, as in the *Ion*, the 'tragic', or 'serious', poets,[65] with Homer in first place because of his dominant position in Athenian culture. (Socrates speaks – again in

Republic X – of the loving respect for him that he has had since his childhood; even the greatest poet of all, and teacher, is not to be exempted.) But comedy gets its share of attention too; and of course, Socrates specifically claimed to be talking in *Republic* X about all poets, poets of all kinds. Paradoxically, comedy gets a warmer welcome than tragedy in the the imaginary city of Magnesia constructed in the *Laws*. The tragedians would come in and set up in the agora in competition with the lawgivers (in this imaginary case, the philosophical participants in the conversation), using the fine voices of their actors to say about the same practices and institutions, 'not the same things as we do, but for the most part actually the opposite' (*Laws* 817a–c). They would be allowed in only if they could show that they were saying the right things. Comic playwrights, on the other hand, will be useful, even necessary, to provide the citizens with an insight into the ridiculous. At first sight this allows the possibility of a distancing, an intellectual detachment on the part of the audience from dramatic productions, which Plato rarely acknowledges elsewhere.[66] His standard interpretation of audience reaction is exclusively in terms of emotional involvement; and in fact the *Laws* passage is no exception.

The question is about *how* comedy would give us its insights. We get an answer to this question from the *Philebus*, in which Plato develops what may be termed a theory of the dramatic emotions. Socrates is involved in establishing the posssibility of pleasures which are mixed with pain, and finds one of his star examples in tragedy: 'Shall we not find [anger, fear, longing, sorrow, love, envy, spite[67] and so on: i.e. the feelings in general] full of inexpressible pleasures?' So *anger* is undeniably pleasant, as is wailing and lamenting similarly when audiences watch tragedies, and 'enjoy weeping' (*Philebus* 47e–49a). (It is because we enjoy them, of course, that such experiences have the capacity to draw us in.) With comedies too, Socrates goes on, our state of mind is the same: a combination of pleasure and pain. The feeling that comedy arouses in us is 'spite' (*phthonos*),[68] which along with other feelings has been agreed to be a 'pain of the soul' (or, as we might put it, a 'mental pain': one which does not have its source in the body). What we find comic or absurd is other people suffering misfortune, and especially the misfortune of not knowing their own limitations. They can think they are richer than they are, or better physical specimens than they really are. But the commonest delusion they suffer is about 'the things of the soul', especially wisdom. Now those in this last condition, if they are strong and powerful, are not objects of amusement at all, but dangerous and frightening, whether we encounter them in real life or in the theatre; it is only if they are weak and unable to defend themselves that they are amusing. So, Socrates concludes, 'our argument now indicates to us that in laments, in tragedies and in comedies,[69] not only on the stage but in the whole tragedy and comedy of life, pains are mixed in together with pleasures.'[70]

By this point, it has become obvious that what he is talking about is not actual comedy and comic audiences, but what comedy should be, and what its audience can and should get from it. By learning to laugh at the right things in the theatre, we will laugh at them, and avoid them, in life itself (and for Plato's Socrates, nothing is more to be avoided than ignorance and the pretence of wisdom). We will learn it through our feelings, by the same sort of process of habituation that the children of Callipolis in the *Republic* learned how to react to death and loss. But this will entail a new kind of comedy, which actually knows what is truly ridiculous. So also in the *Laws*: the comic play-wrights will have to change their act as much as the tragedians would have to change theirs. But there is no need for them, as there is for their comic counterparts, because a substitute is available: '*we* are ourselves poets, according to our ability,' says the Athenian who leads the conversation, 'of the finest and best tragedy there is; so our whole constitution is established as a *mimēsis* of the finest and best life, the very thing we for our part say is genuinely a tragedy of the truest kind.'[71]

No existing poet, then, whether tragic (or 'serious') or comic, knows the truth which his medium is potentially able to convey. This is one of the themes of the *Symposium*, in which Socrates meets, among others, two playwrights: Aristophanes, on the one hand, pre-eminent among writers of comedy, and Agathon, who has just won a victory with his tragedies (the occasion for the dinner-party). By the end of the proceedings, most of the company is asleep, but Socrates is still talking to the two poets, and 'compelling them to agree that it belongs to the same man to know how to write comedy and tragedy, and that the one who has the expertise to write tragedy will also be able to write comedy' (*Symposium* 223c–d). He has to 'compel' them to agree (by means of argument, of course) because, by and large, tragedians of the day did not write comedies nor comic writers tragedies,[72] and Agathon and Aristophanes were certainly cases in point. What lies behind Socrates' proposition is that anyone who knows about one member of a pair of opposites or contraries in a given sphere will know about the other. In just this way, he argues against Ion (in the *Ion*) that if he is an expert on Homer, best of poets, he ought to be equally expert on those who handle the same things in an inferior way; good and bad poetry must be objects of the same knowledge. The implication is that neither Agathon nor Aristophanes really knows his trade, and this has been demonstrated at length in the course of the dialogue, both through the juxtaposition of their speeches with Socrates' (every person at the feast has to make a contribution on the subject of *erōs*) and, in Agathon's case, through the demolition by Socrates of virtually everything he says.[73]

This represents a striking and paradoxical extension of the argument of the *Ion* and *Republic*. Socrates' claim – and since it seems to be given special emphasis, it is a claim that Plato evidently wants us to take seriously – is not only that poets are ignorant about the sorts of matters about which they pretend to teach, but that they do not even know about *poetry*. In fact, this second point follows directly from the first: existing poets are ignorant about poetry just because they are ignorant about the things they ought to be teaching. Poetry, for Plato, cannot avoid its teaching role, because it is so powerful; it must therefore get things right (for there is only one way of being right, certainly in the most important matters), and if it does not, then it must be at best bowdlerized and at the worst rooted out and replaced with something more reliable. What that might be is directly indicated by the Athenian in the *Laws*, when he describes the account that he and his partners in the conversation have given of the constitution of Magnesia as 'the finest and best tragedy we can write'. The *Symposium* itself will be a mixture of tragedy and comedy: comedy, because it puts comic figures like Aristophanes and Agathon on the stage,[74] and 'tragic' to the extent that, through its portrayal of Socrates (both as a character in the dialogue and as the object of Alcibiades' encomium) it is a '*mimēsis* of the finest and best life', which the *Laws* passage declared to be the truest kind of tragedy.

The consequence is that Plato himself is the true poet – not that he himself ever claims it, since he was not there to claim anything (he is mentioned only twice, with apparent casualness, in the whole corpus, and never appears as a character). But this in itself raises a familiar question. If poetry is such a bad thing, and he attacks it so regularly, why does he so regularly borrow (or appropriate) its methods? That he does so will be true even without the argument just derived from the *Symposium* and the *Laws*, if it is an essential feature of poetry that it appeals to the irrational in us,[75] since the dialogues themselves frequently combine reasoned argument with techniques which rely directly on an emotional response from the reader (stories, persuasive descriptions, analogies, and so on).[76] The answer is straightforward enough: Plato uses such methods precisely because he recognizes their power, and because he is in business to persuade us. In any case he repeatedly suggests that poetry itself might be useful. It is only because existing poetry embraces ideals and teaches notions which are so different from his own that he must reject it (reluctantly, if he is anything like his Socrates). In particular, it portrays life in all its complexity and plurality, when – as he sees it – it should be describing the single, simple, best life.[77]

445

In the *Phaedrus*, Plato formulates a theory of philosophical writing in terms of 'rhetoric', the art of addressing audiences through the spoken and written word. In the ideal Platonic world, rhetoric too – normally the property of politicians and others allegedly more interested in style than in substance – would be reformed and become the ally rather than the opponent of philosophy.[78] The ideal writer will be someone who knows about both his subject and the nature of the soul, who is able to 'discover the form [of discourse] which fits each nature, and so arrange and order his *logos* [i.e. what he speaks or writes], offering a complex soul complex *logoi* containing all the modes, and simple *logoi* to a simple soul' (*Phaedrus* 277b–c). The 'simple' soul here appears to be the one dominated by reason, while the 'complex' or 'variegated' (*poikilos*, 'many-coloured') soul for its part recalls the democratic type of individual in *Republic* VIII, in whom no single element or desire is in firm control; for the latter, Plato acknowledges that a purely rational mode of address will not be sufficient, and will need to be supplemented by other means. Playing on the emotions of one's audience will cause nothing but trouble in the hands of the ignorant, whether he is an orator or a poet; for the knowledgeable writer and teacher, it is an indispensable tool if he is to address any but those already persuaded of the value of philosophy.

A distinction of the sort in the *Phaedrus* passage, between the simple and the 'many-coloured' is central to Plato's thinking about literature and art in general. The simple, straightforward, and unmixed tends to be identified as good; the varied, and especially what is *innovative*, as bad. The most extreme statement of such an idea is probably in the *Philebus*, where Socrates is identifying 'true', i.e. pure and unmixed, pleasures. These are related to beautiful colours and shapes; they include 'most pleasures of smell, and those of hearing', all those cases where there is no antecedent or concomitant pain. He then explains what he means by a beautiful shape in this context. It is not what 'the many' would mean by it, pointing to a living creature or a painting, but rather

> something straight – so my account goes – and (something) round, and then from these the planes and solids that are produced with lathes and with rulers and squares. For these I say are not beautiful in relation to something, like other things,[79] but are always beautiful in themselves, and have their own peculiar pleasures ... and colours too which have this characteristic ...
>
> (*Philebus* 51c–d)

Also included are smooth, clear sounds, which issue in some single pure tune; these too are beautiful 'in themselves'. This simplicity is what delights the rational mind, the mind of the Platonic mathematician;

446

to it are opposed the intense and numerous pleasures of 'the many', the non-philosophical. Behind the whole idea is perhaps the contrast between the uniqueness of truth, in the Platonic view, and the multiple ways available for going wrong (we may think of the image in *Republic* X, which represents reason as a man, the appetitive part as a many-headed beast). It follows, of course, that innovation must mean deviation; the *Laws* deplores the decline in standards of literature and music at Athens, caused by too much attention to what the audience demands. But what ignorant people demand is no proper criterion of excellence in art of any kind. Art sinks deep into our souls;[80] if we are to live in an ordered society, peopled by ordered souls, art must be controlled by the best element in us.[81]

 NOTES

1 As will become clear, our word 'mind' and the Greek word traditionally translated as 'soul' (*psuchē*) are not synonymous. But they are closely related, and what Plato says about *psuchai* or 'souls' will often have equal plausibility if applied to 'minds'; and both terms are in any case fairly elastic.

2 There is certainly a gulf between the conception of 'soul' with which Socrates operates in the 'early' dialogues at large and the 'soul' which, in the traditional, Homeric picture, flits off into the underworld at death. 'Soul', with Socrates, seems generally to refer to human beings in their moral aspect: so, for example, he urges us to 'care for our souls' by acquiring knowledge and virtue. A soul or 'shade' in the Homeric underworld, by contrast, is merely a mindless, insubstantial image of our physical selves.

3 In a traditional context, the idea of an *immortal* soul – one which continues to be alive, permanently, despite the intervention of death – has no place (see preceding note); and the exchanges between the characters of the *Symposium*, for all their intellectual and artistic pretensions, are firmly embedded in such a context: even Socrates frames his decidedly radical ideas in (deceptively) familiar language.

4 'Soul' in this medical context covers the 'mental' aspects of the human organism, as opposed to those physical aspects which are more immediately accessible to the doctor's art. For the evidence from the doctors, see Claus [12.4]; and for another, but somewhat different, philosophical development of this contrast, see Vlastos [6.47].

5 In Homer, the existence of the dead is famously unenviable; the *Odyssey* portrays the once proud Achilles there in the underworld, openly declaring that he would rather be alive and a hired labourer than a king and dead. But there is also an equivalent to the Platonic philosopher's heaven, in the shape of the Isles of the Blessed; quite what the criteria are for entry is unclear, though Menelaus qualifies by having been the husband of a daughter of Zeus.

6 For Plato, as for Socrates, virtue – or at any rate premium grade virtue – probably always remains conditional on philosophical knowledge.

7 Mystery religions, such as the one associated with Eleusis in Attica, promised not so much immortality as *something*, and something desirable, for the initiated after death; but immortality, and an immortal soul, certainly played a role in Pythagoreanism, along with other ideas like that of the soul's transmigration, after the death of the original organism, into another body.

8 Plato's attitudes towards women are ambivalent: on the one hand, he has a low opinion of women as they actually are, comparing them for their irrationality with slaves and children; on the other, he is prepared to admit that some women have the potential to become philosophers, and there is some scattered, but good, evidence that women attended the Academy.

9 See especially *Timaeus* 89d–90d.

10 In some places, e.g. in the myth at the end of the *Phaedo* (114 c; see also 82 b–c), there are hints that exceptional souls may escape altogether. But it would be hard to distinguish between this kind of fate and becoming a god; and in general the dialogues seem to maintain a firm distinction between human and divine. One of the *loci classici* is at *Phaedrus* 278d, where Socrates says that to his mind, the title 'wise' (*sophos*) belongs only to gods, and the most to which human beings can aspire is to be called 'lovers of/seekers for wisdom', i.e. philosophers (*philo-sophoi*). That appears to be contradicted by the *Republic*, which describes a city where philosophers have attained wisdom, and are thus qualified to rule; but that should probably count as part of the evidence for treating that central dialogue primarily – in its political aspects – as a thought-experiment.

11 Wisdom is 'what we desire and say we are lovers of' (*Phaedo* 66e), where 'lover' is *erastēs*, the person who experiences *erōs* or sexual love for someone else.

12 The *Phaedo* is subtitled 'On Soul', which is certainly of fairly late origin, but is a reasonable indication of the main emphasis of the dialogue; at any rate, no other Platonic work has more to say directly about the subject.

13 See especially *Phaedo* 66b–68b.

14 Thus at 68e–69d wisdom has value because of its role in the production of the (other) virtues; and in the myth at the end of the dialogue, the catalogue of the rewards and punishments of the dead includes philosophers at one end and the worst criminals at the other.

15 The idea of the body as the prison of the soul was evidently in origin Pythagorean; the negative view of life which it implies is certainly not maintained consistently in Plato's dialogues. For him, the universe we know is not only the best of all possible universes, but also, in so far as it can be described as the work of reason, *good* (as the *Timaeus* tells us at length; cf. also *Phaedo* 98b–99c), and it seems to follow that life within such a universe must have positive value.

16 Although the *Phaedo* does include talk of the desires etc. 'of the body', it is unlikely that we should take this at face value. Without soul to bring life to it, the body is merely inert matter, and unable either to do or to feel anything.

17 The issue arises specifically in relation to the third argument for immortality, the so-called 'affinity' argument: see Rowe [12.18] and [12.2], 189.

18 In so far as that content would be memorable, in a Platonic world, it would

be *true*; but in that case it would not distinguish any one excellent soul from another.

19 The chief difference will be that in the one case the soul can evidently lose its irrationality altogether, while in the other it must permanently retain it – if irrationality is part of its essence. Yet a soul which is both out of a body and has been trained to separate itself from 'bodily influences' might perhaps be said to have irrational elements only *potentially*, and then only if it is bound to be reincarnated. It might be partly this that Plato has in mind when in the *Timaeus* he calls the two lower parts 'mortal' (69e).

20 *Republic* 498d suggests that arguments heard in a previous life might affect a soul in a subsequent one; and evidently, if what was a human soul passes into the body of a donkey, that must have something to do with what that soul had become in its previous occupation of a body (i.e. donkey-like). But neither that soul nor any other will have any evidence to connect it with the earlier human person; it cannot even be inferred that Ned (the donkey) was previously Fred (a man), since donkeys' souls may presumably also have previously animated donkeys.

21 Elsewhere (*Phaedrus* 249b–c) it looks as if Plato may envisage a partial recollection of the Forms, which explains the formation of concepts presupposed by the ordinary, everyday use of language; but in the *Phaedo* what is being talked of is an experience which is evidently restricted to philosophers.

22 *Phaedrus* 246dff. According to the *Meno* (86a), the soul is perpetually in a state of *having* learned the knowledge in question, which seems to imply that there never was a point at which we actually acquired it.

23 In the *Meno*, the theory of recollection is introduced to resolve the general question about how one can look for something one doesn't know, or recognize it when one has found it. It is evidently the vividness of the experience in question, together with the way that what we remember allows things to *make sense*, which is supposed to rule out the possibility of false memory.

24 This expression should not be pressed too hard. The Forms, which are the objects of knowledge for the soul, are apparently 'outside' time and space altogether; divine souls (gods), on the other hand, appear to be part of the natural universe (except in the case of the creator god of the *Timaeus* – but whether we are supposed to believe literally in his existence is unclear), which is where all discarnate souls also seem to be located; on death souls simply move to some less well-known, but nevertheless physical, location.

25 An underlying assumption of the *Timaeus* is that if the world is as good as it can be, it cannot be any other way than it is, and will include all possible types of creatures.

26 From this perspective, the description of these two parts as 'mortal' (see n. 19) looks natural enough, in so far as their presence is a consequence of the soul's function in relation to the body, and the compound of soul and body is itself mortal. They would be actually mortal if a soul finally and permanently escaped the bodily condition.

27 The word is *sumphutos* (246a).

28 As Johansen points out to me, on the account in the *Phaedo* it is perhaps only the presence of the irrational or the 'bodily' which prevents the full flowering of the rational soul. But elsewhere, e.g. in the *Republic*, the removal of (undue)

irrational influences is only a necessary, not a sufficient, condition of the acquisition of wisdom; training is required, and even if this is translated into terms of *anamnēsis*, it is not obviously just a matter of seeing off the irrational parts.

29 This is the traditional, and unsatisfactory, English rendering of the Greek *thumos*, which is connected primarily with anger and indignation.

30 For Plato, what is natural is not what is normally the case, but rather what should be the case, even if it rarely or never is.

31 Spirit, it seems, can and may listen to reason, like an animal adapted for domestication, and yet speaks the same language as the appetitive part, pitching emotion (especially shame, the reverse side of honour) against emotion. (The appetitive part is summed up in the image of the many-headed beast in *Republic* IX: even if it has some tame or domesticated heads, it cannot be reliably domesticated as a whole, only restrained and cut back.) Yet reason too has its own desires (see later in this section), and if so, it can apparently control the appetites directly, by opposing its own drives to them. In that case, it is not clear why it needs its alliance with the spirited part, however appropriate the corresponding idea might be on the political level; there reason, in the shape of the philosopher-rulers, will need a police force, for fear of being overwhelmed by the sheer numbers of the lowest group in society.

32 This analysis, in Books VIII and IX of the *Republic*, may be compared with the simpler one at the end of the *Statesman*, where the king or statesman's chief role is identified as the weaving together of the more aggressive and competitive type of citizen with the quieter and milder.

33 249d–e. It is in this sort of context that the description of Plato as *appropriating* other forms of discourse (see earlier in this section) seems particularly apt: the philosopher does everything the ordinary lover does (251dff.), but for entirely different reasons, and his experience is far more fulfilling than anything that ordinarily goes under the heading of *erōs* or sexual love.

34 The description – in the main part of Socrates' contribution to the banquet, which he puts in the mouth of the imaginary priestess Diotima – is couched in terms of an initiation, and an initiate would no doubt have had an instructor. If we see the 'ascent of love' as in part an allegory of a philosophical education, the guide will be the master-dialectician (I owe this suggestion to Robin Hard).

35 The reasoning part, by contrast, seems to be adaptable: *it* can be corrupted, and be pressed into the service of either of the other two parts (cf. *Republic* 587a). On the possibility of a different model of the relationship between reason and the irrational, in the *Symposium*, see especially n. 37 below.

36 *Republic* 485d; Socrates is here talking of the philosopher, and the way in which his preoccupation with 'the pleasure of the soul' will lead him to neglect 'those through the body', i.e. those which reach the soul through the senses.

37 It may be objected (and Penner in fact objected) that if Socrates does not introduce the topic of tripartition in the *Symposium*, we have no particular justification for introducing it ourselves, apart from what we think we can derive from conclusions about the relative chronology of the dialogues (the *Symposium* is normally classified as 'middle', along with the *Phaedrus* and the *Republic*). If so, then we might in principle try interpreting the *Symposium* in terms of the ('Socratic') *Lysis*, which treats of *erōs* without bringing in irrational desires: there are only beliefs about what is good, together with a generalized

desire for what is in fact good. This option is attractive, particularly in so far as the lover's advance in the *Symposium* is described in strikingly intellectual terms (there is at any rate little blind passion in evidence in the context). However, since an alternative explanation of this feature is available, namely in terms of the chosen metaphor of initiation, there is ultimately no more justification for importing this model of the Platonic soul than for importing the other one. What the *Symposium* offers, through the figure of Socrates, is above all a picture of how an individual's concerns may be redirected from (in Platonic terms) a lower to a higher level – a picture which is short on philosophy but long on persuasion.

38 'It is not easy . . . for what is put together out of many parts, and that not in the finest way, to be eternal': so Socrates says, having offered another attempt at proof of the immortality of the soul. He then makes his suggestion that the tripartite analysis applies to the soul as it appears in this life, encumbered with a body and its accoutrements as the sea-god Glaucus is with barnacles and seaweed (611bff.).

39 As Crombie points out ([10.36] 1: 354), it is a necessary consequence of the argument of *Republic* IV that the parts are genuinely independent, since otherwise the principle (that the same thing cannot act or be acted upon in opposite ways at the same time) will be broken. But in that case there will be no such thing as a person's soul (in the singular), or even a person, or self. (In the next section, we shall discover a further problem with Plato's use of the principle in question.)

40 The clinching point is the low position of the poet in the grading of lives at *Phaedrus* 248d–e (sixth, after e.g. the earthbound gymnastic trainer and doctor, only just before the craftsman and farmer, then the sophist and the demagogue, and finally the tyrant). Lyric poetry, singled out in 245a, also figured earlier in the dialogue, at 235c, in the shape of the 'beautiful' Sappho and the 'wise' Anacreon, love-poets whom Socrates identified as possible sources for his own (inspired, poetic: 238c–d) praise of the *non*-lover. So much for his view of their 'divine inspiration'.

41 See e.g. Hesiod, *Theogony* 22–8.

42 The dialogue as a whole falls into three parts: (1) Socrates argues that Ion cannot perform or lecture on Homer through skill or understanding; (2) he must therefore be able to do it by divine gift (i.e. by being inspired or maddened); then (3) when Ion protests that what he has to say about Homer is anything but crazy, Socrates presses him to say what knowledge it is that he has about his subject, and when he cannot identify this knowledge, he has to choose between either saying he is no good at what he does, or that he does it in the way Socrates has suggested, i.e. by virtue of a kind of madness.

43 *Ion* 535d–e. There is a considerable degree of sleight of hand in Socrates' handling of Ion at this point. He first asks whether 'we should call sane a person who, adorned in colourful dress and golden crowns, weeps at sacrifices and festivals, when he hasn't lost any of these [namely, valuable possessions], or who is afraid when he's standing among more than twenty thousand people who like him, and no one has stripped him or done him wrong?' I suppose you must have a point, replies Ion. Socrates' next move is then to suggest that performers like Ion 'do the same' to the majority of their audience – which

Ion understands to refer to his ability to move them to emotion, while Socrates takes it as referring to his making them *mad*.

44 I.e. *mousikē*, which is broadly that part of human culture which belongs to the Muses, though usually it covers poetry and music, with or without dance, all three of which might be combined in performance (as for example in the theatre).

45 386b–c. Given that Plato himself fails to follow the instructions he puts into Socrates' mouth, e.g. to 'throw away all the horrible and frightening names, like Cocytus and Styx' (deployed to magnificent effect e.g. in the eschatological myth of the *Phaedo*), there must be more than a suspicion that the second criterion is more important than the first.

46 Or, alternatively, on those few occasions when a bad character happens to be behaving well. The asceticism of Socrates' approach to literature is mitigated slightly at this point (396d–e), when he is allowed to acknowledge that the listener might adopt an unworthy persona 'for the sake of amusement'. Occasionally, too, he hints at a feeling for the 'poetic' which is separate from the question about poetic 'truth': so e.g. at 387b, when he is talking about descriptions of Hades (though the concession 'not unpoetic' is immediately taken away by 'and pleasant for the many, *hoi polloi*, to listen to').

47 These are, interestingly, the two sorts of character that reappear at the end of the *Statesman* (cf. n. 32), but as two sorts of character-*types*, needing to be reconciled.

48 See especially 401c.

49 In 400cff., Socrates broadens out the argument to make it apply to all craftsmen: they must not make 'bad character, lack of self-control, meanness or unshapeliness' part of their productions, whether these are paintings or buildings or anything else; we must look for those craftsman who are 'able by their natural disposition to track down the nature of the beautiful and the well-formed' (401a). Growing up among beautiful things will encourage conformity with the true beauty of wisdom. All of this hints at, without fully articulating, a kind of theory of beauty.

50 600e. For the sense in which what the poets recreate are already *images*, see following paragraph.

51 They must be insubstantial and false because they are based on ignorance; poets go only by superficial appearances, Plato suggests – and by offering images of images (see following paragraph).

52 The word is again *eidē*, 'kinds of thing'.

53 It is not that the lower parts are necessarily bad, of course (though the image of the human soul at 588b might give one cause for doubt at least about the lowest part, which is represented as a many-headed monster with some tame heads). Rather it is that the effect of poetry is so strong that it encourages the development of the irrational in us, which it is our business to keep in check.

54 596e–597b. The Form of bed is somehow *the* bed ('what [a] bed is', which is represented as *the real thing*: 597d), while the carpenter simply makes *a* bed, which 'something of the same sort as' the Form; the painter only 'makes' his bed 'in a certain way'.

55 Or again (600a), if he knew anything about generalship, he would have fought wars rather than writing about them. (That is, so Socrates implies, he would

have been a truly expert general – or doctor, or lawgiver – who 'looks to' the relevant Forms, like the carpenter.) This is one of many clear echoes of the *Ion* in this part of *Republic* X: what finally induces Ion's capitulation is his inability to explain why he hasn't actually been elected a general, if he knew about generalship (from Homer).

56 I.e. the majority of mankind. Plato begins from the assumption that poetry appeals to a mass audience, not just to a few; Greek epic and drama are from his perspective (and, on the evidence, in fact) parts of mass culture.

57 The painter may paint a picture of something useful, like a bridle. Now in this sort of case, it is the person who actually uses the thing who really knows about it; the craftsman who makes it just follows the instructions of the user, and so – as Socrates puts it – has merely 'belief' about what makes a good example of whatever it is in question (we should call it 'second-hand knowledge'). The painter, for his part, will be able to paint it without having either knowledge or 'belief'. Once again, the painter stands in for all *mimētai*, and what holds true of him is extended to all the rest; so the poet too, in so far as he is a *mimētēs*, will have a 'charming (lack of) relationship to wisdom', and his only criterion of success will be what appeals to the many. (But we know from earlier parts of the dialogue – see e.g. 590c–d – that the many are controlled by their appetites . . .)

58 In fact, Socrates works throughout without once using the term 'part' (*meros* or *morion*). Perhaps he is already looking forward to 611aff., when he will express doubts about whether the soul, in its essential nature, can really possess 'parts' at all. But it may also suit his purpose not to identify too precisely the element in the soul to which poetry is supposed to appeal; see following paragraph.

59 This translation of *phaulos* is borrowed from Waterfield [10.15].

60 Literally, the Greek says 'to this very (thing) of the mind (*dianoia*) with which the mimetic (art) of poetry associates' (603b–c), where *dianoia* suggests some kind of rational or intellectual capacity.

61 I.e. as the context shows, the 'aspects of the soul' ('aspects' is supplied, for the plain neuter plural of adjectives in the Greek) to do with lower desires and pleasures.

62 'We said, didn't we, that it was impossible to think (*doxazein*) opposite things simultaneously with the same (thing) simultaneously?' 'And we were correct to say it.' 'Then what in the soul thinks contrary to the (actual) measurements [i.e. the thing as measured by the reasoning part] will not be the same as what thinks in accordance with them' (602e–603a).

63 Specifically, that reason moves in circles (or can be represented figuratively as doing so, on the model of the motions of the heavens), and that the head is adapted to containing circular movements in virtue of its roughly spherical shape; see *Timaeus* 34bff., 42eff.

64 Even with the bent stick, it seems unnecessary to insist that the soul at any point both thinks that it is straight and thinks that it is bent; either it is confused (*tarachē*, 602c), or one belief comes to replace the other. The capacity of the 'best part' to see that the stick is straight, if only the 'appearance' were absent, seems to be treated as itself an enduring belief in its straightness. This is intelligible, in so far as the rational part is thought of as our essential selves.

65 These are defined, in Plato, primarily by contrast with the comic poets, who deal in the ridiculous or absurd (see following paragraph).

66 At *Republic* 396e, the concession that good citizens might sometimes impersonate inferior types 'for the sake of amusement' may refer to jesting in ordinary life rather than to the theatre. (For the idea that they must *recognize* inferior or aberrant behaviour, see *Republic* 396a.)

67 The term is *phthonos*, which normally means something like envy, jealousy, or the feeling of someone who begrudges something; later in the *Philebus* it will be used specifically to mean taking pleasure in other people's misfortunes.

68 See n. 67.

69 'And in comedies' is not in the transmitted text, but seems indispensable to the sense of the argument.

70 *Philebus* 50b. Quite where the pain comes in is something of a puzzle; why should *phthonos* be treated as a 'pain of the soul', rather than simply a pleasure?

71 *Laws* 817b. The negative connotations of the term *mimēsis* which were present in *Republic* X are clearly absent here.

72 Cf. *Republic* 394e: 'the same people, I imagine, cannot even produce good examples of *mimēsis* in those cases where the genres seem close to one another, such as when they write tragedy and comedy'. Tragedians certainly wrote satyr-plays, which have strong comic elements but were evidently still regarded as a distinct form.

73 No such demolition of Aristophanes' speech takes place, and many readers find his whimsical, moralizing tale so sympathetic that they look for a positive role for it within the argument of the dialogue. Its main point from Plato's perspective, however, seems to be the way in which it stresses the incompleteness of mere physical union, while being unable to suggest anything to replace it. It is Socrates, of course, who fills the gap.

74 According to the criterion suggested by the *Philebus*, both are ridiculous or laughable (*geloios*) in so far as they lay claim to a wisdom which they in fact lack.

75 See earlier discussion of *Republic* X; cf. also 387b.

76 The use of dialogue form is itself another case in point; even where its dramatic possibilities are not developed to any great extent, elements like the perceived relationship between the interlocutors help to shape our attitude to what is being said, and make it more than a matter of the simple assessment of the strength and weakness of the arguments.

77 See Gould [12.6].

78 The new theory of writing in the *Phaedrus* cannot of course be developed explicitly in relation to Plato's own writing, since from the perspective of the fiction itself it is a spoken and not a written context. But that the lessons taught do apply to the dialogues is assured by the generality of the terms in which they are framed.

79 I.e. in this context, relative to some preceding lack or deprivation.

80 *Republic* 401dff. (with reference to all forms of art, including 'music', painting, sculpture, embroidery and so on).

81 I am grateful to Thomas Johansen for his comments on an earlier draft of the first section of this chapter, and to Terry Penner for his, on a second draft of

the whole. Both helped to remove some errors and infelicites; neither may be supposed to be completely content with the final version.

 BIBLIOGRAPHY

Editions

12.1 Dover, K. J. *Plato, Symposium* (Cambridge Greek and Latin Classics), Cambridge, Cambridge University Press, 1980. Greek text with introduction and commentary.

12.2 Rowe, C. J. *Plato, Phaedo* (Cambridge Greek and Latin Classics), Cambridge, Cambridge University Press, 1993. Greek text with introduction and commentary.

Studies

12.3 Bremmer, J. *The Ancient Greek Concept of the Soul*, Princeton, NJ, Princeton University Press, 1983.

12.4 Claus, D. B. *Toward the Soul: An Enquiry into the Meaning of ψυχή before Plato*, New Haven, Conn., Yale University Press, 1981.

12.5 Ferrari. G. R. F. 'Plato and poetry', in G. A. Kennedy (ed.) *The Cambridge History of Literary Criticism*, Cambridge, Cambridge University Press, 1989: 92–148.

12.6 Gould, J. 'Plato and performance', in A. Barker and M. Warner (eds) *The Language of the Cave (Apeiron* 25(4), 1992): 13–26.

12.7 Griswold, C. L., Jr. (ed.) *Platonic Writings, Platonic Readings*, New York and London, Routledge, 1988.

12.8 Keuls, E. C. *Plato and Greek Painting*, Leiden, Brill, 1978.

12.9 Klagge, J. C. and Smith, N. D. (eds) *Methods of Interpreting Plato and his Dialogues (Oxford Studies in Ancient Philosophy* suppl. vol.), 1992.

12.10 Lovibond, S. 'Plato's theory of mind', in S. Everson (ed.) *Companions to Ancient Thought 2: Psychology* (see [3.39]): 35–55.

12.11 Moravcsik, J. and Temko, P. (eds) *Plato on Beauty, Wisdom, and the Arts*, Totowa, NJ, Rowman and Littlefield, 1982.

12.12 Murdoch, I. *The Fire and the Sun: Why Plato Banished the Artists*, Oxford, Clarendon Press, 1977.

12.13 Murray, P. 'Inspiration and *mimēsis* in Plato', in Barker and Warner (see [12.6]): 27–46.

12.14 Nussbaum [11.11].

12.15 Penner, T. 'Socrates on virtue and motivation', in Lee, Mourelatos and Rorty (see [3.43]): 133–51.

12.16 Price [11.14].

12.17 Robinson, T. M. *Plato's Psychology*, Toronto, Toronto University Press, 1970.

12.18 Rowe, C. J. 'L'argument par "affinité" dans le *Phédon*', *Revue Philosophique* 181 (1991): 463–77.

Glossary

Academy: Plato's 'school', which he founded about 387 BC; perhaps, at least in its original conception, mainly a kind of research institute rather than a place of formal teaching.

akrasia: ('weakness of will') a state of moral character, excluded by Socrates but admitted by Plato, whereby passions or pleasures either corrupt practical judgement or cause action contrary to it.

anamnēsis: see 'recollection'.

anthropomorphism: the practice of understanding the gods on the model of humankind, either in physical form or behaviour.

anthuphairesis, antanairesis ('alternate subtraction'): technique (now sometimes called the Euclidean algorithm) used to find the greatest common measure of two magnitudes (if they have one). Given two magnitudes a_1 and a_2, one subtracts the lesser a_2 from a_1 until one has a remainder a_3 less than a_2. If there is no remainder, a_2 is the greatest common measure of a_1 and a_2. If there is a remainder, one applies the same technique to a_3 and a_2, and continues until a common measure is found. It is not difficult to show that if there is a common measure this technique will find the greatest one. Twentieth-century scholars have argued that *anthuphairesis* was the basis of a pre-Euclidean theory of proportion, which they usually associate with Theaetetus. See also 'Commensurable'.

antilogic: see 'dialectic'.

application (*parabolē*) of areas: technique of constructing on a given straight line a figure having a given area and satisfying other conditions (e.g. being a square); one speaks of excess (*hyperbolē*) or deficiency (*elleipsis*) if the construction requires a straight line longer or shorter than the given one. See also 'geometrical algebra'.

aretē: virtue or excellence, a quality possession of which is partly constitutive of the good life. Also used collectively for the totality of such qualities.

aristocracy: (lit. 'rule by the best') rule by an elite, as opposed to democracy ('rule by the people').

Aristotelian: pertaining to Aristotle, the fourth-century BC philosopher.

atom: a necessarily indivisible physical particle.

atomism: the theory which maintains that atoms are the basic constituents of the physical universe.

atomist: an adherent of atomism.

capacity, Socratic: the translation of *dunamis* in Plato's early dialogues. A capacity or power, according to Socrates, is associated with a particular type of activity and a unique object or subject-matter. E.g. the capacity or power of sight is associated with the activity of seeing and its unique object is colour.

collection and division, method of: a method of classification, expounded in some of Plato's later dialogues, in which a general kind or concept is defined by systematically dividing it into its constituent sub-kinds, into which the particulars falling under the kind or concept are grouped or 'collected'.

commensurable (*summetros*): having a common measure, as 24 and 16 have the common measure 8; applied mainly to geometrical magnitudes. See also '*dunamis*'.

concord (*sumphōnia*): harmonious musical interval, the most important being the fourth, fifth and octave.

cosmogony: an account of or theory about the origin or creation of the world order (*cosmos*).

cultural relativism: the awareness that values and conventional practices may be specific to a particular society.

Cynic: pertaining to the Cynic sect, a school of philosophers originating in the fourth century BC, characterized by austerity of life and extreme rejection of conventional social norms. An adherent of that sect.

definitional knowledge: see ' "What is F-ness?" question'.

dialectic: from its original meaning 'discussion' the term 'dialectic' (*dialektikē*) acquired technical senses as follows: (1) (Pre-Platonic) a method of refutation by opposition of contrary theses, also called 'antilogic' (see ch. 7); (2) (Platonic) the preferred method for acquiring knowledge of the Forms (q.v.). In the dialogues of Plato's middle period it is a method of critical argument operating independently of the senses, involving question and answer. When a proposal is found that resists criticism, one may try to further confirm it by deducing it from a 'higher' hypothesis. In the *Republic* the process is somehow grounded in the Form of the Good, but this is not clearly explained. In later dialogues 'dialectic' refers to the method of collection and division (q.v.), but also to argumentation exploring the interrelations between the most general kinds or concepts, such as Being and Difference.

doxography, doxographer: a second-hand compilation of reports about the views of a number of philosophers on some topic or topics. An author of such a compilation.

dunamis: (lit. 'power, capacity, potentiality') as a mathematical term, translated both 'square' and (with some anachronism) 'square root'. Euclid uses the word only adverbially in the dative, speaking of straight lines as being commensurable in *dunamis* (*dunamei*, literally 'in potentiality') when the squares on the lines are commensurable.

eidōlon: (lit. 'image') (1) a technical term of atomism (q.v.) denoting a film of atoms emitted from the surface of, and reproducing the appearance of, a physical object. The impact of streams of *eidōla* on the sense-organs and on the atoms constituting the mind was responsible for perception and thought. (2) (Platonic) an insubstantial image or 'phantom', especially what is produced by inexpert, ignorant *mimētai* (q.v.).

Eleatic: pertaining to the fifth-century BC philosophers Parmenides and Zeno of Elea in South Italy, and to their followers. An adherent of Eleatic doctrine.

elenchus (*elenchos*): (lit. 'refutation, test, cross-examination') a method of argumentation characteristic of Socrates, in which the beliefs of an interlocutor are shown to contain an inconsistency. It is debated whether Socrates is represented as attempting to show by this method that some particular belief of the interlocutor's is false, or merely that the set of his beliefs is inconsistent.

elenctic mission: Socrates' mission, which he appears to have believed to have been divinely inspired, to show by elenchus that his contemporaries lacked the moral wisdom which they claimed.

Epicurean: pertaining to a philosophical school founded by Epicurus at Athens at the end of the fourth century BC, which developed and popularized the doctrines of atomism (q.v.). An adherent of that school.

epimoric (*epimorios*): standing in a ratio of $n + 1$ to n, as three halves, four thirds, etc.

eristic: argument with the aim of defeating one's opponent, independently of truth.

Euclidean geometry: elementary plane geometry, as discovered in the Greek world in the fifth and fourth centuries BC, and expounded in the *Elements* of Euclid (*c*.300 BC). The geometrical constructions permitted are those using straight edge and compass only.

eudaimonism: (from *eudaimonia*, 'happiness, well-being') the view that the good is happiness or faring well. Once articulated by Socrates in the early dialogues of Plato it became a mainstay of ancient moral thought.

exhaustion, method of: modern (somewhat inappropriate) term applied to a rigorous technique of argumentation in which use is made of the possibility of constructing a figure which approximates the area of a given figure within any pre-assigned degree of accuracy. The method is applied in Book XII of Euclid's *Elements* and is thought to have been developed rigorously by Eudoxus in the fourth century.

expertise: a translation of *technē* (also 'art, skill, craft') in the early dialogues of Plato. An instance of expertise must satisfy the following conditions: rationality or regularity, teachability and learnability, explicability, inerrancy, uniqueness, distinctness of subject-matter and knowledge or wisdom. E.g. the expertise of medicine is the special ability to reach in all cases correct judgements concerning health and to engage in health-producing activities.

figurate numbers: modern term used to refer to the representation of positive integers as arrays of dots in simple geometric configurations. E.g. a triangular number would be represented by a sequence of n rows containing in order 1, 2, 3, 4, ... n dots.

final causation: the causation of an event or process by a goal or end towards which the event or process is directed.

Form: (Platonic) an imperceptible, immaterial, eternal, changeless, perfect, intelligible and divine entity which exists apart from and independently of the sensible world. Plato posited Forms in order to explain various aspects of the world and our experience connected with the existence of generality.

geometrical algebra: modern interpretive term applied primarily to the application of areas: the term expresses the idea that underlying the geometric formulation of much of Greek mathematics are concerns familiar from modern algebra.

happiness: see 'eudaimonism'.

heroic code: the range of behaviour held to be acceptable among the heroes of Greek epic poetry.

Hesiodic: pertaining to the archaic Greek poet Hesiod (c.700 BC), author of the *Theogony*, a poem describing the origins and family relationships of gods and goddesses.

Homeric: pertaining to Homer, the poet (?late eighth-cent. BC) to whom the authorship of the two great verse epics, the *Iliad* and the *Odyssey*, was traditionally ascribed.

homoeomerous: (Aristotelian technical term) having all parts of the same nature as the whole. E.g. flesh is a homoeomerous substance, since every part of a piece of flesh is a piece of flesh.

459

incommensurable (*assumetros*): not commensurable.

indifference reasoning: reasoning relying on the Principle of Sufficient Reason. See 'Sufficient Reason, Principle of'.

instrumental, intrinsic: a good is instrumental if it serves as a means towards some distinct end, but intrinsic if it constitutes an end (or part of an end) in itself.

intellectualism, Socratic: a central tenet of Socratic morality, the doctrine that virtue is the expertise (q.v.) of the good, more frequently expressed as 'Virtue is knowledge'.

interval (*diastēma*): loosely defined term corresponding to the 'distance' between two musical pitches, often applied to the ratios associated with those distances.

Ionians: the collective term for those pre-Socratics (q.v.) who came from the Greek cities of Ionia, the central area of the coast of Asia Minor.

irrational: see 'rational'.

logos: this Greek term conveys a range of meanings related to language, calculation, proportion, rationality and system. It can mean 'speech' or 'discourse', or the reason or argument offered in support of a claim. It can also refer to the definition, or formula, that characterizes a thing.

mean (*meson*): a magnitude or number intermediate in size between two others and satisfying some other condition. The most frequently mentioned means between a and b are the geometric, where a is to m as m is to b, the arithmetic, where $a + b = m + m$, and the harmonic or subcontrary where a is to b as $a-b$ is to $m-b$. Sometimes means are referred to as proportionals.

mimēsis: imitation or representation, especially artistic; in Plato generally associated with the production of inaccurate, misleading and insubstantial images or *eidōla* (q.v.).

mimētēs (pl. *mimētai*): a producer of *mimēsis*, e.g. (in Plato) a poet.

moral paradox: the view maintained by Socrates in Plato's early dialogues that no one ever acts viciously except out of ignorance of the good.

natural and unnatural motion: in Aristotelian theory, the natural motion of a substance is that motion which is intrinsic to it, i.e. with which it will move unless prevented (e.g. the motion of earth to the centre of the universe). Unnatural motion is motion contrary to natural motion, imposed on a substance by external force (e.g. the upward motion of a stone when thrown up).

nature (*phusis*): the characteristic nature of a particular natural object or species. By extension the term also comes to mean the nature of things in general, i.e. the characteristic behaviour of the natural world as a whole. Generally opposed to *nomos*, law or convention.

Neoplatonism: a philosophical movement of late antiquity (second century AD on) which saw itself as expounding Plato, and gave an essentially Platonist interpretation of Aristotle and other early philosophers.

nominalist: (opposed to 'realist') adherent of a view that denies the reality of general properties or universals answering to general terms.

oral tradition: the body of stories told by a society or group in which they account for how they arrived at their current position.

Orphic poems: poems with esoteric religious content, related to Pythagoreanism (q.v.), which circulated from the sixth century BC on, and were ascribed to the mythical figure of Orpheus. 'Orphism', a supposedly well-defined set of beliefs or practices independent of Pythagoreanism, is not well attested.

participation: the relation between an individual and a Form (q.v.) which explains why the individual possesses the property answering to the Form.

Platonic: pertaining to Plato.

Platonism, Platonist: the doctrines of a range of schools of thought owing their inspiration to the work of Plato, including the Middle Platonist and Neoplatonist schools of the first to sixth centuries AD. (See also 'Neoplatonism'.) Pertaining to Platonism; an adherent of Platonism.

pre-Socratic: pertaining to the philosophers of the sixth and fifth centuries BC. Strictly speaking, the term is inaccurate, since a number of those philosophers, including Anaxagoras, Democritus and the sophists, were contemporaries of Socrates.

proportion (*analogia*): an expression of the form '*a* is to *b* as *c* is to *d*' (*a* : *b* :: *c* : *d*). See also 'mean'.

Protagorean: pertaining to Protagoras, the fifth-century BC sophist.

protreptic: a method whose aim is to encourage the reader or hearer to seek wisdom.

prudential paradox: the view maintained by Socrates in Plato's early dialogues that no one ever intentionally acts contrary to his or her own good.

Pythagoreanism, Pythagorean: the religious and philosophical doctines and communal life-style traditionally said to have been initiated by Pythagoras (sixth century BC). Pertaining to Pythagoreanism; an adherent of Pythagoreanism.

quadrature (*tetragōnismos*) of a figure: production of a square equal in area to a given figure.

ratio (*logos*): a loosely defined term for the relation of one magnitude to another; if *a* is to *b* as *c* is to *d*, then *a* is said to have the same ratio to *b* as *c* has to *d*.

rational (*rhētos*) and **irrational** (*alogos*): In Book X of Euclid's *Elements*, the terms are defined for straight lines relative to a given straight line *l* in such a way that a straight line is called rational if it is commensurable (q.v.) with *l* or if the square with it as side is commensurable with the square with side *l*; otherwise the line is called irrational. This means that, for example, the diagonal of the square with side *l* is irrational. The ancient terms closest to the modern mathematical terms 'rational' and 'irrational' are 'commensurable' and 'incommensurable', but even in their case one has to note differences in style and content between ancient and modern mathematics.

realist: see 'nominalist'.

recollection (*anamnēsis*): Plato's belief, expressed in the *Phaedo*, that we are born with latent knowledge of the Forms (q.v.) acquired before birth, and that we can recover this knowledge through enquiry. In the *Phaedo* recollection explains our possession of general concepts, while in the *Meno* it explains our ability to discover general non-empirical truths. The *Meno* does not, however, explicitly connect recollection to the theory of Forms.

regular solids: the convex polyhedra contained by congruent equilateral and equiangular plane figures: the triangular pyramid contained by four equilateral triangles, the octahedron contained by eight such triangles, the icosahedron contained by twenty, the cube contained by six squares, and the dodecahedron contained by twelve regular pentagons. These solids are sometimes called cosmic or Platonic solids because of their cosmological role in Plato's *Timaeus*. They are investigated in the last book of Euclid's *Elements*, a book taken to derive from work by Theaetetus in the fourth century BC.

rhapsode: a professional performer of poetry, particularly that of Homer.

roots (*rizōmata*): Empedocles' term for the four basic elements, earth, air, fire and water.

Sceptic: an adherent of one of the various schools of philosophers who, in the period after Aristotle, questioned the possibility of attaining knowledge. These schools, which include the Academic Sceptics (successors of the Platonic school) and Pyrrhonian Sceptics (followers of Pyrrho of Elis, fourth century BC) are collectively known as the Sceptics. Our main source for their interpretation of pre-Socratic (q.v.) philosophy is Sextus Empiricus, a Pyrrhonian Sceptic of the second or third century AD.

secondary qualities: qualities consisting in powers or dispositions to evoke a particular kind of sensory experience in an observer. The traditional list of secondary qualities includes colours, tastes, smells, and acoustic and tactile qualities.

seeds (*spermata*): Anaxagoras' term for the primitive constituents from which stuffs and substances develop.

self-predication: Plato's doctrine that a Form (q.v.) exemplifies, to a superlative degree, the property which it is. For example, in the *Symposium* the Form of Beauty is the most beautiful thing there is, and therefore the supreme object of love.

Socratic: pertaining to Socrates; an associate of Socrates.

Socratic problem: the problem of determining which of the three portraits of Socrates, those by Plato, Xenophon and Aristophanes, is historically accurate. Many scholars believe that the problem is insoluble and so should be ignored in favour of explorations of the literary character, Socrates, in the works of our three main sources. Others have argued that the problem can be solved in favour of one or more of the three.

sophist: an intinerant intellectual. The fifth-century philosophers known collectively as 'The sophists' (see ch. 7) taught a wide range of subjects, including science and mathematics, but were particularly associated with the teaching of techniques of persuasion (rhetoric) and argument, and with rationalistic and critical attitudes towards traditional morality and religion.

soul (*psuchē*): the Greek word is widely used to refer to the life-force which characterizes animate beings as opposed to the lifeless parts of nature. Animals and plants have souls in this sense. The soul also constitutes the identity or personality of a living individual, and can include intellectual and other mental capacities. In the traditional (Homeric, q.v.) conception, the soul is separated from the body at death and survives in Hades as a shadowy wraith, without mentality or consciousness. In Plato's thought, on the other hand, the claim that the soul survives death amounts to the claim that the mind is separable from the body and can survive independently of it.

Stoic: pertaining to a philosophical school founded by Zeno of Citium (third century BC), influential throughout the Hellenistic and Roman periods. An adherent of that school.

substrate: the underlying subject of predication or bearer of attributes.

Sufficient Reason, Principle of: the principle that for everything that there is, and for every event that occurs, there must be something that grounds a complete explanation for its being just as it is (and, in the case of an event, for its occurring just as it does) and not otherwise.

syllabary: a system of writing which employs a single different sign to represent each syllable.

symposium: a strictly regulated male drinking party at which those present compete in various ways: by singing poetry, making speeches, playing games, etc. Many Greek vases were made for and reflect the activities of the symposium, and both Plato and Xenophon set philosophical dialogues at a symposium.

temperance (*sōphrosunē*): in general, a sane and healthy state of the soul; in particular, the virtue of being properly disposed in respect of one's appetite for pleasure. Within his tripartition (q.v.) of the soul in the *Republic* Plato defines it artificially as agreement between the parts of the soul as to which shall rule.

tetraktus: Pythagorean representation of the number 10 as a triangular number. See 'figurate numbers'.

Third Man Argument: the argument given in Plato's *Parmenides* for the conclusion that there is an infinite number of Forms (q.v.) corresponding to every property (so called because its application to the example of 'man' requires the acknowledgement of a 'Third Man', i.e. a further Form of Man in addition to particular men and the Form of Man). The conclusion of this argument contradicts Plato's belief that there is only one Form of F for every property F. His attitude to this argument is considered crucial for the question of whether the Theory of Forms underwent significant changes in the later dialogues.

transcendental argument: as used by Kant, an argument claiming to show that some feature of the world is necessary because it is a necessary precondition of our having experience of the world in the way we do.

transmigration or **metempsychosis**: the relocation of a soul (*psuchē*) from one body into another (an originally Pythagorean idea, appropriated by Empedocles and Plato).

tripartition: in Plato, the theory that the soul (*psuchē*) has three 'parts' or aspects (distinguished by contrasted aspirations but with a tendency to enter into conflict); reason, which pursues truth and the good of the whole soul, the 'spirited' part (*thumos* or *to thumoeides*), responsible for the higher emotions such as pride and self-respect, and appetite, which pursues bodily pleasure.

tyrant: a ruler who has achieved pre-eminence in a city by irregular means.

virtue, Socratic: the translation of *aretē* (q.v.) in Plato's early dialogues. For Socrates, virtue is the expertise (q.v.) of living well. See also 'eudaimonism'.

virtues, unity of: the view espoused by Socrates, but more doubtfully by Plato after his tripartition (q.v.) of the soul, that to have one virtue (*aretē*, q.v.) is to have all the virtues.

well ordered: of a set, having a linear ordering in which every subset has a first member.

'What is F-ness?' question: the question, generally asked about a particular *aretē* (q.v.), e.g. courage (*Laches*), piety (*Euthyphro*), or *aretē* in general (*Meno*), which preoccupies the early dialogues of Plato.

wisdom, Socratic: Socrates' recognition that he alone among his contemporaries is aware that he lacks the expertise of virtue (q.v.).

Index of topics

Extended discussions are indicated by bold type.

Index locorum

Fragment numbers are those of DK unless otherwise indicated. Commentators on Aristotle are cited by page and line of the editions in *Commentaria in Aristotelem Graeca*, Berlin, G. Reimer, 23 vols + supplements, 1881–1907 (various editors).

Achilles
Introduction 4 69
Aetius
  I.3.3 81n33
  I.3.4 65
  I.5.2 186
  I.25.3 240
  I.26.2 224, 226, 240
  I.29.7 225–6
  II.4.1 67
  II.13.3 (DK 59 A 71) 219
  II.13.10 79n8
  II.15.6 81n29
  II.16.5 81n29
  II.20.1 57–8
  II.22.1 50
  II.23.1 81n41
  II.24.9 77
  II.25.1 81n27
  III.1.2 58
  III.3.2 81n39
  III.4.4 77
  III.7.1 58
  IV.19.3 227
  IV.19.4 56
Albert the Great
On Vegetables VI.2.14 122n70
Alcmaeon
  fr. 1 83n59
Alexander of Aphrodisias

On Fate 6 118n21
Commentary on Aristotle Meteorology
  67.3–12 81n28
  67.11 63
Commentary on Aristotle Topics
  545.15–17 283
Ammonius
Commentary on Porphyry Introduction
  28.10–12 385n39
  29.18–19 385n39
  82.5–10 385n39
Anaxagoras
  fr. 1 210, 211, 218
  fr. 3 213, 218
  fr. 4 210, 211
  fr. 6 211
  fr. 8 214
  fr. 10 211
  fr. 11 217
  fr. 12 213, 217–9
  fr. 14 218
  fr. 16 68
  fr. 17 209–10, 218
  fr. 21 216
  fr. 21a 216
Anaximander
  fr. 1 19
Anonymous works
On Music 266
Nomima Barbarika 266

473

Index of proper names

Extended discussions are indicated by bold type.